Florence & Tuscany

Northwestern Tuscany (p213)

Florence (p56)

Eastern Tuscany (p255)

Central Coast & Elba (p187)

Siena & Central Tuscany (p120)

Southern Tuscany (p168)

Elba

THIS EDITION WRITTEN AND RESEARCHED BY

Nicola Williams, Belinda Dixon

Feb 2016

Contents

FLORENCE P56

EAT & DRINK LIKE A LOCAL
P36

Contents

BOTTICELLI'S *BIRTH OF VENUS*,
UFFIZI GALLERY, FLORENCE P61

Welcome to Florence & Tuscany

With its lyrical landscapes, world-class art and a superb cucina contadina (farmer's kitchen), the Tuscan experience is perfectly in symbiosis with the land.

Postcard-Perfect Landscapes

Tuscany has a timeless familiarity, with its iconic Florentine cathedral dome, gently rolling hills dipped in soft morning mist and sculptural cypress alleys – the whole of this central Italy *regione* is postcard material. Golden wheat fields, silver olive groves and pea-green vineyards marching in sharp terraced rows on hillsides form a graceful prelude to soul-soaring medieval hilltop villages, mountain ranges and fecund forests in the north, and a garland of bijou islands beaded along the coastal south. Get out, explore, hike, bike and ding your bicycle bell, as this rousing postcard-perfect landscape demands.

Sensational Slow Food

No land is more caught up with the fruits of its fertile earth than Tuscany, the gourmet destination for foodies where locals spend an inordinate amount of time thinking, talking and consuming food and wine. Produce sourced locally, seasonally and sustainably is the Holy Trinity and Tuscans share an enormous pride in the quality of their produce and culinary tradition. Tuscan travel is grass-roots: to wineries to taste blockbuster wines like Brunello di Montalcino and Vino Nobile di Montepulciano; to a family-run *pastificio tradizionale* where artisans still cut pasta by hand; or on road trips in quest of the best *bistecca alla fiorentina* (chargrilled T-bone steak). *Buon appetito!*

Living History

Ever since the Etruscans dropped by to party and stayed on, Tuscany has seduced. The Romans stocked their grain silos here, Christians walked stages of a medieval pilgrimage route, and Napolean plundered art (and suffered terribly in exile in a beautiful neoclassical villa with fig trees and sea views on the paradise island of Elba). Florence's historic churches, chapels and monuments were a key stop for British aristocrats on the Grand Tour in the 19th century – and remain so today. And at sundown when the River Arno turns pink, whether you like things old-fashioned simple or so boutique chic you even get to pick your sheets before checking in, know that this achingly handsome city will oblige.

An Artistic Powerhouse

Then there's the art. And oh, what art! The Etruscans indulged their fondness for a classy send-off with exquisite funerary objects, and the Romans, always partial to puffing up their own importance, left their usual legacy of monumental sculptures. But it was during the medieval and Renaissance periods that Tuscany really struck gold with painters, sculptors and architects creating world-class masterpieces. Squirrelled away and safeguarded today in churches, museums and galleries all over the region, art in Tuscany is truly unmatched.

Why I Love Florence & Tuscany

By Nicola Williams, Author

Tuscany won me over at a *farro* farm in the Garfagnana. We were tucking into dinner when the farmer's wife rushed into the kitchen mid-*secondi* and wildly urged us to join her in the stable to watch a calf being born. Later, when she joyfully declared 'We'll call her Kaya after your daughter!' I was speechless. So my five-year-old now has a cow in Tuscany and I the honour of being privy to yet another intimacy of this diverse, soulful, passionately earth-driven region. This (and its white truffles, Florence, *aperitivi* tradition, Renaissance art, Chianti wine touring and glorious farmhouses) is why I love Tuscany.

For more about our authors, see page 352.

Above: Monticchiello (p162)

Florence & Tuscany

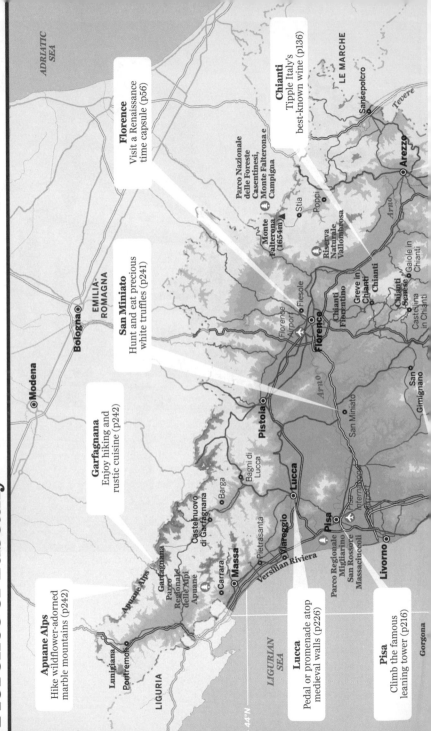

Apuane Alps
Hike wildflower-adorned marble mountains (p242)

Garfagnana
Enjoy hiking and rustic cuisine (p242)

San Miniato
Hunt and eat precious white truffles (p241)

Florence
Visit a Renaissance time capsule (p56)

Chianti
Tipple Italy's best-known wine (p136)

Lucca
Pedal or promenade atop medieval walls (p226)

Pisa
Climb the famous leaning tower (p216)

ADRIATIC SEA

LIGURIAN SEA

LE MARCHE

EMILIA-ROMAGNA

LIGURIA

0   25 miles
0   50 km

— 44°N

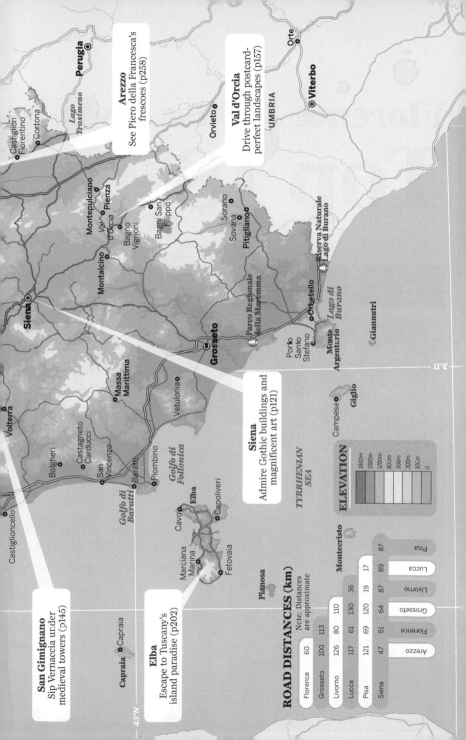

Florence & Tuscany's
Top 18

Uffizi Gallery, Florence

1 Few art galleries evoke such an overwhelming sense of awe and wonderment as the world-class Uffizi (p61), at home in a 16th-century Medici *palazzo* in Florence. Vast, labyrinthine, architecturally magnificent and rich in history, the building alone is stunning. Add to this an art collection chock-full of Renaissance masterpieces with works by Giotto, Botticelli, Michelangelo, da Vinci, Raphael, Titian and Caravaggio all jostling for the limelight, and know you've arrived in artlover heaven. Allow ample time to savour slowly, in several bite-sized visits if needs be. Below left: Botticelli's *Birth of Venus* (p64)

Piazza del Campo, Siena

2 Horses race around it twice a year, local teens picnic on it, tourists inevitably gasp on seeing it for the first time – Siena's strangely sloping, perfectly paved central piazza (p124) is the city's geographical and historical heart, staked out since the 12th century. Presided over by the graceful Palazzo Comunale and fringed with bustling cafe terraces, Piazza del Campo is the finest spot in Siena to promenade, take photographs and lap up the soul-soaring magic of this unique, gloriously Gothic and architecturally harmonious city.

DAMIEN SIMONIS/GETTY IMAGES ©

RICHARD I'ANSON/GETTY IMAGES ©

Chianti

3 This ancient wine region is the Tuscany of postcards, where cypress alleys give way to pea-green vineyards, silver olive groves, honey-coloured stone farmhouses and secluded Renaissance villas built for Florentine and Sienese counts and countesses. Luxurious accommodation and the very best of modern Tuscan cuisine provide the ingredients for an idyllic short escape – peppered with romantic walks and road trips along narrow green lanes to wine cellars for tastings of Italy's best-known wine, the ruby-red violet-scented Chianti Classico (p136).

Flavours of Tuscany

4 'To cook like your mother is good, but to cook like your grandmother is better' says the Tuscan proverb. And indeed, it is in foodie Tuscany that age-old recipes are passed between generations and form the backbone of local cuisine – a highlight of any Tuscan trip. Devour feisty T-bone steak in a family-run *trattoria* such as Mario (p101) by Florence's central food market, savour modern Tuscan fare amid a sea of ancient Antinori vines at Rinuccio 1180, shop at local markets bursting with seasonal produce and wish fellow diners *'Buon appetito!'*

Country Life on an Agriturismo

5 Whether you want to wallow in the beauty of a Tuscan landscape from an infinity pool on an estate or get your hands dirty in the fields, an *agriturismo* (rural accommodation on a working farm or winery) is a five-star way of experiencing country life in Tuscany. Home-cooked dinners of farm produce and mountains of green space are a given. Barbialla Nuova (p241) has just the right mix of adventure (unpaved country roads) and panache (stylish decor and staggering views). Top: Countryside near Pienza (p158)

Truffle Hunting

6 The most precious product in the Italian pantry, the white truffle is snuffed out by dogs in damp autumnal woods around the town of San Miniato. Much secrecy and cut-throat rivalry between local *tartufaio* (truffle hunters) surrounds the business – making a bite into a truffle-laced omelette all the more glam. October to December join the excitement of a truffle hunt (p242), or follow your nose to San Miniato on November weekends when the Mostra Mercato Nazionale del Tartufo Bianco (National White Truffle Market) takes over the town.

MAREMAGNUM/GETTY IMAGES ©

PETER ZELEI/GETTY IMAGES ©

Medieval Festivals

7 Throw yourself into local life with an exuberant festival – a snapshot of Tuscan culture, washed down with much food, wine and merrymaking. Come the warm days of spring and summer, almost every town hosts their own fest: locals don medieval costumes and battle with giant crossbows or lances, often re-enacting ancient political rivalry between different *contrada* (neighbourhoods). The prize? Wonderful trophies evocative of medieval pageantry such as the golden arrow and silk banners of Massa Marittima's Balestro del Girifalco (p173). Top left: Scoppio del Carro parade, Florence (p91)

Val d'Orcia Road Trip

8 Cruise along gently rolling roads along this valley laced with vines, the medieval abbeys of Sant'Antimo and San Galgano, splendidly Renaissance Pienza and the blockbuster wine towns of Montepulciano and Montalcino. Explore abbeys where pilgrims once overnighted en route along the Via Francigena from Canterbury to Rome, indulge in a long lazy Brunello-fuelled lunch, and congratulate yourself on uncovering one of Tuscany's finest road trips – there's good reason why the Val d'Orcia (p157) is a Unesco World Heritage site. Top right: Farm and vineyard, Val d'Orcia

Duomo, Florence

9 The Duomo (p65) isn't just the most spectacular structure in Florence – it's up there with Rome's Colosseum and Pisa's Leaning Tower as Italy's most recognisable icons. Its polychrome marble facade is vast, striking and magnificent. But what makes the building so extraordinary is Filippo Brunelleschi's distinctive red-brick dome, one of the greatest architectural achievements of all time. Scale the steep narrow staircase up to the base of the dome and peer down on the toy-like cathedral interior far below – then climb some more for a stunning city panorama.

Garfagnana

10 Head to the hills north of Lucca to feast on chestnuts, mushrooms, honey and other fruits of the forest in this corner of Tuscany, Hike through fields of wildflowers and meander slowly along bumpy backroads, from one laid-back medieval mountain village to another. Stay in an *agriturismo* and spend your days hiking, mountain biking and devouring homemade dinners around a shared farmhouse table. From the Garfagnana (p242), the beaches and artistic enclaves of the Versilian coast aren't too far away should the need for civilisation kick in. Right: Serchio river, Garfagnana

10

UNIVERSAL IMAGES GROUP/DEAGOSTINI/ALAMY ©

Piazza dei Miracoli, Pisa

11 History resonates when you stand in the middle of this piazza (p216). Showcasing structures built to glorify God and flaunt civic riches (not necessarily in that order), this cluster of Romanesque church buildings possesses an architectural harmony that is remarkably refined and very rare. Hear the acoustics in the baptistry, marvel at Giovanni Pisano's marble pulpit in the *duomo* and confirm that, yes, the famous tower does lean. Living up to its name, this square really is a field full of miracles.

Island Life, Elba

12 Elba (p202) is the Tuscan paradise no one imagines. A Mediterranean island woven with scented orange trees, olive groves and century-old palms, Elba is a sensory landscape designed for beach lounging, heady coastal hikes and hairpin motoring from hilltop village to bijou fishing cove. Napoleon was banished here in 1814, so the island has a few historic sights to visit. And then there's the wine and olive oil, two glorious nectars crafted with pride and passion on family estates unchanged for centuries. Bottom: Portoferraio (p205)

Church Art in Arezzo

13 It is a step off the tourist trail but this only adds to the charm of laid-back Arezzo (p258), a small town in eastern Tuscany which shows Siena a thing or two when it comes to cinematically sloping central squares. Medieval churches safe-guarding precious crucifixes, frescoes and sacred works of art staccato Arezzo's streets and, should you be in the market for an artwork of your own, one of Italy's best-known antiques fairs is held here on the first weekend of each month. Top: Piero's *Legend of the True Cross*, Basilica di San Francesco (p258)

Pedalling Lucca

14 Hire a bike, stock up on picnic supplies and freewheel along the cobbled streets of Lucca (p226) in northwestern Tuscany, zooming through tree-shaded piazzas and stone alleys secreting medieval churches, a Romanesque cathedral and 17th-century *palazzi* (palaces). End with a lunch of local produce atop the city walls, slicked with a circular cycling path (a sweet loaf of *buccellato* from pastry shop Taddeucci is a Lucchese must); or hit the open road to swoon over villas in the countryside. Bottom: Piazza Anfiteatro, Lucca (p226)

DAMIEN SIMONIS/GETTY IMAGES ©

GARY YEOWELL/GETTY IMAGES ©

Exploring the Apuane Alps

15 This rugged mountain range, protected within the Parco Regionale delle Alpi Apuane (p242), beckons hikers, bikers and drivers with a peaceful trail of isolated farmhouses, medieval hermitages and hilltop villages. Its most spectacular sights are the slopes backing the town of Carrara, scarred with marble quarries worked since Roman times. Come here to visit a quarry and sample *lardo di Colonnata* (wafer-thin slices of local pig fat), one of Tuscany's greatest gastronomic treats, in the tiny village of Colonnata.

Aperitivo

16 *Aperitivo* (predinner drinks accompanied by cocktail snacks) is one of Tuscany's finest food and wine rituals, best partaken after a *passeggiata* (early evening stroll) with seemingly half of town along Florence's Via de' Tornabuoni, Lucca's Via Fillungo or any other car-free urban strip. People-watching is an essential part of both elements. Grab a pew on the pavement terrace of Florence wine bar Le Volpi e l'Uva (p108) or between Florentine hipsters sipping gin cocktails at Ditta Artiginiale and enjoy. Above right: Bruschetta

The Franciscan Pilgrim Trail

17 Offering a heady mix of scenery, art, history and religion, the Santuario della Verna (p269) in eastern Tuscany and the hilltop town of Assisi in neighbouring Umbria are two of the most significant Christian pilgrimage sites in the world. Visit the monastery in the Casentino where St Francis is said to have received the stigmata, and then move on to his birthplace, where Giotto's famous fresco series in the upper church stuns beholders with its beauty and narrative power. Far top right: Basilica di San Francesco, Assisi (p274)

17

Medieval Towers, San Gimignano

18 They form one of the world's most enchanting skylines, squirrel away everything from family homes to contemporary art galleries, and bring history alive for every visitor – San Gimignano's medieval towers (p145) are an iconic Tuscan sight. Few can be scaled these days – Torre Grossa in the Palazzo Comunale is a notable exception – but you can explore in their shadows and reflect on the civic pride and neighbourhood rivalry that prompted their construction and have given this hilltop town its unique appearance.

18

Need to Know

For more information, see Survival Guide (p323)

Currency
Euro (€)

Language
Italian

Visas
Not needed for residents of Schengen countries or for many visitors staying for less than 90 days.

Money
ATMs widely available. Credit cards accepted in most hotels and many restaurants.

Mobile (Cell) Phones
Local SIM cards can be used in European and Australian phones. Other phones must be set to roaming.

Time
One hour ahead of GMT/UTC; clocks are put forward one hour during daylight saving time (late March to late October).

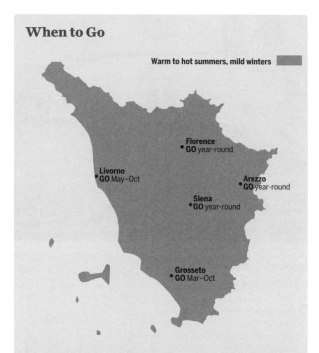

When to Go

Warm to hot summers, mild winters

Florence
• GO year-round

Livorno
• GO May–Oct

Arezzo
•GO year-round

Siena
•GO year-round

Grosseto
• GO Mar–Oct

High Season
(May, Jun, Sep, Oct)

➡ Accommodation prices rise by up to 50%.

➡ Perfect weather for travelling, but it can be crowded.

➡ Major festivals fall June to September.

Shoulder
(Apr, Jul & Aug)

➡ April weather is pleasant and prices are reasonable.

➡ High summer can be hot away from the coast and too crowded on it.

➡ Most attractions stay open to sundown during summer.

Low Season
(Nov–Mar)

➡ Accommodation bargains abound, but many hotels close for the season.

➡ Some tourist information offices close.

➡ Many restaurants close for annual holidays.

Useful Websites

Turismo in Toscana (www.turismo.intoscana.it) Official site of the Tuscan region.

Toscana & Chianti News (www.toscanaechiantinews.com) Magazine features, news, lifestyle and culture.

The Florentine (www.thefloren tine.net) English-language newpaper covering Florence and much of Tuscany.

Il Sole 24 Ore (www.italy24.il sole24ore.com) Digital, English-language edition of Italian newspaper *Il Sole 24 Ore*.

Lonely Planet (www.lonelyplanet.com/italy/tuscany) Loads of practical information.

Important Numbers

Italy country code	⟁39
International access code	⟁00
Ambulance	⟁118
Police	⟁113
Pan-European emergency & emergency from mobile phone	⟁112

Exchange Rates

Australia	A$1	€0.67
Canada	C$1	€0.70
Japan	¥100	€0.73
New Zealand	NZ$1	€0.59
UK	UK£1	€1.43
US	US$1	€0.91

For current exchange rates, see www.xe.com.

Daily Costs

Budget: Less than €80

➡ Dorm bed: €16–36

➡ Sandwich: €5–8

➡ Trattoria dinner: €20

➡ Coffee standing at bar: €1

Midrange: €80–200

➡ Midrange-hotel double room: €110–200

➡ Restaurant meal: €35

➡ *Aperitivo:* €10

➡ Admission to museums: €5–20

Top End: More than €200

➡ Top-end-hotel double room: €200 and over

➡ Dinner of Modern Tuscan cuisine: €50

➡ Coffee sitting on a cafe terrace: €4

➡ Tour guide for two hours: €140

Opening Hours

Opening hours vary throughout the year. We've provided summer (high-season) and winter (low-season) opening hours, but be aware that hours might differ in the shoulder seasons.

Banks 8.30am to 1.30pm and 3.30pm to 4.30pm Monday to Friday

Restaurants 12.30pm to 2.30pm and 7.30pm to 10pm

Cafes 7.30am to 8pm

Bars & pubs 10am to 1am

Shops 9am to 1pm and 3.30pm to 7.30pm (or 4pm to 8pm) Monday to Saturday

Arriving in Tuscany

Pisa International Airport (p225) Buses run to central Pisa (€1.80) and central Florence (€4.99). PisaMover automated trains run to Pisa's Stazione Pisa Centrale (€1.30), regular trains run to Florence's Stazione di Santa Maria Novella (€8). Taxis cost €10 to central Pisa.

Florence Airport (p118) Buses cost €6 to central Florence. Taxis cost €20 to central Florence (€23 on Sundays and holidays, €22 between 10pm and 6am), plus €1 per bag and €1 supplement for fourth passenger.

Getting Around

Car Undoubtedly the best option, allowing you to explore scenic countryside and small hill towns. Drive on the right, overtake on the left, give way to the right at roundabouts. Many towns and cities have a Zona a Traffico Limitato (ZTL; Limited Traffic Zone) in their historic centre; keep your car outside the ZTL or be hit with a hefty fine.

Bus There's a reasonably extensive regional bus network. *Corse rapide* (express) services link Florence and Siena; other routes can involve long trips. In towns and cities, tickets must be time-stamped on public buses (or risk a €50 on-the-spot fine).

Train High-speed trains link Florence, Arezzo and Cortona, as well as Grosseto, Livorno and Pisa. *Regionale* (regional) trains link Florence, Lucca and Pisa. Always time-stamp your ticket before boarding or risk an immediate €50 fine.

For much more on **getting around**, see p332.

First Time Florence & Tuscany

For more information, see Survival Guide (p323)

Checklist

➡ Check passport validity and visa requirements

➡ Arrange travel insurance

➡ Confirm airline baggage restrictions

➡ Book ahead for accommodation and high-profile restaurants

➡ Buy tickets online for Florence's Uffizi and Pisa's Leaning Tower

➡ Reserve guided tours (Vasaraian Corridor) and museum passes (Firenze Card)

➡ Organise international roaming on your phone if needed

What to Pack

➡ Sturdy walking shoes – cobbled and unpaved streets abound

➡ Italian phrasebook

➡ Travel plug (adaptor)

➡ Driving map and GPS for the car (or equivalent phone App)

➡ Sunscreen, sunhat and sunglasses (summer)

➡ Umbrella and/or raincoat (except in high summer)

➡ Corkscrew – Italian winemakers don't approve of screw-tops

Top Tips for Your Trip

➡ Always carry some cash. Unattended petrol (gas) stations don't always accept foreign credit cards, and some restaurants and hotels operate on a cash-only basis.

➡ Don't rely solely on a GPS (which can occasionally lead you too far off the beaten track) – cross-check your route on a printed road map.

➡ You will often find that there is free wi-fi access in or around *palazzi comunale* (town halls) and tourist offices.

➡ To cut costs in Florence, plan your stay for the first Sunday of the month when admission to state museums is free.

➡ Foodies should invest in *Osterie d'Italia* published by Slow Food Editore as an App (iPhone and Android) or printed book, in English or Italian.

What to Wear

A sense of style is vital to Tuscans, who take great pride in their dress and appearance. Maintaining *la bella figura* (ie making a good impression) is extremely important. Steer clear of shorts, mini skirts and flip-flops unless you're at the beach; and always dress up – not down – at restaurants, clubs and bars. Smart-casual outfits will cover you in most situations; trainers are definitely frowned upon after dark.

Cover yourself when entering a church (no shorts, short skirts or sleeveless or off-the-shoulder tops). Topless and nude bathing are unacceptable at most beaches.

Sleeping

Book accommodation in advance, particularly in spring, summer and autumn (fall) when the best addresses fill up fast. Check online for cheaper rates. See p33 for more information.

➡ **Agriturismi** Accommodation on farms, wineries and rural estates: perfect for those with a car, and usually highly practical for those travelling with children.

➡ **Palazzo hotels** Historic 'palace' designer hotels are the boutique option for those in towns and cities with a midrange to top-end budget.

➡ **B&Bs** Small family-run guesthouses with a handful of rooms, offering bed and breakfast; bathrooms are occasionally shared.

Money

Credit and debit cards are widely accepted. Visa and MasterCard are the most popular; American Express is only accepted by international chain hotels, luxury boutiques and major department stores, and few places take Diners Club and JCB. Always check if restaurants take cards before you order; most bars and cafes do not. Chip-and-pin is the norm for card transactions.

Bancomats (ATMs) are widespread; most offer withdrawal from overseas savings accounts and cash advances on credit cards. Both transactions will incur international transaction fees. If you don't want to rely on plastic, you can usually change cash and travellers cheques at a bank, post office or *cambio* (exchange office).

For more information, see p327.

Bargaining

Tuscans don't bargain, so neither should you.

Tipping

➡ **Taxis** Round the fare up to the nearest euro.

➡ **Restaurants** Many locals don't tip waiters, but most visitors leave 10% to 15% if there's no service charge.

➡ **Cafes** Leave a coin (as little as €0.10 is acceptable) if you drank your coffee at the counter or 10% if you sat at a table.

➡ **Hotels** Bellhops usually expect €1 to €2 per bag; it's not necessary to tip the concierge, cleaners or front-desk staff.

Language

Many locals in towns and cities speak at least one language other than Italian – usually English or French. But delve into the Tuscan countryside and you'll need that Italian phrasebook. Regionwide, many traditional places to eat have no written menu or only a menu penned in Italian in spidery handwriting. See Language (p336) for more information.

 What's the local speciality?
Qual'è la specialità di questa regione?
kwa·*le* la spe·cha·lee·*ta* dee *kwes*·ta re·jo·ne

A bit like the rivalry between medieval Italian city-states, these days the country's regions compete in speciality foods and wines.

 Which combined tickets do you have?
Quali biglietti cumulativi avete?
kwa·lee bee·*lye*·tee koo·moo·la·tee·vee a·ve·te

Make the most of your euro by getting combined tickets to various sights; they are available in all major Italian cities.

 Where can I buy discount designer items?
C'è un outlet in zona? che oon *owt*·let in zo·na

Discount fashion outlets are big business in major cities – get bargain-priced seconds, samples and cast-offs for *la bella figura*.

 I'm here with my husband/boyfriend.
Sono qui con il mio marito/ragazzo.
so·no kwee kon eel *mee*·o ma·ree·to/ra·ga·tso

Solo women travellers may receive unwanted attention in some parts of Italy; if ignoring fails have a polite rejection ready.

 Let's meet at 6pm for pre-dinner drinks.
Ci vediamo alle sei per un aperitivo.
chee ve·dya·mo a·le say per oon a·pe·ree·tee·vo

At dusk, watch the main piazza get crowded with people sipping colourful cocktails and snacking the evening away: join your new friends for this authentic Italian ritual!

Etiquette

➡ **Greetings** Shake hands, make eye contact and say *buongiorno* (good morning) or *buonasera* (good afternoon/evening). If you know someone well, air-kissing on both cheeks (starting with their left) is standard.

➡ **Polite language** Say *mi scusi* ('I'm sorry') to attract attention, *grazie (mille)* to say 'thank you (very much)', *per favore* to say 'please', *prego* to say 'you're welcome' or 'please, after you' and *permesso* if you need to push past someone in a crowd.

➡ **Cafes** Don't hang around at an espresso bar; drink your coffee and go. It's called espresso for a reason.

➡ **Body language** Be wary of making a circle with two hands ('I'll kick your ass'), an A-OK signal ('You might be gay'), or the devil horns with your hand ('Your wife is cheating on you').

➡ **In churches** Never intrude on a mass or service.

What's New

Urban Deli Dining

Slow Food is a natural in agricultural Tuscany, but a new take on the concept has been spawned with the arrival of urban deli dining. Stroll from stall to stall or between counters at the market or deli, then grab a table and watch your lunch being cooked. Produce is seasonal, local and invariably organic. Top Florentine addresses include the Mercato Centrale (p100), Eataly (p116) and Michelin-starred La Bottega del Buon Caffè (p105); in Lucca try Local Food Market (p235).

Oltrarno chic sleeps, Florence

Staying in Florence's increasingly gentrified Oltrarno is at last chic: enter designer hostel-bar Ostello Tasso (p97) and superstylish *palazzo* B&B SoprArno Suites (p98), a boutique address brimming with vintage objets d'art and collectibles.

Coffee & Tea, Florence

The quest for perfect *caffè* is gaining ground in Florence where hipster roastery Ditta Artigianale (p110) is shaking up the drinks scene big time. L'Arte del Sogno (p109) is doing the same with tea.

Cathedral museums, Pisa & Florence

A brand new design awaits in revamped museums in Pisa (p222) and Florence (p69), safeguarding sacred treasures from the *duomo* – together one of the world's foremost collections of sacred art after the Vatican.

Hotel Italia, Siena

This budget hotel in Siena eschews *palazzo*-style to main-stage the modern. Now it's added another string to its (cupid's) bow: a Love Room with bubbles, love cookies and romantic tunes. (p131)

Museo di Palazzo Pretorio, Prato

Tuscany's most contemporary cutting-edge local history museum, inside Prato's 13th-century prison and courthouse, is open after a record-breaking 20-year-long renovation job. (p240)

New Moon Walking Tour, Volterra

Twilight fans are skulking around ancient alleyways in Volterra, setting of Stephenie Meyer's *New Moon* novel and proud possessor of a new vampire-themed tour. (p154)

Creative Kids, Pistoia & Florence

Always creative, Pistoia's Museo Marino Marini (p237) has launched get-your-hands-dirty tours in English for families with kids. Equally inspiring are Molly McIlWrath's (p88) artsy tours and workshops for children in Florence.

Palazzo Comunale, San Gimignano

Gazing at medieval frescoes takes a high-tech turn in this 12th-century *palazzo*: augmented reality glasses superimpose digital medieval characters regaling pithy tales over the paintings. Informative and fun! (p147)

Silver Spoon Dining, Florence

Dine after dusk at In Fabbrica, a speakeasy canteen – with silver cutlery, candlesticks etc – where, by day, workers from Florence's Pampaloni silversmith workshop have lunch. (p103)

For more recommendations and reviews, see http://lonelyplanet.com/italy/tuscany

If You Like...

Food

There are so many ways to enjoy Tuscan food: from dining at one of the region's many fabulous restaurants to trawling local food markets or learning how to do it yourself.

Bistecca alla fiorentina Florence's iconic T-bone steak hails from the Val di Chiana: dig in at **Ristorante Da Muzzicone**. (p273)

Antipasto toscano Go local: open your meal with a mixed platter of cured meats, *pecorino* (sheep's-milk cheese) and toast topped with chicken liver pâté.

White truffles Decadent, unique and utterly memorable: hunt them at **Barbialla Nuova**. (p241)

Colonnata Discover *lardo* (pig fat) ageing in marble vats of olive oil in this mountain village near Carrara. (p249)

Fashionable gastronomy Dine with one of Tuscany's top chefs **farm-to-table in Florence** (p105), on **seafood** or in **Brunello wine country**. (p160) (p186) (p158)

Wine

Aperitivi A pre-dinner glass of wine with nibbles is a cornerstone of Florentine culture – indulge at **Le Volpi e l'Uva** or **Il Santino**. (p108) (p108)

Antinori nel Chianti Classico The king of Chianti wine cellars: tasting and dining James Bond–style. (p138)

Strade del Vino Motor through wine country, visiting vineyards, *cantine* (cellars) and local artisan food producers.

Super Tuscans Target **Bolgheri**, home of the groundbreaking Sassicaia, on the Etruscan Coast. (p196)

Montalcino Time visits to coincide with the release of the new vintage of Brunello in February. (p157)

Castello di Brolio Visit Italy's oldest winery, with museum, garden, tasting cellars and restaurant. (p141)

Renaissance Art

Uffizi Gallery It doesn't get any better than this Medici art collection in Florence. (p61)

Museo di San Marco No frescoes better portray the humanist spirit of the Renaissance than Fra Angelico's. (p77)

Cattedrale di Santo Stefano Gorge on Filippo Lippe frescoes in crowd-free Prato. (p240)

Museo dell'Opera Eyeball cool-as-cucumber Madonnas by Renaissance maestros in Siena. (p127)

Museo Diocesano Small but sensational collection of Renaissance art in Cortona. (p271)

Museo Civico Siena's most famous museum is a feast of secular art. (p125)

Piero della Francesca Trail eastern Tuscany's greatest Renaissance painter. (p266)

Caprese Michelangelo Art aficionados adore this village in the remote Tuscan outback of Casentino where *David*'s creator was born. (p267)

Contemporary Art & Sculpture

Museo Novecento Modern and contemporary Italian art, brilliantly at home in a 13th-century Florentine *palazzo*. (p75)

Tuttomondo Who would guess that the last wall mural painted by American pop artist Keith Haring adorns a Pisan church facade? (p223)

Palazzo Fabroni Get acquainted with Pistoian contemporary artists at this riveting art museum. (p237)

Fattoria di Celle Allow four hours to tour this extraordinary alfresco collection of installation art. (p237)

Castello di Ama Ancient winemaking traditions meet cutting-edge contemporary art on this Chianti wine estate. (p144)

Parco Sculture del Chianti
Track down coloured cows, cub
clusters and abstract humans in
a 13-acre wood in Chianti. (p144)

Galleria Continua Ogle at
world-class contemporary art in
medieval San Gimignano. (p149)

Giardino dei Tarocchi Franco-
American artist Niki de Saint
Phalle brings the tarot-card pack
to life. (p186)

Borgo Corsignano Sleep in a
Tuscan farmhouse in northeastern Tuscany, with grounds peppered with fabulous art. (p267)

Natural Landscapes

Parco Nazionale dell'Arcipelago
Europe's largest marine-protect-
ed area has the magical island of
Elba at its heart. (p202)

Golfo di Baratti Tuscany's 'tropical paradise': sandy beaches,
parasol pines and picture-postcard fishing ports. (p202)

Apuane Alps Not snow but
marble whitens these dramatic
mountains peaks around famous
mining town Carrara. (p242)

Garfagnana A trio of remote
valleys in northwestern Tuscany
forested with chestnut groves
and *porcini* mushrooms. (p242)

**Parco Nazionale delle Foreste
Casentinesi, Monte Falterona
e Campigna** Dense forests,
sparkling rivers and medieval
monasteries in Tuscany's
northeast. (p269)

**Parco Regionale della Marem-
ma** Spectacular regional park
protecting pine forests, marshy
plains, unspoilt coastline and the
Uccellina mountains. (p184)

**Riserva Naturale Provinciale
Diaccia Botrona** Follow tens of
thousands of migrating birds
to coastal marshlands around
Castiglione della Pescaia. (p184)

Top: Capella de' Pazzi (p79), Florence.
Bottom: Autumn hues in Chianti (p136)

Scenic Drives

Passo del Vestito Cruise down this hair-raising mountain pass from Castelnuovo di Garfagnana to Massa on the Versilian coast. (p247)

Colle d'Orano & Fetovaia Twinset of gorgeous golden-sand beaches and a dramatic drive linking the two, on Elba's western coast. (p208)

Monte Argentario Bring along nerves of steel to motor the narrow Via Panoramica encircling this rugged promontory. (p186)

Val d'Orcia Take your foot off the pedal in this serene World Heritage–listed valley of rolling hills and Romanesque abbeys. (p159)

Chianti Bump along age-old backroads woven through vineyards, olive groves and photogenic avenues of cypress trees. (p136)

Strada del Vino e dell'Olio From hilltop towns to the Etruscan Coast, via cypress alleys and *enoteche,* this drive is gourmet. (p197)

Gorgeous Gardens

Giardino Torrigiani Explore Europe's largest privately owned green space within the historic centre of Florence. (p87)

Giardino Bardini Quintessential Florentine garden with orangery, marble maidens and Tuscany's finest **garden restaurant**. (p86) (p105)

Museo dell'Opera del Duomo Find peace – and the perfect snap of the Leaning Tower – in this elegant cloister garden in Pisa. (p222)

Villa Grabau Skip around potted lemon trees and fountains in ornate villa gardens near Lucca. (p234)

Palazzo Pfanner Invite romance to a chamber-music concert in the baroque-styled garden of this Luccese 17th-century palace. (p232)

Orto de' Pecci Find peace, tranquility, organic farm, medieval garden and experimental vineyard in this Sienese oasis. (p128)

Museo di Casa Vasari Few know about the bijou Renaissance rooftop garden atop Georgio Vasari's childhood home in Arezzo. (p260)

Pilgrimage Sites

Via Francigena Walk the Tuscan chunk of one of Europe's most important medieval pilgrimages – **Abbazia di Sant'Antimo** is a highlight. (p46) (p161)

Assisi In neighbouring Umbria, the birthplace of St Francis of Assisi makes for a soulful day trip. (p274)

Santuario della Verna Visit the windswept monastery where St Francis received the stigmata – see his bloody gown. (p269)

Cattedrale di San Martino Pay your respects to the Volto Santo, Lucca's revered religious icon carried through the streets by torchlight each September. (p227)

Siena Trail Saint Catherine in her hometown; see where she was born (p121), her embalmed head and desiccated thumb. (p130)

Medieval Towers

Campanile Scale 414 steps to the top of the cathedral's bell-tower for an uplifting panorama of rooftop Florence. (p69)

Torre d'Arnolfo Admire one of Europe's most beautiful cities atop this 94m-tall crenellated tower at 14th-century Palazzo Vecchio in Florence. (p71)

Hotel Torre Guelfa Savour *aperitivi* at sundown in the tiny bar atop Florence's tallest, privately owned *torre* (tower). (p93)

Leaning Tower The bell tower of Pisa's cathedral leaned from the moment it was unveiled in 1372. (p216)

Torre Guinigi What impresses most about this 14th-century red-brick tower, one of 130 that peppered medieval Lucca, are the oak trees that sprout out its sky-high crown! (p232)

Torre del Mangia Views of Siena's iconic Piazza del Campo from atop this graceful tower are predictably swoon-worthy; count 500 steps up. (p125)

Torre Grossa Gorge on spectacular views of centuries-old streets and picture-postcard countryside beyond San Gimignano. (p147)

Torre del Candeliere Quintessential Tuscan views of a hilltop town and rolling hills beyond is the treat that awaits atop Massa Marittima's cute Candlestick Tower. (p172)

Month by Month

February

It's only towards the end of this month that locals are coaxed out of their winter hibernation. Weather conditions can be bone-chillingly cold in mountainous areas and windswept hill towns can appear all but deserted.

Festa di Anna Maria Medici

Anna Maria Louisa de' Medici, the last Medici, bequeathed Florence its vast cultural heritage, hence this feast on 18 February marking her death in 1743: costumed parade from Palazzo Vecchio to her tomb in the Cappelle Medicee; free admission to state museums.

Carnevale di Viareggio

The seaside resort of Viareggio goes wild during carnival (http://viareggio.ilcarnevale.com), an annual festival that kicks off 40 days before Ash Wednesday. The famous month-long street party revolves around fireworks, floats featuring giant satirical effigies of political and other topical personalities, parades and around-the-clock revelry.

March

Locals start to get into the springtime swing of things in the weeks leading up to Easter. Many regular visitors time their trips for this period to take advantage of low-season prices and uncrowded conditions.

Torciata di San Giuseppe

An evocative, torch-lit procession down Pitigliano's mysterious, Etruscan-era *vie cave* which ends in a huge bonfire in the town. Held each spring equinox (19 March), it's a symbol of purification and of winter's end.

Settimana Santa

Easter Week is celebrated in neighbouring Umbria with processions and performances in Assisi. Other Easter celebrations in the region include Florence's dramatic Scoppio del Carro (Explosion of the Cart) in front of the Duomo on Easter Sunday.

April

Wildflowers carpet the countryside, market stalls burst with new-season produce and classical music is staged in wonderfully atmospheric surrounds. Easter sees the tourist season kicking off in earnest.

☆ Maggio Musicale Fiorentino

Italy's oldest arts festival (www.operadifirenze.it), a 1933 creation, brings world-class performances of theatre, classical music, jazz and dance to Florence's sparkling new opera house and other venues in the city. Concerts continue through April into June.

May

Medieval pageants take over the streets of towns and cities across the region from late spring to early autumn, highlighting ancient neighbourhood rivalries and the modern-day love of street parties.

⭐ Balestro del Girifalco

Cinematic flag-waving opens this archery festival, held in Massa Marittima on the fourth Sunday in May and again on 14 August. Marksmen from the town's three *terzieri* (districts) don medieval garb and, armed with 15th-century crossbows, compete for a symbolic golden arrow and painted silk banner.

June

It's summertime and, yes, the living is easy. The start of the month is the perfect time to tour the paradisiacal isle of Elba, and any time is right to gorge on seafood and strawberries.

⭐ Luminaria di San Ranieri

After dark on 16 June, Pisans honour their city's patron saint, San Ranieri, with thousands upon thousands of candles on window sills and doorways, and blazing torches along the banks of the Arno, climaxing at 11pm with a spectacular fireworks display.

⭐ Festa di San Giovanni

The feast of Florence's patron saint, San Giovanni (St John), on 24 June is a fantastic opportunity to catch a match of *calcio storico* (historic football) – head-butting, punching, elbowing, choking et al – on Piazza di Santa Croce. The grand finale is fireworks over Piazzale Michelangelo.

⭐ Giostra del Saracino

A grandiose affair deep-rooted in good old-fashioned neighbourhood rivalry, this medieval jousting tournament sees the four *quartieri* (quarters) of Arezzo put forward a team of knights to battle on one of Tuscany's most beautiful and unusual city squares, Piazza Grande; third Saturday in June and first Sunday in September.

⭐ Medieval in San Gimignano

Battles between knights in shining armour, archery contests, falconry displays, fiery tugs of war and theatre performances evoke all the fun and madness of San Gimignano's medieval heritage during the Ferie delle Messi (www.cavalieridisantafina.it), usually held the third weekend in June.

⭐ Battle of the Bridge

The atmosphere is electric during Pisa's Il Gioco del Ponte (Battle of the Bridge; www.giocodelpontedipisa.it), the last Sunday in June, when two teams in elaborate 16th-century costume battle to capture the city bridge, Ponte di Mezzo.

July

Cyclists and walkers take to the mountains but everyone else heads to the beach, meaning that accommodation prices in inland cities and towns drop as a result. Summer music and arts festivals abound.

⭐ Musical Cortona

The hill town of Cortona is alive with music during the Festival of Sacred Music (www.cortonacristiana.it). Late July ushers in the Cortona Mix Festival (www.mixfestival.it), an enticing cocktail of classical music, rock, theatre, literature and film. Watch for the winter edition in February.

⭐ Pistoia Blues

BB King, Miles Davis, David Bowie, Sting and Santana have all taken to the stage at Pistoia's annual blues festival (www.pistoiablues.com), an electric alfresco fest around since 1980 that packs out central square Piazza del Duomo.

⭐ Puccini Festival

Opera buffs from around the world make a pilgrimage to the small town of Torre del Lago for this annual event in July and August (www.puccinifestival.it). Performances are staged in an open-air lakeside theatre next to the great man's house.

⭐ Palio

The most spectacular event on the Tuscan calendar, on 2 July and 16 August in Siena. Featuring colourful street pageants, a wild horse race and generous doses of civic pride, it exemplifies the living history that makes Tuscany so brilliantly compelling.

☆ Lucca Summer Festival

This month-long music festival (www.summer-festival.com) lures big-name international pop, rock and blues acts to lovely Lucca, where they serenade crowds under the stars in some of the city's most atmospheric piazzas.

⚜ Medieval Evenings

Oh, how apt for Suvereto, one of Tuscany's most beautiful medieval villages on the Etruscan Coast, to be the charming host to July's Serate Medioevali (Medieval Evenings). The festival transforms the serene, red-brick cloister of 13th-century Convento di San Francesco into a bustling medieval marketplace.

☆ Joust of the Bear

Medieval jousting and other equestrian pranks fill Piazza del Duomo during Pistoia's Giostra dell'Orso (Joust of the Bear), a celebration of its patron saint San Giacomo on 25 July.

August

Locals take their annual holidays and the daily tempo of life in the cities slows to a snail's pace. The weather can be oppressively hot and beaches are inevitably crowded.

⚜ Volterra AD 1398

On the third and fourth Sundays of August, locals in Volterra roll back the calendar some 600 years, take to the streets in period costume and party like it's 1398 (www.volterra1398.it).

⚜ Bravio delle Botti

Thick-armed men from Montepulciano's eight *contrade* (districts) flex their muscles and bust a gut to push 80kg wine barrels uphill in this compelling race (www.braviodellebotti.com), held in the wine-producing town on the last Sunday in August.

🔒 Shop for Antiques

Head to eastern Tuscany in late August or early September for antiques market Cortonantiquaria (www.cortonantiquaria.it), inside Cortona's 18th-century Palazzo Vagnotti. Twin it with Tuscany's most famous antiques fair, Fiera Antiquaria di Arezzo, held in Arezzo the first Sunday and preceding Saturday of every month.

September

Gourmets, this is the Tuscan month for you. Autumn (fall) ushers in La Vendemmia (the grape harvest) and a bounty of scented *porcini* mushrooms and creamy chestnuts in the forests.

🍷 Settembre diVino di Pitigliano

Wine aficionados, prepare your tasting palate for plenty of dry and lively white Bianco di Pitigliano at this popular *festa delle cantine* (wine-cellar festival), held the first weekend of September in the spectacular hilltop town of Pitigliano in southern Tuscany.

🍷 Chianti Classico Wine Fair

There is no finer or more fun opportunity to taste Chianti Classico than at Greve in Chianti's annual Chianti Classico Expo (www.expochianticlassico.com), the second weekend in September. Festivities begin the preceding Thursday. Buy a glass and swirl, sniff, sip and spit your way around.

⚜ Palio della Ballestra

Sansepolcro's party-loving locals don medieval costumes and peacock around town on the second Sunday of September while hosting a crossbow tournament between local archers and rivals from the nearby Umbrian town of Gubbio.

☆ Festival Barocco di San Gimignano

Lovers of baroque music will be in their element during this classical-music fest that graces the town of San Gimignano with a wonderful series of concerts (www.accademiadeileggieri.org) on September weekends.

November

This is when restaurateurs and truffle tragics come from every corner of the globe to sample and purchase Tuscany's bounty of strong-smelling and delicious white truffles.

✗ Mostra Mercato Nazionale del Tartufo Bianco

The old stone streets of San Miniato are filled with one of the world's most distinctive aromas at the National White Truffle Market, held on the last three weekends in November.

Itineraries

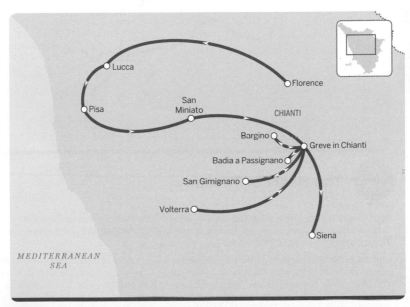

Lucca

Florence

Pisa

San Miniato

CHIANTI

Bargino

Greve in Chianti

Badia a Passignano

San Gimignano

Volterra

Siena

MEDITERRANEAN SEA

 Tuscan Greatest Hits

This road trip takes in a classic Tuscan mix of world-class art, medieval architecture, gorgeous rolling countryside and outstanding food and wine.

Devote three days to exploring Renaissance **Florence**. Visit the Uffizi and meander the Arno riverbanks. Spend day two discovering opulent Medici chapels, extraordinary frescoes and Michelangelo's *David* in San Marco and San Lorenzo. Third day, lose yourself in the Oltrarno's ancient web of squares and alleys laced with artists' workshops.

Day four, shift down a gear to go slow in 16th-century walled **Lucca**. Rent a bicycle to leisurely explore enchanting cobbled streets and graceful, butter-coloured piazzas. Day five, head to **Pisa** early to climb the Leaning Tower then hit the east-bound road to Chianti with a break in foodie town **San Miniato** for lunch. Use a Tuscan farmhouse around **Greve in Chianti** as a base for three days to gorge on the magically preserved medieval town of **San Gimignano**, artistic enclave **Volterra** and Antinori wine cellars in **Bargino** and **Badia a Passignano**. End in Gothic **Siena** for a two-day dose of breathlessly beautiful piazzas, churches, museums and eateries.

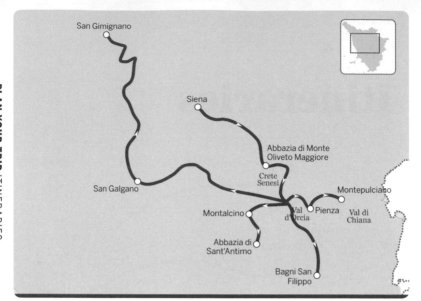

 The Heart of Tuscany

For those in the region for a limited amount of time, this itinerary through central Tuscany more than lives up to the Tuscan dream of gently rolling hills, medieval towns, Renaissance splendour and some very fine wine indeed.

Start in **Siena**, historic rival to Florence, with a walking tour of the city, the perfect prelude to the Gothic symphony this iconic Tuscan city is. Gravitate towards the Museo Civico and Opera della Metropolitana di Siena to explore each in greater depth. Break with a *caffè* on a pavement terrace on famously sloping Piazza del Campo, or nip down the street for Sienese biscuits at nearby Panificio Il Magnifico. Continue your city exploration: Siena's intact *centro storico* (historic centre) is a Unesco World Heritage site for good reason.

Day two (or three if Siena begs you to linger), motor south through the rolling hills and cypress alleys of Crete Senesi to monastery **Abbazia di Monte Oliveto Maggiore**, a wonderful monastery with spectacular frescoes. Continue southeast to Unesco-loved **Pienza**, a stroke of Renaissance architectural genius which, with its many sleeping and eating options in and around town, is a brilliant base for exploring this neck of the Tuscan woods. Spend the next three days pandering to your culture-hungry soul and appetite for world-class wine and food. In the Val d'Orcia tour vineyards around **Montalcino**, listen to Gregorian chants at **Abbazia di Sant'Antimo,** wander through the ruined Cistercian abbey of **San Galgano**, and soak in hot cascades at **Bagni San Filippo**. In the gourmet Val di Chiana, anchored by wine town **Montepulciano**, sink your teeth into a slab of local Chianina beef, slicked in fragrant olive oil and accompanied by a glass of Brunello di Montalcino or Vino Nobile di Montepulciano (two of Italy's greatest wines).

End your sojourn in this idyllic area by looping back along scenic secondary roads to romantic **San Gimignano**, home to medieval tower houses, lavishly frescoed *duomo* (cathedral) and cutting-edge contemporary art. Dine on delicate pasta dishes scented with locally grown saffron, drink the town's golden-hued Vernaccia wine and, whatever you do, don't miss out on the superb saffron-and-Vernaccia sorbet by former gelato world champion Sergio Dondoli.

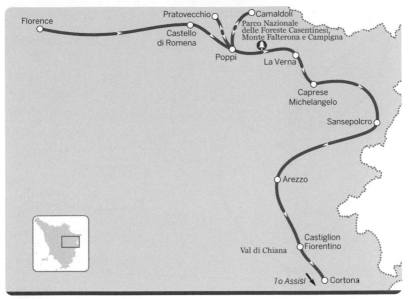

Into the East

The perfect trip for Tuscan connoisseurs, this itinerary varies the pace with an edgy mix of well-known destinations and intriguing off-the-beaten-track alternatives.

Spend three days admiring the Renaissance splendour of **Florence** before motoring east into the Casentino region, home to the isolated Parco Nazionale delle Foreste Casentinesi, Monte Falterona e Campigna. Base yourself around the fortified hill town of **Poppi** for three days (Borgo Corsignano in the hamlet of Corsignano is a grand choice) and visit medieval monasteries in **Camaldoli** and **La Verna**, wander evocative ruins at **Castello di Romena**, hike trails in the national park, and dine well after dark in **Pratovecchio**.

Next head southeast. Stop in the village of **Caprese Michelangelo** to see where *David*'s creator grew up. Then continue to **Sansepolcro**, proud possessor of masterpieces by the Renaissance painter, Piero della Francesca.

Tear yourself away after two nights and continue to your final destination, the Val de Chiana, where you can spend a few days eating, drinking and sightseeing your way around the valley. Allow a full day for provincial capital **Arezzo**, with its sloping square and cafe life. Get acquainted with the architect who designed Florence's Uffizi gallery at the Museo di Casa Vasari, and spend a quiet moment in the town's churches – Cappella Bacci, Pieve di Santa Maria and the *duomo* are highlights. Join locals for lunch at Antica Osteria Agania, then walk it off with a late afternoon *passeggiata* (stroll) on shop-lined Corso Italia.

Foodies are obliged to make the medieval hilltop town of **Castiglion Fiorentino** a port of call. Tuscany's famed Chianina cow hails from this valley and the *bistecca fiorentina* (T-bone steak) served at Ristorante Da Muzzicone is the best there is.

Devote at least a half-day to **Cortona**. Walk up steep cobbled streets to its Fortezza Medicea, and admire the collections at the Museo dell'Accademia Etrusca and the Museo Diocesano. From Cortona, it is an easy day trip to Assisi, one of Italy's most famous pilgrimage centres in the neighbouring region of Umbria. Fans of Giotto's extraordinary frescoes will have a field day.

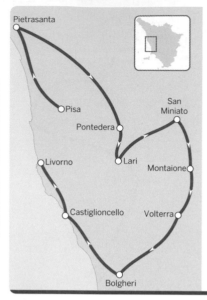

1 WEEK — Pisa to Livorno

This part of Tuscany is not as well trodden as others. Tick off Pisa's icon before indulging in a crowd-free road south to the coast.

Start in **Pisa**, allowing time for the Museo Nazionale di San Matteo as well Piazza dei Miracoli. Scale the famous engineering project gone horribly wrong, aka the Leaning Tower. Come dusk, hit art town **Pietrasanta** for an excellent dinner and overnight stay. Day two, pay homage to Italy's Vespa scooter at **Pontedera**'s Museo Piaggio or skip the scooters to see spaghetti being made in **Lari**. Lunch in the village then motor to gourmet town **San Miniato**. Overnight at Barbialla Nuova at **Montaione** and, if the season's right, hunt white truffles.

From here, head to spectacularly sited **Volterra** in the Val di Cecina to visit alabaster ateliers and Etruscan art. Fourth day, move to the coast where wine lovers can meander south to taste Super Tuscan Sassicaias in **Bolgheri**; overnight in the walled village or at La Cerreta in nearby Pian delle Vigne. Then drive north along the Etruscan Coast, lingering in the old-fashioned seaside resort of **Castiglioncello** should the hustle and bustle of port city **Livorno** not appeal straight away.

1 WEEK — The Maremma

Outdoor lovers will have a field day in southern Tuscany, where dramatic landscapes etched out of volcanic porous rock, local cowboy culture and a heap of wild activities provide a welcome adrenalin boost.

Revel in the great outdoors in southern Tuscany. Start in the delightful medieval town of **Massa Marittima** and spend a couple of days visiting its museums and sampling Maremmese food and wine in its rustic eateries. On day three, check out an archaeological dig, Etruscan tombs and an impressive museum at the ancient hilltop settlement of **Vetulonia**; overnight in a local *agriturismo*. From here, head down the coast to the wild and wonderful **Parco Regionale della Maremma** to walk, canoe, cycle or horse ride alongside the famous cowboys known as the *butteri*. End your journey inland amid the surrounds of the Città del Tufa (City of the Tufa), where you should visit the towns of **Pitigliano**, **Sovana** and **Sorano**. Here you can sample the local Morellino di Scansano wine at **Società Agricola Terenzi**; explore the Etruscan necropolises at the **Parco Archeologico 'Città del Tufa'**; and spend a day taking an 8km walk along the sunken roads known as *vie cave*.

Plan Your Trip
Staying in Tuscany

Selecting the right Tuscan crashpad for you is the first step towards a fabulous holiday. Tuscany is blessed with accommodation styles and options to suit every taste, budget and energy level – in cities and hilltop towns, by the sea and deep in the lush green countryside at the end of a bumpy dirt track.

Choosing Your Accommodation

Tuscany spoils you for choice when it comes to places to stay, so it pays to research thoroughly. Always check hotel websites for good-value internet deals – the cheapest rates require advance payment, are non-reimbursable and non-exchangeable. The following price ranges refer to a double room with private bathroom; unless otherwise stated, breakfast is included in the price.

€ less than €110

€€ €110–200

€€€ more than €200

Accommodation Types

Affittacamere A budget room in a private house.

Agriturismo A working farm or winery with rooms; family-run and often with evening dining. By definition, an *agriturismo* is required to grow at least one commercial crop, but beyond this common thread they run the gamut from a rustic country house with a handful of olive trees to a luxurious country estate with an attached vineyard to a fully functioning farm where guests can help with the harvest.

Albergo A hotel, be it budget or business, luxurious or a characterful midrange choice.

Accommodation Highlights

Best Agriturismi

Il Paluffo (p151) Luxurious ecological oasis near San Gimignano.

Sant' Egle (p181) Organic retreat with bio pool, hot tub, and bread- and cheese-making classes.

Podere San Lorenzo (p155) Idyllic olive farm.

Agriturismo Due Palme (p209) Citrus-scented sleep in an Elba olive grove.

Best Palazzi

Antica Torre di Via de' Tornabuoni 1 (p92) Views of Florence at breakfast don't get better.

Palazzo Magnani Feroni (p99) Opulent furnishings and a sky-high roof terrace in Florence.

Pensione Palazzo Ravizza (p132) Sienese cocktail of heritage and luxury.

La Corte di Ambra (p273) Cortona *palazzo* B&B with every mod-con (lift included).

Best on a Budget

Hotel Scoti (p92) *Palazzo* living in Florence on fashionable Via de' Tornabuoni.

Hotel Alma Domus (p131) Sleeping in a Siena aka (stylish) convent.

Albergo Bartoli (p195) Impeccably kept villa with garden by the sea.

Il Tufo Rosa (p179) Kip countess-style in the bastion of a fortress in Pitigliano.

TOP TIPS

➡ Print out location information from your hotel's website; many places in cities are hidden in hard-to-find laneways, and country retreats are often in obscure locations that don't appear on standard road maps. GPS can be unreliable when it comes to navigating un-named lanes and Tuscan dirt tracks.

➡ If driving, check with the hotel as to the most convenient and cost-effective place to park. In towns and cities with pedestrian-only old towns, beware the infamous Zona a Traffico Limitato (ZTL; Limited Traffic Zones).

➡ Ask hotel staff for restaurant recommendations – they often know about great local eateries and will usually be happy to make reservations for you.

➡ If you're allergic to animals, mention this when booking. Many country hotels have cats and dogs.

➡ It's often possible to negotiate a discount if you stay five nights or more.

B&B A small guesthouse offering bed and breakfast; double rooms have private bathroom.

Boutique hotel Small stylish hotel, midrange to top end, with a select, intimate vibe.

Castello Literally a castle but in reality anything from a converted outbuilding on a farm (such as Castello di Bolgheri (p196)) to a fully fledged castle with crenellated towers like the swoonworthy Castello delle Serre (p132). Whatever it's architectural shape, bags of charm and atmosphere are guaranteed.

Country hotel Tuscan rural retreat ranging from wonderful self-catering properties in a *borgo* (medieval hamlet) such as Borgo Corsignano (p267) to luxurious spa hotels and large country resorts like Montebelli Agriturismo & Country Hotel (p176) with every facility imaginable.

Locanda A country inn offering B&B in rustic surrounds; most provide dinner.

Ostello A hostel offering dorm beds and rooms to budget travellers.

Palazzo hotel Many hotels in towns and cities languish in century-old *palazzi* – literally 'palaces' but in reality historic mansions; some have original frescoes and furnishings, others are thoroughly contemporary in design.

Pensione A small, family-run guesthouse offering B&B; the owners live on site.

Rifugio A mountain hut kitted out with bunk rooms sleeping two to a dozen or more people; half-board; open mid-June to mid-September.

Villa Self-catering villas and *fattorie* (farmhouses) can be rented in their entirety; most have swimming pools and dreamy green surrounds.

Booking Your Accommodation

It is wise to book well ahead for all accommodation in this region, particularly in Florence and Siena and along the coast in summer. During busy periods, some hotels may impose a multinight stay (this usually applies at beach hotels over July and August, and always applies in Siena during the Palio). Country hotels, *locande,* villas and *agriturismi* often close in winter.

Most hotels will give you the choice of a *camera doppia* (room with twin beds) or a *camera matrimoniale* (room with double bed). Many hotels do not have *camera singola* (single rooms); instead, lone travellers will pay a slightly reduced price for a double room.

Credit cards are accepted at many – but not all – places to stay. MasterCard and Visa are more widely accepted than American Express or Diners Club International. When booking directly with the hotel, a deposit of up to 30% may be requested by the establishment.

BOOK YOUR STAY ONLINE

For more accommodation reviews by Lonely Planet authors, check out lonelyplanet.com/hotels/. You'll find independent reviews, as well as recommendations on the best places to stay. Best of all, you can book online.

USEFUL RESOURCES

When it comes to scouting out the accommodation of your Tuscan dreams, there's ample online resources to aid, abet and inspire.

Associazione Italiana Alberghi per la Gioventù (www.aighostels.com) Association of Italian Youth Hostels, affiliated with Hostelling International (HI).

Camping.it (www.camping.it) Directory of camp sites in Tuscany.

Club Alpino Italiano (www.cai.it) Database of CAI-operated *rifugi* (mountain huts).

Lungarno Collection (www.lungarnocollection.com) Boutique collection of luxurious hotels owned by the Ferragamo fashion empire, ranging from penthouse suites in Florence to tropical paradise resorts on the Tuscan coast.

Monastery Stays (www.monasterystays.com) A well-organised online booking centre for monastery and convent stays.

Turismo in Toscana (www.turismo.intoscana.it) Work out where to stay with the website of the Tuscany tourist board; sort by destination, type of stay (countryside, seaside, mountains, spa), or theme (family travel, architecture, gay friendly).

Wtb Hotels (www.whythebesthotels.com) Florence-based hotel group.

What to Expect

You can expect a warm welcome, particularly when staying in rural areas. Whether they be cosy *pensioni,* grand villas or sleek boutique hotels, Tuscan sleeping choices inevitably have personable and professional staff and offer clean and comfortable rooms.

Hotels are nonsmoking by national law and many offer accommodation for mobility-impaired guests. Most offer free wi-fi and/or an internet kiosk.

Leisure Facilities

Country hotels often offer some leisure activities. Swimming pools are commonplace (usually open May to September), and many hotels have mountain bikes for guests to borrow. Tennis courts, horse stables and wellness centres are less common; horse-riding and certain spa and wellness treatments incur an extra charge.

Dining

Breakfast is generally included in hotel rates and can be anything from a coffee and *cornetto* (croissant) to a full Western-style buffet with ham, salami, cheese, cakes, fruit, yoghurt and so on. Breakfast in *agriturismi* tends to be a lavish feast of farm products and home cooking. Many also cook up dinner, as do some boutique hotels and B&Bs, usually in the form of a set dinner menu that changes daily depending on what's hot at the market that morning. Some favourites with recommended evening dining:

Podere San Lorenzo (p155) Gourmet dining in an old 12th century chapel

La Bandita (p163) Sophisticated urban chic melds with stupendous scenery in the Val d'Orcia.

La Cerreta (p198) Biodynamic estate with farm-produce dining, spa and quintessential 'Tuscan hills' panorama.

Fattoria San Martino (p166) Vegetarian dining in a restored 12th-century farmhouse.

Villa Sassolini (p145) Intimate dining in a romantic villa in Chianti.

Grand Hotel Palazzo (p192) Stunning palace rooftop dining with seaview in Livorno.

Hotel Tax

Cities and towns in Tuscany (and Italy) charge a *tassa di soggiorno* (hotel occupancy tax) on top of advertised hotel rates. It is always charged on top of your hotel bill and must generally be paid in cash. The exact amount, which varies from city to city, depends on how many spangly stars your hotel is endowed with and the time of year. Expect to pay €1.50 per person per night in a one-star hotel or hostel, €2.50 in a B&B, €1.50 to €3.50 in an *agriturismo*, €3.50 in a three-star hotel and up to €5 in a four- or five-star hotel. Children under 10 or 12 are generally not taxed; those aged 11 to 16 are usually charged 50% of the adult tax.

Florentine delicatessen

Plan Your Trip

Eat & Drink Like a Local

For Tuscans, eating and drinking is as much a fine art as their masterpiece surrounds. And exceedingly well, seated around a shared table, is how they eat, thanks to an ancient cuisine sourced in the family farmstead from seasonal fruits of the land and sea. Titillate your tastebuds with these food-trip essentials.

BRENDA THARP/GETTY IMAGES ©

The Year in Food

Feasting is year-round, with foodie festivals galore.

Spring (Mar–May)

Markets burst with baby violet artichokes, asparagus, fresh garlic and – towards the season's end – cherries, figs and courgette flowers begging to be stuffed.

Summer (Jun–Aug)

Strawberries, peppers and the start of San Gimignano's saffron harvest (July to November). Beat the heat by the sea with seafood, elsewhere with a gelato – chestnut, fig and honey, or saffron and pine-nut flavour.

Autumn (Sep–Nov)

Olives and grapes are harvested, forest fruits like chestnuts and *porcini* mushrooms (August to October) gathered, and game hunted. Oenophiles head to Greve in Chianti in September for Chianti's biggest wine fair. Mid-October opens the white truffle season near Pisa.

Winter (Dec–Feb)

The truffle season, which continues until mid-December, peaks with San Miniato's truffle market in November. Montalcino wine producers crack open the new vintage at February's Benvenuto Brunello.

Food Experiences

Dining in Tuscany covers the whole gamut of street food to chic farm tables and posh-frock gastronomic temples. Plan ahead to cover all delicious bases.

Meals of a Lifetime

Enoteca Pinchiorri, Florence (p103) Tuscany's only Michelin three-star address, stratospheric and smug in a 16th-century Florentine *palazzo*.

Peperino, San Miniato (p242) Dinner for two at the world's smallest, and possibly most romantic, restaurant.

Barbialla Nuova, Montaione (p241) Hunt white truffles in damp musky woods, then head to a village trattoria to eat it shaved over steak.

Il Pellicano, Monte Argentario (p186) Sensational seafood dishes and glorious sea views.

Il Leccio, Sant'Angelo in Colle (p158) Simple but spectacular cuisine sourced from the garden, washed down with extraordinary Brunellos.

Osteria di Passignano, Chianti (p140) Elegant, wine-fuelled dining on an Antinori estate. It doesn't get more Tuscan glam than this.

Cheap Treats

Pecorino Ewe's-milk cheese perfect in fresh, crunchy *pane* (bread).

Porchetta rolls Warm sliced pork (roasted whole with fennel, garlic and pepper) in a crispy roll.

Torta di ceci Savoury chickpea pancake.

Castagnaccio Hybrid cake-crepe, sweet and made from chestnut flour.

Gelato The best Tuscan ice cream uses seasonal, natural ingredients: figs, chestnuts, pine nuts, honey, saffron, wild strawberries...

Dare to Try

Bistecca alla fiorentina Blue and bloody is the only way to eat Florence's iconic T-bone steak; Trattoria Mario (p101) is the best address.

Lampredotto Cow's fourth stomach, chopped, simmered and cooked up at every Florentine *trippaio*.

Trippa alla fiorentina Tripe in tomato sauce, once eaten, never forgotten at Da Nerbone (p101) in Florence's Mercato Centrale.

Lardo di Colonnata Carrara's luscious pig lard, aged in marble vats, keeps cardiologists in the black.

Biroldo Local version of haggis, included in tastings at Osteria Vecchia Mulino (p243) in Castelnuovo di Garfagnana.

Mallegato San Miniato's Slow Food–accredited blood sausage, always on the menu at Podere del Grillo (p241).

Local Specialities

Spicy green olives, extra-virgin olive oils, full-bodied red wines, smoky *porcini* mushrooms and bags of beans are culinary trademarks across the Tuscan board, but delve deeper to discover geographic differences every gourmand will revel in.

Florence

Tuscany's leading lady is a born-and-bred gourmet. Be it slow food or fine dining, *panino* in a piazza or tripe at a street cart, Florence meets every gastronomic taste with style and panache.

The day's end ushers in **aperitivi** (predinner drinks), a sacrosanct ritual big and buzzing in Tuscany's largest city: so copious are the complimentary buffets of snacks and nibbles laid out to accompany drinks that savvy young Florentines increasingly forgo dinner for **apericena** (*aperitivi* and dinner rolled into one).

Northwestern Tuscany

Wedged between wind-whipped sea and mountain, this unexpected culinary nestegg is known for its fresh *pecorino* cheese, *zuppe di cavolo* (cabbage soup) and other humble farm fare. Slow Food town San Miniato, near Pisa, is the source of Tuscany's exceptional white truffles.

White truffles

WHITE TRUFFLES

They're not a plant, they don't spawn like mushrooms and cultivating them is impossible. Pig-ugly yet precious, these wild knobs of fungus excite and titillate. Said to have aphrodisiacal qualities, one whiff of their pungent aroma is enough to convince: the smell of truffles, especially the more pungent white truffle, is seductive. Or rather, the smell is the taste (think fresh mint without its smell).

Truffles grow in symbiosis with oak trees and are *bianco* (white – actually a mouldy old yellowish colour) or *nero* (black – a gorgeous velvety tone). They are sniffed out by dogs from mid-October to late December, in San Giovanni d'Asso near Siena, and San Miniato, between Florence and Pisa. Truffles are typically served raw and thinly shaved over simple, mild-tasting dishes to give the palate full opportunity to revel in the subtle flavour. Our favourite truffle tastings:

Barbialla Nuova, Montaione (p241) Tuscany's golden ticket for hunting white truffles.

Pepenero, San Miniato (p242) Celebrity chef Gilberto Rossi gives truffles a creative spin.

Ristorante Da Ventura, Sansepolcro (p266) Nothing beats a simple omelette sprinkled with fresh truffle shavings.

Locanda Sant'Agostino, San Gimignano (p150) Glorious white truffles in an Italian grandma's kitchen.

Il Pino, San Gimignano (p150) Truffle dining in an elegant, vaulted eatery.

I Sette Consoli, Orvieto (p167) Special dishes of the day celebrate the truffle season.

Olio & Convivium (p105), Florence

In **Castelnuovo di Garfagnana**, fresh *porcini*, chestnuts and sacks of farm-grown *farro* (spelt) fill autumnal markets. Sweet *castagnaccio* (chestnut cake) is to locals in Garfagnana what *buccellato* (a sugared bread loaf studded with sultanas and aniseed) is to those in Lucca.

Not far from the coast, pig fat is aged in Carrara-marble vats and eaten 12 or 24 months later as wafer-thin, aromatic slices of *lardo di Colonnata*.

Central Coast & Elba

Two words: sensational seafood. The grimy port of **Livorno** is the place to feast on superb affordable dining and **cacciucco,** a zesty fish stew swimming with octopus, rock fish and a shoal of other species.

Inland, vineyards around the walled village of **Bolgheri** produce Super Tuscan Sassicaia and other legendary full-bodied reds – a perfect match for *cinghiale* (wild boar). On **Elba**, sweet red Aleatico Passito DOCG is the nectar amid the raft of sun-drenched wines grown on the island; spunky olive oils, too.

Siena & Central Tuscany

Siena is the GPS coordinate where Tuscan cuisine originates, say locals, for whom *caffè* (coffee) and a slice of *panforte* (a rich cake of almonds, honey and candied fruit) is a mandatory part of their weekend diet.

Chianti is for serious foodies: cheery, dry, full red wines; butcher legend Dario Cecchini in Panzano in Chianti; tip-top Chianti Classico DOP olive oils; *finocchiona briciolona* (pork salami made with fennel seeds and Chianti) from Antica Macellerìa Falorni (p137) in Greve in Chianti; and some of Tuscany's most exciting, Modern Tuscan cuisine.

BEST COOKING CLASSES

➡ Desinare (p89), Florence

➡ Cucina Lorenzo de' Medici (p89), Florence

➡ Pepenero (p242), San Miniato

➡ Podere San Lorenzo (p155), near Volterra

➡ Strada del Vino Nobile di Montepulciano (p165), Montepulciano

Different flavours of gelati

tasty *primo* (first course) of *pici* (a type of local hand-rolled pasta).

Something of a culinary curiosity, fiery red **San Gimignano** saffron was the first in Europe to get its own DOP (protected origin) stamp of quality. Saffron gelato at San Gimignano's Gelateria Dondoli (p150) is predictably memorable.

Southern Tuscany

When it comes to quality-guaranteed beef, chicken and game, Maremma is the byword. **Grosseto** is the Mecca for the sweet-toothed thanks to handmade biscuits (including traditional Jewish honey-and-walnut pastry, *lo sfratto*) from Dolci Tradizioni dalla Maremma Toscana (p183).

Then there's Pitigliano's very own DOC Bianco di Pitigliano, a fresh and fruity, Trebbiano-based white wine.

Montalcino is famed for red Brunello wine, the consistently good Rosso di Montalcino and prized extra-virgin olive oils. **Montepulciano,** home of Vino Nobile red and its equally quaffable second-string Rosso di Montepulciano, also produces fine beef and Terre di Siena DOP extra-virgin olive oil.

Cheese aficionados make a beeline for **Pienza,** where some of Italy's finest *pecorino* is crafted; and the **Val di Chiana** where sheep cheese is wrapped in fern fronds to become *ravaggiolo.* The same gorgeous rolling green valley is also where the world-famous Chianina beef comes from, making it the perfect place to sample *bistecca alla fiorentina,* perhaps after a

BEST WINES

- ➡ Brunello di Montalcino
- ➡ Vino Nobile di Montepulciano
- ➡ Chianti
- ➡ Vernaccia di San Gimignano
- ➡ Super Tuscan Sassicaia

How to Eat & Drink

It pays to know what and how much to eat, and when – adopting the local pace is key to savouring every last exquisite gastronomic moment of the Tuscan day. For an explanation of the dishes you'll find on Italian menus, see p337.

When to Eat

Colazione (breakfast) is a quick dash into a bar or cafe for a short sharp espresso and *cornetto* (croissant) or *brioche* (pastry) standing at the bar.

Pranzo (lunch) is traditionally the main meal of the day, though Tuscans now tend to share the main family meal in the evening. Standard restaurant times are noon or 12.30pm to 2.30pm; locals rarely lunch before 1pm.

Aperitivo (*aperitif*) is the post-work, early-evening drink that takes place any time between 5pm and 10pm when the price of your cocktail (€8 to €10 in Florence) includes a copious buffet of nibbles, finger foods, or even salads, pasta and so on.

Cena (dinner) has traditionally been lighter than lunch. The traditional Tuscan belt-busting, five-course whammy only happens on Sunday and feast days. Standard restaurant times are 7.30pm to around 10pm (often later in Florence and across the board in summer); locals never eat before 8pm.

RIBOLLITA
TOSCANA
8000 Kg.

Top: Ingredients for *ribollita*, a thick vegetable , bread and bean soup

Bottom: A selection of cheeses for sale

RUSSELL MOUNTFORD/GETTY IMAGES ©

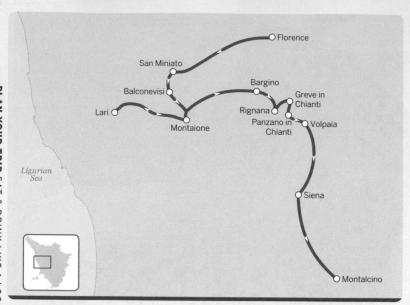

Foodie Itinerary: Florence to Siena

1 WEEK

To taste, drink and dine exceedingly well, take your tastebuds on this tasty road trip through the gourmet heart of Tuscany.

No city plays the gourmet better than **Florence** (p99): shop for olive oils at La Bottega Della Frutta and Mercato Centrale, then nip across the road for lunch at Trattoria Mario. If you need an espresso to round off the meal, gin and coffee bar Ditta Artigianale is a first-class address. Later, indulge in chocolate *degustazione* (tasting) with local foodie Alessandro Frassica at 'Ino and a gelato across the river at Gelateria La Carraia. At dusk join Florentine gastronomes for *aperitivo* at Il Santino, All'Antico Vinaio (superb salami and cheese tasting platters) or Culinaria Bistrot. Florence's fabulous *enoteche* (wine bars) such as Le Volpi e l'Uva and Coquinarius make tip-top *aperitif* stops. Round off the evening with a light mozzarella and violet-artichoke supper at Obicà; super modern Tuscan dinner at iO Osteria Personale; or a theatrical supper with legendary Florentine chef Fabio Picchi at Il Teatro del Sale.

Day two, motor 30km into rolling hills around **San Miniato** (p241), a Slow Food town with superb lunch options. Afterwards, pick up an afternoon tasting itinerary from Slow Food. Indulge in an *aperitif* at Podere del Grillo and dinner at Osteria Il Papero in the hilltop hamlet of Balconevisi (p241). Overnight on white-truffle estate Barbialla Nuova in **Montaione** (p241).

Next morning, drive one hour west to **Lari** (p194) to watch artisan pasta makers at work at Martelli; or dive into **Chianti** for a cellar visit and lunch at the stunning flagship Antinori nel Chianti Classico in **Bargino** (p138). Eat and overnight at **Rignana** (p138).

It's a short drive next day to **Greve in Chianti** (p137) for Enoteca Falorni, the biggest wine cellar in Chianti, stocking more than 1000 wines. Buy *finocchiona briciolona* (fennel-pork salami) for a picnic lunch at Antica Macelleria Falorni and end the day at Badia a Passignano.

Day five, drive south to **Panzano in Chianti** (p144). Lunch with Tuscany's celebrity butcher Dario, and take a cooking class at wine and olive oil estate **Castello di Volpaia** (p144). Overnight in **Siena** (p121) with Enoteca I Terzi for dinner. Next day, shop for *panforte* to take home at Panificio Il Magnifico, then drive to **Montalcino** (p157) for a cellar tour and lunch with award-winning Brunellos at Poggio Antico. End on a culinary high at La Bandita.

Wood-fired pizza, fresh out of the oven

Where to Eat

In a **ristorante** (restaurant) expect to find crisp linen, classic furnishings, formal service and refined dishes. A **trattoria** is a restaurant, often family-owned with cheaper prices, more relaxed service and classic regional specialities. Intimate and relaxed, the **osteria** has its origins in a traditional inn serving wine with a little food on the side; these days it's hard to differentiate between an *osteria* and trattoria. For a cheap feed, cold beer and a buzzing, convivial vibe, head for a **pizzeria**.

Wine bars (**enoteca**) are increasingly casual, atmospheric places to dine and taste Tuscan wines by the glass.

Dining on a farm at an **agriturismo** (farm stay) is the best of Tuscany – a never-ending feast of homemade cooking with local produce, against a quintessential Tuscan backdrop of old stone farmhouse, cypress alley and pea-green rolling hills.

At the **gelateria** (ice-cream shop), rain, hail or shine, a queue outside the door marks the best of ice-cream shops. The astonishing choice of flavours will have you longing for an Italian ice cream long after you've left Tuscany.

Menu Decoder

Menù di degustazione Tasting menu.

Coperto Cover charge, €1 to €3 per person, for bread.

Piatto del giorno Dish of the day.

Antipasto A hot or cold appetiser; for a mix of appetisers go for *antipasto misto* (mixed antipasto).

Primo First course, usually pasta, rice or *zuppa* (soup).

Secondo Second course, *carne* (meat) or *pesce* (fish).

Contorno Vegetable side dish.

Dolce Dessert, often *torta* (cake) or *cantucci* (dry almond-studded biscuits) dunked into a glass of sweet Vin Santo wine.

Acqua minerale (mineral water) Jugs of tap water aren't in, but a bottle of *frizzante* (sparkling) or *naturale* (still) with a meal is a Tuscan standard.

Vino della casa (house wine) Wine in restaurants is reasonably priced and good; the cheapest is house wine, ordered in carafes of 25cl, 50cl, 75cl or a litre.

Plan Your Trip
Outdoor Experiences

High mountains, gentle hills, pristine shores. Tuscany's natural environments deliver irresistible activities. Hiking, cycling, sailing; kayaking, diving, riding – you can do them all here amid superb scenery. In fact, along with the culture, food and wine, it's these memorable outdoor adventures that make Tuscany a must-come-back-to place.

Top Outdoor Experiences

Best Short Walks

Vie cave, along Etruscan sunken roads below **Pitigliano** (p178)

Guided nature walks in the hills around **San Gimignano** (p148)

Montalcino to Abbazia di Sant'Antimo, **Val d'Orcia** (p161)

Best Easy Bike Rides

With elegance atop the city walls of **Lucca** (p227)

Around vineyards and olive groves in **Chianti** (p141)

Island touring in **Elba** (p205)

Best on the Water

Slicing silent waterways with a canoe, **Parco Regionale della Maremma** (p184)

Sea kayaking and diving offshore from **Elba** (p203)

Best Spa Towns

Old English literati fave **Bagni di Lucca** (p246)

Ancient Roman soak **Terme di Saturnia** (p181)

Puccini's favourite: **Terme di Montecatini** (www.termemontecatini.it)

When to Go?

Lapping up all that sea and mountain air, heady with scents of wild sage and pine, is an integral part of the Tuscan outdoor experience. Spring and autumn, with their warm dry days, wildflowers and forest fruits, are the most picturesque times to be outdoors. July (less hot and crowded than August) is the best month for water-sports and hiking in the Apuane Alps. Autumn, when the wine and olive harvests start, has a particularly mellow appeal and, with summer's warmth lingering well into October, there's plenty of daylight for dewy-morning hikes through mushroom-rich forests and crunchy leaves.

Avoid

Easter The first key period of the Italian holiday year, this two-week slot in late-March or April sees too many people jostle for too little trail space.

August Italians take their summer holidays, crowding paths, cycle routes and roads. On lower terrain, August's intense heat can be oppressive.

Winter Often means wet, slippery roads and poor visibility for cyclists.

Where to Go

Chianti Tuscany's key wine-growing area enables easy walking and cycling between achingly pretty vine and olive groves (p141).

Apuane Alps & Garfagnana Ruggedly scenic and remote with the region's most dramatic mountains, marble quarries and forested valleys: hiking, caving, mountain biking and horse riding (p242).

Etruscan Coast Hit the beach in July and August, for sand, sea and water-sport action. Cycling varies from dirt track to silky smooth terrain (p194).

Elba A summer island idyll with stunning sea kayaking, sailing, diving and snorkelling; beautiful hiking between coves through scented *macchia* (herbal scrub) and parasol pines (p203).

Val d'Orcia Family walking and cycling near **Siena** (p157).

Maremma Hiking, biking, horse riding and backwater canoeing on Tuscany's southern coast (p184).

Activity specialists include **Toscana Adventure Team** (☏348 791 12 15; www. tateam.it; Casa Carbonaia, Via di Santa Lucia 11, Vinci), which organises everything from mountain biking and horse riding to coasteering, heli biking, abseiling, hiking and caving. Also try **Hedonistic Hiking** (☏Australia +61 3 5755 2307, UK +44 1858 565148; www.hedonistichiking.com.au), which offers treks around Volterra, Pisa, Elba, Lucca, Chianti and Siena with luxurious villa accommodation and gourmet meals.

Maps

Florentine cartographer Edizioni Multigraphic (www.edizionimultigraphic. it) publishes maps featuring *sentieri* (walking trails), *mulattiere* (mule tracks, especially good for mountain bikes) and mountains huts. Its *Carte dei Sentieri* (1:25,000) and *Carte Turistica e dei Sentieri* (1:25,000 or 1:50,000) series are both available online at Omnimap (www.omnimap.com).

Information

The tourist-board website (www.turismo.intoscana.it) features background information, interactive maps and inspiring walking, cycling and horse-riding routes. It also covers caving, spas and water sports.

Throughout Tuscany, tourist offices and national-park offices have mountains of activity-related information, including lists of guides as well as accommodation options near trails. It's best to buy maps and guidebooks before leaving your home country.

Walking & Hiking

Hiking in Tuscany takes you straight to its soul. People have been criss-crossing this region on foot for millennia, and tracing those heritage-rich trails reveals the best of Tuscany today, opening up wine estates, town-crowned hills, mountains, marshes and sandy shores.

The Apuane Alps

On the spine of the Apennines, the challenging Apuane Alps and the stunning Garfagnana **valleys** (p242) are for seri-

---

BEST WALKS IF YOU LIKE ...

Etruscan ruins – Golfo di Baratti (p202), Pitigliano (p178)

Birdwatching – Riserva Naturale Provinciale Diaccia Botrona (p184), Laguna di Orbetello (p185)

Geology – Monterotondo Marittimo (p176)

Wine – Chianti, Montalcino, Montepulciano

Pilgrim paths – Marciana (p209), Abbazia di Sant'Antimo (p161)

Coastal panoramas – Monte Capanne (p209), Marciana (p209)

Art & Sculpture – Parco Sculture del Chianti (p144), Fattoria di Celle (p237)

Cowboys – Parco Regionale della Maremma (p184)

NATIONAL & REGIONAL PARKS

PARK	FEATURES
Parco Nazionale dell'Arcipelago Toscano	Europe's largest marine park, covering 180 sq km of land and 600 sq km of sea; typical Mediterranean island flora and fauna
Parco Nazionale delle Foreste Casentinesi, Monte Falterona e Campigna	source of the river Arno and Italy's most extensive, best-preserved forest: ancient pines, beech, five maple types and the rare yew; deer, wild boar, mouflon, wolves and 97 nesting bird species
Parco Regionale delle Alpi Apuane	mountainous regional park cascading to the sea from the Garfagnana; golden eagles, peregrine falcons, buzzards and the rare chough (the park's symbol)
Parco Regionale Migliarino, San Rossore, Massaciuccoli	coastal reserve stretching from Viareggio to Livorno; extraordinary birdlife (over 200 species) in its marshes, dunes and wetland
Parco Regionale della Maremma	regional park comprising the Uccellina mountains, pine forest, agricultural farmland, marshland and 20km of unspoiled coastline; oak and cork oak, herbal maquis (scrubland); Maremma cows, horses and wild boar

ous hikers. Hundreds of trails encompass everything from half-day hikes to long-distance treks. The main town, Castelnuovo di Garfagnana, is the best base camp and the place to pick up information on *rifugi* (mountain huts with dorm-style accommodation). The website of the Parco Regionale delle Alpi Apuane (www.parcapuane.it) has detailed hiking information.

Grande Escursione Appenninica

This epic 400km trek takes in the Due Santi pass situated up above La Spezia, Sansepolcro in eastern Tuscany and the Tuscan–Emilian Apennines. The route of ridge and valley hiking is split up into 23 day-long stages, peaks at 2000m and can normally be tackled between the months of April and October. Cicerone Press (www.cicerone.co.uk) publishes the guidebook *The GEA - The Grande Escursione Appenninica* (€17).

Via Francigena

Stretching from English cathedral city Canterbury to Rome, the **Via Francigena** (www.viefrancigene.org) was one of Europe's most important medieval pilgrimage routes. In north Italy it wound from the Magra river valley via the coast before cutting inland to turn south.

Thousands still walk 'Legs' (sections) of the trail today along tracks that meander beside hills and through farmland.

Tuscan highlights:

San Miniato to Gambassi Terme (Leg 29; 24km)

San Gimignano to Monteriggioni (Leg 31; 31km)

Monteriggioni to Siena (Leg 32; 20km)

Globalmap publishes the hiking map *Via Francigena in Toscana* (€8; 1:50,000), which includes routes and accommodation options; it's available from tourist offices and bookshops throughout Tuscany. The Via Francigena website above also sells guides; www.francigenalibrari.beniculturali.it features route maps and GPS coordinates.

Chianti

For some this wine- and vine-laden region is the big hiking favourite. It'll see you rambling between vineyards, wine cellars and century-old farms, then sitting down at a shared table to dine on homemade pasta, oil and wine.

One of the most popular walks is between Florence and Siena. Routes head south out of Florence, across Chianti (often via Greve and Rada in Chianti) to Siena. Handily, there are plenty of restaurants, *enoteche* and *agriturismi* along the way. Factor in distances of around 80km to 120km between the two cities (five to seven days), depending on your chosen route.

Il Mugello

Starting a few kilometres northeast of Florence, the Mugello region is ideal for half- and full-day hikes among gentle hills,

ACTIVITIES	BEST TIME TO VISIT	WEBSITE
sea kayaking, sailing, diving, snorkelling, water sports, walking, cycling, wine tasting	spring and summer	www.islepark.it
walking, hiking, birdwatching	spring and autumn	www.parcoforestecasentinesi.it
hiking, mountain biking, caving	summer and autumn	www.parcapuane.it
easy walking, cycling, horse riding, birdwatching, canoeing	spring, summer and autumn	www.parcosanrossore.org
walking, hiking, cycling, horse riding, canoeing	spring and autumn (mid-Jun–mid-Sep visits largely by guided tour only)	www.parco-maremma.it

river valleys and low mountains. See the website www.mugellotoscana.it.

Elba

A prime hiking spot for dramatic scenery, the only really stiff hike is up Monte Capanne (p209).

Practicalities

Depending on the terrain and time of year, you'll need to pack extra clothing layers and wet-weather gear. Sunblock, sunglasses and a hat are essential. Factor in carrying at least 1.5L of water per walker for a summer's day, plus high-nutrition energy foods.

Map and compass are essential off the beaten track. Wild camping isn't permitted in the high mountains; plan overnight stops around the availability of *rifugi* beds and bring a sleeping bag. Many *rifugi* can only be reached on foot from June to September, and have basic kitchen facilities and/or serve meals. Some are privately run; many are part of Italy's national alpine association Club Alpino Italiano (www.cai.it).

Cycling

Whether you're out for a day's gentle pedal around Florence, a sybaritic Chianti weekend winery tour, or a serious two-week-long workout, Tuscany offers bags of cycling scope.

Regions & Routes

Via Francigena Cyclists are also welcome on this medieval pilgrimage trail (p46).

Chianti The picturesque **Strada Chiantigiana** (SS222) waltzes through Chianti en route from Florence to Siena, opening up smooth cycling and short, challenging climbs. If you're fairly fit and have a multigear mountain bike, consider peeling off the SS222 onto Chianti's tranquil back roads (sometimes just gravel tracks), which snake between hamlets and vineyards. Either way, farmstay accommodation abounds.

Etruscan Coast Relatively gentle coastal cycling south from Livorno. Ask at the town's tourist office (p193) for the 20-route *Costa degli Etruschi: Cycling Itineraries* booklet.

Strada del Vino e dell'Olio A wine- and olive-oil-themed 150km tourist itinerary, winding south from Livorno to Piombino and then across to Elba. The 36km stretch from Bolgheri to Suvereto via the hill towns of Castagneto Carducci and Sassetta is particularly scenic; expect switchbacks galore. The San Guido visitor centre (p196) has more information.

Le Crete & Val d'Orcia Offer extensive, hilly itineraries where bursts of hill-climbing are interspersed with cruises amid golden wheat fields and cypress alleys.

Monte Amiata A 1700m volcanic dome in southern Tuscany whose roads are a test for aspiring hill climbers.

GUIDED BIKE TOURS
....

Florence is a top spot to hook up with a cycling guide and venture into Chianti. On the following guided tours everything is supplied, including bike and helmet. Expect to pedal around 20km a day.

➡ Florence By Bike (p141) Tour of northern Chianti (one day) with lunch and wine tasting (€83).

➡ I Bike Italy (p141) Two-day tour including accommodation, breakfast, lunch and dinner (€375).

➡ I Bike Tuscany (p141) One-day tours (€155) for all levels, includes transports from Florence to Chianti.

Florence by Bike also rents bikes and suggests self-guided itineraries; while FiesoleBike (p97) runs a guided, 21km sunset pedal from Fiesole to Florence (€45).

Practicalities

Bike types All-terrain bikes, suitable for both paved and country routes, are the most versatile for Tuscan roads.

Equipment You'll need sun, wind and rain protection, plus a helmet. Carry enough liquids if you're heading into the high hills.

Bike transportation If bringing your own bike from home, check with your airline whether there's a fee and how much disassembly it requires. Bikes can be transported by train in Italy, either with you or to arrive within a couple of days (p332).

Bike hire Hire outlets are common in Tuscany. Book through EcoRent (www.ecorent.net), or on arrival in towns including Florence, Pisa, Lucca and Siena. Hotels and *agriturismi* often have bike rental.

Access While most historic town and city centres are closed to cars, cyclists are often free to enter – double-check the ZTL signs locally.

Horse Riding

Sauntering serenely on horseback through chestnut and cork-oak woods, between vines and past fields of bright yellow sunflowers and wild red poppies is hypnotically calming, aromatic and oh-so-Tuscan.

Holidays

Several farms specialise in equestrian holidays, offering treks of one or several days. Often combining the intimacy of eat-with-the-family *agriturismi* and the formality of a riding school, they're an atmospheric way to experience Tuscany.

The following places offer both accommodation and riding lessons or treks:

La Cerreta (p198)

Circolo Ippico Uccellina (p184)

Il Gelsomino (p184)

Montebelli Agriturismo & Country Hotel (p176)

Regions

Maremma Riding is particularly high-profile in this rural slice of southern Tuscany – it's also home to the famous *butteri* (Maremmese cowboys); experienced riders can sign up for a day herding cows with them at the Agienza Regionale Agricola di Alberese (p184). Or opt for two- to four-hour guided horseback tours (suitable for all experience levels); the Parco Regionale della Maremma (p184) can advise.

Etruscan Coast A horseback itinerary takes riders from Livorno, 170km southeast to Sassetta along sun-scorched coastal paths (best in spring and autumn) and shaded cart tracks. It recommends targeted accommodation en route; the tourist office in Livorno has more info.

Elba The Parco Nazionale dell'Arcipelago Toscano (p202) features old military and forest tracks which double as equestrian pathways; Portoferraio tourist office has maps, brochures and trail details.

Water Sports

You could say Tuscany's best-kept secret is its coast, where a horizon of shimmering blue water is speckled with islands. Add sea kayaks, sailboats and sandy coves reached only from the sea, and you have the source of great outdoor action.

Diving & Snorkelling

Elba is among Italy's top year-round diving spots. Wreck-diving sites include Pomonte, where the *Elvisco* cargo boat sits on the seabed 12m down, and the German WWII plane *Junker 52,* wrecked at a more challenging 38m near Portoferraio.

Aquatic flora and fauna is protected and dramatic. Several Elba diving schools rent gear and organise guides and courses (p203). Less intrepid water lovers can snorkel.

You can also dive along the mainland **Etruscan Coast** and in Porto Ercole on **Monte Argentario**.

Kayaking & Canoeing

Hot summer afternoons are best spent lapping up the slow rhythm of Tuscan travel in a sea kayak or canoe – especially along **Elba's** cove-clad coast. Sea Kayak Italy (p203) runs a wide range of excursions.

The Parco Regionale della Maremma (p184) has a fabulous guided canoe trail.

Sailing & Surfing

The coves of the Tuscan archipelagos and around **Monte Argentario** are superb for sailing, windsurfing and kite surfing. Rent equipment and receive instruction at all the major resorts. **Viareggio** holds several annual sailing regattas.

White-Water Rafting

A handful of outfits in the spa town of **Bagni di Lucca** in northwestern Tuscany organise white-water rafting expeditions on the Lima River.

Ballooning

Drifting noiselessly over Tuscany's vineyards and silvery olive groves is slow, serene and cinematic.

The ballooning season is late spring to early autumn. Take-off is around 6am, flights last 1¼ hours, and cost €240 to €280 per person, often including a 'sparkling wine' breakfast.

Tuscany Ballooning (☑0558 24 91 20; www. tuscanyballooning.com; Via del Masso 14, San Casciano in Val di Pesa) Near Florence.

Ballooning in Tuscany (☑338 146 29 94; www. ballooningintuscany.com) South of Siena.

BEST BEACHES

➡ **Sansone & Sorgente, Elba** White shingle and turquoise waters equals snorkeling bliss (p208).

➡ **Golfo di Baratti, Etruscan Coast** Sandy coves fringed by parasol pines (p202).

➡ **Innamorata, Elba** A wild sand-meets-pebble cove backed by eucalyptus trees (p208).

➡ **Castiglioncello, Etruscan Coast** A sandy strip on the town's northern fringe (p194).

Chianti Ballooning (☑0558 07 79 40; www. chiantiballooning.com) Chianti-based.

Caving

Typically it's a sport that's inaccessible without the gear and expertise. But deep in the Apuane Alps, seasonal three-hour tours of the Grotta del Vento (p247) – 1200 steps past subterranean rivers and crystal-brimmed lakes – are an extraordinary experience.

Spas

Tuscany is one of Italy's thermal activity hot-spots, with the province of Siena particularly rich in mineral-packed waters. Ranging from swish indoor spas to natural woodland pools, tracking them down – and trying them out – is a delight.

Terme di Saturnia (p181) A stunning, cascading cluster of free, open-air pools near Pitigliano.

Bagni di Lucca Terme (p246) Thermal swims and massages in a northwestern spa town.

Bagni San Filippo (p162) Free, alfresco backwoods bathing at its best in the Val d'Orcia.

Calidario Terme Etrusche (p198) Spa treatments and atmospheric outdoor swims on the Etruscan Coast.

Plan Your Trip

Travel with Children

There is far more to Tuscany than churches and museums. The region is a quietly child-friendly destination and, with savvy planning, families can revel in a wonderful choice of creative, educational, culinary and old-fashioned fun things to see, do and experience.

Best Regions for Kids

Florence

Fascinating museums – some interactive, others with creative workshops and tours for children – make Florence a favourite for families with children school-age and older. For the under fives, gentle riverside ambles, fantastic *gelaterie* (ice-cream shops) and a vast choice of dining options add appeal.

Southern Tuscany

Marammese cowboys, archaeological ruins, sandy beaches, snowy mountains: this region might be rural, but it's a cracker when it comes to farmstay accommodation, outdoor action and quirky sights to pique kids' natural curiosity.

Central Coast & Elba

Beaches and boats; Livorno's aquarium and 'Venetian' waterways to explore; and the paradise island of Elba to sail to.

Northwestern Tuscany

Head to the Apuane Alps and Garfagnana to stay on Tuscan farms, see marble being mined, explore subterranean lakes and caverns. Then there's Pisa's Leaning Tower to climb and Lucca's fairy-tale city walls to cycle.

Tuscany for Kids

Tuscany for children is wonderfully varied. Buckets, spades and swimming are a natural element of coastal travel (hit the Etruscan Coast or the island of Elba for the best sandy beaches), but there are mountains of things to see and do inland, too. Urban centres such as Florence and Siena are finer (and more fun) than any school textbook when it comes to learning about Renaissance art, architecture and history – an increasing number of museums are catering to younger-generation minds by offering many superb multimedia displays, touchscreen gadgets, audioguides and creative tours.

The pace slows down in the countryside. Rural farmsteads and *agritursimi,* wineries and agricultural estates inspire and excite young minds with traditional pastimes such as olive picking, feeding the black pigs, bread making in ancient stone ovens and saffron cultivation. There's bags of space to run around in, nature trails to explore, alfresco art sculptures and installations to gawp at, plus sufficient outdoor activities to keep children entertained for weeks.

Museums & Activities

Many museums and monuments are free for children – but there is no single rule about until what age kids get free admission (often up to six years). In Florence state museums are free to EU passport holders aged under 18. Otherwise, museums offer a reduced admission fee – usually half the adult price – for children, usually six and older. Some exceptions make no concession: the Leaning Tower of Pisa has a fixed flat rate of €18 for everyone aged eight and over (under eights are not allowed up the tower).

Most sights offer multilingual audioguides (usually for a fee of €3 to €5) – an instant way to catch the interest of children from eight years (it really does not matter if they don't understand or listen to every last word). Only museums in Florence and other larger towns tend to organise guided tours and workshops for children in English.

Food & Drink

Appeasing most children's natural love of gelato, pizza and pasta is easy in Tuscany, a region that couldn't be easier when it comes to family dining. Children are warmly welcomed in restaurants, especially in casual *trattorie* and *osterie* – often family-owned with overwhelmingly friendly and indulgent waiting staff and a menu featuring simple pasta dishes as well as more elaborate items. If you really cannot find anything on the menu that your child will eat – many restaurants have a *menù bambini* (children's menu) – ask for a plate of pasta with butter or olive oil and parmesan cheese.

Getting Around

Distances are not particularly long and there are plenty of 'count the churches' opportunities to entertain while driving; children under 150cm or 36kg must be in an appropriate child seat for their weight and are not allowed in the front.

On public transport, a seat on a bus costs the same for everyone (toddlers and babies on laps are free). Children under 12 pay half-fare on trains.

Children's Highlights
Towers to Climb

➤ **Torre del Mangia** (p125), **Siena** Steep steps and awesome views at the top.

➤ **Duomo** (p65) **& Campanile** (p69), **Florence** Climb up Giotto's bell tower or into Brunelleschi's dome.

➤ **Torre d'Arnolfo, Florence** Clamber up 418 steps to reach the Palazzo Vecchio (p70) battlements.

➤ **Leaning Tower** (p216), **Pisa** Accessible to children from eight years; otherwise have fun taking photos of your kids propping up the tower.

➤ **Torre Civica delle Ore** (p233), **Lucca** Beware the resident ghost in this 13th-century clock tower.

➤ **Torre Guinigi** (p232), **Lucca** Count 230 steps to the top of this 45m-high tower crowned with seven oak trees.

Medieval to Modern Art

➤ **Parco Sculture del Chianti** (p144), **Central Tuscany** A 1km walking trail and lots of peculiar artworks to gawk at.

➤ **Giardino dei Tarocchi** (p186), **Southern Tuscany** Giant sculptures tumbling down a hillside.

PLANNING

Travelling with children to Florence and Tuscany involves little extra predeparture planning. Your most important decisions will be about the time of year you visit – perhaps timing your visit with one of Tuscany's many vibrant kid-appealing festivals such as Siena's **Palio** (⊙2 Jul & 16 Aug), Viareggio's carnival (p251) or Florence's Scoppio del Carro (p91) – and accommodation. *Agriturismi* and country resorts, such as Borgo Corsignano (p267) and Fattorie de Celli (p267) near Poppi in eastern Tuscany, are invariably the best option for families, often with self-catering facilities and plenty of kid-friendly activities like swimming, tennis, horse riding and mountain biking.

→ **Museo Civico** (p164), **Montepulciano** Explore art by Caravaggio with innovative, touch-screen gadgets.

→ **Palazzo Comunale & Torre Grossa** (p147), **San Gimignano** Learn about medieval frescoes wearing augmented-reality glasses.

→ **Museo Novecento** (p75) **& Palazzo Strozzi** (p72), **Florence** Hands-on art workshops for children and families.

→ **Museo Marino Marini** (p237), **Pistoia** Monthly family tours and hands-on activities in English.

Best Museums

→ **Museo Galileo** (p72), **Florence** Astronomical and mathematical treasures, with ample hands-on opportunities to explore how they work.

→ **Palazzo Vecchio** (p70), **Florence** Guided tours for children and families through secret staircases and hidden rooms; led by historical personages.

→ **Museo Piaggio** (p226), **Pontedera** Learn about Italy's iconic Vespa scooter at this fun museum near Pisa.

→ **Parco Minerario Naturalistico Gavorrano** (p176), **Southern Tuscany** Museum in a huge pyrite mine, with underground galleries and interactive displays.

→ **Museo Stibbert** (p75), **Florence** Life-sized horses and knights in suits of armour from Europe and the Middle East.

In the Making

→ **Curious Appetite** (p91), **Florence** Learn how to make gelato (and eat it).

→ **Martelli** (p194), **Lari** Watch spaghetti being made at this artisanal pasta workshop.

→ **Antonio Mattei** (p240), **Prato** Watch bakers working the ovens at Tuscany's most famous *biscottificio* (biscuit shop).

→ **La Citadella di Carnevale** (p251), **Viareggio** Meet artists and watch them crafting giant-sized clowns, kings etc for carnival floats; papier-mâché workshops for families, too.

→ **Barbialla Nuova** (p241), **Montaione** Dirty hands with a bread- or pizza-making workshop on an idyllic Tuscan cattle farm and truffle estate.

Cool Stuff Outdoors

→ **Cava di Fantiscritti** (p248), **Carrara** Take a Bond-style 4WD tour of the open-cast quarry or follow miners inside 'marble mountain'.

→ **City walls** (p227), **Lucca** Hire a bike and ride along the top of the walls.

→ **Grotta del Vento** (p247), **Northwestern Tuscany** Go underground to explore subterranean abysses, lakes and caverns.

→ **Cabinovia Monte Capanne** (p209), **Elba** Ride a 'bird cage' up Elba's highest peak.

→ **Pistoia Sotterranea** (p237), **Pistoia** Discover subterranean rivers underneath a 13th-century hospital.

→ **Bagni San Filippo, Val d'Orcia** Free backwoods bathing in hot thermal springs.

→ **Terme di Saturnia** (p181), **Southern Tuscany** Not the plush luxe spa; rather the hidden cluster of natural pools by the actual springs, at the end of a dirt path.

Wildlife Encounters

→ **Museo di Storia Naturale del Mediterraneo** (p190), **Livorno** Meet Annie, the whale skeleton.

→ **Riserva Naturale Provinciale Diaccia Botrona** (p184), **Southern Tuscany** Spot flamingos and herons on a boat tour through the marshes.

→ **Parco Regionale della Maremma** (www.parco-maremma.it; park admission adult/reduced €10/5), **Southern Tuscany** Hike, cycle or canoe through this huge coastal park.

→ **Acquario di Livorno** (p190), **Livorno** Thoroughly modern aquarium by the seaside.

Walks with Kids

→ **Le Biancane** (p176), **Monterotondo Maritime** Geothermal park with trails through steam-belching woods.

→ **Vie cave** (p178), **Southern Tuscany** Excite young historians with a trail along sunken Etruscan roads.

→ **Parco Archeologico di Baratti e Populonia** (p202), **Golfi di Baratti** Incredible trails around quarries and ruined tombs.

→ **Elba** (p202) Tuscany's largest island is walk-perfect, with plenty of capes and beaches.

→ **Fortezza del Girifalco** (p273), **Cortona** Kids love the stiff scamper uphill to this ruined Medici fortress atop the town's highest point.

Regions at a Glance

Florence

Food
Art
Shopping

Gourmet Paradise

The city's exceptional dining scene encompasses everything from *enoteche* (wine bars) bursting with cured meats and cheeses to no-nonsense trattorias, bustling food markets and the only restaurant in Tuscany to possess three Michelin stars.

Renaissance Beauty

The Uffizi is one of the world's most famous art galleries, but it's not the only repository of artistic masterpieces in the city (the expression 'an embarrassment of riches' seems appropriate). Churches, chapels and a bevy of lesser-known museums showcase masterpieces galore.

Fashion & Artisan Crafts

From the designer boutiques on shopping strip Via de' Tornabuoni to artisan workshops hidden down alleys and back streets in the traditional artisan district of Oltrarno: the city where Gucci was born really is the last word in quality shopping.

p56

Siena & Central Tuscany

Food
Wine
Hill Towns

Sweet Temptations

Sample Siena's famous cakes and biscuits, accompanied by a coffee or dunked in a glass of sweet Vin Santo wine at the end of a meal.

In Vino Veritas

Tuscan wine hot shots Brunello, Vino Nobile, Chianti Classico and Vernaccia all hail from this rich part of Tuscany, with estates throughout the region opening their cellar doors and vine-laced estates for tastings and visits.

Take to the Hills

Explore scenic hill towns such as Montalcino, Montepulciano, Volterra and San Gimignano where medieval architecture is as impressive as the panoramic views that reward those who hike to the top.

p120

Southern Tuscany

Food
Archaeology
Nature

Slow Food

This is a no-fuss zone when it comes to cuisine. Local chefs buy local, stick to the season and subscribe to the concept of Slow Food. And the results are superb.

Waves of Civilisation

The Etruscans certainly left their mark here, and the countryside of the extraordinary Città del Tufa (City of the Tufa) is littered with their tombs. The Romans didn't shirk in this respect either, as a visit to the archaeological sites of Roselle or Vetulonia will attest.

Land of the Big Sky

Europe's bird species stop here on their migration to North Africa for good reason – huge tracts of pristine landscape boast an impressive range of flora and fauna.

p168

Central Coast & Elba

Food
Beaches
History

Seafood in Livorno

Feisty locals in this waterside port city are staunchly proud of *cacciucco,* a remarkable seafood stew swimming with at least five types of fish. It's best enjoyed with a glass or two of locally produced Sassicaia wine.

Coastal Capers

Visit Elba, the palm-tree-clad paradise where Napoleon was banished. This bijou island offers a sensational mix of sunbathing, sea kayaking, snorkelling and swimming.

Etruscan Heritage

Exploring the remains of ancient Etruscan tombs and temples hidden beneath sky-high parasol pines on the Golfo di Baratti's sandy shoreline is an extraordinary experience. Pair it with gentle walking and a picnic lunch for the perfect day.

p187

Northwestern Tuscany

Food
Mountains
Outdoors

White Truffles

No single food product is lusted over quite as much as the perfumed fresh white truffle – hunted in autumn forests around San Miniato and eaten with gusto during the autumn truffle season.

Majestic Marble

Take a drive from the Garfagnana through rugged peaks and richly forested valleys laced with walking trails to witness the majestic marble mountains of the Apuane Alps in their full glory.

Outdoor Treasures

The trio of valleys that form the Garfagnana region suits holiday-makers keen on hiking, biking and eating. Trails criss-cross chestnut woods and forests rich in berries and *porcini* mushrooms.

p213

Eastern Tuscany

Food
Holy Shrines
Art

Real McCoy T-bone

Come to the Val di Chiana to eat Italy's best *bistecca alla fiorentina,* the succulent, lightly seared piece of locally raised Chianina beef that is Tuscany's signature dish.

Holy Places

St Francis is closely associated with this part of Tuscany. Born in nearby Assisi, he is said to have received the stigmata at the Santuario della Verna in the wonderfully wild Casentino forest.

Arty Itineraries

The old adage 'quality before quantity' applies here. Follow a trail highlighting the works of Piero della Francesca, but also look out for works by Cimabue, Fra' Angelico, Signorelli, Rosso Fiorentino, the Lorenzettis and the della Robbias.

p255

On the Road

Northwestern Tuscany (p213)

Florence (p56)

Eastern Tuscany (p255)

Central Coast & Elba (p187)

Siena & Central Tuscany (p120)

Southern Tuscany (p168)

Elba

Florence

POP 377,200

Best Places to Eat

➡ Trattoria Mario (p101)

➡ Mercato Centrale (p100)

➡ La Leggenda dei Frati (p105)

➡ Il Teatro del Sale (p102)

➡ 5 e Cinque (p103)

➡ La Bottega del Buon Caffè (p105)

Best City Panoramas

➡ Dome (p68) & Campanile (p69), Duomo (p65)

➡ Torre d'Arnolfo, Palazzo Vecchio (p70)

➡ Piazzale Michelangelo (p89)

➡ La Reggia degli Etruschi, Fiesole (p97)

Why Go?

Return time and again and you still won't see it all. Stand on a bridge over the Arno river several times in a day and the light, mood and view changes every time. Surprisingly small as it is, this riverside city looms large on the world's 'must-sees' list. Cradle of the Renaissance and of tourist masses that flock here to feast on world-class art, Florence (Firenze) is magnetic, romantic and busy. Its urban fabric has hardly changed since the Renaissance, its narrow streets evoke a thousand tales, and its food and wine are so wonderful the tag 'Fiorentina' has become an international label of quality assurance.

Fashion designers parade on Via de' Tornabuoni. Gucci was born here, as was Roberto Cavalli, who, like many a smart Florentine these days, hangs out in wine-rich hills around Florence. After a while in this absorbing city, you might want to do the same.

Road Distances (km)

	Florence	Pisa	Lucca	San Miniato
Pisa	69			
Lucca	61	23		
San Miniato	37	47	70	
Siena	51	87	30	77

History

Florence's history stretches to the time of the Etruscans, who based themselves in Fiesole. Julius Caesar founded the Roman colony of Florentia around 59 BC, making it a strategic garrison on the narrowest crossing of the Arno in order to control the Via Flaminia linking Rome to northern Italy and Gaul.

After the collapse of the Roman Empire, Florence fell to invading Goths, followed by Lombards and Franks. The year AD 1000 marked a crucial turning point in the city's fortunes, when Margrave Ugo of Tuscany moved his capital from Lucca to Florence. In 1110 Florence became a free *comune* (city-state) and by 1138 it was ruled by 12 consuls, assisted by the Consiglio di Cento (Council of One Hundred), whose members were drawn mainly from the prosperous merchant class. Agitation among differing factions in the city led to the appointment in 1207 of a foreign head of state called the *podestà,* aloof in principle from the plotting and wheeling and dealing of local cliques and alliances.

Medieval Florence was a wealthy, dynamic *comune,* one of Europe's leading financial, banking and cultural centres, and a major player in the international wool, silk and leather trades. The sizeable population of moneyed merchants and artisans began forming guilds and patronising the growing number of artists who found lucrative commissions in this burgeoning city.

Struggles between the pro-papal Guelphs (Guelfi) and the pro–Holy Roman Empire Ghibellines (Ghibellini) started in the mid-13th century, with power yo-yoing between the two for almost a century. Into this fractious atmosphere were born revolutionary artist Giotto and outspoken poet Dante Alighieri, whose family belonged to the Guelph camp. After the Guelphs split into two factions, the Neri (Blacks) and Bianchi (Whites), Dante went with the Bianchi – the wrong side – and was expelled from his beloved city in 1302, never to return.

In 1348 the Black Death spirited away almost half the population. The history of Medici Florence begins in 1434, when Cosimo the Elder (Cosimo de' Medici), a patron of the arts, assumed power. His eye for talent and tact in dealing with artists saw Alberti, Brunelleschi, Luca della Robbia, Fra' Angelico, Donatello and Fra' Filippo Lippi flourish under his patronage.

Under the rule of Cosimo's popular and cultured grandson, Lorenzo il Magnifico (1469–92), Florence became the epicentre of the Renaissance (Rebirth), with artists such as Michelangelo, Botticelli and Domenico Ghirlandaio at work. Lorenzo's court, filled with Humanists (a school of thought begun in Florence in the late 14th century affirming the dignity and potential of mankind and

THREE PERFECT DAYS

Day 1: David Tour
Follow the world's most famous naked man: start with Michelangelo's original in the **Galleria dell'Accademia** (p77), saunter past the famous copy at **Piazza della Signoria** (p70), then hit **Museo del Bargello** (p80) for versions by Donatello and Andrea Verrocchio. Enjoy other Michelangelos in the **Biblioteca Medicea Laurenziana** (p75), **Basilica di Santo Spirito** (p82) and **Museo delle Cappelle Medicee** (p76); enjoy sunset on **Piazzale Michelangelo** (p88).

Day 2: Both Sides of the Arno
Devote the morning to the **Uffizi** (p61). If you have a reservation, take a guided tour of the **Vasarian Corridor** (p83); otherwise, wander through the heart of Florence. Window-shop on **Via de' Tornabuoni** (p72) with a break for a truffle *panino* at **Procacci** (p106). At 7pm indulge in a gourmet *aperitivo* with hipsters over gin cocktails at **Ditta Artigianale** (p110), then cross the Arno for dinner on **Piazza della Passera** (p103).

Day 3: No Art Please!
Breakfast on views of Piazza della Signoria at **Caffè Rivoire** (p108) then visit **Gucci Museo** (p72). By the river, **Museo Galileo** (p72) enthrals. Cross **Ponte Vecchio** (p82) for lunch at a **Piazza Santa Spirito** (p103) eatery, then meander to **Palazzo Pitti** (p83). Flop afterwards in **Giardino di Boboli** (p86). At dusk head east to San Niccolò for dinner at **La Bottega del Buon Caffè** (p105).

Florence Highlights

❶ Visiting the world's finest collection of Renaissance paintings at the **Uffizi Gallery** (p61).

❷ Climbing inside Brunelleschi's **dome** (p68), crowning glory of Florence's **Duomo** (p65).

❸ Contemplating the artistic genius of Fra' Angelico at **Museo di San Marco** (p77); no fresco better portrays the humanist spirit of the Renaissance than his *Annunciation*.

❹ Admiring sculptural tombs of Florentine luminaries and a Brunelleschi chapel inside **Basilica di Santa Croce** (p79).

❺ Hiking uphill to **Piazzale Michelangelo** (p89) to meet *David*'s lookalike and enjoying the most magnificent sunset show and city panorama.

❻ Escaping the city heat for a day between olive groves and Roman ruins in hilltop **Fiesole**; lunching at **La Reggia degli Etruschi** (p97) and cycling back to Florence with the setting sun and local guide Giovanni.

❼ Dipping into Florentine cafe culture at timeless classic **Caffè Giacosa** (p108), trendsetter **Ditta Artigianale** (p110) or a backstreet address in artisanal **Oltrarno** (p108).

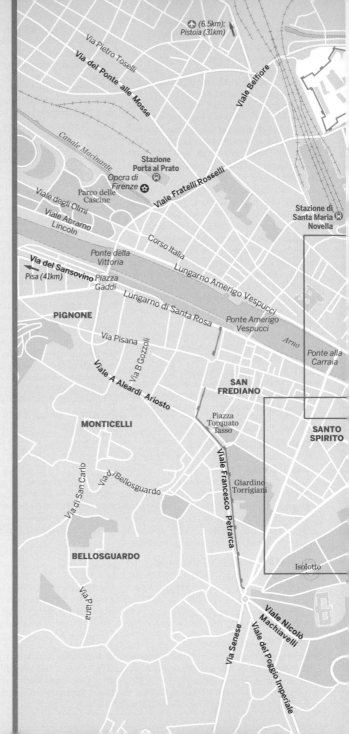

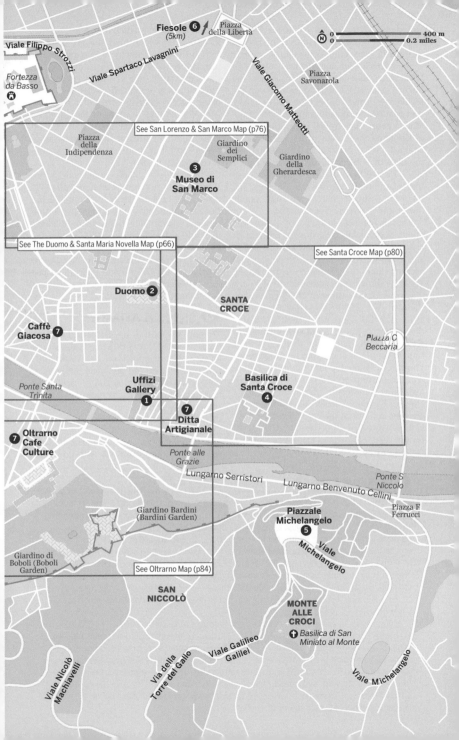

Fiesole **6** *(5km)* Piazza della Libertà

Viale Filippo Strozzi

Fortezza da Basso

Viale Spartaco Lavagnini

Viale Giacomo Matteotti

Piazza Savonarola

N 0 ——————— 400 m
0 ——————— 0.2 miles

See San Lorenzo & San Marco Map (p76)

Piazza della Indipendenza

Giardino dei Semplici

Giardino della Gherardesca

Museo di San Marco **3**

See The Duomo & Santa Maria Novella Map (p66)

See Santa Croce Map (p80)

Duomo 2

SANTA CROCE

Caffè Giacosa 7

Piazza C Beccaria

Ponte Santa Trinita

Uffizi Gallery 1

Basilica di Santa Croce 4

7
Ditta Artigianale

7 Oltrarno Cafe Culture

Ponte alle Grazie

Lungarno Serristori

Lungarno Benvenuto Cellini

Ponte S Niccolo

Piazza F Ferrucci

Giardino Bardini (Bardini Garden)

Piazzale Michelangelo 5

Viale Michelangelo

Giardino di Boboli (Boboli Garden)

See Oltrarno Map (p84)

SAN NICCOLÒ

MONTE ALLE CROCI

Basilica di San Miniato al Monte

Viale Nicolò Machiavelli

Via della Torre del Gallo

Viale Galileo Galilei

Viale Michelangelo

embracing Latin and Greek literary texts), fostered a flowering of art, music and poetry, turning Florence into Italy's cultural capital.

Florence's golden age effectively died with Lorenzo in 1492. Just before his death, the Medici bank failed and two years later the Medici were driven out of Florence. In a reaction against the splendour and excess of the Medici court, the city fell under the control of Girolamo Savonarola, a Dominican monk who led a stern, puritanical republic. In 1497 the likes of Botticelli gladly consigned their 'immoral' works and finery to the flames of the infamous 'Bonfire of the Vanities'. The following year Savonarola fell from public favour and was burned as a heretic.

The pro-French leanings of the subsequent republican government brought it into conflict with the pope and his Spanish allies. In 1512 a Spanish force defeated Florence and the Medici were reinstated. Their tyrannical rule endeared them to few and when Rome, ruled by the Medici pope Clement VII, fell to the emperor Charles V in 1527, the Florentines took advantage of this low point in the Medici fortunes to kick the family out again. Two years later though, imperial and papal forces besieged Florence, forcing the city to accept Lorenzo's great-grandson, Alessandro de' Medici, a ruthless transvestite whom Charles made Duke of Florence. Medici rule continued for another 200 years, during which time they gained control of all of Tuscany, though after the reign of Cosimo I (1537–74), Florence drifted into steep decline.

The last male Medici, Gian Gastone, died in 1737, after which his sister, Anna Maria, signed the grand duchy of Tuscany over to the House of Habsburg-Lorraine (at the time effectively under Austrian control). This situation remained unchanged, apart from a brief interruption under Napoleon from 1799 to 1814, until the duchy was incorporated into the Kingdom of Italy in 1860. Florence briefly became the national capital a year later, but Rome assumed the mantle permanently in 1871.

Florence was badly damaged during WWII by the retreating Germans, who blew up all of its bridges except the Ponte Vecchio. Devastating floods ravaged the city in 1966, causing inestimable damage to its buildings and artworks. Since 1997, amid a fair amount of controversy, the world-class Uffizi Gallery has been engaged in its biggest-ever expansion – a €65 million investment project, dubbed the 'New Uffizi project'. Its end date remains a mystery.

◉ Sights & Activities

Florence's wealth of museums and galleries house many of the world's most exquisite examples of Renaissance art, and its architecture is unrivalled. Yet don't feel pressured to see everything: combine your personal pick of sights with ample meandering through the city's warren of narrow streets broken by cafe and *enoteca* (wine bar) stops.

Churches enforce a strict dress code for visitors: no shorts, sleeveless shirts or plunging necklines. Photography with no flash is

---

❶ MUSEUM PASSES

The **Firenze Card** (€72) is valid for 72 hours and covers admission to some 70 museums, villas and gardens in Florence, as well as unlimited use of public transport and free wi-fi across the city. Its biggest advantage is reducing queueing time in high season – museums have a separate queue for card-holders. The downside of the Firenze Card is it only allows one admission per museum, plus you need to visit an awful lot of museums to justify the cost. Buy the card online (and collect upon arrival in Florence) or in Florence at tourist offices or ticketing desks of the Uffizi (Entrance 2), Palazzo Pitti, Palazzo Vecchio, Museo del Bargello, Cappella Brancacci, Museo di Santa Maria Novella and Giardini Bardini. If you're an EU citizen, your card also covers under 18 year olds travelling with you.

If you prefer to split your Uffizi forays into a couple of visits and/or you're not from the EU and are travelling with kids, the annual **Friends of the Uffizi Card** (adult/reduced/family of 4 €60/40/100) is a better deal. Valid for a calendar year (expires 31 December), it covers admission to 22 Florence museums (including Galleria dell'Accademia, Museo del Bargello and Palazzo Pitti) and allows return visits (have your passport on you as proof of ID to show at each museum with your card). Buy online or from the **Amici degli Uffizi Welcome Desk** (Map p66; ☑ 055 28 56 10; www.amicidegliuffizi.it; Piazzale degli Uffizi 6; ☺10am-5pm Tue-Sat) next to Entrance 2 at the Uffizi.

ℹ MUSEUM TICKETS

In July, August and other busy periods such as Easter, unbelievably long queues are a fact of life at Florence's key museums – if you haven't prebooked your ticket, you could well end up standing in line queuing for four hours or so.

For a fee of €3 per ticket (€4 for the Uffizi and Galleria dell'Accademia), tickets to nine *musei statali* (state museums) can be reserved, including the Uffizi, Galleria dell'Accademia (where *David* lives), Palazzo Pitti, Museo del Bargello and the Medicean chapels (Cappelle Medicee). In reality, the only museums where prebooking is vital are the Uffizi and Accademia – to organise your ticket, go online or call **Firenze Musei** (Florence Museums; ☑ 055 29 48 83; www.firenzemusei.it), with ticketing desks (open 8.30am to 7pm Tuesday to Sunday) at the Uffizi and Palazzo Pitti.

At the Uffizi, signs point prebooked ticket holders to the building opposite the gallery where tickets can be collected; once you've got the ticket you go to Door 1 of the museum (for prebooked tickets only) and queue again to enter the gallery. It's annoying, but you'll still save hours of queuing time overall. Many hotels in Florence also prebook museum tickets for guests.

Admission to all state museums, including the Uffizi and Galleria dell'Accademia, is free on the first Sunday of each month and also on 18 February, the day Anna Maria Louisa de' Medici (1667–1743) died. The last of the Medici family, it was she who bequeathed the city its vast cultural heritage.

EU passport holders aged under 18 and over 65 get into Florence's state museums for free, and EU citizens aged 18 to 25 pay half price. Have your ID with you at all times. Note that museum ticket offices usually shut 30 minutes before closing time.

---

allowed in museums, but leave the selfie stick at home.

⊙ Duomo to Piazza della Signoria

Florence's big-hit sights lie in the geographic, historic and cultural heart of the city – the tight grid of streets between Piazza del Duomo and cafe-strung Piazza della Signoria.

★ **Galleria degli Uffizi**   GALLERY

(Uffizi Gallery; Map p66; www.uffizi.firenze.it; Piazzale degli Uffizi 6; adult/reduced €8/4, incl temporary exhibition €12.50/6.25; ⊗8.15am-6.50pm Tue-Sun) Home to the world's greatest collection of Italian Renaissance art, Florence's premier gallery occupies the vast U-shaped Palazzo degli Uffizi, built between 1560 and 1580 to house government offices. The collection, bequeathed to the city by the Medici family in 1743 on the condition that it never leave Florence, contains some of Italy's best-known paintings including Piero della Francesco's profile portaits of the Duke and Duchess of Urbino and a room full of masterpieces by Sandro Botticelli.

The gallery is undergoing a €65 million refurbishment (the Nuovi Uffizi project) that will eventually see the doubling of exhibition space and possibly a new exit loggia (balcony) designed by Japanese architect Arato Isozaki. A number of revamped rooms

are open, but until the project is completed (date unknown) expect some halls to be closed and the contents of others changed.

The world-famous collection, displayed in chronological order, spans the gamut of art history from ancient Greek sculpture to 18th-century Venetian paintings. But its core is the Renaissance collection.

Visits are best kept to three or four hours maximum. When it all gets too much, head to the rooftop cafe (aka the terraced hanging garden, where the Medici clan listened to music performances on the square below) for fresh air and fabulous views.

➔ *Tuscan Masters: 13th to 14th Centuries*

In the *Primo Corridoio* (First Corridor) on the 2nd floor, the first seven rooms – closed for renovation at the time of writing – are dedicated to pre-Renaissance Tuscan art. Among the 13th-century Sienese works displayed are three large altarpieces from Florentine churches by Duccio di Buoninsegna, Cimabue and Giotto. These clearly reflect the transition from the Gothic to the nascent Renaissance style. Note the overtly naturalistic realism overtones in Giotto's portrayal of the Virgin Mary and saints in the *Madonna di Ognissanti*.

Moving into Siena in the 14th century, the highlight is Simone Martini's shimmering *Annunciazione* (1333), painted with Lippo Memmi and setting the Madonna in a sea of

The Uffizi

JOURNEY INTO THE RENAISSANCE

Navigating the Uffizi's chronologically-ordered art collection is straightforward enough: knowing which of the 1500-odd masterpieces to view before gallery fatigue strikes is not. Swap coat and bag (travel light) for floor plan and audioguide on the ground floor, then meet 16th-century Tuscany head-on with a walk up the *palazzo's* magnificent bust-lined staircase (skip the lift – the Uffizi is as much about masterly architecture as art).

Allow four hours for this journey into the High Renaissance. At the top of the staircase, on the 2nd floor, show your ticket, turn left and pause to admire the full length of the first corridor sweeping south towards the Arno river. Then duck left into room 2 to witness first steps in Tuscan art – shimmering altarpieces by **Giotto** ❶ et al. Journey through medieval art to room 8 and **Piero della Francesca's** ❷ impossibly famous portrait, then break in the corridor with playful **ceiling art** ❸. After Renaissance heavyweights **Botticelli** ❹ and **da Vinci** ❺, meander past the Tribuna (potential detour) and enjoy the daylight streaming in through the vast windows and panorama of the **riverside second corridor** ❻. Lap up soul-stirring views of the Arno, crossed by Ponte Vecchio and its echo of four bridges drifting towards the Apuane Alps on the horizon. Then saunter into the third corridor, pausing between rooms 25 and 34 to ponder the entrance to the enigmatic Vasari Corridor. End on a high with High Renaissance maestro **Michelangelo** ❼.

The Ognissanti Madonna
Room 2
Draw breath at the shy blush and curvaceous breast of Giotto's humanised Virgin (*Maestà;* 1310) – so feminine compared with those of Duccio and Cimabue painted just 25 years before.

Portraits of the Duke & Duchess of Urbino
Room 8
Revel in realism's voyage with these uncompromising, warts-and-all portraits (1472–75) by Piero della Francesca. No larger than A3 size, they originally slotted into a portable, hinged frame that folded like a book.

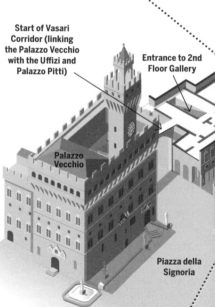

Start of Vasari Corridor (linking the Palazzo Vecchio with the Uffizi and Palazzo Pitti)

Entrance to 2nd Floor Gallery

Palazzo Vecchio

Piazza della Signoria

Grotesque Ceiling Frescoes
First Corridor
Take time to study the make-believe monsters and most unexpected of burlesques (spot the arrow-shooting satyr outside room 15) waltzing across this eastern corridor's fabulous frescoed ceiling (1581).

JUERGEN RIC-TTER/GETTY IMAGES ©

The Genius of Botticelli
Room 10–14

The miniature form of *The Discovery of the Body of Holofernes* (c 1470) makes Botticelli's early Renaissance masterpiece all the more impressive. Don't miss the artist watching you in *Adoration of the Magi* (1475), left of the exit.

View of the Arno

Indulge in intoxicating city views from this short glassed-in corridor – an architectural masterpiece. Near the top of the hill, spot one of 73 outer towers built to defend Florence and its 15 city gates below.

Second Corridor

Tribuna

First Corridor

Arno River

Entrance to Vasari Corridor

VALUE LUNCHBOX

Try the Uffizi rooftop cafe or – better value – gourmet *panini* at 'Ino (www.ino-firenze.com; Via dei Georgofili 3-7r).

Doni Tondo
Room 35

The creator of *David*, Michelangelo, was essentially a sculptor and no painting expresses this better than *Doni Tondo* (1506–08). Mary's muscular arms against a backdrop of curvaceous nudes are practically 3D in their shapeliness.

Third Corridor

Tribuna

No room in the Uffizi is so tiny or so exquisite. It was created in 1851 as a 'treasure chest' for Grand Duke Francesco and in the days of the Grand Tour, the Medici Venus here was a tour highlight.

Annunciation
Room 15

Admire the exquisite portrayal of the Tuscan landscape in this painting (c 1472), one of few by Leonardo da Vinci to remain in Florence.

MATTER OF FACT

The Uffizi collection spans the 13th to 18th centuries, but its 15th- and 16th-century Renaissance works are second to none.

ℹ SAVVY ADVANCE PLANNING

➡ To cut costs, visit on the first Sunday of the month, when admission to state museums, including the Uffizi and Galleria dell'Accademia, is free.

➡ Cut queues by booking tickets in advance for the Uffizi and Galleria dell'Accademia.

➡ Reserve a tour of the Vasarian Corridor; also reserve for Cappella Brancacci and Cappella dei Magi.

➡ Book family-friendly tours and/or art workshops at Palazzo Vecchio and Museo Novecento.

➡ Buy tickets for springtime's Maggio Musicale Fiorentino.

➡ The Uffizi, Galleria dell'Accademia and most other state museums are shut on Mondays – the perfect day for visiting hidden-gem museum Museo di Orsanmichele.

➡ Catch contemporary art (for free) on Thursday evening at Palazzo Strozzi.

➡ One ticket gets into all the cathedral-related sights (Cripta Santa Reparata, Campanile, Cupola del Brunelleschi, Battistero di San Giovanni, Museo dell'Opera del Duomo), known collectively as Il Grande Museo del Duomo. Buy it at Piazza di San Giovanni 7 and use within 24 hours.

gold. Also of note is the *Madonna in trono con il Bambino in trono e otto angeli* (Madonna with Child and Saints; 1340) by Pietro Lorenzetti, which demonstrates a realism similar to Giotto's; unfortunately both Pietro and his artistic brother Ambrogio died from the plague in Siena in 1348.

Masters in 14th-century Florence paid as much attention to detail as their Sienese counterparts: savour the realism and extraordinary gold-leaf work of the *Pietà di San Remigio* (1360–65) by gifted Giotto pupil, Giottino.

➡ *Renaissance Pioneers*

In Room 8, Piero della Francesca's famous profile portraits (1465) of the crooked-nosed, red-robed duke and duchess of Urbino are wholly humanist in spirit: the former painted from the left side as he'd lost his right eye in a jousting accident, and the latter painted a deathly stone-white, reflecting the fact the portrait was painted posthumously. Don't miss the reverse side featuring the duke and duchess eternalised with the Virtues.

Carmelite monk Fra' Filippo Lippi had an unfortunate soft spot for earthly pleasures, scandalously marrying a nun from Prato. Search out his self-portrait as a podgy friar in *Incoronazione Maringhi* (Coronation of the Virgin; 1439–47) and don't mss his later *Madonna con Bambino e due angeli* (Madonna and Child with Two Angels; 1460–65), an exquisite work that clearly influenced his pupil, Sandro Botticelli.

Another related pair, brothers Antonio and Piero del Pollaiolo, fill Room 9, where

their seven cardinal and theological values of 15th-century Florence – commissioned for the merchant's tribunal in Piazza della Signoria – radiate energy. More restrained is Piero's *Portrait of Galeazzo Maria Sforza* (1471).

The only canvas in the theological and cardinal virtues series not to be painted by the Pollaiolos is *Fortitude* (1470), the first documented work by Botticelli.

➡ *Botticelli Room*

The spectacular Sala del Botticelli, numbered as Rooms 10 to 14 but in fact one large hall, is one of the Uffizi's hot spots and is always packed. Of the 15 works by the Renaissance master known for his ethereal figures, *La nascita di Venere* (The Birth of Venus; c 1485), *Primavera* (Spring; c 1482), the deeply spiritual *Annunciazione di Cestello* (Cestello Annunciation; 1489–90), the *Adorazione dei Magi* (Adoration of the Magi; 1475) featuring the artist's self-portrait (look for the blond-haired guy, extreme right, dressed in yellow), and the *Madonna del Magnificat* (Madonna of the Magnificat; 1483) are the best known. True aficionados rate his twin set of miniatures depicting a sword-bearing Judith returning from the camp of Holofernes and the discovery of the decapitated Holofernes in his tent (1495–1500) as being among his finest works.

➡ *Leonardo Room*

Room 15 displays three early Florentine works by Leonardo da Vinci: the incomplete *Adorazione dei Magi* (Adoration of the Magi; 1481–82), drawn in red-earth pigment (removed for restoration at the time of writing); his *Annunciazione* (c 1475–80); and *The Baptism of Christ* (1470–75).

➡ *La Tribuna*

The Medici clan stashed away their most precious masterpieces in this exquisite octagonal-shaped treasure trove (Room 18), created by Francesco I between 1581 and 1586. Designed to amaze and perfectly restored to its original exquisite state, a small collection of classical statues and paintings adorns its walls, upholstered in crimson silk, and 6000 mother-of-pearl shells painted with crimson varnish encrust the domed ceiling.

➡ *High Renaissance to Mannerism*

Passing through the loggia or Secondo Corridoio (Second Corridor), visitors enjoy wonderful views of Florence before entering the Terzo Corridoio (Third Corridor). Rooms 24 to 34 were closed at the time of writing as part of the massive ongoing expansion and reorganisation of the Uffizi.

Michelangelo dazzles with the *Doni Tondo*, a depiction of the Holy Family that steals the High Renaissance show in Room 35. The composition is unusual – Joseph holding an exuberant Jesus on his muscled mother's shoulder as she twists round to gaze at him, the colours as vibrant as when they were first applied in 1506–08. It was painted for wealthy Florentine merchant Agnolo Doni (who hung it above his bed) and bought by the Medici for Palazzo Pitti in 1594.

➡ *1st-Floor Galleries*

As part of the ongoing New Uffizi expansion project, the Uffizi has already added 1800 sq metres of gallery space to its vast repertoire. Head downstairs to the 1st-floor galleries where Rooms 46 to 55 display the Uffizi's collection of 16th- to 18th-century works by foreign artists, including Rembrandt (room 49); Rubens and Van Dyck share room 55. The next 10 rooms give a nod to antique sculpture, before moving back into the 16th century with Andrea del Sarto (Rooms 57 and 58) and Raphael (Room 66) whose *Madonna del cardellino* (Madonna of the Goldfinch; 1505–06) steals the show. Raphael painted it during his four-year sojourn in Florence.

Rooms 90 to 94 feature works by Caravaggio, deemed vulgar at the time for his direct interpretation of reality. *The Head of Medusa* (1598–99), commissioned for a ceremonial shield, is supposedly a self-portrait of the young artist who died at the age of 39. The biblical drama of an angel steadying the hand of Abraham as he holds a knife to his

son Isaac's throat in Caravaggio's *Sacrifice of Isaac* (1601–02) is glorious in its intensity.

★ **Duomo**   CATHEDRAL

(Cattedrale di Santa Maria del Fiore; Map p66; www.operaduomo.firenze.it; Piazza del Duomo; ⏱10am-5pm Mon-Wed & Fri, to 4.30pm Thu, to 4.45pm Sat, 1.30-4.45pm Sun) FREE Florence's Duomo is the city's most iconic landmark. Capped by Filippo Brunelleschi's red-tiled cupola, it's a staggering construction whose breathtaking pink, white and green marble facade and graceful *campanile* (bell tower) dominate the medieval cityscape. Sienese architect Arnolfo di Cambio began work on it in 1296, but construction took almost 150 years and it wasn't consecrated until 1436. In the echoing interior, look out for frescoes by Vasari and Zuccari and up to 44 stained-glass windows.

The Duomo's neo-Gothic facade was designed in the 19th century by architect Emilio de Fabris to replace the uncompleted original, torn down in the 16th century. The oldest and most clearly Gothic part of the cathedral is its south flank, pierced by Porta dei Canonici (Canons' Door), a mid-14th-century High Gothic creation (you enter here to climb up inside the dome).

After the visual wham-bam of the facade, the sparse decoration of the cathedral's vast interior, 155m long and 90m wide, comes as a surprise – most of its artistic treasures have been removed over the centuries according to the vagaries of ecclesiastical fashion, and many will be on show in the sparkling new Grande Museo del Duomo. The interior is also unexpectedly secular in places (a reflection of the sizeable chunk of the cathedral not paid for by the church): down the left aisle two immense frescoes of equestrian statues portray two *condottieri* (mercenaries) – on the left Niccolò da Tolentino by Andrea del Castagno (1456), and on the right Sir John

> ℹ **LESSER-KNOWN GEMS**
>
> When the Uffizi, *David* and Ponte Vecchio crowd gets too much, flee to one of Florence's faintly lesser-known gems: Palazzo Strozzi (blockbuster art exhibitions), Museo del Bargello (early Michelangelos), Chiesa di Orsanmichele (medieval statuary), Biblioteca Medicea Laurenziana (Michelangelo staircase), Museo Marino Marini (Rucellai Chapel) and Chiesa di Santa Trinita (frescoes).

The Duomo & Santa Maria Novella

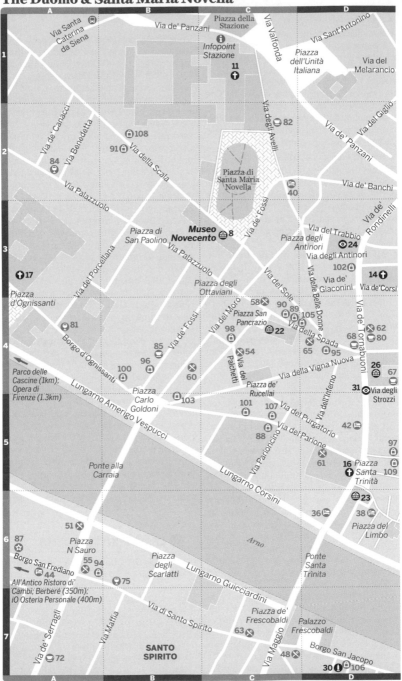

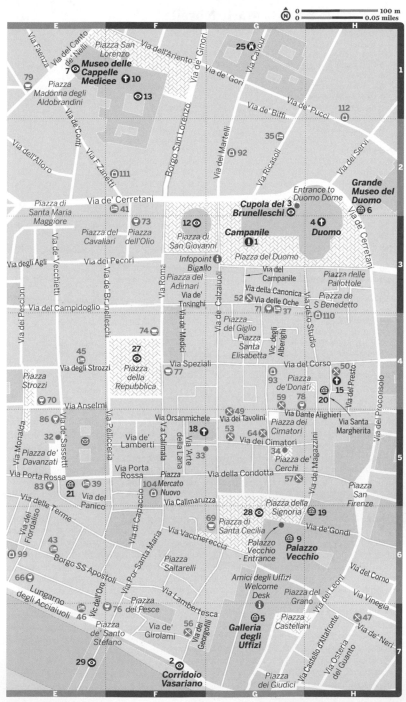

The Duomo & Santa Maria Novella

Hawkwood (who fought in the service of Florence in the 14th century) by Uccello (1436).

Between the left (north) arm of the transept and the apse is the **Sagrestia delle Messe** (Mass Sacristy), its panelling a marvel of inlaid wood carved by Benedetto and Giuliano da Maiano. The fine bronze doors were executed by Luca della Robbia – his only known work in the material. Above the doorway is his glazed terracotta *Resurrezione* (Resurrection).

A stairway near the main entrance of the cathedral leads down to the **Cripta Santa Reparata** (crypt), where excavations between 1965 and 1974 unearthed parts of the 5th-century Chiesa di Santa Reparata that originally stood on the site.

★ **Cupola del Brunelleschi**   LANDMARK
(Brunelleschi's Dome; Map p66; www.operaduomo. firenze.it; Duomo, Piazza del Duomo; adult/child incl campanile & baptistry €15/3; ◎ 8.30am-7pm Mon-Fri, to 5.40pm Sat) When Michelangelo went to work on St Peter's in Rome, he reportedly said: 'I go to build a greater dome, but not a fairer one.' One of the finest masterpieces of the Renaissance, the cupola crowning the Duomo is a feat of engineering and one that cannot be fully appreciated without climbing its 463 interior stone steps. It was built between 1420 and 1436 to a design by Filippo Brunelleschi, and is a staggering 91m high and 45.5m wide.

Taking his inspiration from Rome's Pantheon, Brunelleschi arrived at an innovative engineering solution of a distinctive octagonal shape of inner and outer concentric domes resting on the drum of the cathedral rather than the roof itself, allowing artisans to build from the ground up without needing a wooden support frame. Over four million bricks were used in the construction, all of them laid in consecutive rings in horizontal courses using a vertical herringbone pattern.

The climb up the spiral staircase is relatively steep, and should not be attempted if you are claustrophobic. Make sure to pause when you reach the balustrade at the base of the dome, which gives an aerial view of the octagonal *coro* (choir) of the cathedral below and the seven round stained-glass windows (by Donatello, Andrea del Castagno, Paolo Uccello and Lorenzo Ghiberti) that pierce the octagonal drum.

Look up and you'll see flamboyant late-16th-century frescoes by Giorgio Vasari and Federico Zuccari, depicting the *Giudizio Universale* (Last Judgement).

As you climb, snapshots of Florence can be spied through small windows. The final leg – a straight, somewhat hazardous flight up the curve of the inner dome – rewards with an unforgettable 360-degree panorama of one of Europe's most beautiful cities.

Buy tickets from the Duomo ticket office at Piazza San Giovanni 7, opposite the baptistry's northern entrance.

★**Campanile**   TOWER
(Map p66; www.operaduomo.firenze.it; Piazza del Duomo; adult/child incl cathedral cupola & baptistry €15/3; ⊙8.30am-7.30pm) The 414-step climb up the cathedral's 85m-tall *campanile*, begun by Giotto in 1334, rewards with a staggering city panorama. The first tier of

bas-reliefs around the base of its elaborate Gothic facade are copies of those carved by Pisano depicting the Creation of Man and the *attività umane* (arts and industries). Those on the second tier depict the planets, the cardinal virtues, the arts and the seven sacraments. The sculpted Prophets and Sibyls in the upper-storey niches are copies of works by Donatello and others.

★**Grande Museo del Duomo**   MUSEUM
(Cathedral Museum; Map p66; www.ilgrande museodelduomo.it; Piazza del Duomo 9; adult/child incl cathedral campanile, cupola & baptistry €15/3; ⊙9am-7pm) This impressive museum safeguards sacred and liturgical treasures from the Duomo, baptistry and bell tower. Awe-inspiring highlights include Ghiberti's original 15th-century masterpiece *Porta del Paradiso* (Gates of Paradise) – gloriously golden, 16m-tall gilded bronze doors designed for the eastern entrance to the Baptistry – as well as those he sculpted for the northern entrance. The best-known work is Michelangelo's

La Pietà, a work he sculpted when he was almost 80 and intended for his own tomb.

Vasari recorded in his *Lives of the Artists* that, dissatisfied with both the quality of the marble and of his own work, Michelangelo broke up the unfinished sculpture, destroying the arm and left leg of the figure of Christ. A student of Michelangelo's later restored the arm and completed the figure.

The museum's spectacular main hall, the **Room of the First Facade**, is dominated by a life-size reconstruction of the original facade of Florence's Duomo, decorated with some 40 14th- and early-15th-century statues carved for the facade by 14th-century masters. Led by Arnolfo di Cambio, building work began in 1296 but it was never finished and in 1586 the facade was eventually dismantled.

In the Gallery of Brunelleschi's Dome, look at 15th-century tools used to build the cathedral's groundbreaking cupola. Brunelleschi's funeral mask is also here.

Look out for the pair of exquisitely carved *cantorie* (singing galleries) or organ lofts – one by Donatello, the other by Luca della Robbia. Originally in the cathedral's sacristy, their scenes of musicians and children at play add a refreshingly frivolous touch amid so much sombre piety. Don't miss the same sculptor's wooden representation of a gaunt, desperately desolate Mary Magdalene in the same room, a work completed late in his career.

Battistero di San Giovanni   LANDMARK

(Baptistry; Map p66; Piazza di San Giovanni; adult/child incl cupola, campanile & museum €15/3; ⊘8.15-10.15am & 11.15am-7pm Mon-Sat, 8.30am-2pm Sun & 1st Sat of month) This 11th-century baptistry is a Romanesque, octagonal striped structure of white-and-green marble with three sets of doors conceived as panels on which to tell the story of humanity and the Redemption. Most celebrated of all are Lorenzo Ghiberti's gilded bronze doors at the eastern entrance, the *Porta del Paradiso* (Gate of Paradise). What you see today are copies – the originals are in the Grande Museo del Duomo.

Andrea Pisano executed the southern doors (1330), illustrating the life of St John the Baptist, and Lorenzo Ghiberti won a public competition in 1401 to design the northern doors, likewise replaced by copies today.

Dante counts among the famous dunked in the Baptistry's baptismal font.

Buy tickets from the Duomo ticket office at Piazza San Giovanni 7, opposite the baptistry's northern entrance.

Piazza della Signoria   PIAZZA

(Map p66; Piazza della Signoria) The hub of local life since the 13th century, Florentines flock here to meet friends and chat over early-evening *aperitivi* at historic cafes. Presiding over everything is **Palazzo Vecchio**, Florence's city hall, and the 14th-century **Loggia dei Lanzi**, an open-air gallery showcasing Renaissance sculptures, including Giambologna's *Rape of the Sabine Women* (c 1583), Benvenuto Cellini's bronze *Perseus* (1554) and Agnolo Gaddi's *Seven Virtues* (1384–89).

In centuries past, townsfolk congregated on the piazza whenever the city entered one of its innumerable political crises. The people would be called for a *parlamento* (a people's plebiscite) to rubber-stamp decisions that frequently meant ruin for some ruling families and victory for others. Scenes of great pomp and circumstance alternated with those of terrible suffering: it was here that vehemently pious preacher-leader Savonarola set fire to the city's art – books, paintings, musical instruments, mirrors, fine clothes and so on – during his famous 'Bonfire of the Vanities' in 1497, and where he was hung in chains and burnt as a heretic, along with two other supporters a year later.

The same spot where both fires burned is marked by a bronze plaque embedded in the ground in front of Amannati's **Fontana de Nettuno** (Neptune Fountain) with pin-headed bronze satyrs and divinities frolicking at its edges. More impressive are the equestrian statue of Cosimo I by Giambologna in the centre of the piazza, the much-photographed copy of Michelangelo's *David* guarding the western entrance to the Palazzo Vecchio since 1910 (the original stood here until 1873), and two copies of important Donatello works – *Marzocco*, the heraldic Florentine lion (for the original, visit the Museo del Bargello), and *Giuditta e Oloferne* (Judith and Holofernes; c 1455; original inside Palazzo Vecchio).

The Loggia dei Lanzi at the piazza's southern end owes its name to the Lanzichenecchi (Swiss bodyguards) of Cosimo I, who were stationed here.

★ Palazzo Vecchio   MUSEUM

(Map p66; ☑055 276 82 24; www.musefirenze.it; Piazza della Signoria; museum adult/reduced €10/8, tower €10/8, archaeology tour €2, museum & tower €14/12; ⊘museum 9am-midnight Fri-Wed, to 2pm Thu summer, 9am-7pm Fri-Wed, to 2pm Thu winter; tower 9am-9pm Fri-Wed, to 2pm Thu summer, 10am-5pm Fri-Wed, to 2pm Thu winter) This fortress palace, with its crenellations and 94m-high tower, was designed by Arnolfo di Cambio between 1298 and 1314 for the *signoria* (city government). It remains the seat of the city's power, home to the mayor's office and the municipal council. From the top of the **Torre d'Arnolfo** (tower), you can revel in unforgettable rooftop views.

During their short time in office the nine *priori* (consuls) – guild members picked at random – of the *signoria* lived in the palace. Every two months nine new names were pulled out of the hat, ensuring ample comings and goings.

In 1540 Cosimo I made the palace his ducal residence and centre of government, commissioning Vasari to renovate and decorate the interior. What impresses is the 53m-long, 22m-wide **Salone dei Cinquecento**, a magnificent painted hall created for the city's 15th-century ruling Consiglio dei Cinquecento (Council of 500). It's decorated with swirling battle scenes, painted floor to ceiling by Vasari and his apprentices. These scenes glorify Florentine victories by Cosimo I over arch-rivals Pisa and Siena: unlike the Sienese, the Pisans are depicted bare of armour (play 'Spot the Leaning Tower'). To top off this unabashed celebration of his own power, Cosimo had himself portrayed as a god in the centre of the exquisite panelled ceiling – but not before commissioning Vasari to raise the original ceiling 7m in height. It took Vasari and his school, in consultation with Michelangelo, just two years (1563–65) to construct the ceiling and paint the 34 gold-leafed panels. The effect is mesmerising. The hall is also graced by Michelangelo's *Genio della Vittoria* (Genius of Victory) sculpture.

Off this huge space is the **Chapel of SS Cosmas and Damian**, home to Vasari's 1557–58 triptych panels of the two saints depicting Cosimo the Elder as Cosmas (right) and Cosimo I as Damian (left). Next to the chapel is the **Sala di Leo X**, the private suite of apartments of Cardinal Giovanni de'

PALAZZO VECCHIO TOURS & ART WORKSHOPS

To get the most out of one of Florence's most dynamic, well-thought-out museums, join one of its excellent guided tours that take you into parts of the building otherwise inaccessible; many of the tours are in English.

The best of the adult bunch is probably the 'Secret Passages' tour (adult/reduced €12/10, 1½ hours, twice daily), which leads small groups along the secret staircase built between the palace's super-thick walls in 1342 as an escape route for French Duke of Athens Walter de Brienne, who seized the palace and nominated himself Lord of Florence, only to be sent packing back to France by the Florentines a year later. It follows this staircase to the **Tesoretto** (Treasury) of Cosimo I – a tiny room no larger than a cupboard for his private collection – and the equally intimate, sumptuous **Studiolo** (Study) of his introverted, alchemy-mad son Francesco I. Cosimo commissioned Vasari and a team of Florentine Mannerist artists to decorate the study, Francesco appearing in one of the 34 emblematic paintings covering the walls not as a prince, but as a scientist experimenting with gunpowder. The lower paintings concealed 20 cabinets in which the young prince hid his shells, crystals and other treasures. The tour ends in the palace **roof** above the Salone dei Cinquecento, where you can see the huge wooden trusses supporting Vasari's ornate ceiling.

The 'Invitation to Court' tour (adult/child €12/2, 1¼ hours) is open to visitors aged eight years and upwards. Actors dressed in Renaissance costume rope young participants into the performance. A sumptuously attired Eleonora of Toledo, clearly shocked by the casual attire of today's children, has been known to give advice about proper grooming for young ladies, and Cosimo I is happy to lay down the law about the proper age for a Medici to take on duties as a cardinal (the answer is 14, the age of his son Ferdinando when he became a cardinal). Other engaging tours specifically designed with children in mind include 'At Court with Donna Isabelle' (adult/child €12/2, 1¼ hours) for kids from age 10, led by a gregarious Spanish Isabel de Reinoso; and 'Life at Court' (adult/child €12/2, 70 minutes) for four to seven year olds, which ends with a 16th-century dressing-up session. There are also story-telling sessions for children and hands-on fresco- and panel-painting workshops (adult/child €12/2, 1¼ hours) led by an actor dressed up as Giorgio Vasari.

Reserve tours and workshops in advance by telephone (☎ 055 276 82 24, ☎ 055 276 85 58) or email info@muse.comune.fi.it.

Medici, the son of Lorenzo Il Magnifico, who became pope in 1513.

Upstairs, the private apartments of Eleonora and her ladies-in-waiting bear the same heavy-handed decor, blaring the glory of the Medici. The ceiling in the **Camera Verde** (Green Room) by Ridolfo del Ghirlandaio was inspired by designs from Nero's Domus Aurea in Rome. The **Sala dei Gigli**, named after its frieze of fleur-de-lis, representing the Florentine Republic, is home to Donatello's original *Judith and Holofernes*.

The **Sala delle Carte Geografiche** (Map Room) houses Cosimo I's fascinating collection of 16th-century maps charting everywhere in the known world at the time, from the polar regions to the Caribbean.

On rain-free days, end with a 418-step hike up the palace's striking **Torre d'Arnolfo**. No more than 25 people are allowed at any one time and you have just 30 minutes to lap up the brilliant city panorama.

Gucci Museo
MUSEUM

(Map p66; www.gucci.com; Piazza della Signoria 10; adult/child €7/free, after 5pm €5; ⊙10am-8pm, to 11pm Thu) Strut through the chic cafe and icon store to reach this museum. It tells the tale of the Gucci fashion house, from the first luggage pieces in Gucci's signature beige fabric emblazoned with the interlocking 'GG' logo to the 1950s red-and-green stripe and beyond. Don't miss the 1979 Cadillac Seville with gold Gs on the hubcaps and Gucci fabric upholstery. Displays continue to present day. In the final room exhibiting men's loafers, look in the mirrors (to admire your own feet and inferior footwear).

Piazza della Repubblica
PIAZZA

(Map p66) The site of a Roman forum and heart of medieval Florence, this busy civic space was created in the 1880s as part of a controversial plan of 'civic improvements' involving the demolition of the old market, Jewish ghetto and slums, and the relocation of nearly 6000 residents. Vasari's lovely *Loggia del Pesce* (Fish Market) was saved and re-erected on Via Pietrapiana.

Museo Galileo
MUSEUM

(Map p84; ☑055 26 53 11; www.museogalileo.it; Piazza dei Giudici 1; adult/reduced/family €9/5.50/22; ⊙9.30am-6pm Wed-Mon, to 12.30pm Tue) On the river next to the Uffizi in 12th-century Palazzo Castellani – look for the sundial telling the time on the pavement outside – is this state-of-the-art science museum, named after the great Pisa-born sci-

entist who was invited by the Medici court to Florence in 1610 (don't miss two of his fingers and a tooth displayed here).

A visit of the museum unravels a mesmerising curiosity box of astronomical and mathematical treasures (think telescopes, beautiful painted globes, barometers, watches, clocks and so on) collected by Cosimo I and other Medicis from 1562 and, later, the Lorraine dynasty. Allow plenty of time for the interactive area where various hands-on exhibits allow visitors to discover first-hand how and why some of the historic instruments actually work. Temporary exhibitions are equally compelling. Save your ticket to get €3 discount on admission to Museo di Storia Naturale – Zoologia La Specola (p87).

Chiesa e Museo di Orsanmichele
CHURCH, MUSEUM

(Map p66; Via dell'Arte della Lana; ⊙church 10am-5pm, museum 10am-5pm Mon) **FREE** This unusual and inspirational church, with a Gothic tabernacle by Andrea Orcagna, was created when the arcades of an old grain market (1290) were walled in and two storeys added during the 14th century. Its exterior is decorated with niches and tabernacles bearing statues. Representing the patron saints of Florence's many guilds, the statues were commissioned in the 15th and 16th centuries after the *signoria* ordered the city's guilds to finance the church's decoration.

These statues represent the work of some of the greatest Renaissance artists. Only copies adorn the building's exterior today, but all the originals except one are beautifully displayed in the church's little-known, light and airy museum, open only on Mondays, over two floors above the church.

Via de' Tornabuoni
LANDMARK

(Map p66) Renaissance palaces and Italian fashion houses border Via de' Tornabuoni, the city's most expensive shopping strip. Named after a Florentine noble family (which died out in the 17th century), it is referred to as the Salotto di Firenze (Florence's Drawing Room). At its northern end is **Palazzo Antinori** (Map p66; Piazza Antinori 3), 1461–69, owned by the aristocratic Antinori family (known for wine production) since 1506. Opposite, huge stone steps lead up to 17th-century **Chiesa di San Gaetano** (Map p66).

Palazzo Strozzi
GALLERY

(Map p66; ☑055 246 96 00; www.palazzostrozzi.org; Piazza degli Strozzi; adult/reduced €10/8,

2 tickets for price of 1 6-11pm Thu; ☺ 9am-8pm Tue, Wed & Fri-Sun, to 11pm Thu) This 15th-century Renaissance mansion was built for wealthy merchant Filippo Strozzi, one of the Medicis' major political and commercial rivals. Today it hosts exciting art exhibitions. There's always a buzz about the place, with young Florentines congregating in the courtyard Café Apollo (run by Florentine designer Roberto Cavalli). Art workshops and other activities aimed squarely at families make the gallery a firm favourite with pretty much everyone.

Chiesa di Santa Trìnita   CHURCH
(Map p66; Piazza Santa Trinita; ☺ 8am-noon & 4-5.45pm Mon-Sat, 8-10.45am & 4-5.45pm Sun) Built in Gothic style and later given a Mannerist facade, this 14th-century church shelters some of the city's finest frescoes: Lorenzo Monaco's *Annunciation* (1422) in **Cappella Bartholini Salimbeni** and eye-catching frescoes by Ghirlandaio depicting the life of St Francis of Assisi in **Cappella Sassetti**, right of the altar. The frescoes were painted between 1483 and 1485 and feature portraits of illustrious Florentines of the time; pop a €0.50 coin in the slot to illuminate the frescoes for two minutes.

Look out for the crest of the Bartholini Salimbeni family on the floor of the chapel – it features poppies and the motto *'Per Non Dormire'* (For Those Who Don't Sleep), a reference to the fact that the family fortune resulted from the acquisition of an important cargo of wool from Northern Europe, a deal scaled unbeknown to their business rivals, who had been doped with opium-laced wine at a lavish party the night before the cargo was due to arrive in Florence.

Museo Salvatore Ferragamo   MUSEUM
(Map p66; www.museoferragamo.it; Via de' Tornabuoni 2; adult/child €6/free; ☺ 10am-7.30pm) The splendid 13th-century **Palazzo Spini-Feroni** has been the home of the Ferragamo fashion empire since 1938. Anyone with even the faintest tendency towards shoe addiction or with an interest in the socio-historical context of fashion should not miss the esoteric but oddly compelling shoe museum.

Museo di Palazzo Davanzati   MUSEUM
(Map p66; Via Porta Rossa 13; adult/reduced €2/1; ☺ 8.15am-1.50pm, closed 1st, 3rd & 5th Mon, 2nd & 4th Sun of month) Tucked inside a 14th-century warehouse and residence, home to the wealthy Davanzati merchant family from 1578, this *palazzo* museum with wonderful central loggia is a gem. Peep at the carved faces of the original owners on the pillars in the inner courtyard and don't miss the 1st-floor **Sala Madornale** (Reception Room) with its painted wooden ceiling. Other highlights include the exotic **Sala dei Pappagalli** (Parrot Room) and **Camera dei Pavoni** (Peacock Bedroom).

Museo Marino Marini   GALLERY
(Map p66; Piazza San Pancrazio 1; adult/reduced €6/4; ☺ 10am-5pm Wed-Sat & Mon) Deconsecrated in the 19th century, Chiesa di San Pancrazio is home to this small art museum displaying sculptures, portraits and drawings by Pistoia-born sculptor Marino Marini (1901-80). But the highlight is the **Cappella Rucellai** with a tiny scale copy of Christ's Holy Sepulchre in Jerusalem – a Renaissance gem by Leon Battista Alberti. The chapel was built between 1458 and 1467 for the tomb of wealthy Florentine banker and wool merchant, Giovanni Ruccellai.

Alberti chose white marble from Carrara and green marble from Prato to craft the sepulchre, an exquisite work of art with its classical mouldings, decorative geometric motifs and lantern crown. Visits are limited to 25 people, every 30 minutes.

◉ Santa Maria Novella

Radiating west and south from the venerable basilica, the neighbourhood of Santa Maria Novella is blessed with chic boutiques, impressive palaces and art-adorned churches.

Basilica di Santa Maria Novella   CHURCH
(Map p66; www.chiesasantamarianovella.it; Piazza di Santa Maria Novella 18; adult/reduced €5/3.50; ☺ 9am-5.30pm Mon-Thu, 11am-5.30pm Fri, 9am-5pm Sat, 1-5pm Sun) The striking green-and-white marble facade of 13th- to 15th-century Basilica di Santa Maria Novella fronts an entire monastical complex, comprising romantic church cloisters and a frescoed chapel. The basilica itself is a treasure chest of artistic masterpieces, climaxing with frescoes by Domenico Ghirlandaio. The lower section of the basilica's striped marbled facade is transitional from Romanesque to Gothic; the upper section and the main doorway (1456–70) were designed by Leon Battista Alberti.

As you enter, look straight ahead to see Masaccio's superb fresco *Holy Trinity* (1424–25), one of the first artworks to use the then newly discovered techniques of perspective and proportion. Hanging in the central nave is a luminous painted *Crucifix* by Giotto (c 1290).

The first chapel to the right of the altar, **Cappella di Filippo Strozzi**, features spirited late-15th-century frescoes by Filippino Lippi (son of Fra' Filippo Lippi) depicting the lives of St John the Evangelist and St Philip the Apostle.

Behind the main altar is the **Cappella Maggiore** with Domenico Ghirlandaio's frescoes. Those on the right depict the life of John the Baptist; those on the left illustrate scenes from the life of the Virgin Mary. The frescoes were painted between 1485 and 1490, and are notable for their depiction of Florentine life during the Renaissance. Spot portraits of Ghirlandaio's contemporaries and members of the Tornabuoni family, who commissioned them.

To the far left of the altar, up a short flight of stairs, is the **Cappella Strozzi di Mantova**, covered in 14th-century frescoes by Niccolò di Tommaso and Nardo di Cione depicting paradise, purgatory and hell. The altarpiece (1354–57) here was painted by the latter's brother Andrea, better known as Andrea Orcagna.

From the church, walk through a side door into the serene **Chiostro Verde** (Green Cloister; 1332–62), part of the vast monastical complex occupied by Dominican friars who arrived in Florence in 1219 and settled in Santa Maria Novella two years later. The tranquil cloister takes its name from the green earth base used for the frescoes on three of the cloister's four walls. On its north side is the spectacular **Cappellone degli Spagnoli** (Spanish Chapel), originally the friars' chapter house and named as such in 1566 when it was given to the Spanish colony in Florence. The chapel is covered in extraordinary frescoes (c 1365–67) by Andrea di Bonaiuto. The vault features depictions of the Resurrection, Ascension and Pentecost, and on the altar wall are the *Via Dolorosa, Crucifixion* and *Descent into Limbo*. On the right wall is a huge fresco of *The Militant and Triumphant Church* – look in the foreground for a portrait of Cimabue, Giotto, Boccaccio, Petrarch and Dante. Other frescoes in the chapels depict the *Triumph of Christian Doctrine*, 14 figures symbolising the Arts and Sciences, and the Life of St Peter.

By the side of the chapel, a passage leads into the **Chiostro dei Morti** (Cloister of the Dead), a cemetery existent well before the arrival of the Dominicans to Santa Maria Novella. The tombstones embedded in the walls and floor date to the 13th and 14th centuries.

On the west side of the Chiostro Verde, another passage leads to the 14th-century **Cappella degli Ubriachi** and a large **refectory** (1353–54) featuring ecclesiastical relics and a 1583 *Last Supper* by Alessandro Allori.

There are two entrances to the Santa Maria Novella complex: the main entrance to the basilica or through the tourist office opposite

---

DON'T MISS

BACKSTREET FLORENCE: DANTE
··

Italy's most divine poet was born in 1265 in a wee house down a narrow lane in the back-streets of Florence. Tragic romance made him tick and there's no better place to unravel the medieval life and times of Dante than the **Museo Casa di Dante**. (Map p66; ☑ 055 21 94 16; Via Santa Margherita 1; adult/reduced €4/2; ☉ 10am-5pm Tue-Sun).

When Dante was just 12 he was promised in marriage to Gemma Donati. But it was another Florentine gal, Beatrice Portinari (1266–90), that was his muse, his inspiration, the love of his life (despite only ever meeting her twice in his life): in *Divina Commedia* (Divine Comedy) Dante broke with tradition by using the familiar Italian, not the formal Latin, to describe travelling through the circles of hell in search of his beloved Beatrice.

Beatrice, who wed a banker and died a couple of years later aged just 24, is buried in 11th-century **Chiesa di Santa Margherita** (Map p66; Via Santa Margherita 4), in an alley near Dante's house; note the wicker basket in front of her grave filled with scraps of paper on which prayers and dedications evoking unrequited love have been penned. This chapel was also where the poet married Gemma in 1295. Dimly lit, it remains much as it was in medieval Florence. No wonder novelist Dan Brown chose it to set a scene in his most recent Dante-themed thriller, *Inferno* (2013), which takes place in Florence.

Crown the old-world experience with a traditional tripe *panino* (sandwich) from hole-in-the-wall **Da Vinattieri** (p100), best eaten squatting on a simple wooden stool in this old-fashioned alley in backstreet Florence.

the train station on Via de' Partzani; Firenze Card holders are obliged to use the latter.

★ Museo Novecento   MUSEUM

(Museum of the 20th Century; Map p66; ☑055 28 61 32; www.museonovecento.it; Piazza di Santa Maria Novella 10; adult/reduced €8.50/4; ☉10am-6pm Mon-Wed, to 2pm Thu, to 9pm Fri, to 8pm Sat & Sun) Don't allow the Renaissance to distract from Florence's fantastic modern art museum, in a 13th-century *palazzo* previously used as a pilgrim shelter, hospital and school. A well-articulated itinerary guides visitors through modern Italian painting and sculpture from the early 20th century to the late 1980s. Installation art makes effective use of the outside space on the 1st-floor loggia. Fashion and theatre get a nod on the 2nd floor, and the itinerary ends with a 20-minute cinematic montage of the best films set in Florence.

A highlight of Room 10 is Arturo Martini's exquisite sculpture *La Pisana* (1933), next to one of Marino Marini's signature bronze horses – both representative of the archaeological rediscovery of the ancient world expressed by artists in Italy in the 1920s and 1930s.

Captivating guided tours and activities for children and families cap off the museum's first-class portfolio.

Chiesa d'Ognissanti   CHURCH

(Map p66; Borgo d'Ognissanti 42; ☉9am-12.30pm & 4-6pm Mon-Sat, 9-10am & 4-5.30pm Sun) Stroll along Borgo d'Ognissanti, from Piazza Carlo Goldoni towards the ancient city gate Porta al Prato, past antiques shops and designer boutiques to reach this 13th-century church, built as part of a Benedictine monastery. Its highlight is Domenico Ghirlandaio's fresco of the *Madonna della Misericordia* protecting members of the Vespucci family, the church's main patrons.

Amerigo Vespucci, the Florentine navigator who gave his name to the American continent, is supposed to be the young boy whose head peeks between the Madonna and the old man.

Also here are a *Crucifixion* by Taddeo Gaddi, Ghirlandaio's *St Jerome* (1480) and Botticelli's pensive *St Augustine* (also 1480). Botticelli, who grew up in a house on Borgo d'Ognissanti, is buried here (look for the simple round tombstone marked 'Sandro Filipepe' in the south transept).

Museo Stibbert   MUSEUM

(www.museostibbert.it; Via Federigo Stibbert 26; adult/reduced €8/6; ☉10am-2pm Mon-Wed, to 6pm Fri-Sun) Anglo-Italian, Florence-born Frederick Stibbert (1838–1906) was one of the grand 19th-century wheeler-dealers on the European antiquities market and amassed an intriguing personal collection of furnishings, tapestries and 16th- to 19th-century paintings, showcased in this villa museum. Fun for kids is the **Sala della Cavalcata** (Parade Room) with life-sized figures of horses and their riders in suits of armour from Europe and the Middle East. Take bus 4 from Stazione di Santa Maria Novella to the 'Gioia' stop on Via Fabroni, from where it is a short walk.

◉ San Lorenzo

This is Medici territory – come here to see their palace, church, library and mausoleum, all decorated with extraordinary works of art.

Basilica di San Lorenzo   BASILICA

(Map p66; Piazza San Lorenzo; admission €4.50, incl Biblioteca Medicea Laurenziana €7; ☉10am-5.30pm Mon-Sat, plus 1.30-5pm Sun winter) Considered one of Florence's most harmonious examples of Renaissance architecture, this unfinished basilica was the Medici parish church and mausoleum. It was designed by Brunelleschi in 1425 for Cosimo the Elder and built over an earlier 4th-century church. In the solemn interior look out for Brunelleschi's austerely beautiful **Sagrestia Vecchia** (Old Sacristy) with its sculptural decoration by Donatello. Michelangelo was commissioned to design the facade in 1518, but his design in white Carrara marble was never executed, hence the building's rough unfinished appearance.

Inside, columns of *pietra serena* (soft grey stone) crowned with Corinthian capitals separate the nave from the two aisles. Donatello, who was still sculpting the two bronze pulpits (1460–67) adorned with panels of the Crucifixion when he died, is buried in the chapel featuring Fra' Filippo Lippi's *Annunciation* (c 1450).

Biblioteca Medicea Laurenziana   LIBRARY

(Medici Library; Map p66; www.bml.firenze.sbn.it; Piazza San Lorenzo 9; admission €3, incl basilica €7; ☉9.30am-1.30pm Mon-Sat) Beyond the Basilica di San Lorenzo ticket office lie peaceful cloisters framing a garden with orange trees. Stairs lead up the loggia and the Biblioteca Medicea Laurenziana, commissioned by Giulio de' Medici (Pope Clement VII) in 1524 to house the extensive Medici library (started by Cosimo the Elder and greatly added to by Lorenzo il Magnifico). The extraordinary staircase in the vestibule,

San Lorenzo & San Marco

San Lorenzo & San Marco

intended as a 'dark prelude' to the magnificent **Sala di Lettura** (Reading Room), was designed in by Michelangelo.

★ Museo delle Cappelle Medicee
MAUSOLEUM

(Medici Chapels; Map p66; ☑ 055 29 48 83; www.polomuseale.firenze.it; Piazza Madonna degli Aldobrandini; adult/reduced €6/3; ⏱ 8.15am-1.50pm, closed 2nd & 4th Sun, 1st, 3rd & 5th Mon of month) Nowhere is Medici conceit expressed so explicitly as in the Medici Chapels. Adorned with granite, marble, semiprecious stones and some of Michelangelo's most beautiful sculptures, it is the burial place of 49 dynasty members. Francesco I lies in the dark, impos-

ing **Cappella dei Principi** (Princes' Chapel) alongside Ferdinando I and II and Cosimo I, II and III. Lorenzo il Magnifico is buried in the graceful **Sagrestia Nuova** (New Sacristy), which was Michelangelo's first architectural work.

It is also in the sacristy that you can swoon over three of Michelangelo's most haunting sculptures: *Dawn and Dusk* on the sarcophagus of Lorenzo, Duke of Urbino; *Night and Day* on the sarcophagus of Lorenzo's son Giuliano (note the unfinished face of 'Day' and the youth of the sleeping woman drenched in light aka 'Night'); and *Madonna and Child*, which adorns Lorenzo's tomb.

Palazzo Medici-Riccardi   PALACE
(Map p66; ☑ 055 276 03 40; www.palazzo-medici.it; Via Cavour 3; adult/reduced €7/4; ⊙ 8.30am-7pm Thu-Tue) Cosimo the Elder entrusted Michelozzo with the design of the family's townhouse in 1444. The result was this palace, a blueprint that influenced the construction of Florentine family residences such as Palazzo Pitti and Palazzo Strozzi. The upstairs chapel, **Cappella dei Magi**, is covered in a wonderfully detailed frescoes (c 1459-63) by Benozzo Gozzoli, a pupil of Fra' Angelico, and is one of the supreme achievements of Renaissance painting.

Gozzoli's ostensible theme of *Procession of the Magi to Bethlehem* is but a slender pretext for portraying members of the Medici clan in their best light; spy Lorenzo il Magnifico and Cosimo the Elder in the crowd. The chapel was reconfigured to accommodate a baroque staircase, hence the oddly split fresco. The mid-15th-century altarpiece of the *Adoration of the Child* is a copy of the original (originally here) by Fra' Filippo Lippi. Only 10 visitors are allowed in at a time; in high season reserve in advance at the ticket desk.

The Medici lived at Palazzo Medici until 1540, making way for the Riccardi family a century later. They remodelled the palace and built the 1st-floor **Sala Luca Giordano**, a sumptuous masterpiece of baroque art. Giordano adorned the ceiling with his complex *Allegory of Divine Wisdom* (1685), a rather overblown example of late baroque dripping with gold leaf and bursting with colour.

◉ San Marco

This part of the city boasts far more than the city's most famous resident, one Signore *David*. The frescoes in the Museo di San Marco are nothing short of superb.

★ Galleria dell'Accademia   GALLERY
(Map p76; www.polomuseale.firenze.it; Via Ricasoli 60; adult/reduced €8/4; ⊙ 8.15am-6.50pm Tue-Sun) A queue marks the door to this gallery, built to house one of the Renaissance's most iconic masterpieces, Michelangelo's *David*. But the world's most famous statue is worth the wait. The subtle detail of the real thing – the veins in his sinewy arms, the leg muscles, the change in expression as you move around the statue – *is* impressive. Carved from a single block of marble, Michelangelo's most famous work was his most challenging – he didn't choose the marble himself and it was veined.

And when the statue of the nude boy-warrior, depicted for the first time as a man in the prime of life rather than a young boy, assumed its pedestal in front of Palazzo Vecchio on Piazza della Signoria in 1504, Florentines immediately adopted it as a powerful emblem of Florentine power, liberty and civic pride.

Michelangelo was also the master behind the unfinished *San Matteo* (St Matthew; 1504-08) and four *Prigioni* ('Prisoners' or 'Slaves'; 1521-30), also displayed in the gallery. The Prisoners seem to be writhing and struggling to free themselves from the marble; they were meant for the tomb of Pope Julius II, itself never completed. Adjacent rooms contain paintings by Andrea Orcagna, Taddeo Gaddi, Domenico Ghirlandaio, Filippino Lippi and Sandro Botticelli.

★ Museo di San Marco   MUSEUM
(Map p76; www.polomuseale.firenze.it; Piazza San Marco 1; adult/reduced €4/2; ⊙ 8.15am-1.50pm Mon-Fri, 8.15am-4.50pm Sat & Sun, closed 1st, 3rd & 5th Sun, 2nd & 4th Mon of month) At the heart of Florence's university area sits **Chiesa di San Marco** and adjoining 15th-century Dominican monastery where both gifted painter Fra' Angelico (c 1395-1455) and the sharp-tongued Savonarola (1452-98) piously served God. Today the monastery, aka one of Florence's most spiritually uplifting museums, showcases the work of Fra' Angelico. After centuries of being known as 'Il Beato Angelico' (literally 'The Blessed Angelic One') or simply 'Il Beato' (The Blessed), the Renaissance's most blessed religious painter was made a saint by Pope John Paul II in 1984.

Enter via Michelozzo's **Cloister of Saint Antoninus** (1440). Turn immediately right to enter the **Sala dell'Ospizio** (Pilgrims' Hospital) where Fra' Angelico's attention to perspective and the realistic portrayal of nature comes to life in a number of major paintings, including the *Deposition of Christ* (1432).

Giovanni Antonio Sogliani's fresco *The Miraculous Supper of St Domenic* (1536) dominates the former monks' **refectory** in the cloister; and Fra' Angelico's huge *Crucifixion and Saints* fresco (1441-42) decorates the former chapterhouse. But it is the 44 monastic **cells** on the 1st floor that are the most haunting: at the top of the stairs, Fra' Angelico's most famous work, *Annunciation* (c 1440), commands all eyes.

A stroll around each of the cells reveals snippets of many more religious reliefs by the Tuscan-born friar, who decorated the

WHO'S THAT BLOKE?

Name *David*

Occupation World's most famous sculpture.

Vital statistics Height: 516cm tall; weight: 19 tonnes of mediocre-quality pearly white marble from the Fantiscritti quarries in Carrara.

Spirit Young biblical hero in meditative pose who, with the help of God, defeats an enemy more powerful than himself. Scarcely visible sling emphasises victory of innocence and intellect over brute force.

Commissioned In 1501 by the Opera del Duomo for the cathedral, but subsequently placed in front of the Palazzo Vecchio on Piazza della Signoria, where it stayed until 1873.

Famous journeys It took 40 men four days to transport the statue on rails from Michelangelo's workshop behind the cathedral to Piazza della Signoria in 1504. Its journey from here, through the streets of Florence, to its current purpose-built tribune in the Galleria dell'Accademia in 1873 took seven long days.

Outstanding features (a) His expression which, from the left profile, appears serene, Zen and boy-like, and from the right, concentrated, manly and highly charged in anticipation of the gargantuan Goliath he is about to slay; (b) the sense of counterbalanced weight rippling through his body, from the tension in his right hip on which he leans to his taut left arm.

Why the small penis? In classical art a large or even normal-sized packet was not deemed elegant, hence the daintier size.

And the big head and hands? *David* was designed to stand up high on a cathedral buttress in the apse, from where his head and hands would have appeared in perfect proportion.

Beauty treatments Body scrub with hydrochloric acid (1843); clay and cellulose pulp 'mud pack', bath in distilled water (2004).

Occupational hazards Over the centuries he's been struck by lightning, attacked by rioters and had his toes bashed with a hammer. The two pale white lines visible on his lower left arm is where his arm got broken during the 1527 revolt when the Medici were kicked out of Florence. Giorgio Vasari, then a child, picked up the pieces and 16 years later had them sent to Cosimo I who restored the statue, so the story goes.

cells between 1440 and 1441 with deeply devotional frescoes to guide the meditation of his fellow friars. Most were executed by Fra' Angelico himself, others by aides under his supervision, including Benozzo Gozzoli. Among several masterpieces is the magnificent *Adoration of the Magi* in the cell used by Cosimo the Elder as a meditation retreat (Nos 38 to 39). Quite a few of the frescoes are gruesome: the cell of San Antonino Arcivescovo features Jesus pushing open the door of his sepulchre, squashing a nasty-looking devil in the process.

Contrasting with the pure beauty of these frescoes are the plain rooms that Savonarola called home from 1489. Rising to the position of prior at the Dominican convent, it was from here that the fanatical monk railed against luxury, greed and corruption of the clergy. Kept as a kind of shrine to the turbulent priest, they house a portrait, a few personal items, the linen banner Savonarola carried in processions and a grand marble monument erected by admirers in 1873.

Piazza della Santissima Annunziata PIAZZA
(Map p76) Giambologna's equestrian statue of Grand Duke Ferdinando I de' Medici commands the scene from the centre of this majestic square, dominated by the facades of **Chiesa della Santissima Annunziata** (Map p76), 1250, rebuilt by Michelozzo et al in the mid-15th century, and the **Ospedale degli Innocenti** (Hospital of the Innocents; Map p76; Piazza della SS Annunziata 12), Europe's first orphanage founded in 1421. Look up to admire Brunelleschi's classically influenced portico, decorated by Andrea della Robbia (1435–1525) with terracotta medallions of babies in swaddling clothes.

At the north end of the portico, the false door surrounded by railings was once a revolving door where unwanted children were left. You can pay €3 to visit its lovely courtyard (open 9am to 6.30pm Monday to Saturday), but the interior is closed for major restoration works; when it reopens (date unknown) it will host a new **Museum of Childhood**.

About 200m southeast of the piazza is the **Museo Archeologico** (Map p76; Piazza Santissima Annunziata 9b; adult/reduced €4/2; ☻8.30am-7pm Tue-Fri, to 2pm Sat-Mon), whose rich collection of finds, including most of the Medici hoard of antiquities, plunges you deep into the past and offers an alternative to Renaissance splendour. On the 1st floor you can either head left into the ancient Egyptian collection or right for the smaller section of Etruscan and Graeco-Roman art.

◉ Santa Croce

Presided over by the massive Franciscan basilica of the same name on the neighbourhood's main square, this area has a slightly rough veneer to it

Piazza di Santa Croce   PIAZZA

(Map p80) This square was cleared in the Middle Ages to allow the faithful to gather when the church itself was full. In Savonarola's day, heretics were executed here. Such an open space inevitably found other uses, and from the 14th century it was often the colourful scene of jousts, festivals and *calcio storico* matches. The city's 2nd-century amphitheatre took up the area facing the western end of Piazza di Santa Croce: Piazza dei Peruzzi, Via de' Bentaccordi and Via Torta mark the oval outline of its course.

Still played in this square in the third week of June each year, *calcio storico* (www.calciostorico.it) is like a combination of football and rugby with few rules (headbutting, punching, elbowing and choking are allowed, but sucker-punching and kicks to the head are forbidden).

Basilica di Santa Croce   CHURCH, MUSEUM

(Map p80; www.santacroceopera.it; Piazza di Santa Croce; adult/reduced €6/4; ☻9.30am-5.30pm Mon-Sat, 2-5.30pm Sun) The austere interior of this Franciscan basilica is a shock after the magnificent neo-Gothic facade enlivened by varying shades of coloured marble. Most visitors come to see the tombs of Michelangelo, Galileo and Ghiberti inside this church, but frescoes by Giotto in the chapels right of the altar are the

real highlights. The basilica was designed by Arnolfo di Cambio between 1294 and 1385 and owes its name to a splinter of the Holy Cross donated by King Louis of France in 1258.

Some of its frescoed chapels are much better preserved than others – Giotto's murals in the **Cappella Peruzzi** are in particularly poor condition. Those in the **Cappella Bardi** (1315–20) depicting scenes from the life of St Francis have fared better. Giotto's assistant and most loyal pupil, Taddeo Gaddi, frescoed the neighbouring **Cappella Majeure** and nearby **Cappella Baroncelli** (1332–38); the latter takes as its subject the life of the Virgin.

Taddeo's son Agnolo painted the **Cappella Castellani** (1385), with frescoes depicting the life of St Nicholas, and was also responsible for the frescoes above the altar.

From the transept chapels a doorway designed by Michelozzo leads into a corridor, off which is the **Sagrestia**, an enchanting 14th-century room dominated on the left by Taddeo Gaddi's fresco of the Crucifixion. There are also a few relics of St Francis on show, including his cowl and belt. Through the next room, the church bookshop, you can access the Scuola del Cuoio (p116), a leather school where you can see bags being fashioned and buy the finished products.

At the end of the corridor is a Medici chapel with a fine two-tone altarpiece in glazed terracotta by Andrea della Robbia.

Brunelleschi designed the second of Santa Croce's two serene cloisters just before his death in 1446. His unfinished **Cappella de' Pazzi** at the end of the first cloister is notable for its harmonious lines and restrained terracotta medallions of the Apostles by Luca della Robbia, and is a masterpiece of Renaissance architecture. It was built for, but never used by, the wealthy banking family destroyed in the 1478 Pazzi Conspiracy – when papal sympathisers sought to overthrow Lorenzo il Magnifico and the Medici dynasty.

Located off the first cloister, the **Museo dell'Opera di Santa Croce** features a Crucifixion by Cimabue, restored to the best degree possible after flood damage in 1966, when more than 4m of water inundated the Santa Croce area. Other highlights include Donatello's gilded bronze statue *St Louis of Toulouse* (1424), originally placed in a tabernacle on the Orsanmichele facade; a wonderful terracotta bust of St Francis receiving the stigmata by the della Robbia workshop; and frescoes by Taddeo Gaddi, including *The Last Supper* (1333).

Santa Croce

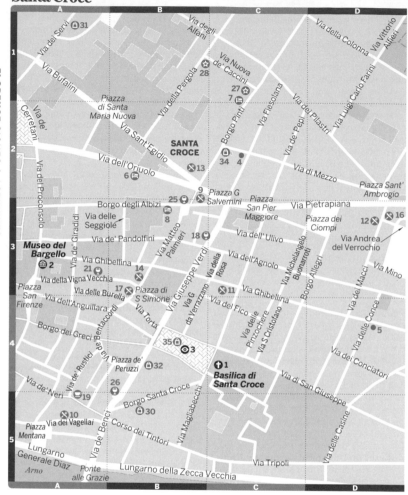

★ **Museo del Bargello** MUSEUM
(Map p80; www.polomuseale.firenze.it; Via del Proconsolo 4; adult/reduced €4/2; ☉8.15am-4.50pm summer, to 1.50pm winter, closed 1st, 3rd & 5th Sun, 2nd & 4th Mon of month) It was behind the stark walls of Palazzo del Bargello, Florence's earliest public building, that the *podestà* meted out justice from the late 13th century until 1502. Today the building safeguards Italy's most comprehensive collection of Tuscan Renaissance sculpture with some of Michelangelo's best early works and a hall full of Donatello's. Michelangelo was just 21 when a cardinal commissioned him to create the drunken grape-adorned Bacchus (1496-97), displayed in Bargello's downstairs **Sala di Michelangelo**.

Unfortunately the cardinal didn't like the result and sold it to a banker. Other Michelangelo works to look out for here include the marble bust of *Brutus* (c 1539-40), the *David/Apollo* from 1530-32 and the large, uncompleted roundel of the *Madonna and Child with the Infant St John* (aka the *Tondo Pitti*; 1503-05).

After Michelangelo left Florence for the final time in 1534, sculpture was dominated by Baccio Bandinelli (his 1551 *Adam and*

Eve, created for the Duomo, is displayed in the Sala di Michelangelo) and Benvenuto Cellini (look for his playful 1548–50 marble *Ganimede* in the same room).

On the 1st floor, to the right of the staircase, is the **Sala di Donatello**. Here, in the majestic Salone del Consiglio Generale where the city's general council met, works by Donatello and other early-15th-century sculptors can be admired. Originally on the facade of Chiesa di Orsanmichele and now within a tabernacle at the hall's far end, Donatello's wonderful *St George* (1416–17) brought a new sense of perspective and movement to Italian sculpture. Also look for the bronze bas-reliefs created for the Baptistry doors competition by Brunelleschi and Ghiberti.

Yet it is Donatello's two versions of *David,* a favourite subject for sculptors, which really fascinate: Donatello fashioned his youthful dressed image in marble in 1408 and his fabled bronze between 1440 and 1450. The latter is extraordinary – the more so when you consider it was the first freestanding naked statue to be sculpted since classical times.

Criminals received their last rites before execution in the 1st-floor **Cappella del Podestà** (Mary Magdalene Chapel), where Hell and Paradise are frescoed on the walls, as are stories from the lives of Mary of Egypt, Mary Magdalene and John the Baptist. These remnants of frescoes by Giotto were not discovered until 1840, when the chapel was turned into a storeroom and prison.

The 2nd floor moves into the 16th century with a superb collection of terracotta pieces by the prolific della Robbia family, including some of their best-known works, such as Andrea's *Ritratto idealizia di fanciullo* (Bust of a Boy; c 1475) and Giovanni's *Pietà* (1514). Instantly recognisable, Giovanni's works are more elaborate and flamboyant than either father Luca's or cousin Andrea's, using a larger palette of colours.

◉ Oltrarno

Literally 'other side of the Arno', atmospheric Oltrarno is the traditional home of the city's artisanal workshops. It embraces the area south of the river and west of Ponte Vecchio and its backbone is busy Borgo San Jacopo, clad with restaurants, shops and a twinset of 12th-century towers, **Torre dei Marsili** (Map p66) and **Torre de' Belfredelli** (Map p84).

When you reach the stage of museum overload and need to stretch your legs and see some sky, the tiers of parks and gardens behind Palazzo Pitti – not to be missed at sunset when its entire vast facade is coloured a vibrant pink – are just the ticket.

Should you notice something gone awry with street signs in Oltrarno – on a No Entry sign, a tiny black figure stealthily sneaking away with the white bar for example – you can be sure it is the work of **CLET** (Via dell'Olmo 8r; ⊙variable), Florence's most talked-about and admired street artist who quietly beavers away in his Oltrarno studio on Via dell'Olmo creating stickers that end up on street signs all over the city. In 2011 the French-born artist created quite a stir in his adopted city by installing, in

Santa Croce

the black of night, a life-sized figurine entitled *Uomo Comune* (Common Man) on Ponte alle Grazie (to which the city authorities turned a blind eye for a week before removing it).

Ponte Vecchio BRIDGE
(Map p66) Dating to 1345, Ponte Vecchio was the only Florentine bridge to survive destruction at the hands of retreating German forces in 1944. Above the jewellers' shops on the eastern side, the **Corridoio Vasariano** (Vasari corridor) is a 16th-century passageway between the Uffizi and Palazzo Pitti that runs around, rather than through, the medieval **Torre dei Mannelli** at the bridge's southern end. The first documentation of a stone bridge here, at the narrowest crossing point along the entire length of the Arno, dates from 972.

Floods in 1177 and 1333 destroyed the bridge, and in 1966 it came close to being destroyed again. Many of the jewellers with shops on the bridge were convinced the floodwaters would sweep away their livelihoods; fortunately the bridge held.

They're still here. Indeed, the bridge has twinkled with the glittering wares of jewellers, their trade often passed down from generation to generation, ever since the 16th century, when Ferdinando I de' Medici ordered them here to replace the often malodorous

presence of the town butchers, who used to toss unwanted leftovers into the river.

★**Basilica di Santo Spirito** CHURCH
(Map p84; Piazza Santo Spirito; ◒9.30am-12.30pm & 4-5.30pm Thu-Tue) FREE The facade of this Brunelleschi church, smart on Florence's most shabby-chic piazza, makes a striking backdrop to open-air concerts in summer. Inside, the basilica's length is lined with 38 semicircular chapels (covered with a plain wall in the 1960s), and a colonnade of grey *pietra forte* Corinthian columns injects monumental grandeur. Artworks to look for include Domenico di Zanobi's *Madonna of the Relief* (1485) in the Cappella Velutti, in which the Madonna wards off a little red devil with a club.

Filippino Lippi's poorly lit *Madonna with Child and Saints* (1493–94) is in the **Cappella Nerli** in the right transept.

The main altar, beneath the central dome, is a voluptuous baroque flourish, rather out of place in Brunelleschi's spare interior.

Don't miss the door next to **Capella Segni** in the left aisle leading to the **sacristy**, where you'll find a poignant wooden crucifix attributed by some experts to Michelangelo. Michelangelo used to visit the hospital inside the neighbouring monastery at night to study the anatomy of corpses yet to be buried, hence his donation of the exquisitely sculptured Christ, or so the story goes.

Cenacolo di Santo Spirito   MUSEUM
(Map p84; ☑055 28 70 43; Piazza Santo Spirito 29; adult/child €4/free; ⊙10am-4pm Sat-Mon) For a change of pace from the Renaissance, head to this former refectory decorated with a grand fresco by Andrea Orcagna depicting the *Last Supper and the Crucifixion* (c 1370). Inside, a collection of rare 11th-century Romanesque sculpture woos.

★ Cappella Brancacci   CHAPEL
(Map p84; ☑055 276 82 24; http://museicivici fiorentini.comune.fi.it; Piazza del Carmine 14; adult/ reduced €6/4.50; ⊙10am-5pm Wed-Sat & Mon, 1-5pm Sun) Fire in the 18th century all but destroyed 13th-century **Basilica di Santa Maria del Carmine**, but fortunately it spared the magnificent frescoes in this chapel – a treasure of paintings by Masolino da Panicale, Masaccio and Filippino Lippi commissioned by rich merchant Felice Brancacci upon his return from Egypt in 1423. The entrance to the chapel is to the right of the main church entrance. Only 30 people are allowed in at any one time and visits are limited to 30 minutes in high season.

Masaccio's fresco cycle illustrating the life of St Peter is considered among his greatest works, representing a definitive break with Gothic art and a plunge into new worlds of expression in the early stages of the Renaissance. *The Expulsion of Adam and Eve from Paradise* and *The Tribute Money,* both on the left side of the chapel, are his best-known works. Masaccio painted these frescoes in his early 20s, taking over from Masolino, and interrupted the task to go to Rome, where he died, aged only 27. The cycle was completed some 60 years later by Filippino Lippi. Masaccio himself features in his *St Peter Enthroned;* he's the one standing beside the Apostle, staring out at the viewer. The figures around him have been identified as Brunelleschi, Masolino and Alberti. Filippino Lippi also painted himself into the scene of *St Peter's Crucifixion,* along with his teacher, Botticelli.

★ Palazzo Pitti   MUSEUM
(Map p84; www.polomuseale.firenze.it; Piazza dei Pitti; ⊙8.15am-6.50pm Tue-Sun, reduced hours winter) Commissioned by banker Luca Pitta and designed by Brunelleschi in 1457, this

---

THE EXTRAORDINARY VASARIAN CORRIDOR

Bathed in mystery, this must be the world's most infamous and enigmatic corridor. Look above the jewellery shops on the eastern side of Ponte Vecchio to see Florence's **Corridoio Vasariano** (Vasarian Corridor; Map p66; ⊙by guided tour; 🚇B), an elevated covered passageway joining the Palazzo Vecchio on Piazza della Signoria with the Uffizi and Palazzo Pitti on the other side of the river. Around 1km long, it was designed by Vasari for Cosimo I in 1565 to allow the Medicis to wander between the two palaces in privacy and comfort. From the 17th century, the Medicis strung it with self-portraits – today the collection of 700-odd artworks includes self-portraits of Andrea del Sarto (the oldest), Rubens, Rembrandt, Canova and others.

The original promenade incorporated tiny windows (facing the river) and circular apertures with iron gratings (facing the street) to protect those who used the corridor from outside attacks. But when Hitler visited Florence in 1941, his chum and fellow dictator Benito Mussolini had big new windows punched into the corridor walls on Ponte Vecchio so that his guest could enjoy an expansive view down the Arno from the famous Florentine bridge.

On the Oltrarno, the corridor passes by **Chiesa di Santa Felicità** (Map p84; www.santa felicita.it; Piazza di Santa Felicità; ⊙9.30am-noon & 3.30-5.30pm Mon-Sat), thereby providing the Medici with a private balcony in the church where they could attend Mass without mingling with the minions. Stand in front of the Romanesque church on Piazza di Santa Felicità and admire the trio of arches of the Vasarian Corridor that runs right above the portico outside the otherwise unnotable church facade. Inside, walk towards the altar and look backwards to see the Medici balcony up high (and imagine the corridor snaking behind it). Oh, and before leaving the church, don't miss Ghirlandaio's *Meeting of St Anne and St Joachim* hung at the end of its right transept.

The Vasarian Corridor is open to just a privileged few by guided tour: **Florence Town** (p226) and **Caf Tour & Travel** (Map p76; ☑055 28 32 00; www.caftours.com; Via degli Alfani 151r; ⊙8am-7pm Mon-Sat, to 3pm Sun) organise morning tours (adult €85) covering Uffizi and corridor. Reserve in advance.

Oltrarno

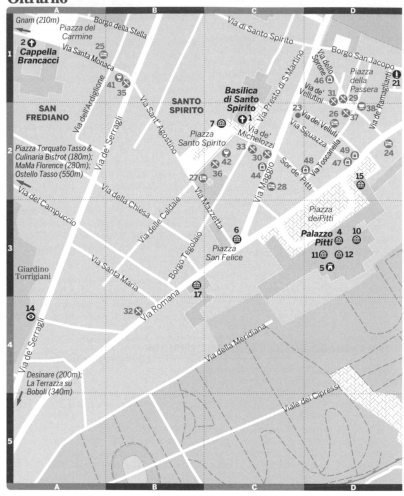

vast Renaissance palace was later bought by the Medici family. Over the centuries it served as the residence of the city's rulers until the Savoys donated it to the state in 1919. Nowadays it houses an impressive silver museum, a couple of art museums and a series of rooms re-creating life in the palace during House of Savoy times.

➡ *Ground Floor*

Exquisite amber carvings, ivory miniatures, glittering tiaras and headpieces, silver pill boxes and various other gems and jewels are displayed in the **Museo degli Argenti** (Silver Museum; Map p84; adult/reduced incl Museo delle

Porcellane, Galleria del Costume & Giardino di Boboli €7/3.50; ⊙ 8.15am-6.50pm summer, reduced hours winter, closed 1st & last Mon of month), a series of elaborately frescoed audience chambers, some of which host temporary exhibitions. Notable (but not always open) is the **Sala di Giovanni da San Giovanni**, which sports lavish head-to-toe frescoes (1635–42) celebrating the life of Lorenzo Il Magnifico – spot Michelangelo giving Lorenzo a statue. 'Talk little, be brief and witty' is the curt motto above the painted staircase in the next room, the public audience chamber, where the grand duke received visitors in the presence of his court.

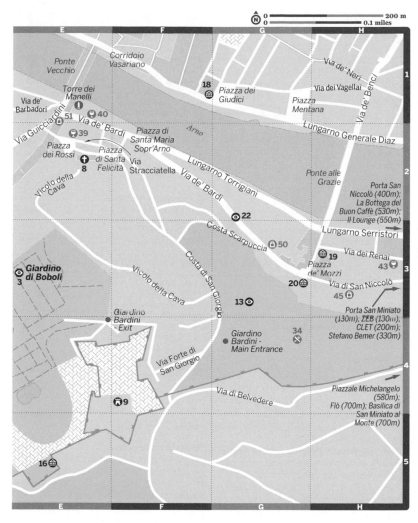

➡ *1st Floor*

Raphaels and Rubens vie for centre stage in the enviable collection of 16th- to 18th-century art amassed by the Medici and Lorraine dukes in the **Galleria Palatina** (Map p84; adult/reduced incl Appartamenti Reali & Galleria d'Arte Moderna €8.50/4.25; ⊙ 8.15am-6.50pm Tue-Sun summer, reduced hours winter), reached by several flights of stairs from the palace's central courtyard. This gallery has retained the original display arrangement of paintings (squeezed in, often on top of each other), so can be visually overwhelming – go slow and focus on the works one by one.

Highlights include Fra' Filippo Lippi's *Madonna and Child with Stories from the Life of St Anne* (aka the *Tondo Bartolini*; 1452–53) and Botticelli's *Madonna with Child and a Young Saint John the Baptist* (c 1490–95) in the **Sala di Prometeo**; Raphael's *Madonna of the Window* (1513–14) in the **Sala di Ulisse**; and Caravaggio's *Sleeping Cupid* (1608) in the **Sala dell'Educazione di Giove**. Don't miss the **Sala di Saturno**, full of magnificent works by Raphael, including the *Madonna of the Chair* (1511) and portraits of Anolo Doni and Maddalena Strozzi (c 1506). Nearby, in the **Sala di Giove**, the

Oltrarno

same artist's *Lady with a Veil* (aka *La velata;* c 1516) holds court alongside Giorgione's *Three Ages of Man* (c 1500).

Past the **Sala di Venere** are the **Appartamenti Reali** (Royal Apartments; Map p84; adult/reduced incl Galleria Palatina & Galleria d'Arte Moderna €8.50/4.25; ☺8.15am-6.50pm Tue-Sun summer, reduced hours winter), a series of rooms presented as they were c 1880–91 during House of Savoy times.

➡ *2nd Floor*

The **Galleria d'Arte Moderna** (Map p84; adult/reduced incl Appartamenti Reali & Galleria Palatina €8.50/4.25; ☺8.15am-6.50pm Tue-Sun summer, reduced hours winter) curates 18th- and 19th-century works. Paintings of the Florentine Macchiaioli school (the local equivalent of Impressionism) dominates the collection.

Crowning the palace is the **Galleria del Costume** (Costume Gallery; Map p84; admission incl Museo degli Argenti, Museo delle Porcellane & Giardino di Boboli adult/reduced €7/3.50; ☺8.15am-6.50pm summer, reduced hours winter, closed 1st & last Mon of month), a parade of

fashions from the times of Cosimo I to the haute-couture 1990s.

★ **Giardino di Boboli** GARDENS
(Map p84; Piazza dei Pitti; adult/reduced incl Museo degli Argenti, Museo delle Porcellane & Galleria del Costume €7/3.50; ☺8.15am-7.30pm summer, reduced hours winter) Behind Palazzo Pitti, the Boboli Gardens were laid out in the mid-16th century to a design by architect Niccolò Pericoli. At the upper, southern limit, beyond the box-hedged rose garden and **Museo delle Porcellane** (Porcelain Museum; Map p84; Giardino di Boboli; admission incl Giardino di Boboli, Museo delgi Argenti & Museo del Costume adult/reduced €7/3.50; ☺8.15am-7.30pm summer, reduced hours winter), fantastic views over the Florentine countryside unfold.

Giardino Bardini GARDENS
(Map p84; www.bardinipeyron.it; entrances at Via de' Bardi 1r & Costa di San Giorgio 2; adult/reduced €8/6; ☺10am-7pm Tue-Sun) This garden was named after art collector Stefano Bardini (1836–1922), who bought the villa in 1913 and

restored its medieval garden. It has all the features of a quintessential Tuscan garden including artificial grottos, an orangery, marble statues and fountains. Inside the villa is the 2nd-floor **Museo Pietro Annigoni** displaying works by the Italian painter Pietro Annigoni (1910–88), the **Museo Roberto Capucci** showcasing Capucci-designed haute couture on the 4th floor; and temporary exhibitions plus a wonderful **roof terrace** to gaze down on the city on the 3rd floor.

April and May, with the garden's flower beds of azaleas, peonies and wisteria in bloom, are lovely months to visit, as is June with its flowering irises. The garden restaurant, La Leggenda Dei Frati (p105), with stone loggia overlooking the Florentine skyline, is one of the most romantic spots in the city to dine.

Museo Stefano Bardini
MUSEUM

(Map p84; www.bardinipeyron.it; Via dei Renai 37; adult/reduced €6/4.50; ⊙11am-5pm Fri-Mon) To learn about 19th-century antiquarian and art collector and restorer Stefano Bardini, visit this lesser-known *palazzo* museum. Through his work as one of Italy's most authoritative antiquarians, Bardini amassed a small fortune and his own expansive collection of Renaissance art, displayed here, is one of Florence's unspoken-about delights. Bardini bought the former church and convent of San Gregorio della Pace in 1881 and converted it into a neo-Renaissance *palazzo* to house both his collection and laboratories in which to restore artworks.

Giardino Torrigiani
GARDENS

(Map p84; ✆055 22 45 27; www.giardino torrigiani.it; Via de' Serragli 144; 1½hr guided tours by donation; ⊙advance reservation via email) Astonishing. Behind the unassuming facades of Via de' Serragli lies a vast, secret garden – Europe's largest privately owned green space within a historic centre, owned by the Torrigiani Malaspina and Torrigiani di Santa Cristina families. Well-kept and loved, it's possible to visit this leafy retreat in the engaging company of the charismatic Marquis Vanni Torrigiani Malaspina and his wife Susanna. Tours (in English or Italian) are intimate and proffer a rare glimpse into a very different and privileged Florentine world.

Designed at the height of the Romantic movement in the early 19th century, the idyllic oasis of green wrapped around the original 16th-century villa and subsequent early-19th-century house includes rare tree species, wide English-style lawns, herb and vegetable gardens, sculpted lions, a beautifully restored greenhouse, and remains of city walls built under Cosimo I in 1544 (one of six sets of walls to be built around Florence at different times – spot the segment of older, 14th century walls outside the garden).

The garden design is laden with complex Masonic symbology, climaxing with an elegant neo-Gothic tower spiralling to the heavens; the three levels allude to the three stages of the initiation process from the profane world to the world of Freemasonry.

In the restored antique greenhouse and garden known as **Serra Torrigiani**, the marquis Vanni and Susanna run gardening and painting courses and workshops.

Casa Guidi
MUSEUM

(Map p84; www.browningsociety.org; Piazza San Felice 8; ⊙3-6pm Mon, Wed & Fri Apr-Nov) **FREE** It was on the ground floor of 15th-century Palazzo Guidi, across from Palazzo Pitti, that Robert and Elizabeth Browning rented an apartment in 1847, a year after their marriage. Robert wrote *Men and Women* in the apartment they called home for 14 years and poet Elizabeth both gave birth to their only child here and died here.

Museo di Storia Naturale – Zoologia La Specola
MUSEUM

(Map p84; www.msn.unifi.it; Via Romana 17; adult/reduced €6/3; ⊙9.30am-4.30pm Tue-Sun winter, to 5.30pm summer) One of several sections of Florence's natural history museum dating to 1775, La Specola showcases 5000-odd animals (out of an unbelievable depository of 3.5 million). The big highlight, not recommended for the squeamish or young children, is the collection of wax models of bits of human anatomy in varying states of bad health.

Via de' Bardi
STREET

(Map p84) Walking east from Ponte Vecchio, the first stretch of Via de' Bardi shows clear signs of its recent history. This entire area was flattened by German mines in 1944, and hastily rebuilt in questionable taste after the war. The street spills into Piazza di Santa Maria Sopr'Arno. Follow narrow Via de' Bardi away from the square and you enter

---

❶ GARDEN STROLL

An easy footpath leads from Giardino di Boboli to Giardino Bardini; the gate between the two – a mere five-minute walk – shuts at 5pm.

FLORENCE FOR CHILDREN

Children are welcomed anywhere, anytime, in Florence. Families frequently go out with young children in the evenings, strolling riverside with a gelato or dining alfresco on summertime terraces. That said, Florence is not the easiest city to visit with very young children: green spaces and playgrounds are scarce and, while some of the pricier hotels can provide babysitters, there's no organised service for tourists.

For parents with a baby in tow, there is no easier, more central spot to stop for a break than **Gucci Museo Caffè** (p107). The clean toilets are equipped with changing mats, mums can breastfeed without anyone batting an eyelid, and there are plenty of art books and free iPads in the cafe to amuse tots.

Teems of locally published books help children discover Florence – museum bookshops in Palazzo Vecchio and the Uffizi have the widest selections.

Art Tours & Workshops

Florence, being the arty city it is, encourages children to discover its astonishing artistic heritage with engaging themed tours and workshops for children from aged four years upwards at **Palazzo Vecchio** (p70) and **Museo Novecento** (p75); book online via www.musefirenze. it. **Palazzo Strozzi** (p72) organises monthly family weekend activities. Out of town in Fiesole, the **Museo Primo Conti** (p96) organises a couple of fabulous art workshops for children a month.

For a private tour with children (hourly rate €70), contact professional licensed guide **Molly McIlwrath** (http://letterartemente.com) who leads family tours and organises creative art workshops for kids which parents can also participate in. Her hands-on workshops range from calligraphy and frescoes to the art of mosaics, book-making and creating Arcimboldo-inspired self-portraits in vegetables and fruits. Many of Molly's city tours wind up in a local artisan workshop in the Oltrarno.

Context Travel (www.contexttravel.com) organises small-group family tours, including a 2½-hour 'Florence art' tour (from six years) focusing on the Uffizi, a two-hour 'Dissection Expedition' (from eight years), which zooms in on science in the city, and a two-hour Renaissance Life–themed city walk (from six years).

Hands-On Cooking

Consider a pizza, pasta or other Italian cookery course for your child – almost every cooking school runs classes for kids. **Curious Appetite** (p91) organises gelato-making workshops and **Freya's Florence** (p91) arranges pizza-making classes (1½ hours, €45 per person).

Museums & Monuments

Hopeless for pushchairs, yes, but older kids love scaling new Florentine heights with an energy-burning hike up **Palazzo Vecchio's Torre d'Arnolfo** (p70), the Duomo bell-tower or around the inside of its astonishing dome. Recommended museums for those over six years include the **Museo di Storia Naturale – Zoologia La Specola** (p87), **Museo Stibbert** (p75) and state-of-the-art science museum **Museo Galileo** (p72).

Parks & Playgrounds

The best playgrounds for children under six years are near the Duomo on Piazza Massimo d'Azeglio and across the river on Lungarno Santa Rosa and Piazza Torquato Tasso. The vintage **carousel** on Piazza della Repubblica never stops turning.

Children over six years can play hide-and-seek between statues in **Giardino di Boboli** (p86) or tear round 118-hectare **Parco delle Cascine** (Viale degli Olmi), with an open-air swimming pool in summer.

a quiet corner of Florence once practically owned by the powerful Bardi family.

By the time Cosimo the Elder wed Contessina de' Bardi in 1415, the latter's family was on the decline. Via de' Bardi ends on Piazza de' Mozzi, surrounded by the sturdy facades of grand residences. Pope Gregory X stayed at **Palazzo de' Mozzi** (Map p84; Piazza de' Mozzi 2) when brokering peace between the Guelphs and Ghibellines.

Forte di Belvedere   FORTRESS, GALLERY
(Map p84; www.museicivicifiorentini.comune.
fi.it; Via di San Leonardo 1; adult/reduced €5/3;
⊙variable) Forte di Belvedere is a rambling
fort designed by Bernardo Buontalenti for
Grand Duke Ferdinando I at the end of the
16th century. From the massive bulwark soldiers kept watch on four fronts – as much
for internal security to protect the Palazzo
Pitti as against foreign attack. Today the fort
hosts seasonal art exhibitions, well worth a
peek if only to revel in the sweeping city
panorama that can be had from the fort.

To get here from Piazza de' Mozzi, turn
east down Via dei Renai, past leafy Piazza
Nicola Demidoff, dedicated to the 19th-
century Russian philanthropist who lived
nearby in Via di San Niccolò. At the end of
Via dei Renai, turn right onto Via di San
Niccolò; walk east to emerge at the tower
marking **Porta San Niccolò**, all that is left
of the city walls. To get an idea of what the
walls were once like, walk south from Chiesa
di San Niccolò Oltrarno through **Porta San
Miniato**. The wall extends a short way to
the east and for a stretch further west, up a
steep hill that leads you to the fortress.

Piazzale Michelangelo   VIEWPOINT
(🚌13) Turn your back on the bevy of ticky-
tacky souvenir stalls flogging *David* statues
and boxer shorts and take in the spectacular
city panorama from this vast square, pierced
by one of Florence's two *David* copies.
Sunset here is particularly dramatic. It's a
10-minute uphill walk along the serpentine
road, paths and steps that scale the hillside
from the Arno and Piazza Giuseppe Poggi;
from Piazza San Niccolò walk uphill and
bear left up the long flight of steps signposted Viale Michelangelo. Or take bus 13 from
Stazione di Santa Maria Novella.

Basilica di San Miniato al Monte   CHURCH
(www.sanminiatoalmonte.it; Via Monte alle Croci;
⊙8am-7pm summer, 8am-noon & 3-6pm winter)
Five minutes uphill from Piazzale Michelangelo is this wonderful Romanesque church,
dedicated to St Minius, an early-Christian
martyr in Florence said to have flown to this
spot after his death down in the town (or, if
you want to believe an alternative version,
walked up the hill with head tucked underneath his arm). The church dates to the early 11th century, although its typical Tuscan
multicoloured marble facade was tacked on
a couple of centuries later.

Inside its unlit interior, 13th- to 15th-
century frescoes adorn the south wall and
intricate inlaid marble designs line the nave,
leading to a fine Romanesque crypt. The sacristy in the southeast corner features frescoes by Spinello Arentino depicting the life
of St Benedict. Slap-bang in the middle of
the nave is the bijou **Capella del Crocefis-
so**, to which Michelozzo, Agnolo Gaddi and
Luca della Robbia all contributed.

🍴 Courses

Florence has zillions of schools running
courses in Italian language, culture and cuisine. **Context Travel** (www.contexttravel.com)
organises fresco-painting workshops.

Desinare   COOKING COURSE
(🖉055 22 11 18; www.desinare.it; Via dei Serragli 234r) Shop for and cook a typical Tuscan
meal, learn about Italian cheeses or master
the art of pasta-making at this recommended (and super-stylish) school near the Boboli
Gardens. Superb kitchen shop and tastings
at the 'chef's table' in the showroom of interior designer Riccardo Barthel.

Cucina Lorenzo de' Medici   COOKING COURSE
(Map p76; www.cucinaldm.com; Via dell'Ariento,
Piazza del Mercato Centrale) Shiny new state-of-
the-art cooking school with 16 work stations
in the fabulously bustling food mall above
Florence's central food market; cooking
classes (€90 to €130, three hours) and cooking demonstrations with tastings (€38, 1½
hours) around the chef's table. Sign up online
or at the information desk in the food mall.

MaMa Florence   COOKING COURSE
(🖉055 22 01 01; www.mamaflorence.com; Viale
Petrarca 12) From Florence market tours to
wine-tasting classes, gluten-free cooking to
pasta-making and meaty mains, this dynamic cooking school has every base covered.

**Scuola di Arte Culinaria
Cordon Bleu**   COOKING COURSE
(Map p80; 🖉055 234 54 68; www.cordonbleu-it.
com; Via Giusti 7) Serious cooking school for
amateurs and professionals with heaps of
short-term, long-term and one-off courses.

In Tavola   COOKING COURSE
(Map p84; 🖉055 21 76 72; www.intavola.org; Via dei
Velluti 18r) Dozens of carefully crafted courses for beginners and professionals, such as
pizza and gelato, pasta-making, easy Tuscan
dinners etc.

FLORENCE COURSES

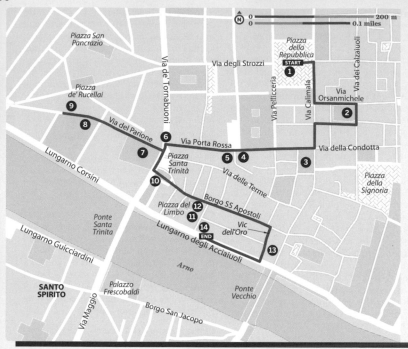

City Walk
Through the Heart of Florence

START PIAZZA DELLA REPUBBLICA
END AMBLÉ
LENGTH 2KM; TWO HOURS

Start with coffee on **❶ Piazza della Repubblica** (p72) then walk one block south along Via Calimala and turn left onto Via Orsanmichele to **❷ Chiesa e Museo di Orsanmichele** (p72), a unique church with ornate statuary adorning its facade and a fascinating museum inside. Backtrack to Via Calimala and continue walking south until you see the loggia of **❸ Mercato Nuovo** (p111), the 16th-century 'New Market'. Florentines know it as 'Il Porcellino' (The Piglet) after the bronze statue of a wild boar on its southern side. Rub its snout to ensure your return to Florence.

Walk past the market and along Via Porta Rossa to **❹ Palazzo Davanzati** (p73) with its magnificent studded doors and fascinating museum. A few doors down, next to **❺ Slowly** (p107) bar, peep through the sturdy iron gate and look up to admire the ancient brick vaults of this dark alley – this is

hidden Florence of 1001 fabulous doors and lost alleys at its best!

Continue to **❻ Via de' Tornabuoni** (p72) with its luxury designer boutiques. Swoon over frescoed chapels in **❼ Chiesa di Santa Trìnita** (p73), then wander down Via del Parione to visit paper marbler **❽ Alberto Cozzi** (p112) and puppet maker **❾ Letizia Fiorini** (p112).

Backtrack to Via de' Tornabuoni and turn right, past 13th-century **❿ Palazzo Spini-Feroni** (p73), home of Salvatore Ferragamo's flagship store, to Borgo Santissimi Apostoli. A short way ahead on Piazza del Limbo is the Romanesque **⓫ Chiesa dei Santissimi Apostoli**, in a sunken square once used as a cemetery for unbaptised babies.

After browsing for Tuscan olive oil in **⓬ La Bottega dell'Olio** (p116), continue east and turn right into Vicolo dell' Oro, home to the **⓭ Hotel Continentale**, whose sleek rooftop terrace is the perfect spot for a sundowner with a Ponte Vecchio view. If hipster Florence is more your cup of tea, indulge in an alfresco aperitivo at **⓮ Amblé** (p106).

☞ Tours

De Gustibus   TOUR
(☑340 579 62 07; www.de-gustibus.it) This umbrella association for local farms in the surrounding Florentine countryside organises extremely tasty tours to small family-run organic farms. Tours are invariably themed – wine, truffles, olive oil – and can be by car, on foot or bicycle. Check its website or Facebook page for details of upcoming tours.

City Sightseeing Firenze   BUS TOUR
(Map p76; ☑055 29 04 51; www.firenze.city-sightseeing.it; Piazza della Stazione 1; adult 1/2/3 days €20/25/30) Explore Florence by red open-top bus, hopping on and off at 15 bus stops around the city. Tickets, sold by the driver, are valid for 24 hours.

Tuscany Bike Tours   BICYCLE TOUR
(Map p80; ☑055 386 02 53; www.tuscany-bike-tours.com; Via Ghibellina 34r) One-day, 23km-long bike tours in Chianti with lunch, castle tour, wine and oil tasting (€80); transfer to Chianti by minibus.

Italy by Segway   TOUR
(Map p66; www.italysegwaytours.com; Via dei Cimatori 9r; ☉9am-1pm & 2-6pm Mon-Sat, closed Sat winter) Three-hour segway tours with a tour leader and audioguide (€75) or live guide (€90). Summertime night tours departing at 8pm (2½ hours, €65) are easier to navigate (fewer crowds to steer around). Reserve in advance online.

ArtViva   WALKING TOUR
(Map p66; ☑055 264 50 33; www.italy.artviva.com; Via de' Sassetti 1; per person from €25) One- to three-hour city walks led by historians or art history graduates: tours include the Uffizi, the Original David tour and an adult-only 'Sex, Drugs and the Renaissance' art tour.

Freya's Florence Tours   WALKING TOUR
(☑349 074 89 07; www.freyasflorence.com; per hr €70-90) Australian-born, Florence-based tour guide; admission not included in fee.

Curious Appetite   TOUR
(www.curiousappetitetravel.com) Private and group food and wine tastings led by Italian-American Coral Lelah. Tastings last 3½ hours, cost from €65 per person (minimum four people) and are themed: at the market, craft cocktails and *aperitivi*, Italian food and wine pairings, artisan gelato.

Accidental Tourist   TOUR
(☑055 69 93 76; www.accidentaltourist.com) Become an Accidental Tourist (membership

OFF THE BEATEN TRACK

VINTAGE MOTORING
....

500 Touring Club (www.500touring club.com; Via Gherardo Silvani 149a) Hook up with Florence's 500 Touring Club for a guided tour in a vintage motor – with you behind the wheel! Every car has a name in this outfit's fleet of gorgeous vintage Fiat 500s from the 1960s (Giacomo is the playboy, Anna the feminist girl and so on). Motoring tours are guided – hop in your car and follow the leader – and themed – families love the picnic trip, couples wine tasting.

March to November tours need to be booked well in advance.

€10), then sign up for a wine tour (€60), cooking class (€70), gourmet picnic (€35) and so on; tours happen in and around Florence.

★☆ Festivals & Events

Festa di Anna Maria Medici   CULTURAL
(☉18 Feb) Florence's Feast of Anna Maria Medici marks her death in 1743 with a costumed parade from Palazzo Vecchio to her tomb in the Cappelle Medicee.

Scoppio del Carro   FIREWORKS
(☉Easter Sun) A cart of fireworks is exploded in front of the cathedral at 11am on Easter Sunday.

Maggio Musicale Fiorentino   PERFORMING ARTS
(www.operadifirenze.it; ☉Apr-Jun) Italy's oldest arts festival features world-class performances of theatre, classical music, jazz and dance.

Festa di San Giovanni   RELIGIOUS
(☉24 Jun) Florence celebrates its patron saint, John, with a *calcio storico* match on Piazza di Santa Croce and fireworks over Piazzale Michelangelo.

Festa delle Rificolone   RELIGIOUS
(☉7 Sep) During the Festival of the Paper Lanterns, lantern-carrying children, accompanied by drummers, *sbandieratori* (flag throwers), musicians and others in medieval dress, process through the streets from Piazza di Santa Croce to Piazza della Santissima Annunziata to celebrate the Virgin Mary's birthday.

🛏 Sleeping

Florence is unexpectedly small, rendering almost anywhere in the centre convenient. Budget hotels are clustered around the Santa

TOP FIVE: LOSE THE CROWD

➡ Florence can be overwhelming: flee to Fiesole in the Florentine hills for peace, quiet and lunch with a spectacular view.

➡ Lunch with a panoramic city view in the manicured gardens of **Giardino Bardini** (p86).

➡ Join the privileged few in an exclusive, cross-river stroll along the enigmatic **Vasarian Corridor** (p83).

➡ Motor out of the city through vineyards and olive groves in a vintage Fiat 500 with the **500 Touring Club** (p91).

➡ Lose yourself among rare trees and sculpted lions in Florence's secret garden, aka **Giardino Torrigiani** (p87), Europe's largest private walled garden right in the heart of Florence.

Maria Novella train station and Mercato Centrale in neighbouring San Lorenzo. Hip Santa Croce and increasingly gentrified Oltrarno are packed with great dining addresses.

🛏 Duomo to Piazza della Signoria

Incredibly, for such a dead-central part of Florence, this area has some excellent budget addresses.

Hotel Cestelli HOTEL **€**
(Map p66; ☎ 055 21 42 13; www.hotelcestelli.com; Borgo SS Apostoli 25; d €70-100, without bathroom s €40-60, d €50-80; ⊘ closed 4 weeks Jan-Feb, 2-3 weeks Aug; 🛜) Housed in a 12th-century *palazzo* a stiletto hop from fashionable Via de' Tornabuoni, this intimate eight-room hotel is a gem. Rooms reveal an understated style, tastefully combining polished antiques with spangly chandeliers, vintage art and silk screens. Owners Alessio and Asumi are a mine of local information and are happy to share their knowledge. No breakfast.

⭐ **Hotel Scoti** PENSION **€€**
(Map p66; ☎ 055 29 21 28; www.hotelscoti.com; Via de' Tornabuoni 7; s/d €75/130; 🛜) Wedged between the designer stores on Florence's smartest shopping strip, this hidden *pensione* is a splendid mix of old-fashioned charm and value for money. Its 16 traditionally styled rooms are spread across the 2nd floor of a towering 16th-century *palazzo*, with some offering lovely rooftop views.

The star of the show, though, is the frescoed lounge from 1780. Breakfast €5.

⭐ **Hotel Davanzati** HOTEL **€€**
(Map p66; ☎ 055 28 66 66; www.hoteldavanzati.it; Via Porta Rossa 5; s/d €132/199; 🖳 @ 🛜) Twenty-odd steps lead up to this swish hotel. A labyrinth of 27 enchanting rooms, frescoes and modern comforts, it has bags of charisma – and that includes Florentine brothers Tommaso and Riccardo, and father Fabrizio, who run the show (Grandpa Marcello surveys proceedings). Laptop, Nespresso coffee machine and 300 free movies on the TV in every room; iPads and playstations to borrow at reception.

Hotel Benivieni HOTEL **€€**
(Map p66; ☎ 055 238 21 33; www.hotelbenivieni.it; Via delle Oche 5; d/tr/q €170/195/215; 🖳 @ 🛜) Superbly located on a narrow lane in the heart of historic Florence, this hotel really is a hop and a skip to all the major sights and tempting after-dark dining options. Rooms are three-star with a comforting classical decor, complimentary slippers, blackout drapes and decent soundproofing. Tip-top family rooms, too.

Hotel Perseo HOTEL **€€**
(Map p66; ☎ 055 21 25 04; www.hotelperseo.it; Via de' Cerretani 1; s €130, d €155-210; 🖳 @ 🛜 🍴) Perseo is a perfect family choice with its 20 large rooms, down-to-earth decor and friendly hosts, New Zealander Louise and Italian husband Giacinto. Top-floor rooms smooch with the rooftops and gorgeous Duomo views. Should you not find the (black) No 1 on the street, look for red No 23. Book online for the cheapest rates.

⭐ **Antica Torre di Via de' Tornabuoni 1** BOUTIQUE HOTEL **€€€**
(Map p66; ☎ 055 265 81 61; www.tornabuoni1.com; Via de' Tornabuoni 1; d from €200; 🛜) Footsteps from the Arno, inside the beautiful 14th-century Palazzo Gianfigliazzi, is this raved-about hotel. Its 20 rooms are stylish, spacious and contemporary. But what steals the show is the rooftop breakfast terrace – easily the best in the city. Sip a cappuccino and swoon over Florence graciously laid out at your feet.

Portrait Firenze DESIGN HOTEL **€€€**
(Map p66; ☎ 055 2726 8000; http://portrait-firenze. hotel-rn.com; Lungarno degli Acciaiuoli 4; d from €450) This luxury 44-room hotel stands out for its exceptional riverside location, a stone's throw from Ponte Vecchio – deluxe studios and balcony-clad suites on the higher floors have an eagle-eye view of the bridge. Equally dazzling is the interior design, inspired by

1950s haute couture design, with vintage photos on the wall starring Italy's *dolce vita* (sweet life). Every bespoke room in this lifestyle ensemble has a state-of-the-art kitchenette.

Palazzo Vecchietti　　　DESIGN HOTEL €€€
(Map p66; ☑ 055 230 28 02; www.palazzovecchietti. com; Via degli Strozzi 4; d from €429; ✳ @ 🤍) This *residenza d'epoca* (period residence) with 14 hopelessly romantic rooms and loggia in a 15th-century *palazzo* between designer shops is a buzzword for hotel chic. Tapestries, bookshelves and artworks adorn stone walls and colour schemes mix traditional hues with bolder blues, reds and violets. Three rooms have a terrace to breakfast between rooftops. No surprise: this is the handiwork of Florentine designer Michele Bönan.

Hotel Torre Guelfa　　　HISTORIC HOTEL €€€
(Map p66; ☑ 055 239 63 38; www.hoteltorreguelfa.com; Borgo SS Apostoli 8; d/tr €240/270; P ✳ @ 🤍) If you wanna kip in a Real McCoy Florentine *palazzo* without breaking the bank, this 31-room hotel with fortress-style facade is the address. Scale its 13th-century, 50m-tall tower – Florence's tallest privately owned *torre* – for a sundowner overlooking Florence and you'll be blown away. Rates are practically halved in low season. To lose yourself in a mind-blowing Florence panorama from your bed, check into the deluxe suite with private terrace (€310). Parking €26 per 24 hours.

🛏 Santa Maria Novella

Ostello Archi Rossi　　　HOSTEL €
(Map p76; ☑ 055 29 08 04; www.hostelarchirossi. com; Via Faenza 94r; dm €25-32; ◷ closed Dec; @ 🤍) Guests' paintings and artwork brighten this busy hostel near Santa Maria Novella train station. Bright white dorms have three to nine beds and must be evacuated between 10.30am and 2.30pm for cleaning. Guests can use washing machines, frozen meal dispensers and microwaves. No curfew but guests have to ring the bell after 2am.

Hotel Azzi　　　HOTEL €€
(Locanda degli Artisti; Map p76; ☑ 055 213 806; www. hotelazzi.com; Via Faenza 56/88r; d €120-150, tr €160-180, q €180-210; ✳ 🤍 🐾) The five-minute walk from the train station only adds to the convenience of this 24-room hotel. It has been around a while and furnishings are old-style. But triple and quadruple rooms in particular are enormous – brilliant for families – and the kids' corner with toys in

the lounge, library full of books and summer terrace are welcome touches.

Hotel L'O　　　DESIGN HOTEL €€€
(Map p66; ☑ 055 27 73 80; www.hotelorologio florence.com; Piazza di Santa Maria Novella 24; d from €375; P ✳ @ 🤍) The type of seductive address James Bond would feel right at home in, this super-stylish hotel oozes panache. Designed as a showcase for the (very wealthy) owner's (exceedingly expensive) luxury wristwatch collection, L'O (the hip take on its full name, Hotel L'Orologio) has four stars, rooms named after watches and clocks pretty much everywhere. Don't be late...

🛏 San Lorenzo & San Marco

★ **Academy Hostel**　　　HOSTEL €
(Map p66; ☑ 055 239 86 65; www.academyhostel. eu; Via Ricasoli 9r; dm €32-36, s/d €42/100, d without bathroom €85; ✳ @ 🤍) This classy 10-room, 40-bed hostel sits on the 1st floor of Baron Ricasoli's 17th-century *palazzo*. The inviting lobby area was once a theatre and 'dorms' sport maximum four or six beds, high moulded ceilings and brightly coloured lockers. The terrace is a perfect spot to chill. No credit cards for payments under €100.

Hotel Orto de' Medici　　　HOTEL €€
(Map p76; ☑ 055 48 34 27; www.ortodeimedici. it; Via San Gallo 30; d from €184; ✳ @ 🤍) This three-star hotel in San Marco redefines elegance with its majestic high ceilings, chic oyster-grey colour scheme and contemporary furnishings, offset to perfection by the historic *palazzo* in which it languishes. Hunt down the odd remaining 19th-century fresco, and don't miss the garden complete with lemon trees in terracotta pots and rambling ivy. To really splurge, go for a room with its own flowery terrace.

Antica Dimora Johlea　　　B&B €€
(☑ 055 463 32 92; www.johanna.it; Via San Gallo 80; d €90-220; ✳ @ 🤍) A walk from the centre, this impeccable residence is a lovely retreat. There's an air of old-world elegance about the six guest rooms with their four-poster beds, creaking parquet floors, high ceilings and period furniture. Help yourself to a drink from the honesty bar and head up to the small terrace to enjoy views over the Duomo.

Hotel Morandi alla Crocetta　　　BOUTIQUE HOTEL €€
(Map p76; ☑ 055 234 47 47; www.hotel morandi.it; Via Laura 50; s/d €105/170; P ✳ 🤍)

SUPERSTOCK/ALAMY ©

JOHN HARPER/GETTY IMAGES ©

1. Di Banco's *Four Crowned Martyrs*, Chiesa e Museo di Orsanmichele (p72)

This unusual church is decorated with sculptures by some of the greatest Renaissance artists.

2. Fra' Angelico's *Deposition of Christ*, Museo di San Marco (p77)

Previously a monastery where Fra' Angelico served God, the Museo di San Marco is one of Florence's most spiritually uplifting museums.

3. Michelangelo's *David*, Galleria dell'Accademia (p77)

A lengthy queue marks the door to this gallery, but the world's most famous statue is worth the wait.

4. Uffizi Gallery (p61)

The Galleria degli Uffizi is the jewel in Florence's crown. Its collection spans the gamut of art history, but its core is the masterpiece-rich Renaissance collection.

FIESOLE DAY TRIPPER

One of the joys of Florence is leaving it behind and Fiesole provides the perfect excuse. Perched in the hills 9km northeast of the city, this bijou hilltop village has seduced for centuries with its cooler air, olive groves, scattering of Renaissance-styled villas and spectacular views of the plain. Boccaccio, Marcel Proust, Gertrude Stein and Frank Lloyd Wright, among others, raved about it.

10am

Founded in the 7th century BC by the Etruscans, Fiesole was the most important city in northern Etruria and its **Area Archeologica** (www.museidifiesole.it; Via Portigiani 1; adult/reduced Fri-Sun €10/6, Mon-Thu €8/4; ⊙ 10am-7pm summer, shorter hours winter), off central square Piazza Mino di Fiesole, provides the perfect flashback. Buy a ticket from the tourist office a couple of doors away then meander around the ruins of an Etruscan temple, Roman baths and archaeological museum. Later, pause for thought on the stone steps of the 1st-century-BC Roman amphitheatre, summer stage to Italy's oldest open-air festival, **Estate Fiesolana**.

Afterwards pop into neighbouring **Museo Bandini** (www.museidifiesole.it; Via Dupré; adult/reduced €5/3, with Area Archeologica ticket free; ⊙ 10am-7pm summer, shorter hours winter) to view early Tuscan Renaissance art, including fine medallions (c 1505–20) by Giovanni della Robbia and Taddeo Gaddi's luminous *Annunciation* (1340–45).

Noon

From the museum, a 300m walk along Via Giovanni Dupré brings you to the **Museo Primo Conti** (☑ 055 59 70 95; www.fondazioneprimoconti.org; Via Giovanni Dupré 18; admission €3; ⊙ 9am-2pm Mon-Fri), where the eponymous avant-garde 20th-century artist lived and worked. Inside hang more than 60 of his paintings and the views from the garden are inspiring. Ring to enter.

1pm

Meander back to **Piazza Mino di Fiesole**, host to an antiques market on the first Sunday of each month, where cafe and restaurant terraces tempt. The pagoda-covered terrace of **Villa Aurora** (☑ 055 5 93 63; www.villaaurora.net; Piazza Mino da Fiesole 39; meals €30; ⊙ noon-2.30pm & 7-10.30pm), around since 1860, is the classic choice for its view. For rustic Tuscan

---

This medieval-convent-turned-hotel away from the madding crowd in San Marco is a stunner. Rooms are refined and traditional in look – think antique furnishings, wood beams and oil paintings – with a quiet, old-world ambience. Pick of the bunch is frescoed room No 29, the former chapel.

🛏 Santa Croce

★ Hotel Dalí   HOTEL €
(Map p80; ☑ 055 234 07 06; www.hoteldali.com; Via dell'Oriuolo 17; d €90, s/d without bathroom €40/70, apt from €95; ℗ 🛜) A warm welcome from hosts Marco and Samantha awaits at this lovely small hotel. A stone's throw from the Duomo, it has 10 sunny rooms, some overlooking a leafy inner courtyard, decorated in a low-key modern way and equipped with kettles, coffee and tea. No breakfast, but – miraculous for downtown Florence – free parking in the rear courtyard.

The icing on the cake is a trio of gorgeous self-catering apartments – one with a Duomo view – sleeping two, four or six.

Hotel Orchidea   HOTEL €
(Map p80; ☑ 055 248 03 46; www.hotelorchidea florence.it; Borgo degli Albizi 11; s/d with shared bathroom €60/80) This old-fashioned *pensione* in the mansion where the Donati family roosted in the 13th century (Dante's wife, Gemma, was allegedly born in the tower) is charm personified. Its seven rooms with sink and shared bathroom are simple, but their outlook is five-star. Many guests return each May/June simply to enjoy the 100-year-old wisteria in bloom. No breakfast.

Rooms 5, 6 and 7 have huge windows overlooking a gorgeous garden and No 4 spills out onto an old stone terrace.

Villa Landucci   B&B €€
(☑ 055 66 05 95; www.villalanducci.it; Via Luca Landucci 7; d/tr €130/150; ℗ 🛜) Five elegant and refreshingly spacious rooms are named after

partaken at a shared table, **Vinandro** (☑ 055 5 91 21; www.vinandrofiesole.com; Piazza Mino da Fiesole 33; meals €25; ☺ noon-midnight) is popular, but not a patch on **La Reggia degli Etruschi** (☑ 055 5 93 85; www.lareggiadeglietruschi.com; Via San Francesco; meals €30; ☺ 7-9.30pm Mon-Wed, 12.30-1.30pm & 7-9.30pm Thu-Sun), an outstanding dine with swoon-worthy views where knowing Florentines lunch on Sunday.

3pm

Stagger around **Cattedrale di San Romolo** (Piazza Mino di Fiesole; ☺ 7.30am-noon & 3-5pm) FREE, begun in the 11th century. A glazed terracotta statue of San Romolo by Giovanni della Robbia guards the entrance inside. Afterwards, make your way up steep walled **Via San Francesco** and be blown away by the staggeringly beautiful panorama of Florence that unfolds from the terrace adjoining 15th-century **Chiesa e Convento di San Francesco**. Grassy-green afternoon-nap spots abound and the tourist office has brochures outlining walking trails (1km to 3.5km) from here.

5pm

Enjoy an *aperitivo* with Florentines at local hangout **JJ Hill** (☑ 055 5 93 24; Piazza Mino da Fiesole 40; ☺ 6pm-midnight Mon-Wed, 5pm-1am Thu-Sat, 5-11pm Sun), an atmospheric Irish pub with a tip-top beer list, excellent burgers and other quality pub grub. Or fire up the romantic in you with a 2½-hour, 21km guided bike ride (€45 including bike hire) by sunset back to Florence with **FiesoleBike** (☑ 345 33 50 926; www.fiesolebike.it; Piazza Mino da Fiesole), a creative bike rental/guiding outfit run with passion by local Fiesole lad Giovanni Crescioli (a qualified biking and hiking guide to boot). His sunset tour departs daily from Piazza Mino di Fiesole at 5pm in season; book in advance online.

Practicalities

The **tourist office** (☑ 055 596 13 11, 055 596 13 23; www.fiesoleforyou.it; Via Portigiani 3, Fiesole; ☺ 10am-6.30pm summer, to 5.30pm winter) has local information.

ATAF bus 7 (€1.20, 20 minutes, every 15 minutes) runs from Florence's Piazza San Marco uphill to Fiesole's central square, Piazza Mino di Fiesole.

Tuscan wines at this gourmet-themed B&B, a short walk away from Santa Croce. The best in the house, 'Bolgheri' and 'Chianti', open onto the well-tended garden with veggie patch, magnolia tree, age-old palm and kids' play area. Breakfast is predominantly organic and free parking is a rarity.

Borrow a bicycle (reserve in advance) to pedal the 500m to Piazza del Duomo. Debora, a sommelier, and partner Matteo, who created the place, are fonts of knowledge when it comes to dining well, and they can organise wine-tasting and food tours for guests.

Hotel Monna Lisa   HOTEL €€€
(Map p80; ☑ 055 247 97 51; www.monnalisa.it; Borgo Pinti 27; s/d €59/152; ☎; ▯) At home in a Renaissance *palazzo* endowed with beautiful paintings and sculptures, Monna Lisa is one chic dame. Her 45 rooms are old-world and four-star, but what really stuns are the communal spaces – the loggia with painted ceiling, the extraordinary garden with gravel paths, jasmine and lime trees.

🛏 Oltrarno

★**Ostello Tasso**   HOSTEL €
(☑ 055 060 20 87; www.ostellotassofirenze.it; Via Villani 15; dm €30-32, s/d €37/70; @ 🛜) Hostelling in Florence got a whole load more stylish with the opening of this chic crash pad, a two-minute walk from the tasty eateries of Piazza Tasso. Coloured bed linen and floor rugs give three- to six-bed dorms a boutique charm, the courtyard garden is a dream and DJs spin tunes in the hip lounge bar (open to nonguests too). Rates include breakfast, locker, sheets and towel.

Ostello Santa Monaca   HOSTEL €
(Map p84; ☑ 055 26 83 38; www.ostellosanta monaca.com; Via Santa Monaca 6; dm €19-22; @ 🛜) A convent until the 1860s, this 112-bed hostel first opened in 1966 to give shelter to flood victims. It has a great little terrace from which to contemplate the stars on summer nights, well-equipped kitchen, free safe deposits and bike rental. Girls-only

FLEE THE CROWD

Should you want to get away from it all and stay out of town, two remarkable 'prince and pauper' addresses leap out.

Villa Camerata (☎ 055 60 14 51; www.ostellofirenze.it; Viale Augusto Righi 2-4; dm €19-21; ☒ @ ☜) In a 17th-century villa framed by extensive grounds, HI-affiliated Villa Camerata is among Italy's most beautiful hostels (and oh so typically Tuscan!). Bus 17 from Stazione di Santa Maria Novella stops 400m from the hostel; count on 30 minutes' travel time.

Il Salviatino (☎ 055 904 11 11; www.salviatino.com; Via del Salviatino 21; d from €430; ☒ ✲ @ ☜ ☒) Hidden among cypress trees in the hills 3.5km east of Florence, this villa really is the stuff of Tuscan dreams. Italian literati gathered here in the 17th and 18th centuries, and today it is Europe's moneyed hipsters who check in to spoil themselves rotten in the spa, lounge in the cascading infinity pool or perfectly manicured Italian gardens, and ogle smugly at the dome of Florence's cathedral from the terrace bar.

Il Salviatino is named after the Salviati family who transformed the 14th-century villa into the ravishing, swoon-worthy 17th-century ode to luxury it is today. The dreamy view of the dome of Florence's cathedral from the terrace bar is not to be scoffed at.

or mixed dorms sleep eight to 22 and are closed for cleaning between 10am and 2pm. Curfew 2am.

La Terrazza su Boboli   B&B €
(☎ 055 233 73 94; www.laterrazzasuboboli.com; Via Petrarca 122; d/ste from €80/120; ✲ @ ☜) Across from the old city walls and traffic-busy Porta Romana is this elegant B&B, a mere hop and a skip from Boboli Gardens, hence its name. Its six rooms are comfortable and spacious, with plenty of books, ornaments and knick-kacks to make guests feel at home. The best have their own pocket-sized terrace to breakfast on.

★**Palazzo Guadagni Hotel**   HOTEL €€
(Map p84; ☎ 055 265 83 76; www.palazzoguadagni.com; Piazza Santo Spirito 9; d €150, extra bed €45; ✲ ☜) This romantic hotel overlooking Florence's liveliest summertime square is legendary – Zefferelli shot scenes from *Tea with Mussolini* here. Housed in an artfully revamped Renaissance palace, it has 15 spacious if old-fashioned rooms and an impossibly romantic loggia terrace with wicker chairs and predictably dreamy views. Off season, double room rates drop to as low as €90.

Hotel La Scaletta   HOTEL €€
(Map p84; ☎ 055 28 30 28; www.hotellascaletta.it; Via Guicciardini 13; d €124-174, ste €194-214) An austere air wafts through this maze of a hotel, hidden in a 15th-century *palazzo* near Palazzo Pitti. But rooms – the priciest ones peeping down on Boboli Gardens – are spacious, and the view from the dreamy roof terrace is

absolutely fabulous. Savour a summertime breakfast or early evening drink here and congratulate yourself on finding one of the best deals in town.

Palazzo Belfiore   APARTMENT €€
(Map p84; ☎ 055 26 44 15; www.palazzobelfiore.it; Via dei Velluti 8; d €160-185; ☜) The smartly painted taupe door with shiny black knocker reflects the contemporary twist on the historic at this stylish residence, at home in a Renaissance *palazzo* on the Oltrarno. Its seven apartments with kitchen are spacious and swish, with a complimentary newspaper of your choice to start each day. Upon request, breakfast can be delivered (for an additional cost).

★**SoprArno Suites**   GUESTHOUSE €€€
(Map p84; ☎ 055 046 87 18; www.soprarnosuites.com; Via Maggio 35; d from €230; ☜) A brilliant addition to the hotel scene, this boutique address squirrelled away in an Oltrarno courtyard creates an intimate home-from-home vibe while making it very clear each guest is special. Each of the 11 designer rooms are exquisitely dressed in vintage objets d'art and collectibles – the passion of Florentine owner Matteo and his talented Florence-born, British-raised wife Betty Soldi (herself a calligrapher and graphic designer).

Several have bathtubs with clawed feet, some are inspired by what remains of original 19th-century ceiling frescoes, and every room has a kettle, a fridge, a mini-bar and a DVD player (no telly). Breakfast around the shared table makes a grand start to the day.

Palazzo Magnani Feroni   HISTORIC HOTEL €€€
(Map p66; ☑ 055 239 95 44; www.florence palace.com; Borgo San Frediano 5; d from €430; 🅿❋@🛜) This extraordinary old *palazzo* is simply gorgeous. Its 12 suites, which occupy four floors with the family's private residence wedged in between, are vast and elegant with period furnishings, rich fabrics and Bulgari toiletries. The 360-degree city view from the rooftop is unbeatable.

✖ Eating

Quality ingredients and simple execution are the hallmarks of Florentine cuisine, climaxing with the *bistecca alla fiorentina,* a huge slab of prime T-bone steak rubbed with olive oil, seared on the char grill, garnished with salt and pepper and served beautifully *al sangue* (bloody). Other typical dishes include *crostini* (toasts typically topped with chicken-liver pâté), *ribollita* (thick vegetable, bread and bean soup), *pappa al pomodoro* (bread and tomato soup) and *trippa alla fiorentina* (tripe cooked in a rich tomato sauce).

✖ Duomo to Piazza della Signoria

An excellent choice for dining in this tourist-busy 'hood – for both outstanding pasta and meal-sized salads when traditional Tuscan tires – is ever-charming wine bar Coquinarius (p106).

★Osteria Il Buongustai   OSTERIA €
(Map p66; Via dei Cerchi 15r; meals €15; 🕙11.30am-3.30pm Mon-Sat) Run with breathtaking speed and grace by Laura and Lucia, this place is unmissable. Lunchtimes heave with locals who work nearby and savvy students who flock here to fill up on tasty Tuscan homecooking at a snip of other restaurant prices. The place is brilliantly no frills – expect to share a table and pay in cash; no credit cards.

★Trattoria Marione   TRATTORIA €
(Map p66; ☑055 21 47 56; Via della Spada 27; meals €25; 🕙noon-3pm & 7-11pm) For the quintessential Italian dining experience, Marione is gold. It's busy, it's noisy, it's 99.9% local and the cuisine is right out Nonna's Tuscan kitchen. No one appears to speak English so go for Italian – the tasty excellent-value traditional fare is worth it.

Cantinetta dei Verrazzano   TUSCAN €
(Map p66; Via dei Tavolini 18-20; focaccia from €3; 🕙8am-9pm summer, 8am-4pm Mon-Sat, 10am-4.30pm Sun winter) A *forno* (baker's oven) and *cantinetta* (small cellar) make a heavenly match. Sit down at a marble-topped table, sip wine from the Verrazzano family's Chianti estate and tuck into traditional focaccia or a mixed cold-meat platter.

La Spada   TRATTORIA €
(Map p66; ☑055 21 87 57; www.laspadaitalia.com; Via della Spada 62r; meals €35; 🕙noon-3pm & 7-10.30pm) This trattoria and *rosticceria* (rotisserie) has been here for aeons but its traditional fare and old-school attitude safeguards a faithful clientele. Its lunchtime fixed €15 menu is exceptional value and its meats roasted over an open fire are the evening highlight.

Obicà   ITALIAN €€
(Map p66; ☑055 277 35 26; www.obica.com; Via de' Tornabuoni 16; 1/2/3 mozzarella €13/20/30, pizza €9.50-17, taglierini €4.50-19.50; 🕙noon-4pm & 6.30-11.30pm Mon-Fri, noon-11pm Sat & Sun) Given its exclusive location in Palazzo Tornabuoni, this designer address is naturally ubertrendy – even the table mats are upcycled from organic products. Taste different mozzarella cheeses

FLORENCE EATING

in the cathedral-like interior or snuggle beneath heaters on sofa seating in the elegant, star-topped courtyard. At *aperitivo* hour nibble on *taglierini* (tasting boards loaded with cheeses, salami, deep fried veg and so on).

La Canova di Gustavino   TUSCAN €€
(Map p66; ☑ 055 239 98 06; Via della Condotta 29r; meals €45; ⊙ noon-midnight) The rear dining room of this atmospheric *enoteca* is lined with shelves of Tuscan wine – the perfect accompaniment to homemade black tagliolini in a seafood and pesto sauce, salt-encrusted sea bass or grilled quail with polenta and red *radicchio* crème brulée. Yes, cuisine is creative Tuscan and, yes, one eats as well as drinks exceedingly well here.

✖ Santa Maria Novella

Il Latini   TRATTORIA €€
(Map p66; ☑ 055 21 09 16; www.illatini.com; Via dei Palchetti 6r; meals €30; ⊙ 12.30-2.30pm & 7.30-10.30pm Tue-Sun) A veteran guidebook favourite built around traditional *crostini* (toast), Tuscan meats, fine pasta and roasted meats served at shared tables. There are two dinner seatings (7.30pm and 9pm), with service ranging from charming to not so charming. Reservations mandatory.

★ **L'Osteria di Giovanni**   TUSCAN €€€
(Map p66; ☑ 055 28 48 97; www.osteriadigiovanni.it; Via del Moro 22; meals €50; ⊙ 7-10pm Mon-Fri, noon-3pm & 7-10pm Sat & Sun) Cuisine at this smart neighbourhood eatery is sumptu-

ously Tuscan. Imagine truffles, tender steaks and pastas such as *pici al sugo di salsicccia e cavolo nero* (thick spaghetti with a sauce of sausage and black cabbage). Throw in a complimentary glass of *prosecco* and you'll want to return time and again.

✖ San Lorenzo & San Marco

★ **Mercato Centrale**   TUSCAN €
(Map p76; ☑ 055 239 97 98; www.mercatocentrale.it; Piazza del Mercato Centrale 4; dishes €7-15; ⊙ 10am-1am, food stalls noon-3pm & 7pm-midnight; 🛜) Meander the maze of stalls rammed with fresh produce at Florence's oldest and largest food market, on the ground of a 19th-century iron-and-glass structure. Then head up to the shiny new 1st floor – a vibrant food fair with dedicated bookshop, cookery school, bar and stalls cooking up steaks, grilled burgers, vegetarian dishes, pizza, gelato, pastries and pasta. Load up and find a free table.

Pugi   BAKERY €
(Map p76; www.focacceria-pugi.it; Piazza San Marco 9b; ⊙ 7.45am-8pm Mon-Sat, closed 2 weeks mid-Aug) The line outside the door says it all. This bakery is a Florentine favourite for pizza slices and *schiacciata* (Tuscan flatbread) baked, spiked with salt and rosemary, or topped or stuffed with delicious edible goodies in season. Grab a number, drool over the savoury (and sweet) treats, and wait for your number to be called.

Should you be queueing to see *David*, Pugi is a perfect two-minute hop from the Galleria dell'Accademia.

TRIPE: FAST-FOOD FAVOURITE

When Florentines fancy a fast munch-on-the-move, they flit by a *trippaio* – a cart on wheels or mobile stand – for a tripe *panini* (sandwich). Think cow's stomach chopped up, boiled, sliced, seasoned and bunged between bread.

Those great bastions of good old-fashioned Florentine tradition still going strong include the cart on the southwest corner of Mercato Nuovo, **L'Antico Trippaio** (Map p66; Piazza dei Cimatori; ⊙ variable); **Pollini** (Map p80; Piazza Sant' Ambrogio; ⊙ variable) in Santa Croce; and hole-in-the-wall **Da Vinattieri** (Map p66; Via Santa Margherita 4; panini €4.50; ⊙ 10am-7.30pm Mon-Fri, to 8pm Sat & Sun) tucked down an alley next to Dante's Chiesa di Santa Margherita. Pay between €3.50 and €4.50 for a *panini* with tripe doused in *salsa verde* (pea-green sauce of smashed parsley, garlic, capers and anchovies) or garnished with salt, pepper and ground chilli. Alternatively, opt for a meaty-sized bowl (€5.50 to €7) of *lampredotto* (cow's fourth stomach that is chopped and simmered for hours).

The pew-style seating at staunchly local **Osteria del Cocotrippone** (☑ 055 234 75 27; Via Vincenzo Gioberti 140; meals €25; ⊙ noon-2.30pm & 7-10.30pm) in the off-centre Beccaria neighbourhood is not a coincidence: Florentines come here to venerate the offal side of their city's traditional cuisine. The *trippa alla fiorentina* (tripe in tomato sauce) and *L'Intelligente* (fried brain and zucchini) are local legends.

TOP GELATERIE

Florentines take gelato seriously and there's healthy rivalry among local *gelaterie artigianale* (makers of handmade gelato) who strive to create the city's creamiest, most flavourful and freshest ice cream. Flavours are seasonal and a cone or tub costs around €2/3/4/5 per small/medium/large/maxi.

Vivoli (Map p80; Via dell'Isola delle Stinche 7; tubs €2-10; ⊘ 7.30am-midnight Tue-Sun summer, to 9pm winter) Inside seating makes this ice-cream and cake shop stand out. Pistachio, pear and caramel, and chocolate with orange are crowd favourites. Pay at the cash desk then trade your receipt for ice. No cones, only tubs.

Grom (Map p66; www.grom.it; cnr Via del Campanile & Via delle Oche; cones €2.50-4.50, tubs €2.50-5.50; ⊘ 10am-midnight summer, to 11pm winter) Rain, hail or shine, queues run halfway down the street at this sweet address; many ingredients organic. Tasty hot chocolate and milkshakes too.

Gelateria La Carraia (Map p66; Piazza Nazario Sauro 25r; cones/tubs €1.50-6; ⊘ 11am-11pm summer, to 10pm winter) One glance at the constant line out the door of this bright green-and-citrus shop with exciting flavours (ricotta and pear, English soup, the best mint in town), and you know you're at a Florentine favourite.

Carabé (Map p76; www.gelatocarabe.com; Via Ricasoli 60r; ⊘ 10am-midnight, closed mid-Dec–mid-Jan) Traditional Sicilian gelato, granita (sorbet) and brioche (Sicilian ice-cream sandwich); handy address if you're waiting in line to see *David*.

★ **Trattoria Mario** TUSCAN €
(Map p76; www.trattoria-mario.com; Via Rosina 2; meals €20; ⊘ noon-3.30pm Mon-Sat, closed 3 weeks Aug; ⌹) Arrive by noon to ensure a shared table at this noisy, busy, brilliant trattoria – a legend that retains its soul (and allure with locals) despite being in every guidebook. Charming Fabio, whose grandfather opened the place in 1953, is front of house while big brother Romeo and nephew Francesco cook with speed in the kitchen.

Monday and Thursday are tripe days, and Friday is fish. Whatever the day, local Florentines flock here for a brilliantly blue *bistecca alla fiorentina*. No advance reservations, no credit cards.

Da Nerbone MARKET €
(Map p76; Piazza del Mercato Centrale, Mercato Centrale; ⊘ 7am-2pm Mon-Sat) Forge your way past cheese, meat and sausage stalls on the ground floor of Florence's Mercato Centrale to join the lunchtime queue at Nerbone, in the biz since 1872. Order *trippa alla fiorentina* (tripe and tomato stew) or follow the crowd with a feisty *panini con bollito* (a hefty boiled-beef bun, dunked in the meat's juices before serving). Eat standing up or fight for a table.

Clubhouse AMERICAN, PIZZA €
(Map p76; ☑ 055 21 14 27; www.theclubhouse.it; Via de' Ginori 6r; pizza €6-15, pasta €10-14; ⊘ noon-midnight) This cavernous American bar, pizzeria and restaurant is handily close to *David* and makes for the perfect dining-drinking hybrid any time of day (including Sunday brunch). Design buffs will appreciate its faintly industrial vibe. Foodies will love its pizza-making courses. Gluten-free menu and cocktail *aperitivi* from 6pm.

Antica Trattoria da Tito TRATTORIA €€
(☑ 055 47 24 75; www.trattoriadatito.it; Via San Gallo 112r; meals €30; ⊘ lunch & dinner Mon-Sat) The 'No well done meat here' sign, strung in the window, says it all: the best of Tuscan culinary tradition is the only thing this iconic trattoria serves. In business since 1913, da Tito does everything right – tasty Tuscan dishes like onion soup and wild boar pasta, served with friendly gusto and hearty goodwill to a local crowd. Don't be shy to enter.

La Cucina del Garga TUSCAN €€
(Map p76; ☑ 055 47 52 86; www.garga.it; Via San Zanobi 33r; meals €30; ⊘ 7.30-10.20pm Mon-Sat) Alessandro Gargani, former New York chef and son of Giuliano 'Garga' Gargani whose San Frediano trattoria wooed Florentine tastebuds for more than three decades, is at the helm of this bold and original restaurant crammed with modern art. *Tagliatelle de magnifico* (pasta ribbons with mint and citrus zest in a creamy brandy sauce) is a Garga classic. Reservations essential at weekends.

✗ Santa Croce

Brac
VEGETARIAN €

(Map p80; ☑ 055 094 48 77; www.libreriabrac.net; Via dei Vagellai 18r; meals €20; ☺ noon-midnight, closed 2 weeks mid-Aug; ✈) This cafe-bookshop – hybrid dining-*aperitivi* – cooks up inventive, home-style and strictly vegetarian and/or vegan cuisine. Its decor is recycled vintage with the odd kid's drawing thrown in for that intimate homey touch. Dine at the front-room bar, in the interior courtyard, or around a candlelit table in the back dining room. Reserve in advance at weekends. Brac can be tricky to find – there is no sign outside, just an inconspicuous doorway a block back from the river with a jumble of books in the window – but persevere.

Antico Noè
OSTERIA €€

(Map p80; Volta di San Piero 6r; meals €30; ☺ noon-midnight Mon-Sat) Don't be put off by the dank alley in which this old butcher's shop with white marble-clad walls and wrought-iron meat hooks is found. The drunks loitering outside are generally harmless and the down-to-earth Tuscan fodder served is a real joy. For a quick bite, go for a *panini* (€4.50 to €5) at its adjoining *fiaschetteria* (small tavern). No credit cards.

★ Il Teatro del Sale
TUSCAN €€

(Map p80; ☑ 055 200 14 92; www.teatrodelsale.com; Via dei Macci 111r; lunch/dinner/weekend brunch €15/20/30; ☺ 11am-3pm & 7.30-11pm Tue-Sat, 11am-3pm Sun, closed Aug) Florentine chef Fabio Picchi is one of Florence's living treasures who steals the Sant' Ambrogio show with this eccentric, good-value members-only club (everyone welcome, annual membership €7) inside an old theatre. He cooks up weekend brunch, lunch and dinner, culminating at 9.30pm in a live performance of drama, mu-

---

TOP SANDWICH SHOPS

Count on paying between €5 and €8 for a lavishly filled *panino* (sandwich). Vintage bakery **S.Forno** (p116) in Oltrarno is a hip new address.

Mariano (Map p66; Via del Parione 19r; panini €3-5; ☺ 8am-3pm & 5-7.30pm Mon-Fri, 8am-3pm Sat) Our favourite for its simplicity, around since 1973. Sunrise to sunset this brick-vaulted, 13th-century cellar gently buzzes with Florentines propped at the counter sipping coffee or wine or eating salads and *panini*. Come here for a coffee-and-pastry breakfast, light lunch, *aperitivo* or *panino* to eat on the move. Look for the green neon 'pizzicheria' up high on the outside facade and the discrete '*Alimentari*' sign above the entrance.

Semel (Map p80; Piazza Ghiberti 44r; panini €3.50-5; ☺ 11.30am-3pm) Florentines swear by this pocket-sized sandwich bar opposite Sant' Ambrogio food market. There is no fixed menu, rather an impossible-to-decide choice of six gourmet combos, crafted with love by passionate owner and *panini* king Marco Paparozzi. Wash it down with a glass of water or wine, and pride yourself on snagging one of the cheapest, tastiest lunches in town.

'Ino (Map p66; www.inofirenze.com; Via dei Georgofili 3r-7r; panini €5-8; ☺ 11.30am-4.30pm summer, noon-3.30pm Mon-Fri, 11.30am-4.30pm Sat & Sun winter) Artisan ingredients sourced locally and mixed creatively by passionate gourmet Alessandro Frassica is the secret behind this gourmet sandwich bar near the Uffizi. Create your own combo, pick from dozens of fun house specials or go for a tasting platter (salami, cheese, pecorini). End with chocolate *degustazione* (tasting) – the chocolate peppered with olive oil and lemon zest is sensational.

All'Antico Vinaio (Map p66; ☑ 055 238 27 23; www.allanticovinaio.com; Via dei Neri 65r; tasting platters €8-30, focaccia €5-7; ☺ 10am-4pm & 6-11pm Tue-Sat, noon-3.30pm Sun) The crowd spills out door of this noisy Florentine thoroughbred. Push your way to the tables at the back and pray for a pew to taste cheese and salami in situ. Or join the queue at the deli counter for a well-stuffed focaccia (€5 to €7) wrapped in waxed paper to take away – quality is outstanding. Pour yourself a glass of wine (€2) while you wait.

I Due Fratellini (Map p66; www.iduefratellini.com; Via dei Cimatori 38r; panini €3; ☺ 9am-8pm Mon-Sat) This hole-in-the-wall has been in business since 1875. Wash *panini* down with a beaker of wine and leave the empty on the wooden shelf outside.

Oil Shoppe (Map p80; Via Sant'Egidio 22r; panini €3.50-4.50; ☺ 11am-5pm Mon-Fri) Queue at the back of the shop for hot subs, at the front for cold, at this busy student favourite. Choose your own or let chef Alberto Scorzon take the lead with his 10-filling wonder.

sic or comedy arranged by his wife, artistic director and comic actress Maria Cassi.

Dinners are hectic: grab a chair, serve yourself water, wine and antipasti and wait for the chef to yell out what's about to be served before queuing at the glass hatch for your *primo* (first course) and *secondo* (second course). Note this is the only Picchi restaurant to serve pasta! Dessert and coffee are laid out buffet-style just prior to the performance.

Trattoria Cibrèo
TUSCAN €€

(Map p80; www.edizioniteatrodelsalecibreofirenze. it; Via dei Macci 122r; meals €30; ⊘12.50-2.30pm & 6.50-11pm Tue-Sat, closed Aug) Dine here and you'll instantly understand why a queue gathers outside before it opens. Once inside, revel in top-notch Tuscan cuisine: perhaps *pappa al pomodoro* (a thick soupy mash of tomato, bread and basil) followed by *polpettine di pollo e ricotta* (chicken and ricotta meatballs). No reservations, no credit cards, no coffee, no pasta and arrive early to snag a table.

Enoteca Pinchiorri
TUSCAN €€€

(Map p80; ☑055 24 27 77; www.enoteca pinchiorri.com; Via Ghibellina 87r; 6-79-course tasting menu €175/250; ⊘lunch & dinner Tue-Sat, closed Aug) Chef Annie Féolde applies French techniques to her versions of refined Tuscan cuisine and does it so well that this is the only restaurant in Tuscany to brandish three shiny Michelin stars. The setting is a 16th-century palace hotel and the wine list is mind-boggling in its extent and excellence. A once-in-a-lifetime experience.

✕ Oltrarno

New places to eat are forever popping up in this increasingly gentrified neighbourhood the 'other side' of the Arno. Several gourmet choices frame Piazza del Passera, a bijou square with no passing traffic.

★5 e Cinque
VEGETARIAN €

(Map p84; ☑055 274 15 83; Piazza della Passera 1; meals €25; ⊘10am-10pm Tue-Sun) The hard work and passion of a photography and antique dealer is behind this highly creative, intimate eating space adored by every savvy local. Cuisine is vegetarian with its roots in Genova's kitchen – '5 e Cinque' (meaning '5 and 5') is a chickpea sandwich from Livorno, and the restaurant's *cecina* (traditinal Ligurian flat bread made from chickpea flour) is legendary.

Find 5 e Cinque sitting sweet on one of Florence's cutest old-world squares, pedestrian to boot.

DON'T MISS

SILVER SPOON DINING

In Fabbrica (☑347 5145468; http://www. pampaloni.com/restaurant/; Via del Gelsomino 99; meal €45; ⊘8-10.30pm Wed-Sat) In Fabbrica, 1.5km south of Porto Romana along Via Senese in the Oltrarno, fuses Florence's outstanding tradition of craftsmanship with its equally fine cuisine. Meaning 'In the Factory', In Fabbrica is just that. By day, workers from third-generation Florentine silver house **Pampaloni** (Map p66; www.pampaloni. com; Via Porta Rossa 97; ⊘10am-1.30pm & 3-7.30pm Mon-Sat) lunch here. Come dusk, the speakeasy canteen opens its doors to culturally curious diners.

Tables are laid with silver cutlery and majestic candelabras, waiters wear white gloves, and there are two fixed menus – one Italian, one Japanese. Advance reservations essential.

★Gnam
BURGERS €

(☑055 22 39 52; www.gnamfirenze.it; Via di Camaldoli 2r; meals from €10; ⊘noon-3pm & 6pm-midnight) Bread arrives at the table in a brown paper bag and fries are served in a miniature copper cauldron at this green, artisanal burger joint in San Frediano. Ingredients are seasonal, locally sourced and organic – and there are vegetarian and gluten-free burgers as well as the traditional beefy variety. Delicous homemade soups also, to eat in or takeway.

Tamerò
ITALIAN €

(Map p84; ☑055 28 25 96; www.tamero.it; Piazza Santa Spirito 11r; meals €20; ⊘noon-3pm & 7pm-2am Tue-Sun) A happening address on Florence's hippest square: admire pasta cooks at work in the open kitchen while you wait for a table – the chances are you'll have to. A buoyant, party-loving crowd flocks here to fill up on imaginative fresh pasta, giant salads and copious cheese/salami platters. Decor is trendy industrial and weekend DJs spin sets from 10pm.

La Casalinga
TRATTORIA €

(Map p84; ☑055 21 86 24; www.trattoria lacasalinga.it; Via de' Michelozzi 9r; meals €25; ⊘noon-2.30pm & 7-10pm Mon-Sat) Family run and locally loved, this busy unpretentious place is one of Florence's cheapest trattorias. Don't be surprised if Paolo, the patriarch figure who conducts the mad-busy show from behind the bar, relegates you behind locals in the queue: it's a fact of life, and

TIP-TOP PIZZERIE

Berberé (☑ 055 238 29 46; www.berberepizza.it; Piazza dei Nerli 1; pizza €6.50-13; ⊗ noon-2.30pm & 7pm-midnight Fri-Sun, 7pm-midnight Mon-Thu) Florence's stunning new kid on the block, this modern pizza space in San Frediano is an inspirational cocktail of perfect pizza, delicious craft beers brewed by small producers and striking contemporary interior design. Grab a stool at the white marble bar and pick from 14 pizza types – several are vegetarian – made with organic flour and live yeast. Reservations essential.

Gustapizza (Map p84; Via Maggio 46r; pizza €4.50-8; ⊗ 11.30am-3pm & 7-11pm Tue-Sun) This unpretentious pizzeria near Piazza Santa Spirito redefines the word 'packed'. Arrive early to grab a bar stool at a wooden-barrel table and pick from seven pizza types.

Pizzeria del' Osteria del Caffè Italiano (Map p80; ☑ 055 289 368; Via dell'Isola delle Stinche 11-13r; pizza €8; ⊗ 7-11pm Tue-Sun, closed lunchtime) Simplicity is the buzz word at this pocket-sized pizzeria that makes just three pizza types – margherita, napoli and marinara. No credit cards.

Il Pizzaiuolo (Map p80; ☑ 055 24 11 71; Via dei Macci 113r; pizzas €5-10; ⊗ 12.30-2.30pm & 7.30pm-midnight Mon-Sat, closed Aug) Young Florentines flock to the Pizza Maker to nosh Neapolitan thick-crust pizzas hot from the wood-fired oven. Bookings essential for dinner.

eventually you'll be rewarded with hearty Tuscan dishes, cooked to exacting perfection. Think *bollito misto con salsa verde* (mixed boiled meats with green sauce), spaghetti *al pomodoro* and *ribollita* just like *nonna* (grandma) and her *nonna* and her *nonna* made.

★ **Il Santo Graal** TUSCAN €€
(Map p84; ☑ 055 228 65 33; www.ristorante santograal.it; Via Romana 70r; 2-/4-course lunch €20/35, meals €45; ⊗ noon-3pm Fri-Sun, 7-10.30pm Thu-Tue) Its name is no concidence. The Holy Grail, with young chef Simone Cipriani at the helm, is rapidly becoming just that when it comes to superb Tuscan cuisine with an inventive twist. Think kale-dressed spaghetti in a *ribollita* broth or orange-spiced chickpea soup. Exposed red bricks and low vaulted ceilings add atmosphere, and its location makes it perfect for lunch after visiting Palazzo Pitti.

★ **Il Santo Bevitore** TUSCAN €€
(Map p66; ☑ 055 21 12 64; www.ilsantobevi tore.com; Via di Santo Spirito 64-66r; meals €40; ⊗ 12.30-2.30pm & 7.30-11pm, closed Aug) Reserve or arrive dot-on 7.30pm to snag the last table at this ever-popular address, an ode to stylish dining where gastronomes dine by candlelight in a vaulted, whitewashed, bottle-lined interior. The lunch and dinner menus are a creative reinvention of seasonal classics: purple cabbage soup with mozzarella cream and anchovy syrup, acacia honey bavarese (firm, creamy mousse) with Vin Santo–marinated dried fruits.

All'Antico Ristoro di' Cambi TUSCAN €€
(☑ 055 21 71 34; www.anticoristorodicambi.it; Via Sant'Onofrio 1r; meals €35; ⊗ noon-2.30pm & 6-10.30pm Mon-Sat) Founded as a wine shop in 1950, this Oltrarno institution sticks closely to the traditional, with its long list of fine Tuscan wines, dried meats hanging from brick-vaulted ceilings and a glass case proudly displaying its highly regarded *bistecca alla fiorentina* – it's one of the best places in town to try the city's iconic T-bone steak. Meat aficionados will also enjoy the succulent *tagliata di cinta senese* (Senese pork steak).

Trattoria 4 Leoni TUSCAN €€
(Map p84; ☑ 055 21 85 62; www.4leoni.com; Piazza della Passera 2/3; meals €40; ⊗ noon-midnight) A faithful byword for decent Tuscan fare, older Florentines in particular mention this place with a satisfied smile. And indeed, 4 Leoni is a reliable choice for meats, seafood and fish dishes, not to mention Florence's famed *bistecca alla fiorentina* cooked up here since 1550. The summertime terrace here spilling across Piazza della Passera only adds to the charm. Reservations essential.

Il Magazzino OSTERIA €€
(Map p84; ☑ 055 21 59 69; www.tripperiailmagaz zino.com; Piazza della Passera 2/3; meals €32; ⊗ noon-3pm & 7.30-11pm) This unassuming brick-walled *osteria* on one of Oltrarno's prettiest car-free squares is a top choice for foodies in search of the Florentine tripe experience. Begin with *tagliatelle con ragù di lampredotto* (ribbon pasta with a tripe-

based sauce) followed by *trippa alla fiorentina* (tripe simmered with tomatoes and herbs) or *lampredotto* (tripe boiled with carrots and herbs). Bookings recommended.

Olio & Convivium   TUSCAN €€

(Map p66; ☑ 055 265 81 98; www.conviviumfirenze.it; Via di Santo Spirito 4; meals €35; ⊙ lunch & dinner Tue-Sat, lunch Mon) A key address on any gastronomy agenda: your tastebuds will tingle at the sight of the legs of ham, conserved truffles, wheels of cheese, artisan-made bread and other delectable delicatessen products sold in its shop. Dine out the back.

★ La Leggenda dei Frati   TUSCAN €€€

(Map p84; ☑ 055 068 05 45; www.laleggendadeifrati.it; Costa di San Giorgio 6, Villa Bardini; menus €55 & €70, meals €60; ⊙ lunch & dinner Tue-Sun) This is summer's hottest address. At home in the historic garden house of Villa Bardini, the Legend of Friars (run by the highly regarded Saporito brothers, previously in Castellina in Chianti) enjoys the most romantic terrace with view in Florence. Veggies are plucked fresh from the vegetable patch, tucked between waterfalls and ornamental beds in Giardino Bardini, and contemporary art jazzes up the classical interior.

Cuisine is Tuscan, gastronomic and well worth the vital advance reservation.

Camillo   TRATTORIA €€€

(Map p66; ☑ 055 21 24 27; Borgo San Jacopo 57r; meals €45; ⊙ lunch & dinner Thu-Mon) *Crostini* topped with aphrodisiacal white-truffle shavings, deep-fried battered green tomatoes or zucchini (courgette) flowers and homemade walnut liqueur are a few of the seasonal highlights served beneath a centuries-old red-brick vaulted ceiling at this much-loved trattoria. The quality of products used is exceptional and service is endearingly old-fashioned.

iO Osteria Personale   TUSCAN €€€

(☑ 055 933 13 41; www.io-osteriapersonale.it; Borgo San Frediano 167r; 4-/5-/6-course tasting menus €40/48/55, meals €45; ⊙ dinner from 8pm Mon-Sat) Persuade everyone at your table to order the tasting menu to avoid the torture of picking just one dish – everything on the menu at this fabulously contemporary and creative *osteria* is to die for. Pontedera-born chef Nicolò Baretti uses only seasonal products, natural ingredients and traditional flavours – to sensational effect.

LOCAL KNOWLEDGE

FARM TO TABLE

Culinaria Bistrot (☑ 055 22 94 94; www.de-gustibus.it/en; Piazza Torquato Tasso 13; meals €20; ⊙ 12.30-2.30pm & 6-11.30pm Wed-Mon) No dining address in Florence captures the culinary magic of 'farm to table' dining quite like this San Frediano bistro, an instant charmer with its exposed red-brick vaulted ceiling. French chef Jacques Pachoud only works with organic produce from local farms to cook up memorable Tuscan and Mediterranean dishes.

Titillate tastebuds with a traditional Tuscan tasting platter of local salami and/or cheese (€10 to €13), then move onto a chicken and prune tajine perhaps or a pork cheek and bean *cocotte* (casserole).

Also known as Culinaria di De Gustibus, the bistro is the business card of **De Gustibus** (p91), an organisation established to promote sustainable food and wine tourism through tastings, lunches, tours and other tempting foodie events and happenings. Farmers in the network supply the bistro with its astonishing choice of superb-quality local products.

La Bottega del Buon Caffè (☑ 055 553 56 77; www.borgointhecity.com; Lungarno Benvenuto Cellini 69r; 4-course lunch menu €60, 6-course tasting menus €80 & €95, incl wine €125 & €145); ⊙ 12:30-3pm & 7.30-10.30pm Tue-Sat, 12:30-3pm Sun) At this Michelin-starred restaurant head chef Antonello Sardi mesmerises diners from the stunning open kitchen. Veg and herbs arrive from the restaurant's own farm, Borgo Santa Pietro, in the Sienese hills. Breads and focaccia (the nut version is heavenly) are homemade and the olive oil used (special production from Vinci) is clearly only the best.

From the complimentary amuse-bouche (pecorino cheese mousse served on a broad bean leaf with rosemary blossom) to the leapy pink radish dipped in salted butter that accompanies Sardi's creative take on traditional chicken-liver pâté, ingredients are overwhelmingly fresh, green and natural.

ℹ APERICENA

Apericena, a brilliant cent-saving trick and trend among students and 20-somethings in Florence, translates as an *aperitivo* buffet so copious it doubles as *cena* (dinner). Firm Florentine favourites known for their exceptionally generous buffets include Kitsch (p109) and Slowly (p107).

Imagine sea bass tartare with ricotta cheese, pine kernels and spinach salad; or sweetbreads with marjoram-scented artichokes. The grand finale is dessert, climaxing with warm white chocolate and olive oil cream served with lavender slush and passionfruit aspic. Culinary heaven on earth.

✗ Out of Town

When the summer city heat stifles, do what Florentines do – get out of town for an alfresco lunch between flowers or riverside.

Targa   TUSCAN €€
(☑ 055 67 73 77; www.targabistrot.net; Lungarno Colombo 7; meals €30; ☻noon-3pm & 7-11.30pm Mon-Sat) 'Friendly food' is the strapline of this sleek address, a modern *bistrot Fiorentino* (Florentine bistro) bursting with green foliage on the banks of the Arno just over 1km east of Ponte San Niccolò. Dining is around Parisian-style wooden bistro tables – in or out on the wooden-decked verandah – and the wine list is superb. Advance reservations essential.

Trattoria Bibe   TRATTORIA €€
(☑ 055 204 00 85; www.trattoriabibe.com; Via della Bagnese 1r, Galuzzo; meals €35; ☻12.30-2.30pm & 7.30-9.30pm Sat & Sun, 7.30-9.30pm Mon, Tue, Thu & Fri Dec-Jan & Mar-Oct; ☑46) Pigeon, frogs legs, hare and guineafowl are among the roasts (count at least 40 minutes) at this old-fashioned inn – so legendary that Italian poet Eugenio Montale wrote a poem about Grandfather 'Bibe' in 1927. Dine elegantly inside or amid flowers out. Find it 3km south of Florence.

Trattoria le Cave di Maiano   TRATTORIA €€
(☑ 055 5 91 33; Via Cave di Maiano 16, Maiano; meals €35; ☻12.30-2.30pm & 7.30-10.30pm, closed Mon winter) Florentines flock to this restaurant in Maiano, a village 8km north of Florence near Fiesole, at weekends to indulge in long lunches on its outdoor terrace. Huge servings are the rule of thumb, everything is homemade, and the rustic inclination of the chef

is reflected in the abundance of rabbit, boar and suckling pig dishes – all of which go wonderfully well with the quaffable house wine.

🍷 Drinking & Nightlife

Florence's drinking scene is split between *enoteche* (increasingly hip wine bars that invariably make great eating addresses too), trendy bars with lavish *aperitivo* buffets and straightforward cafes that quite often double as lovely lunch venues. For craft beer Berberé (p104) is an excellent address.

🍷 Duomo to Piazza della Signoria

★**Coquinarius**   WINE BAR
(Map p66; www.coquinarius.com; Via delle Oche 11r; crostini & carpacci €4, meals €35; ☻noon-10.30pm) With its old stone vaults, scrubbed wooden tables and refreshingly modern air, this *enoteca* run by the dynamic and charismatic Nicolas is spacious and stylish. The wine list features bags of Tuscan greats and unknowns, and outstanding *crostini* and *carpacci* (cold sliced meats) ensure you don't leave hungry.

The meal-sized salads (€12 to €15) and the ravioli with burrata cheese and pistachio pesto are particularly outstanding.

Café Apollo   CAFE
(Map p66; Piazza Strozzi; ☻8.30am-8pm Fri-Wed, to 11pm Thu) High-vaulted ceiling, sleek black Panton chairs, excellent coffee and unelevated prices seduce a mixed crowd at this artsy hangout in Palazzo Strozzi on Florence's most designer-chic street. It's run by the same team as Caffè Giacosa (p108) of Roberto Cavalli fame across the road, and the chocolate-swirled cappuccino is among the best in town.

Amblé   BAR, CAFE
(Map p66; ☑ 055 26 85 28; Piazzetta dei del Bene 7a; ☻10am-10pm Mon-Sat, noon-10pm Sun) You need to know about this cafe-bar, a hop and a skip from Ponte Vecchio, to find it. Vintage tables and chairs – all for sale – create a shabby-chic look and the tiny terrace feels well away from the crowds on summer evenings. From the river head down Viccolo Oro to the Continentale hotel, and turn left along the alleyway that runs parallel to the river.

La Terrazza   BAR
(Map p66; www.continentale.it; Vicolo dell Oro 6r; ☻2.30-11.30pm Apr-Sep) This rooftop bar with wooden-decking terrace accessible from the 5th floor of the Ferragamo-owned Hotel

Continentale is as chic as one would expect of a fashion-house hotel. Its *aperitivo* buffet is a modest affair, but who cares with that fabulous, drop-dead-gorgeous panorama of one of Europe's most beautiful cities.

Sei Divino
WINE BAR

(Map p66; Borgo d'Ognissanti 42r; ⊙6pm-2am Wed-Mon) This stylish wine bar tucked beneath a red-brick vaulted ceiling is privy to one of Florence's most happening *aperitivo* scenes. It plays music, hosts occasional exhibitions and in summertime the pavement action kicks in. *Aperitivi* 'hour' (with copious banquet) runs 7pm to 10pm.

Open Bar
LOUNGE, BAR

(Map p84; www.goldenviewopenbar.com; Via de' Bardi 58; ⊙7.30am-1.30am) Of course it is touristy given its prime location near Ponte Vecchio, but it is worth a pit stop nonetheless – preferably at *aperitivo* hour (glass of wine/champagne €10/14, cocktail €10 to €15) from 6.30pm to 9pm when chic Florentines sip cocktails, slurp oysters and enjoy the 'golden view' of the Arno swirling below their feet. Stand by the bar rather than sitting down to keep costs down.

Fiaschetteria Nuvoli
WINE BAR

(Map p66; Piazza dell'Olio 15r; ⊙7am-9pm Mon-Sat) Pull up a stool on the street and chat with a regular over a glass of *vino della casa* (house wine) at this old-fashioned *fiaschetteria,* a street away from the Duomo.

Procacci
CAFE

(Map p66; www.procacci1885.it; Via de' Tornabuoni 64r; ⊙10am-9pm Mon-Sat & 11am-8pm Sun, closed 3 weeks Aug) The last remaining bastion of genteel old Florence on Via de' Tornabuoni, this tiny cafe was born in 1885 opposite an English pharmacy as a delicatessen serving truffles in its repertoire of tasty morsels. Bite-sized *panini tartufati* (truffle pâté rolls) remain the thing to order, best accompanied by a glass of *prosecco* (€5).

Cuculia
CAFE

(Map p66; www.cuculia.it; Via dei Serragli 11; ⊙10am-midnight Tue-Fri, to 1am Sat) This hybrid bookshop-cafe is a wonderfully serene spot to while away a few hours in the company of classical music and shelves loaded with books. The vibe is very much old-world refinement and the tiny candlelit nook out back is perfect for a romantic moment over a cocktail *aperitivo*. Food too and excellent weekend brunch.

Colle Bereto
LOUNGE, BAR

(Map p66; Piazza Strozzi 5; ⊙8am-5am Tue-Sun; 🛜) The local fashion scene's bar of choice, uberstylish Colle Bereto is where the bold and the beautiful come to see or be seen for breakfast, lunch, dinner or at *aperitivo* hour.

Slowly
LOUNGE, BAR

(Map p66; www.slowlycafe.com; Via Porta Rossa 63r; ⊙6.30pm-3am Mon-Sat, closed Aug) Sleek and sometimes snooty, this lounge bar with a candle flickering on every table is known for its glam interior, Florentine Lotharios and lavish fruit-garnished cocktails – €10 including buffet during the bewitching *aperitivo* 'hour' (6.30pm to 10pm). Ibiza-style lounge tracks dominate the turntable.

Gucci Museo Caffè
CAFE

(Map p66; Piazza della Signoria 10; meals €25; ⊙10am-11pm; 🛜) Everything from the crockery to G-shaped sugar 'cubes' might be emblazoned with the Gucci monogram. But over-zealous branding aside, this laid-back cafe is one of the city's hippest places to hang over coffee, lunch, *aperitivo*, newspapers or in-house iPads. A huge table hooked up with plugs makes it a laptop-user favourite.

La Terrazza
CAFE

(Map p66; La Rinascente, Piazza della Repubblica 1; ⊙9am-9pm Mon-Sat, 10.30am-8pm Sun) Three canvas parasols and a dozen tables make this hidden terrace on the roof of Florence's central department store a privileged spot. Gloat with the birds over coffee or a cocktail at achingly lovely views of the Duomo, Piazza della Repubblica and Florentine hills beyond.

Todo Modo
CAFE

(Map p66; ☎055 239 91 10; www.todomodo.org; Via dei Fossi 15r; ⊙10am-8pm Tue-Sun) This contemporary bookshop with cafe-bar and pocket theatre out back makes a refreshing change from the *caffè* norm. A salvaged mix of vintage tables and chairs sits between book- and bottle-lined shelves in the relaxed cafe, actually called 'UqBar' after the fictional place of the same name in a short story by Argentinian writer Jorges Luis Borges.

YAB
CLUB

(Map p66; www.yab.it; Via de' Sassetti 5r; ⊙9pm-4am Oct-May) Pick your night according to your age and tastes at this disco club, around since the 1970s behind Palazzo Strozzi.

DON'T MISS

TOP THREE: HISTORIC CAFES

Few cafes have seen or heard as much as these fabulous old Florentine beauties.

Caffè Giacosa (Map p66; www.caffegiacosa.it; Via della Spada 10r; ⏱ 7.45am-8.30pm Mon-Fri, 8.30am-8.30pm Sat, 12.30-8pm Sun) This small cafe with 1815 pedigree was the inventor of the Negroni cocktail and hub of Anglo-Florentine sophistication during the interwar years. Today it is the hip cafe of local hotshot designer Roberto Cavalli, whose flagship boutique is next door. Giacosa is known for its refreshingly unelevated prices, excellent coffee and hip cafe across the street in Palazzo Strozzi.

Drink-list standouts include the herbal infusions, ginseng cappuccino and Caffè de' Medici aka a shaken espresso topped with whipped cream, granola and chocolate.

Caffè Rivoire (Map p66; Piazza della Signoria 4; ⏱ 7am-11pm Tue-Sun) This golden oldie with unbeatable people-watching terrace has produced some of the city's most exquisite chocolate since 1872. Black-jacketed barmen with ties set the formal tone.

Gilli (Map p66; www.gilli.it; Piazza della Repubblica 39r; ⏱ 7.30am-1.30am) The most famous of historic cafes on the city's old Roman forum, Gilli has been serving utterly delectable cakes, chocolates, fruit tartlets and *millefoglie* (sheets of puff pastry filled with rich vanilla or chocolate Chantilly cream) to die for since 1733 (it moved to this square in 1910 and sports a beautifully preserved art-nouveau interior).

🍷 Oltrarno

⭐ Le Volpi e l'Uva   WINE BAR

(Map p84; www.levolpieluva.com; Piazza dei Rossi 1; ⏱ 11am-9pm Mon-Sat) This unassuming wine bar hidden away by Chiesa di Santa Felicità remains as appealing as the day it opened over a decade ago. Its food and wine pairings are first class – taste and buy boutique wines by 150 small producers from all over Italy, matched perfectly with cheeses, cold meats and the best *crostini* (toasts with various toppings) in town. Wine-tasting classes too.

Il Santino   WINE BAR

(Map p66; Via di Santo Spirito 60r; ⏱ 12.30-11pm) This pocket-sized wine bar is packed every evening. Inside, squat modern stools contrast with old brick walls, but the real action is outside, from around 9pm, when the buoyant wine-loving crowd spills onto the street.

⭐ Volume   BAR

(Map p84; www.volumefirenze.com; Piazza Santo Spirito 3r; ⏱ 9am-1.30am) Armchairs, recycled and upcycled vintage furniture, books to read, juke box, crepes and a tasty choice of nibbles with coffee or a light lunch give this hybrid cafe-bar-gallery real appeal – all in an old hat-making workshop with tools and wooden moulds strewn around. Watch for various music, art and DJ events and happenings.

ZEB   WINE BAR

(www.zebgastronomia.com; Via San Miniato 2r; ⏱ noon-3pm Sun-Tue, noon-3pm & 7.30-10.30pm Thu-Sat) Local gastronomes adore this modern, minimalist *enoteca* at the foot of the hill leading up to Piazzale Michelangelo, in village-like San Niccolò. Post-panorama, sit around the deli-style counter and indulge in a delicious choice of cold cuts and creative Tuscan dishes prepared by passionate chef Alberto Navari and his *mamma,* Giuseppina.

Flò   LOUNGE

(⏱ 055 65 07 91; www.flofirenze.com; Piazzale Michelangelo 84; ⏱ 7.30pm-late summer) Without a doubt the hottest and hippest place to be seen in the city on hot sultry summer nights is Flò, a truly ab fab seasonal lounge bar that pops up each May on Piazzale Michelangelo. Different themed lounge areas include a dance floor, and VIP area (where you have no chance of reserving a table unless you're in the Florentine in-crowd).

Il Lounge   LOUNGE

(Lungarno Benvenuto Cellini 69r; ⏱ 2pm-midnight Tue-Sat, noon-3pm Sun) When the madding crowd and raucous Tuscan *fiaschetteria* get too much, recharge your batteries in this stylish lounge – a chic haven of peace and tranquillity. The wine list is outstanding, a fireplace makes it winter cosy, and bar snacks are straight out the gourmet kitchen of Michelin-starred chef Antonella Sardi (his restaurant is next door). Watch for live music, readings and art happenings at weekends.

Zoé BAR

(Map p84; Via dei Renai 13r; ⊗9am-3am; 🛜)
Bright white and shiny, this savvy Oltrarno bar knows exactly what its hip punters want – a relaxed, faintly industrial space to hang out in all hours (well, almost). Be it breakfast, lunch, cocktails or an after-dinner party, Zoé is your woman. Come springtime's warmth, the scene spills out onto a wooden decking street terrace in front. Watch for DJs spinning tunes and parties.

Vivanda WINE BAR

(Map p84; ☑ 055 238 12 08; www.vivandafirenze.it; Via Santa Monaca 7r) The focus of this modern *enoteca*, small interior packed jaw to jowl with tables, is organic wine. Locally sourced products ensure a delightful early-evening tasting of different organic wines perfectly paired with ash-aged pecorino, *bufala* ricotta cheese and Cienta Senese salami. Table reservations recommended.

Caffè degli Artigiani CAFE

(Map p84; www.caffedegliartigiani.it; Via dello Sprone 16r; ⊗7am-7pm Mon, to 1am Tue-Sat, closed Aug)
Sitting on one of the most atmospheric little piazzas in Florence, this quaintly countrified cafe pulls in local artisans in need of an espresso hit or a nip of brandy to complete a day's work. In the back room, which seems to have been plucked from a Provençal farmhouse, you can enjoy quick eats such as sandwiches and homemade cakes. Even more inviting is the handful of outdoor tables.

James Joyce PUB

(☑ 055 658 08 56; Lungarno Benvenuto Cellini 1r; ⊗6pm-2am Sun-Thu, to 3am Fri & Sat) Neither as Irish nor as literary as the name suggests, this veteran pub with beer garden attracts a gregarious student and post-grad crowd thanks to its fabulous and large riverside terrace, Guinness on tap, table football and requisite U2 soundtrack.

🍺 Santa Croce

⭐**L'Arte del Sogno** CAFE, TEAHOUSE

(Map p80; ☑ 055 012 02 93; Borgo La Croce 24-26r; ⊗9am-7.30pm Mon-Fri, to 11pm Sat) Be it a mug of cinnamon-spiced milk, cappuccino or the most outrageous coffee imagineable with every cream-nut-chocolate topping going, this contemporary coffee-house and tearoom is just divine, darling. The choice of hot chocolate, tea and infusions – not to mention cookies, cakes, muffins and tarts – is equally impressive. Tables strung together

from upcycled gilded picture frames and driftwood add an appealing artsy vibe.

Kitsch BAR

(Map p80; www.kitschfirenze.com; Viale A Gramsci 5; ⊗6.30pm-2.30am; 🛜) Cent-conscious Florentines love this American-styled bar for its lavish spread at *aperitivi* time – €10 for a drink and sufficient nibbles to not need dinner. It sports a dark-red theatrical interior and a bright 20s- to early-30s crowd on for a good time. DJ sets set the place rocking after dark. **Kitsch Devx** (Map p76; Via San Gallo 22r; ⊗6pm-2am) is its twin sister.

Moyo BAR

(Map p80; www.moyo.it; Via de' Benci 23r; ⊗8am-2am Sun-Thu, 9am-3am Fri & Sat; 🛜) This trendy all-rounder pulls in a moneyed younger set with its endless stream of DJ sets, themed *aperitivi* and late-night drinks, different types of breakfast, quick-fix lunches and American-style weekend brunches. Cocktails are particularly big – cranberry martini with lemon juice and triple sec is the house speciality.

Drogheria LOUNGE, BAR

(Map p80; www.drogheriafirenze.it; Largo Annigoni 22; ⊗10am-2am) Be it rain, hail or shine, this is a lovely contemporary address in Santa Croce. Inside, it is a large space with dark-wood furnishings and comfy leaf-green

---

DON'T MISS

CRAFT COCKTAILS

Mayday (Map p66; ☑ 055 238 12 90; Via Dante Alighieri 16; cocktails €8; ⊗7pm-2am Tue-Sat) Strike up a conversation with passionate mixologist Marco at Mayday. Within seconds you'll be hooked on his homemade mixers and astonishing infusions, all handmade using wholly Tuscan ingredients. Think pancetta-infused whisky, saffron limoncello and porcini liqueur. Marco's cocktail list is equally impressive – or tell him your favourite flavours and let yourself be surprised.

Beer lovers will enjoy the pale ales, bitter and other artisanal brews from Tuscany's Birrificio Artigianale Ororo microbrewery.

Surf Ventura (☑ 055 68 85 89; Via Ser Ventura Monachi 21r ; ⊗5pm-2am Thu-Tue) If half a scooped out papaya filled with alcohol is your cup of tea, hit underground cocktail club Surf Ventura.

armchairs, perfect for lounging for hours on end. Come spring, the action moves outside onto the terrace on the huge square across from Sant' Ambrogio market. The kitchen cooks up various bar-style dishes including burgers – beef, veggie, tofu or falafel.

Lion's Fountain
IRISH PUB

(Map p80; www.thelionsfountain.com; Borgo degli Albizi 34r; ⊙10am-2am) If you have the urge to hear more English than Italian – or local bands play for that matter – this is the place. Plump on a pretty pedestrian square, Florence's busiest Irish pub buzzes in summer when the beer-loving crowd spills across most of the square. Live music.

Bamboo
CLUB

(Map p80; ☑335 43 44 84; www.bamboolounge club.com; Via Giuseppe Verdi 59r; ⊙7pm-4am Thu-Sat) A hipster crowd looks beautiful in this Santa Croce newcomer, a lounge and dance club with chintzy red seating, steely grey bar and a mix of hip hop and R&B on the turntable. Dress up, look good to get in.

Full Up
CLUB

(Map p80; Via della Vigna Vecchia 21r; ⊙11pm-4am Mon-Sat Sep-Jun) A variety of sounds energises the crowd at this popular Florentine nightclub where 20-somethings dance until dawn.

San Lorenzo & San Marco

News Cafe
CAFE

(Map p66; ☑055 21 11 68; Via del Giglio 59) There is one fun reason to have a coffee at this San Lorenzo cafe – for a bespoke cappuccino

---

DON'T MISS

THE PERFECT HANGOUT

Ditta Artigianale (Map p80; ☑055 274 15 41; www.dittaartigianale.it; Via dei Neri 32r; ⊙8am-10pm Mon-Thu, 8am-midnight Fri, 9.30am-midnight Sat, 9.30am-10pm Sun; 🛜) With industrial decor and welcoming laid-back vibe, ingenious coffee roastery–cafe-bar Ditta Artigianale rocks. Behind the bar is well-travelled Florentine barrista Francesco Sanapo and gin queen Cecilia who together shake and mix what the city's most compelling hybrid is famed for – first-class coffee and outstanding gin cocktails. Brunch is served from 10am to 4pm, and a gourmet *aperitivo* kicks in at 7pm, making it a perfect place to hang out whatever the time of day.

---

made by barista Marco. Designs drawn on the frothy milk depend on mood and whim, but the unelevated price is a constant – €1.20/2.10 standing up/sitting down.

Un Cafe
CAFE, BAR

(Map p76; Via Cesare Battisti 3; ⊙variable) A bohemian air wafts through this cafe-bar overlooking San Marco's Piazza della Santissima Annunziata. It is the size of a shoebox but its jaunty vibe and vintage bric-a-brac decor instantly charms. The bar has no fixed hours – the door shuts when the last punter's left.

Santa Maria Novella

Shake Café
CAFE

(Map p66; ☑055 29 53 10; www.shakecafe.bio; Via degli Avelli 2r; ⊙7am-8pm) Close to the train station, this self-service juice bar has a perfect people-watching pavement terrace on car-free Piazza Santa Maria Novella. Its fruit juices and smoothies include fabulous combos such as pineapple, fennel, celery, mint, chicory and liquorice. Unusually for Florence, Shake Café also makes cappuccinos with soya, almond or rice milk. Salads, wraps, sandwiches and gelato stave off hunger pangs.

Space Club
CLUB

(Map p66; www.spaceclubfirenze.com; Via Palazzuolo 37r; admission incl 1 drink €16; ⊙10pm-4am) Sheer size alone at this vast club in Santa Maria Novella impresses – dancing, drinking, video-karaoke in the bar, and a mixed student-international crowd.

Out of Town

Tenax
CLUB

(www.tenax.org; Via Pratese 46; admission varies; ⊙10pm-4am Thu-Sun Oct-Apr) The only club in Florence on the European club circuit, with great international guest DJs and wildly popular 'Nobody's Perfect' house parties on Saturday night; find the warehouse-style building out of town near Florence airport. Take bus 29 or 30 from Stazione di Santa Maria Novella.

☆ Entertainment

Hanging out on warm summer nights on cafe and bar terraces aside, Florence enjoys a vibrant entertainment scene thanks in part to its substantial foreign-student population. The city has highly regarded theatres, a bounty of festivals and – from around midnight once *aperitivi* and dinner is done – a fairly low-key but varied dance scene.

GO TO JAIL!

Florence's old city jail (1883–1985) and 15th-century nunnery behind the Mercato di Sant'Ambrogio is one of the city's most interesting cultural spaces. Arranged around an interior courtyard, the historic red-brick complex is, in itself, compelling: there's absolutely no mistaking the thick sturdy doors leading to the old prison cells, many of which now open onto a bookshop, wine bar, art gallery and so on. The *pièce de résistance* is Le Murate Caffè Letterario (Map p80; ☑ 055 234 68 72; www.lemurate.it; Piazza delle Murate Firenze; ◷ 9am-1am), an artsy cafe-bar in the heart of the complex where Florence's literati meet to talk, create and perform over coffee, drinks and light meals. Intended as a melting pot for writers, the literary cafe hosts everything from readings and interviews with authors – Florentine, Italian and international – to film screenings, debates, live music and art exhibitions. Its funky interior embraces a series of retro rooms with vintage chairs and table tops built from recycled window frames. In summer everything spills outside in the wonderful brick courtyard. Check upcoming events online.

Live Music

Most venues are outside town and closed in July and/or August.

La Cité   LIVE MUSIC
(Map p66; www.lacitelibreria.info; Borgo San Frediano 20r; ◷ 8am-2am Mon-Sat, 3pm-2am Sun; 🛜) A hip cafe-bookshop with an eclectic choice of vintage seating, La Cité makes a wonderful, intimate venue for live music – jazz, swing, world music – and book readings.

Jazz Club   JAZZ
(Map p80; Via Nuovo de' Caccini 3; ◷ 10.30pm-2am Tue-Sat, closed Jul & Aug) Catch salsa, blues, Dixieland and world music as well as jazz at Florence's top jazz venue.

Theatre, Classical Music & Ballet

Opera di Firenze   OPERA
(☑ 055 277 9350; www.operadifirenze.it; Piazzale Vittorio Gui, Viale Fratelli Rosselli; ◷ box office 2-6pm Mon, 10am-6pm Tue-Sat) Florence's striking new opera house with glittering contemporary geometric facade sits on the green edge of city park Parco delle Cascine. Its three thoughtfully designed and multifunctional concert halls seat an audience of 5000 and play host to the springtime Maggio Musicale Fiorentino.

Teatro della Pergola   THEATRE
(Map p80; ☑ 055 2 26 41; www.teatrodellapergola.com; Via della Pergola 18) Beautiful city theatre with stunning entrance; host to classical concerts October to April.

🛍 Shopping

Tacky mass-produced souvenirs (boxer shorts emblazoned with *David's* packet) are everywhere, not least at the city's two main markets, Mercato Centrale (p100) and Mercato Nuovo (Map p66; Loggia Mercato Nuovo; ◷ 8.30am-7pm Mon-Sat), awash with cheap imported handbags and other leather goods. But for serious shoppers keen to delve into a city synonymous with craftsmanship since medieval times, there are plenty of workshops and boutiques to visit. Leather goods, jewellery, hand-embroidered linens, designer fashion, perfume, marbled paper, wine, puppets and gourmet foods all make quality souvenirs.

🛍 Duomo to Piazza della Signoria

Grevi   FASHION
(Map p66; www.grevi.it; Via della Spada 11-13r; ◷ 10am-2pm & 3-8pm Mon-Sat) It was a hat made by Siena milliner Grevi that actress Cher wore in the film *Tea with Mussolini* (1999); ditto Maggie Smith in *My House in Umbria* (2003). So if you want to shop like a star for a hat by Grevi, this hopelessly romantic boutique is the address. Hats range in price from €30 to unaffordable for many.

Officina de' Tornabuoni   BEAUTY
(Map p66; http://odtshop.com; Via del Parione 52r; ◷ 10am-7pm Mon-Sat) This Florentine house has pampered well-heeled locals with its natural skincare, fragrance and wellbeing products since 1843 (when it first opened its doors on nearby via' de Tornabuoni). Be it a rose and Sicilian orange face toner or Tornabuoni travel kit concocted from dandelion extract and sage oil, this crisp white boutique promises to spoil.

Fabriano Boutique   GIFTS, HANDICRAFTS
(Map p66; www.fabrianoboutique.com; Via del Corso 59r; ◷ 10am-7.30pm Mon-Sat, 11am-7pm Sun) Luxurious writing paper, origami and pop-up

greeting cards, and other lovely paper products entice customers into this modern stationery boutique. It also organises card-making, calligraphy and origami workshops.

★ Letizia Fiorini
GIFTS, HANDICRAFTS
(Map p66; Via del Parione 60r; ☺10am-7pm Tue-Sat) This charming shop is a one-woman affair; Letizia Fiorini sits at the counter and makes her distinctive puppets by hand in between assisting customers. You'll find Pulcinella (Punch), Arlecchino the clown, beautiful servant girl Colombina, Doctor Peste (complete with plague mask), cheeky Brighella, swashbuckling Il Capitano and many other characters from traditional Italian puppetry.

Alberto Cozzi
HANDICRAFTS
(Map p66; Via del Parione 35r; ☺9am-1pm & 2.30-7pm Mon-Fri, 3-7pm Sat) Florence is famous for its exquisite marbled paper and this fourth-generation bookbinder and restorer has been making sheets of the stuff by hand since 1908. Come here to buy paper, leather-bound journals, colourful cards and stationery.

Scriptorium
CRAFTS
(Map p66; Via dei Pucci 4; ☺9.30am-7.30pm Mon-Fri, 9.30am-1pm Sat) A mooch around this up-market boutique is worth it, if only to dip into the utterly cinematic courtyard of Palazzo Pucci in which it's hidden. Scriptorium crafts exquisite leather boxes and books, calligraphy nibs and pens, and old-world wax seals in every colour under the sun.

Il Papiro
SOUVENIRS
(Map p66; www.ilpapirofirenze.it; Via Porta Rosso 76; ☺10am-7pm) One of several branches around town, this elegant boutique specialises in books, journals, writing paper, cards and other stationery made from Florence's signature, hand-decorated marbled paper.

Marioluca Giusti
HOMEWARES
(Map p66; www.mariolucagiusti.com; Via della Vigna Nuova 88r; ☺10am-7.30pm Mon-Sat, 11am-7pm Sun) The jugs, beakers, glasses and other elegant tableware items in this eye-catching boutique look like glass – but are not! Everything created by Florentine designer Marioluca Giusti is, in fact, crafted from acrylic, melamine or other synthetic material. Fresh with a mix of pop and vintage in style, the homewares here make great gifts to take home.

Bartolini
HOMEWARES
(Map p80; ☑055 29 14 97; www.dinobartolini.it; Via dei Servi 72r; ☺10am-7pm Mon-Sat) Foodies with even the mildest interest in cooking

will find Florence's most famous kitchen shop absolutely fascinating. Don't miss the collection of pasta-making tools.

Mrs Macis
FASHION
(Map p80; Borgo Pinti 38r; ☺4-7.30pm Mon, 10.30am-1pm & 4-7.30pm Tue-Sat) Workshop and showroom of the talented Carla Macis, this eye-catching boutique – dollhouse-like in design – specialises in very feminine 1950s, '60s and '70s clothes and jewellery made from new and recycled fabrics. Every piece is unique and fabulous.

★ Street Doing
FASHION, VINTAGE
(Map p76; ☑055 538 13 34; www.streetdoing vintage.it; Via dei Servi 88r; ☺2.30-7.30pm Mon, 10.30am-7.30pm Tue-Sat) Vintage couture for men and women is what this extraordinary rabbit warren of a boutique – surely the city's largest collection of vintage – is about. Carefully curated garments and acessories are in excellent condition and feature all the top Italian designers: beaded 1950s Gucci clutch bags, floral 1960s Pucci dresses, Valentino shades from every decade. Fashionists, *this* is heaven.

Il Cancello
ANTIQUES, FASHION
(Map p66; www.antiquariatoilcancello.com; Via dei Fossi 13r; ☺10am-7pm Tue-Sat) The glitz, glam and romance of bygone eras are evoked at this wonderful antiquarian boutique specialising in vintage fashion. Garments and accessories from the 1920s to 1980s are beautifully arranged, complete with a tantalising display of 1940s duck-feather hats and travelling trunks in the window. Find several more antiquarians on the same street.

Angela Caputi
JEWELLERY
(Map p66; www.angelacaputi.com; Borgo SS Apostoli 42-46; ☺10am-1pm & 3.30-7.30pm Mon-Sat) The bold and colourful resin jewellery of Angela Caputi, at work in Florence since the 1970s, is much loved by Florentines. Eye-catching costume gems and jewels are her forte, shown off to perfection against one-of-a-kind women's fashion labels uncovered during her worldwide travels.

Aprosio & Co
ACCESSORIES, JEWELLERY
(Map p66; www.aprosio.it; Via della Spada 38; ☺10am-7pm Mon-Fri, 10.30am-7.30pm Sat) Ornella Aprosio fashions teeny tiny glass and crystal beads into dazzling pieces of jewellery, hair accessories, animal-shaped brooches, handbags, even glass-flecked cashmere. It is all quite magical.

DESIGNER OUTLET STORES

Pick up previous-season designer pieces at low prices at Florence's out-of-town outlets.

Barberino Designer Outlet (☎055 84 21 61; www.mcarthurglen.it; Via Meucci, Barberino di Mugello; ☺10am-8pm Mon-Fri, to 9pm Sat & Sun) Previous season's collections by D&G, Prada, Roberto Cavalli, Missoni et al at discounted prices, 40km north of Florence. A shuttle bus (adult/reduced return €15/8, 30 minutes) departs from Piazza della Stazione 44 (in front of Zoppini) two to four times daily. Check seasonal schedules online.

The Mall (☎055 865 77 75; www.themall.it; Via Europa 8, Leccio; ☺10am-8pm summer, to 7pm winter) Shop for last season's Gucci, Ferragamo, Ermenegildo Zegna, Fendi, Valentino et al at this mall, 30km from Florence. Buses (€5, up to eight daily) depart daily from the SITA bus station.

Desii Lab
FASHION
(Map p66; Via della Spada 40r; ☺11am-1.30pm & 2-7.30pm Mon, 10.30am-1.30pm & 2.30-7.30pm Tue-Sat) Be it a pair of glittering lilac and turquoise sequinned Uggs, patent yellow Doc Martens or the latest Converse, this shoe shop – new and vintage – is the place to go. The street fashion specialist sells scarves and other accessories too.

Mio Concept
HOMEWARES
(Map p66; www.mio-concept.com; Via della Spada 34r; ☺3-7pm Mon, 10am-1.30pm & 2.30-7pm Tue-Sat) A stunning and fascinating range of design objects for the home – some recycled or upcycled – as well as jewellery, T-shirts and so on cram this stylish boutique created by German-born globetrotter Antje. A real highlight is the street sign artworks by Florence-based street artist CLET.

Loretta Caponi
FASHION
(Map p66; www.lorettacaponi.com; Piazza degli Antinori 4r; ☺3-7pm Mon, 10am-7pm Tue-Sat) An old family name dressing the aristocracy for aeons, this utterly gorgeous shop sells hand-embroidered sleepwear, bed and table linen, as well as slippers, bathrobes and exquisitely smocked children's clothes. Think posh boudoir vibe.

Famarcia SS Annunziata
BEAUTY
(Map p76; ☎055 21 07 38; www.farmacia ssannunziata1561.it; Via dei Servi 80r; ☺9am-1pm & 3.30-7.30pm Mon-Fri, 9.30am-1pm Sat) Step into old-world Florence at this family-run, 16th-century pharmacy and herbalist – an elegant mirage of dark-wood cabinets, colourful tiled floor and vaulted ceiling (all from the 18th century). Beauty products are as old and appealing as the shop interior: this is the spot to pick up a natural bamboo toothbrush, whitening toothpaste with sage, or ginseng and gingko hair tonic.

🏠 Santa Maria Novella

★ Officina Profumo-Farmaceutica di Santa Maria Novella
BEAUTY, GIFTS
(Map p66; www.smnovella.it; Via della Scala 16; ☺9.30am-7.30pm) In business since 1612, this perfumery-pharmacy began life when the Dominican friars of Santa Maria Novella began to concoct cures and sweet-smelling unguents using medicinal herbs cultivated in the monastery garden. The shop today sells a wide range of fragrances, skin-care products, ancient herbal remedies and preparations alongside teas, herbal infusions, liqueurs, scented candles, organic olive oil, chocolate, honey and cookies.

A real treasure, it has touchscreen catalogues and a state-of-the-art payment system, yet still manages to ooze vintage charm. After a day battling crowds at the Uffizi or Accademia, you may want to come here for some Aqua di Santa Maria Novella, said to cure hysterics.

Midinette
FASHION
(Map p76; Piazza della Stazione 5; ☺10.30am-7.30pm Mon-Sat, 11am-7.30pm Sun) From the shabby-chic floor – partly original tiles, partly bare paint – to the retro-inspired fashion, this clothing and accessory boutique for women is impossibly romantic. The same French stylist is also the creative spirit behind sister boutique Le Poème, two doors down on the same street.

Penko
JEWELLERY
(Map p66; Via Ferdinando Zannetti 14-16r; ☺9.30am-7pm Mon-Sat) Renaissance jewels and gems inspire the designs of third-generation jeweller Paolo Penko who works with his son in the atelier his grandfather opened in the 1950s. Everything is handmade, as the mass of vintage

Florence for Shoppers

Florence is naturally stylish – the city did spawn the Renaissance and Gucci after all – which translates as inspirational shopping. Be it the hottest big-name label to strut down the catwalk or something handmade and unique by a smaller designer, fashion is what many people come to Florence for. Big-name Florentine fashion designers to look for in multi-brand stores include Michele Negri, Enrico Coveri, Patrizia Pepe and Ermanno Daelli. For wonderful leather designs, staunch crusader of artisanal talent Jennifer Tattanelli of Casini Firenze is a good starting point (p117).

Shopping Streets

The world's luxury brands sit smart on **Via de' Tornabuoni**, Florence's main shopping strip with a dazzling line-up of designers – everyone from Prada to Cartier and home-grown players Gucci, Roberto Cavalli and Ferragamo (with glittering shoe museum to boot). From here, it is a stiletto hop to **Via della Vigna Nuova** and **Via della Spada**, a twin-set of impossibly charming, old-world back streets where some of the city's smartest and most creative designers can be found: milliner Grevi (p111) from Siena and bead designer Ornella Aprosio (p112) are two of many stylish boutiques to have legged it here in the last couple of years. Move east into **Santa Croce** to mingle with Florentine designers specialising in vintage and recycled fashion – Borgo degli Albizi, Borgo Pinti and Via di Mezzo are key streets.

Across the river, **Oltrarno** is the traditional 'working' part of the city, the quarter where the Florentine artisan was born and had his tiny workshop. Borgo

1. Mercato Nuovo (p111)
2. Leather craftsman, Santa Croce
3. High-end fashion, Via de' Tornabuoni

RICHARD I'ANSON/GETTY IMAGES ©

LONELY PLANET/GETTY IMAGES ©

HEMIS/ALAMY ©

San Jacopo and Via Santo Spirito remain great streets for avant-garde fashion, shoes, hand-crafted wood and dazzling jewellery; while steps from the river on Via dell'Olmo, Florence's most playful (and wildly popular) street artist CLET (p81) quietly works in his studio on yet another street sign guaranteed to make you grin.

Handmade

Watching artisans cut bags from tanned calf skin, bookbinders marble paper with peacock patterns, puppeteers stitch, and jewellers pore over gold is what Florence shopping is about: Scuola del Cuoio (p116), Letizia Fiorini (p112) and Giulio Giannini e Figlio (p118) are key addresses to do just that.

Markets

Meandering the sea of open-air stalls at the city's two main markets, **Mercato de San Lorenzo** (Piazza San Lorenzo; ⊙9am-7pm Mon-Sat) and Mercato Nuovo (p111), is fun but shoppers on the prowl for a handbag, belt or jacket, be aware: Florence's street markets only hawk cheap, imported leather. For quality Florentine leather head to an old family-run boutique.

BEST SPECIALIST BOUTIQUES

➡ Grevi (p111)
➡ Street Doing (p112)
➡ & Company (p117)
➡ Byørk (p117)
➡ Mio Concept (p113)

SHOP TO EAT

Shopping for culinary products is a sheer joy in foodie Florence, a city where locals live to eat. Mercato Centrale (p100) aside, these are Florentines' favourites for food shopping. In addition, don't miss the splendid array of conserved vegetables and other homemade treats on sale at Il Teatro del Sale (p102).

La Bottega Della Frutta (Map p66; Via dei Federighi 31r; ☺8.30am-7.30pm Mon-Sat, closed Aug) Follow the trail of knowing Florentines, past the flower-and-veg-laden bicycle parked outside, into this enticing food shop bursting with boutique cheeses, organic fruit and veg, biscuits, chocolates, conserved produce, excellent-value wine et al. Mozzarella oozing raw milk arrives fresh from Eboli in Sicily every Tuesday, and if you're looking to buy olive oil this is the place to taste. Simply ask Elisabeta or husband Francesco.

Pegna (Map p66; www.pegnafirenze.com; Via dello Studio 8; ☺9.30am-7.30pm Mon-Sat, 11am-7pm Sun) This historic *salumeria* (delicatessen) and *drogheria* (grocers') store dating to 1860 is a quality stop for everything from gourmet cheeses, cold meats and biscuits to Florence-made cinnamon- or ginseng-mint toothpaste and handmade Martelli pasta.

Alla Sosta dei Pipi (Map p80; ☎055 234 11 74; www.sostadeipapi.it; Via Borgo la Croce 81r; ☺4-8pm Mon, 9am-1.30pm & 4-8pm Tue-Sat) This tiny *enoteca* is a wine-buff's one-stop shop. Vats of wine and shelves of bottles pack its tiny interior, Tuscan wines ranging from as cheap as chips (bring your own bottle and fill her up for €2.30/L) to the very best.

Eataly (Map p66; ☎055 015 36 01; Via de' Martelli 22r; ☺10am-10.30pm) Eataly shops are as much about learning about food as shopping for it, and the Florence branch is no exception. Grab a free audioguide at the information desk (near the exit) and peruse aisles laden with coffee, biscuits, conserved vegetables, pasta, rice, olive oil etc while listening to Renaissance tales. Many products are local and/or organic; most are by small producers.

S.Forno (Map p84; Via Santa Monaco 3r; ☺7.30am-7.30pm) Fresh breads, *panini* and gourmet products are stacked on vintage shelves at this hip bakery with baker Angelo at the helm.

Dolce Forte (Map p66; www.dolceforte.it; Via della Scala 21; ☺10am-1pm & 3.30-7.45pm Wed-Sat & Mon, 3.30-7.45pm Tue) Elena is the passion and knowledge behind this chocolate shop that sells only the best. Think black-truffle-flavoured chocolate; an entire cherry, stone and all, soaked in grappa and wrapped in white chocolate; or – for the ultimate taste sensation – *formaggio di fossa* (a cheese from central Italy) soaked in sweet wine and enrobed in dark chocolate.

Obsequium (Map p66; www.obsequium.it; Borgo San Jacopo 17-39r; ☺11am-7.30pm) Tuscan wines, wine accessories and gourmet foods, including truffles, on the ground floor of one of Florence's best-preserved medieval towers.

La Bottega dell'Olio (Map p66; Piazza del Limbo 2r; ☺2.30-6.30pm Mon, 10am-1pm & 2-6.30pm Tue-Sat) This boutique displays olive oils, olive oil soaps, platters made from olive wood and skincare products made with olive oil (the Lepo range is particularly good).

Mercato di Sant'Ambrogio (Map p80; Piazza Ghiberti; ☺7am-2pm Mon-Sat) Outdoor food market with an intimate, local flavour.

---

tools strewn on the workbench attests. Drop in at the right moment and Paolo can mint you your very own Florentine florin in bronze, silver or gold (€10 to €30).

🔒 Santa Croce

Aquaflor　　　　　　　　　BEAUTY
(Map p80; ☎055 234 34 71; www.florenceparfum. com; Via Borgo Santa Croce 6; ☺10am-7pm) This elegant Santa Croce perfumery in a vaulted 15th-century *palazzo* exudes romance

and exoticism. Scents are crafted here with tremendous care and precision by master perfumer Sileno Cheloni, who works with precious essences from all over the world, including the Florentine iris. Organic soaps, cosmetics and body care products make equally lovely gifts to take back home.

Scuola del Cuoio　　　　ACCESSORIES
(Map p80; www.scuoladelcuoio.com; Via San Giuseppe 5r; ☺10am-6pm) Hidden in a courtyard behind Santa Croce church, this store

and workshop features a long corridor where craftspeople stand at their stations fashioning their leathergoods by hand.

Boutique Nadine
VINTAGE

(Map p80; www.boutiquenadine.com; Via de' Benci 32r; ⊙ 2.30-7.30pm Mon, 10.30am-7.30pm Tue-Sat, 2-7pm Sun) There is no more elegant and quaint address to shop for vintage clothing, jewellery, homewares and other pretty little trinkets. From the wooden floor and antique display cabinets to the period changing cabin, Nadine's attention to detail is impeccable. Find a second, riverside boutique near Ponte Vecchio at Lungarno Acciaiuoli 22r.

🏠 Oltrarno

Lorenzo Villoresi
BEAUTY

(Map p84; ☑ 055 234 11 87; www.lorenzovilloresi.it; Via de' Bardi 14; ⊙ 10am-7pm Mon-Sat) Villoresi's perfumes and potpourris meld distinctively Tuscan elements such as laurel, olive, cypress and iris with essential oils and essences from around the world. His bespoke fragrances are highly sought after. Visiting his showroom, which occupies his family's 15th-century *palazzo*, is quite an experience. Drop-ins welcome but it's better to call in advance to arrange your visit.

★ & Company
ARTS, CRAFTS

(Map p84; http://andcompanyshop.tumblr.com/; Via Maggio 60r; ⊙ 10.30am-1pm & 3-6.30pm Mon-Sat) This mesmerising Pandora's box of beautiful objects and paper creations is the love child of Florence-born, British-raised callligrapher and graphic designer Betty Soldi and her vintage-loving husband, Matteo Perduca. Together the pair have created an extraordinary boutique showcasing their own customised cards and upcycled homewares alongside work by other designers. Souvenir shopping at its best!

Byørk
FASHION

(Map p84; Via della Sprone; ⊙ 2.30-7.30pm Mon, 10.30am-1.30pm & 2.30-7.30pm Tue-Fri, 10.30am-1pm & 2.30-7.30pm Sat) Cutting-edge fashion plus zines, books and magazines are sold at this trendy lifestyle shop, incongruously wedged between tatty old artisan workshops on an Oltrarno backstreet. It's the creation of well-travelled fashionist Filippo Anzaione, whose taste in Italian and other contemporary European designers is impeccable.

Le Gare 24
FASHION

(Map p66; Borgo d'Ognissanti 24r; ⊙ 10am-8pm Mon-Sat) Waltz into this retro boutique near the river, note the bright turquoise sofa with hairy fuschia-pink cushions and know you're in one of the best addresses in town for cutting-edge fashion.

Casini Firenze
FASHION

(Map p84; www.casinifirenze.it; Piazza dei Pitti 30-31r; ⊙ 10am-7pm Mon-Sat, 11am-6pm Sun) One of Florence's oldest and most reputable fashion houses, this lovely boutique across from Palazzo Pitti keeps its edge thanks to American-Florentine designer and stylist Jennifer Tattanelli (she does personal wardrobe consultations).

Stefano Bemer
SHOES

(www.stefanobemersrl.com; Via di San Niccolò 2; ⊙ 10am-7pm Mon-Sat) Bespoke shoes for gents – complete with an original six pence coin embedded in the sole of the left shoe for good luck – is what this Florentine shoemaker does best. Pick from 40 basic styles, fashioned in a remarkable choice of leather, including deer, bull, shark, hippopotamus or Russian reindeer, preserved since 1786 using traditional tanning methods.

Francesco
SHOES

(Map p66; www.francescodafirenze.it; Via di Santo Spirito 62r; ⊙ 10am-1pm & 3.30-7.30pm Mon-Sat, 10am-1pm Sun, closed 2 weeks Aug) Hand-stitched leather is the cornerstone of this tiny family business specialising in ready-to-wear – and indeed made-to-measure – men's and women's shoes.

Madova
ACCESSORIES

(Map p84; www.madova.com; Via Guicciardini 1r; ⊙ 9.30am-7.30pm Mon-Sat, 10.30am-7pm Mon-Fri Aug) Cashmere lined, silk lined, lambs'-wool lined, unlined – gloves in whatever size, shape, colour and type of leather you fancy by Florentine glovemakers in the biz since 1919.

Alessandro Dari
JEWELLERY

(Map p84; www.alessandrodari.com; Via di San Niccolò 115r; ⊙ 10am-7pm Mon-Sat) Jeweller and classical guitarist Alessandro Dari creates unique pieces in his 15th-century workshopshowroom in San Niccolò. 'Sculpture that you can wear' is how he describes his work.

Geraldine Tayar
FASHION

(Map p84; Sdrucciolo de' Pitti 6r; ⊙ 10am-6pm Mon-Sat) Bags, belts, capes and cushions are among the many items designer Geraldine Tayar crafts in her Oltrarno workshop near Palazzo Pitti. Her mix of unusual knits and colourful fabrics is particularly eye-catching.

Giulio Giannini e Figlio HANDICRAFTS
(Map p84; www.giuliogiannini.it; Piazza dei Pitti 37r; ⊙10am-7pm Mon-Sat, 11am-6.30pm Sun) This quaint old shopfront has been around since 1856. One of Florence's oldest artisan families, the Gianninis – bookbinders by trade – make and sell marbled paper, beautifully bound books, stationery and so on.

ℹ Information

EMERGENCY

Police Station (Questura; ☑ English-language service 055 497 72 68, 055 4 97 71; http://questure.poliziadistato.it; Via Zara 2; ⊙24hr) Should you have a theft or other unfortunate incident to report, the best time to visit the city's police station is between 9am and 2pm weekdays when the foreign-language service – meaning someone speaks English – kicks in.

MEDICAL SERVICES

24-Hour Pharmacy (Stazione di Santa Maria Novella) This pharmacy inside Florence's central train station opens 24 hours. There is usually at least one member of staff who speaks English.

Dr Stephen Kerr: Medical Service (☑ 055 28 80 55, 335 8361682; www.dr-kerr.com; Piazza Mercato Nuovo 1; ⊙3-5pm Mon-Fri, or by appointment 9am-3pm Mon-Fri) Resident British doctor.

Hospital (Ospedale di Santa Maria Nuova; ☑ 055 2 75 81; Piazza di Santa Maria Nuova 1)

TOURIST INFORMATION

Airport Tourist Office (☑ 055 31 58 74; www.firenzeturismo.it; Via del Termine, Aeroporto Vespucci; ⊙9am-7pm Mon-Sat, to 2pm Sun)

Infopoint Stazione (Map p66; ☑ 055 21 22 45; www.firenzeturismo.it; Piazza della Stazione 5; ⊙9am-7pm Mon-Sat, to 2pm Sun)

Central Tourist Office (Map p76; ☑ 055 29 08 32; www.firenzeturismo.it; Via Cavour 1r; ⊙9am-6pm Mon-Sat)

Infopoint Bigallo (Map p66; ☑ 055 28 84 96; www.firenzeturismo.it; Piazza San Giovanni 1; ⊙9am-7pm Mon-Sat, to 2pm Sun)

Centro Visite Parco delle Cascine (Piazzale delle Cascine, Parco delle Cascine; ⊙9am-7pm Mon-Sat, to 5pm Sun)

ℹ Getting There & Away

AIR

Tuscany's international airport (p225) is in Pisa and offers flights to most major European cities.

Florence Airport (Aeroport Vespucci; ☑ 055 306 13 00; www.aeroporto.firenze.it; Via del Termine) Also known as Amerigo Vespucci or Peretola airport, 5km northwest of the city centre; domestic and European flights.

BUS

Services from the **SITA bus station** (Autostazione Busitalia-Sita Nord; Map p66; ☑ 800 37 37 60; Via Santa Caterina da Siena 17r; ⊙5.30am-8.30pm Mon-Sat, 6am-8pm Sun), just west of Piazza della Stazione, are limited; the train is better. Destinations include the following:

Greve in Chianti (€4.20, one hour, hourly)

San Gimignano (via Poggibonsi; €7.20, 1¼ hours, 14 daily)

Siena (€7.80, 1¼ hours, at least hourly)

CAR & MOTORCYCLE

Florence is connected by the A1 northwards to Bologna and Milan, and southwards to Rome and Naples. The Autostrada del Mare (A11) links Florence with Pistoia, Lucca, Pisa and the coast, but most locals use the FI-PI-LI – a superstrada (dual carriageway, hence no tolls); look for blue signs saying FI-PI-LI (as in Firenze-Pisa-Livorno). Another dual carriageway, the S2, links Florence with Siena. The much more picturesque SS67 connects the city with Pisa to the west, and Forli and Ravenna to the east.

TRAIN

Florence's central train station is **Stazione di Santa Maria Novella** (Piazza della Stazione). The **left-luggage counter** (deposito bagagliamano; Stazione di Santa Maria Novella; first 5hr €6, then per hr €0.90; ⊙6am-11pm) is located on platform 16. Tickets for all trains are sold in the main ticketing hall, but skip the permanently long queue by buying tickets from the touch-screen automatic ticket-vending machines; machines have an English option and accept cash and credit cards.

Florence is on the Rome–Milan line. Services include the following:

DESTINATION	COST	DURATION
Bologna	€24	1–1¾ hr
Lucca	€7.20	1½–1¾hr
Milan	€50–60	2¼–3½hr
Pisa	€8	45min–1hr
Pistoia	€4.30	45min–1hr
Rome	€43–52	1¾–4¼hr
Venice	€45	2¾–4½hr

ℹ Getting Around

Regular buses link both Florence and Pisa airports with the bus and train stations, both in the centre of town. Florence itself is small and

PARKING IN FLORENCE

There is a strict Limited Traffic Zone in Florence's historic centre between 7.30am and 7.30pm Monday to Friday and 7.30am to 6pm Saturday for all nonresidents, monitored by cyclopean cameras positioned at all entry points. The exclusion also applies on Thursday, Friday and Saturday nights from 11pm to 3am late May to mid-September. Motorists staying in hotels within the zone are allowed to drive to their hotel to drop off luggage, but must tell reception their car registration number and the time they were in no-cars-land (there's a two-hour window) so that the hotel can inform the authority and organise a permit. If you transgress, a fine of around €150 will be sent to you (or the car-hire company you used). For more information see www.comune.fi.it.

There is free street parking around Piazzale Michelangelo and plenty of car parks costing between €2 and €3 per hour around town, including at Santa Maria Novella train station, by Fortezza da Basso and in the Oltrarno beneath Piazzale di Porta Romana. Find a complete list of car parks on www.firenzeparcheggi.it.

best navigated on foot, with most major sights within easy walking distance. There are bicycles for rent and an efficient network of buses and trams. Unless you're mad, forget a car.

TO/FROM THE AIRPORTS
Bus

ATAF operates a Volainbus shuttle (single/return €6/8, 20 minutes) between Florence airport and Florence bus station every 30 minutes between 6am and 8pm, then hourly from 8.30pm until 11.30pm (from 5.30am to 12.30am from the airport). To get to/from Pisa airport, daily buses are operated by **Terravision** (www.terravision.eu; one way €4.99, 70 minutes) and **Autostradale** (www.airportbusexpress.it; one way €5, 80 minutes, hourly) between Pisa International Airport and the bus stops outside Florence's Stazione di Santa Maria Novella on Via Luigi Alamanni (under the digital station clock). For either company, buy tickets online, on board and in Pisa at the Pisa Airport Information Desk in the arrrivals hall.

Taxi

A taxi between Florence's Vespucci airport and town costs a flat rate of €20 (€23 on Sundays and holidays, €22 between 10pm and 6am), plus €1 per bag and €1 supplement for a fourth passenger. Exit the terminal building, bear right and you'll come to the taxi rank.

Train

Regular trains link Florence's Stazione di Santa Maria Novella with the central train station in Pisa, Pisa Centrale (€8, 1½ hours, at least hourly from 4.30am to 10.25pm), from where the Pisa-Mover shuttle bus (€1.30, 8 minutes) continues to Pisa International Airport.

CAR & MOTORCYCLE
Nonresident traffic is banned from the centre of Florence for most of the week and our advice, if

you can, is to avoid the whole irksome bother of having a car in the city.

BICYCLE & SCOOTER
Milleunabici (www.bicifirenze.it; Piazza della Stazione; 1hr/5hr/1 day €2/5/10; ⏰10am-7pm Mar-Oct) Violet-coloured bikes to rent in front of Stazione di Santa Maria Novella; leave ID as a deposit.

Florence by Bike (Map p76; www.florencebybike. com; Via San Zanobi 54r; 1hr/5hr/1 day €3/9/14; ⏰9am-1pm & 3.30-7.30pm Mon-Sat, 9am-5pm Sun summer, closed Sun winter) Top-notch bike shop with bike rental (city, mountain, touring and road bikes), itinerary suggestions and organised bike tours (two-hour photography tours of the city by bike, and day trips to Chianti).

PUBLIC TRANSPORT
Buses and electric minibuses run by public transport company ATAF serve the city. Most buses – including bus 13 to Piazzale Michelangelo – start/terminate at the ATAF bus stops opposite the southeastern exit of Stazione di Santa Maria Novella. Tickets valid for 90 minutes (no return journeys) cost €1.20 (€2 on board – drivers don't give change!) and are sold at kiosks, tobacconists and at the **ATAF ticket & information office** (Map p76; ☎199 10 42 45, 800 42 45 00; www.ataf.net; Piazza della Stazione, Stazione di Santa Maria Novella; ⏰6.45am-8pm Mon-Sat) inside the main ticketing hall at Santa Maria Novella train station. A travel pass valid for one/three/seven days is €5/12/18. Upon boarding, time-stamp your ticket (punch on board) or risk an on-the-spot €50 fine. One tramline is up and running; more are meant to follow in 2017.

TAXI
For a taxi, call ☎055 42 42.

Siena & Central Tuscany

Best Places to Eat

➡ Il Leccio (p158)

➡ Enoteca I Terzi (p133)

➡ Osteria di Passignano (p140)

➡ Osteria Acquacheta (p166)

➡ Locanda Sant'Agostino (p150)

Best Places to Stay

➡ Il Paluffo (p151)

➡ La Bandita (p163)

➡ Pensione Palazzo Ravizza (p132)

➡ Podere San Lorenzo (p155)

➡ Fattoria di Rignana (p138)

Why Go?

This swathe of Tuscany has a landscape to fall in love with. Rugged Chianti's bumpy backroads reveal a timeless terrain traced with cypress avenues and criss-crossing vines. In vineyards innovative and ancient you'll hear people talking of wine having a soul; taste it and see if you agree. Verdant western valleys shelter San Gimignano, where 14 medieval towers stretch for the sky. Nearby, Volterra's alleys deliver ancient hill-town atmosphere and 21st-century vampire tales.

Rolling and vine-lined, the gentle Val d'Orcia is dotted with Romanesque abbeys and thermal springs. Pienza presents a unique Renaissance cityscape; blockbuster wine towns Montepulciano and Montalcino wait in the wings. And then there's Siena: rich in spectacular architecture and exquisite art, it's both Gothic time capsule and vibrant city, where good food and drink and taking time for conversations are still cornerstones of everyday life. All in all, it's very easy to love.

Road Distances (km)

	Montepulciano	Siena	San Gimignano	Volterra
Siena	70			
San Gimignano	112	46		
Volterra	120	50	30	
Greve in Chianti	102	48	33	53

SIENA

POP 54,100

In Siena the architecture soars, and could well lift your soul. Effectively a giant, open-air museum to the Gothic, its spiritual and secular medieval monuments still sit in harmony, many filled with collections of Sienese art. Add vibrant streets where every third door (literally) opens into a restaurant, *enoteca* or deli, and you're in for a very fine time indeed. This is Italy before the Renaissance, magically transported to the modern day.

History

Legend tells us Siena was founded by the son of Remus, and the symbol of the wolf feeding the twins Romulus and Remus is as ubiquitous in Siena as it is in Rome. In reality the city was probably of Etruscan origin, although it didn't begin growing into a proper town until the 1st century BC, when the Romans established a military colony here called Sena Julia.

In the 12th century, Siena's wealth, size and power grew along with its involvement in commerce and trade. Its rivalry with neighbouring Florence grew proportionately, leading to numerous wars during the 13th century between Guelph Florence and Ghibelline Siena. In 1230 Florence besieged Siena and catapulted dung and donkeys over its walls. Siena's revenge came at the Battle of Montaperti in 1260, when it defeated its rival decisively. But victory was short-lived.

Only 10 years later, the Tuscan Ghibellines were defeated by Charles of Anjou and Siena was forced to ally with Florence, the chief town of the Tuscan Guelph League.

In the ensuing century, Siena was ruled by the Consiglio dei Nove (Council of Nine), a bourgeois group constantly bickering with the feudal nobles. It enjoyed its greatest prosperity during this time, and the Council commissioned many of the fine buildings in the Sienese-Gothic style that give the city its striking appearance, including lasting monuments such as the *duomo* (cathedral), Palazzo Comunale and Piazza del Campo.

The Sienese school of painting also had its origins at this time and reached its peak in the early 14th century, when artists such as Duccio di Buoninsegna and Ambrogio Lorenzetti were at work.

A plague outbreak in 1348 killed two-thirds of Siena's 100,000 inhabitants, leading to a period of decline that culminated in the city being handed over to Florence's Cosimo I de' Medici, who barred inhabitants from operating banks, thus severely curtailing its power.

But this centuries-long economic downturn was a blessing in disguise, as lack of funds meant that Siena's city centre was subject to very little redevelopment or new construction. In WWII the French took Siena virtually unopposed, sparing it discernible damage. Hence the historic centre's listing on Unesco's World Heritage list as the living embodiment of a medieval city.

THREE PERFECT DAYS

Day 1: Chianti Food & Wine

Prime your palate by touring the ultra-modern **Antinori nel Chianti Classico** winery (perhaps lunching at **Rinuccio 1180**) before exploring a historic one; try **Badia a Passignano** or **Castello di Verrazzano**. Next navigate vine-backed backroads to Greve in Chianti to browse the **Antica Macellerìa Falorni**. Motor south to Panzano in Chianti, dining at a **Dario Cecchini** eatery, then check into your chosen sleep spot: **Locanda La Capannuccia** or **Il Colombaio** might appeal.

Day 2: Val d'Elsa

Explore Volterra's cobbled streets, admiring artefacts in the **Museo Etrusco Guarnacci** and visiting the workshops of alabaster artisans. Lunch might be at **Ristorante-Enoteca Del Duca** (fine dining) or **L'Incontro** (cafe-style). Next, to the perfectly preserved medieval town of San Gimignano for art that balances the gravitas of the old (**Collegiata**) with the exhilaration of the new (**Galleria Continua**).

Day 3: Around Montalcino

At the medieval abbey of **Sant'Antimo**, you'll hopefully hear the monks chanting during mass. Drive beside sangiovese grape vines for lunch alongside local winemakers at **Il Leccio**. Next comes Montalcino, home to blockbuster Brunello wines; climb the **Fortezza's battlements**, taste vintages in its *enoteca*, then stroll to **Osticcio** to sample some more.

Siena & Central Tuscany Highlights

1 Feasting on fine food and touring vineyards at high-tech **Antinori** (p138), and age-old **Badia a Passignano** (p138) – in the wine region of Chianti.

2 Delighting in the **Duomo** (p126), people-watching in one of Italy's finest squares and encountering world-class art: all in sublime Siena.

3 Glorying in the Gregorian chanting at the Romanesque **Abbazia di Sant'Antimo** (p161).

4 Climbing the 218 steps of the medieval **Torre Grossa** (p147) to gaze down on the centuries-old streets of San Gimignano.

5 Clambering up **Il Corso** (p163), fuelled by Vino Nobile; the steep, winding central street of Montepulciano.

6 Discovering Etruscan artefacts and alabaster workshops in the artistic enclave of **Volterra** (p151).

7 Taste-testing Brunello, Tuscany's most famous wine, in Montalcino's historic **Fortezza** (p157).

8 Detouring onto scenic back roads in the World Heritage–listed **Val d'Orcia** (p159).

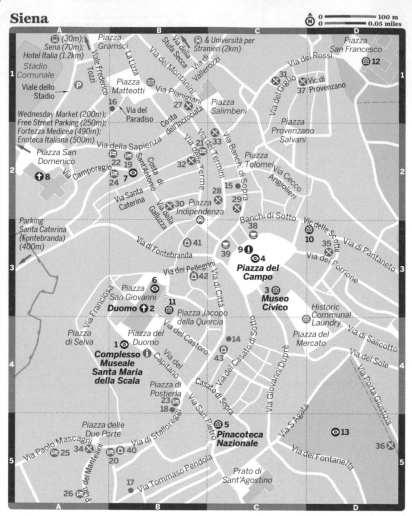

◎ Sights

★ Piazza del Campo · SQUARE

This sloping piazza, popularly known as Il Campo, has been Siena's civic and social centre since being staked out by the ruling Consiglio dei Nove in the mid-12th century. It was built on the site of a Roman marketplace, and its pie-piece paving design is divided into nine sectors to represent the number of members of that ruling council.

In 1346 water first bubbled forth from the **Fonte Gaia** (Happy Fountain; Piazza del Campo) in the upper part of the square. Today, the fountain's panels are reproductions; the severely weathered originals, sculpted by Jacopo della Quercia in the early 15th century, are on display in the Complesso Museale Santa Maria della Scala (p128).

The Campo is the heart of the city. Its magnificent pavement acts as a carpet on which students and tourists picnic and relax, and the cafes around the perimeter are the most popular *aperitivo* spots in town.

Palazzo Comunale · HISTORIC BUILDING

(Palazzo Pubblico; Piazza del Campo; ⊙10am-7pm summer, to 6pm winter) The restrained, 14th-century Palazzo Comunale serves as the

Siena

grand centrepiece of the square in which it sits – notice how its concave facade mirrors the opposing convex curve. From the *palazzo* soars a graceful bell tower, the **Torre del Mangia** (Palazzo Comunale, Piazza del Campo; admission €10; ☉10am-7pm summer, to 4pm winter), 102m high and with 500-odd steps. The views from the top are magnificent.

Entry to the ground-floor central courtyard is free.

★ **Museo Civico**   MUSEUM
(Palazzo Comunale, Piazza del Campo; adult/ reduced €9/8; ☉10am-7pm summer, to 6pm winter) Siena's most famous museum occupies rooms richly frescoed by artists of the Sienese school. Commissioned by the governing body of the city, rather than by the Church, many – unusually – depict secular subjects. The highlight is Simone Martini's celebrated *Maestà* (Virgin Mary in Majesty; 1315) in the **Sala del Mappamondo** (Hall of the World Map). It features the Madonna beneath a canopy surrounded by saints and angels, and is Martini's first known work.

After purchasing your ticket, head upstairs to the **Sala del Risorgimento**, where impressive late-19th-century frescoes serialise key events in the Risorgimento (reunification period). Continue through to the **Sala di Balia** (Rooms of Authority), where frescoes recount episodes in the life of Pope Alexander III (the Sienese Rolando Bandinelli), including his clashes with the Holy Roman Emperor Frederick Barbarossa. Straight ahead is the **Sala del Concistoro** (Hall of the Council of Clergymen), dominated by the allegorical ceiling frescoes of the Mannerist Domenico Beccafumi. Through a vestibule to the left are the **Anticappella** (Chapel entrance hall) and **Cappella** (Chapel). The Anticappella features frescoes painted in 1415 by Taddeo di Bartolo. These include figures representing the virtues needed for the proper exercise of power (Justice, Magnanimity, Strength, Prudence, Religion), and depictions of some of the leading Republican lights of ancient Rome. The Cappella contains a fine *Holy Family* and *St Leonard* by Il Sodoma. Next to the Anticappella is the

ℹ SIENA COMBINED PASSES

If you're planning to visit Siena's major monuments several combined passes can save you money.

➡ OPA SI Pass (includes the *duomo*, Libreria Piccolomini, Museo dell'Opera, Battistero di San Giovanni, Cripta and Oratorio di San Bernardino); March to October €12, November to February €8, valid for three days. Available along with individual tickets for all the above sights from the *duomo* ticket office beside the Museo dell'Opera.

➡ Museo Civico and Museale Santa Maria della Scala pass; €13 (tickets available at the museums).

➡ Museo Civico, Museale Santa Maria della Scala and Torre del Mangia pass; €20 (tickets available at the museums).

Vestibolo (Vestibule), whose star attraction is a bronze wolf, the symbol of the city.

The vestibule leads into the Sala del Mappamondo which houses Simone Martini's powerful and striking *Maestà*. On the other side of the room is Martini's oft-reproduced fresco (1328–30) of Guidoriccio da Fogliano, a captain of the Sienese army.

The next room, the **Sala dei Nove** (Hall of the Nine), is where the ruling Council of Nine was based. It's decorated with Ambrogio Lorenzetti's fresco cycle, the *Allegories of Good and Bad Government* (c 1338–40). The central allegory portrays scenes with personifications of Justice, Wisdom, Virtue and Peace, all unusually depicted as women, along with scenes of criminal punishment and rewards for righteousness. Set perpendicular from it are the frescoes *Allegory of Good Government* and *Allegory of Bad Government*, which feature intensely contrasting scenes clearly set around Siena. The good depicts a sunlit, idyllic, serene city, with joyous citizens and a countryside filled with crops; the bad city is filled with vices, crime and disease. These frescoes are often described as the most important secular paintings of the Renaissance, and are worth the admission alone.

★ **Duomo**   CATHEDRAL
(www.operaduomo.siena.it; Piazza del Duomo; summer/winter €4/free, when floor displayed €7; ⏱ 10.30am-7pm Mon-Sat, 1.30-6pm Sun summer, 10.30am-5.30pm Mon-Sat, 1.30-5.30pm Sun winter) Siena's cathedral is one of Italy's most awe-inspiring churches. Construction started in 1215 and over the centuries many of Italy's top artists have contributed: Giovanni Pisano designed the intricate white, green and red marble facade; Nicola Pisano carved the elaborate pulpit; Pinturicchio painted some of the frescoes; Michelangelo, Donatello and Gian Lorenzo Bernini all produced sculptures.

This triumph of Romanesque-Gothic architecture has a truly stunning interior. Walls and pillars continue the exterior's striped theme, while the vaults are painted blue with gold stars. The intricate **floor** is inlaid with 56 panels depicting historical and biblical scenes executed by about 40 artists over 200 years from the 14th century on. The older rectangular panels, including the *Wheel of Fortune* (1372) and *The She-Wolf of Siena with the Emblems of the Confederate Cities* (1373), are graffiti designs by unknown artists. Domenico di Niccoló dei Cori was the first known artist to work on the cathedral, contributing several panels between 1413 and 1423, followed by renowned painter Domenico di Bartolo, who contributed *Emperor Sigismund Enthroned* in 1434. In the 15th century, director Alberto Aringhieri and celebrated Sienese artist Domenico Beccafumi created the dramatic expansion of the floor scheme. These later panels feature more advanced multicoloured marble, inlaid with hexagon and rhombus frames. Unfortunately, many panels are covered for much of the year, only being revealed between mid-August and October when the cathedral is open longer (from 10.30am to 7pm Monday to Saturday, and 9.30am to 6pm Sunday).

Other drawcards include the exquisite marble and porphyry **pulpit** created by Nicola Pisano, assisted by Arnolfo di Cambio, who later designed Florence's Duomo. Intricately carved with realistic crowd scenes, it's one of the masterpieces of Gothic sculpture. Over from the pulpit to the right of the transept, the **Cappella del Voto** harbours two marble statues of St Jerome and Mary Magdalene by baroque maestro Gian Lorenzo Bernini.

Donatello's famous bronze of St John the Baptist headlines in the **Cappella di San Giovanni Battista**, next to the **Libreria Piccolomini**. This enchanting library, accessible through a door from the north aisle, was built to house the books of Enea Silvio Piccolomini, better known as Pius II. The walls of the small hall are decorated with vividly coloured narrative frescoes painted between 1502 and 1507 by Bernardino Pinturicchio depicting events in the life of Piccolomini. Nearby, on the **Piccolomini altar**, you can admire four saintly sculptures by the young Michelangelo.

The *duomo* could have been grander still: in 1339 the city's medieval rulers drew up plans to enlarge it, creating one of Italy's biggest churches. The remains of this project, known as the Duomo Nuovo (New Cathedral), are on Piazza Jacopo della Quercia, on the eastern side of the cathedral. The daring plan to build an immense new nave with the present church becoming the transept was scotched by the plague of 1348. Buy tickets from the **duomo ticket office** (www.operaduomo.siena.it; Piazza del Duomo; ⊘10.30am-7pm summer, to 5.30pm winter).

Museo dell'Opera del Duomo MUSEUM
(www.operaduomo.siena.it; Piazza del Duomo 8; admission €7; ⊘10.30am-7pm summer, to 5.30pm winter) The collection here showcases artworks that formerly adorned the cathedral, including 12 statues of prophets and philosophers by Giovanni Pisano that originally stood on the facade. Many of the statues were designed to be viewed from ground level, which is why they look so distorted as they crane uncomfortably forward. The museum's highlight is Duccio di Buoninsegna's striking *Maestà* (1311), which was painted on both sides as a screen for the *duomo*'s high altar. Buy tickets from the *duomo* ticket office

SIENA & CENTRAL TUSCANY SIENA

ST CATHERINE OF SIENA

One of the two patron saints of Italy (with St Francis) and one of only three female Doctors of the Church (with St Teresa of Avilà and St Thérèse of Liseux), St Catherine was born in Siena in 1347, the 23rd child out of 25. A true prodigy, she had religious fixations at an early age. She's said to have entertained plans to impersonate a man so she could be a Dominican friar and occasionally raced out to the road to kiss the place where Dominicans had walked.

When she was seven, Catherine consecrated her virginity to Christ, much to her family's despair. At 18 she assumed the life of a Dominican Tertiary (lay affiliate) and lived as a recluse in the family's basement, focusing her attention on devotion and spiritual ecstasy. She was noted for her ability to fast for extended periods, living only on the Blessed Sacrament, which, as nutritionists might attest, probably contributed to a delirium or two. Catherine described one such episode as a 'mystical marriage' with Jesus. Feeling a surge of humanity, she emerged from her cloistered path and began caring for the sick and poor at the Ospedale Santa Maria della Scala.

Another series of visions (this time set in Hell, Purgatory and Heaven) compelled Catherine to begin an ambitious and fearless letter-writing campaign to influential people, including lengthy correspondence with Pope Gregory XI. She beseeched royalty and religious leaders for everything from peace between Italy's republics to reform within the clergy. This go-getting early activism was considered highly unusual for a woman at the time and her no-holds-barred style, sometimes scolding cardinals and queens like naughty children, was gutsy by any standard. And yet, rather than being persecuted for her insolence, she was admired; her powers of persuasion often winning the day where so many others had failed. She is said to have experienced the stigmata, but this event was suppressed as it was considered bad form then to associate the stigmata with anyone but St Francis.

Acting as an ambassador to Florence, Catherine went to Avignon and convinced Gregory XI to bring the papacy back to Rome after a 73-year reign in France. A few years later she was invited to Rome by newly elected Pope Urban VI to campaign on his behalf during the pope/anti-pope struggle (the Great Western Schism), where she did her best to undo the effects that his temper and shortcomings were having on Rome. This heroic, utterly exhausting effort likely contributed to her untimely death in 1380 at the age of 33.

Catherine's abundant post-mortem accolades started soon after her death, with Pope Pius II canonising her in 1461. More recently, in 1970, Pope Paul VI bestowed Catherine with the title of Doctor of the Church, while Pope John Paul II made her one of Europe's patron saints in 1999. She is also one of Siena's three patron saints (the others being Sts Ansanas and Ambrose).

For information about guided and self-guided walking tours of St Catherine's Siena, go to www.viaesiena.it.

OFF THE BEATEN TRACK

ORTO DE' PECCI

In this urban **oasis** (www.ortodepecci.it; ⊘24hr) FREE geese, goats, ducks and donkeys live amid green spaces that are perfect for picnics or an afternoon snooze (locals can often be found here, hiding from the crowds). There's a medieval garden, a vineyard with clones of medieval vines, and a cooperative organic farm that supplies the on-site **restaurant** (Orto de' Pecci; dishes €8, 4-course lunch/dinner €30/45; ⊘12.30-2.30pm & 7.30-10.30pm, closed Sun eve summer, closed Sun eve & Mon-Thu winter). On summer evenings, concerts are sometimes held here, too.

Duccio's main painting portrays the Virgin surrounded by angels, saints and prominent contemporary Sienese citizens; the rear panels (sadly incomplete) portray scenes from the Passion of Christ. Duccio also designed and painted the vibrant stained-glass window downstairs; it was originally in the *duomo*.

Battistero di San Giovanni   LANDMARK
(Piazza San Giovanni; admission €4; ⊘10.30am-7pm summer, to 5.30pm winter) The Baptistery is lined with frescoes and centres around a hexagonal marble font by Jacopo della Quercia, decorated with bronze panels depicting the life of St John the Baptist by artists including Lorenzo Ghiberti (*Baptism of Christ* and *St John in Prison*) and Donatello (*The Head of John the Baptist Being Presented to Herod*). Buy tickets from the *duomo* ticket office.

Cripta   CHRISTIAN SITE
(Piazza San Giovanni; admission incl audioguide €6; ⊘10.30am-7pm summer, to 5.30pm winter) Remarkably, this now-atmospheric, vaulted space was filled with debris until 1999 (with the rubbish having been deposited in the 1300s). Now you'll see 180 sq metres of 13th century *pintura a secco*; these 'dry paintings' (also called 'mural paintings') contrast with frescoes which are painted on wet plaster, making them more durable. Buy tickets from the *duomo* ticket office.

Panorama del Facciatone   TOWER
(Piazza del Duomo 8; ⊘10.30am-7pm summer, to 5.30pm winter) For an unforgettable view of Siena's unique cityscape, haul yourself up the 131-step, narrow corkscrew stairway to the **Panorama del Facciatone**. Entrance is included in the Museo dell'Opera ticket.

★Complesso Museale
Santa Maria della Scala   BUILDING
(www.santamariadellascala.com; Piazza del Duomo 1; adult/reduced €9/8; ⊘10.30am-6.30pm Wed-Mon summer, to 4.30pm winter) This former hospital, parts of which date from the 13th century, was built as a hospice for pilgrims travelling the Via Francigena pilgrimage trail. Its highlight is the upstairs *Pellegrinaio* (Pilgrim's Hall), with vivid 15th-century frescoes by Lorenzo Vecchietta, Priamo della Quercia and Domenico di Bartolo lauding the good works of the hospital and its patrons.

The building is now a cultural centre and houses three museums. The pick is the Archaeological Museum set in the basement tunnels. Also don't miss the medieval *fienile* (hayloft) on level three, which showcases Jacopo della Quercia's original sculptures from Siena's central Fonte Gaia fountain.

★Pinacoteca Nazionale   GALLERY
(Via San Pietro 29; adult/reduced €4/2; ⊘8.15am-7.15pm Tue-Sat, 9am-1pm Sun & Mon) An extraordinary collection of Gothic masterpieces from the Sienese school sits inside the once grand but now sadly dishevelled 14th-century Palazzo Buonsignori. The pick of the collection is on the 2nd floor, including magnificent works by Duccio di Buoninsegna, Simone Martini, Niccolò di Segna, Lippo Memmi, Ambrogio and Pietro Lorenzetti, Bartolo di Fredi and Taddeo di Bartolo.

The collection demonstrates the gulf cleaved between artistic life in Siena and Florence in the 15th century. While the Renaissance flourished 70km to the north, Siena's masters and their patrons remained firmly rooted in the Byzantine and Gothic precepts borne of the early 13th century. Religious images and episodes predominate, typically pasted lavishly with gold and generally lacking any of the advances in painting (perspective, emotion, movement) that artists in Florence were exploring. That's not to say that the works here are second-rate – many are among the most beautiful and important creations of their time.

Artworks to hunt out include Duccio's *Madonna and Child* (Room 2), *Madonna with Child and Four Saints* (Room 4) and *Santa Maria Maddalena* (Room 5); Simone Martini's *Madonna della Misericordia* and *Madonna with Child* (both in Room 4), *Madonna and Child* (Room 6) and *Blessed*

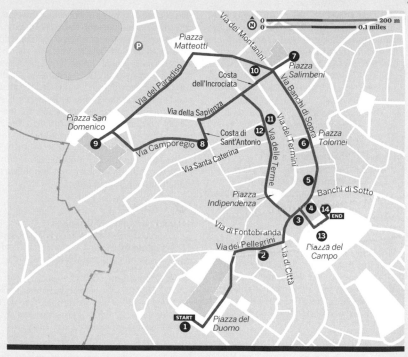

City Walk
Siena: Sights, Streets & Eats

START COMPLESSO MUSEALE SANTA
MARIA DELLA SCALA
END BAR IL PALIO
LENGTH 2KM; TWO HOURS

Be the only one turning your back on the *duomo's* brilliant facade; instead, admire the austere lines of the **❶ Complesso Museale Santa Maria della Scala** (p128) opposite; one of the world's oldest hospitals, the door-side plaque attests to its role. Head right beside the *duomo*, under the towering arch and down steep steps to Via del Pellegrini, where **❷ Panificio Il Magnifico** (p134) offers sweet treats. Casting glances at the Campo ahead, turn into Via di Città for a stand-up coffee in historic **❸ Caffè Fiorella** (p133). Then comes the arches and carved stone of 13th century **❹ Loggia della Mercanzia**. In main shopping street Via Banchi di Sopra, if ice cream appeals, **❺ Grom** (p133) is nearby. Next, spot **❻ Palazzo Tolomei**, a towering Gothic structure with double lancet windows. It belonged to the Tolomei family, Guelph bankers

who were sworn enemies of the Ghibelline Salimbeni clan; their stately fortified home, **❼ Palazzo Salimbeni**, is in the next square.

Time to trace medieval lanes to the soothing **❽ Casa Santuario di Santa Caterina** (p130). Emerging, climb a few steps back up the hill, then cut immediately left up two steps into an unsigned lane. This leads past superb Siena panoramas to the **❾ Chiesa di San Domenico** (p130); St Catherine's head sits inside. Next, walk up Via del Paradiso and across Piazza Matteotti until the rich aromas of the **❿ Consorzio Agrario di Siena** (p133) draw you inside, perhaps to munch pizza at the bar. Double back into Costa dell'Incrociata, then head along Via delle Terme. If thirsty, try a rough and ready glass of wine at **⓫ Osteria da Trombicche** or a classy one at **⓬ La Compagnia dei Vinattieri** (p133). Pass scores of delis, enotec and pastry shops before emerging into Via di Città . From there it's some 20 paces (either left or right) to a lane leading into **⓭ Il Campo** (p124). Here, join the crows sitting on the slo paving or stump up for a drink at **⓮ Bar Il P** (p134), marveling at the utter glory of the s

Agostino altarpiece (Room 6); Lippo Memmi's *Adoration of the Magi* (Room 6); Ambrogio Lorenzetti's *Annunciation* and *Madonna with Child* (both in Room 8); Pietro Lorenzetti's *Madonna Enthroned with Saint Nicholas and the Prophet Elijah* and *Crucifixion* (both in Room 8); and Taddeo di Bartolo's *The Annunciation of the Virgin Mary* (Room 11).

The gallery occasionally rearranges its exhibits; we've cited the room numbers at time of writing.

Chiesa di San Domenico CHURCH

(Piazza San Domenico; ⊘9am-12.30pm & 3-7pm) FREE St Catherine was welcomed into the Dominican fold within this imposing church and its **Cappella di Santa Caterina** is adorned with frescoes by Il Sodoma depicting events in her life. Catherine died in Rome but her head was returned to Siena – it's clearly visible in a 15th-century tabernacle above the altar in a signed *cappella* near the gift shop.

Also here are her desiccated thumb (in a small window box on the chapel's right) and a nasty-looking chain that the saint is said to have flagellated herself with.

Casa Santuario di Santa Caterina RELIGIOUS SITE

(Costa di Sant'Antonio 6; ⊘9am-6.30pm Mar-Nov, 10am-6pm Dec-Feb) FREE An air of serenity pervades this pilgrimage site which is the former home of the eponymous saint, her parents and 24 siblings (locals joke her mother must have been a saint, too). The rooms were converted into small chapels in the 15th century. The lower-level bedroom, frescoed in 1893 by Alessandro Franchi, includes her untouched, nearly bare cell.

The largest of the chapels is minded by nuns, and closes during their lunchtime (12.30pm to 3pm).

Oratorio di San Bernardino GALLERY

(Piazza San Francesco 10; admission €3; ⊘10.30am-1.30pm & 3-5.30pm mid-Mar–Oct) Nestled in the shadow of the huge Gothic church of **San Francesco**, this 15th-century oratory is dedicated to St Bernardino and decorated with Mannerist frescoes by Il Sodoma, Beccafumi and Pacchia. Upstairs, the small **Museo Diocesano di Arte Sacra** has some lovely paintings, including *Madonna del Latte* (Nursing Madonna, c 1340) by Ambrogio Lorenzetti.

Museo delle Tavolette di Biccherna MUSEUM

(www.archiviostato.si.it; Banchi di Sotto 52; ⊘guided tours 9.30am, 10.30am & 11.30am Mon-Sat) FREE

Siena's state archives are housed in the magnificent Renaissance-era **Palazzo Piccolomini**. Enter from the courtyard and take the elevator to the 4th floor to visit this charming museum, which takes its name from the pride of its collection; a series of small late-13th-century painted and gilded wooden panels known as the Tavolette di Biccherna.

Originally created as covers for the municipal accounts books, the *tavolette* were painted by Sienese artists including Ambogio Lorenzetti. They and other evocative, historically significant documents (many medieval) can be seen on the compulsory guided tour (in Italian only).

Courses

Accademia Musicale Chigiana COURSE

(⊘0577 22 09 1; www.chigiana.it; Via di Città 89; from €145) Competitive-entry, summer classical-music masterclasses and workshops.

Fondazione Siena Jazz COURSE

(⊘0577 27 14 01; www.sienajazz.it; Fortezza Medicea 1; from €250) One of Europe's foremost institutions of its type, offering courses and workshops for experienced jazz musicians.

Scuola Leonardo da Vinci LANGUAGE COURSE

(⊘0577 24 90 97; www.scuolaleonardo.com; Via del Paradiso 16; per 1/2 weeks €200/360) Italian-language school with supplementary cultural programs.

Società Dante Alighieri LANGUAGE COURSE

(⊘0577 4 95 33; www.dantealighieri.com; Via Tommaso Pendola 37; per 1/2 weeks €210/380) Language and cultural courses southwest of the city centre.

Tuscan Wine School COURSE

(⊘0577 22 17 04; www.tuscanwineschool.com; Via di Stalloreggi 26; ⊘11am-6.30pm Mon-Sat Mar-Oct) Daily two-hour wine-tasting classes introducing Italian and Tuscan wines (€40).

Università per Stranieri LANGUAGE COURSE

(University for Foreigners; ⊘0577 24 01 00; www.unistrasi.it; Piazza Carlo Rosselli 27; per month €520) Offers courses in Italian language and culture from a base near the train station.

Tours

Centro Guide Turistiche Siena e Provincia CULTURAL TOUR

(⊘0577 4 32 73; www.guidesiena.it; Galleria Odeon, Via Banchi di Sopra 31; ⊘10am-1pm & 3-5pm Mon-Fri) The pick of the tours offered by this association of accredited guides are the 90-minute

Classical Siena Walking Tour (€20, 11am Monday to Saturday), which features key historical and cultural landmarks, and the 90-minute Secret Siena Walk (€20, 11am Sunday), which takes in both Siena's streets and the *duomo*'s crypt. Prices include admission fees.

The tours, in English and Italian, depart from outside the tourist office in the Piazza Duomo. You can buy tickets from the guide, there's no need to book and children under 12 are free. The centre also operates private guided tours in Siena and throughout the region (three/six hours €140/260).

✪ Festivals & Events

Accademia Musicale Chigiana   MUSIC
(www.chigiana.it) The Accademia Musicale Chigiana presents three highly regarded concert series featuring classical musicians from around the world: **Micat in Vertice** from November to April, **Settimana Musicale Senese** in July and **Estate Musicale Chigiana** in July and August.

🛏 Sleeping

★Hotel Alma Domus   HOTEL €
(☑0577 4 41 77; www.hotelalmadomus.it; Via Camporegio 37; s €40-52, d €60-€122; ▣ 🛜) Your chance to sleep in a convent: Alma Domus is owned by the church and is still home to several Dominican nuns. The economy rooms, although supremely comfortable, are styled very simply. But the superior ones are positively sumptuous, with pristine bathrooms, paired-down furniture and bursts of magenta and lime. Many have mini-balconies with uninterrupted *duomo* views. Families are welcome. Note the 1am curfew.

Antica Residenza Cicogna   B&B €
(☑0577 28 56 13; www.anticaresidenzacicogna.it; Via delle Terme 76; s €70-95, d €95-115, ste €120-155; ▣ @ 🛜) You get a true feel for Siena's history in this exquisite 13th-century *palazzo*. Tiled floors, ornate lights and painted ceilings meet tones of yellow ochre and (suitably) burnt sienna. The best of the fabulous suites is named after landscape painter Paesaggi, where bucolic views sit in panels above your head, and a tiny blue passageway winds to the bathroom.

There's also a lounge where you can relax over complimentary Vin Santo and *cantuccini* (hard, sweet almond biscuits).

Alle Due Porte   B&B €
(☑0577 28 76 70; www.sienatur.it; Via di Stalloreggi 51; d/tr €85/110; ▣ 🛜) Taking its name from the nearby city gate, this well-located B&B has loads of character and a real 'home away from home' vibe. It's set on the 1st floor of a rebuilt 12th-century tower house and offers three rooms (two with air-con) full of Tuscan features such as beams and metal bed frames.

Hotel Italia   HOTEL €
(☑0577 4 45 54; www.hotelitalia-siena.it; Viale Camillo Benso Conte di Cavour 67; d €59-120; 🅿 ▣ 🛜) While most Siena hotels plump for 'heritage-*palazzo*' style, swish Hotel Italia majors on the modern. The bar and breakfast area are all bright colours and clean lines; sleek bedrooms feature candy-stripes and contemporary checks – except the Love Room, which overflows with hearts, pillows and romantic music. It's 20 minutes' walk from the historic centre, near the train station. Parking is €10, but there's also free parking in the streets nearby.

THE PALIO

Dating from the Middle Ages, this spectacular annual event includes a series of colourful pageants and a frenetic horse race on 2 July and 16 August. Ten of Siena's 17 *contrade* (town districts) compete for the coveted *palio* (silk banner). Each *contrada* has its own traditions, symbols and colours plus its own church and *palio* museum.

The race is staged in the Campo. From about 5pm, representatives from each *contrada* parade in historical costume, all bearing their individual banners. For scarcely one exhilarating minute, the 10 horses and their bareback riders tear three times around a temporarily constructed dirt racetrack with a speed and violence that makes spectators' hair stand on end.

The race is held at 7.45pm in July and 7pm in August. Join the crowds in the centre of the Campo at least four hours before the start if you want a place on the rails, but be aware that once there you won't be able to leave for toilet or drink breaks until the race has finished. Alternatively, the cafes in the Campo sell places on their terraces; these cost between €350 and €400 per ticket, and can be booked through the tourist office up to one year in advance.

Note that during the Palio, hotels raise their rates between 10% and 50% and enforce a minimum-stay requirement.

Casa del Conte
B&B €

(☎0577 4 30 41; www.bbsienaincentro.com; Via di Stalloreggi 14; s €40-50, d €60-80) Despite satiny furnishing, brass bedsteads and exposed rafters this B&B has a homely air, plus a good range of rooms and a galley kitchen for guest use. The same family runs two other B&Bs (one nearby, the other on the northwest side of the old town); this is the reception address, the B&B itself is hidden in a lane nearby.

Albergo Bernini
PENSION €

(☎0577 28 90 47; www.albergobernini.com; Via della Sapienza 15; d €85, without bathroom €65; 🛜) The tiny terrace alone might prompt you to stay at this welcoming, family-run hotel – it sports grandstand views across to the *duomo* and is a captivating spot for breakfast or drinks later in the day. The bedrooms are traditional affairs and only two – the single and triple – have air-con. Breakfast costs €9. Room rates fall in winter; payment is cash only.

Casa Mastacchi
B&B €

(☎0577 22 39 38; www.casamastacchi.com; Via Camollia 52; d €100) Wood beams, patterned floors and artfully draped curtains lend this B&B extra character, although some of the rooms are small. It's set away from the tourist bustle to the north of the old town, a pleasant 10-minute stroll to the Campo.

★Pensione Palazzo Ravizza
BOUTIQUE HOTEL €€

(☎0577 28 04 62; www.palazzoravizza.it; Pian dei Mantellini 34; d €80-220, ste €180-320; P🛜@🛜) Heritage features and luxurious flourishes combine at this Renaissance-era *palazzo* to create an irresistible hotel. Frescoed ceilings, stone staircases and gilt mirrors meet elegant furnishings, wooden shutters and (from some bedrooms) captivating views. The greenery-framed rear garden is utterly delightful; settle down in a wicker chair here, gaze out towards the hills and you may never want to leave.

★Castel Pietraio
HISTORIC HOTEL €€

(☎0577 30 00 20; www.castelpietraio.it; Strada di Strove 33 , Monteriggioni; s €90, d €120-165) Castel Pietraio is a sleep spot that's simply too good to miss. The medieval castle is owned by Barone Neri Del Nero and bedrooms, in the adjoining outhouses, are rich in aristocratic trappings with Carrara-marble bathrooms and chestnut beams. The wine cellar is stocked with the Baron's own DOCG Chianti and DOC Vin Santo. It's 15km west of Siena.

Hotel Athena
HOTEL €€

(☎0577 28 63 13; www.hotelathena.com; Via Paolo Mascagni 55; s €70-140, d €80-250; P🛜@🛜) A recent refurbishment means all the bedrooms at this superbly run hotel are stately affairs in warm red and gold. Executive rooms differ only in size and views (cracking ones where cityscapes meet fields). The terrace bar and restaurant overlook the Tuscan hills and are the stuff of which lasting holiday memories are made.

★Campo Regio Relais
BOUTIQUE HOTEL €€€

(☎0577 22 20 73; www.camporegio.com; Via della Sapienza 25; d €220-400, ste €450; 🛜🛜) The decor in each of the six, individually styled rooms here is exquisite – expect anything from old mahogany to fine linen, 18th-century antiques to art nouveau. Breakfast is served in the sumptuously decorated lounge or on the terrace, with a sensational view across a valley of higgledy-piggledy rooftops to Torre del Mangia and the *duomo*.

★Castello delle Serre
BOUTIQUE HOTEL €€€

(☎338 5040811; www.castellodelleserre.com; Piazza XX Settembre 1, Serre di Rapolano; d €225-265, ste €275-395; P🛜@🛜🛜) The prospect of spending the night in this fabulous medieval castle makes the 40km trip east from Siena well worth the effort. Meticulously restored by the Italian-American Gangale family, it features huge rooms and a swish pool area. For a once-in-a-lifetime experience, book into the deluxe suite in the turret where a private terrace commands suitably regal views.

Villa Scacciapensieri
BOUTIQUE HOTEL €€€

(☎0577 4 14 41; www.villascacciapensieri.it; Via Scacciapensieri 10; s €65-140, d €100-275, ste €220-450; P🛜🛜🛜) Just 2km north of Siena, this 19th-century villa with two annexes is set in formal gardens and has plenty of amenities, including a swimming pool, a restaurant (dinner €45, Thurday to Tuesday) and a tennis court. Handily, if you're driving you can leave the car here and catch the bus into Florence for day trips (the bus stop is right outside).

🍴 Eating

Among many Sienese dishes are *panzanella* (salad of soaked bread, basil, onion and tomatoes), *ribollita* (a rich vegetable, bean and bread soup), *pappardelle con la lepre* (ribbon pasta with hare) and *panforte* (a rich cake of almonds, honey and candied fruit). Keep an eye out for dishes featuring the region's signature *cinta senese* (indigenous Tuscan pig).

★**Morbidi** DELI €
(www.morbidi.com; Via Banchi di Sopra 75; lunch buffet €12; ☺8am-8pm Mon-Thu, to 9pm Fri & Sat) Possibly the classiest cheap feed in Siena: set in the stylish basement of Morbidi's deli, the lunch buffet on offer here is excellent. For a mere €12, you can join the well-dressed locals sampling antipasti, salads, risottos, pastas and a dessert of the day. Bottled water is supplied, wine and coffee cost extra. Buy your ticket upstairs before heading down.

Consorzio Agrario di Siena DELI €
(www.capsi.it; Via Pianigiani 13; ☺8am-8.30pm Mon-Sat, 9.30am-8pm Sun) Operating since 1901, this farmer's co-op is a rich emporium of food and wine, much of it locally produced. There's a small bar area where you can purchase and eat a slab of freshly cooked pizza (€12 to €14.30 per kg).

Grom GELATERIA €
(www.grom.it; Via Banchi di Sopra 11; gelato €2.50-5.50; ☺11am-midnight summer, to 11pm winter) Delectable gelato with flavours that change with the seasons; many of the ingredients are organic or Slow Food accredited. They do milkshakes too.

Kopa Kabana GELATERIA €
(www.gelateriakopakabana.it; Via dei Rossi 52-55; gelato €1.90-4.50; ☺11am-8pm mid-Feb–mid-Nov, later hours in warm weather) Come here for fresh gelato made by self-proclaimed ice-cream master Fabio (we're pleased to concur).

★**Enoteca I Terzi** TUSCAN €€
(☎0577 4 43 29; www.enotecaiterzi.it; Via dei Termini 7; meals €35-40; ☺11am-1am summer, 11am-4pm & 6.30pm-midnight winter, closed Sun) A favourite for many locals who head to this historic *enoteca* to linger over lunches, *aperitivi* and casual dinners featuring top-notch Tuscan *salumi* (cured meats), delicate handmade pasta and wonderful wines.

Nonna Gina OSTERIA €€
(☎0577 28 72 47; www.osterianonnagina.com; Pian dei Mantellini 2; meals €25-35; ☺12.30-2.30pm & 7.30-10.30pm Tue-Sun) The atmosphere is pure Siena-neighbourhood-*osteria*: gingham tablecloths, postcards tacked to the rafters and pictures of Palio jockeys on the walls. The menu speaks of fine local traditions too: piles of local meat form the *antipasto Toscano*, the house red is a very decent Chianti, while the ingredients of the 'secret sauce' covering the plump, cheese-filled gnocchi will never be revealed.

La Compagnia dei Vinattieri TUSCAN €€
(☎0577 23 65 68; www.vinattieri.net; Via delle Terme 79; antipasto platter €7-9, meals €35; ☺noon-10pm, closed late Feb-late Mar) Duck down the stairs to enjoy a quick glass of wine and a meat or cheese platter in this cellar, or settle in for a leisurely meal, perhaps trying *radicchio* pie with Gorgonzola and walnuts, guinea fowl ravioli, or Tuscan-style cuttlefish stuffed with spinach. To drink? Choose something from a wine list 1000-strong.

Grotta Santa Caterina da Bagoga TUSCAN €€
(☎0577 28 22 08; www.bagoga.it; Via della Galluzza 26; meals €35; ☺noon-3pm & 7-10pm Tue-Sat, 12-3pm Sun) Pierino Fagnani ('Bagoga'), one of Siena's most famous Palio jockeys, swapped saddle for apron in 1973 and has been operating this much-loved restaurant ever since. Traditional Tuscan palate-pleasers feature on the menu, and are perhaps best showcased in the four-course *tipico* (€35) or *degustazione* (€50 with wine) menus. Book ahead.

★**Tre Cristi** SEAFOOD €€€
(☎0577 28 06 08; www.trecristi.com; Vicolo di Provenzano 1; 4-course tasting menus €35-45. 6-course menus €65; ☺12.30-2.30pm & 7.30-10pm Mon-Sat) Seafood restaurants are thin on the ground in this meat-obsessed region, so the long existence of Tre Cristi (it's been around since 1830) should be heartily celebrated. The menu here is as elegant as the decor, and touches such as a complimentary glass of *prosecco* (dry sparkling wine) at the start of the meal add to the experience.

Osteria Le Logge TUSCAN €€€
(☎0577 4 80 13; www.osterialelogge.it; Via del Porrione 33; meals €55; ☺noon-2.30pm & 7-10.30pm Mon-Sat) The menu of creative Tuscan cuisine served here changes almost daily. The best tables are in the downstairs dining room – once a pharmacy and still retaining handsome display cabinets – or on the streetside terrace. We've found that the antipasti and *primi* (first courses) are consistently delicious, but the mains aren't always as strong.

🍸 Drinking & Nightlife

Caffè Fiorella CAFE
(www.torrefazionefiorella.it; Via di Città 13; ☺7am-8pm Mon-Sat) Squeeze into this tiny, heart-of-the-action space to enjoy some of Siena's best coffee. In summer, the coffee granita with a dollop of cream is a wonderful indulgence.

Enoteca Italiana
WINE BAR

(www.enoteca-italiana.it; Fortezza Medicea, Piazza Libertà 1; ☺ noon-midnight Wed-Sat, to 7.30pm Mon & Tue) The former munitions cellar and dungeon of this Medici fortress has been artfully transformed into a classy *enoteca* that carries more than 1500 Italian labels. You can take a bottle with you, ship a case home or just enjoy a glass in the attractive courtyard or vaulted interior. There's usually food available, too.

Bar Il Palio
CAFE

(Piazza del Campo 47; ☺ 8am-midnight) Arguably the best coffee on the central Campo square; drink it standing at the bar or suffer the financial consequences.

🛍 Shopping

Panificio Il Magnifico
FOOD

(www.ilmagnifico.siena.it; Via dei Pellegrini 27; ☺ 7.30am-7.30pm Mon-Sat) Lorenzo Rossi is Siena's best baker, and his *panforte, ricciarelli* (sugar-dusted chewy almond biscuits) and *cavallucci* (almond biscuits made with Tuscan millefiori honey) are a weekly purchase for most local households. Try them at his bakery and shop behind the *duomo*, and you'll understand why.

Bottega d'Arte
ARTS

(☎ 349 2928636; www.arteinsiena.it; Via di Stalloreggi 47; ☺ hours vary) Inspired by the works of Sienese masters of the 14th and 15th centuries, artists Chiara Perinetti Casoni and Michelangelo Attardo Perinetti Casoni create exquisite icons in tempera and 24-carat gold leaf. Expensive? Yes. Worth it? You bet.

Il Pellicano
CERAMICS

(☎ 340 5974038; www.siena-ilpellicano.it; Via Diacceto 17a; ☺ 10.30am-7pm summer, hours vary in winter) Elisabetta Ricci has been making traditional hand-painted Sienese ceramics for over 30 years. She shapes, fires and paints her creations, often using Renaissance-era styles or typical *contrade* designs. Elisabetta also conducts lessons in traditional ceramic techniques.

Wednesday Market
MARKET

(☺ 7.30am-1pm) Spreading around Fortezza Medicea and towards the Stadio Comunale, this is one of Tuscany's largest markets and is great for cheap clothing; some food is also sold. An antiques market is held here on the third Sunday of each month.

Pizzicheria de Miccoli
FOOD

(Via di Città 93; ☺ 9am-9pm Mon-Sat, 10am-6pm Sun) A stuffed boar's head sits above de Miccoli's entrance, fine aromas waft from the doorway, and the windows are festooned with sausages, stacks of cheese and sacks of *porcini* mushrooms. It also sells filled *panini* to go.

ℹ Information

Hospital (☎ 0577 58 51 11; www.ao-siena. toscana.it; Viale Bracci) Just north of Siena at Le Scotte.

Police Station (☎ 0577 20 11 11; Via del Castoro 6)

Tourist Office (☎ 0577 28 05 51; www.terre siena.it; Piazza del Duomo 1; ☺ 9am-6pm daily summer, 10am-5pm Mon-Sat, to 1pm Sun winter) Provides free Siena city maps, reserves accommodation, organises car and scooter hire, and sells train tickets (commission applies). Also takes bookings for a range of day tours.

OFF THE BEATEN TRACK

ABBAZIA DI MONTE OLIVETO MAGGIORE

This **medieval abbey** (☎ 0577 70 76 11; www.monteolivetomaggiore.it; Monte Oliveto Maggiore; admission free, library donation requested; ☺ 9am-noon & 3-5pm Mon-Sat, to 6pm in summer, to 12.30pm Sun), 39km southeast of Siena, was founded in 1313 by John Tolomei, although construction didn't begin on the monastery itself until 1393. Today it is still a retreat for Benedictine monks. Visitors come here for the wonderful fresco series in the Great Cloister, painted by Luca Signorelli and Il Sodoma, which illustrates events in the life of St Benedict, founder of the order.

You can also visit the church, which features magnificent choir stalls of inlaid wood; the refectory, frescoed by Paolo Novelli; the magnificent library, built in 1518; the pharmacy; and the chapter house.

Downhill from the main building is the abbey's 14th-century **Cantina Storica** (Historic Wine Cellar; www.agricolamonteoliveto.com; Monte Oliveto Maggiore; ☺ 10am-1pm & 2-6pm), where it is possible to take a guided tour and enjoy a wine tasting.

ABBAZIA DI SAN GALGANO

About 45km southwest of Siena via the SS73 are the evocative ruins of the 13th-century Cistercian **Abbazia di San Galgano** (www.sangalgano.info; San Galgano; adult/reduced €2/1; ☉9am-7pm summer, 9.30am-5.30pm winter), in its day one of the country's finest Gothic buildings. Today, it's roofless ruins are a compelling sight, with remarkably intact walls interspersed with soaring arches and empty, round spaces where the windows would have been.

On a hill overlooking the abbey is the tiny, round Romanesque **Cappella di Monte Siepi**, home to badly preserved frescoes by Ambrogio Lorenzetti depicting the life of local soldier and saint, San Galgano, who lived his last years here as a hermit.

Near the approach to the abbey is a **fattoria** (farmhouse) with a **cafe** (*panino* €3.50 to €4) and **restaurant** (meals €22).

If you are heading towards Siena, Montalcino, Pienza or Montepulciano after your visit here, be sure to take the SS73 south and then veer east onto the SP delle Pinete (direction San Lorenzo a Merse), a scenic drive through protected forest.

ⓘ Getting There & Away

BUS

Siena Mobilità (☏800 922984; www.siena mobilita.it), part of the Tiemme network, links Siena with the rest of Tuscany. It has a **ticket office** (☏0577 20 42 25; www.tiemmespa.it; Piazza Gramsci; ☉6.30am-7.30pm Mon-Fri, 7am-7.30pm Sat & Sun) underneath the main bus station in Piazza Gramsci; there's also a left-luggage office here (per 24 hours €5.50).

Bus services often run to dramatically reduced timetables on Sundays and holidays.

Routes operated by Siena Mobilità from Monday to Saturday include the following:

Arezzo (€6.60, 1½ hours, eight daily)

Colle di Val d'Elsa (€3.40, 30 minutes, hourly) With onward connections for **Volterra** (€2.75, four daily).

Florence (€7.80, 1¼ hours, frequent) 'Corse Rapide' (Express) service.

Montalcino (€4.90, 70 minutes, six daily) Leaves from the train station.

Montepulciano (€6.60, 1½ hours, two daily) Leaves from the train station.

Pienza (€5.50, 70 minutes, two daily) Leaves from the train station.

Pisa Airport (one way/return €13/26, two hours) Departs Siena at 7.10am and Pisa at 11.45am. Buy tickets at least one day in advance from the bus station or online.

Poggibonsi (€4.35, one hour, hourly)

Rome's Fiumicino Airport (€22, 3¾ hours, two daily)

San Gimignano (€6, one to 1½ hours, 10 daily) Either direct or changing in Poggibonsi.

The firm **Sena** (www.sena.it) also has a **ticket office** (☏0861 1991900; Piazza Gramsci; ☉8.30am-7.45pm Mon-Sat) underneath the bus station in Piazza Gramsci. Its routes include the following:

Milan (€25, 4¼ hours, three daily)
Perugia (€15, 1½ hours, two daily)
Rome (€20, 3½ hours, nine daily)
Turin (€20, 7¼ hours, two daily)
Venice (€20, 5½ hours, two daily)

CAR & MOTORCYCLE

For Florence, take the Siena–Florence *S2 superstrada* or the more scenic SR222.

TRAIN

Siena's rail links aren't that extensive; buses can be a better option.

Rome requires a change of train, often at Grosseto or Chiusi. For Pisa, change at Empoli.

Direct services include the following:

Florence (€10, 1½ hours, hourly)
Grosseto (€9, 1½ hours, eight daily)

ⓘ Getting Around

BUS

Siena Mobilità operates city buses (€1.10 per 90 minutes). Buses 3 and 9 run between the train station and Piazza Gramsci.

CAR & MOTORCYCLE

There's a ZTL (Limited Traffic Zone) in the historic centre, although visitors can often drop off luggage at their hotel; ask reception to report your licence number in advance, or risk a hefty fine.

There are large car parks at the Stadio Comunale and around the Fortezza Medicea, both just north of Piazza San Domenico. Hotly contested free street parking (look for white lines) is available in Viale Vittorio Veneto on the Fortezza Medicea's southern edge. The paid car parks at San Francesco and Santa Caterina (aka Fontebranda) each have an escalator going up into the centre.

Most car parks charge €2 per hour. You'll find further parking information online at www.siena parcheggi.com.

CHIANTI

The ancient vineyards in this postcard-perfect region of Tuscany produce the grapes used in Chianti and Chianti Classico, the world-famous red wines sold under the Gallo Nero (Black Cockerel/Rooster) trademark. As well as giving this region its identity, wine also shapes the landscape – immaculately maintained rows of vines snake down hillsides; criss-crossing vineyards hug contrasting contour lines. In spring, amid the pruning, the air is scented by wood smoke; during the autumn harvests it's perfumed with wine. In this ancient, almost unchanged landscape you'll encounter historic olive groves, stone farmhouses, dense forests, graceful Romanesque *pieve* (rural churches), Renaissance villas and stone castles built in the Middle Ages by Florentine and Sienese warlords.

Though it's now part of the province of Siena, the southern section of Chianti was once the stronghold of the Lega del Chianti, a military and administrative alliance within the city-state of Florence that comprised Castellina, Gaiole and Radda. Chianti's northern part sits in the province of Florence; a popular day trip from the city, with visitors arriving by bus, car and bicycle.

Chianti is usually accessed via the SR222 (Via Chiantigiana) and is traced by a picturesque network of *strade provinciale* (provincial roads) and *strade secondaria* (secondary roads), some of which are unsealed, narrow and difficult to navigate. A good map is *Le strade del Gallo Nero* (€2.50), which shows both major and secondary routes and is available at news stands in the region.

★ Festivals & Events

Chianti Classico E FOOD
A popular 10-day festival featuring wine tastings and culinary and arts events. It's held in May and June and is organised by the Consorzio Vino Chianti Classico (www. chianticlassico.com).

Chianti

Chianti Festival PERFORMING ARTS
(www.chiantifestival.com) An eclectic, high-quality program of arts events, staged in June and July.

Greve in Chianti

POP 14,000

Some 26km south of Florence, Greve in Chianti is the main town in the Chianti Fiorentino. It's the hub of the local wine industry and has an amiable market-town air, an attractive central square and eateries and *enoteche* that truly showcase the best Chianti food and drink.

Greve's annual **wine fair** is held in the first or second week of September – book accommodation then well in advance.

◉ Sights & Activities

Enoteca Falorni WINE BAR
(www.enotecafalorni.it; Galleria delle Cantine 2; ⊙11.30am-5.30pm Mon, Thu & Fri, to 7.30pm Sat & Sun) Enoteca Falorni is the biggest in Chianti, stocking more than 1000 wines, with 100 different varieties available for tasting, including Toscana IGTs (Super Tuscans), top DOCs and DOCGs, Vin Santo and grappa. Buy a prepaid wine card costing €10 to €25 from the central bar, stick it into one of the many taps and out trickles your tipple of choice.

You can also buy bottles to take away and ship home. Enoteca Falorni is down a staircase opposite the entrance of the supermarket on the main road through Greve.

🛏 Sleeping & Eating

★Casa al Sole PENSION €
(☑0558 54 64 29; www.casaalsole.net; Via Vittorio Veneto 82; s €60-90, d €70-135) Cosy rooms done out in mellow colours and a superbly warm welcome make this small family-run hotel an excellent choice if you fancy being in the heart of town.

Giovanni da Verrazzano HOTEL €
(☑0558 5 31 89; Piazza Matteotti 28; s €68-86, d €90-105; ⊙dining room noon-2pm & 7-9.30pm, closed Mon) There's such an established feel to this *albergo* that it's almost like entering someone's home. Appealingly old-fashioned bedrooms feature chunky furniture and traditional fabrics, while squishy armchairs adjoin a beamed dining room. Bag a terrace table for views onto Greve's central square and feast on hearty classics such as ravioli with artichokes and cheese, or wild boar stew (meals €35).

★Mangiando Mangiando TUSCAN €€
(☑0558 54 63 72; www.mangiandomangiando.it; Piazza Matteotti 80; meals €30; ⊙noon-3pm & 7-10pm Feb-Dec, closed Thu) When an eatery gives as proud prominence to its list of producers as it does its menu, you know the dishes should be local and good. So it proves in this cheerful, casual eatery, where Tuscan standards (think rich beef pasta) accompany flavoursome soups, and Chianti Classico (€4.50) and Riserva (€5.50) come by the glass.

🛍 Shopping

Antica Macellerìa Falorni FOOD
(www.falorni.it; Piazza Matteotti 71; ⊙9.30am-1.30pm & 3.30-7.30pm) This atmospheric *macellerìa* (butcher shop) in the main square was established by the local Falorni family way back in 1729. Known for its *finocchiona briciolona* (pork salami made with fennel seeds and Chianti), it's the perfect picnic pit stop.

ℹ Information

Tourist Office (☑0558 54 62 99; info@ turismo.greveinchianti.eu; Piazza Matteotti 11; ⊙10am-7pm summer, reduced hours winter) On Greve's main square.

ℹ Getting There & Around

BUS
Buses travel between Greve in Chianti and Florence (€3.30, one hour, hourly).

CAR & MOTORCYCLE
Greve is on the Via Chiantigiana. Find free parking in the two-level, open-air car park on Piazza della Resistenza, on the opposite side of the main road to Piazza Matteotti. On Fridays, don't park overnight in the paid spaces in Piazza Matteotti – your car will be towed away to make room for Saturday market stalls.

Around Greve in Chianti

The hills around Greve are idyllic – vine-etched undulations reach as far as the eye can see. It's classic wine-making territory and provides prime opportunities to explore ancient villages and prestigious wine estates.

◉ Sights & Activities

Montefioralle VILLAGE
Medieval Montefioralle crowns a rise 1km east of Greve. An atmospheric huddle of homes with wraparound views, it was home to Amerigo Vespucci (1415–1512), an explorer who followed Columbus' route to America. He wrote

so excitedly about the New World that he inspired cartographer Martin Waldseemüller (creator of the 1507 Universalis Cosmographia) to name the new continent in his honour.

★**Antinori nel Chianti Classico**   WINERY
(✆0552 35 97 00; www.antinorichianticlassico.it; Via Cassia per Siena 133, Località Bargino; tour & tasting €25-50; ⊙10am-6pm summer, to 5pm winter) Visiting this cellar complex is a James Bond-esque experience. Get cleared at the gated, guarded entrance, approach a sculptural main building that's set into the hillside then explore an exquisitely designed winery full of architectural flourishes and state-of-the-art equipment. Your one-hour guided tour (English and Italian; bookings essential) finishes with a tutored tasting of three Antinori wines beside the family museum.

At the stylish bar beside the shop you can taste 16 different wines (€4 to €9 per tasting) have a sommelier-led 'guided tasting' of three wines (€9 or €12), or simply drink a glass of wine (ranging from €7 for a Marchese Antinori 2009 to €35 for a Solaia 2009). Afterwards, you can also enjoy lunch in the Rinuccio 1180 restaurant.

Bargino is 20km northwest of Greve via the SS222, SP3 and SS2.

Badia a Passignano   WINERY
(www.osteriadipassignano.com; Badia a Passignano) It doesn't get much more atmospheric: an 11th-century abbey owned by Benedictine monks set amid vineyards run by the legendary Antinori dynasty. The four-hour 'Antinori at Badia a Passignano' tour (€150, two daily, Monday to Saturday) includes a vineyard and cellar visit and a meal in the estate's Osteria di Passignano (p140) restaurant, accompanied by four signature Antinori wines.

Other options include visits to the Tignanello vineyard (where the grapes for the Tignanello and Solaia Super Tuscans are grown), and tours of the cellars with tastings of four wines (€80; one tour daily Monday to Saturday). Bookings are essential for tours.

Or, just turn up at the estate's wine shop, La Bottega (p140), to taste and buy Antinori wines and olive oil. Badia à Passignano is 7km west of Greve.

Castello di Verrazzano   WINERY
(✆0558 5 42 43; www.verrazzano.com; Via Citille, Greti; tours €16-115) This castle 3km north of Greve was once home to Giovanni da Verrazzano (1485–1528), who explored the North American coast and is commemorated in New York by the Verrazano Narrows bridge (the good captain lost a 'z' from his name somewhere in the mid-Atlantic). Today it presides over a 220-hectare historic wine estate offering a wide range of tours.

Each tour incorporates a short visit to the historic wine cellar and gardens and tastings of the estate's wines (including its flagship Chianti Classico) and other products; perhaps honey, olive oil or balsamic vinegar. The 'Classic Wine Tour' (€16, 1½ hours, 10am to 3pm Monday to Friday) includes a tasting of several wines; the 'Chianti Tradition Tour' (€34, 2½ hours, 11am Monday to Friday) includes a tasting of wine and gastronomic specialities; while the 'Wine and Food Experience' (€58, three hours, noon Monday to Friday) includes a four-course lunch with estate wines. Tour bookings are essential.

🛏 Sleeping

Ostello del Chianti   HOSTEL €
(✆0558 05 02 65; www.ostellodelchianti.it; Via Roma 137, Tavarnelle Val di Pesa; dm €16, d/q €50/70; ⊙reception 8.30-11am & 4pm-midnight, hostel closed Nov–mid-Mar; ⓟ@🛜) This is one of Italy's oldest hostels and though it occupies an ugly building in the less-than-scenic town of Tavarnelle Val di Pesa, the friendly staff and bargain prices compensate. Dorms max out at six beds and bike hire can be arranged for €8 per day. Breakfast costs €2. Florence is easily accessed by SITA bus (€3.30, one hour).

★**Fattoria di Rignana**   AGRITURISMO €€
(✆0558 5 20 65; www.rignana.it; Via di Rignana 15, Rignana; fattoria d €110, without bathroom €95, villa

d €140; P@🛜🏊) A chic, historic farmhouse with its very own bell tower rewards you for the drive up the long, rutted road. You'll also find glorious views, a large swimming pool and a very decent eatery. Choose between elegant rooms in the 17th-century villa and rustic ones in the *fattoria* (farmhouse). It's 4km from Badia a Passignano and 10km west of Greve.

Villa Il Poggiale   BOUTIQUE HOTEL €€

(📋0558 2 83 11; www.villailpoggiale.it; Via Empolese 69, San Casciano in Val di Pesa; d €150-170, ste €195-350; P@🛜🏊) Accommodation in Chianti is often prohibitively expensive, but this hilltop Renaissance-era villa bucks the trend. Spacious rooms have four-poster beds and frescoed ceilings, a spa sits downstairs and the swimming pool commands wraparound views. Just the place, after a day's sighseeing, to savour the complimentary afternoon tea. Villa Il Poggiale is 20km northwest of Greve.

Villa Le Barone   BOUTIQUE HOTEL €€€

(📋055 85 26 21; www.villalebarone.com; Via San Liolino 19, Panzano in Chianti; r €195-370; P🛜🏊) Encircled by a rose garden and panoramic views, this tasteful manor house 8km south of Greve was once home to the famous Della Robbia family of Renaissance sculptors, so its historical pedigree is as impressive as the luxurious facilities, which include a swimming pool, a tennis court and a top restaurant (dinner €35). Choose to sleep in the villa, cottages or converted barn.

Villa I Barronci   HOTEL €€€

(📋0558 2 05 98; www.ibarronci.com; Via Sorripa 10, San Casciano in Val di Pesa; d €190-250; P❄@🛜🏊) Exemplary service, superb amenities and high comfort levels ensure this modern country hotel is one to remember. You can relax in the bar, rejuvenate in the spa, laze by the pool or head off for easy day trips to Volterra, San Gimignano and Siena. The villa is 20km northwest of Greve, and 15km south of Florence.

🍴 Eating & Drinking

⭐ Rinuccio 1180   TUSCAN €€

(📋0552 35 97 20; www.antinorichianticlassico.it; Via Cassia per Siena 133, Bargino; meals €35, tasting platters €10-15; ⏰noon-4pm) Imagine lunching inside a glass box on a terrace with an intoxicating 180-degree Dolby-esque surround of hills, birdsong and pea-green vines. This is what the starlet of the Chianti dining scene, set on the uber-high-tech Antinori wine estate in Bargino, is all about. Cuisine is Tus-

can, modern, seasonal and sassy. The wine list is (naturally) fabulous. Book ahead.

Bargino is 20km northwest of Greve.

La Cantinetta di Rignana   TUSCAN €€

(📋0558 5 26 01; www.lacantinettadirignana.com; Rignana; meals €40; ⏰noon-3pm & 7-10pm Wed-Mon summer, hours vary winter) As you settle onto the terrace here, you might wonder whether you've found your perfect Chianti lazy lunch location. A historic mill forms the backdrop, vine-lined hills roll off to the horizon and rustic dishes are full of local ingredients and packed with flavour. It's 4km from Badia a Passignano at the end of an unsealed road.

La Castellana   TUSCAN €€

(📋0558 5 31 34; www.ristorantelacastellana.it; Montefioralle; meals €30; ⏰noon-2pm & 7.30-9.30pm Tue-Sun summer, hours vary winter) Rough wooden tables and rough stone walls set the scene for some fabulous home-style Tuscan cooking – it might include fragrant ravioli stuffed with mushrooms and truffles, or succulent sliced, rosemary-studded beef. The wine list reads like a map of Chianti's highlights, vintages best sampled on the hillside terrace where views are full of cypresses and vines.

La Castellana is in the hilltop village of Montefioralle, 1km west of Greve.

CHIANTI: THE WINES

The ruby-red Chianti and Chianti Classico DOCGs have a minimum Sangiovese component: 75% for Chianti and 80% for Chianti Classico. They're undoubtedly the region's blockbuster wines, but they're not the only quality vintages produced here: the Colli dell'Etruria Centrale, Pomino, Vin Santo del Chianti and Vin Santo del Chianti Classico DOCs are top local drops too.

The biggest wine-producing estates have *cantine* (cellars) where you can taste and buy wine, but few vineyards – big or small – can be visited without reservations. For a comprehensive list and map of wine estates, buy *Le strade del Gallo Nero* (€2.50) from local newsstands.

The **Consorzio Vino Chianti Classico** (www.chianticlassico.com) is a high-profile consortium of local producers; its website has more information on its 600 members, the wines themselves and related events.

BEST WINE TASTINGS

....

Book ahead to be sure of a space on these prestigious vineyard tours.

Antinori nel Chianti Classico (p138) Admire cutting-edge architecture at this flagship wine estate.

Castello di Ama (p144) Wander through a sculpture garden and enjoy world-class wines.

Poggio Antico (p157) Taste award-winning Brunellos and tour high-tech cellars.

Fattoria Le Capezzine (p166) Sample Vino Nobile di Montepulciano on this Avignonesi estate.

La Locanda di Pietracupa TUSCAN €€
(☑ 0558 07 24 00; www.locandapietracupa.com; Via Madonna di Pietracupa 31, San Donato in Poggio; meals €40; ☺ 12.30-2.30pm & 7.30-9.30pm daily summer, closed Tue winter; ℗ 🛜) Exquisitely presented dishes showcasing local ingredients are the hallmarks of this elegant but unstuffy eatery 20km southwest of Greve in Chianti. The regularly changing menu might feature beef with a Chianti Classico reduction, pigeon with truffle vinaigrette or *tagliolini* studded with courgette flowers. The bedrooms (single/double €80/95) are also suitably refined; expect candy-striped satins and paired-down wrought iron beds.

L'Antica Scuderia TUSCAN €€
(☑ 0558 07 16 23; www.ristorolanticascuderia.com; Via di Passignano 17, Badia a Passignano; meals €45, pizzas €8-15; ☺ 12.30-2.30pm & 7.30-10.30pm Wed-Mon) If you fancy eating on a garden terrace overlooking one of the Antinori vineyards, this casual eatery may well fit the bill. Lunch features antipasti, pastas and traditional grilled meats, while dinner sees plenty of pizza-oven action. Kids love the playground set; adults love the fact that it's at the opposite end of the garden.

⭐ **Osteria di Passignano** TUSCAN €€€
(☑ 0558 07 12 78; www.osteriadipassignano.com; Via di Passignano 33, Badia a Passignano; meals €60; ☺ 12.15-2.15pm & 7.30-10pm Mon-Sat) Badia a Passignano sits amid a landscape scored by row upon row of vines and the elegant eatery in the centre of the village has long been one of Tuscany's most glamorous dining destinations. Intricate, Tuscan-inspired dishes

fly the local produce flag and the wine list is mightily impressive, with Antinori offerings aplenty (by the glass €7 to €35).

There's also an epic six-course *menù degustazione* for €80, or €130 with a flight of wine.

La Bottega WINE BAR
(www.osteriadipassignano.com; Badia di Passignano; ☺ 10am-7.30pm, closed Sun) At this *enoteca* beside the prestigious Osteria di Passignano restaurant, tasting three top-quality wines by the glass will cost €25 to €55.

Castellina in Chianti & Around

POP 2900

Established by the Etruscans and fortified by the Florentines in the 15th century as a defensive outpost against the Sienese, sturdy Castellina in Chianti is now a major centre of the wine industry, as the huge silos brimming with Chianti Classico on the town's approaches attest.

⊙ Sights & Activities

Museo Archeologico del Chianti Senese MUSEUM
(www.museoarcheologicochianti.it; Piazza del Comune 18; adult/reduced €5/3; ☺ 10am-6pm daily Apr, May, Sep & Oct, 11am-7pm Jun-Aug, 10am-5pm Sat & Sun Nov-Mar) Etruscan archaeological finds from the local area are on display at this museum in the town's medieval *roccca* (fortress). Room 4 showcases artefacts found in the 7th-century-BC **Etruscan Tombs of Montecalvario** (Ipogeo Etrusco di Monte Calvario; ☺ 24hr) **FREE**, which are located on the northern edge of town off the SR222.

Via delle Volte WALKING
From Castellina's southern car park, follow Via Ferruccio or the panoramic path next to the town's eastern defensive walls. These lead to the atmospheric Via delle Volte, an arched medieval passageway that was originally used for ancient sacred rites and later enclosed with a roof and incorporated into the Florentine defensive structure.

🛏 Sleeping

Il Colombaio B&B €
(☑ 0577 74 04 44; www.albergoilcolombaio.it; Via Chiantigiana 29; d €90; ℗ 🛜 🏊) A tasteful conversion has turned this 14th-century farmhouse on the edge of Castellina into

a stylish *albergo* with a rich heritage feel: tapestry-covered chairs frame lace curtains and oil paintings a vast stone sink graces the lounge. Breakfast is served in the vaulted wine cellar or on the terrace; perhaps linger over it before a dip in the pool.

Locanda La Capannuccia INN €€
(☑ 0577 74 11 83; www.lacapannuccia.it; Borgo di Pietrafitta; s €80-90, d €96-130, 2-night minimum; ⊘ closed Nov-Feb; [P][🛜][🏊]) If you don't fancy some rally-style driving, you might want to give this true Tuscan getaway a miss; it's at the end of a steep, twisting, 1.5km dirt road. The atmosphere is pure country inn, rooms are restrained and comfortable, and they'll cook you dinner if you book. It's situated 5km north of Castellina, off the SR222 on the Pietrafitta road.

✗ Eating

Ristorante Albergaccio TUSCAN €€€
(☑ 0577 74 10 42; www.albergacciocast.com; Via Fiorentina 63, Castellina in Chianti; 4/5 courses €58/68, 3-course kids menu €27; ⊘ 12.30-2.30pm & 7.30-9.30pm, closed parts of Dec-Mar; 🅿) Albergaccio bills its culinary approach as 'the territory on the table' and local, seasonal and organic produce certainly hold sway here. The style is innovative and upmarket, the 320-strong wine list is well priced and the eatery is rightly popular with local and international foodies. It's located 1km northeast of Castellina on the San Donato in Poggio road.

🛍 Shopping

Antica Fattoria la Castellina WINE
(Via Ferruccio 26; ⊘ 10.30am-12.30pm & 2.30-5.30pm) The town's best-known wine shop will let you sample the local product too.

❶ Information

Tourist Office (☑ 0577 74 13 92; www.turismo.comune.castellina.si.it; Via Ferruccio 40; ⊘ 10am-noon & 3-6pm daily Jun-Oct, Tue, Thu, Sat & Sun only Mar-May, reduced hours winter) Has maps and books visits to wineries and cellars.

❶ Getting There & Around

BUS
Tiemme (www.tiemmespa.it) buses link Castellina in Chianti with Siena (€3.40, 35 minutes, seven daily Monday to Saturday).

CAR & MOTORCYCLE
The most convenient car park is at the southern edge of town off Via IV Novembre (€1/5 per hour/day).

Radda in Chianti & Around

POP 1670

Pretty Radda's age-old streets fan out from its central square, where the shields and escutcheons of the 16th-century Palazzo del Podestà add a touch of drama to the scene. A historic wine town, it's an appealing if low-key base for visits to some classic Tuscan vineyards and some striking sculpture parks.

👁 Sights & Activities

★ **Castello di Brolio** CASTLE
(☑ 0577 73 02 80; www.ricasoli.it; garden, chapel & crypt €5, guided tours €8; ⊘ 10am-7pm Apr-Oct, guided tours every 30min 10.30am-12.30pm & 2.30-5pm Tue-Sun) The ancestral estate of the aristocratic Ricasoli family dates from the 11th century and is the oldest winery in Italy. Currently home to the 32nd baron, it opens its formal garden, panoramic terrace and museum to day-trippers, who often adjourn to the

---

CYCLING CHIANTI

Exploring Chianti by bicycle is a true highlight. The Greve in Chianti tourist office publishes a brochure listing local cycling and walking routes. You can rent bicycles from **Ramuzzi** (☑ 055 85 30 37; www.ramuzzi.com; Via Italo Stecchi 23; touring bike per day/week €35/220, scooter per day/week €55/290; ⊘ 9am-1pm & 3-7pm Mon-Fri, 9am-1pm Sat) in the town.

A number of companies offer guided cycling tours leaving from Florence:

Florence By Bike (☑ 0554 8 89 92; www.florencebybike.it) Tour of northern Chianti (one day) with lunch and wine tasting (€83; four per week March to October).

I Bike Italy (☑ 342 9352395; www.ibikeitaly.com) Two-day tour including accommodation, breakfast, lunch and dinner (€375; mid-March to October).

I Bike Tuscany (☑ 335 812 07 69; www.ibiketuscany.com) Year-round, one-day tours (€155) for all levels. Includes transports from Florence to Chianti.

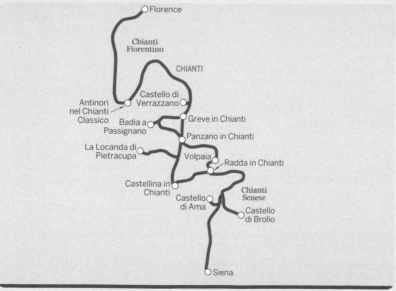

Florence

Chianti Fiorentino

CHIANTI

Castello di Verrazzano

Antinori nel Chianti Classico

Badia a Passignano

Greve in Chianti

Panzano in Chianti

La Locanda di Pietracupa

Volpaia

Radda in Chianti

Castellina in Chianti

Castello di Ama

Chianti Senese

Castello di Brolio

Siena

JOHN ELK/GETTY IMAGES ©

Wine Tour of Chianti

4 DAYS

Tuscany has more than its fair share of highlights, but few can match the glorious indulgence of a leisurely drive through Chianti. On offer is an intoxicating blend of scenery, acclaimed restaurants and ruby-red wine.

From **Florence**, take the *superstrada* (expressway) towards Siena, exit at Bargino and follow the signs to **Antinori nel Chianti Classico** (p138), a state-of-the-art wine estate featuring an architecturally innovative ageing cellar. Take a tour, prime your palate with a wine tasting and enjoy lunch in the estate's Rinuccio 1180 restaurant.

Head southeast along the SS2, SP3 and SS222 (Via Chiantigiana) towards Greve in Chianti. Stop at historic **Castello di Verrazzano** (p138) for a tasting en route.

On the next day, make your way to **Greve in Chianti** to test your new-found knowledge over a self-directed tasting at Enoteca Falorni (p137). For lunch, eat a Tuscan-style burger at Dario DOC (p144) in **Panzano in Chianti** or linger over lunch at La Locanda di Pietracupa (p140). Your destination in the afternoon should be **Badia a Passignano** (p138), an 11th-century, still-functioning Vallombrosian abbey surrounded by an Antinori wine estate. Enjoy a tasting in the *enoteca* (wine bar) and consider staying for an early pizza dinner at L'Antica Scuderia (p140) opposite the abbey, where you'll be able to watch the sun set over the vineyards.

On day three, pop into the pretty hilltop hamlet of **Volpaia** near **Radda in Chianti** and take a tour of the Castello di Volpaia (p144) cellars before relaxing over lunch at Bar Ucci (p145) or heading to the innovative Ristorante Albergaccio (p141) in **Castellina in Chianti**.

On the final day, head towards **Siena**. Along the way, take a guided tour of the **Castello di Brolio** (p141), ancestral home of the aristocratic Ricasoli family. Their wine estate is the oldest in Italy, so be sure to sample some Baron Ricasoli Chianti Classico at the estate's *cantina* (cellar) or over lunch in its *osteria* (casual tavern). Afterwards, investigate award-winning wines and contemporary art at **Castello di Ama** (p144).

ROCCO FASANO/GETTY IMAGES ©

Top: Vineyards in Chianti
Bottom: Generations of winemakers at work

L'ANTICA MACELLERÌA CECCHINI

The small town of Panzano in Chianti, 10km south of Greve in Chianti, is known through-out Italy as the location of **L'Antica Macelleria Cecchini** (www.dariocecchini.com; Via XX Luglio 11; ⊙9am-4pm), a butcher's shop owned and run by the ever-extrovert **Dario Cecchini**. This Tuscan celebrity has carved out a niche for himself as a poetry-spouting guardian of the *bistecca* (steak) and other Tuscan meaty treats, and he operates three eateries clustered around the *macelleria*: **Officina della Bistecca** (☑0558 5 21 76; Via XX Luglio 11; set menu €50; ⊙sittings at 1pm & 8pm), with a set menu built around the famous *bistecca*; **Solociccia** (☑0558 5 27 27; Via Chiantigiana 5; set menus €30 & €50; ⊙sittings at 1pm, 7pm & 9pm daily), where guests sample meat dishes other than steak; and **Dario DOC** (Via XX Luglio 11; burger €10-15, light menu €20; ⊙noon-3pm Mon-Sat), his casual lunchtime-only eatery. Book ahead for the Officina and Solociccia.

on-site *osteria* for lunch after a guided tour of the castle's small but fascinating museum.

Occupying three rooms in the castle's tower, the museum is dedicated to documenting the life of the extravagantly mustachioed Baron Bettino Ricasoli (1809–80), the second prime minster of the Republic of Italy and a true polymath (scientist, farmer, winemaker, statesman, businessman). A leading figure in the Risorgimento, one of his other great claims to fame is inventing the formula for Chianti Classico that is enshrined in current DOC regulations.

The *castello's* chapel dates from the early 14th century; below it is a crypt where generations of Ricasolis are interred. The estate produces wine and olive oil, and the huge terrace commands a spectacular view of the vineyards and olive groves. The Classic Tour (€25, two hours, 10am Monday, Wednesday and Friday, plus 3pm March to June) takes in the wine-making facilities and features a tasting, while the Vineyard Tour (€45, two hours, 3.30pm Tuesday and Thursday) sees you exploring the estate's different *terroirs* and sampling vintages beside the vines.

A *bosco Inglese* (English garden) surrounds the estate, in it (near the car park) you'll find the estate's **Osteria del Castello** (☑0577 73 02 90; 4-course tasting menu with wines €50; ⊙noon-2.30pm & 7.30-9.30pm Fri-Wed late-Mar–Oct). Just outside the estate's entrance gates, on the SP484, is a modern **cantina** (⊙9am-7.30pm Mon-Fri, 10am-7pm Sat & Sun Apr–mid-Oct) where you can taste the Castello di Brolio's well-regarded Chianti Classico.

★ Castello di Ama   SCULPTURE
(☑0577 74 60 31; www.castellodiama.com; Località Ama; guided tours €15, with wine & oil tasting €35; ⊙by appointment year-round) At Castello di Ama centuries-old wine-making traditions

meet cutting-edge contemporary art. As well as producing internationally famous wines such as 'L'Apparita' Merlot, this estate also features a sculpture park showcasing 13 impressive site-specific pieces by artists including Louise Bourgeois, Chen Zhen, Anish Kapoor, Kendell Geers and Daniel Buren. It's 9km south of Radda, near Lecchi in Chianti.

Guided tours (in English, French, Italian or German) take in the sculpture park, villa and cellar – as well as 'L'Apparita', wines to keep an eye out for are the 'Haiku' Sangiovese/cabernet Franc/merlot blend and a delicious 'Vigneto Bellavista' Chianti Classico.

Parco Sculture del Chianti   SCULPTURE
(Chianti Sculpture Park; ☑0577 35 71 51; www.chianti sculpturepark.it; Località La Fornace; adult/child €10/5; ⊙10am-dusk Apr-Oct, by appointment Nov-Mar; 📶) More than 25 site-specific contemporary artworks are tucked into this 13-acre wood, meaning you'll encounter abstract humans, cube clusters and multicoloured cows amid the foliage. Between June and August weekly sunset jazz and opera **concerts** are staged in the park's white Carrara marble and black Zimbabwean granite amphitheatre. Look out for Hitchcock, Fellini and Charlie Chaplin amid the 'spectators'.

The park is 16km south of Radda. While here, detour to the nearby village of **Pievasciata**, whose streets are home to an ever-growing number of site-specific contemporary international artworks (check to see if Yu Zhaoyang's hilarious Town Ostriches are still next to the cypress trees).

Castello di Volpaia   WINERY
(☑0577 73 80 66; www.volpaia.it; Località Volpaia) Wines, olive oils, vinegars and honey have been produced for centuries at this wine estate based in the medieval hill-top hamlet of Volpaia (the name is misleading, as there's no actual castle

here). Book ahead to enjoy a tasting and tour of the estate's cellars (€11), or pop into its *enoteca* (noon to 7pm Thursday to Tuesday), which is inside the hamlet's main tower.

🛏 Sleeping

★Villa Sassolini   BOUTIQUE HOTEL €€€
(✆0559 70 22 46; www.villasassolini.it; Largo Moncioni, Località Moncioni; d €200-345, ste €325-443, dinner €50; ⊙closed Nov–mid-Mar; ❀🛜🏊) It's hard to top the romantic credentials of this gorgeous hotel set in dense forest on the border of Chianti and the Valdarno. Luxe rooms, an intimate restaurant and a spectacular pool terrace are three of many elements contributing to an utterly irresistible package; proximity to the Valdarno's designer clothing outlet stores is another. It's 25km east of Radda.

La Locanda   BOUTIQUE HOTEL €€€
(✆0577 73 88 32; www.lalocanda.it; Montanino di Volpaia; s €200-245, d €220-290, ste €290-310; ⊙closed Nov–mid-Apr; P❀🛜🏊) Overlooking the medieval village of Volpaia, 7km north of Radda in Chianti, this country hotel offers seven charming rooms in the converted 16th-century farmhouse, as well as a lounge, a library and a dining room (dinner Monday, Wednesday and Friday, €35) in the former stables.

🍴 Eating

Bar Ucci   TUSCAN, WINE BAR €
(www.bar-ucci.it; Piazza Della Torre 9, Volpaia; crostoni €4.50-6, antipasti plates €7-12, salads €4-8; ⊙8am-9pm Tue-Sun) The philosophy behind this bar-cafe is to use good ingredients and a warm welcome to create special moments – and it works. The house salami is made by the owner's father, dishes range from *crostoni* to wild boar stew, and there's a tempting range of Chianti by the bottle or Volpaia's own Chianti Classico and Riserva by the glass. Volpaia is 7km north of Radda in Chianti.

★Ristorante La Bottega   TUSCAN €€
(✆0577 73 80 01; www.labottegadivolpaia.it; Piazza della Torre 1, Volpaia; meals €25; ⊙noon-2.30pm & 7.30-9.30pm Wed-Mon Easter-Jan) *Cucina contadina* (food from the farmers' kitchen) is the mainstay of this pretty restaurant run by the Barucci family – the kitchen garden is right outside and Mum Gina is likely to have made the soup or pasta (her *ribollita* is famous). And what better place to eat it than an outdoor, tree-shaded terrace with sweeping views of Chianti's hills.

Osteria Le Panzanelle   TUSCAN €€
(✆0577 73 35 11; www.lepanzanelle.it; Lucarelli; meals €35; ⊙12.30-2pm & 7.30-9pm Tue-Sun, closed part of Jan & Feb) An ideal lunch stop en route from Chianti to Siena, this roadside inn serves traditional Tuscan dishes in its garden and downstairs bar-dining room. The menu changes monthly, reflecting what is in season. Find it 5km south of Panzano in Chianti, right next to the SP2 to Radda in Chianti. Bookings are advisable.

ℹ Information

Tourist Office (✆0577 73 84 94; proradda@chiantinet.it; Piazza Castello 2, Radda in Chianti; ⊙10am-1pm & 3-7pm summer, 10.30am-12.30pm & 3.30-6.30pm winter) The tourist office can book accommodation and tours for this pocket of Chianti, and also supplies information about walks in the area.

VAL D'ELSA

A convenient base for visiting the rest of Tuscany, this valley stretching from Chianti to the Maremma can be relied upon to tick many of the boxes on your Tuscan 'must-do' list, with plenty of opportunities to enjoy food, wine, museums and scenery. The valley's major towns are Colle di Val d'Elsa and Poggibonsi, but the major tourist drawcard is the medieval splendour of San Gimignano. Note that we have included nearby Volterra in this section despite the fact that it is officially located in the Val di Cecina, a province of Pisa.

San Gimignano

POP 7770

As you crest the nearby hills, the 14 towers of this walled town rise up like a medieval Manhattan. Originally an Etruscan village, the settlement was named after the bishop of Modena, San Gimignano, who is said to have saved the city from Attila the Hun. It became a *comune* (local government) in 1199, prospering in part because of its location on the Via Francigena. Building a tower taller than their neighbours' (there were originally 72) became a popular way for prominent families to flaunt their power and wealth. In 1348 plague wiped out much of the population and weakened the local economy, leading to the town's submission to Florence in 1353. Today, not even the plague would deter the swarms of summer day-trippers, who are lured by a palpable

San Gimignano

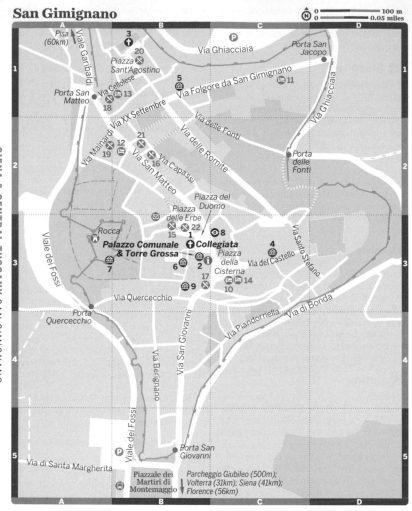

sense of history, intact medieval streetscapes and enchanting rural setting.

◉ Sights

Triangular **Piazza della Cisterna** is named after the 13th-century cistern at its centre. In Piazza del Duomo, the cathedral looks across to the late-13th-century **Palazzo Vecchio del Podestà** (Piazza del Duomo) and its tower, the **Torre della Rognosa**.

★ Collegiata   CHURCH
(Duomo or Basilica di Santa Maria Assunta; Piazza del Duomo; adult/reduced €4/2; ⊙10am-7pm Mon-Fri, to 5pm Sat, 12.30-7pm Sun summer, to 4.30pm daily winter) Parts of San Gimignano's Romanesque cathedral were built in the second half of the 11th century, but its remarkably vivid frescoes, depicting episodes from the Old and New Testaments, date from the 14th century. Look out too for the Cappella di Santa Fina, near the main altar – a Renaissance chapel adorned with naive and touching frescoes by Domenico Ghirlandaio depicting the life of one of the town's patron saints. These featured in Franco Zeffirelli's 1999 film *Tea with Mussolini*.

San Gimignano

Entry is via the side stairs and through a loggia (balcony) that was originally covered and functioned as the baptistry. Once in the main space, face the altar and look to your left (north). On the wall are scenes from Genesis and the Old Testament by Bartolo di Fredi, dating from around 1367. The top row runs from the creation of the world through to the forbidden fruit scene. This in turn leads to the next level and fresco, the expulsion of Adam and Eve from the Garden of Eden, which has sustained some war damage. Further scenes include Cain killing Abel, and the stories of Noah's ark and Joseph's coat. The last level continues with the tale of Moses leading the Jews out of Egypt, and the story of Job.

On the right (south) wall are scenes from the New Testament by the workshop of Simone Martini (probably led by Lippo Memmi, Martini's brother-in-law), which were completed in 1336. Again, the frescoes are spread over three levels, starting in the six lunettes at the top. Starting with the Annunciation, the panels work through episodes such as the Epiphany, the presentation of Christ in the temple and the massacre of the innocents on Herod's orders. The subsequent panels on the lower levels summarise the life and death of Christ, the Resurrection and so on. Again, some have sustained damage, but most are in good condition.

On the inside wall of the front facade, extending onto adjoining walls, is Taddeo di Bartolo's striking depiction of the Last Judgment – on the upper-left side is a fresco depicting *Paradiso* (Heaven) and on the upper-right *Inferno* (Hell). The fresco of San Sebastian under them is by Benozzo Gozzoli.

The church is commonly known as the Collegiata, a reference to the college of priests which originally managed it.

★ **Palazzo Comunale & Torre Grossa**   MUSEUM

(Museo Civico; ☑ 0577 99 03 12; Piazza del Duomo 2; adult/reduced €6/5, ☉ 9am 6.30pm summer, 11am-5pm winter) The 12th-century Palazzo Comunale is home to the **Camera del Podestà**, with its meticulously restored and slightly saucy cycle of frescoes by Memmo di Filippuccio – in this morality tale the rewards of marriage are shown in the scenes of the husband and wife naked in the bath and in bed. Be sure to climb the 218 steps of the *palazzo*'s 54m Torre Grossa for a spectacular view over the town and surrounding countryside.

The *palazzo*'s **Sala di Dante** is where the great poet addressed the town's council in 1299, urging it to support the Guelph cause. The room (also known as the Sala del Consiglio) is home to Lippo Memmi's early 14th-century *Maestà,* which portrays the enthroned Virgin and Child surrounded by angels, saints and local dignitaries – the kneeling noble in red-and-black stripes was the *podestà* (chief magistrate) of the time. Other frescoes portray jousts, hunting scenes and castles. Gadget fans are likely to enjoy the augmented reality glasses which superimpose digital medieval characters over the frescoes; hire them from the gift shop.

Upstairs is a small but charming pinacoteca. Highlights are two large *Annunciation* panels (1482) by Filippino Lippi, *Madonna of Humility Worshipped by Two Saints* (1466) and *Madonna and Child with Saints* (1466) by Benozzo Gozzoli, and an altarpiece by Taddeo di Bartolo (1401) illustrating the life of St Gimignano.

Chiesa di Sant'Agostino CHURCH

(Piazza Sant'Agostino; ⊙ 7am-noon & 3-7pm summer, to 6pm winter) FREE This late-13th-century church is best known for Benozzo Gozzoli's charming fresco cycle illustrating the life of St Augustine. You'll find it behind the altar – putting €0.50 in the slot provides better illumination. Gozzoli also painted the San Sebastian fresco on the north wall, which shows the saint protecting the citizens of San Gimignano during the 1464 plague. What makes the image highly unusual is that he's helped by a bare-breasted Virgin Mary; this symbolises her maternal love for humanity.

On Sundays at 11am an English-language mass is celebrated in a chapel off the cloister.

Museo del Vino MUSEUM

(www.sangimignanomuseovernaccia.com; Parco della Rocca; ⊙ 11.30am-6.30pm Apr-Oct) FREE San Gimignano's famous wine, Vernaccia, is celebrated in this small museum next to the *rocca* (fortress). Exhibits trace the history of the product and the surrounding land; there's also an *enoteca* where you can buy glasses of local vintages to enjoy on a terrace with a panoramic view.

Museo Archeologico & Speziera di Santa Fina MUSEUM

(Via Folgore da San Gimignano 11; adult/reduced €6/5; ⊙ 9.30am-6.30pm summer, 11am-5pm winter) The Speziera di Santa Fina, one of two museums on the same site, features a part-reconstructed 15th- to 18th-century pharmacy, complete with shelves stacked with brightly painted ceramic jars, half-empty potion bottles, terracotta bowls full of ingredients and leather-bound inventories containing elaborate script. The Museo Archeologico showcases some fine pottery, huge serving platters with heraldic crests and Roman finds including tiny bronze figurines, etched mirrors and piles of brightly coloured mosaic tiles.

Upstairs, you'll find the **Galleria d'Arte Moderna E Contemporanea**, a modern art gallery whose permanent works include Renato Guttuso's impressive *Marina* (1970).

Museo d'Arte Sacra MUSEUM

(Piazza Pecori 1; adult/child €3.50/2; ⊙ 10am-7pm Mon-Fri, to 5pm Sat, 12.30-7pm Sun summer, 10am-4.30pm Mon-Sat, 12.30-4.30pm Sun winter) Works of medieval religious art from San Gimignano's key churches are on display in this modest museum. Particularly beautiful items made from precious metals include crafted chalices and *thuribles* (censers); there are also some exquisitely embroidered textiles.

San Gimignano del 1300 MUSEUM

(www.sangimignano1300.com; Via Costarella 3; adult/child €3/free; ⊙ 10am-6pm summer only) Youngsters love this handmade ceramic re-creation of the medieval city, complete with houses, streets, towers and people as they would have looked in 1300. It's quite likely to inspire junior visitors to bigger and better Lego projects once home.

🕝 Tours

⭐ Vernaccia di San Gimignano Vineyard Visit WINERY

(tastings €20; ⊙ 5-7pm Tue & Thu Apr-Oct) Highly enjoyable tastings of local foods and wines delivered by English-language guides. Book at the tourist office at least a day in advance.

Nature Walk WALKING TOUR

(tours €22-25; ⊙ times vary) Offers a range of English-language nature walks amid the hills surrounding San Gimignano, along 6km to 9km stretches of the Via Francigena and through the Riserva Naturale di Castelvecchio to the southwest of town. Book at the tourist office.

🎊 Festivals & Events

Ferie delle Messi CULTURAL

(www.cavalieridisantafina.it) A June pagent (usually the third weekend) evoking the town's medieval past through re-enacted battles, archery contests and plays.

Festival Barocco di San Gimignano MUSIC

A high-quality season of Baroque music concerts in September and early October. Check www.sangimignano.com for details.

ℹ SAN GIMIGNANO COMBINED TICKETS

Two combined tickets can save you money. The first (adult/reduced €6/5) gives admission to the Museo Civico, the Museo Archeologico, the Speziera di Santa Fina and the town's small ornithological museum. The second (adult/reduced €6/3) gets you into the Collegiata and Museo d'Arte Sacra.

🛏 Sleeping

★ Al Pozzo dei Desideri   APARTMENT €
(📞 370 3102538, 0577 90 71 99; www.alpozzodeidesi deri.it; Piazza della Cisterna 32; d/tr/q €110/120/160; ❄️ 🛜) Three rooms with a view (two over the countryside and one over the town's main piazza) are on offer in this gorgeous 13th-century building; expect marble bathrooms, drapes and warm stone walls. All rooms have a fridge and tea- and coffee-making facilities. There's no breakfast, but this is town-centre Tuscany: there's a good cafe close by.

Il Pino   B&B €
(📞 0577 94 04 15; www.locandailpino.it; Via Cellolese 6; s/d €52/70; 🛜) Exposed rafters and well-worn terracotta floors enhance the atmosphere at this superb-value *locanda* (inn); patchwork quilts and smart modern bathrooms ensure it's cosy and comfortable too. The location is excellent – in one of the quieter parts of town, but still well within the ancient walls.

Foresteria Monastero di San Girolamo   HOSTEL €
(📞 0577 94 05 73; www.monasterosangirolamo.it; Via Folgore da San Gimignano 30; s/tw €43/75; 🅿) This is a first-rate backpacker choice. Run by friendly Benedictine Vallumbrosan nuns, it has basic but comfortable rooms sleeping two to five people; all have attached bathrooms. Parking and kitchen use are available for a small fee. Book in advance at www. monasterystays.com, as it's usually full.

If you don't have a reservation, arrive between 9am and noon or between 3.30pm and 5.30pm and ring the monastery bell (the one closer to the town centre), rather than the Foresteria one, which is never answered.

Hotel L'Antico Pozzo   BOUTIQUE HOTEL €€
(📞 0577 94 20 14; www.anticopozzo.com; Via San Matteo 87; s €80-95, d €90-180; ❄️ @ 🛜) The sense of heritage here is irresistible: stone arches and winding stairs lead to an intimate breakfast terrace; chic, spacious bedrooms are often replete with cornices and crowned with networks of beams. The posher rooms are named after poets and graded – Dante, a high-ceilinged beauty rich in polished woods, is the best. Naturally.

La Cisterna   HOTEL €€
(📞 0577 94 03 28; www.hotelcisterna.it; Piazza della Cisterna 24; s €72-78, d €96-150; ❄️ @ 🛜) They bill the views as panoramic from the pricier

balcony rooms at La Cisterna and they're not wrong: 180-degree vistas over tiled roofs, tiny vegetable gardens and vineyards to the hazy hills beyond. Inside arches frame iron bedsteads and hand-painted furniture. The cheaper rooms, although very comfy, are sadly nowhere near as fine.

🍴 Eating & Drinking

San Gimignano is known for its *zafferano* (saffron). You can purchase meat, vegetables, fish and takeaway food at the **Thursday morning market** (Piazza delle Erbe) in and around Piazzas Cisterna, Duomo and Erbe.

Dal Bertelli   SANDWICHES €
(Via Capassi 30; panini €4-6, glasses of wine €2; ⏰ 1-7pm Mar-early Jan) The Bertelli family has lived in San Gimignano since 1779, and its current patriarch is fiercely proud of both his heritage and his sandwiches. Salami, cheese, bread and wine is sourced from local artisan producers, it's sold in generous portions in a determinedly un-gentrified space with marble work surfaces, wooden shelves and curious agricultural implements dangling from stone walls.

Caffè Delle Erbe   CAFE €
(📞 0577 94 04 78; www.caffedelleerbesangimig nano.it; Piazza delle Erbe; panini €5, platters €6-13; ⏰ 9am-7pm Wed-Mon) Skip the *panini* and plump for the *piatto misto* for tasty bruschetta, salads and a fine selection of Tuscan meats and cheese. Best enjoyed with a glass of Vernaccia at a pavement table with views of San Gimignano's famous towers.

Gelateria Dondoli GELATERIA €
(www.gelateriadipiazza.com; Piazza della Cisterna 4; gelati €2.50-5; ⊙9am-11pm summer, to 7.30pm winter) Think of it less as ice cream, more as art. Former gelato world champion Sergio Dondoli is a member of Italy's Ice Cream World Championship team (of course there's such a thing). Among his most famous creations are *Crema di Santa Fina* (saffron cream) gelato and Vernaccia sorbet.

★ **Locanda Sant'Agostino** TUSCAN €€
(⊋0577 94 31 41; www.locandasantagostino.net; Piazza Sant'Agostino 15; meals €30; ⊙12.30-2.30pm & 7-10pm Thu-Tue) It's a bit like eating in an Italian grandmother's kitchen: bundles of wheat hang from the ceiling; knick-knacks stack the shelves; and the cooking is sublime. Homemade *pici* (thick, hand-rolled pasta) might come with wild boar ragù, while truffles feature strongly – like the servings of Vernaccia wine, they're dished out with an admirably generous hand.

Perucà TUSCAN €€
(⊋0577 94 31 36; www.peruca.eu; Via Capassi 16; meals €30; ⊙12.30-2pm & 7.30-10pm Tue-Sun mid-Feb–early Dec, Mon Apr-Sep) The owner is as knowledgeable about regional food and wine as she is enthusiastic, and the food is excellent. Try the house speciality of *fagottini del contadino* (ravioli with *pecorino*, pears and saffron cream) with a glass of Fattoria San Donato's Vernaccia – it's a match made in heaven.

OFF THE BEATEN TRACK

THE VIA FRANCIGENA

Devise a holiday with a difference by walking or driving parts of the **Via Francigena**, a medieval pilgrimage route connecting Canterbury with Rome. In Central Tuscany, the route goes past or through towns including San Gimignano, Monteriggioni, San Quirico d'Orcia and Radicófani. Globalmap publishes *Via Francigena in Toscana* (€8), an excellent hiking map (1:50,000) with detailed routes and information about accommodation for pilgrims. You'll find it for sale in tourist offices and bookshops throughout the region. You can also check www.franci genalibrari.beniculturali.it for route maps and GPS coordinates.

La Mangiatoia TUSCAN €€
(⊋0577 94 15 28; Via Mainardi 5; meals €20; ⊙12.30-2.30pm & 7.30-9.30pm Wed-Mon) There's confidence in their craft among the chefs at La Mangiatoia – they offer only five options in each antipasto, *primo* and *secondo*. Luckily they're all good, with assured treatments of traditional Tuscan ingredients such as beef, venison and wild boar.

Il Pino TUSCAN €€
(⊋0577 94 04 15; www.ristoranteilpino.it; Via Cellolese 8; meals €25-50; ⊙noon-2.30pm & 7-9.30pm Fri, Sat & Mon-Wed, noon-2.30pm Sun) Truffles pop up everywhere in the dishes at this elegant, vaulted eatery; the one with marinated Chianina beef and *pecorino* is memorable. The bread is homemade, the ingredients are seasonal and the four-course set menus (ranging from €25 to €50) are a steal.

❶ Information

Tourist Office (⊋0577 94 00 08; www. sangimignano.com; Piazza del Duomo 1; ⊙9am-1pm & 3-7pm summer, 9am-1pm & 2-6pm winter) An extremely helpful office which organises tours, supplies maps and has information on the *Strada del Vino Vernaccia di San Gimignano* (Wine Road of the Vernaccia of San Gimignano). It also offers accommodation booking on its website.

❶ Getting There & Away

BUS

The bus station is next to the Carabinieri (Police Station) at Porta San Giovanni. The tourist office sells bus tickets. Routes include the following:

Florence (€6.80, 1¼ to two hours, 14 daily) Change at Poggibonsi.

Siena (€6, one to 1½ hours, 10 daily Monday to Saturday)

Volterra (€6, 1½ hours, four daily Monday to Saturday) Change at Colle di Val d'Elsa.

CAR & MOTORCYCLE

From Florence and Siena, take the Siena–Florence *superstrada*, then the SR2 and finally the SP1 from Poggibonsi Nord. From Volterra, take the SR68 east and follow the turn-off signs north to San Gimignano on the SP47.

Parking is expensive here. The cheapest option (per hour/24 hours €1.50/6) is at Parcheggio Giubileo on the southern edge of town; the most convenient is at Parcheggio Montemaggio next to Porta San Giovanni (per hour/24 hours €2/20).

TRAIN

The closest train station is Poggibonsi (by bus €2.50, 30 minutes, frequent).

OFF THE BEATEN TRACK

IL PALUFFO

Hidden in the hills 20km north of San Gimignano sits the kind of luxurious, innovative, ecological *agriturismo* (farm stay accommodation) that you remember for a very, very long time. At **Il Paluffo** (☑ 0571 66 42 59; www.paluffo.com; via Citerna 144 , near Lucardo; B&B d €160, 4-/6-person apt per week €1890/2300; P 🌐 @ 🛜 🛏) an inspired conversion of a centuries-old olive farm has seen the former fermentation room transformed into a book-packed, two-story lounge with vast sofas and a kooky feature fireplace.

Bedrooms feature 18th-century frescoes, polished wooden shutters and age-speckled mirrors. Bathrooms are jaw-dropping, with circular tubs, mezzanine showers, and wood from old wine barrels lining the floors.

Staff can arrange wine tasting and truffle hunting, and cookery courses covering everything from pasta making to Tuscan dinner parties. Add a luscious bio-filtered swimming pool, an honesty bar stacked with Tuscan wines, a courtyard dotted with lemon trees, and terraces where valley views stretch as far San Gimignano's towers, and you have a dream stay.

Volterra

POP 10,800

Volterra's well-preserved medieval ramparts give the windswept town a proud, forbidding air that author Stephanie Meyer deemed ideal for the discriminating tastes of the planet's principal vampire coven in her wildly popular *Twilight* book series. Fortunately, the reality is considerably more welcoming, as a wander through the winding cobbled streets attests.

The Etruscan settlement of Velathri was an important trading centre and a senior partner of the Dodecapolis. It's believed that as many as 25,000 people lived here in its Etruscan heyday. Partly because of the surrounding inhospitable terrain, the city was among the last to succumb to Rome – it was absorbed into the Roman confederation around 260 BC and renamed Volaterrae. The bulk of the old city was raised in the 12th and 13th centuries under a fiercely independent free *comune*. The city first entered Florence's orbit in 1361, but the people of Volterra fought hard against Medici rule – their rebellion was brought to a brutal end when Lorenzo Il Magnifico's soldiers sacked the city in 1472. There was another rebellion in 1530 – again brutally crushed by the Florentines – but Volterra would never again achieve self-government, moving from Florentine rule to that of the Grand Duchy of Tuscany before unification in 1860. Since Etruscan times the people of Volterra have been famous for carving alabaster mined from nearby quarries, artistry that's still in evidence locally today.

◉ Sights & Activities

★**Museo Etrusco Guarnacci**   MUSEUM

(Via Don Minzoni 15; adult/reduced incl Pinacoteca Comunale & Ecomuseo dell'Alabastro €10/6; ⊙ 9am-7pm summer, 10am-4.30pm winter) The vast collection of Etruscan artefacts exhibited here makes this one of Italy's most impressive collections. Found locally, they include some 600 funerary urns carved mainly from alabaster and tufa – perhaps the pick is the Urn of the Sposi, a strikingly realistic terracotta rendering of an elderly couple. The finds are displayed according to subject and era; the best examples (those dating from later periods) are on the 2nd and 3rd floors.

Make sure you track down the crested helmet excavated from the Tomba del Guernero at nearby Poggio alle Croci, and the *L'Ombra della Sera* (Shadow of the Evening), an elongated bronze nude figurine that bears a striking resemblance to the work of the Swiss sculptor Alberto Giacometti.

★**Cattedrale di
Santa Maria Assunta**   CATHEDRAL

(Duomo di Volterra; Piazza San Giovanni; ⊙ 8am-noon & 2-7pm summer, to 5pm winter) A handsome coffered ceiling is the most striking single feature of the *duomo*, which was built in the 12th and 13th centuries and remodelled in the 16th. The **Chapel of Our Lady of Sorrows**, on the left as you enter from Piazza San Giovanni, has two sculptures by Andrea della Robbia and a small fresco of the *Procession of the Magi* by Benozzo Gozzoli.

In front of the *duomo*, a 13th-century **baptistry** (Piazza San Giovanni) features a small marble font (1502) by Andrea Sansovino.

LEEMAGE/GETTY IMAGES ©

1. Di Buoninsegna's *Maestà* **2.** Piazza dei Priori, Volterra
3. Abbazia di Sant'Antimo **4.** Palazzo Comunale, Siena

TINO SORIANO/GETTY IMAGES ©

Medieval Masterpieces

We reckon the Middle Ages get a bad rap in the history books. This period may have been blighted by famines, plagues and wars, but it also saw an extraordinary flowering of art and architecture. Cities such as Siena, San Gimignano and Volterra are full of masterpieces dating from this time.

Palazzo Comunale, Siena

Built on the cusp of the Middle Ages and the Renaissance, Siena's city hall (p124) is a triumph of Gothic secular architecture. Inside, the Museo Civico showcases a collection that is modest in size but monumental in quality.

Abbazia di Sant'Antimo

Benedictine monks have been performing Gregorian chants in this Romanesque abbey (p161) near Montalcino ever since the Middle Ages. Dating back to the time of Charlemagne, its austere beauty and idyllic setting make it an essential stop on every itinerary.

Piazza dei Priori, Volterra

Ringed by medieval palaces, Volterra's central square (p154) is presided over by the handsome Palazzo dei Priori and Palazzo Pretorio, the latter crowned by the Torre del Porcellino (Piglet's Tower), named for the wild boar protruding from its upper section.

Duccio di Buoninsegna's *Maestà*, Siena

Originally displayed in Siena's *duomo* (cathedral) and now the prize exhibit in the Museo dell'Opera, Duccio's altarpiece (p127) portrays the Virgin surrounded by angels, saints and prominent Sienese citizens of the period.

Collegiata, San Gimignano

Don't be fooled by its modest facade. Inside, the walls of this Romanesque cathedral (p146) are adorned with brightly coloured frescoes resembling a vast medieval comic strip.

Palazzo dei Priori
HISTORIC BUILDING

(Piazza dei Priori; adult/reduced €4/3; ⊙10.30am-5.30pm summer, 10am-4pm Sat & Sun winter) Volterra's 13th-century town hall is the oldest seat of local government in Tuscany. The staircase bears a fresco of the Crucifixion by Piero Francesco Fiorentino and there's a magnificent cross-vaulted council hall. The soaring **bell tower** was significantly rebuilt in the 19th century; get to the top either by lift or stairs.

Palazzo Pretorio
PALACE

(Piazza del Priori; ⊘not open to the public) Forming one side of Volterra's central square, the Palazzo Pretorio was the seat of the local mayor. From it sprouts one of the town's oldest towers, the **Torre del Porcellino** (Piglet's Tower). Look out for the wild boar, protruding from its upper section, which gives the structure its name.

Pinacoteca Comunale
GALLERY

(Via dei Sarti 1; adult/reduced incl Museo Etrusco Guarnacci & Ecomuseo dell'Alabastro €10/6; ⊙ 9am-7pm summer, 10am-4.30pm winter) Local, Sienese and Florentine art holds sway in this modest collection in the Palazzo Minucci Solaini. Taddeo di Bartolo's *Madonna Enthroned with Child* (1411) is exquisite, while Rosso Fiorentino's *Deposition from the Cross* (1521) appears strikingly, surprisingly, modern.

Ecomuseo dell'Alabastro
MUSEUM

(Via dei Sarti 1; adult/reduced incl Museo Etrusco Guarnacci & Pinacoteca Comunale €10/6; ⊘9am-7pm summer, 10am-4.30pm winter) As befits a town that's hewn the material from nearby quarries since Etruscan times, Volterra is the proud possessor of an alabaster museum. It's an intriguing exploration of everything related to the rock, from production and working to commercialisation. Contemporary creations feature strongly; there are also choice examples from Etruscan times onwards as well as a re-created artisan's workshop.

Roman Theatre
ARCHAEOLOGICAL SITE

(Via Francesco Ferrucci; admission €3.50; ⊙10.30am-5.30pm summer, 10am-4.30pm winter)

> ### ⓘ VOLTERRA COMBINED TICKET
>
> A *biglietto cumulativo* (adult/reduced €10/6) gives admission to Volterra's Museo Etrusco Guarnacci, the Pinacoteca Comunale and the Ecomuseo dell'Alabastro.

One of Italy's finest and best-preserved Roman theatres makes for an evocative site, with its grassy ranks of seating and towering columns. It was commissioned in the 1st century BC and could hold up to 2000 spectators. Today the sloping seating area (*cavea*), orchestra pit and stage are still clearly discernible. If you're not that keen on Roman ruins, though, do note there's a great view of the theatre from (free to access) Via Lungo Le Mura del Mandorlo.

⫸ Tours

★ Volterra by Night
WALKING TOUR

(www.volterratur.it/en; adult/child €10/free; ⊘weekly mid-Jun–mid-Sep) Fabulously atmospheric, in-the-dark meanderings amid Volterra's improbably small alleyways and Gothic archetecture. Tours last 90 minutes, start at 9.30pm, and have to be booked by 4pm the same day.

New Moon Tour
WALKING TOUR

(⫏0588 8 60 99; www.newmoonofficialtour.com; tours €30) Fans of Stephanie Meyer's *Twilight* series adore discovering the clock tower, alleyways and arches that Edward and Bella career around in the *New Moon* vampire novel. These evening tours tend to run twice-monthly in April and May, and weekly in July and August. Tickets must be prebooked – the price includes an *aperitivo* and a surprise or two...

Volterra Walking Tour
WALKING TOUR

(⫏0588 08 62 01; www.volterrawalkingtour.com; tours €10; ⊘6pm Apr-Jul & Sep-Oct) An enjoyable one-hour English-language exploration of the city's Etruscan, Roman and Medieval past. It leaves from Piazza Martiri della Libertà. Bookings aren't necessary; payment is cash only.

⫸ Festivals & Events

Volterra AD 1398
CULTURAL

(www.volterra1398.it; day pass adult/reduced €10/6) On the third and fourth Sundays of August, the citizens of Volterra roll back the calendar some 600 years, take to the streets in period costume and celebrate all the fun of a medieval fair.

Volterragusto
FOOD

(www.volterragusto.com) Events in mid-March, late-October and early-November showcase local produce, including cheese, white truffles, olive oil and chocolate.

Volterra

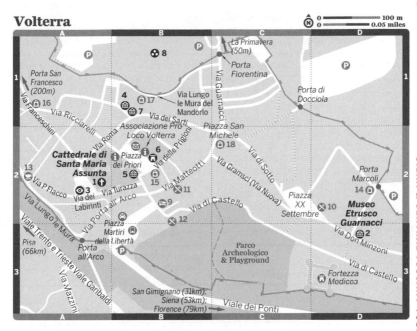

Volterra

◎ Top Sights

◎ Sights

🛏 Sleeping

✖ Eating

🍷 Drinking & Nightlife

🛍 Shopping

🛏 Sleeping

★ Podere San Lorenzo
AGRITURISMO €

(☎ 0588 3 90 80; www.agriturismo-volterra.it; Via Allori 80; B&B d €100, 2-/3-/4-bed apt without breakfast €105/135/160; 🛜 🏊) In this tranquil model of slow tourism you dip straight into a rural idyll. An alluring spring-fed biological swimming pool sits steps away from an enviable veg garden. Apartments (two with private terraces) and rooms are chock-full of history – in the oldest the 'new' beams are 500 years old. Gourmet dinners (per person €30 including wine) are served in a former 12th-century chapel.

Walking, biking and hands-on olive-oil production opportunities are available, as are cooking classes given by chef Mariana (per person €100). It's set on an olive farm some 3km outside Volterra. Arriving on the SS68 from Siena, Florence and San Gimignano, you'll pass a sculpture of a red circle at the entrance to town and should then turn right into the narrow lane after the car saleyard.

★ La Primavera
B&B €

(☎ 0588 8 72 95; www.affittacamere-laprimavera. com; Via Porta Diana 15; s/d/tr €50/75/100; ☺ mid-Apr–mid-Nov; 🅿 🛜) Fittingly for a former alabaster workshop, some of the bedrooms in this home-style B&B feature vast carved fireplaces. Otherwise this is a cosy affair, with a communal lounge, pretty garden, polished parquet floors and soothing pastel colour schemes – choose from violet, yellow, green or blue. It's just outside the city walls, a 10-minute walk from Piazza dei Priori. No credit cards.

Molina d'Era HOTEL €
(☑ 0588 3 32 20; www.molinodera.com; Molina d'Era; SR439; s €59-69, d €69-79; ☺ closed Jan, Feb and Sun-Thu Mar; Ⓟ ☎) Sometimes people make the place. A pink-painted, 1990s construction, this building won't win heritage Tuscan farmhouse of the year. But the warmth of the welcome from the exuberant sisters who run it, the community feel of the restaurant and the quality of the home-cooking make it absolutely worth staying. And the coffee and homemade *amaretti* are gorgeous. Love it.

Nazionale PENSION €
(☑ 0588 8 62 84; www.hotelnazionale-volterra.it; Via Dei Marchesi 11; s/d €65/88; ☎) A proper old-fashioned *pensione*, complete with smiling *signora*, creaking lift, basic but clean rooms, decent breakfast spread and a great, in-town location.

Chiosco delle Monache HOSTEL €
(☑ 0588 8 66 13; www.ostellovolterra.it; Via del Teatro 4, Località San Girolamo; dm €18, B&B s/d €53/69; ☺ mid-Mar–Oct; Ⓟ ☎) Opened in 2009 after a major renovation, this excellent private hostel occupies a 13th-century monastery complete with a frescoed refectory where breakfast is served. Airy rooms overlook the cloisters and have good beds and bathrooms; dorms sleep up to six. Breakfast (for those in dorms) costs €6. It's 1km away from the centre of town.

Local buses from Piazza Martiri della Libertà stop right outside the entrance (€1). Reception is open 8am to noon and 5pm to 11pm.

🍴 Eating & Drinking

L'Incontro CAFE €
(Via G Matteotti 18; sandwiches €2.50-3.50; ☺ 7am-1am Thu-Tue; ☎) L'Incontro's rear *salone* is a top spot to grab a quick antipasto plate or *panino* for lunch, and its front bar area is always crowded with locals enjoying a coffee or *aperitivo*. The house-baked biscuits are noteworthy – try the chewy and nutty *brutti mai buoni* ('ugly but good') or its alabaster-coloured cousin, *ossi di morto* (bones of the dead). There's a short but sound selection of Tuscan wines by the glass (€3 to €8).

La Carabaccia TUSCAN €€
(☑ 0588 8 62 39; www.lacarabacciavolterra.it; Piazza XX Settembre 4-5; meals €25; ☺ noon-2.30pm & 7.30-9.30pm, closed Mon Oct-Easter; ☑) Sisters Sara, Lalla and Patrizia have put their heart and soul into this fantastic trattoria with a coutry-style interior and attractive front terrace. It's the city's best lunch option and is named after a humble Tuscan vegetable soup (one of the specialities of the house). The small menu changes daily according to the pick of the offerings from local producers.

⭐ **Ristorante-Enoteca Del Duca** TUSCAN €€
(☑ 0588 8 15 10; www.enoteca-delduca-ristorante. it; Via di Castello 2; 5-course tasting menus €45; ☺ 12.30-3pm & 7.30-10pm Wed-Mon; ☑) Volterra's acclaimed fine-dining establishment serves traditional Tuscan dishes in its vaulted dining areas and lovely rear courtyard. It has an excellent wine list – not surprising considering the owner has his own vineyard (try his Giusto Alle Balze merlot).

Caffè dei Fornelli CAFE, BAR
(☑ 0588 8 05 96; www.caffedeifornelli.it; Piazza dei Fornelli 3; ☺ 9am-11pm, closed Thu in winter) A bohemian set congregates here, drawn by genial host Carlo Bigazzi, cheap house wine (€1.50 per glass), live jazz, poetry readings and exhibitions. The cafe interior is pleasant, but the most sought-after tables are on the street outside.

🛍 Shopping

Volterra's centuries-old heritage as an alabaster mining and working town ensures plenty of shops specialise in hand-carved alabaster items. The **Cooperativa Artieri dell'Alabastro** (www.artierialabastro.it; Piazza dei Priori 5; ☺ 10am-6pm) showcases the impressive work of 23 local alabaster artisans in a roomy town-centre shop. The showroom of craftsman **Paolo Sabatini** (www.paolosabatini.com; Via G Matteotti 56; ☺ variable) is a smaller, more intimate affair. To watch alabaster being carved, head to **alab'Arte** (www.alabarte.com; Via Orti San Agostino 28; ☺ 10am-12.30pm & 3-6pm Mon-Sat).

For more information about artisans in Volterra, see www.arteinbottegavolterra.it.

Emporio del Gusto FOOD
(Via San Lino 2; ☺ 7.30am-1pm Tue, 7.30am-1pm & 5-8pm Wed-Fri, 9.30am-1pm Sat) A feast of local goodies stacks the shelves in this *comune*-sponsored food co-op. Look out for olive-oil products (including toiletries), fresh milk and yoghurt, cheese, vegetables, locally grown saffron, truffles, pasta, bread and wine.

Fabula Etrusca JEWELLERY
(www.fabulaetrusca.it; Via Lungo Le Mura del Mandorlo 10; ☉10am-7pm Easter-Christmas) Distinctive pieces in 18-carat gold – many based on Etruscan designs – are handmade in this workshop on the city's northern walls.

ⓘ Information

Tourist Office (☏ 0588 8 60 99; www.volterratur.it; Piazza dei Priori 19; ☉9.30am-1pm & 2-6pm) The extremely efficient tourist office provides free maps, offers a free hotel-booking service and rents out an audioguide tour of the town.

ⓘ Getting There & Around

BUS

The bus station is in Piazza Martiri della Libertà. Buy tickets at *tabacchi* or the volunteer-run **Associazione Pro Loco Volterra** (☏ 0588 8 61 50; www.provolterra.it; Piazza dei Priori 10; ☉9.30am-12.30pm & 3-6pm, hours can vary) office. Note bus services are greatly reduced on Sundays.

CPT (☏ 800 570530; www.cpt.pisa.it) buses connect Volterra with Pisa (€6.10, two hours, up to 10 Monday to Saturday).

You'll need to go to Colle di Val d'Elsa (€2.75, 50 minutes, four Monday to Saturday) to catch one of four connecting services (Monday to Saturday) to San Gimignano (€3.40, 35 minutes), Siena (€3.40, two hours) and Florence (€8.35, two hours).

CAR & MOTORCYCLE

Volterra is accessed via the SR68, which runs between Cecina on the coast and Colle di Val d'Elsa, just off the Siena–Florence *superstrada*.

A ZTL applies in the historic centre. The most convenient car park is beneath Piazza Martiri della Libertà (per hour/day €1.50/11). Whether charges apply in other car parks encircling the town is seasonal and subject to change. The tourist office can advise on the latest.

VAL D'ORCIA

This picturesque agricultural valley is a Unesco World Heritage site, as is the town of Pienza on its northeastern edge. Its distinctive landscape features flat chalk plains out of which rise almost conical hills topped with fortified settlements and magnificent abbeys that were once important staging points on the Via Francigena.

Montalcino & Around

POP 5130

This town is defined by the fruit of vines. Known globally as the home of one of the world's great wines, Brunello di Montalcino, a remarkable number of *enoteche* line its medieval streets. There's history to explore too; the town's efforts to hold out against Florence even after Siena had fallen earned it the title 'the Republic of Siena in Montalcino'.

◉ Sights & Activities

Fortezza HISTORIC BUILDING
(Piazzale Fortezza; courtyard free, ramparts adult/child €4/2; ☉9am-8pm Apr-Oct, 10am-6pm Nov-Mar) This imposing 14th-century structure was expanded under the Medici dukes and now dominates the town's skyline. You can sample and buy local wines in its *enoteca* (tasting of two/three/five Brunellos €9/13/19) and also climb up to the fort's ramparts.

Museo Civico e Diocesano d'Arte Sacra MUSEUM
(☏0577 84 60 14; Via Ricasoli 31; adult/reduced €4.50/3; ☉10am-1pm & 2-5.30pm Tue-Sun) Occupying the former convent of the neighbouring **Chiesa di Sant'Agostino**, this collection of religious art from the town and surrounding region includes a triptych by Duccio and a *Madonna and Child* by Simone Martini. Other artists represented include the Lorenzetti brothers, Giovanni di Paolo and Sano di Pietro.

★Poggio Antico WINERY
(☏0577 84 80 44; www.poggioantico.com; ☉cantina 10am-6pm, restaurant noon-2.30pm & 7-9.30pm Tue-Sun, closed Sun evening winter) Located 5km outside Montalcino on the road to Grosseto, Poggio Antico is a superb foodie one-stop-shop. It makes award-winning wines (try its Brunello Altero or Riserva), conducts free cellar tours in Italian, English and German, offers paid tastings (approx €25 depending on wines) and has an on-site restaurant (meals €40). Book tours in advance.

> ## ⓘ MONTALCINO COMBINED TICKET
> To save a couple of euro for the wine fund, purchase a combined ticket (€6) for entry to the *fortezza*'s ramparts and the Museo Civico e Diocesano d'Arte Sacra. These are available from the tourist office.

SIENA & CENTRAL TUSCANY MONTALCINO & AROUND

✖️ Festivals & Events

International Chamber Music Festival
MUSIC

(www.musica-reale.com) Usually held in July, but postponed for a few years due to finances and damage to the venue. Organisers hope to stage it again from 2016.

Sagra del Tordo
CULTURAL

(www.comunedimontalcino.it; ⊘Oct) A procession and traditional archery competition held on the last weekend in October.

🛏️ Sleeping

★ Il Palazzo
B&B €

(✐ 0577 84 91 10; www.ilpalazzomontalcino.it; Via Panfilo Dell'Oca 23; d €75-80; P 🛜) Il Palazzo manages to both immerse you in aristocratic surroundings and make you feel cosily at home. The rambling 500-year-old building features ornate tile floors, beams, sumptuous tapestries and antique chairs. But it's the friendly welcome and the almost incidental nature of the splendour that really delights. The rates are ridiculously good too.

Hotel Vecchia Oliviera
HOTEL €€

(✐ 0577 84 60 28; www.vecchiaoliviera.com; Via Landi 1; s €70-85, d €120-190; P ❄️ 🛜 ≋) Chandeliers, elegant armchairs, polished wooden floors and rich rugs lend this converted oil mill a refined air. The pick of the 11 rooms comes with hill views and a jacuzzi, the pool is in an attractive garden setting, and the terrace has wraparound views.

Hotel Il Giglio
HOTEL €€

(✐ 0577 84 65 77; www.gigliohotel.com; Via Soccorso Saloni 5; s €95, d €138-148, apt 2/4 people €100/150; P 🛜) There's a real old-world feel here, something enhanced by the traditional Tuscan fireplace in the lounge and the brass bedsteads and arched ceilings upstairs. The views from the windows, looking out over the plains from on high, are captivating.

🍴 Eating & Drinking

★ Il Leccio
TUSCAN €€

(✐ 0577 84 41 75; www.illeccio.net; Costa Castellare 1, Sant'Angelo in Colle; meals €40; ⊘noon-3pm & 7-10pm) Sometimes simple dishes are the hardest to perfect, and perfection is the only term to use when discussing this trattoria in Brunello heartland. Watching the chef make his way between his stove and kitchen garden to gather produce for each order puts a whole new spin on the word 'fresh', and

both the results and the house Brunello are spectacular. Sant'Angelo in Colle is 10km southwest of Montalcino (along Via del Sole) along an unsealed but signed road through vineyards.

★ Osticcio
WINE BAR

(www.osticcio.it; Via Matteotti 23; antipasto plates €7-18, meals €37; ⊘noon-4pm & 7-11pm Fri-Wed, plus noon-7pm Thu summer) In a town overflowing with *enoteche*, this is definitely one of the best. A huge selection of Brunello and its more modest sibling Rosso di Montalcino accompanies tempting dishes such as marinated anchovies, *cinta senese* (Tuscan pork) crostini, and pasta with pumpkin and pecorino. The panoramic view, meanwhile, almost upstages it all.

Fiaschetteria Italiana 1888
CAFE

(Piazza del Popolo 6; ⊘7.30am-midnight, closed Thu winter) You could take a seat in the slender square outside this atmosphere-laden *enoteca*-cafe, but then you'd miss its remarkable 19th-century decor – all brass, mirrors and ornate lights. It's been serving coffee and glasses of Brunello to locals since 1888 (hence the name) and is still chock-full of charm.

ℹ️ Information

Tourist Office (✐ 0577 84 93 31; www.prolocomontalcino.com; Costa del Municipio 1; ⊘10am-1pm & 2-5.50pm) The tourist office is just off the main square and can book cellar-door visits and accommodation.

ℹ️ Getting There & Away

BUS

Siena Mobilità buses (€5, 1½ hours, six daily Monday to Saturday) run to/from Siena.

CAR & MOTORCYCLE

From Siena, take the SS2 (Via Cassia); after Buonconvento, turn off onto the SP45. There's plenty of parking around the *fortezza* (€1.50 per hour 8am to 8pm).

Pienza

POP 2130

Pretty Pienza is a true one-off. This once sleepy hamlet was transformed when, in 1459, Pope Pius II began turning his home village into an ideal Renaissance town. The result is magnificent – the church, papal palace, town hall and accompanying buildings in and around Piazza Pio II went up in just four years and haven't been remodelled

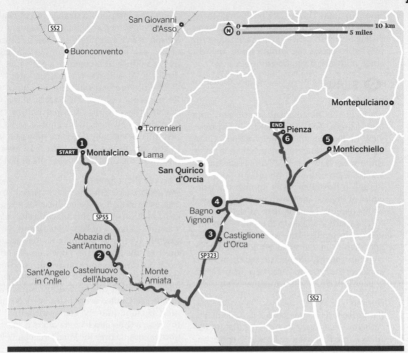

🏃 Driving Tour
Exploring the Val d'Orcia

START MONTALCINO
END PIENZA
LENGTH 55KM; ONE DAY

From ❶ **Montalcino**, perhaps having breakfasted in Fiaschetteria Italiana 1888, pick up the SP55 south, which undulates past vineyards and olive groves. Soon the elegant ❷ **Abbazia di Sant'Antimo** (p161) appears on your right. Park up beside it to drink in its beauty and wander the grounds. Then, from the crossroads by the abbey entrance, pick up the SP55 (signed Castiglione d'Orcia), then the SP323. These roads ride a ridge providing sweeping Val d'Orcia views, before twisting down then up through a quintessentially Tuscan landscape: honey-yellow farmhouses set amid rows of cypress trees and vines.

Near Castiglione d'Orcia the crisply geometric lines of the ❸ **Rocca d'Orcia** (also called the Rocca di Tentennano) loom into view. This part-13th-century fortress clings to a limestone spur: follow signs to park beneath it and clamber up for a closer look, both at the castle and the landscape laid out like a living map far below.

Next, the SP323 swoops down amid more panoramic views. Motor to ❹ **Bagno Vignoni** to stroll the fine town square, which frames a vast thermal water-filled basin. If you haven't booked for lunch at the next stop, Monticchiello, consider one of the *osterie* here. Back on the road, take the (signed) right turn towards Monticchiello to enter the valley you saw from the high hills. Here a series of minor roads, straight as arrows and lined with cypresses, sweep past farms.

At tiny ❺ **Monticchiello** (p162) take in the narrow streets, picturesque squares and panoramic views of the Val d'Orcia; best appreciated from the terrace of the Osteria La Porta (note: it's best to book).

Pick up signs for ❻ **Pienza** (p161); a comfortable cruise that sees the town's turreted skyline become ever more impressive as you climb nearer. Park then explore this extraordinary piece of 15th-century town planning. Check into the excellent La Bandita Townhouse, then settle down for an alfresco meal at Osteria Sette di Vino where, at last, the driver can also enjoy the wine.

since. In 1996 Unesco added Pienza to its World Heritage list, citing the revolutionary vision of urban space. Pienza's uniqueness inevitably draws big summertime crowds; come midweek if you possibly can.

◉ Sights

Piazza Pio II   PIAZZA
Stand in this magnificent square and spin 360 degrees. You've just taken in an overview of Pienza's major monuments. Gems of the Renaissance constructed in a mere three years between 1459 and 1462, they're arranged according to the urban design of Bernardo Rossellino, who applied the principles of Renaissance town planning devised by his mentor, Leon Battista Alberti.

The space available to Rossellino was limited, so to increase the sense of perspective and dignity of the great edifices he'd been commissioned to design, he set them off at angles to the cathedral around a magnificently paved piazza. It was a true masterstroke.

Duomo   CATHEDRAL
(Piazza Pio II; ⊙8.30am-1pm & 2.15-6.30pm) The cathedral that forms Pienza's focal point features a fine Renaissance facade in travertine stone. The interior is a strange mix of Gothic and Renaissance styles and contains a collection of five altarpieces painted by Sienese artists, as well as a superb marble tabernacle by Rossellino – this contains a relic of St Andrew the Apostle, Pienza's patron saint.

The *duomo* was built on the site of the Romanesque Chiesa di Santa Maria, of which little remains. A papal bull of 1462 forbade any changes to the church, so its appearance is virtually the same now as it was in the Middle Ages. The Casa dei Canonici (House of the Church Canons) sits next door.

Palazzo Piccolomini   PALACE
(www.palazzopiccolominipienza.it; guided tours adult/reduced €7/5; ⊙10am-6.30pm Tue-Sun summer, to 4.30pm winter) This magnificent palace was the residence of Pope Pius II, and is considered Bernardo Rossellino's masterpiece. Built on the site of the pope's family houses, it features a fine courtyard, handsome staircase and the former papal apartments, which are filled with period furnishings and minor art. Guided tours leave every 30 minutes; peeking into the courtyard is free. To the rear, a three-level loggia offers a spectacular panorama over the Val d'Orcia far below.

BRUNELLOPOLI

In 2008 Montalcino drew the attention of the international wine world when allegations emerged that a number of local producers had secretly adulterated their vintages of Brunello di Montalcino with 'foreign' grapes such as merlot and cabernet sauvignon. The Disciplinare di Produzione dei Vini a Denominazione di Origine Controllata (Law Controlling Wine Appellations in Italy) decrees, by law, that Brunello must be 100% Sangiovese, so suggestions of a breach were taken extremely seriously by the government, wine industry and international wine media.

A huge investigation followed, with some vineyards quarantined and thousands of litres of wine seized for inspection. Those under investigation denied any wrongdoing and there were no suggestions of any health risks, but as a result of the claims the US temporarily blocked some imports of Brunello, hitting Montalcino's economy hard (approximately 25% of each vintage ends up in the States). The local industry's reputation suffered dramatically as a consequence.

The Consorzio del Vino Brunello, the peak consortium of local producers, has since taken steps to prevent future allegations, including increasing the monitoring of wine sales and drafting a code of ethics. The scandal – known as Brunellopoli or Brunellogate – also raised the whole question of whether winemakers should be able to vary the DOCG decree and add other grapes to broaden Brunello's appeal, particularly for palates attuned to New World wines. Heated debates have occurred about whether upholding tradition equates to halting progress.

The vast majority of the consortium's 700-odd members voted to keep the 100% local Sangiovese rule, arguing that it is the purest expression of *terroir* and the wine's strongest claim to quality and marketability. They also say that allowing blending would simply be another step towards global wine homogenisation. Proponents of change argue that blending with other varieties makes economic sense and leads to the creation of better wines.

Only one thing is sure: the debate is unlikely to be resolved any time soon.

ABBAZIA DI SANT'ANTIMO

The beautiful, Romanesque **Abbazia di Sant'Antimo** (www.antimo.it; Castelnuovo dell'Abate; ☉10.15am-12.30pm & 3-6.30pm Mon-Sat, 9.15-10.45am & 3-6pm Sun) `FREE` lies in an isolated valley just below the village of Castelnuovo dell'Abate, 11km from Montalcino. It's best visited in the morning, when the sun, streaming through the windows, creates an almost surreal atmosphere. It's impressive too at night, when it's lit up like a beacon.

Tradition tells us Charlemagne founded the original monastery here in 781. The exterior, built in pale travertine stone, is simple except for the stone carvings, which include various fantastical animals. Inside, study the capitals of the columns lining the nave, especially the one representing Daniel in the lion's den (second on the right as you enter). Below it is a particularly intense polychrome 13th-century Madonna and Child and there's a haunting 12th-century Crucifixion above the main altar. The real highlight, though, is when the monks perform Gregorian chants during daily services – check the website for times.

Three to four buses per day (€1.50, 15 minutes, Monday to Saturday) connect Montalcino with the village of Castelnuovo dell'Abate.

It's a two- to three-hour walk from Montalcino to the abbey. The route starts next to the police station near the main roundabout in town; many visitors choose to walk there and return by bus – check the timetable with the tourist office (p158).

Palazzo Borgia PALACE
(Palazzo Vescovile; Piazza Pio II) The future Pope Alexander VI, then just Cardinal Roderigo Borgia, modified and enlarged this *palazzo* in 1492. It's home to **Museo Diocesano** (☑0578 74 99 05; Corso Rossellino 30; adult/reduced €4.50/3; ☉10am-1pm & 2-5pm Wed-Mon summer, 10am-4pm Sat & Sun winter), which displays an intriguing miscellany of artworks, illuminated manuscripts, tapestries and miniatures. The tourist office is here as well. Enter via the courtyard onto Corso Rossellino.

Pieve di Corsignano CHURCH
(☉9am-6pm summer, from 10am winter) Look out for this edge-of-town Romanesque church, which dates from the 10th century, when Pienza was called Corsignano, and boasts a strange circular bell tower with eight arched windows. Close inspection reveals the carving of a two-headed siren over the main doorway and scenes of the Three Kings and Nativity over the side door to the right. Inside the church is the baptismal font where Pope Pius II was christened.

🛏 Sleeping

★ Cavalierino AGRITURISMO €
(☑0578 75 87 33; www.cavalierino.it; Via di Poggiano 17; 4-person apt per night/week from €180/1100; P🛏🖥) The first thing that strikes you about Cavalierino is the peace. In this supremely stylish, organic, hilltop *agriturismo*, wicker furniture and contemporary paintings blend artfully with bright rooms and terracotta floors. The top-floor bedrooms offer bewitching views of snaking rows of vines. The pool and sauna add to the appeal, as do the washing machines, well-stocked kitchens (including coffee makers) and racks of luxury smellies. Cavalierino is midway between Pienza and Montepulciano.

★ La Bandita Townhouse BOUTIQUE HOTEL €€€
(☑0578 74 90 05; www.labanditatownhouse.com; Corso Il Rossellino 111; r €250-495, ste €350-695; P🌡@🖥) There's something irresistible about La Bandita, where 12 dreamily luxurious rooms sit inside a Renaissance-era convent – here age-old stone walls meet sleek leather sofas and suspended beds. But the real joy is the ambition: to give guests a taste of Tuscan village life. Its heart-of-Pienza setting helps, as does a gorgeous communal lounge and a laid-back wine bar.

🍴 Eating

Osteria Sette di Vino TUSCAN €
(☑0578 74 90 92; Piazza di Spagna 1; meals €20; ☉12.30-2.30pm & 7.30-10pm Thu-Tue) Known for its *zuppa di pane e fagioli* (bread and white-bean soup), bruschetta and range of local *pecorino* cheese, this simple place is run by the exuberant Luciano, who is immortalised as Bacchus in a copy of Caravaggio's famous painting hanging above the main counter. There's a clutch of tables inside and a scattering outside – book ahead.

Pummarò PIZZA €
(Via del Giglio 4; slice €2.50, pizza €6-10; ☉noon-11pm Tue-Sun; 🖥🍴) Look for brightly painted

LOCAL KNOWLEDGE

BAGNI SAN FILIPPO

Medieval pilgrims walking the Via Francigena from Canterbury to Rome loved pausing in this part of central Tuscany to enjoy a long therapeutic soak in its thermal springs. If you're keen to do the same, consider avoiding the famous thermal institute in Bagno Vignoni and instead head to the open-air cascades in this tiny village 16km southwest of Pienza. You'll find them just uphill from Hotel le Terme – follow signs to 'Fosso Bianco' down a lane for about 150m, or if driving park on the right as you enter the village and take one of the (less steep) well-worn paths down the hillside. Either way your destination is a series of mini pools, fed by hot, tumbling cascades of water. Not unlike a free, alfresco spa.

bicycles in a laneway off Via Rossellino and you'll find this teensy pizzeria, which is a great place to source a cheap and quick snack. There's an innovative range of all-vegetable offerings; the *pizza pummarò* (with cherry tomatoes, *mozzarella di bufala* and basil) is superb.

Townhouse Caffè TUSCAN €€
(☑ 0578 74 90 05; www.labanditatownhouse.com; Via San Andrea 8; dishes €15-20, meals €40; ⊙noon-2.30pm Tue-Sun, 7-10pm daily) The owners believe chefs should chat with diners and shop daily – hence the open kitchen and freshest of ingredients. Your meal might feature battered zucchini flowers stuffed with ricotta and mint, asparagus topped by an egg and truffle shavings, or flavourful Tuscan meats roasted or grilled. The medieval courtyard setting is a delight.

Il Rossellino TUSCAN €€
(☑ 0578 74 90 64; Piazza di Spagna 4; meals €40; ⊙12.30-2.30pm & 7.30-9.30pm Fri-Wed) This old-fashioned place has a small number of tables and a big reputation for its handmade pasta and perfectly cooked meat dishes. The house speciality is handmade *pici* (short pasta) with porcini mushrooms in a rich ragù. There's a great wine list.

🛍 Shopping

La Bottega del Cacio FOOD
(Corso Il Rossellino 64 ; ⊙10am-7.30pm, closed winter) Open the door here and encounter extraordinary aromas – the shelves are piled high with an astonishing 20 to 30 different types of *pecorino* cheese. A selection of salami and wine makes the picnic shopping complete.

❶ Information

Tourist Office (☑ 0578 74 99 05; info.turismo@comune.pienza.si.it; Corso Rossellino 30; ⊙10am-1pm & 2-5pm Wed-Mon summer, 10am-4pm Sat & Sun winter) Located on the ground floor of Palazzo Borgia.

❶ Getting There & Away

BUS

Two Siena Mobilità buses run Monday to Saturday between Siena and Pienza (€5.50, 70 minutes) and nine travel to/from Montepulciano (€2.50). The bus stops are just off Piazza Dante Alighieri. Buy tickets at one of the nearby bars.

CAR & MOTORCYCLE

On summer weekends finding a parking space can be a real challenge as the car park near the centre (€1.50 per hour) fills quickly.

Monticchiello

Semi-comatose and pretty-as-a-picture, the medieval village of Monticchiello crowns a hill 10km south of Pienza.

🛏 Sleeping & Eating

★ La Casa di Adelina B&B €
(☑ 0578 75 51 67; www.lacasadiadelina.eu; Piazza San Martino 3; s €55, d €85-105, 4-bed apt €204; @ 🛜) Laden with art and atmosphere, this place has friendly hosts, a communal lounge with wood stove (a joy in winter) and four delectable, rustic-chic rooms done out in accents of dove-gray and aquamarine. There's also a similarly styled two-bedroom apartment with all the mod-cons that's perfect for an extended stay (when discounts apply).

Osteria La Porta TUSCAN €€
(☑ 0578 75 51 63; www.osterialaporta.it; Via del Piano 3; meals €40; ⊙cafe 9am-12.30pm & 3-7pm, restaurant 12.30-3pm & 7.30-10.30pm, closed Thu winter) When somewhere is this good, it's best to book. Set just inside the town's main gate, the highly regarded eatery has a terrace with panoramic Val d'Orcia views and a legion of local fans. The €23 fixed-lunch menu is stylish and wonderful value, while *spuntini* (snacks) such as bruschetta, olives and cheese plates are served outside usual meal hours.

VAL DI CHIANA

Straddling the provinces of Siena and Arezzo, the scenic Val di Chiana is known for its exquisite food and wine. Dining in its major town, Montepulciano, is a highlight – particularly if you opt for the local Chianina beef with a glass or two of the famous Vino Nobile.

Montepulciano

POP 14,300

Exploring this reclaimed narrow ridge of volcanic rock will push your quadriceps to failure point. When this happens, self-medicate with a generous pour of the highly reputed Vino Nobile while drinking in the spectacular views over the Val di Chiana and Val d'Orcia.

A late-Etruscan fort was the first in a series of settlements here. During the Middle Ages, the town was a constant bone of contention between Florence and Siena. Florence eventually won the day in 1404 and the Marzocco, or lion of Florence, came to replace the she-wolf of Siena as the city's symbol. The new administration invited architects including Michelozzo and Sangallo il Vecchio to design new buildings and endow this Gothic stronghold with some Renaissance grace and style. That intriguing mix alone makes the steep climbs worthwhile.

◉ Sights & Activities

Il Corso
STREET

Montepulciano's main street – called in stages Via di Gracciano, Via di Voltaia, Via dell'Opio and Via d'Poliziano – climbs up the eastern ridge of the town from **Porta al Prato** and loops to meet Via di Collazzi on the western ridge. To reach the centre of town (Piazza Grande) take a dog-leg turn into Via del Teatro.

In Piazza Savonarola, up from the Porta al Prato, is the **Colonna del Marzocca** (Piazza Savonarola), erected in 1511 to confirm Montepulciano's allegiance to Florence. The splendid stone lion, squat as a pussycat atop this column is, in fact, a copy; the original is in the town's Museo Civico. The late-Renaissance **Palazzo Avignonesi** (Via di Gracciano nel Corso 91) is at No 91; other notable buildings include the **Palazzo di Bucelli** (Via di Gracciano nel Corso 73) at No 73 (look for the recycled Etruscan and Latin inscriptions and reliefs on the lower facade), and **Palazzo Cocconi** (Via di Gracciano nel Corso 70) at No 70.

Continuing uphill, you'll find Michelozzo's **Chiesa di Sant'Agostino** (Piazza Michelozzo; ☉ 9am-noon & 3-6pm), with its lunette above the entrance holding a terracotta Madonna and Child, John the Baptist and St Augustine. Opposite, the **Torre di Pulcinella** (Piazza Michelozzo), a medieval tower house, is topped by the town clock and the hunched figure of Pulcinella (Punch of Punch and Judy fame), which strikes the hours. After passing historic Caffè Poliziano (p167), the Corso continues straight ahead and Via del Teatro veers off to the right.

Piazza Grande
PIAZZA

Elegant Piazza Grande is the town's highest point and if you think it looks familiar, it might be because it featured in *New Moon*, the second movie in the *Twilight* series based on Stephanie Meyer's vampire novels. They shot the main crowd scene here, despite the book being set in Volterra.

★ Palazzo Comunale
PALACE

(Piazza Grande; terrace/tower €3/5; ☉ 10am-6pm summer) Built in the 14th-century in Gothic style and remodelled in the 15th century by Michelozzo, the Palazzo Comunale still functions as the town hall. The main reasons to head inside are the extraordinary views from the panoramic terrace and the tower – from the latter you can see as far as Pienza, Montalcino and even, on a clear day, Siena.

Duomo
CATHEDRAL

(Piazza Grande; ☉ 8am-6pm) Montepulciano's late-16th-century *duomo* is striking, largely

---

LA BANDITA

Sophisticated urban style melds with stupendous scenery at **La Bandita** (☎ 333 4046704; www.la-bandita.com; d €195-600; ☉ Mar-Dec; P ✳ @ ☎ ✉), a rural retreat set amid working sheep farms in one of the most stunning sections of the Val d'Orcia. Owned and operated by former NYC music executive John Voigtmann and his travel-writer wife (non–Lonely Planet, we hasten to add), it offers supremely stylish rooms, amenities galore (we love the Ortigia toiletries), wonderful meals and impressive levels of personalised service.

Put simply, it's the type of retreat we all fantasise about owning, but perhaps can't quite afford. It's also the perfect base for nearby Pienza, Montepulciano and Montalcino.

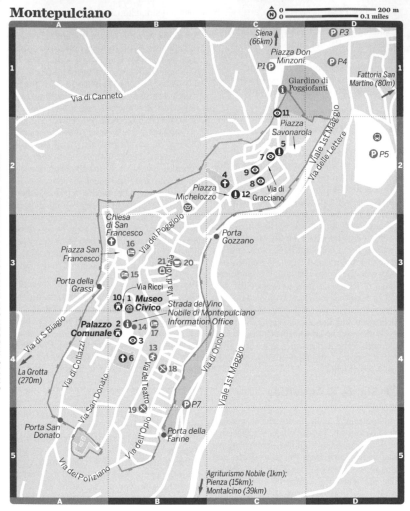

because its unfinished facade gives the building an organic, heavily weathered look. Inside track down Taddeo di Bartolo's ornate *Assumption* triptych (1401), behind the high altar.

★**Museo Civico** MUSEUM, ART GALLERY
(www.museocivicomontepulciano.it; Via Ricci 10; adult/reduced €5/3; ☉10am-1pm & 3-6pm Tue-Sun summer, Sat & Sun only winter) Montepulciano's modest museum and pinacoteca have recently had a curatorial dream come true: a painting in their collections has been attributed to Caravaggio. The masterpiece is a characteristic *Portrait of a Gentleman*. Worth the entrance fee alone, it's accompanied by high-tech, touch-screen interpretation, which allows you to explore details of the painting, its restoration and diagnostic attribution.

Via Ricci STREET
From the Piazza Grande, Via Ricci runs past **Palazzo Ricci** (www.palazzoricci.com; Via Ricci 9-11), now home to a German music academy. The street ends in **Piazza San Francesco**, where you can admire views of the Val di Chiana.

★**Cantina del Redi** WINE TASTING
(Via Ricci; fees for tastings; ☉10.30am-7pm mid-Mar–early Jan, Sat & Sun only early Jan–mid-Mar) Arguably the most evocative of the town's wine cellars,

Montepulciano

Redi's lie at the foot of a steep winding staircase. Here immense vaulted stone encasements surround two-storey-high barrels. Dimly lit and hushed, it's like a cathedral of wine. Entry is free; fees only apply if you opt for tastings – the prices depend on your choices.

Cantine Contucci   WINE TASTING
(www.contucci.it; Via del Teatro 1; fees for tastings; ☉9.30am-12.30pm & 2.30-6pm Mon-Fri, from 9.30am Sat & Sun) The cellars of Contucci, one of the first producers of Vino Nobile, provide an atmospheric insight into this region's rich heritage. Entry is free and leads into arched enclaves stacked high with vast barrels of wine. There's supposed to be a fee for tasting, but – happily – you're quite likely to be offered a few samples for free.

🎓 Courses & Tours

Strada del Vino Nobile di Montepulciano   TOUR
(☎0578 71 74 84; www.stradavinonobile.it; Piazza Grande 7) The office of the Strada del Vino Nobile di Montepulciano organises tours and courses, including cooking courses (€60 to €180), vineyard tours (€30 to €115), Slow Food tours (€100 to €155), wine-tasting lessons (€40) and walking tours in the vineyards culminating in a wine tasting (€45 to €60).

🎉 Festivals & Events

Fondazione Cantiere   PERFORMING ARTS
(www.fondazionecantiere.it; Jul) Performances of opera, theatre and classical and contemporary music, in venues throughout the town.

Bruscello Festival   MUSIC
(www.bruscello.it; Aug) This four-day, open-air theatre and music festival is held in Piazza Grande, in front of Montepulciano's *duomo*, in mid-August.

Bravio delle Botti   CULTURAL
(www.braviodellebotti.com; ☉Aug) Members of the city's eight *contrade* push 80kg wine barrels uphill in this race held on the last Sunday in August. There are also Renaissance-themed celebrations during the week before.

Festival of Chamber Music   MUSIC
(www.palazzoricci.com; Aug & Sep) Held at Palazzo Ricci in late-August and September.

🛏 Sleeping

Camere Bellavista   HOTEL €
(☎0578 75 73 48; www.camerebellavista.it; Via Ricci 25; d €75-100; P🖥) As this excellent budget hotel is four stories tall and sits on the edge of the old town, the views live up to its name. The styling is heritage rustic with exposed beams, hefty wooden furniture, brass bedsteads and smart new bathrooms. The owner isn't resident, so phone ahead to be met with the key. No breakfast.

★**Locanda San Francesco**   B&B €€
(☎0578 75 87 25; www.locandasanfrancesco.it; Piazza San Francesco 3; d €160-250; P❄@🖥) There's only one downside to this B&B: once you check into this supremely welcoming, 14th century *palazzo*, you might never want to go. The feel is elegant but also homely: refined furnishings meet well-stocked bookshelves; restrained fabrics are teamed with

fluffy bathrobes. The best room has superb views over the Val d'Orcia on one side and the Val di Chiana on the other.

★**Fattoria San Martino**   AGRITURISMO **€€**

(☑0578 71 74 63; www.fattoriasanmartino.it; Via di Martiena 3; r €140-180; ⊘closed Dec-Easter; **P**🐾🛋️) 🐾 Dutch-born Karin and Italian Antonio met when working in Milan's high-velocity fashion industry, but eventually decided organic farming was more to their liking than haute couture. The homespun-chic rooms in this rebuilt 12th-century farmhouse and purpose-built annexe are sure to please, as will the all-vegetarian meals (dinner €35 plus wine), pretty garden, biological filtered pool and emphasis on sustainability.

Meublé Il Riccio   B&B **€€**

(☑0578 75 77 13; www.ilriccio.net; Via Talosa 21; s €80, d €100-110, ste €150-180; **P**❄️@🛋️) It's hard to imagine a more atmospheric place to stay: at Il Riccio you're surrounded by centuries-old stone, inner courtyards, heritage furniture and creaking doors. It's been in the same family since the 1200s and is right in the heart of the upper old town. There's an impressive breakfast salon and a terrace with a spectacular view. Breakfast €8.

Agriturismo Nobile   AGRITURISMO **€€**

(☑0578 75 73 98; www.agriturismonobile.it; Strada per Chianciano; d €90-99, 2-/4-/6-person apt per week €780/870/1250; **P**🛋️) In the 15th century they were sheds and hen houses; now they're five rustic-chic apartments with lofty ceilings

---

FATTORIA LE CAPEZZINE
·······················

Fattoria Le Capezzine (☑0578 72 43 04; www.avignonesi.it; Via Colonica 1, Valiano di Montepulciano; ⊘9am-5pm Mon-Fri, from 11am Sat & Sun, no tours Dec-Feb) wine estate, 15km northeast of Montepulciano, is part of the legendary Avignonesi company, which produces Vino Nobile di Montepulciano, Rosso di Montepulciano, Vin Santo, grappa and olive oil. Spread over 19 hectares, the estate is known for its 'Round Vineyard', which was designed to establish to what extent the quality of wine is influenced by density of planting and type of rootstock.

Book in advance to enjoy a two-hour **tour** (www.avignonesi.it; standard/premium tasting €18/40; ⊘tours Mon-Fri Mar-Nov, plus Sat May-Oct) of the vineyards, ageing cellars and *vinsantaia* (where Vin Santo is aged), followed by a tasting of Avignonesi wines.

---

and pared-down bathrooms. Some have big open fireplaces, many feature grandstand views of Montepulciano, and families will love the table tennis and table-football. It's around 1km south of town, beside the main road, so it's not totally tranquil. There are also five cheaper, simpler (and noisier) rooms in the 15th-century farmhouse itself.

✖️ Eating & Drinking

★**Osteria Acquacheta**   TUSCAN **€€**

(☑0578 71 70 86; www.acquacheta.eu; Via del Teatro 2; meals €25; ⊘12.15-4pm & 7.30-10.30pm Wed-Mon) Hugely popular with locals and tourists alike, this bustling *osteria* specialises in *bistecca alla fiorentina* (chargrilled T-bone steak), which comes to the table in huge, lightly seared and exceptionally flavoursome slabs (don't even *think* of asking for it to be served otherwise). Lunch sittings are at 12.15pm and 2.15pm; dinner at 7.30pm and 9.15pm.

Cagnano   TRATTORIA **€€**

(☑0578 75 87 57; www.trattoriadicagnano.it; Via dell'opio 30; meals €30; ⊘noon-2.30pm & 7.30-10pm Tue-Sat) An unfussy dining room sets the scene for hearty Tuscan cooking – homemade soups include potato and *pici*; polenta comes with wild boar that's been steeped in Montepulciano Nobile. Meanwhile DOC versions of the wine itself can be sampled by the glass (from €3).

★**La Grotta**   RISTORANTE **€€€**

(☑0578 75 74 79; www.lagrottamontepulciano. it; Via San Biagio 15; meals €44, 6-course tasting menu €48; ⊘12.30-2.30pm & 7.30-10pm Thu-Tue, closed mid-Jan–mid-Mar) The ingredients, and sometimes dishes, may be traditional, but the presentation is full of refined flourishes – artfully arranged Parmesan shavings and sprigs of herbs crown delicate towers of pasta, vegetables and meat. The service is exemplary and the courtyard garden divine. It's just outside town on the road to Chiusi.

E Lucevan Le Stelle   WINE BAR

(www.locandasanfrancesco.it; Piazza San Francesco 5; ⊘noon-11pm mid-Mar–Dec; 🛋️) The decked terrace here is the top spot in Montepulciano to watch the sun go down. Inside squishy sofas, modern art and jazz on the sound system give the place a chilled-out vibe. Dishes (antipasto plates €4.50 to €8, *piadinas* (flatbreads) €6, pastas €6.50 to €9) are simple but tasty, and there's Montepulciano Nobile

ORVIETO

This Umbrian city looms over the A1 *superstrada* (expressway) in spectacular fashion. Perched on a craggy volcanic landform, its skyline is dominated by a huge **cathedral** (☑ 0763 34 24 77; www.opsm.it; Piazza Duomo 26; admission €3; ⊙ 9.30am-6pm Mon-Sat, 1-5.30pm Sun, shorter hours winter), one of the great masterpieces of medieval architecture. Construction of the cathedral commenced in 1290 and took three centuries to complete. Its facade is perhaps the most beautiful to grace any Italian church and inside the stark but ethereally beautiful interior is Luca Signorelli's *The Last Judgment* fresco cycle. Signorelli began work on these extraordinary frescoes in 1499, and Michelangelo is said to have taken inspiration from them.

The **tourist office** (☑ 0763 34 17 72; www.orvieto.regioneumbria.eu; Piazza Duomo 24; ⊙ 8.15am-1.50pm & 4-7pm Mon-Fri, 10am-1pm & 3-6pm Sat & Sun) is opposite the cathedral; nearby sits **I Sette Consoli** (☑ 0763 34 39 11; www.isetteconsoli.it; Piazza Sant'Angelo 1a; meals around €45, 6-course tasting menu €42; ⊙ 12.30-3pm & 7.30-10pm, closed Wed & dinner Sun), one of Umbria's best restaurants – it specialises in intensely flavoured pasta, meat and fish creations; the six-course tasting menu is a treat.

Orvieto is a mere one-hour drive from both Montepulciano and Arezzo, so can easily be visited in a day if you're staying in the Val di Chiana. Trains run to/from Florence (*regionale veloce*, €15, 2¼ hours, eight daily) and Rome (*regionale veloce* €8, 80 minutes, eight daily). From the train station you'll need to take the *funicolore* (cable car; €1 each way, €0.80 with train ticket; every 10 minutes 8.15am to 8pm daily) up to the town centre. The car park next to the *funicolore* station in the upper town charges €1.50 per hour between 8am and 8pm.

by the glass (€5 to €7). Or opt for a tasting flight featuring three wines (€15), choose from Tuscany (Chianti, Montepulciano Nobile and Brunello) or Montepulciano (Rosso, Nobile and Nobile Riserva).

Caffè Poliziano   CAFE
(Via di Voltaia 27; ⊙ 7am-8pm Mon-Thu, to 10pm Fri, to 11pm Sat, to 9pm Sun; 🛜) Established as a cafe in 1868, Poliziano was lovingly restored to its original form 20 years ago and is the town's favourite cafe. A sit-down coffee is expensive, but is worth the outlay if you score one of the tiny, precipitous balcony tables.

🛍 Shopping

Maledetti Toscani   ACCESSORIES
(Via di Voltaia 44-46; ⊙ 10.30am-1.30pm & 3.30-6.30pm) In the leather goods business since 1848, local Maledetti manufactures good-quality shoes, bags, coats and belts. This is the women's store; the men's store is at number 40.

❶ Information

Strada del Vino Nobile di Montepulciano Information Office (☑ 0578 71 74 84; www.stradavinonobile.it; Piazza Grande 7; ⊙ 10am-1pm & 3-6pm Mon-Fri) Books accommodation and arranges courses and tours.
Tourist Office (☑ 0578 75 73 41; www.proloco montepulciano.it; Piazza Don Minzoni 1; ⊙ 9.30am-12.30pm & 3-6pm Mon-Sat, 9.30am-

12.30pm Sun) Reserves last-minute accommodation (in person only), offers internet access (€3.50 per hour), supplies town maps, can advise on mountain bike and scooter rental (€25 to €50) and sells bus and train tickets (€1 commission applies for train tickets).

❶ Getting There & Around

BUS
The bus station is next to Car Park No 5. Siena Mobilità runs four buses daily between Siena and Montepulciano (€6.60, one hour) stopping at Pienza (€2.50) en route. There are three services per day to/from Florence (€11.20, 90 minutes).

Regular buses connect with Chiusi-Chianciano Terme (€3.40, 40 minutes), from where you can catch a train to Florence (€12.50, two hours, frequent) via Arezzo (€6.40, 50 minutes).

CAR & MOTORCYCLE
Coming from Florence, take the Valdichiana exit off the A1 (direction Bettolle–Sinalunga) and then follow the signs; from Siena, take the Siena–Bettolle–Perugia *superstrada*.

A 24-hour ZTL applies in the historic centre between May and September. In October and April it applies from 8am to 8pm, and from November to March it applies from 8am to 5pm. Check whether your hotel can supply a permit. The most convenient car park is at Piazza Don Minzoni (€1.30 per hour April to October, free November to March), from where minibuses (€1) weave their way up the hill to Piazza Grande.

Southern Tuscany

Best Places to Eat

➡ Il Tufo Allegro (p179)

➡ Il Pellicano (p186)

➡ Grantosco (p183)

➡ La Tana del Brillo Parlante (p173)

➡ La Vecchia Hosteria (p177)

Best Places to Stay

➡ Sant'Egle (p181)

➡ Le Camere del Ceccottino (p179)

➡ La Fattoria di Tatti (p173)

➡ Pieve di Caminino (p177)

➡ Villa Fattoria Granducale (p185)

Why Go?

Despite being barely a blip on many visitors' radars, Southern Tuscany is really a region for the Italy connoisseur. Here you'll encounter the intensely atmospheric Città del Tufa, a trio of still-inhabited hill towns that have been sculpted from volcanic rock since Etruscan times. All around archaeological sites, Renaissance settlements, churches and museums lie waiting to be explored.

Locals are fiercely proud of the traditions and food culture of this, the Maremma region. So you can dine at an innovative Michelin-starred eatery or feast on dishes perfected over the generations, washed down with fine local wine. An embarrassment of natural riches means you can travel from sandy beaches to snowy mountains in just a few hours, passing wildlife-packed marshes and vine-covered slopes. The activities on offer are irresistible: swim, hike, horse ride and mountain bike by day before recharging in secluded *agriturismi* by night.

Road Distances (km)

	Vetulonia	Massa Marittima	Grosseto	Pitigliano
Massa Marittima	38			
Grosseto	52	48		
Pitigliano	129	120	75	
Parco Regionale della Maremma	28	67	20	56

THE ALTA MAREMMA

The Alta (Upper) Maremma starts south of Livorno and continues down to Grosseto, incorporating Massa Marittima and the surrounding Colline Metallifere (metal-producing hills) that are now part of Unesco's European Geopark Network. It also covers inland territory including the hill towns south of the Crete Senesi and the mountainous terrain surrounding Monte Amiata.

Massa Marittima

POP 8670

Drawcards at this tranquil hill town include an eccentric yet endearing jumble of museums, an extremely handsome central piazza and largely intact medieval streets that are blessedly bereft of tour groups.

Briefly under Pisan domination, Massa Marittima became an independent *comune* (city-state) in 1225 but was swallowed up by Siena a century later. A plague in 1348 was followed by the decline of the region's lucrative mining industry, reducing the town to the brink of extinction, a situation made even worse by the prevalence of malaria in surrounding marshlands. Fortunately, the draining of marshes in the 18th century and the re-establishment of mining shortly afterwards brought it back to life.

The town is divided into three districts: the Città Vecchia (Old Town), Città Nuova (New Town) and Borgo (Borough).

◎ Sights & Activities

★ **Cattedrale di San Cerbone** CATHEDRAL
(Piazza Garibaldi; ⊘ noon-7pm summer, to 6pm winter) Presiding over photogenic Piazza Garibaldi (aka Piazza Duomo), Massa Marittima's asymmetrically positioned 13th-century *duomo* is dedicated to St Cerbonius, the town's patron saint, who's always depicted surrounded by a flock of geese. Inside, don't miss the freestanding *Maestà* (Madonna and Child enthroned in majesty; 1316) attributed by some experts to Duccio di Buoninsegna.

The *duomo's* other treasures include a carved marble urn known as the *Arca di San Cerbone* (St Cerbone's Ark; 1324) behind the high altar and an early 14th-century polychrome wooden crucifix carved by Giovanni Pisano on the altar itself.

The facade's main doorway is topped by carved panels depicting scenes from St Cerbonius' life.

★ **Museo di Arte Sacra** MUSEUM
(Museum of Sacred Art; ☑ 0566 90 19 54; www.museiartesacra.net; Corso Diaz 36; adult/reduced €5/3; ⊘ 10am-1pm & 3-6pm Tue-Sun summer, 11am-1pm & 3-5pm Tue-Sun winter) Housed in the former monastery of San Pietro all'Orto,

---

THREE PERFECT DAYS

Day 1: Città del Tufa
In Pitigliano wander centuries-old streets and an **ancient Jewish enclave** before sampling unique regional cuisine: try **La Rocca** or **Hostaria del Ceccottino**. Next, to Sorano and Sovana for Etruscan necropolises and mysterious *vie cave* (sunken roads). Hot and dusty? Detour to **Terme di Saturnia** to soak in free, alfresco thermal pools. Sovana's **Taverna Etrusca** is a classy place to stay.

Day 2: Parco Regionale della Maremma
Head west to **Terenzi** to sample award-winning Morellino di Scansano wine, then hit the **Parco Regionale della Maremma** to walk, cycle or canoe through wild scenery. Enjoy farm experiences at **Agienza Regionale Agricola di Alberese**, perhaps joining the famous Maremmese cowboys on the range. Detour south to the super-quirky **Giardino dei Tarocchi** sculpture garden or make straight for **Il Pellicano** for top-notch eats and sleeps.

Day 3: Massa Marittima
Cruise north to this medieval hill town for narrow streets, handsome piazzas and the **Cattedrale di San Cerbone**, heading to **La Tana del Brillo Parlante** for lunch. Work off some calories exploring the geological sites around **Monterotondo Marittimo** or the Etruscan-era settlement near **Vetulonia**. Where to sleep? **Pieve di Caminino** and **La Fattoria di Tatti** are idyllic Tuscan hideaways.

Southern Tuscany Highlights

1 Riding the range with Maremmese cowboys in the **Parco Regionale della Maremma** (p184).

2 Soaking up thousands of years of history at **Pitigliano** (p177), a hilltop stronghold built from volcanic rock.

3 Embarking on a hike with a difference amid the otherworldly geothermal landscape of **Monterotondo Marittimo** (p176).

4 Taking a free dip in mineral-rich, open-air waters at **Terme di Saturnia** (p181).

5 Walking in the footsteps of Etruscans along the mysterious rock-carved **sunken roads** (p178) around Sovana.

6 Admiring a saucy fresco and one of Tuscany's most magnificent piazzas in **Massa Marittima** (p169).

7 Following tens of thousands of migrating birds to the unspoilt landscapes of the **Riserva Naturale Provinciale Diaccia Botrona** (p184).

8 Exploring exciting **Etruscan excavations** (p177) at the archaeological sites near Vetulonia.

Massa Marittima

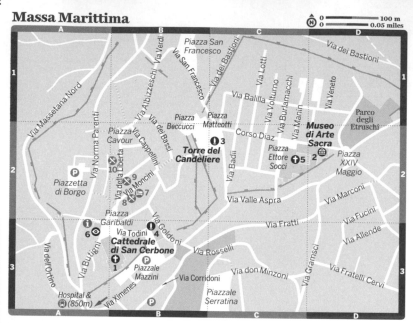

Massa Marittima

this museum houses a splendid *Maestà* (c 1335–37) by Ambrogio Lorenzetti and sculptures by Giovanni Pisano that originally adorned the *duomo's* facade. The collection of primitive grey alabaster bas-reliefs also came from the *duomo*, but originally date from an earlier era.

Some local maps feature the museum as Complesso museale di San Pietro all'Orto.

Museo Archeologico   MUSEUM
(Piazza Garibaldi 1; adult/reduced €3/1.50; ⊘10am-12.30pm & 3.30-7pm Tue-Sun summer, 10am-12.30pm & 3-5pm Tue-Sun winter) The 13th-century **Palazzo del Podestà** houses a dusty archaeological museum where the noteworthy exhibit is *La Stele del Vado all'Arancio,* a simple but compelling stone stela (funeral or commemorative marker) dating from the 3rd millennium BC.

Albero della Fecondità   MONUMENT
(Via Ximenes, off Piazza Garibaldi) FREE A rather risqué surprise lurks underneath this 13th-century former wheat store. Its loggia (balcony) shelters the Fonte dell'Abbondanza (Fountain of Abundance), a now decommissioned public drinking fountain. But it's the extraordinary fresco known as the *Albero della Fecondità* (Fertility Tree) that might make you blush. Look closely to see what type of fruit the tree bears!

★ Torre del Candeliere   TOWER
(Candlestick Tower; Piazza Matteotti; adult/child €3/2; ⊘10am-1pm & 3-6pm Tue-Sun summer, 11am-1pm & 2.30-4.30pm Tue-Sun winter) Climb to the top of this 13th-century, 74m-high tower for stupendous views over the old town.

Arco Senese ARCHITECTURE

(Piazza Matteotti) Massa Marittima's immense, medieval Arco Senese (Sienese Arch) peels away from the old city walls to soar overhead as you pass between the Città Vecchia and Città Nuova.

🎋 Festivals & Events

Balestro del Girifalco CULTURAL

(Contest of the Falcon's Heart; www.societaterzieri massetani.it) This crossbow competition is held twice yearly on the first Sunday after 20 May and on a Sunday in either July or August (usually the second Sunday in August). Twenty-four crossbowmen from the town's three *terzieri* (districts) dress in medieval costume and compete for a golden arrow.

🛏 Sleeping

⭐ La Fattoria di Tatti B&B €

(☑ 0566 91 20 01; www.tattifattoria.it; Via Matteotti 10, Tatti; s €60-80, d €90-115; ⊘ closed Nov–mid-Mar; 🅿 @) La Fattoria di Tatti is imposing – one of those stately Tuscan farmhouses that ranges over four floors. Its weathered 18th-century walls shelter eight simple but stylish rooms, while its position at the summit of the hilltop village of Tatti, 25km southeast of Massa Marittima, ensures mesmerising valley views.

Manager Maria prepares a delicious breakfast and guests are welcome to use the kitchen at other times. A nearby playground and pizzeria/trattoria make it an ideal choice for families.

Residenza d'Epoca Palazzo Malfatti APARTMENT €

(☑ 0566 90 41 81; www.palazzomalfattiresidenza depoca.com; Via Moncini 10; d €68-127, tr €95-148, 6-bed €149-220; 🕾) These seven apartments in an 13th-century *palazzo* overlooking Piazza Garibaldi are an attractive choice for self-catering guests wanting to stay a while (rates drop by 10/15% for the second/third week of stay). The building is brim-full of heritage features, with stone staircases, mullioned windows, wrought-iron furniture and bright rugs on tile floors.

Podere Riparbella AGRITURISMO €€

(☑ 0566 91 55 57; www.riparbella.com; Località Sopra Pian di Mucini; s €82-92, d €164; ⊘ closed early Jan–mid-Apr; 🅿🕾) 🍴 The Swiss owners of this 46-hectare estate, 5km outside town, have built an ecologically sustainable farm operation where they cultivate grapes and olives, and make jams. The 11 guest rooms

are in a charming old building with communal lounge and terrace. A delicious four-course dinner uses home-grown and local products and is included in the price. No credit cards.

🍴 Eating & Drinking

Il Bacchino DELI €

(Via Moncini 8; ⊘ 9am-10pm summer, 10am-1pm & 4-7.30pm Tue-Sat winter) Owner Magdy Lamei may not be a local (he's from Cairo), but it would be hard to find anyone else as knowledgeable and passionate about local artisanal produce. Come here to taste local wines, or to stock up on picnic provisions including jams, cheese and cured meats.

⭐ La Tana del Brillo Parlante TUSCAN €€

(☑ 0566 90 12 74; www.latanadeibrilli.it; Vicolo del Ciambellano 4; meals €32; ⊘ noon-2.30pm & 7-10pm Thu-Tue Dec-Oct) In this enchanting space rustic trinkets are lit by fairy lights. It's billed as the 'smallest *osteria* in Italy' and seats a mere 10 people (another six can squeeze onto tiny alley tables outside). The food ticks every box on the Slow Food checklist, featuring deliciously authentic Maremmese dishes. In summer and at weekends, book well in advance. No credit cards.

L'Osteria da Tronca TUSCAN €€

(☑ 0566 90 19 91; Vicolo Porte 5; meals €32; ⊘ 7.30-10.30pm Thu-Tue Mar-Jul & Sep–mid-Dec, 7.30-10pm Aug; 🍴) Squeezed into a side street, this stone-walled restaurant specialises in the rustic dishes of the Maremma. Specialities include *acquacotta* (a hearty vegetable soup with bread and egg), *tortelli alla maremma* (pasta parcels filled with ricotta and spinach) and *coniglio in porchetta* (roasted stuffed rabbit). It's open for dinner only.

ℹ Information

Tourist Office (☑ 0566 90 27 56; www.alta maremmaturismo.it; Via Todini 3; ⊘ 9.30am-1pm & 2-6.30pm Tue-Sun) Down a side street beneath the Museo Archeologico.

1. Pitigliano (p177)
This spectacular hilltop village sprouts from a volcanic rocky outcrop that towers over the surrounding country.

2. Massa Marittima (p169)
This tranquil hill town boasts an eccentric yet endearing jumble of museums, an extremely handsome central piazza and largely intact medieval streets.

3. Near Porto Ercole, Monte Argentario (p186)
Porto Ercole, on the less-crowded, southern side of Monte Argentario, has a small and attractive harbour nestled between Spanish forts.

THE COLLINE METALLIFERE

Massa Marittima's handsome buildings and artistic treasures are the legacy of the town's location in the centre of Tuscany's Colline Metallifere (metal-producing hills). Mining occurred here for three millennia, and has shaped the region's physical and cultural landscapes – something acknowledged by the addition of the **Parco Nazionale Technologico Archeologico delle Colline Metallifere Grossetane** (National Technological and Archaeological Park of the Colline Metallifere; www.parcocollinemetallifere.it) to Unesco's European Geopark Network.

The national park incorporates many sites, including **Le Biancane** (☑0566 91 70 39; via Poggiarello, Monterotondo Maritime; ⊘information office 10.30am-12.30pm Tue-Fri) **FREE** in Monterotondo Marittimo, a geothermal park 21km north of Massa Marittima where steam has been transformed into power by vapour turbines since 1916, supplying electricity to one million Tuscan households (meeting 25% of Tuscany's energy needs). Visitors can take a two-hour walk through wooded terrain, where steam belches from the earth's crust and clumps of sulphur crystals form.

The **Parco Minerario Naturalistico Gavorrano** (☑0566 84 62 31; www.parco minerario.it; Località Ex Bagnetti, Gavorrano; adult/reduced €8/4; ⊘10am-1pm & 4-7pm Tue-Sun mid-Jun–mid-Sep, Sat & Sun only May–mid-Jun & mid-Sep–Dec) is a museum and education centre in a huge former pyrite mine that operated from 1898 to 1984 and was once Europe's largest mine. A section of the mine's 180km of underground galleries can be visited on a fascinating guided tour incorporating social history commentary and interactive displays.

ⓘ Getting There & Away

BUS
The bus station is near the hospital on Piazza del Risorgimento, 1km down the hill from Piazza Garibaldi. There are four buses, Monday to Saturday, to Grosseto (€4, 1¼ hours) and one, Monday to Saturday, to Siena (€5.50, two hours) at 7.10am. To get to Volterra you'll need to change at Monterotondo Marittima. **Massa Veternensis** (Piazza Garibaldi 18) sells both bus and train tickets.

CAR
There's a convenient car park (€1 per hour during the day, free at night) close to Piazza Garibaldi; head up the hill and you'll find it on your left. There's also a free car park at Piazzetta di Borgo further down the hill.

TRAIN
The nearest train station is in Follonica, 22km southwest of Massa, and is served by a regular shuttle bus (€2.60, 25 minutes, 10 daily).

Vetulonia & Around

Originally an important Etruscan settlement, this windswept hilltop village 23km northwest of Grosseto was colonised by the Romans in 224 BC. It retains important traces of both eras.

⊙ Sights & Activities

★**Museo Civico Archeologico 'Isidoro Falchi'**   MUSEUM
(www.museidimaremma.it; Piazza Vatluna; adult/reduced €4.50/2.50; ⊘10am-1pm & 4-9pm Tue-Sun Jun-Sep, 10am-1pm & 3-6pm Tue-Sun Mar-May) Vetulonia's main piazza boasts spectacular views over the surrounding countryside and is home to this small but extremely impressive museum bringing Etruscan history to life through rich display of artefacts excavated from local Etruscan tombs and settlements. Highlights include the furnishings of the tomb of the *Fibula d'Oro* (Golden Brooch), including the precious brooch itself.

🛏 Sleeping

★**Montebelli Agriturismo & Country Hotel**   AGRITURISMO €€
(☑0566 88 71 00; www.montebelli.com; Località Molinetto Caldana; agriturismo r €110-145, country hotel r €178-225; ⊘closed Jan-end Mar; ℗❋🛜🏊) A country-club feel prevails on this sprawling biodynamic wine and olive-oil estate 10km north of Vetulonia. The facilities are sensational: tennis court, two swimming pools (one indoor, one outdoor), horse-riding lessons, restaurant (five-course dinner adult/child €30/15) and sleek health centre. Choose between cheaper

(but more atmospheric) rooms in the *agriturismo* or deluxe air-con rooms in the modern 'country hotel'.

★ **Pieve di Caminino** AGRITURISMO €€
(📋 0564 56 97 36; www.caminino.com; Via Provinciale di Peruzzo, Roccatederighi; ste €90-180, 4-person apt €180-250; P❄🅿🛏) Few sleeping options can boast a historic atmosphere to equal this now-decommissioned 11th-century monastery 25km northeast of Vetulonia. Set on a 500-hectare estate planted with olive trees and vines, it offers six charmingly decorated two-person suites and two apartments. Each has a panoramic terrace, sitting area and basic kitchen, some also have wi-fi and air-conditioning. Breakfast costs €5 to €10.

✘ Eating

★ **La Vecchia Hosteria** TUSCAN €€
(📋 0566 84 49 80; Viale Marconi 249, Bagno di Gavorrano; meals €31; ⊙ noon-2.30pm & 7-10pm Fri-Wed Feb-Dec) The unassuming exterior of this neighbourhood eatery on Bagno di Gavorrano's main street gives no clue as to the excellence of its kitchen. The handmade pasta is sensational (especially the *tortelli di ricotta*) and the rustic mains pack a flavoursome punch. You'll find the town 14km north of Vetulonia, near the Parco Minerario Naturalistico Gavorrano.

❶ Getting There & Away

Driving to Vetulonia, exit the SS1 at Montepescali/Braccagni (heading towards Braccagni) and follow the SP152 and SP72 uphill to the village.

CITTÀ DEL TUFA

The picturesque towns of Pitigliano, Sovana and Sorano form a triangle enclosing a dramatic landscape where local buildings have been constructed from the volcanic porous rock called tufa since Etruscan times. This area is known as the Città del Tufa (City of the Tufa) or, less commonly, the Paese del Tufa (Land of the Tufa).

Pitigliano

POP 3880

Check your car mirrors before screeching to a halt and indulging in an orgy of photography on the approach to this spectacularly sited hilltop stronghold. Organically sprout-

---

❶ COMBINED TICKET

For Etruscan heritage savings, buy the combined ticket (adult/reduced €6/3) giving entry to the Museo Civico Archeologico di Pitigliano and the Museo Archeologico all'Aperto 'Alberto Manzi' outside town.

---

ing from a volcanic rocky outcrop towering over the surrounding country, Pitigliano is surrounded by gorges on three sides, constituting a natural bastion completed to the east by a fort. Within the town, twisting stairways disappear around corners, cobbled alleys bend tantalisingly out of sight beneath graceful arches and quaint stone houses are crammed next to each other in higgledy-piggledy fashion.

Originally built by the Etruscans, Pitigliano came under Roman rule before becoming a fiefdom of the wealthy Aldobrandeschi and Orsini families. The Orsinis enlarged the fortress, reinforced the defensive walls and built the imposing aqueduct. Their rule came to an end in 1608 when the town was absorbed into the grand duchy of Tuscany under Cosimo I de' Medici.

In 1944, 88 local residents were killed and many buildings were damaged during Allied bombings. A plaque near Piazza della Repubblica commemorates the victims.

◉ Sights & Activities

La Piccola Gerusalemme MUSEUM
(Little Jerusalem; 📋 0564 61 42 30; www.lapiccolagerusalemme.it; Vicolo Manin 30; adult/reduced €4/3; ⊙ 10am-1pm & 2.30-6pm summer, 10am-noon & 3-5pm winter) Head down Via Zuccarelli

---

ETRUSCAN EXCAVATIONS

Scavi di Città (⊙ 10.10am-6.50pm summer, 8.30am-5pm winter, closed Tue & Fri) In 2009 a small team of archaeologists began excavating these foundations of a 2300-year-old Etruscan *domus* (house), located on the main road just below Vetulonia. The team uncovered dry-stone walls, a brick floor, a small terracotta altar, plenty of amphorae and a small fragment of wall fresco. It's thought this is the most intact Etruscan-Roman era villa in existence, and there may be other undiscovered sites nearby.

---

and turn left at a sign indicating 'La Piccola Gerusalemme' to visit this fascinating time capsule of Pitogliano's rich but sadly near-extinct Jewish culture. It incorporates a tiny, richly adorned synagogue (established in 1598 and one of only five in Tuscany), ritual bath, kosher butcher, bakery, wine cellar and dyeing workshops.

Interpretative panels recount the history: in the course of the 16th century, a Jewish community settled in Pitigliano, increasing notably when Pope Pius IV banned Jews from Rome in 1569. Under Medici rule, its members were moved into this tiny ghetto, where they remained until 1772. From then until well into the following century, the local community of 400 flourished, forming the largest Jewish community in Italy and leading to the town being dubbed 'Little Jerusalem'. By the time the Fascists introduced the race laws in 1938, most Jews had moved away; only 80 or so were left and precious few survived the war. Those that did were hidden from the Fascists by locals.

Palazzo Orsini MUSEUM
(0564 61 60 74; www.palazzo-orsini-pitigliano.it; Piazza della Fortezza; adult/reduced €4.50/3.50; 10am-1pm & 3-8pm Tue-Sun summer, 10am-1pm & 3-5pm Tue-Sun winter) Interlinked Piazza Petruccioli and Piazza Garibaldi provide a majestic walkway towards this 13th-century castle, which was enlarged by the ruling Orsinis in the 16th century; became the residence of the local bishop; and is now a museum. Its rooms are filled with an eclectic collection of artworks and local ecclesiastic oddments.

Museo Civico Archeologico di Pitigliano MUSEUM
(0564 61 40 67; Piazza della Fortezza; adult/reduced €3/2; 10am-5pm Mon, Thu & Fri, to 6pm Sat & Sun Jun-Aug, 10am-5pm Sat & Sun Easter-May) Head up the stone stairs to this small but well-run museum which has rich displays of finds from local Etruscan sites. Highlights include some huge intact *bucchero* (black earthenware pottery) urns dating from the 6th century BC and a collection of charming pinkish-cream clay oil containers in the form of small deer.

★ Festivals & Events

Settembre diVino – Festa delle Cantine WINE
(Festival of the Wine Cellars; Sep) The first weekend in September (from Thursday to Sunday) sees the town celebrating its signature Bianco di Pitigliano, a dry and lively white. Local *cantine* (cellars) open specially for tastings; check www.comune.pitigliano.gr.it for details.

VIE CAVE

There are at least 15 *vie cave* (sunken roads) hewn out of tufa in the valleys below Pitigliano. These enormous passages – up to 20m deep and 3m wide – are popularly believed to be sacred routes linking Etruscan necropolises and other religious sites. A more mundane explanation is that these strange prehistoric corridors were used to move livestock or as some kind of defence, allowing people to flit from village to village unseen. Whatever the reason, every spring on the night of the equinox (19 March) there is a torch-lit procession down the Via Cava di San Giuseppe, which culminates in a huge bonfire in Pitigliano's Piazza Garibaldi. Known as the **Torciata di San Giuseppe**, the procession serves as a symbol of purification and renewal marking the end of winter.

Two particularly good examples of *vie cave*, the Via Cava di Fratenuti and the Via Cava di San Giuseppe, are found 500m west of Pitigliano on the road to Sovana. Fratenuti has high vertical walls and Etruscan markings, and San Giuseppe passes the Fontana dell'Olmo, a fountain carved out of solid rock. From it stares the sculpted head of Bacchus, the god of fruitfulness.

There's a fine walk from Pitigliano to Sovana (8km) that incorporates parts of the *vie cave*. For a description and map, go to www.trekking.it and download the pdf in the Maremma section. There's also an enjoyable 2km walk from the small stone bridge in the gorge below Sorano along the Via Cava San Rocco (2km) to the **Necropoli di San Rocco**, another Etruscan burial site.

The open-air **Museo Archeologico all'Aperto 'Alberto Manzi'** (Alberto Manzi Open-Air Archaeology Museum; 0564 61 40 67; Strada Provinciale 127 Pantano, off SS74; adult/reduced €4/2.50; 11am-7pm Tue-Sun Apr-Oct), south of Pitigliano on the road to Saturnia, contains sections of *vie cave* and several necropolises.

Sleeping

Il Tufo Rosa PENSION €

(☎0564 61 70 19; www.iltuforosa.com; Piazza Petruccioli 97-101; s €42-48, d €55-75; ❄📶) There's a resolutely old-fashioned feel to these appealing bedrooms which are set in a bastion of the fortress on Piazza Petruccioli, on the edge of the old town. Each room is named after an Aldobrandeschi, Orsini or Medici countess and features silky throws, dainty cushions and filmy fabrics. No breakfast, and air-con is only available in a few rooms.

★**Le Camere del Ceccottino** PENSION €€

(☎0564 61 42 73; www.ceccottino.com; Via Roma 159; r €80-150; ❄📶) Owned and operated by the extremely helpful Chiara and Alessandro, who also run a nearby *osteria* and *enoteca* of the same name, this *pensione* boasts an excellent location near the *duomo* and four immaculately maintained and well-equipped rooms. Opt for the superior or prestige room if possible, as the standard versions are a little small. No breakfast.

Eating & Drinking

★**La Rocca** TUSCAN, WINE BAR €

(Piazza della Repubblica 92; panino €4, meals €28; ⏲10am-3am Tue-Sat, to midnight Sun) Generous pourings of local wine, including Pitigliano's very own DOC white, are on offer at this cavernous wine bar tucked away at the far end of Piazza della Repubblica, near the panoramic viewpoint. The range of *prodotti tipici* (typical local products) is impressive – choose from rustic pastas, antipasti platters and *panini* stuffed with cured meats and *pecorino* cheese.

Enoteca La Corte del Cechcottino TUSCAN, WINE BAR €

(Via Vignoli 202; plates from €9; ⏲variable hours Fri-Wed mid-Mar–mid-Jan) This sunken courtyard is an atmospheric spot to sample a glass or two of the local *vino,* accompanied by a simple antipasto plate or a bowl of pasta.

★**Il Tufo Allegro** TUSCAN €€

(☎0564 61 61 92; www.iltufoallegro.com; Vicolo della Costituzione 5; meals €22-70; ⏲noon-2.30pm & 8-10.30pm Wed-Sun, 7.30-9.30pm Tue Mar-Dec) The aromas emanating from the kitchen door off Via Zuccarelli should be enough to draw you down the stairs and into the cosy dining rooms, which are carved out of tufa. Chef Domenico Pichini's menus range from traditional to modern and all of his creations rely heavily on local produce for inspiration. It's near Piccola Gerusalemme.

Hostaria del Ceccottino ITALIAN €€

(☎0564 61 42 73; www.ceccottino.com; Piazza San Gregorio VII 64; meals €45; ⏲noon-3pm & 7-9.30pm mid-Mar–mid-Jan, closed Thu Oct-May; 🖉) Carla, the chef here, has been cooking traditional local dishes for 30 years – famously, none of her recipes are written down. Pitigliano's Jewish heritage is reflected in the food, which also features prime local produce, so expect beef from certified Chianina and Maremmana cows as well as *Sfratto Pitiglianese,* a Jewish sweet majoring on honey and walnuts.

> **OFF THE BEATEN TRACK**
>
> **TERENZI**
>
> Awarded the prestigious 'Emerging Winery of the Year' accolade in Gambero Rosso's 2013 *Vini d'Italia* (Wines of Italy) guide, **Terenzi** (☎0564 59 96 01; www.terenzi.eu; Località Montedonico, Scansano) wine estate is located on a scenic road just outside the town of Scansano, a 50-minute drive from Pitigliano on a secondary route to Grosseto.
>
> It's best known for its Morellino di Scansano DOCG, a ruby-red Sangiovese with berry and violet overtones that can be tasted over a meal at the winery's **restaurant** (meals €35; ⏲noon-3pm, closed Wed in winter) or purchased at its **cantina** (per 3 wines €10-20; ⏲9.30am-7.30pm summer, 9.30am-1pm & 2-5.30pm Mon-Fri, 10am-6pm Sat & Sun winter). There's even a **locanda** (d €110-155, ste €140-175; P❄📶🏊) for travellers wanting to soak up wonderful views and wine over a few days.

Information

Tourist Office (☎0564 61 71 11; www.comune.pitigliano.gr.it; Piazza Garibaldi 12; ⏲10am-12.30pm & 3.30-6pm Tue-Sat summer, 10am-12.30pm & 3-5.30pm Fri & Sat, 10am-12.30pm Sun winter) In the piazza just inside the Old City's main gate.

Getting There & Away

BUS

Tiemme (www.tiemmespa.it) buses leave from Via Santa Chiara, just off Piazza Petruccioli. They tend to operate Monday to Saturday only; buy tickets at Bar Guastini in Piazza Petruccioli. Services include the following:

Grosseto (€6, two hours, three per day)
Siena (€8.50, three hours, one per day)
Sorano (€1.50, 10 to 20 minutes, four per day)
Sovana (€1.50, 10 to 20 minutes, one per day)

CAR
There are plenty of free car parks around town; look for white lines. Alternatively, the car park near Piazza Petruccioli charges €0.50 per hour from 8am to 1pm and from 3pm to 8pm.

Sovana

The main attractions at this postcard-pretty town are a cobbled main street that dates from Roman times, two austerely beautiful Romanesque churches and a museum showcasing a collection of ancient gold coins.

◉ Sights

Duomo   CATHEDRAL
(Concattedrale dei Santi Pietro e Paolo; ☉10am-1pm & 2.30-6pm summer, 11am-1pm & 2.30-5pm winter) Built over a 200-year period starting in the 1100s, this Romanesque cathedral was commissioned by local boy-made-big Pope Gregory VII (Hildebrand of Sovana; c 1015–85). Its strangely positioned doorway is decorated with carvings of people, animals and plants, and its huge interior has a beauty that owes nothing to artworks and everything to the genius of its architect.

Museo di San Mamiliano   MUSEUM
(Piazza del Pretorio; adult/child €4/2; ☉10am-1pm & 3-7pm Thu-Tue (open daily in Aug), to 6pm Oct, 10am-1pm & 2-5pm Sat & Sun Nov & Dec) In 2004 archaeologists excavating beneath the ruined 9th-century Church of St Mamiliano made the discovery of a lifetime – a cache of 498 gold coins buried in a vase under the church floor in the 5th century AD. Most are now displayed in this small museum of Roman times, which occupies the restored church.

Santa Maria Maggiore   CHURCH
(Piazza Pretorio; ☉9am-5pm) Designed in a Romanesque-Gothic transitional style, the

---

ⓘ COMBINED TICKET
....

If you're planning to visit the Museo di San Mamiliano, Parco Archeologico 'Città del Tufa', outside town, and Fortezza Orsini, in Sorano, a combined ticket (adult/ reduced €8/5) will save you money.

16th-century frescoes in the apse of this church are perhaps the main reason to head inside; there's also an unusual stone *ciborium* (vaulted canopy over the altar) dating from the 9th century.

🍽 Sleeping & Eating

★**Taverna Etrusca**   HOTEL €
(☑0564 61 41 13; www.tavernaetrusca.com; Piazza del Pretorio 16; d €80-90, meals €20-60; 🛜) Sovana's rich heritage can certainly be felt in these stylish lodgings. Twisting wooden stairs lead to stately rooms made atmospheric by artful lighting and stone walls. Downstairs, refined modern Tuscan cuisine is served in a shaded courtyard garden and brick-and-beam dining room. The 30-page *carta dei vini* features both Sovana and Morellino di Scansano DOC wines.

La Tavernetta   TRATTORIA €
(www.latavernettasovana.it; Via del Pretorio 3; meals €20, pizzas €4-7; ☉12.30-2.30pm & 7-9pm daily summer, Wed-Mon winter; 🛜) Bag a table on the street-side terrace of this casual eatery near the tourist office for simple, traditional local dishes by day (try the *Tortelli alla Maremmana* or *salumi Toscana*) and pizzas from a wood-fired oven by night.

ⓘ Information

Tourist Office (☑0564 61 40 74; ☉10am-1pm & 3-7pm Fri-Wed summer only) The helpful tourist office is in the Palazzo Pretorio on the main piazza.

ⓘ Getting There & Away

BUS
Between Monday and Saturday, **Tiemme** (www. tiemmespa.it) buses travel to/from Pitigliano (€1.50, 10 to 20 minutes, one per day) and Sorano (€1.50, 15 minutes, once or twice daily).

CAR
The car park at the entrance to town charges €0.50 per hour.

Parco Archeologico 'Città del Tufa'

**Parco Archeologico
'Città del Tufa'**   ARCHAEOLOGICAL SITE
(Necropoli di Sovana; www.leviecave.it; admission €5; ☉10am-7pm summer, to 5pm Sat & Sun Nov & Mar) At Tuscany's most significant Etruscan tombs, 1.5km east of town, signs in Italian

TERME DI SATURNIA

The sulphurous thermal baths at **Terme di Saturnia** (☑0564 60 01 11; www.termedi saturnia.it; day admission €25, after 2pm €20; ☺9.30am-7pm summer, to 5pm winter) are some 3km downhill from the village of the same name, which is 35km from Sorano and 26km from Pitigliano. You can happily imitate the Romans and spend a whole day indulging in hot pools and spa treatments at this luxury resort, or take the econo-bather option and track down the springs themselves. Just south of the Terme di Saturnia turn-off, look for the telltale sign of bathers' cars parked beside the road (or spy the *Cascate del Gorello* signs), then forage down the dirt path until you find this cluster of gratis, open-air pools, where temperatures are a constant 37.5°C. Alternatively, overnight in the **Hotel Saturno Fontepura** (☑0564 60 13 13; www.hotelsaturnofontepura.com; Località la Croce; r €135-190; Ⓟ❋☎☀), a spa resort with its own thermal pool overlooking the *terme*.

and English guide you around four elaborate burial sites. The headline exhibit is the **Tomba Ildebranda**, named after Gregory VII, which still preserves traces of its carved columns and stairs. The **Tomba dei Demoni Alati** (Tomb of the Winged Demons) features a headless terracotta recumbent figure.

The carving of a sea demon with huge wings that was the original centrepiece of that tomb is now protected in a roofed enclosure nearby. The **Tomba del Tifone** (Tomb of the Typhoon) is about 300m down a trail running alongside a rank of tomb facades cut from the rock face. Two arresting lengths of *via cave* (one known as 'Cavone' and the other 'Poggio Prisca') are nearby.

On the opposite side of the site is the **Tomba della Sirena** and another *via cava* ('San Sebastiano'), which remains closed due to safety concerns at the time of research.

Sorano & Around

POP 3510

Sorano's setting is truly dramatic – sitting astride a rocky outcrop, its weatherworn stone houses are built along a ridge overlooking the Lente river and gorge. Below the ridgeline are *cantine* dug out of tufa, as well as a tantalising series of terraced gardens, many part-hidden from public view.

⊙ Sights & Activities

Fortezza Orsini   FORT
(☑0564 63 34 24; admission €4; ☺10am-1pm & 3-7pm Tue-Sun summer, open daily Aug), till 6pm Oct, 10am-1pm & 2-5pm Sat & Sun Mar) Work on this massive fortress started in the 11th century. Today it still stands sentinel over the town, its sturdy walls linking two bastions surrounded by a dry moat. The highlight of any visit is undoubtedly a guided tour of the evocative subterranean passages (11am and 3.30pm), which are noticeably chilly even in the height of the Tuscan summer.

Area Archeologica di Vitozza   ARCHAEOLOGICAL SITE
(☺10am-dusk) **FREE** More than 200 caves pepper a high rock ridge here, making it one of the largest troglodyte dwellings in Italy. The complex was first inhabited in prehistoric times. To explore the site, you'll need two hours and sturdy walking shoes. It's 3 miles due east of Sorano, near the hamlet of San Quírico; follow signs from the SR74.

🛏 Sleeping

★Sant'Egle   AGRITURISMO €€
(☑329 4250285; www.santegle.it; Case Sparse Sant'Egle 18; d/tr €112/150; ⓅⓈ☀) ⏀ Here the organic, Tuscan dream comes true. Exquisite bedrooms fill a 17th-century customs house that's rich in exposed rafters and dotted with home-crafted quirks: expect rickety ladders as clothes racks, and rough-hewn wood as shelves. One bedroom is in a former kitchen with a fireplace big enough to sleep in (but perhaps opt for the four-poster bed instead).

Almost everything is organic, from the bedding and the toiletries (made with extra virgin olive oil) to the gourmet breakfast and evening meals (four courses €30). There are also tranquil grounds, a tiny bio-pool and an alfresco hot tub, while the owners stage cookery classes on bread and cheese making, and Tuscan cuisine. Highly recommended.

Hotel della Fortezza
HOTEL €€

(☎ 0564 63 35 49; www.fortezzahotel.it; Piazza Cairoli 5; d €100-120, ste €115-140; P) Fancy the idea of sleeping in a medieval castle? If so, this comfortable hotel inside one of the fortress' bastions is just what you're looking for. Many of its 16 rooms have spectacular views, but the best is undoubtedly the massive 'La Torre' (Tower) suite.

Eating & Drinking

Cantina L'Ottava Rima
WINE BAR

(www.cantinaottavarima.com; Via del Borgo 25; ☺ noon-3pm & 6pm-midnight daily summer, Thu-Sun only winter) Here you'll sup your drink surrounded by carved rock walls – this casual *cantina* has been hacked out of the tufa. Add rickety tables and it's an atmospheric spot to sample local wines and simple dishes (antipasto plates €12) that highlight quality Maremmese produce. It's on a terraced walkway towards the foot of town.

Information

Tourist Office (☎ 0564 63 30 99; ☺ 10am-1pm & 3-7pm Tue-Sun) Sorano's handiest tourist office is at the *fortezza*.

Getting There & Away

BUS

Tiemme (www.tiemmespa.it) services include those to Pitigliano (€1.50, 10 to 20 minutes, four per day) and Sovana (€1.50, 15 minutes, once or twice daily).

CAR

The car park outside the Town Hall charges €0.50 per hour from 8am to 1pm and 3pm to 8pm daily. Parking at the *fortezza* is free.

THE BASSA MAREMMA

The Bassa (Lower) Maremma starts at Grosseto and sweeps along the coast, incorporating the peninsula of Monte Argentario and the mountains and marshes of the Parco Regionale della Maremma.

Grosseto

POP 81,540

Poor Grosseto. Its uninviting name, unattractive surrounds and lack of headline sights lead to it being ignored by most tourists, relegated to a mere navigational marker for those taking the coastal highway to Rome. But an appealing if low-key old town, some lively places to eat and drink and a vaguely counter-culture vibe may prompt you to stop.

One of the last Sienese-dominated towns to fall into Medici hands (in 1559), Grosseto's bastions, fortress and hexagonal-shaped, 2.5km-long walls were raised by the Florentines in order to protect what was then an important grain and salt depot for the grand duchy. Today, the city is the provincial capital of the Maremma and its *centro storico* (historic centre) is a perfect place to stroll and experience the *passeggiata* (evening stroll) along Corso Carducci.

The city is renowned for its heavy winter rainfalls, which have caused catastrophic floods in the past.

Sights & Activities

Cattedrale di San Lorenzo
CATHEDRAL

(Piazza del Duomo; ☺ 7.30am-noon & 3.30-7pm) Grosseto's late-13th-century *duomo* has a distinctive Sienese character and a particularly beautiful rose window. Much of the facade was renewed along neo-Romanesque lines during the 19th century. Inside, look for Matteo di Giovanni's *Madonna delle Grazie* in the left transept, the 1470 baptismal font and the 15th-century stained-glass windows depicting saints.

Museo Archeologico e d'Arte della Maremma
MUSEUM

(http://maam.comune.grosseto.it/; Piazza Baccarini 3; adult/reduced €5/2.50; ☺ 10am-5.30pm Tue-Fri, 10am-1pm & 5-8pm Sat & Sun Jun–mid-Sep, 9am-3pm Tue-Fri, 10am-1pm & 4-7pm Sat & Sun mid-Sep–May) Grosseto's major tourist drawcard features an archaeological museum on the ground floor and a museum of ecclesiastical art upstairs. Items unearthed from Roselle and Vetulonia feature among the Etruscan and Roman artefacts, which include some fine examples of 6th-century-BC Etruscan writing. Artworks spanning the 13th to 19th centuries include striking illuminated manuscripts dating from the 1200s.

Festivals & Events

Festa di San Lorenzo
CULTURAL

(☺ Aug) Grosseto's patron saint, St Lawrence, is celebrated in this festival, held on 9 and 10 August.

🛏 Sleeping

Appennino PENSION €
(☎ 0564 2 30 09; www.albergoappennino.it; Viale Goffredo Mameli 1; s/d €40/80; 🅿 🕿) The basic but cheerful rooms in this two-star *albergo*, 10 minutes' walk from the *centro storico*, are a good short-stay option. No breakfast.

Grand Hotel Bastiani HOTEL €€
(☎ 0564 2 00 47; www.hotelbastiani.com; Piazza Gioberti 64; s from €82, d from €120, ste from €180; 🅿 ❋ @ 🕿) Housed within an imposing old building, complete with marble floors and a *Gone with the Wind*–style dance-down-me staircase, the Grand offers swish but stately rooms (expect polished wood, sedate fabrics and glinting bathrooms) and a lavish breakfast buffet. It's set just inside the main gate into the *centro storico*.

🍴 Eating & Drinking

Vineria da Romolo TUSCAN €
(Via Vinzaglio 3; meals €20; ☺ 10am-3.30pm & 6pm-midnight, closed lunch Tue & Wed) There's a decidedly boho vibe at this chilled-out *osteria* where wine barrels have been turned into tables and benches and terracotta tablets frame the front. Inside it's a mass of bottles, plastic grapes and the odd fake parrot. The food is flavourful and traditional – expect country-style pastas and platters piled-high with meat and cheese.

★ Grantosco TUSCAN €€
(☎ 0564 2 60 27; www.grantosco.it; Via Solferino 4; meals €35; ☺ noon-2.30pm & 7-10pm) Succulent meat dishes including Maremmese beef, *cinta senese* (Tuscan pork) and *cinghiale* (wild boar) marinated in Morellino di Scansano wine are the show-stoppers here, but the pastas and desserts are pretty darned fine, too. Soft lighting and walls adorned with wine bottles ensure an atmospheric setting.

★ Caffè Ricasoli BAR
(www.caffericasoli.it; Strada Ricasoli 20; ☺ 8am-midnight Mon-Sat; 🕿) Old vinyl records may dangle from the ceiling, but the music at Grosseto's best beatnik cafe-bar is bang up to date. DJs spin Italian pop towards the end of the week and it hosts occasional live music. There's an internet cafe at the back and the free wi-fi, like the coffee, comes fast and strong.

🛍 Shopping

Dolci Tradizioni dalla Maremma Toscana FOOD
(Via Garibaldi 60; ☺ 8am-4pm Mon-Sat) Specialising in local delicacies including *lo sfratto*, a traditional Jewish pastry made with honey and walnuts, this wonderful *pasticceria* opposite the Medici fortress makes all of its products by hand and sells them in beautifully wrapped packages.

ℹ Information

Tourism Information Point (☎ 0564 42 79 18; www.turismoinmaremma.it; Piazza del Popolo 3; ☺ 10am-2pm Thu, 4-6pm Fri summer, 9-11.30am Mon, Tue & Thu 3-5.30pm Tue, Wed & Fri winter) Tucked in beside the *Bastione della Rimembranza* on the northwest side of the old town.

ℹ Getting There & Away

BUS
Buses usually leave from the train station. Buy tickets at the Tiemme office nearby. Monday to Saturday services include the following:
Florence (€11, two hours, six daily)
Massa Marittima (€3.70, one hour, four daily)
Pitigliano (€6, two hours, three daily)
Porto Santo Stefano (€3.70, one hour, one daily)
Siena (€7.80, 80 minutes, 10 daily)

CAR
A Limited Traffic Zone (ZTL) applies in the *centro storico*. There's plenty of paid car parking surrounding the city walls; the most convenient is at Porta Corsica, next to the city gate on Viale Zimenes (per hour €1).

TRAIN
The main coastal train line runs between Pisa, Livorno and Rome via Grosseto. Services include the high-speed (Alta Velocità) Frecciabianca. Regular, roughly hourly, connections from Grosseto include the following:
Genoa (Alta Velocità, €22, three hours; Intercity, €17, 3½ hours)
Livorno (Alta Velocità, €20, one hour; Intercity, €10, 70 minutes)
Pisa (Alta Velocità, €20, 75 minutes; Intercity, €10, 90 minutes)
Rome (Alta Velocità, €28, 90 minutes; Intercity, €20, two hours)
Siena (Regionale, €9, 90 minutes, seven daily)

SOUTHERN TUSCANY GROSSETO

Riserva Naturale Provinciale Diaccia Botrona

Riserva Naturale Provinciale Diaccia Botrona PARK

(☑ 0564 2 02 98; www.maremma-online.it) The marshes surrounding the coastal town of Castiglione della Pescaia are an important shelter for migrating birds, and this 1272-hectare nature reserve off the SS322 is a wonderful chance to explore this flat yet fascinating landscape. **Boat tours** (adult/reduced €12/10; ⊙ 5pm & 6.30pm Tue-Sun mid-Jun–mid-Sep) enable you to spot waterfowl, herons, flamingos and other species; book in advance.

Boat tours leave from the **visitor centre** (multimedia display adult/reduced €3.50/2.50; ⊙ 4-8.30pm Tue-Sun mid-Jun–mid-Sep, 3.30pm-sunset Thu-Sun mid-Sep–mid-Jun) in the **Casa Rossa Ximenes**, a handsome sluice-house commissioned in the mid-1700s by Grand Duke Pietro Leopoldo I of Lorriane to help reclaim the marshes for agriculture and reduce the area's horrifyingly high levels of malaria. The visitor centre features a multimedia display (in Italian only) about the reserve's wildlife, the building and the reclamation.

Guided mountain-bike tours (adult/reduced €8/5) of the reserve depart from the nearby town of Castiglione della Pescaia between late May and early October; booking is essential.

Roselle

Roselle ARCHAEOLOGICAL SITE

(SS 223; adult/reduced €4/2; ⊙ 8.30am-7pm May-Aug, to 6.30pm Mar, Apr, Sep & Oct, to 5.30pm Nov-Feb) In the 7th century BC Roselle (Rusellae) was already an Etruscan town; it fell under Roman control in the 3rd century BC. Although there are no great monuments, you do get a clear idea of the town's layout from the remaining Roman defensive walls, amphitheatre, traces of houses, forum and streets. It's around 7km northeast of Grosseto.

Parco Regionale della Maremma

Hundreds of acres of forests, pristine coasts, countless activities and your chance to be a cowboy are all on offer in this national park.

◉ Sights & Activities

★ **Parco Regionale della Maremma** NATURE RESERVE

(☑ 0564 40 70 98; www.parco-maremma.it; adult/reduced €10/5) This spectacular regional park incorporates the Uccellina mountain range, a 600-hectare pine forest, marshy plains and 20kms of unspoilt coast. Park access is limited to 13 signed walking trails of 2.5km to 13km; the most popular is A2 (Le Torri), a 5.8km walk to the beach. From mid-June to mid-September you can only visit on a guided tour because of possible bushfires; call ahead to check times. An entry fee is paid at the main, Alberese visitor centre.

★ **Agienza Regionale Agricola di Alberese Farm Experience** FARM

(☑ 0564 40 71 80; www.alberese.com; Via della Spergolaia, Alberese; farm experience €20-60; ⊙ 10am-1pm Thu Jul & Aug, other times by reservation) Parts of the park are farmed, mainly to graze the Maremma's famous cattle. This experience offers a superb insight into the work of the local *butteri* (traditional cowboys); experienced riders can even practice herding cows themselves. The Agienza is also the regional headquarters of the Slow Food organisation and offers tastings of its produce. Book at least 24 hours ahead.

Canoe Tours CANOEING

(adult/reduced €16/10) Tranquil 2½-hour canoe paddles along peaceful waterways, with the chance of seeing ducks, geese and even beaver. Book at the Alberese visitor centre at least a day in advance.

Mountain Bike Tours BICYCLE TOUR

(bike tours €20-25) These two- to six-hour guided mountain-bike excursions (some are challenging) take you to the park's heart. Book at least 24 hours in advance at the Alberese visitor centre.

Circolo Ippico Uccellina HORSE RIDING

(☑ 334 9797181; www.circoloippicouccellina.it; Località Collecchio 38, Magliano in Toscana; per half/full day from €55/95) Aimed at intermediate to experienced riders, these treks range from 2½-hour trips to five-hour expeditions into the hills where there's a good chance of spotting deer and wild boar.

Il Gelsomino HORSE RIDING

(☑ 0564 40 5 133; www.ilgelsomino.com; Via Strada del Barbicato 4, Alberese; treks from €30) Horse-riding treks through the park suitable for all skill levels – beginners welcome.

Sleeping

★Villa Fattoria Granducale AGRITURISMO €
(☑0564 40 71 00; www.alberese.com/fattoria-granducale; Alberese; B&B d & tr €90-100, self-contained apt €100-14) The Granducale sits on a slight rise just above the village of Alberese, looking every inch the classy 15th-century villa. Inside a careful renovation has resulted in elegant rooms with historic flourishes aplenty: exposed rafters and stone arches meet subtle lighting and sleek chairs. It also rents out simple apartments in surrounding farm buildings. The Granducale has a two-night minimum.

Eating & Drinking

La Bottega Maremmana CAFE €
(Alberese; ⊘7am-1pm & 4-7.30pm Mon Wed, Fri & Sat, 8.30am-12.30pm Sun summer, shorter hours in winter) A cafe opposite the park's Alberese visitor centre that has a range of local produce to try.

Shopping

**Agienza Regionale
Agricola di Alberese Fattoria** FOOD & DRINK
(Via dell'Artigliere 4, Alberese; ⊘8.30am-12.30pm & 4-7pm Tue & Thu-Sun) The local, Slow Food–accredited produce on offer here is irresistible – look out for olive oils, *pecorini* (sheep's cheese), *salumi* (meats), organic bread and DOCG wines. One robust Morellino di Scansano costs a mere €2 per litre, so bring a couple of bottles to fill.

❶ Information

Main Visitor Centre (☑0564 40 70 98; Via del Bersagliere 7-9, Alberese; ⊘8am-6pm mid-Jun–mid-Sep, to 4pm mid-Sep–mid-Nov, to 2pm mid-Nov–mid-Jun) The Parco Regionale della Maremma's main visitor centre.
Seasonal Visitor Centre (☑0564 88 71 73; Via Nizza 12, Talamone; ⊘9am-noon & 3-5pm Jul & Aug) A summer-only visitor centre which adjoins the Talamone Aquarium at the park's southern edge (the aquarium showcases the local lagoon environment and works to safeguard local turtles).

Orbetello
POP 14,900
Set on a balance-beam isthmus running through a lagoon south of the Parco Regionale della Maremma, Orbetello is a relatively laid-back destination with some appealing if

---

OFF THE BEATEN TRACK

MAGLIANO IN TOSCANA

A 23km drive inland from Orbetello leads to this hilltop town, fortified by monumental walls built between the 14th and 16th centuries. Specific sights are limited to the Romanesque churches of **San Martino** and **San Giovanni Battista** (the latter has a remodelled Renaissance facade). But the trip is well rewarded by lunch in the pretty garden at **Antica Trattoria Aurora** (☑0564 59 27 74; Via Chiasso Lavagnini 12, Magliano in Toscana; meals €45; ⊘noon-2.30pm & 7.30-10pm Thu-Tue Mar-Dec), a restaurant serving excellent modern Tuscan cuisine. The attached *cantina* (dishes €8 to €16) offers more casual, less-expensive meals. To get here, take the Albinia exit off the SS1 and then turn left onto the SS323.

---

low-key historic buildings and a bird-packed nature reserve.

◉ Sights

Reminders of the Spanish garrison that was stationed in Orbetello for nearly 150 years include the **viceroy's residence** on Piazza Eroe dei Due Mondi, the **fort** and the **city walls**, parts of which are the original Etruscan fortification.

Cathedral CATHEDRAL
(Piazza della Repubblica; ⊘9am-noon & 3-6pm) **FREE** It may be modest as far as many Tuscan churches go, but Orbetello's *duomo* is still attractive, retaining its 14th-century Gothic facade despite being remodelled in the Spanish style during the 16th century.

L'Oasi WWF di Orbetello NATURE RESERVE
(☑0564 89 88 29; www.wwf.it; SS Aurelia, Località Ceriolo; adult/reduced €5/3; ⊘guided visits 9.30am & 1.30pm Sat & Sun Sep-Apr) An extraordinary 140 species of birds have been seen on Orbetello Lagoon. The best place to spot some of them is at the L'Oasi WWF di Orbetello north of town. As well as winter weekend visits, you can also explore the reserve in July and August, but by appointment only on Tuesdays and Saturdays at 5.30pm.

OFF THE BEATEN TRACK

GIARDINO DEI TAROCCHI

Twenty-two oversized Gaudí-influenced sculptures tumble down a hillside at **Giardino dei Tarocchi Scultura** (www.nikidesaintphalle.com; Località Garavicchio-Capalbio; adult/reduced €12/7; ☉ 2.30-7.30pm summer), a fantastical sculpture garden created by Franco-American artist Niki de Saint Phalle (1930–2002). The whimsical, mosaic-covered creations merge with the surrounding park, creating what the artist called a 'garden of joy'. It's a colossal effort that depicts characters from the tarot card pack (think the Moon, Fool and Justice) and even includes a sculpture lived in by De Saint Phalle while the garden was being built.

Sculptor Jean Tinguely contributed to many of the figures; the visitor centre was designed by Swiss architect Mario Botta. The sculpture garden is 25km east of Orbetello; take the Pescia Fiorentina exit from the SS1.

✕ Eating

La Taverna   TUSCAN €
(☏ 0564 86 79 69; Via Roma 48; meals €20; ☉ 12.30-2pm & 7.30-10pm Wed-Mon) You'll find flavoursome Maremman dishes at this trattoria and pizzeria, with seafood and shellfish at the fore.

❶ Information

Tourist Office (☏ 0564 86 04 47; www.proloco-orbetello.it; Piazza della Repubblica 1; ☉ 10am-1pm & 4-6pm) Opposite the cathedral.

Monte Argentario

POP 12,939

Once an island, this rugged promontory became linked to the mainland by three slender, 6km-long accumulations of sand, one of which now forms the isthmus of Orbetello. Overdevelopment has spoilt the promontory's northern side, particularly around crowded **Porto Santo Stefano**. In summer, high accommodation prices generally make it poor value; you're better off visiting as a day trip and sleeping inland. Several good pebble beaches sit just to the east and west of town.

On the promontory's less-frenetic southern side **Porto Ercole** is a smaller and more attractive harbour, with a relatively clean beach that gets cluttered with deck chairs.

◉ Sights & Activities

Old Town   HISTORIC SITE
(Porto Ercole) Porto Ercole's *centro storico* stretches up the hillside, past sandwiched-in Chiesa di Sant'Erasmo and up towards the largest of the three Spanish forts that surround the town.

Via Panoramica   DRIVING TOUR
Signs point you towards this narrow route that encircles the entire Monte Argentario promontory. It offers sweeping sea views across to the hazy whaleback of the Isola de Giglio. The road can get dangerously busy in summer.

✕ Eating & Drinking

★ Il Pellicano   SEAFOOD €€€
(☏ 0564 85 82 75; www.pellicanohotel.com; Località Lo Sbarcatello, Porto Ercole; menus €85-195; ☉ 7.30pm daily summer; ☏) The proud possessor of a Michelin star, the classy restaurant at the five-star hotel of the same name specialises in intricate, impeccably presented seafood creations and has two outdoor terraces with spectacular views. There's also a more casual and slightly cheaper poolside grill that serves lunch and dinner.

Bar Giulia   CAFE
(Via del Molo 16, Porto Santo Stefano; ☉ 6.30am-2am Tue-Sun, daily summer) The terrace of Bar Giulia is a popular locals' haunt, sitting as it does right beside the sea overlooking a harbour framed by buildings stacked up on the slopes behind. All in all a picturesque spot for a morning coffee, *panino* or late-afternoon *aperitivo*. It's at the far (west) end of the *lungomare* (port promenade).

❶ Information

Porto Santo Stefano Tourist Office (☏ 0564 81 42 08; www.turismoinmaremma.it; Piazzale Sant'Andrea; ☉ 9am-1pm & 4-8pm summer, 10am-1pm & 3-6pm Sat, 10am-1pm Sun, 3-6pm Fri winter) Set at the far eastern end of the port.

❶ Getting There & Away

BUS
Between Monday and Saturday frequent **Tiemme** (www.tiemmespa.it) buses connect most towns on Monte Argentario with central Orbetello (€2.60, 20 minutes), continuing to the train station. They also run to Grosseto (€3.70, one hour, up to four daily).

CAR & MOTORCYCLE
Follow signs for Monte Argentario from the SS1, which connects Grosseto with Rome.

Central Coast & Elba

Best Places to Eat

➡ La Barrocciaia (p192)

➡ del Cacini (p199)

➡ Ristorante Capo Nord (p210)

➡ Il Castagnacciao (p206)

➡ Enoteca Tognoni (p196)

Best Places to Stay

➡ Castello di Bolgheri (p196)

➡ Belvedere di Suvereto (p199)

➡ Podere dell'Orso (p195)

➡ Tenuta La Chiusa (p209)

➡ La Cerreta (p198)

Why Go?

Despite possessing landscapes dreams are made of, much of this part of Tuscany is free from well-known destinations and feels far away from the tourist trails. Here you can revel in the hustle of port-city Livorno, where a gritty harbour borders enchanting canals and restaurants overflowing with fish. Then drive the Strada del Vino e dell'Olio Costa degli Etrischi, whose tiny roads and blind switchbacks wind amid vineyards, olive groves and medieval villages packed with perfect places to sample food and wine.

Flop on the sun-drenched sands of the southern Etruscan Coast then lunch beside the shore, especially around the bijou Golfo di Baratti. And then there's Elba: ripe for alfresco frolics, a Mediterranean island with orange trees, palms and not a single high-rise fronting its beach-laced bays. Tramp its rugged interior, explore by mountain bike, or hop on a sea kayak and discover your very own hidden coves.

Road Distances (km)

	Suvereto	Livorno	Piombino	Bogheri
Livorno	79			
Piombino	24	86		
Bolgheri	39	50	38	
Portoferrario	24+1hr	86+1hr	1hr	38+1hr

Central Coast & Elba Highlights

① Delighting in superb seafood in bustling **Livorno** (p190), promenading along the port's 1920s Terrazza Mascagni, then taking a dip in its 19th-century seaside baths.

② Tasting some of Italy's best wines and marvelling at Tuscany's longest **Cypress Alley** (p196) on the Strada del Vino e dell'Olio at Bolgheri.

③ Picnicking between Etruscan tombs and enjoying majestic sea views in the **Parco Archeologico di Baratti e Populonia** (p202).

④ Setting sail to Napoleon's **Elba** (p202); haggling with fishermen, lunching

---

Ligurian Sea

Gorgona

TYRRHENIAN SEA

Livorno ①

Antignano

Montenero

Gabbro

Quercianella

Castelnuovo
Misericordia

Fortullino

Castiglioncello

Rosignano
Solvay

Rosignano
Marittimo

Vada

Cecina

Marina di
Cecina

Marina di
Bibbona

Forte di
Bibbona

Bibbona

Bolgheri ②

San Guido

Donoratico

Castagneto
Carducci

Monteverdi
Marittimo

Sassetta

Montescudaio

Riparbella

Chianni

Casciana
Terme

Lari

Lorenzana

Crespina

Cresina

A12

SS206

A12

SS206

SS1

SS568

SS243

SS1

in Portoferraio's Old Town then escaping to a historic wine estate scented with orange blooms.

⑤ Exploring an underground mine, soaking in a mineral-rich thermal spa then chilling out on a sandy pine-backed beach at **San Vincenzo** (p198).

Capraia

Monte Castello (447m) ▲ • Capraia
▲ • San Stéfano
⊕
Monte Arpagna (415m)

⑤ San Vincenzo
⊗ Parco Nazionale di San Silvestro
• Belvedere
• Suvereto • Cafaggio
• Campiglia Marittima [SS398]
• Venturina [SS1]
[SP23]
• Baratti
• Populonia
Parco Archeologico di ③
Baratti e Populonia
• Piombino ⊙
• Follonica

Golfo di Follonica

• Cavo
• Rio Marina
• Capoliveri
Le Grotte ⊗ Porto Azzurro
Portoferraio
La Biodcia
Lacona
④ Elba
Marciana Marina
La Pila
Monte Capanne (1018m) ▲
Cavoli
Fetovaia
Chiessi

Punta Brigantina • Pianosa

Ⓝ
0 — 20 km
0 — 10 miles

LIVORNO

POP 160,512

Tuscany's second-largest city is a quintessential port town. Though first impressions are rarely kind, this is a 'real' city that really does grow on you. Its seafood is the best on the Tyrrhenian coast, its shabby historic quarter threaded with Venetian-style canals is uber-cool, and pebbly beaches stretch south from the town's elegant belle époque seafront. Be it a short stay between ferries or a day trip from Florence or Pisa, Livorno (Leghorn in English) is understated but worth the trip.

History

The earliest references to Livorno date from 1017. The port was ruled by Pisa and Genoa for centuries, until Florence took control in 1421. It was still tiny; by the 1550s it had only 480 residents. But all that changed under Cosimo I de' Medici, who converted the scrawny settlement into a heavily fortified bastion – to the point that even today it's known throughout Italy as a 'Medici town'.

The 17th-century declaration of Livorno as a free port sparked swift development. By the late 1800s this now vital, cosmopolitan city of 80,000 souls functioned as a key staging post for British and Dutch merchants trading between Europe and the Middle East. The 19th century again saw the city swell in terms of the economy, arts and culture.

As one of Fascist Italy's main naval bases, Livorno was bombed heavily during WWII then rebuilt with a largely unimaginative face that only a sea captain could love.

◉ Sights & Activities

★ **Terrazza Mascagni**   STREET
(Viale Italia; ⊙24hr) FREE No trip to Livorno is complete without a stroll along (and photo shoot of) this dazzling terrace with stone balustrades that sweeps gracefully along the seafront in a dramatic chessboard flurry of black-and-white checks. When it was built in the 1920s it was called Terrazza Ciano after the leader of the Livorno fascist movement; it now bears the name of Livorno-born opera composer Pietro Mascagni (1863–1945).

Acquario di Livorno   AQUARIUM
(www.acquariodilivorno.it; Terrazza Mascagni; adult/reduced €13/11; ⊙10am-7pm summer (to 9pm Jul & Aug), to 6pm weekends only winter) Livorno's thoroughly modern acquarium swims with 300 different species of Mediterranean fish and sea life. The stars of the show are black-tip reef sharks, seahorses and the huge green sea turtles Ari and Cuba.

★ **Piccola Venezia**   AREA
Piccola Venezia (Little Venice) is crossed with small canals built during the 17th century using Venetian methods of reclaiming land from the sea. At the heart sits the remains of the Medici-era **Fortezza Nuova** (New Fort; ⊙24hr) FREE. Canals link it with the waterfront **Fortezza Vecchia** (Old Fort; ⊙24hr) FREE, built 60 years before the Fortezza Nuova. The waterways are huge fun to explore; either from canal-side footpaths or by tour boat, shabby-chic panoramas emerge of faded, peeling apartments draped with brightly coloured washing, interspersed with waterside cafes.

End Little Venice explorations on a high on **Piazza dei Domenicani**, across the bridge at the northern end of Via Borra. **Chiesa di Santa Catarina** (Piazza dei Domenicani), with its ancient, stone walls, stands sentry on the western side of the square as it did for the Medicis four centuries ago.

Museo Civico Giovanni Fattori   GALLERY
(Via San Jacopo in Acquaviva 65; adult/reduced €4/2.50; ⊙10am-1pm & 4-7pm Tue-Sun) This gallery in a pretty park features works by the 19th-century Italian Impressionist Macchiaioli school led by Livorno-born Giovanni Fattori. The group, inspired by the Parisian Barbizon school, flouted stringent academic art conventions and worked directly from nature, emphasising immediacy and freshness through patches, or 'stains' *(macchia),* of colour.

**Museo di Storia
Naturale del Mediterraneo**   MUSEUM
(Via Roma 234; adult/reduced €6/3; ⊙9am-1.30pm Wed & Fri, 9am-7pm Tue, Thu & Sat, 3-7pm Sun) Livorno's Natural History Museum is an excellent, hands-on affair. The highlight of the permanent collection is a 20m-long whale skeleton called Annie.

Bagni Pancaldi   SWIMMING
(www.pancaldiacquaviva.it; Viale Italia 56, Terrazza Mascagni; adult/reduced €5/4; ⊙8.30am-noon & 3-6pm Sat & Sun summer) The elegant soft-apricot facade of Bagni Pancaldi shelters an old-fashioned baths where you can swim, rent canoes, hang out in coloured canvas cabins and frolic in the sun. The baths were the height of sophistication, host to tea dances and musical soirées, when they first opened in 1846.

Livorno

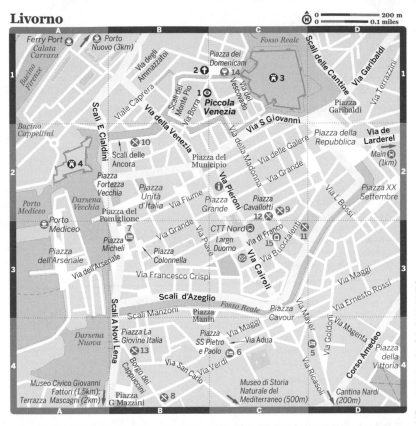

Livorno

◎ Top Sights
1 Piccola Venezia B1

◎ Sights
2 Chiesa di Santa Catarina B1
3 Fortezza Nuova C1
4 Fortezza Vecchia A2

🛏 Sleeping
5 Hotel al Teatro D4
6 Hotel Cavour C4
7 Hotel Gran Duca B3

✖ Eating
8 Cantina Senese B4
9 La Barocciaia C2
10 L'Ancora B2
11 Mercato Centrale C3
12 Mercato di Piazza Cavallotti C2
13 Osteria del Mare B4

🍷 Drinking & Nightlife
14 La Bodeguita C1

🛍 Shopping
15 VAD Formaggi C3

🕝 Tours

Giro in Battello　　　　　　　　BOAT TOUR
(adult/reduced €10/5; ⊙11am, noon & 4pm summer) The tourist office sells tickets for twice-or thrice-daily guided tours by boat (45 minutes) of Livorno's Medicean waterways.

🛏 Sleeping

Camping Miramare　　　　　CAMPGROUND €
(📞0586 58 04 02; www.campingmiramare.it; Via del Littorale 220; camping 2 people, car & tent €32-65; 🛌) Be it tent pitch beneath trees or deluxe version with wooden terrace and sun lounges on the stony beach, this campground – open

THREE PERFECT DAYS

Day 1: Stunning Seafood

Livorno does seafood like nowhere else in Tuscany. Examine raw specimens bright and early at the **Mercato Centrale**, then stroll the black-and-white checked **Terrazza Mascagni** before a seafood lunch – **L'Ancora** and **Osteria del Mare** are top options.

Day 2: Along the Strada del Vino e dell'Olio Costa degli Etruschi

From Livorno head inland, wending your way south through a rolling hinterland strung with medieval villages and vines. Particularly fine wine- and food-tasting stops include **Bolgheri**, where **Enoteca Tognoni** is a top pick. Then it's a wiggly 20km south to **Sassetta**, perhaps overnighting at **La Cerreta**. Next day focus on Val di Cornia DOC wines in **Suvereto** – **Enoteca dei Difficili** will oblige – then head 25km southwest to the **Golfo di Baratti** for a picnic among Etruscan ruins.

Day 3: The Elba Experience

On day three, head across the water to this paradise island. Catch the ferry from Piombino to Portoferraio to explore the waterfront, visit Napoleon-related sites and lunch in the Old Town (try **Osteria Libertaria**). You might also squeeze in a trip up **Monte Capanne**, a *passeggiata* (evening stroll) in **Marciana Marina**, and dinner at **Ristorante Capo Nord**. Either way, the historic wine estate **Tenuta La Chiusa** is a choice place to stay.

year-round thanks to its village of mobile homes, maxi caravans and bungalows – has it all. Rates out of summer are at least 50% lower. Find the site 8km south of town in Antignano.

Hotel Cavour   PENSION €
(☑ 0586 89 96 04; www.hotelcavour-livorno.it; Via Adua 10; d €50-70, tr €70-90) Brightly furnished budget rooms, including triples and quads.

⭐ **Hotel al Teatro**   BOUTIQUE HOTEL €€
(☑ 0586 89 87 05; www.hotelalteatro.it; Via Mayer 42; s/d €85/110; P ✳ @ 🛜) With its marble staircase, antique furniture, tapestries and individually designed rooms, this irresistible eight-room address is one of Tuscany's loveliest urban hotels. The real stunner is the gravel garden out back where guests can lounge on green wicker furniture beneath a breathtakingly beautiful, 350-year-old magnolia tree.

Grand Hotel Palazzo   HISTORIC HOTEL €€
(☑ 0586 26 08 36; www.grandhotelpalazzo.com; Viale Italia 195, near Terrazza Mascagni; d €150-190, ste €350-400; P ✳ @ 🛜 ▨) This shimmering ship of a 19th-century seafront palace, with 123 perfectly thought-out rooms and glistening sea views, is belle époque Livorno relived. Dip into the rooftop infinity pool then indulge in a sunset *aperitivo* and panoramic sea view. Dining in its rooftop garden restaurant, face to face with the sea and the islet of Gorgona, is equally glam. Rooms are 10% cheaper if you book two weeks in advance.

Hotel Gran Duca   HOTEL €€
(☑ 0586 89 10 24; www.granduca.it; Piazza Micheli 16; s €85, d €90-130, ste €120-160; ✳ ✳ @ 🛜) Bag a front-facing room here and (as well as the road) you'll have prime views of Livorno's fishing fleet complete with nets piled up on the quay. The 60 rooms are classic with regal-coloured fabrics. Some have fortress views, while the ones with a private terrace in the red-brick Medici ramparts are straight out of a film set.

🍴 Eating & Drinking

Sampling traditional *cacciucco,* a mixed seafood stew, is reason enough to visit Livorno.

⭐ **La Barrocciaia**   OSTERIA €
(☑ 0586 88 26 37; www.labarrocciaia.it; Piazza Cavallotti 13; meals €20; ☺ 11am-3pm & 6-11pm Tue-Sat) Locals speak of La Barrocciaia with reverence – partly because of a homely interior that's alive with banter, but also because of the simple but superb food. The menu fluctuates, with stews often majoring on wild boar, octopus or squid; the pasta might come smothered in crab, while the chocolate and pear tart is one heck of a dessert.

Cantina Nardi   TUSCAN €
(☑ 0586 80 80 06; Via Cambini 6; meals €20; ☺ 11am-4pm & 6.30-9pm Mon-Sat) They've been in business since 1965, so the friendly Nardis know a thing or three about cooking up hearty, wholly affordable Tuscan fare served

with fabulous wine. As much *enoteca* (wine bar) as Slow Food–hailed restaurant, the bistro organises wine tastings and predinner *aperitivi*. Dine between bottled-filled shelves inside, or on the bijou patio.

Cantina Senese
OSTERIA €

(☑0586 89 02 39; www.ristorantecantinasenese livorno.com; Borgo dei Cappuccini 95; meals €20; ◷noon-2pm & 7-10pm Mon-Sat) Food- and value-conscious harbour workers are the first to fill the long wooden tables at this wonderfully unpretentious eatery, with neighbourhood families arriving later. Ordering is frequently done via faith in your server, rather than by menu. The mussels are exceptional, as is the *cacciucco,* both served with piquant garlic bread.

Surfer Joe's Diner
AMERICAN €

(☑0586 80 92 11; www.surferjoe.it/diner; Terrazza Mascagni; meals €15-30; ◷11am-midnight Sun-Thu, to 1am Fri & Sat, shorter hours winter) What a burst of dynamism this zesty surf bar on the seafront adds to Livorno's drinking and dining scene. American burgers, onion rings, pancakes and smoothies form its culinary core; 1950s diner is its 'look'; and surf music is its idol. A huge terrace licked by the sea breeze and shaded with bamboo huts is the icing on the cake.

By day families pile into Surfer Joe's. After dark, a younger crowd flocks here for DJ and jam sessions, concerts and surf-music.

★ L'Ancora
SEAFOOD €€

(☑0586 88 14 01; www.ristoranteancoralivorno. com; Scali delle Ancora 10; meals €35; ◷noon-2.30pm & 7-10.30pm summer, Wed-Mon winter) L'Ancora's canal-side terrace is the white-hot ticket in good weather, though settling for a table in the 17th-century, barrel-ceilinged, brick boathouse is hardly a hardship. You can get *cacciucco* here, but the *carbonara di mare* (seafood and pasta in white sauce) is the family's pride and joy.

Osteria del Mare
SEAFOOD €€

(☑0586 88 10 27; Borgo dei Cappuccini 5; meals €25-30; ◷12.30-2.30pm & 7.30-10pm Fri-Wed) The list of *secondi* (second courses) is almost purely fish at this smart old-world *osteria* near the water. The traditional, home-style cooking lures the punters: many opt for the signature *riso nero* (black rice) and the catch of the day, or a simple plate of *fritto misto* (a battered and deep-fried mix of thumb-sized fish).

La Bodeguita
BAR

(☑346 6100832; www.labodeguitalivornese.com; Piazza dei Domenicani 20; ◷12.30pm-1.30am Fri-Sun, 6.30pm-1.30am Mon, Wed & Thu) A red-brick cellar bar with sun-drenched wooden-decking terrace afloat the canal in Piccolo Venezia. Enjoy a cocktail and generously topped bruschetta while members of the local rowing club ply the water with oars in front of you, or dance to live music after dark.

ⓘ Information

Tourist office (☑0586 89 42 36; www.costa-deglietruschi.it; Via Pieroni 16; ◷8.30am-5pm summer, 9.30am-3.30pm winter) Hands out free maps and books boat tours.

ⓘ Getting There & Away

BOAT

Livorno is a major port. Regular ferries for Sardinia and Corsica depart from the ferry port at Calata Carrara; and ferries to Capraia use the smaller **Porto Mediceo** (Via del Molo Mediceo) near Piazza dell'Arsenale. Boats to Spain and

---

LIVORNO'S MARKETS

Mercato Centrale (Via Buontalenti; ◷6am-2pm Mon-Sat) For foodie nirvana, get lost in Livorno's magnificent late-19th-century Mercato Centrale, a 95m-long neoclassical food market that miraculously survived Allied WWII bombing. Arresting both gastronomically and architecturally, the market is a gargantuan maze of food stalls bursting with local produce, including the most astonishing fish and seafood.

Mercato di Piazza Cavallotti (Piazza Cavallotti; ◷6am-2pm Mon-Sat) Every Saturday morning, the Mercato di Piazza Cavallotti transforms the otherwise quiet square into a sea of open-air stalls full of baby violet artichokes, golden courgette flowers, hot red peppers and seasonal fruit and veg.

VAD Formaggi (www.vadformaggi.com; Via di Franco 36; ◷7.45am-12.45pm Mon & Wed, 7.45am-12.45pm & 4.40-7.30pm Thu-Sat) The walls of this extraordinary cheese shop, in business since 1955, are lined floor-to-ceiling with giant rounds of Parmesan; market days see the queue spill out the door.

OFF THE BEATEN TRACK

MAKING SPAGHETTI

In the medieval hilltop village of Lari (population 8755), across from the thick red-brick walls of its huge 11th-century fortress, is an address no gastronome should miss: **Martelli** (www.martelli.info; Via San Martino 3; ⊙10am–noon & 3–4pm Mon, Tue, Thu & Fri). Behind the canary-yellow facade of this *pastificio trazionale* (artisanal pasta maker), seven members of the Martelli family beaver away to make 1 tonne of pasta a year – an output any factory would achieve in a matter of hours. Slowly kneaded dough is fed through traditional bronze moulds to create spaghetti and spaghettini, penne, macaroni and fusilli. This is then air-dried for 50 hours (compared to three hours industrially) before being cut and packaged by hand in Martelli's trademark canary-yellow paper packets. These are designed to evoke the pre-1960s paper that loose, market-bought pasta was wrapped in before industrialisation changed it all.

Martelli pasta has been around since 1926. Chewier and coarser in texture than many, it marries particularly well with meat sauces and game, and is shipped all over the world to many a gourmet store, Harrods of London included. In Lari, which is 35km southeast of Pisa, buy it for €4 per kilogram at village cafe and tobacconist, **La Bottega delle Specialità** (Via Diaz 12-14) and taste it for lunch at village restaurants.

To tour the workshops, try sticking your head around the shopfront, asking to visit, then nipping down the neighbouring alley to reach the small room where the spaghetti action takes place.

Sicily, plus some Sardinia services, use Porto Nuovo, 3km north of the city.

Corsica Ferries (☑825 095095 per min €0.15; www.corsica-ferries.it) Two to seven services per week to Bastia, Corsica (from €30, four hours) and Golfo Aranci, Sardinia (from €50, six to 10 hours).

Grimaldi Lines (www.grimaldi-ferries.com) Weekly sailings to/from Barcelona (from €35, 21 hours) and Tangiers, Morocco (from €80, 58 hours).

Moby (www.moby.it) Year-round, runs at least two services a day to Olbia, Sardinia (from €48, seven to 10 hours). Plus in the summer, several crossings a week to Bastia, Corsica (from €30, four hours).

Toremar (www.toremar.it) Several crossings per week, year round to Capraia (€17, 2¾ hours).

CAR

The A12 runs past the city; the SS1 connects Livorno with Rome. There are several car parks near the waterfront.

TRAIN

From the **main train station** (Piazza Dante) walk westwards (straight ahead) along Viale Carducci, Via de Larderel, then Via Grande into central Piazza Grande, Livorno's main square.

Services include the following:

Florence (€10, 1½ hours, hourly)
Pisa (€3, 15 minutes, two to four per hour)
Rome (from €19, three to four hours, 12 daily)

ℹ Getting Around

CTT Nord (www.livorno.cttnord.it; Via Bellatalla 1) has a service (bus 1) from the main train station to Porto Mediceo (€1.20, on board €1.70, valid for 75 minutes), via Piazza Grande. If you're catching a ferry to Sardinia or Corsica, take bus 1 to Piazza Grande then bus 5 from Via Cogorano, just off Piazza Grande.

THE ETRUSCAN COAST

The coastline south from Livorno to just beyond Piombino lives up to its historically charged name, Costa degli Etruschi (Etruscan Coast), thanks to the Etruscan tombs unearthed on its shores. Its basic bucket-and-spade beaches are often unstartling, but saunter inland away from the coast and you'll discover a swathe of pretty hilltop villages and some lesser-known but very good wines.

Piombino is the main port to the island of Elba. The website www.costadeglietruschi.it has lots of useful information, including a list of excellent cycle routes.

Castiglioncello

Diminutive Castiglioncello sits 30km south of Livorno, an agreeably unpretentious seaside resort where Italian art critic Digo Martelli held court in the late 19th century.

He played host to the Florentine Impressionist artists of the period, giving birth to the artistic movement known as La Scuola di Castiglioncello (Castiglioncello School). Castiglioncello's best sandy beaches are on the town's northern fringe.

⊙ Sights & Activities

Centro per l'Arte Diego Martelli GALLERY
(☑ 0586 75 90 12; Piazza della Vittoria; ⊙ 10.30am-1pm & 3.30-7pm Sat & Sun) FREE This gallery reflects on the life and times of the influential patron of the arts Diego Martelli (especially the 1860s) and showcases the work of local painters, filmmakers, writers, actors and dancers who've shaped the town's culture up until the present day.

Castello Pasquini CASTLE
(Piazza della Vittoria; ⊙ 24hr) FREE Crenellated Castello Pasquini was built in the late 19th century. Today it has tree-shaded grounds, a great play park and hosts the town theatre.

🛏 Sleeping

★ **Albergo Bartoli** PENSION €
(☑ 0586 7 52 05; www.albergobartoli.com; Via Martelli 9; s/d €60/80, per person half-board €58-70, full board €70-75; P) For bags of character and superb value, head to this impeccably kept villa with an old-fashioned 'let's stay with grandma' atmosphere and 17 rooms (five with sea views) made characterful by burnished wood, tile floors, photos and knick-knacks. The shaded garden is a treat. In June to August, it's half- or full-board only.

★ **Podere dell'Orso** FARMSTAY €
(☑ 0506 6 26 98; Serre di Sotto 1, Colle Alberti, Lorenzana; d/tr €95/120) The quest for the perfect Tuscan room with a view ends at this classy 15th-century farmhouse, which is surrounded by fruit orchards, olive groves and a peace and tranquility you'll never want to leave. Your hosts serve Tuscan classics laced with own-grown olive oil in the farm *osteria* (dinner on Friday and Saturday, and lunch on Sunday, by reservation only).

From Lorenzana, follow signs to Casciana Terme and after 3km turn left towards the hamlet of Colle Alberti.

La Moriccia AGRITURISMO €
(☑ 333 1283042; lamoriccia@hotmail.net; Via Comunale di Terricciola 107, Casciana Terme; d €50-60; P 🕏) Sharpen your map-reading skills: La Moriccia is hidden high in the hills at the end of a dusty dirt track. Four rustic-chic rooms feature handmade beds, wrought-iron fittings and filmy drapes, and one even has an open fire. Cots, triples and a host of farm animals strengthen the family appeal. It's 35km northeast of Castiglioncello, 1km outside Casciana Terme.

Grand Hotel Villa Parisi DESIGN HOTEL €€€
(☑ 0586 75 16 98; www.villaparisi.com; Via Romolo Monti 10; s €112-135, d €170-235; ⊙ Apr-Sep; P ❄ 🕏 🛎) With its chic cream facade and racing-green wooden shutters, this exquisite seaside villa wouldn't look amiss in a glossy design mag. Refined elegance holds sway inside, while the sea-view terrace and supremely stylish pool might well take your breath away. The top-notch option in town, Villa Parisi oozes panache; there's a gorgeous five-star restaurant too.

🍷 Drinking

Caffè Ginori CAFE
(Piazza della Vittoria; ⊙ 6.30am-9pm) Caffè Ginori is *the* locals' hang-out – join them chatting at the 1940s-era bar or on the shaded terrace and tuck into miniature cakes that look almost too good to eat. This was the favourite haunt of Italian heart-throb Marcello Mastroianni when he had a summer villa in town.

ℹ Information

Tourist Office (☑ 0586 75 48 90; Via Aurelia 632; ⊙ 9.30am-12.30pm & 4-6pm) At the train station; can provide free town maps.

ℹ Getting There & Away

Hourly trains run to Livorno (€3.10, 20 minutes).

OFF THE BEATEN TRACK

THE WINE & OIL ROAD

If tasting wine on the seashore or pedalling between olive groves rocks your boat, then trip it by car or bike along the Strada del Vino e dell'Olio Costa degli Etruschi (www.lastradadelvino.com), a 150km tourist itinerary stretching south from Livorno to Piombino and across to Elba. It maps out cellars, wine estates and farms where you can taste and buy local wine and olive oil, and also recommends places to eat and stay. Its **visitor centre** (p196) is just outside Bolgheri. Wineries are open to the public on a rota system; book at least two days in advance.

BEST WINE TASTING

Cantina Nardi (p192)

Enoteca Tognoni (p196)

Enoteca dei Difficili (p199)

Tenuta La Chiusa (p209)

Fandango (p211)

Bolgheri & Around

Tiny, walled Bolgheri is dominated by a toylike, red-brick castle which takes in the imposing gate and part-Romanesque Chiesa di SS Giacomo e Cristoro. But the main reason people flock to this village, bar browsing pricey tourist shops, is to taste wine – notably the locally produced, internationally famous 'Super Tuscan' Sassicaia.

◉ Sights

Cypress Alley LANDMARK

This dead-straight, 5km-long tree-lined avenue stretches between Bolgheri and San Guido; a stunning, impossibly romantic avenue built from 2540 trees. It was made famous by Tuscan poet Giosuè Carducci in his 1874 poem *Davanti a San Guido.* Each year in July the road creates a green backdrop for the arts festival, **Bolgheri Melody** (www.bolgherimelody.com).

⌕ Sleeping

DallOlivo AGRITURISMO €

(☑347 5423060; www.dallolivo.it; Magazzino 273; 4-person apt per week €510-800; P ✳ 🛜) 🏉 Splashes of yellow and red lend these two modern holiday apartments a jaunty air; their terraces, framed by narrow olive groves, have a chilled-out feel – helped by the outdoor wood-fires and alfresco sunshowers. A welcome bottle of own-grown olive oil is thrown in too. DallOlivo is 5km south of Bolgheri, just off the road to Castagneto. The owners lend guests bikes, too.

★ Castello di Bolgheri APARTMENT €€

(☑0565 76 21 10; www.castellodibolgheri.eu/en; Bolgheri; 2-/4-/6-person farmhouses per week €950/1500/2000; P ✳ 🛜) Your chance to stay within the grounds of an aristocratic estate – the family of the Counts Zileri Dal Verme. In these converted farmhouses smart, bright rooms open onto gardens which in turn lead onto olive groves. Guests get a free tour of the Castello di Bolgheri wine cellars, while gastro village Bolgheri is just a few minutes' stroll away. Prices fall by around €150 out of high season.

Strada Giulia 16 B&B €€

(☑331 2661699; www.stradagiuliabolgheri.it; Strada Giulia 16, Bolgheri; d €150-190; P) Strada Giulia 16 is both the name and address of this hybrid B&B–boutique hotel in a centuries-old house. Location alone, within the historic walls of Bolgheri, renders it instantly charming and its four rooms are glamorously named after famous ladies. Pick from Marilyn, Brigitte, Jaqueline or Lady D.

✕ Eating & Drinking

★ La Taverna del Pittore TUSCAN €€

(☑0565 76 21 84; www.latavernadelpittore.it; Largo Nonna Lucia 4, Bolgheri; meals €30-40; ☺ noon-2.30pm & 7-10pm, closed Mon) At this bewitching eatery, just beyond the north side of the town square, tables spill onto decking and a swirling mass of painted ballerinas grace the dining room. The menu is full of local classics cooked extremely well; its ricotta, mushroom and pheasant *tortello* (square, filled pasta), and stew of beef steeped in Bolgheri are rightly renowned.

★ Enoteca Tognoni WINE BAR

(☑0565 76 20 01; www.enotecatognoni.it; Via Lauretta 5, Bolgheri; meals €30; ☺ noon-2.30pm & 7-10pm Thu-Tue) This serious wine bar on Bolgheri's central piazza is a temple to taste, gastronomic and oenological. Sassicaia (€22 per 100mL) is among dozens of wines to sample, as is Castello di Bolgheri, which is produced just next door. Order a mixed plate of antipasti (€12), a generous feast of salami, cheese, tomato-topped bruschetta and *crostini,* and enter foodie heaven.

ⓘ Information

Strada del Vino e dell'Olio Visitor Centre

(☑0565 74 97 05; www.lastradadelvino.com; Castegneto Carducci 45, San Guido; ☺ 9.30am-7.30pm Mon-Sat summer, 10am-1pm & 2-5pm Mon-Sat winter) This visitor centre has lists of wine estates where you can taste and buy, and also arranges winery visits, olive farms and honey producers. You should aim to book at least a few days in advance. It's just off the SS1.

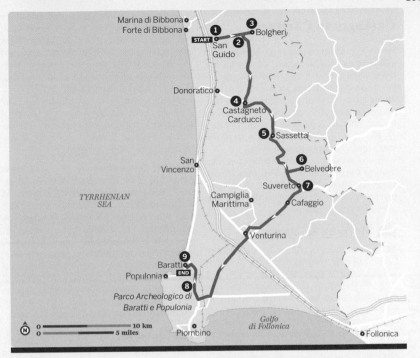

Marina di Bibbona
Forte di Bibbona
START San Guido
Bolgheri ③
② ①
Donoratico
Castagneto ④
Carducci
Sassetta ⑤
San
Vincenzo
Belvedere ⑥
Suvereto ⑦
TYRRHENIAN
SEA
Campiglia
Marittima
Cafaggio
Venturina
⑨
Baratti
END
Populonia
⑧
Parco Archeologico di
Baratti e Populonia
Golfo
di Follonica
Piombino
Follonica
N 0   10 km
   0   5 miles

🏃 Driving Tour
The Wine & Oil Road

START SAN GUIDO
END BARATTI
LENGTH 65KM; ONE DAY

Stock up with info at the Strada del Vino e dell'Olio visitor centre in ① **San Guido** before peeling along the undulating 5km ② **Cypress Alley** (p196) to pretty ③ **Bolgheri**. Park up on the right before town, then stroll through the fortified arch to explore streets lined with trattorias and *enoteche* (wine bars). Next, head 0.8km back down the Cypress Alley, before taking the SP16B, a slender, winding road leading through woods and past vineyards and olive groves. A series of switchbacks later, the pale yellow buildings of ④ **Castagneto Carducci** appear ranged on the ridge above. Park on the village edge and pick a lane heading upwards. Most lead to the 13th-century Propositura di San Lorenzo, a dimly lit affair with faded frescoes and ornate beams inside and a view of the Etruscan Coast from the terrace.

Driving on, towards Sassetta, signs warn of a wealth of hazards: narrow roads, tumbling

rocks, collapsing verges and leaping deer – it's a twisting drive with glimpses of the valley far below. At ⑤ **Sassetta**, park up to wander among improbably narrow, maze-like lanes; hunt out the best vantage points of houses that cling to the hills. Back behind the wheel, head through Sassetta, again onto one-lane hairpins and second-gear chicanes. Eventually olive trees and cypresses replace the dense woods. As you reach the fringes of Suvereto, look out for the minor road, cutting sharp left, up even narrower roads and first-gear bends, to the hamlet of ⑥ **Belvedere** with its extraordinary views and stylish bistro. Snake back down towards ⑦ **Suvereto**, an enchanting hill town with historic buildings aplenty to explore; here del Cacini and Enoteca dei Difficili are prime places to eat and drink. Finally, head southwest to swoop down from the hills to the shore. On the fringes of picturesque port Baratti stop at the ⑧ **archaeological park** (p202) to admire Etruscan ruins then head onto ⑨ **Baratti** itself, to Canessa for sundowners and just-caught fish.

Castagneto Carducci

POP 8906

Set on the high hills amid woods, vineyards and olive groves, Castagneto Carducci's fortified walls shelter a web of steep, narrow lanes crowded with ancient homes. It's dominated by a castle of the Gherardesca clan that once controlled the area, a stronghold turned into a mansion in the 18th century. The 19th-century poet Giosuè Carducci spent much of his childhood here.

From Castagneto, a winding forested road leads to the tiny hamlet of **Sassetta** (population 532), where houses hang on to their perches for dear life. A map at the entrance marks local walking trails.

Sleeping & Eating

★ **La Cerreta**　　　　AGRITURISMO €€

(☑ 0565 79 43 52; www.lacerreta.it; Via Campagna Sud 143, Pian delle Vigne; s/d half-board €85/130; P 🏊) 🍴 There's more than a hint of the Tuscan dream about La Cerreta, a biodynamic estate with sweeping hillside views where four stone cottages are wedged between woods, fig trees and vines. Add horses to ride and tours of the 70-hectare farm, complete with *cinta senese* (indigenous Tuscan pigs), Maremma cows and rare Livornese chickens, and it's a real rural delight.

A whopping 95% of produce served for dinner comes from the estate, while the spirit is 100% in harmony with nature – right down to the state-of-the-art thermal spa (admission €20), where a series of pebble rock pools cascades down the hills.

San Vincenzo & Around

POP 7007

Italian visitors flock to this moderately attractive seaside town in summer to flop on sandy beaches backed by herb-scented *macchia* (wild scrubland) and pine forest. Yachties moor their vessels in the town's smart, modern **Marina di San Vincenzo**, while the plains inland are rich in industrial heritage and soothing thermal springs.

◉ Sights & Activities

Parco Archeominerario di San Silvestro　　ARCHAEOLOGICAL SITE

(www.parchivaldicornia.it; off SP20; adult/reduced €15/11; ⏰ 10am-6pm summer, to 8pm Jul & Aug, shorter hours rest of year, closed Nov & Dec) The area's 3000-year mining history is explored at this intriguing industrial site, which sits a few kilometres inland from San Vincenzo. Here you can explore the ruins of the 14th-century mining town Rocca di San Silvestro, reached via an underground train that passes through the Temperino copper and lead mines. Guided tours depart roughly hourly.

Around 50m before the turn-off to the park entrance, a sunken lane on the right signposted *'forni fusori'* leads to the remains of some Etruscan smelting ovens, once used for copper production.

Calidario Terme Etrusche　　HOT SPRING

(☑ 0565 85 15 04; www.calidario.it; Via del Bottaccio 40, Venturina; pool entry per day adult/reduced €20/10, spa package (pools & 30min massage) from €80) What a treat: a thermal spa where you can just come for a swim and a massage or stay a few days. Magnesium- and calcium-rich waters, at a toasty 36°C, flow into a mini-lake; inside a stone and red-tile pool borders treatment rooms. The bedrooms (doubles from €150), in a converted outbuilding, feature swirling fabrics and soft lights.

Calidario is 15km south of San Vincenzo.

Sleeping

Podere San Michele　　AGRITURISMO €

(☑ 335 7809881; www.poderesanmichele.it; Via della Caduta 3; s/d €45/90; P ❄ 🛜) The warmth of the welcome at this wine estate is superb. Wicker furniture, huge beds and swish bathrooms define bedrooms, breakfast is a vast spread and you can organise tastings of the wine grown just outside. The setting, on the plains just south of San Vincenzo, isn't as picturesque as some, but it's well placed for exploring both hills and coast.

Drinking

Zanzibar　　BAR

(☑ 0565 70 29 27; Piazza del Porto; ⏰ noon-midnight Thu-Tue) Those in the know remain staunchly loyal to shabby-chic Zanzibar, drawn by vintage decor, designer nourishment and DJ sets after dark. It's in a former fisherman's hut at the northern end of the marina.

Suvereto

POP 3115

Suvereto is one of Tuscany's most beautiful medieval villages, hence the crowds that flock here to meander narrow cobbled streets and steep, cream-stone stairways brightened by balconies brimming with flowers. The town, the seat of a bishopric, was only incorporated into the Tuscan grand duchy in 1815.

◎ Sights

Rocca CASTLE
(Via Corta; ⊙9am-6pm or dusk) Suvereto's crowning glory is this part-15th-century *rocca* (castle), abandoned in the 1600s and slowly being restored. The climb to it up winding village streets is steep, but rewards with a magnificent panorama of surrounding fields and olive groves. On dusky pink summer evenings it's particularly enchanting.

Convento di San Francesco RELIGIOUS SITE
(Via del Crocifisso; ⊙times vary) FREE A stroll from the main street, Via Matteoti, uphill along Via del Crocifisso, brings you to all that remains of the 13th century Convento di San Francesco: its beautiful red-brick Chiostro di San Francesco is used today as a stunning stage for summer concerts, theatre performances and cultural events.

⚝ Festivals & Events

Serate Medioevali CULTURAL
Each year in mid-July the Serate Medioevali (Medieval Evenings) transforms the Romanesque cloister of the Convento di San Francesco into a medieval marketplace complete with locals dressed in traditional costume, a medieval banquet, and euro coins being traded for medieval money to spend at art, craft and food stalls.

⏢ Sleeping

★ Belvedere di Suvereto B&B €
(☑0565 82 70 61; www.belvederedisuvereto.it; Piazza San Tommaso 33, Belvedere; s/d €60/90) At this stylish B&B and bistro the views inside are as good as those outside: fresh white walls frame rustic roof supports and minimalist country-crafted furnishings. From the windows (especially the top-floor bedroom) expect a blockbuster *belvedere* (viewpoint) of sweet Suvereto far, far below.

✖ Eating & Drinking

Given the accolades of 'Slow Food town', 'wine town' and 'oil town' that it bears, Suvereto is a predictably wonderful place to discover local Val di Cornia DOC wines and dine well.

LOCAL KNOWLEDGE

BELVEDERE

'Belvedere' in Italian means 'viewpoint', and that's precisely what this eponymous hilltop hamlet proffers anyone who drives this far. Set 280m above sea level 3km north of Suvereto, the homes here were built in the mid-1500s so the rich could escape the malaria-infested plain. Its tiny, unpaved central square remains one of Tuscany's most enchanting and intimate.

★ del Cacini TUSCAN €€
(☑0565 82 83 13; www.ilcacini.it; Via del Crocifisso 3; 3-/4-course lunch €30/40; ⊙noon-3pm & 7-10pm, closed Tue) The best place in town to eat seafood; the fish at this chic eatery is so fresh the menu changes daily. Tables sport driftwood and filmy drapes, while the vine-shaded terrace and garden have sea glimpses – the perfect spots to linger over lunch or the exquisite, seven-course tasting menu (€55).

l'Ciocio TUSCAN €€
(☑0565 82 99 47; www.osteriadisuvereto.it; Piazza dei Giudici 1; meals €40; ⊙noon-2.30pm & 7-10.30pm, closed Mon) There's an appealing mix of old and new at this creative *osteria*. Its beautiful terrace features modern furnishings and views of the exquisite red-brick Palazzo Comunale (town hall) opposite. The menu, meanwhile, is squared firmly at foodies – the 12 different sugar types served after dinner with coffee say it all.

Enoteca dei Difficili WINE BAR
(Via San Leonardo 2; ⊙6pm-2am Tue-Thu, to 3am Fri-Sun; 🖥) Local foodies love this spirited *osteria*. No wonder: the brick ceiling and vintage chairs ensure it's stylish, while tasty treats include soup, *crostini* and €10 *taglieri* (wild boar, salami and cheese platters). Best sampled along with a glass from the stellar wine list in the street outside, looking up to the 18th-century Chiesa della Madonna di sopra la Porta.

ⓘ Information

Tourist Office (www.costadeglietruschi.it; Via Magenta 14; ⊙10.30am-12.30pm & 3.30-6pm summer, 3.30-6pm Sat & 10.30am-12.30pm Sun winter) There's a tourist information point inside the Museo artistico della Bambola.

1. Terrazza Mascagni (p190), Livorno

This elegant promenade sweeps gracefully along Livorno's seafront.

2. Golfo di Baratti (p202)

Golfo di Baratti's sundrenched shoreline is the perfect place for a seaside lunch.

3. Portoferraio (p205), Elba

Portoferraio's Old Town is a spiderweb of narrow streets and alleys that stagger uphill from the old harbour.

Golfo di Baratti

The Baratti Gulf sits at the southern tip of the Etruscan Coast, at the end of a 12km dead-straight road lined by beautiful sandy beaches and sky-high parasol pines. The main draws are the gorgeous little fishing port of Baratti and the area's archaeological sites.

◉ Sights & Activities

★ **Parco Archeologico di Baratti e Populonia** ARCHAEOLOGICAL SITE
(☑ 0565 22 64 45; www.parchivaldicornia.it; Baratti; Necropoli or Acropoli adult/child €9/6, entire park adult/child/family €10/7/25; ⊘ 9.30am-8pm Jul & Aug, 10am-6pm Tue-Sun Apr-Jun & Sep–mid-Oct) The Etruscan sites on display here are some of Tuscany's finest. Five marked walking trails lead through a vast green park, revealing a ruined town and incredibly well-preserved prehistoric tombs. The gigantic circular tumulus tombs in the **Necropoli di San Cerbone** are among the most impressive; the **Tomba dei Carri** is a whopping 28m in diameter.

The two-hour **Via delle Cave trail** leads through shady woodland to ranks of chamber tombs which have been hacked out of the soft ochre sandstone; ancient quarries are also dotted around.

The **Via della Romanella** (Metal Working Trail; 2½ hours) leads to the Etruscan **Acropoli di Populonia** (settlement of Populonia). Digs here have revealed the foundations of a 2nd-century-BC Etruscan temple; you'll see the remains of Roman temples, the city's central square, some towering terracing and an evocative, roughly paved road. Bring a sun hat, sun cream and sturdy shoes.

🛏 Sleeping & Eating

Canessa SEAFOOD €€
(☑ 0565 2 95 30; www.canessacamere.it; Baratti; d €75-105, meals €33; ⊘ noon-2.30pm & 7-10pm, closed Mon Sep-Jun) What makes this contemporary seafood restaurant so unique is the 15th-century watchtower that the modern building is wrapped around. Cuisine is fishy and fresh, and huge windows look onto the lapping waves. Should you fall in love with quaint Baratti (likely), Canessa has four rooms up top with romantic terraces and sea views.

ELBA & THE TUSCAN ARCHIPELAGO

POP 31,000

A local legend says that when Venus rose from the waves seven precious stones fell from her tiara, creating seven islands off the Tuscan coast. These little-known gems range from tiny uninhabited Gorgona, just 2.23 sq km in size, to the biggest and busiest island, 224-sq-km Elba (Isola d'Elba), best known as the place where Napoleon (poor thing) was exiled.

National Parks

The **Parco Nazionale dell'Arcipelago Toscano** (Tuscan Archipelago National Park; www.isle park.it) safeguards the delicate ecosystems of Elba's seven islands as well as the 600 sq km of sea that washes around them. It's Europe's largest protected marine area and is home to rare species such as the Neptune's shaving brush seaweed, unique to the archipelago. Monk seals, driven from other islands by humans, still gambol in the deep underwater ravines off Montecristo. The islands serve as an essential rest stop for birds migrating between Europe and Africa. The shy red partridge survives on Elba and Pianosa and the archipelago supports more than a third of the world's population of the Corsican seagull, adopted as the national park's symbol.

On Elba, the park runs visitors centres in Enfola, Marciana and Rio dell'Elba.

Elba

Napoleon would think twice about fleeing Elba today. Dramatically more congested than when the emperor was charitably dumped here in 1814 (he did manage to engineer an escape within a year), the island is an ever-glorious paradise of beach-laced coves, vineyards, azure waters, hairpin-bend motoring, a 1018m mountain (Monte Capanne) and mind-bending views. All supplemented by a fine seafaring cuisine, lovely island wines, and land and seascapes just made for hiking, biking and sea-kayaking.

BEST FAMILY ADVENTURES

Acquario di Livorno (p190)

Parco Archeominerario di San Silvestro (p198)

Parco Archeologico di Baratti e Populonia (p202)

Museo dei Minerali e dell'Arte Mineraria (p212)

Cabinovia Monte Capanne (p209)

With the exception of high season (actually only August), when the island's beaches and roads are jammed packed, Elba is something of a *Robinson Crusoe* paradise. In springtime, early summer and autumn, when grapes and olives are harvested, there are plenty of tranquil nooks on this stunningly picturesque, 28km-long, 19km-wide island.

History

Elba has been inhabited since the Iron Age and the extraction of iron ore and metallurgy were the island's principal sources of economic wellbeing until well into the second half of the 20th century. In 1917 some 840,000 tonnes of iron were produced, but in WWII the Allies bombed the industry to bits.

Ligurian tribespeople were the island's first inhabitants, followed by Etruscans and Greeks. Centuries of peace under the Pax Romana gave way to more uncertain times during the barbarian invasions, when Elba became a refuge for those fleeing mainland marauders. By the 11th century, Pisa (and later Piombino) was in control and built fortresses to help ward off attacks by Muslim raiders and pirates operating out of North Africa.

In the 16th century, Cosimo I de' Medici grabbed territory in the north of the island, where he founded the port town of Cosmopolis, today's Portoferraio.

Activities

The tourist office in Portoferraio can advise on Elba's many **walking trails**, **biking paths** and other outdoor activities; the visitor centre in Enfola maps out a lovely circular walk around the cape starting from the waterside office. From May to October it organises guided nature-themed walks.

Given its crystal-clear waters, **diving** and **snorkelling** are big on Elba between June and September. Otherwise, explore the island's sea-locked beaches and coves by **motor boat**, **kayak** or **yacht**.

Sea Kayak Italy   KAYAKING
(☑ 348 3337654; www.seakayakitaly.com) Runs sea-kayaking courses (per two days €180), excursions and a sublime two-day trip with a spot of fishing, beach camping and a campfire dinner of just-caught fish (€140, minimum two people). Or encircle the entire island in seven magical days (€550).

Il Viottolo   TREKKING, CYCLING
(☑ 329 7367100; www.ilviottolo.com; Via Fucini 279, Marina di Campo) Adventure specialists offering a wide range of treks, from archaeological and mineralogical to moonlit (from €40/200 per one/two days); mountain biking (€40 per half-day); sailing (per half-day €90) and sea kayaking (€40 per half-day).

Enfola Diving Center   DIVING
(☑ 339 6791367; www.enfoladivingcenter.it; Enfola; ☉ Jun-Sep) Get set up with gear, tuition and guides at this diving and snorkelling school on Enfola beach, 6km west of Portoferraio.

Diving in Elba   DIVING
(☑ 347 3715788; www.divinginelba.com) Ogle at eagle rays, sun fish, barracudas and a couple of Roman wrecks with this school, the island's largest. It operates 25-odd diving sites along Elba's north coast and has offices in Portoferraio, La Biodola and Procchio.

ℹ Information

The Portoferraio tourist office can provide island-wide information.

ℹ Getting There & Away

AIR
Elba's airstrip, **Aeroporto Isola d'Elba** (www.elbaisland-airport.it), is 2km north of Marina di Campo in La Pila. It links to Pisa and Florence, and a fairly wide range of European cities.

BOAT
Year-round, regular car and foot passenger ferries sail at least hourly from the Stazione Marittima (ferry port) in Piombino to Elba's main town, Portoferraio. Unless it's August or a summer weekend, there's no need to book a ticket in advance; simply buy one from a booth at the port. Fares (one way around €14/55 per person/car and driver) vary according to the season. Sailing time is one hour.
Blunavy (www.blunavytraghetti.com)
Moby (www.mobylines.com)
Toremar (www.toremar.it)

ℹ Getting Around

BUS
CTT Nord (www.livorno.cttnord.it) runs reasonably regular services linking all of Elba's main towns. In Portoferraio, buses leave from the bus station, opposite the main Piombino ferry jetty.

CAR
Car is the easiest way to get around Elba, except in August when roads are jammed. The island's southwest coast offers the most dramatic and scenic motoring. With no traffic, expect to take one hour to motor the 35km from Procchio to Cavoli.

Elba

5 km
2.5 miles

Piombino

Piombino

Piombino

Cavo

Rio Marina

Rio dell'Elba

Ortano

Nisportino

Nisporto

Bagnaia

Ottone

Magazzini

Schiopparello

Portoferraio

Le Grotte

Spiaggia la Padulella

Spiaggia di Capo Bianco

Spiaggia di Sansone

Spiaggia di Sorgente

San Giovanni

San Martino

Capo d'Enfola

Enfola

Viticcio

Spiaggia di Scaglieri

La Biodola

Spiaggia di Spartaia

Procchio

Marmi

La Pila

Aeroporto Isola d'Elba

Spiaggia della Paolina

Golfo della Biodola

Monte Perone (630m)

SP37

Monte Maolo (749m)

Sant'Ilario in Campo

San Piero in Campo

Marina di Campo

Marciana Marina

Poggio

Marciana

Santuario della Madonna del Monte

Colle d'Orano

Capo Sant'Andrea

Monte Capanne (1018m)

Chiessi

Pomonte

Fetovaia

Spiaggia delle Tombe

Seccheto

Cavoli

Le Piscine

Punta di Fetovaia

Tyrrhenian Sea

Tyrrhenian Sea

Golfo di Campo

Golfo della Lacona

Lacona

Via Colle Reciso

Cima del Monte (516m)

Porto Azzurro

Capoliveri

Monte Calamita (413m)

Punta della Calamita

Spiaggia di Naregno

Spiaggia di Morcone

Spiaggia di Pareti

Spiaggia dell'Innamorata

Spiaggia di Zuccale

Spiaggia di Barabarca

Spiaggia dello Stagnone

Pianosa

Montecristo (35km)

Capraia

Tyrrhenian Sea

In Portoferraio, **Twn Rent** (☑ 0565 91 46 66; www.twn-rent.it; Viale Elba 32) rents out cars and scooters. Car hire costs around €60 for one day; rates for four days range from €175 in low season to €220 in August.

Portoferraio & Around

POP 12,027

Known to the Romans as Fabricia and later Ferraia (since it was a port for iron exports), this small harbour was acquired by Cosimo I de' Medici in the mid-16th century, when its distinctive fortifications took shape.

Portoferraio can be a hectic place, especially in August when holidaymakers pour off the ferries from Piombino on the mainland every 20 minutes or so. But wandering the streets and steps of the historic centre, indulging in the exceptional eating options and haggling for sardines with fishermen more than makes up for the squeeze.

◎ Sights & Activities

Old Town AREA
The Old Town's spiderweb of narrow streets and alleys staggers uphill from the old harbour to Portoferraio's defining twinset of forts, **Forte Falcone** and the salmon-pink **Forte Stella** (Via della Stella; adult/reduced €2/1.50; ⊙9am-7pm Easter-Sep), revealing deserted 16th-century ramparts to wander and seagulls freewheeling overhead.

From central square Piazza Cavour head uphill along Via Garibaldi to the foot of the monumental **Scalinata Medici**, a fabulous mirage of 140 wonky stone steps cascading up through every sunlit shade of amber to the dimly lit, 17th-century **Chiesa della Misericordia** (Via della Misericordia; ⊙8am-5pm). Inside is Napoleon's death mask. Continue to the top of the staircase to reach the forts and **Villa dei Mulini**, where Napoleon lived when in Elba.

**Museo Nazionale
della Residenza Napoleoniche** MUSEUM
(Villa dei Mulini; Piazzale Napoleone; adult/reduced €5/3; ⊙9am-7pm Mon & Wed-Sat, to 1pm Sun) Villa dei Mulini was home to Napoleon during his stint in exile on this small isle. With its Empire-style furnishings, splendid library, fig-tree-studded Italianate gardens and unbeatable sea view, the emperor didn't want for creature comforts – contrast this with the simplicity of the camp bed and travelling trunk he used when on campaigns.

**Museo Archeologica
della Linguelle** ARCHAEOLOGICAL SITE, MUSEUM
(Torre della Linguella; Calata Buccari; adult/reduced €3/2; ⊙10am-1pm & 3.30-7pm Fri-Wed summer) Napoleon was 'imprisoned' at the start of his fleeting exile on Elba in 1814 in 16th-century **Torre del Martello**. The russet-red, octagonal tower remained a prison until 1877. The archaeological ruins in front of it were part of a luxurious Roman villa between the 1st and 5th centuries AD, and form part of this modest museum today.

**Museo Villa
Napoleonica di San Martino** MUSEUM
(San Martino; adult/reduced €5/2.50; ⊙9am-7pm Tue-Sat, to 1pm Sun summer, 9am-3pm Tue-Sat, to 1pm Sun winter) Napoleon used to drop into this quaintly ornate villa 5km southwest of Portoferraio to escape the summer heat. At heart, it's a remodelled farmhouse topped by a roof terrace bearing Napoleonic stone eagles. In the 1850s a Russian nobleman had the gallery built at its base, now host to temporary Napoleon-related exhibitions.

OFF THE BEATEN TRACK

BIKING & HIKING ON ELBA

A dizzying network of walking and mountain-biking trails blankets Elba. Many start in Portoferraio, but some of the best, far-flung trailheads kick off elsewhere.

Monte Capanne Circular A three-hour, 20km adventure on the slopes of Elba's highest mountain, which sees you cycling on paved and unpaved routes past scented *maquis* and pines. Total climb: 540m.

Marciana to Chiessi A 12km (six-hour) hike starting high up in Marciana, dribbling downhill past ancient churches, sea vistas and granite boulders to the seaside in Chiessi.

The Great Elba Crossing A three- to four-day, 60km east–west island crossing, including Monte Capanne, Elba's highest point (1018m), overnighting on the coast (camping isn't allowed beside paths). The highlight is the final 19km leg from Poggio to Pomonte, passing the Santuario della Madonna del Monte and the Masso dell'Aquila rock formation.

DON'T MISS

HAGGLING FOR FISH

Hanging out with locals, waiting for the fishing boats to come in, is a quintessential Portoferraio pastime. The crowd starts forming on the quay around 9.30am and by the time the first boats dock at 10am there's a line-up of punters waiting to exchange hand-crumpled bank notes for the catch of the day.

The larger industrial fishing boats dock midway between the ferry terminal and the old-town harbour on **Banchina d'Alto Fondale**. Occasionally they'll catch a huge tuna – which draws a real crowd – but in the main it's wooden crates of sardines, mackerel and anchovies the crew sell from the side of their boat (€5 for a plastic-bag full).

Smaller vessels with just one or two fishermen moor alongside **Calata Giacomo Matteotti** at the old harbour each morning any time from 8am onwards. And these are the guys who get the real catch – octopus, lobster, eel and swordfish on good days.

If haggling for fish is simply not your cup of tea, there's always harbourside fishmonger **Pescheria del Porto** (Calata Matteotti 10; ⏲8am-12.30pm Mon-Sat).

Sleeping

Half-board is usually the only option in August and many hotels only open April to October.

Villa Ombrosa HOTEL €
(☎0565 91 43 63; www.villaombrosa.it; Via Alcide de Gasperi 3, Portoferraio; d from €95, half-board per person €60-126; P 📶) One of the few hotels in town and open year-round, three-star Ombrosa looks out to sea and the pinprick islet of Lo Scoglietto. Decor is a jumble of styles, but summer rates include a lounger and umbrella on Ghiaie Beach across the street. Rooms with sea views tout pocket-sized balconies and the breakfast pastries are light as air.

Porta del Mare PENSION €
(☎328 8261441; www.bebportadelmarelba.com; Piazza Cavour 34, Portoferraio; d €70-140, tr €160-170; 📶) If you like being in the heart of things, the 4th-floor rooms in this elegant townhouse could work a treat. Light, bright bedrooms have tall ceilings and filmy drapes; two have cracking harbour views. It's right in the middle of Portoferraio's main square (so expect some night-time noise) and breakfast (€2.50) is served in a sea-view cafe nearby.

Rosselba Le Palme CAMPGROUND €
(☎0565 93 31 01; www.rosselbalepalme.it; Ottone; adult €14-23, tent €6-55, car €1-6; ⏲mid-Apr–Sep; P 📶 🏊) Set around a botanical garden backed by Mediterranean forest, few campsites are as leafy or large. The beach is a 400m walk between trees while accommodation ranges from simple pitches and cute wooden chalets to 'glamping' tents with bathtubs and villa apartments. Find the ground 9km east of Portoferraio near Ottone.

Hotel e Ristorante Mare HOTEL €€
(☎0565 93 30 69; www.hotelmare.org; Magazzini; d €125-180, half-board per person €55-110; ⏲summer; ❄ @ 📶 🏊) The setting is secluded and gorgeous: on the edge of a tiny, crab-claw harbour that's 9km east of Portoferraio by car. A crisp blue-and-white striped colour scheme lends things a nautical air, while the rooftop terrace, pool and waterfront restaurant are reminiscent of being on an ocean liner, something enhanced by spectacular views across a grand, sweeping bay.

Villa Ottone HISTORIC HOTEL €€€
(☎0565 93 30 42; www.villaottone.com; Ottone 4; s €94-170, d €234-414, d in villa €199-390, dinner €30; ⏲May-Sep; P ❄ @ 📶 🏊) Elba doesn't get classier than this. The height of elegance and lap of luxury, this aristocratic 19th-century villa looking out to sea 10km east of Portoferraio was home to Tuscan counts until the 1920s. With its own private beach, spa, pool bar, lush gardens and restaurants, guests want for nothing. Cheaper rooms are in a modern block; half-board only.

Eating

★Il Castagnacciao PIZZA €
(Via del Mercato Vecchio 13; pizza €4.50-7; ⏲10am-2.30pm & 5-10.30pm Thu-Tue, to midnight summer) They work the pizza chef so hard here the dining room sometimes has a smoky tinge. To go local, start with a lip-smacking plate of *torta di ceci* (chickpea 'pizza'), then watch your rectangular, thin-crust supper go in to and out of the wood-fired oven. But save space for dessert – *castagnaccio* (chestnut 'cake') baked over the same flames.

Caffescondido
TRATTORIA €€
(Via del Carmine 65; meals €25; ⊘noon-2pm & 7-9.30pm Mon-Sat) This Slow Food–endorsed trattoria, footsteps from pretty Piazza Gramsci, makes for the perfect getaway from the waterfront crowds. Options are simple – just a handful of *primi* (first courses) and *secondi* are chalked on the blackboard, which usually stars a local classic such as *baccacà alla marinese* (salt cod with potatoes) or *polpo brisco* (octopus). No credit cards.

Osteria Libertaria
TUSCAN €€
(☑0565 91 49 78; Calata Giacomo Matteotti 12; meals €30; ⊘noon-2.30pm & 7-9.30pm summer) Fish drives the menu of this traditional *osteria* – no wonder the boats that land it are right outside. Traditional dishes such as fried calamari or *tonno in crosta di pistacchi* (pistachio-encrusted tuna fillet) are super-fresh and cooked to perfection every time. Dine at one of two tile-topped tables on the traffic-noisy street or on the back-alley terrace.

La Lucchetta
TRATTORIA €€
(Piazza della Repubblica 40; meals €30; ⊘11.30am-3pm & 6-11.30pm Wed-Mon) The setting is homely rather than smart (a couple of TVs show the nightly news), but the seafood here is top-notch. The gnocchi or *pappardelle primi* are packed with crustaceans and fishy flavour, while the garlicky catch of the day is superb: chargrilled, dotted with rocket and laced with lemon and olive oil.

Bitta 20
SEAFOOD €€€
(☑0565 93 02 70; Calata Mazzini 20; meals €45; ⊘noon-2.30pm & 7-11pm) Portoferraio's best chef has relocated to this bright, harbour-side eatery, where a long strip of tables overlooks a string of bobbing yachts. White tablecloths and smart service combine with sublime fish and seafood cooked with a fabulous dose of creativity. Which all makes it very popular – book.

Information

Tourist office (☑0565 91 46 71; www.isoleditoscana.it; Calata Italia 44; ⊘9am-7pm Mon-Sat, 10am-1pm & 3-6pm Sun summer, 9am-5pm Mon-Thu, 9am-1pm Fri winter) Helpful staff have abundant information on walking and biking on the island. Find the office on the seafront, near the ferry docks.

Procchio & Around

Just 10km west of Portoferraio, this small bustling beach town draws summertime

---

EMPEROR NAPOLEON

At precisely 6pm on 3 May 1814, the English frigate *Undaunted* dropped anchor in the harbour of Portoferraio on Elba. It bore an unusual cargo. Under the Treaty of Fontainebleau, the emperor Napoleon was exiled to this seemingly safe open prison, some 15km from the Tuscan coast.

It could have been so much worse, but the irony for a conqueror who'd stridden across all Europe and taken Egypt must have been bitter.

Napoleon, ever hyperactive, threw himself into frenetic activity in his new domain. He prescribed a mass of public works, including improving the island's iron-ore mines – whose revenue, it is pertinent to note, now went his way. He also boosted agriculture, built roads, drained marshes and overhauled the legal and education systems.

Some weeks after his arrival, his mother Letizia and sister Paolina rolled up. But he remained separated from his wife, Maria Luisa, and was visited for just two days by his lover, Maria Walewska.

At the Congress of Vienna, the new regime in France called for Napoleon's removal to a more distant location. Some favoured a shift to Malta, but Britain objected and suggested the remote South Atlantic islet of St Helena. The Congress broke up with no agreed decision.

Napoleon was well aware of the debate. A lifelong risk taker, he decided to have another roll of the dice. For months he had sent out on 'routine' trips around the Mediterranean a couple of vessels flying the flag of his little empire, Elba. When one, the *Incostante*, set sail early in the morning of 26 February 1815, no one suspected that the conqueror of Europe was stowed away on board.

Napoleon made his way to France, reassumed power and embarked on the Hundred Days, the last of his expansionist campaigns that would culminate in defeat at Waterloo, after which he got his Atlantic exile after all, dying on St Helena in 1821, from arsenic poisoning – contracted, many believe, from the hair tonic he applied to keep that famous quiff glistening.

ELBA'S BEST BEACH SPOTS

Given the wide range of bays on Elba's 147km-long coast it pays to know your *spiagge* (beaches). You'll find sandy strands on the south coast and in the Golfo della Biodola, on the western side of Capo d'Enfola; **La Biodola** has the nearest sandy beach to Portoferraio. The quietest, prettiest beaches are tucked in bijou rocky coves and often involve a steep clamber down. Parking is invariably roadside and scant.

Enfola

Just 6km west of Portoferraio, it's not so much the grey pebbles as the outdoor action that lures crowds to this tiny fishing port. There are pedalos to rent, a beachside diving school, and a family-friendly 2.5km-long circular **hiking trail** around the green cape. The **Parco Nazionale dell'Arcipelago Toscano visitors centre** (Tuscan Archipelago National Park; ☑ 0565 91 94 11; www.islepark.it; Enfola; ⊙ 10.30am-1.30pm & 2.30-4.30pm summer only) is also here.

Sansone & Sorgente

This twinset of cliff-ensnared, white-shingle and pebble beaches stands out for crystal-clear, turquoise waters just made for **snorkelling**. By car from Portoferraio, follow the SP27 towards Enfola. Parking is challenging.

Morcone, Pareti & Innamorata

Find this trio of charming sandy-pebble coves framed by sweet-smelling pine trees some 3km south of Capoliveri in southeast Elba. Rent a kayak and paddle out to sea on Innamorata, the wildest of the three; or fine dine and overnight on Pareti beach at **Hotel Stella Maris** (☑ 0565 96 84 25; www.albergostellamaris.it; Pareti; half-board per person d €70-125; P ❄), one of the few three-star hotels to be found on the sand.

Colle d'Orano & Fetovaia

The standout highlight of these two gorgeous swathes of golden sand on Elba's western coast is the dramatic drive between the two. Legend has it Napoleon frequented Colle d'Orano to sit and swoon over his native Corsica, which is visible across the water. A promontory covered with heavenly scented *maquis* (herbal scrubland) protects sandy Fetovaia, where nudists flop on nearby granite rocks known as **Le Piscine**.

---

crowds thanks to one of Elba's longest stretches of golden sand. West from Procchio, the road hugs cliffs above **Spiaggia di Spartaia** and **Spiaggia della Paolina**, beautiful little beaches requiring a steep clamber down.

🏃 Activities

Rent Procchio   BICYCLE RENTAL
(☑ 338 7185735; www.rentprocchio.it; Via Provinciale di Procchio; mountain bikes per day €15-30) Rent Procchio's stand on the main street provides both bikes and cycling itineraries.

🛏 Sleeping

Relais Baia Bianca   APARTMENT €€€
(☑ 0565 96 99 16; www.baiabiancarelais.com; La Biodola 16; d €132-600; ⊙ Apr-Sep) A picture-perfect manicured garden, pea-green lawns and wooden decking walkways are the only

things separating these dazzling white, designer-chic apartments from the sand. At this much-raved-about address, each self-catering apartment has its own waterside, bright-white sun veranda. It also offers a series of rooms. Find it all on the golden beach of La Biodola, slightly northeast of Procchio.

There's a minimum stay of seven nights between June and August.

Hotel Hermitage   LUXURY HOTEL €€€
(☑ 0565 97 40; www.hotelhermitage.it; La Biodola; half-board per person €130-365; ⊙ summer; P ❄ @ 🛜 🏊) If James Bond were to parachute onto Elba in a tuxedo, he'd land on the tennis courts here. One of the island's truly luxurious hotels, this gorgeous retreat has a sea-view infinity pool, golf course, beauty centre and countless other spoil-yourself treats. It's in the seaside hamlet of La Biodola, northeast of Procchio.

✕ Eating & Drinking

Scalo 70 GELATERIA €
(Via del Mare 10, Procchio; cones €2.20-4.50; ☺ noon-8pm summer) Arguably Elba's best gelato and Sicilian *granita;* try the rice or nut, fig and caramel gelato.

La Casa del Vino BAR
(Via del Mare 15, Procchio; ☺10am-2pm & 4pm-2am Wed-Mon) Scuffed wooden floorboards, dark wood barrels, and lively DJ sets make this a heart-of-the action place to sip Elban grappa or wines – especially while people-watching from the street-side terrace.

Marciana & Marciana Marina

POP 2250

Unlike many modern cookie-cutter marinas, the attractive resort of Marciana Marina has character and history to complement its pleasant pebble beaches. The port is 18km west along the coast from Portoferraio. From it, a twisting 9km mountain road winds inland up to Marciana, the island's oldest and highest village (375m), which is crowned by a much-knocked-about fort.

Meandering Marciana's stone streets, past arches, flower boxes and petite balconies, reveals drop-offs with views of the coastline below. But the highlight is the short half-day walk from the village to the island's most important pilgrimage site: the Santuario della Madonna del Monte.

⊙ Sights & Activities

Santuario della Madonna del Monte CHAPEL
(☺ dawn-dusk) Park at the entrance to Marciana and head 40 minutes out of the village on foot along Via delle Fonti and its continuations, Via delle Coste and Via dei Monti, to this much-altered 11th-century church. Inside is a stone upon which a divine hand is said to have painted an image of the Virgin, believed to have miraculous powers.

It is an invigorating uphill hike along an old mule track bordered by scented parasol pines, chestnut trees, wild sage and thyme. The coastal panorama that unfolds as you get higher is remarkable. Once you reach the hilltop chapel (627m), drink like Napoleon did from the old stone fountain across from the church – look for the plaque commemorating his visit here on horseback in 1814. Next, continue five minutes along the footpath to play 'I Spy Corsica'.

★ **Cabinovia Monte Capanne** FUNICULAR
(Cableway; ☑ 0565 90 10 20; www.cabinovia-isoladelba.it; single/return €12/18; ☺10am-1pm & 2.20-6pm Apr-Sep, to 5pm Oct) If you only have time for one road trip from Portoferraio, make it this. Some 750m south of Marciana on the Poggio road, this cable car sees you climbing into an open, barred basket – imagine riding in a canary-yellow parrot cage – to be whisked up to the summit of Elba's highest point, **Monte Capanne** (1018m).

CENTRAL COAST & ELBA ELBA

OFF THE BEATEN TRACK

GOURMET ESCAPES

Tenuta La Chiusa (☑ 0565 93 30 46; www.tenutalachiusa.it; Magazzini 93; 2 people per week €450-850, up to 5 people per week €750-1300; ℗) Some 8km east of Portoferraio, Tenuta La Chiusa is Elba's oldest winemaking estate, and is also where Napoleon stayed the night upon landing on Elba in 1814. Right on the seashore, it is stunning – offering a 17th-century farmhouse, 18th-century villa, 8 hectares of vineyards, olive groves, palm trees and 10 apartments; some on the beach in former peasants' cottages.

Self-catering accommodation (minimum stay one week) has a simple charm; guests can buy olive oil and wine at reception; and, should you not fancy cooking, an excellent eatery is a two-minute shore-side stroll away at tiny Magazzini harbour. The estate also organises wine-tasting in its cellar.

Agriturismo Due Palme (☑ 0565 93 30 17, 338 7433736; www.agriturismoelba.it; Via Schiopparello 28, Schiopparello; d €50-70, 4-person house per week €720-900) Utterly tranquil, despite being just a few minutes from the Portoferraio–Magazzini road, this idyllic *agriturismo*'s five traditionally styled former workers' cottages are dotted amid orange and lemon trees and 100 year old olive groves. The estate was founded by the welcoming Fabrizio's grandfather, and is the only olive plantation on Elba to produce quality-stamped IGP olive oil.

Guests can taste and buy the silky fresh-green oil (€19 per litre) and are invariably tempted to sample some oranges. Tree-shaded deck chairs, a BBQ and an astonishingly flowery garden heighten the charm.

MARCIANA MARINA: A TRADITIONAL PASSEGGIATA

The loveliest moment of the day in Marciana Marina is early evening when the entire town seems to wander beside the waterfront for their *passeggiata* (evening stroll).

Start at the seafront's eastern end where the gigantic palm trees and bars of **Piazza della Vittoria** provide prime places to watch the walking get under way. Around the corner, **La Svolta** (www.gelaterialasvolta.it; Via Cairoli 6; ☉2-8pm Tue-Sun) sells creative gelato flavour combos, such as apple and cinnamon, and orange and black pepper.

Walk west a few minutes along waterside Viale Margherita, then make a quick detour a block inland to take in the pretty peach-painted church and pristine carpet cobblestones in **Piazza Vittorio Emanuele**.

Backtrack to the water and continue meandering west past boutiques and a mini marina before, as the sun sinks, you find yourself at the far end of the waterfront on **Spiaggia di Capo Nord**, a handsome beach of large smooth pebbles overlooked by a 12th-century Saracen tower.

Here, **Ristorante Capo Nord** (☑0565 99 69 83; www.ristorantecaponord.it; meals €50; ☉noon-2pm & 7-9.30pm Tue-Sun), an impossibly romantic seafood restaurant with splendid beach-side terrace, is the perfect place to end your *passeggiata*, perhaps while enjoying its octopus risotto or grilled swordfish and gazing out to sea.

After 20 minutes, scramble around the rocky peak to savour an astonishing 360-degree panorama of Elba, the Tuscan Archipelago, Etruscan Coast and Corsica 50km away. The scent of *la macchia* is heavenly. Hikers can buy a one-way ticket and walk back down – a 1½-hour hike along a rocky but well-marked path.

✖ Eating

★ Osteria del Noce   FISH €€
(☑0565 90 12 84; www.osteriadelnoce.it; Via della Madonna 14; meals €25; ☉noon-2pm & 7.30-9.30pm late-Mar–Sep) This family-run bistro in hilltop Marciana is the type of place where the bread is homemade and flavoured with fennel, chestnut flour and other seasonal treats. The *miso mare del Noce* (mixed fish *antipasti*), spaghetti laced with *Granseolo Elbano* (a large crab typical to Elba) and sweeping views are truly memorable.

❶ Information

Casa del Parco di Marciana (☑0565 90 10 30; www.islepark.it; Fortezza Pisana; ☉10am-1pm Mon, 9am-1pm Tue, 9am-1pm & 5.30-7.30pm Wed & Thu, 10am-1pm & 3-7pm Sat, shorter hours mid-season, closed Nov-Mar) The national park visitors centre, just below Fortezza Pisana, has lots of walking and outdoor activity info.

Poggio

A twisting ascent up precipitous ridgebacks brings you to the attractive mountain village of Poggio. Set on the SP25, it's famous for its spring water and is an enchanting little place with steep, cobblestone alleys and stunning coastal views.

◎ Sights & Activities

Monte Perone   MOUNTAIN
Just south of Poggio, the SP37 winds to a well-signed picnic site at the foot of Monte Perone (630m). To the left (east) you can wander up the mountain to take in spectacular views across much of the island. To the right (west) you can scramble fairly quickly to a height affording broad vistas down to Poggio, Marciana and Marciana Marina.

Monte Maolo   MOUNTAIN
At Monte Maolo (749m), slightly south of Poggio village and the peak of Monte Perone, the road descends into the southern flank of the island, passing en route the granite shell of the Romanesque **Chiesa di San Giovanni** and, shortly after, a ruined tower, the **Torre di San Giovanni**. Two small hamlets, Sant'Ilario in Campo and San Piero in Campo, make simple stops to stretch your legs.

✖ Eating

Publius   TUSCAN €€
(☑0565 9 92 08; www.ristorantepublius.it; Piazza del Castagneto 11; meals €35; ☉noon-2.30pm & 7-9.30pm Tue-Sun Mar-Nov) The floor-to-ceiling windows of this formal, hillside restaurant at the lower end of Poggio village create the sense of eating in a classy treehouse, while

the vistas from the stylish roof terrace make you feel you're suspended above the sea. The refined Tuscan menu profiles fish and mountain produce; a popular house speciality is chestnut gnocchi with duck *ragù*.

Marina di Campo

A small fishing harbour on the south side of the island, Marina di Campo is Elba's second-largest town. Here a curling, picturesque bay dotted with bobbing boats adds personality to what is otherwise very much a holiday-oriented town. Its beach of bright, white sand pulls in vacationers by the thousands; coves further west, though less spectacular, are more tranquil.

◉ Sights

Cavoli   BEACH
The shingle-sand beach at Cavoli, just 6km west of Marina di Campo, is particularly family-friendly, thanks to its beach cafe, sun lounges, pedalos and kids' playground.

Acquario dell'Elba   ACQUARIUM
(www.acquarioelba.com; Marina di Campo; adult/child €7/3; ⊙9am-7pm Apr-Oct, to 11.30pm Jun–mid-Sep) More than 150 Mediterranean species inhabit this modest aquarium, making it a good grey-day option. It's 2km northeast of town, signposted off the SP30 to Lacona.

✖ Eating & Drinking

★**Il Cantuccio**   TRATTORIA €
(☑0565 97 67 75; www.ristoranteilcantuccio. eu; Largo Garibaldi 6; pizza €6-9, meals €25; ⊙noon-3pm & 7-11pm) Ignore the waterfront's menu-touting waiters and instead duck into Piazza Della Fontana to find this unassuming trattoria's spearmint-green facade. In business since 1930, the place is excellent value – hence the strong local following which comes here for Tuscan classics, homemade pasta, wood-oven-fired pizza and 18 different varieties of olive oil.

Da Mario   BAR
(Piazza Teseo Tesei 56; ⊙8am-11pm) Da Mario has been around since 1952 and its decking overlooks a cluster of fishing boats and a long curl of sand. Which explains both why it's a local institution and an ideal spot to linger over a cappuccino or something stronger.

Capoliveri

POP 3910

Picturesque Capoliveri sits in the high hills of Elba's southeast corner. Its steep, narrow alleys are lined with squeezed-in houses, while the panorama of rooftops and sea that fans out from the old stone terrace on its central square, **Piazza Matteotti**, is lovely indeed.

🛏 Sleeping

Villa Wanda   HOTEL €€
(☑0565 94 00 25; www.hotelvillawanda.com; Via Generinco 17, Lido di Capoliveri; d €140-200) At this friendly, family-run 15-room hotel, 4km north of Capoliveri, unfussy rooms are bright and fresh while a series of terraces provide plenty of space to lounge around. The best bedrooms have balconies with fine sea views (the terrace attached to 301 is huge), and the sandy beach at Lido di Capoliveri is 10 minutes' walk away.

✖ Eating & Drinking

La Taverna dei Poeti   TUSCAN €€
(☑0565 96 83 06; www.latavernadeipoeti.com; Via Roma 14, Capoliveri; meals €35; ⊙6-11pm daily summer only) Much-loved by locals, this traditional address sees chef Massimo cook up the very best of Tuscan produce with a generous peppering of simplicity. The menu splits dishes into '*mare*' (sea) and '*terre*' (literally 'earth', meaning meat), and a €50 tasting menu pairs each of the four courses with a different wine.

Il Chiasso   SEAFOOD €€€
(☑0565 96 87 09; Nazario Sauro 13, Capoliveri; meals €48; ⊙7-9.30pm Easter-Oct) Tucked down an alley *(chiasso)* enlivened only by the odd line of washing, Il Chiasso serves up seafood classics and excellent wine. For a true taste of Capoliveri go for the fish soup *di Luciano* (€25), cooked up by chef Luciano since time began and swimming with local catch. Advance reservations recommended.

★**Fandango**   WINE BAR
(Via Cardenti 1, Capoliveri; ⊙Tue-Sun Easter-Oct) Steps lead down from the panoramic terrace at the far end of the central Piazza Matteotti to this lively *enoteca*. Sitting beneath its vine-clad pergola in the early evening is particularly atmospheric. Cocktails, live music and *piccolo cucina* (light snacks) add real after-dark flair.

Porto Azzurro

POP 3730

Laid-back Porto Azzurro is pretty much the quintessential small Elban town. Fittingly (considering its name), a glittering blue harbour fronts a palm-dotted pedestrianised square; a compact maze of flower-framed lanes, lined with restaurant and cafe terraces, spreads out behind. It makes for an atmospheric place to sample local seafood and wine, and a sweep of good beaches lies within easy reach by bike.

✖ Eating

★ **La Botte Gaia**   OSTERIA €€
(☑ 0565 9 56 07; www.labottegaia.com; Viale Europa 5, Porto Azzurro; meals €35; ☺ 7-9.30pm Tue-Sun) Slow Food–featured and deservedly so, this is *the* revered dining address in Porto Azzurro. Expect creative use of homemade pasta, just-caught fish and island wines, plus a few relative rarities: slow-cooked salt cod with truffles, octopus *gazpacho* and goose salami. Book ahead.

L'Osteria dei Quattro Gatti   SEAFOOD €€
(☑ 0565 9 52 40; Piazza Mercato 4; meals €35; ☺ 7-9.30pm) In the maze of lanes leading off from the main square (Piazza Matteotti), hunt out this *osteria*'s flower-framed deck, which sets the scene for excellently executed fish-themed dishes, often including a memorable *spaghetti alle vongole*.

Rio dell'Elba & Rio Marina

Mountainous and relatively remote, northeast Elba was the heart of the island's mining operation, and heritage attractions here vividly bring that industrial history to life. The two main towns, hilltop Rio dell'Elba (population 1212) and coastal Rio Marina (population 2233), sit amid a network of plunging, twisting roads that will test your nerve and driving skills.

◉ Sights

Museo dei Minerali e dell'Arte Mineraria   MUSEUM
(☑ 0565 96 20 88; www.parcominelba.it; Via Magenta 26, Rio Marina; adult/reduced €2.50/1.50; ☺ 9.30am-12.30pm & 3.30-6.30pm summer) Rio's mining history dates from Etruscan times, with open-cast working continuing right up until 1982 when the mines closed. This museum charts that story and runs guided tours (adult/child €12/7.50) of the mining area by electric train – these include a chance to dig for minerals (hammers and plastic bags are provided) yourself. Book a few days in advance.

Gorgona, Capraia, Pianosa & Giglio

Pinprick Gorgona is the greenest, northernmost of the Tuscan islands and can only be visited with a guide. Two towers built by the Pisans and Medicis of Florence keep watch over its plunging coastline and beautiful interior, part of which has been off limits as a low-security prison since 1869. **Toscana Trekking** (www.toscanatrekking.it) runs daylong tours (adult/child €68/42), leaving roughly weekly from Livorno.

By contrast the elliptical volcanic island of Capraia (population 400), 31km from the French island of Corsica, is 8km long, 4km wide, peaks with Monte Castello (447m) and has a few hotels and restaurants. The island's great walks include the trail to Lake Stagnone – Capraia's **tourist office** (☑ 0586 90 51 38; www.prolococapraiaisola.it; Via Assunzione 42; ☺ 9am-12.30pm & 4.30-7pm Fri-Wed summer) has maps of hiking and biking routes around the island. A chequered history has seen Genoa, Sardinia, the Saracens from North Africa and Napoleon all have a bash at running Capraia. Once a week, **Aquavision** (www.aquavision.it) runs a day trip (adult/child return €30/15, 2½ hours each way) from Portoferraio on Elba, which leaves you five hours to explore the island. **Toremar** (www.toremar.it) operates ferries from mainland Livorno to Capraia (€38 return, 2½ hours each way; one or two daily in summer, less frequently in winter); in high season schedules can allow a return trip in a day, but triple-check before setting out.

South of Elba, Giglio (population 1500), the second-largest Tuscan island, is 21 km sq and is perhaps now most famous as the place where the cruise ship *Costa Concordia* met its tragic end in 2012. Then there is pinprick Pianosa, a haven of peace 14km southwest of Elba. It served as a penal colony until 1997. To get to Giglio and Pianosa, sign up for a day trip with Aquavision (adult/child return from €20/10). At time of writing services were scheduled to leave one to three times a week and only from its base port of Marina di Campo on Elba.

Northwestern Tuscany

Best Places to Eat

➡ Osteria Vecchia Mulino (p243)

➡ Pepenero (p242)

➡ Magno Gaudio (p239)

➡ Buca di Baldabò (p246)

➡ Osteria Il Papero (p241)

Crowd-free Treasures

➡ Barbialla Nuova (p241)

➡ Museo di Palazzo Pretorio (p240)

➡ Al Benefizio (p245)

➡ Villa Bongi (p233)

➡ Palazzo Pfanner (p232)

Why Go?

There is far more to this green corner of Tuscany than Italy's iconic Leaning Tower. Usually hurtled through en route to Florence and Siena's grand-slam queue-for-hours sights, this is the place to take your foot off the accelerator and go slow – on foot, by bicycle or car. Allow for long lunches of regional specialities to set the pace for the day, before meandering around a medieval hilltop village or along an ancient pilgrimage route.

University hub Pisa and 'love at first sight' Lucca – with its 16th-century walls ensnaring a labyrinth of butter-coloured buildings, Romanesque palaces and gracious piazzas – have an air of tranquillity and tradition that begs the traveller to linger. Lesser-known Pistoia, Prato and Pietrasanta, all off the beaten tourist track, provide a welcome reprieve in high season from the crowds (dead-easy half- or full-day trips by train from Florence, incidentally). This is snail-paced Italy, impossible not to love.

Road Distances (km)

	Pistoia	Pisa	Lucca	San Miniato
Pisa	55			
Lucca	40	23		
San Miniato	64	47	70	
Pietrasanta	68	31	30	77

North-western Tuscany Highlights

❶ Pedalling and picnicking atop the lovely Renaissance city walls of **Lucca** (p226).

❷ Meandering medieval Pisa and scaling its iconic **Leaning Tower** (p216) at sunset.

❸ Hunting white truffles with a dog in autumnal woods at **Barbialla Nuova** (p241) in Montaione, near foodie San Miniato.

❹ Fleeing the crowds in small-town **Pistoia** (p236) and discovering Tuscany's smartest history museum in art-rich **Prato** (p240).

❺ Revelling in exciting contemporary art, cuisine and boutique shopping in **Pietrasanta** (p249).

❻ Losing yourself in green rural Tuscany in chestnut-rich **Garfagnana region** (p243).

❼ Seeing where Michelangelo sourced his marble and visiting the quarries in **Carrara** (p247).

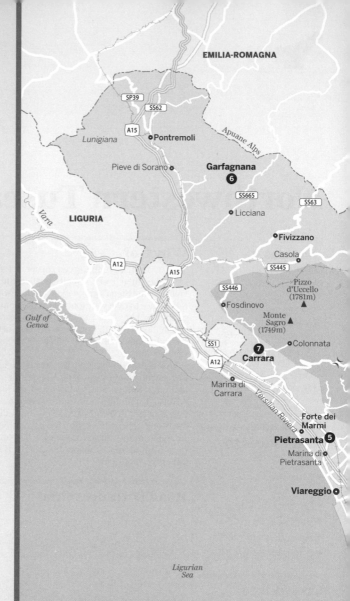

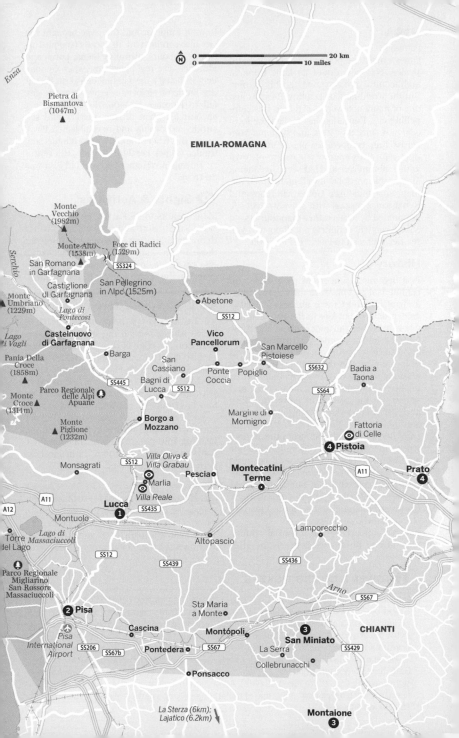

PISA

POP 88,600

Once a maritime power to rival Genoa and Venice, Pisa now draws its fame from an architectural project gone terribly wrong. But the world-famous Leaning Tower is just one of many noteworthy sights in this compelling city. Education has fuelled the local economy since the 1400s, and students from across Italy compete for places in its elite university. This endows the centre of town with a vibrant cafe and bar scene, balancing an enviable portfolio of well-maintained Romanesque buildings, Gothic churches and Renaissance piazzas with a lively street life dominated by locals rather than tourists – a charm you will definitely not discover if you restrict your visit to Piazza dei Miracoli.

History

Pisa became an important naval base and commercial port under Rome and remained a significant port for centuries. The city's golden days began late in the 10th century, when it became an independent maritime republic and a formidable rival of Genoa and Venice. A century on, the Pisan fleet was sailing far beyond the Mediterranean, successfully trading with the Orient and bringing home new ideas in art, architecture and science. At the peak of its power (the 12th and 13th centuries), Pisa controlled Corsica, Sardinia and the Tuscan coast. Most of the city's finest buildings date from this period, when the distinctive Pisan-Romanesque architectural style with its use of coloured marbles and subtle references to Andalucian architectural styles flourished. Many of these buildings sported decoration by the great father-and-son sculptural team of Nicola and Giovanni Pisano.

Pisa's support for the imperial Ghibellines during the tussles between the Holy Roman Emperor and the pope brought the city into conflict with its mostly Guelph Tuscan neighbours, including Siena, Lucca and Florence. The real blow came when Genoa's fleet inflicted a devastating defeat on Pisa at the Battle of Meloria in 1284. After the city fell to Florence in 1406, the Medici court encouraged great artistic, literary and scientific endeavours and re-established Pisa's university, where the city's most famous son, Galileo Galilei, taught in the late 16th century. During WWII about 40% of old Pisa was destroyed.

⊙ Sights & Activities

Many visitors to Pisa arrive by train at Stazione San Rossore and don't get any further than neighbouring Piazza dei Miracoli; those in the know arrive or depart using Pisa's Stazione Centrale, allowing casual discovery of the *centro storico* (historic centre).

⊙ Piazza dei Miracoli

No Tuscan sight is more immortalised in kitsch souvenirs than the iconic tower teetering on the edge of this gargantuan piazza, also known as the **Campo dei Miracoli** (Field of Miracles) or Piazza del Duomo (Cathedral Sq). With two million visitors every year, crowds are the norm, many arriving by tour bus from Florence for a whirlwind visit.

Each year from mid-June until the last Sunday in August or first in September, the Leaning Tower and Camposanta open their doors to visitors until 10pm – a magical experience not to be missed.

★ **Leaning Tower**   TOWER
(Torre Pendente; www.opapisa.it; Piazza dei Miracoli; admission €18; ⊙9am-8pm summer, 10am-5pm winter) One of Italy's signature sights, the Torre Pendente truly lives up to its name, leaning a startling 3.9 degrees off the verti-

---

ℹ TOWER & COMBO TICKETS

Buy tickets for the Leaning Tower from one of two well-signposted ticket offices: the main **ticket office** (www.opapisa.it; Piazza dei Miracoli; ⊙8am-8pm summer, 10am-5pm winter) behind the tower or the smaller office inside Museo delle Sinópie. To guarantee your visit to the tower and cut the long queue in high season, buy tickets in advance online (note tickets can only be bought 20 days before visiting).

Ticket offices in Pisa also sell combination tickets covering admission to the Battistero, Camposanto and Museo delle Sinópie: buy a ticket covering one/two/three sights costing €5/7/8 (reduced €3/4/5). Admission to the cathedral is free, but you need to show a ticket – either for one of the other sights or a cathedral coupon distributed at ticket offices.

THREE PERFECT DAYS

Day 1: Biking Lucca

Hire a bike, stock up on the city's finest picnic fare and free-wheel along the city's medieval streets. Picnic atop the monumental city walls or pedal east to lunch alfresco in Renaissance villa grounds. Come evening enjoy a Puccini recital in a medieval church.

Day 2: Backstreet Pisa

Fall in love with backstreet Pisa, saving **Piazza dei Miracoli** for last – the best tower shots are from the cloister garden of **Museo dell'Opera del Duomo** once it reopens after renovation work. Late afternoon, leave Pisa for Slow Food town **San Miniato**. Sip an *aperitivo* with valley view in a quaint old-world cafe and dine at **Pepenero** or out-of-town **Osteria Il Papero**. Overnight at truffle farm **Barbialla Nuova**.

Day 3: Mountain to Sea

Shop for a picnic of local forest produce in **Castelnuovo di Garfagnana**, then motor up and over the **Apuane Alps** – allow time for pulling over to soak up vistas of monumental marble blocks being cut out of the mountainside. Picnic on the **Passo del Vestito** and visit its botanical garden, then drop down to the sea. In **Massa**, head north to **Carrara** to see a marble quarry or south to **Pietrasanta** for fine art and creative dining.

cal. The 56m-high tower, officially the Duomo's *campanile* (bell tower), took almost 200 years to build, but was already listing when it was unveiled in 1372. Over time, the tilt, caused by a layer of weak subsoil, steadily worsened until it was finally halted by a major stabilisation project in the 1990s.

Building began in 1173 under the supervision of architect Bonanno Pisano, but his plans came a cropper almost immediately. Only three of the tower's seven tiers had been built when he was forced to abandon construction after it started leaning. Work resumed in 1272, with artisans and masons attempting to bolster the foundations, but failing miserably. They kept going, though, compensating for the lean by gradually building straight up from the lower storeys. But once again work had to be suspended – this time due to war – and construction wasn't completed until the second half of the 14th century.

Over the next 600 years, the tower continued to tilt at an estimated 1mm per year. By 1993 it stood 4.47m out of plumb, more than 5 degrees from the vertical. To counter this, steel braces were slung around the 3rd storey and joined to steel cables attached to neighbouring buildings. This held the tower in place as engineers began gingerly removing soil from below the northern foundations. After some 70 tonnes of earth had been extracted from the northern side, the tower sank to its 18th-century level and, in the process, rectified the lean by 43.8cm.

Experts believe that this will guarantee the tower's future for the next three centuries.

Access to the Leaning Tower is limited to 40 people at a time – children under eight are not allowed in/up and those aged eight to 10 years must hold an adult's hand. To avoid disappointment, book in advance online or go straight to a ticket office when you arrive in Pisa to book a slot for later in the day. Visits last 30 minutes and involve a steep climb up 300-odd occasionally slippery steps. All bags, handbags included, must be deposited at the free left-luggage desk next to the central ticket office – cameras are about the only thing you can take up.

★ **Duomo** CATHEDRAL
(www.opapisa.it; Piazza dei Miracoli; ⊙10am-8pm summer, 10am-12.45pm & 2-5pm winter) `FREE`
Pisa's magnificent Romanesque Duomo was begun in 1064 and consecrated in 1118. Its striking tiered exterior, with cladding of green-and-cream marble bands, gives on to a vast columned interior capped by a gold wooden ceiling. The elliptical dome, the first of its kind in Europe at the time, was added in 1380.

Note that while admission is free, you'll need an entrance coupon from the ticket office or a ticket from one of the other Piazza dei Miracoli sights.

The cathedral, which served as a blueprint for subsequent Romanesque churches in Tuscany, was paid for with spoils from a 1063 naval battle that the Pisans fought

NORTHWESTERN TUSCANY PISA

Pisa

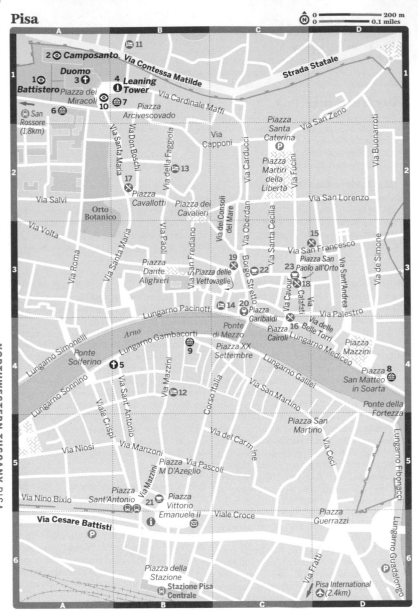

against an Arab fleet off Palermo. To mark the victory, and symbolise Pisa's domination of the Mediterranean, the cathedral was Europe's largest when it was completed.

The main facade – not finished until the 13th century – has four exquisite tiers of columns diminishing skywards, while the echoing interior, 96m long and 28m high, is propped up by 68 hefty granite columns in classical style. The wooden ceiling, decorated with 24-carat gold, is a legacy from the period of Medici rule.

Pisa

Before stepping foot in the cathedral, study the three pairs of 16th-century bronze doors at the main entrance. Designed by the school of Giambologna to replace the wooden originals destroyed (along with most of the cathedral interior) by fire in 1596, the doors are quite spellbinding – hours can be spent deciphering the biblical scenes illustrating the immaculate conception of the Virgin and birth of Christ (central doors), the road to Calvary and crucifixion of Christ, and the ministry of Christ. Kids can play spot the rhino.

Inside, don't miss the extraordinary early 14th-century octagonal pulpit in the north aisle. Sculpted from Carrara marble by Giovanni Pisano and featuring nude and heroic figures, its depth of detail and heightening of feeling brought a new pictorial expressionism and life to Gothic sculpture. Pisano's work forms a striking contrast to the controversial 2001 pulpit and altar by Italian sculptor Giuliano Vangi.

★ **Battistero** RELIGIOUS SITE
(Baptistry; www.opapisa.it; Piazza dei Miracoli; adult/reduced €5/3, combination ticket with Camposanto & Museo delle Sinópie 2/3 sights €7/8 (reduced €4/5); ⊙8am-8pm summer, 10am-5pm Nov-Feb) Pisa's unusual round baptistry has one dome piled on top of another, each roofed half in lead, half in tiles, and topped by a gilt bronze John the Baptist (1395). Construction began in 1152, but it was remodelled and continued by Nicola and Giovanni Pisano more than a century later and finally completed in the 14th century. Inside, the hexagonal marble pulpit (1260) by Nicola Pisano is the highlight.

The lower level of arcades is Pisan-Romanesque; the pinnacled upper section and dome are Gothic.

Pisan scientist Galileo Galilei (who, so the story goes, came up with the laws of the pendulum by watching a lamp in Pisa's cathedral swing), was baptised in the octagonal font (1246). Don't leave without climbing to the **Upper Gallery** to listen to the custodian demonstrate the double dome's remarkable acoustics and echo effects, every half-hour on the hour/half-hour.

★ **Camposanto** CEMETERY
(www.opapisa.it; Piazza dei Miracoli; adult/reduced €5/3, combination ticket with Battistero & Museo delle Sinópie 2/3 sights €7/8 (reduced €4/5); ⊙8am-8pm summer, 10am-5pm winter) Soil shipped from Calvary during the Crusades is said to lie within the white walls of this hauntingly beautiful, final resting place for many prominent Pisans, arranged around a garden in a cloistered quadrangle. During WWII, Allied artillery destroyed many of the cloisters' frescoes, but a couple were salvaged and are now displayed in the **Sala Affreschi** (Frescoes Room). Most notable is the Triumph of Death (1336–41), a remarkable illustration of Hell attributed to 14th-century painter Buonamico Buffalmacco.

Fortunately, the mirrors apparently once stuck next to the graphic, no-holds-barred images of the damned being roasted alive on spits have since been removed – meaning a marginally less uncomfortable visit for visitors who would have once seen their own faces peering out of the cruel wall painting. Buffalmacco's *Last Judgement & Hell* (1336–41), in the same room, is equally brutal.

NORTHWESTERN TUSCANY PISA

Why Pisa Leans

In 1160 Pisa boasted 10,000-odd towers, but no *campanile* (bell tower) for its cathedral. Loyal Pisan, Berta di Bernardo, righted this in 1172 when she died and left a legacy of 60 pieces of silver in her will to the city to get cracking on a *campanile*.

Ironically, when Bonnano Pisano set to work on the world's most famous *campanile* in 1173, he did not realise what shaky ground he was on: beneath Piazza dei Miracoli's lawns lay a treacherous mix of sand and clay, 40m deep. And when work stopped five years on, with just three storeys completed, Italy's stump of an icon already tilted. Building resumed in 1272, workers compensating for the lean by building straight up from the lower storeys to create a subtle banana curve. By the 19th century, many were convinced the tower was a mere whimsical folly of its inventors, built deliberately to lean.

In 1838 a clean-up job to remove muck oozing from the base of the tower exposed, once and for all, the true nature of its precarious foundations. In the 1950s the seven bells inside the tower, each sounding a different musical note and rung from the ground by 14 men since 1370, were silenced for fear of a catastrophic collapse. In 1990 the tower was closed to the public. Engineers placed 1000 tonnes of lead ingots on the north side to counteract the subsidence on the south side. Steel bands were wrapped around the 2nd storey to keep it together.

Then in 1995 the tower slipped a whole 2.5mm. Steel braces were slung

1. Pisa's *duomo* (cathedral) and Leaning Tower **2.** Street view of Leaning Tower and *duomo* **3.** Close-up view of Leaning Tower

around the 3rd storey of the tower and attached to heavy hydraulic A-frame anchors some way from the northern side. The frames were replaced by steel cables, attached to neighbouring buildings. The tower held in place, engineers gingerly removed 70 tonnes of earth from below the northern foundations, forcing the tower to sink to its 18th-century level – and correct the lean by 2011 to 43.8cm. Success...

Every year scientists carry out tests on Pisa's pearly white leaning tower to measure its lean and check it's stable. Ironically, results in 2013 showed that the world's most famous leaning tower had, in fact, lost 2.5cm of its iconic lean, with some scientists even predicting a complete self-straightening by the year 2300. Let's hope not.

LEANING CITY

➡ **Duomo & Baptistry** (p217 & p219) The tower's neighbours lean 25cm and 51cm respectively.

➡ **Chiesa di San Nicola** (Via Santa Maria) Nicola Pisano's octagonal *campanile* (bell tower) is another sacred edifice that is not dead straight.

➡ **Chiesa di San Michele degli Scalzi** (Via San Michele degli Scalzi) Note the wonky red-brick square tower.

PIAZZA DEI MIRACOLI WALKING TOUR

No other square has such expansive lawns or such a concentration of Romanesque buildings. From the **ticket office** (p216) behind the Leaning Tower, walk towards the **Duomo** (p217) – the first structure built on this almighty piazza. Before strolling its length to reach the main entrance, stop by the **Portale di San Ranieri**, the cathedral doorway facing the Leaning Tower. What you see are copies of 12th-century bronze doors illustrating the life of Christ. The doors are named after Pisa's patron saint, Ranieri.

Continue to the Duomo main entrance, pausing to savour the gleaming marbled facade. Inside, recover from the shock of the vast gold ceiling, then walk past the pulpit to the **Cappella di San Cappella Ranieri**. Here lies the preserved skeleton of Ranieri, inside a glass-sided marble 'urn'. Arab sculpted decorative elements in the chapel demonstrate just how influential the Islamic world was on Pisa at this time; the 11th-century bronze griffin that stood atop the cathedral until 1828 was booty, probably Egyptian in origin.

Exit the Duomo and follow the short marble pathway linking it to the **Battistero** (p219), built almost a century later. Walk upstairs to the crowd-free **Upper Gallery**, the perfect place to listen to the singing custodian demonstrate the extraordinary acoustics. Break afterwards with the **tourist souvenir stalls** along the piazza's south side, pose for the ritual 'prop up the tower' photo shoot, then flee the mayhem for the serenity of **Camposanto** (p219). Lose yourself in the wonderful medieval frescoes, and learn how they were executed in the **Museo delle Sinópie** (p222) opposite. This vast building was a shelter for the poor and sick, pilgrims and abandoned children in the 13th century, and was a hospital until 1979.

When it reopens after extensive renovation work, no museum will provide a finer round-up of Piazza dei Miracoli's architectural masterpieces than the **Museo dell'Opera del Duomo** (p222). Close the circle with the original bronze doors of the Portale di San Ranieri and that magnificent griffin that Pisans pilfered to place atop their *duomo*.

This walk takes three to four hours, including monument visits.

Museo delle Sinópie   MUSEUM

(www.opapisa.it; Piazza dei Miracoli; adult/reduced €5/3, combination ticket with Battistero or Camposanto €7/5, Battistero & Camposanto €8/5; ⊗ 8am-7.30pm summer, 10am-4.30pm winter) Home to some fascinating frescoes, this museum safeguards several *sinópie* (preliminary sketches), drawn by the artists in red earth pigment on the walls of the Camposanto in the 14th and 15th centuries before the frescoes were overpainted. The museum is a compelling study in fresco painting, with short films and scale models filling in the gaps.

Museo dell'Opera del Duomo   MUSEUM

(www.opapisa.it; Piazza dei Miracoli) Closed for extensive renovation, this museum is a repository for works of art once displayed in the cathedral and baptistry. Collection highlights include Giovanni Pisano's ivory carving of the *Madonna and Child* (1299), made for the cathedral's high altar, and his mid-13th-century *Madonna del colloquio*, originally from a gate of the Duomo. Possibly even more memorable is the museum's tranquil cloister garden with stunning, crowd-free views of the Leaning Tower.

⊙ Along the Arno

Away from the crowded heavyweights of Piazza dei Miracoli, along the Arno river banks, Pisa comes into its own. Splendid *palazzi* (mansions) painted a multitude of hues, line the southern *lungarno* (riverside embankment), from where shopping boulevard **Corso Italia** legs it to the central train station, Stazione Centrale. Don't miss the waterside, triple-spired **Chiesa di Santa Maria della Spina** (Lungarno Gambacorti), an exquisite Pisan-Gothic church encrusted with tabernacles and statues. It was built between 1230 and 1223 to house a reliquary of a *spina* (thorn) from Christ's crown. Closed for restoration.

Pisa's medieval heart lies north of the water: from **Piazza Cairoli**, with its evening bevy of bars and gelato shops, meander along **Via Cavour** and get lost in the surrounding lanes and alleys. A daily fresh produce market fills **Piazza delle Vettovaglie**, ringed with 15th-century porticoes and cafe terraces.

Palazzo Blu GALLERY
(www.palazzoblu.it; Lungarno Gambacorti 9; ⊙10am-7pm Tue-Fri, to 8pm Sat & Sun) FREE Facing the river is this magnificently restored, 14th-century building that has a striking dusty-blue facade. Inside, its over-the-top 19th-century interior decoration is the perfect backdrop for the Foundation Pisa's art collection – predominantly Pisan works from the 14th to the 20th centuries, plus various temporary exhibitions.

Museo Nazionale di San Matteo MUSEUM
(Piazza San Matteo in Soarta; adult/reduced €5/2.50; ⊙8.30am-7.30pm Tue-Sat, to 1.30pm Sun) This inspiring repository of medieval masterpieces sits in a 13th-century Benedictine convent on the Arno's northern waterfront boulevard. The museum's collection of paintings from the Tuscan school (c 12th to 14th centuries) is notable, with works by Lippo Memmi, Taddeo Gaddi, Gentile da Fabriano and Ghirlandaio. Don't miss Masaccio's *St Paul*, Fra Angelico's *Madonna of Humility* and Simone Martini's *Polyptych of Saint Catherine*.

✵ Festivals & Events

Luminaria di San Ranieri LIGHT SHOW
(⊙16 Jun) The night before Pisa's patron saint's day is magical: thousands upon thousands of candles and blazing torches light up the river and riverbanks while fireworks bedazzle the night sky.

Regata Storica di San Ranieri SPORTS
(⊙17 Jun) The Arno comes to life with a rowing regatta to commemorate the city's patron saint.

Palio delle Quattro Antiche Repubbliche Marinare CULTURAL
(⊙Jun) The four historical maritime rivals – Pisa, Venice, Amalfi and Genoa – take turns to host this historic regatta in early June; in 2017 it sails into Pisa.

Gioco del Ponte CULTURAL
(⊙Jun) During Gioco del Ponte (Game of the Bridge), two teams in medieval costume battle it out over the Ponte di Mezzo; last Sunday in June.

🛏 Sleeping

Hostel Pisa Tower HOSTEL €
(☏050 520 24 54; www.hostelpisatower.it; Via Piave 4; dm €20-25; @🛜) This super-friendly hostel occupies a suburban villa a couple of minutes' walk from Piazza dei Miracoli. It's bright and cheery, with colourful decor, female and mixed dorms, communal kitchen, and a summer-friendly terrace overlooking a small grassy garden. Dorms are named, meaning you can sleep with Galileo, Mona Lisa, Leonardo or Michelangelo.

Royal Victoria Hotel HOTEL €€
(☏050 94 01 11; www.royalvictoria.it; Lungarno Pacinotti 12; d €95-170, tr €105-180; ❄🛜) This doyen of Pisan hotels, run by the Piegaja family since 1837, offers old-world luxury accompanied by warm, attentive service. Its 38 rooms exude a shabby-chic spirit with their Grand Tour antiques, although renovations are imminent. Don't miss an aperitif flopped on a sofa on the 4th-floor terrace, packed with potted plants. Garage parking/bike hire €20/15 per day, breakfast €5.

Hotel Bologna HOTEL €€
(☏050 50 21 20; www.hotelbologna.pisa.it; Via Giuseppe Mazzini 57; d/tr €148/188; P❄🛜) Placed well away from the Piazza dei Miracoli mayhem, this elegant four-star mansion hotel is an oasis of peace and tranquillity. Its big, bright rooms have wooden floors and colour-coordinated furnishings – some are frescoed. Kudos for the small terrace and the cypress-shaded garden out the back – delightful for lazy summertime breakfasts. Reception organises bike/scooter hire; courtyard parking for motorists €12 per night.

Hotel Relais dell'Orologio HOTEL €€€
(☏050 83 03 61; www.hotelrelaisorologio.com; Via della Faggiola 12-14; d €150-240; ❄🛜) Something of a honeymoon venue, Pisa's dreamy five-star hotel occupies a tastefully restored

---

LOCAL KNOWLEDGE

KEITH
···
Trendy cafe, **Keith** (www.keithcafe.com; Via Zandonai 4; ⊙7am-11pm; 🛜), stares face to face with *Tuttomondo* (1989), the last wall mural American pop artist Keith Haring painted on the facade of a Pisan church just months before his death. Sip a coffee or cocktail on the terrace and lament the fading, weather-beaten colours of Haring's 30 signature prancing dancing men.

Free wi-fi, occasional contemporary art exhibitions, superb coffee and a student-friendly €5 *apericena* buffet keeps Keith buzzing.

14th-century fortified tower housed in a quiet backstreet. Some rooms have original frescoes and the flowery patio restaurant is a welcome retreat from the crowds. Book online to bag the cheapest deal – nonrefundable, early booking rates are the best value.

✗ Eating

Being a university town, Pisa has a good range of eating places, especially around Borgo Stretto, the university on cafe-ringed Piazza Dante Alighieri – always packed with students – and south of the river in the trendy San Martino quarter.

Local specialities include fresh *pecorino* (sheep's milk cheese) from San Rossore, *zuppe di cavolo* (cabbage soup), *pan ficato* (fig cake) and *castagnaccio* (chestnut-flour cake enriched by nuts).

★ Pizzeria Il Montino   PIZZA €

(☑ 050 59 86 95; www.pizzeriailmontino.com; Vicolo del Monte 1; pizzas €6-8, focaccine €2.50-4; ⊙ 10.30am-3pm & 5-10pm Mon-Sat) There is nothing flash or fancy about this down-to-earth pizzeria, an icon among Pisans, student and sophisticate alike. Take away or order at the bar then grab a table, inside or out, and munch on house specialities such as *cecina* (chickpea pizza), *castagnaccio* and *spuma* (sweet, nonalcoholic drink). Or go for a *focaccine* (small flat roll) filled with salami, pancetta or *porchetta* (suckling pig).

Hidden in a back alley, the quickest way to find Il Montino is to head west along Via Ulisse Dini from the northern end of Borgo Stretto (opposite the Lo Sfizio cafe at Borgo Stretto 54) to Piazza San Felice where it is easy to spot, on your left, with its telling blue neon 'Pizzeria' sign.

★ L'Ostellino   SANDWICHES €

(Piazza Felice Cavallotti 1; panini €3-6; ⊙ 11.30am-4.30pm Mon-Fri, to 6pm Sat & Sun) For a buster-size gourmet *panino* (sandwich) wrapped in crunchy waxed paper, this miniscule deli and *panineria* (sandwich shop) with just a handful of tables delivers. Take your pick from dozens of different combos written by hand on the blackboard (*lardo di colonnata* with figs or cave-aged pecorino with honey and walnuts are sweet favourites), await construction, then hit the green lawns of Piazza dei Miracoli to picnic with the crowds.

Il Crudo   SANDWICHES €

(www.ilcrudopisa.it; Piazza Cairoli 7; panini €4.50-6; ⊙ 11am-midnight Sun-Thu, to 2am Fri & Sat) A monster baguette stuffed with cured meat and *salsa verde* (green sauce) makes for an ideal lunch at this pocket-sized *panineria*. Order from the bar and sit on the pretty piazza.

Osteria Bernardo   TUSCAN €€

(☑ 050 57 52 16; www.osteriabernardo.it; Piazza San Paolo all'Orto 1; meals €35; ⊙ 8-11pm Tue-Sat, 12.30-2.30pm & 8-11pm Sun) This small bistro on one of Pisa's loveliest squares, well away from the madding Leaning Tower crowd, is the perfect fusion of easy dining and gourmet excellence. Its menu is small – just four or five dishes to choose from for each course – and its cuisine is creative. The wild boar *pappardelle* (wide flat pasta strips) scented with chocolate is a great change from the norm.

biOsteria 050   VEGETARIAN €€

(☑ 050 54 31 06; www.biosteria050.it; Via San Francesco 36; meals €25-30; ⊙ 12.30-2.30pm & 7.30-10.30pm Tue-Sat, 7.30-10.30pm Mon & Sun; ☑) ●

ⓘ HOW TO FALL IN LOVE WITH PISA

Sure, the iconic Leaning Tower is the reason everyone wants to go to Pisa. But once you've put yourself through the Piazza dei Miracoli madness (littered lawns, football-playing school groups, photo-posing pandemonium...) most people simply want to get out of town.

To avoid leaving Pisa feeling oddly deflated by one of Europe's great landmarks, save the Leaning Tower and its oversized square for the latter part of the day – or, better still, an enchanting visit after dark (mid-June to August) when the night casts a certain magic on the glistening white monuments and the tour buses have long gone.

Upon arrival, indulge instead in peaceful meanderings along the Arno river, over its bridges and through Pisa's medieval heart. Discover the last monumental wall **painting** (p223) Keith Haring did before he died, enjoy low-key architectural and art genius at the **Chiesa di Santa Maria della Spina** (p222) and **Palazzo Blu** (p223), and lunch with locals at **Sottobosco** (p225) or **Osteria Bernardo** (p224).

And only once you've fallen in love with the other Pisa, should you head for the tower.

Everything that Marco and Raffaele at Zero Cinquanta cook up is strictly seasonal, local and organic, with products from farms within a 50km radius of Pisa. Feast on dishes like risotto with almonds and asparagus or go for one of the excellent-value lunch specials.

Drinking & Nightlife

Most drinking action takes place on and around Piazza delle Vettovaglie and the university on cafe-ringed Piazza Dante Alighieri, always packed with students.

The local Denominazione d'Origine Controllata e Garantita (DOCG) is Chianti delle Colline Pisane, and though there's no Pisan Denominazione d'Origine Controllata (DOC), Bianco Pisano di San Torpè, which is a Trebbiano-dominated wine with a delicate, dry flavour, is a popular substitute.

Sottobosco CAFE
(www.sottoboscocafe.it; Piazza San Paolo all'Orto; ⊗10am-midnight Tue-Fri, noon-1am Sat, 7pm-midnight Sun) This creative cafe with books for sale and funky furnishings induces love at first sight. Tuck into a doughnut and cappuccino at a glass-topped table filled with artists' crayons perhaps, or a collection of buttons. Lunch dishes (salads, pies and pasta) are simple and homemade, and come dusk, jazz bands play or DJs spin tunes.

Bazeel BAR
(www.bazeel.it; Lungarno Pacinotti 1; ⊗7.30am-2am) A dedicated all-rounder, Bazeel is a hot spot from dawn to dark. Laze over breakfast, save cents with a great-value buffet lunch (two/three courses €8/10) or hang out with the A crowd over a generous *aperitivo* spread, live music and DJs. Its chapel-like interior is nothing short of fabulous, as is its pavement terrace out front. Check its Twitter feed for what's on.

Salza CAFE
(Borgo Stretto 44; ⊗8.15am-8pm Tue-Sun) This old-fashioned cake shop has been tempting Pisans into sugar-induced wickedness since 1898. It's an equally lovely spot for a cocktail – anytime.

❶ Information

Tourist Office (☑050 4 22 91; www.pisaunica terra.it; Piazza Vittorio Emanuele II 16; ⊗10am-1pm & 2-4pm)

❶ SAVVY SLEEP

Pisa is the obvious place to stay, but it is traffic busy and quality accommodation is limited. Opt instead for lovely Lucca (tricky parking), a farm around San Miniato, or stylish art gem Pietrasanta: all three are an easy drive to northwestern Tuscany's key sights.

❶ Getting There & Away

AIR
Pisa International Airport (Galileo Galilei Airport; ☑050 84 93 00; www.pisa-airport. com) Tuscany's main international airport, a 10-minute drive south of Pisa; has flights to most major European cities.

BUS
From its hub on Piazza Sant'Antonio, Pisan bus company **CPT** (☑050 50 55 02; www.cpt.pisa. it; Piazza Sant'Antonio 1; ⊗ticket office 7am-8.15pm Mon-Fri, to 8pm Sat & Sun) runs buses to/from Volterra (€6.10, two hours, up to 10 daily) and Livorno (€2.70, 55 minutes, half-hourly to hourly).

CAR
Pisa is close to the A11 and A12. The SCG FI-PI-LI (SS67) is a toll-free alternative for Florence and Livorno, while the north–south SS1, the Via Aurelia, connects the city with La Spezia and Rome.

TRAIN
There is a handy left-luggage office at **Pisa Centrale** (Piazza della Stazione) train station – not to be confused with north-of-town Pisa San Rossore station. Regional train services to/from Pisa Centrale:

Florence (€8, 1¼ hours, frequent)
Livorno (€2.50, 15 minutes, frequent)
Lucca (€3.40, 30 minutes, every 30 minutes)
Viareggio (€3.40, 15 minutes, every 20 minutes)

❶ Getting Around

TO/FROM THE AIRPORT
PisaMover shuttle buses link the airport with Pisa Centrale (€1.80, eight minutes, every 10 minutes) train station. From December 2015 this shuttlebus service will be replaced by a super-speedy, fully automated rail link called PisaMover; check the Pisa airport website for details.

The LAM Rossa (red) bus line (€1.20, 10 minutes, every 10 to 20 minutes) run by CPT passes through the city centre and the train station en route to/from the airport. Buy tickets from the

OFF THE BEATEN TRACK

VESPA TOUR

There's a certain romance to touring Tuscany on the back of a Vespa, Italy's iconic scooter that revolutionised travel when Piaggio launched it from its factory in **Pontedera**, 25km southeast of Pisa, in 1946. The 'wasp', as the two-wheeled utility vehicle was affectionately known, has been restyled 120 times since, culminating most recently in Piaggio's vintage-inspired GTV and LXV models. Yet the essential design remains timeless.

The complete Vespa story, from the Genovese company's arrival in Tuscany in 1921 to its manufacturing of four-engine aircraft and hydroplanes, WWII destruction and rebirth as Europe's exclusive Vespa producer, is grippingly told in Pontedera's **Museo Piaggio** (☑ 0587 2 71 71; www.museopiaggio.it; Viale Rinaldo Piaggio 7; ⊙ 10am-6pm Tue-Fri, 10am-1pm & 2-6pm Sat) FREE, in a former factory building.

Should Vespa's free-wheeling, carefree spirit take hold, hook up with **Tuscany by Vespa** (www.tuscanybyvespa.com) – operated by **Florence Town** (Map p66; ☑ 055 012 39 94; www.florencetown.com; Via de' Lamberti 1) in Florence – for your very own Hepburn-style Vespa tour.

blue ticket machine, next to the bus stops to the right of the train station exit.

A taxi between the airport and city centre should cost no more than €10. To book, call **Radio Taxi Pisa** (☑ 050 54 16 00; www.cotapi.it).

BICYCLE

Many hotels rent bikes. Otherwise, stands at the northern end of Via Santa Maria and other streets off Piazza dei Miracoli rent touristy four-wheel rickshaws for up to three/six people (€10/15 per hour) and regular bicycles (€3 to €5 per hour).

CAR & MOTORCYCLE

Parking costs around €2 per hour; don't park in the historic centre's Limited Traffic Zone (ZTL). There's a free car park outside the zone on Lungarno Guadalongo, near Fortezza di San Gallo on the south side of the Arno.

LUCCA

POP 89,200

Lovely Lucca endears itself to everyone who visits. Hidden behind imposing Renaissance walls, its cobbled streets, handsome piazzas and shady promenades make it a perfect destination to explore by foot – as a day trip from Florence or in its own right. At the day's end, historic cafes and restaurants tempt visitors to relax over a glass or two of Lucchesi wine and a slow progression of rustic dishes prepared with fresh produce from nearby Garfagnana.

If you have a car, the hills to the east of Lucca demand exploration. Home to historic villas and belle époque Montecatini Terme where Puccini lazed in warm spa waters, they are easy day-trip destinations from Lucca.

History

Founded by the Etruscans, Lucca became a Roman colony in 180 BC and a free *comune* (self-governing city) during the 12th century, when it enjoyed a period of prosperity based on the silk trade. In 1314 it briefly fell to Pisa but regained its independence under the leadership of local adventurer Castruccio Castracani degli Anterminelli, and began to amass territories in western Tuscany, including marble-rich Carrara. Castruccio died in 1328 but Lucca remained an independent republic for almost 500 years.

Napoleon ended all that in 1805 when he created the principality of Lucca and placed one of the seemingly countless members of his family in need of an Italian fiefdom (this time his sister Elisa) in control of all of Tuscany. Ten years later the city became a Bourbon duchy before being incorporated into the Kingdom of Italy. It miraculously escaped being bombed during WWII, so the fabric of the *centro storico* has remained unchanged for centuries.

◎ Sights & Activities

Stone-paved **Via Fillungo**, with its fashion boutiques and car-free mantra, threads its way through the medieval heart of the old city. East is one of Tuscany's loveliest piazzas, oval cafe-ringed **Piazza Anfiteatro**, so-called after the amphitheatre that was here in Roman times. Spot remnants of the amphitheatre's brick arches and masonry on the exterior walls of the medieval houses ringing the piazza.

City Wall
HISTORIC SITE

Lucca's monumental *mura* (wall) was built around the old city in the 16th and 17th centuries and remains in almost perfect condition. It superseded two previous walls, the first built from travertine stone blocks as early as the 2nd century BC. Twelve metres high and 4.2km long, today's ramparts are crowned with a tree-lined footpath looking down on the *centro storico* and out towards the Apuane Alps. This path is a favourite location for the locals' daily *passeggiata* (traditional evening stroll).

Children's playgrounds, swings and picnic tables beneath shady plane trees add a buzz of activity to Baluardo San Regolo, Baluardo San Salvatore and Baluardo Santa Croce – three of the 11 bastions studding the way. Older kids kick footballs around on the green lawns of Baluardo San Donato.

★ Cattedrale di San Martino
CATHEDRAL

(www.museocattedralelucca.it; Piazza San Martino; adult/reduced €3/2, with museum & Chiesa e Battistero dei SS Giovanni & Reparata €7/5; ⏰ 9.30am-5pm Mon-Fri, to 6pm Sat, 11.30am-5pm Sun) Lucca's predominantly Romanesque cathedral dates to the 11th century. Its stunning facade was constructed in the prevailing Lucca-Pisan style and designed to accommodate the pre-existing *campanile*. The reliefs

---

THE PUCCINI TRAIL

Lucca has a particular lure for opera buffs: it was here, in 1858, that the great Giacomo Puccini was born, and baptised the following day in the **Chiesa dei SS Giovanni e Reparata** (p229). The maestro, who came from a long line of Lucchesi musicians, grew up in an apartment at Corte San Lorenzo 9, now the house-museum **Casa Natale di Puccini** (Casa Natale di Giacomo Puccini; ☎ 0583 58 40 28; www.puccinimuseum.org; Corte San Lorenzo 9; adult/reduced €7/5; ⏰ 10am-6pm Wed-Mon summer, 10am-1pm Mon, Wed & Thu, 10am-4pm Fri-Sun winter) – look for the imposing statue of the maestro at the front. During his teenage years, Puccini played the organ in **Cattedrale di San Martino** and performed as a piano accompanist at the **Teatro del Giglio** (www.teatrodelgiglio.it; Piazza del Giglio 13-15), the 17th-century theatre where the curtain would later rise on some of his best-known operas: *La Bohème* (1896), *Tosca* (1900) and *Madame Butterfly* (1907).

In 1880 Puccini left Lucca to study at Milan's music conservatory. After his studies he returned to Tuscany to rent a lakeside house in **Torre del Lago**, 15km west of Lucca on the shore of Lago Massaciuccoli. Nine years later, after the successes of *Manon Lescaut* (1893) and *La Bohème,* he had a villa built on the same lakeshore, undertaking the Liberty-style interior decoration himself. It was here that Puccini with his wife, Elvira, spent his time working, hunting on the lake and carousing with a diverse group of hunters, fishermen and bohemian artists. *Madame Butterfly, La fanciulla del West* (1910), *La Rondine* (1917) and *Il Trittico* (1918) were composed on the Forster piano in his front study, and he wrote his scores on the walnut table in the same room.

Villa di Torre del Lago, now the **Museo Villa Puccini** (☎ 0584 34 14 45; www.giacomo puccini.it; Viale Puccini 266, Torre del Lago; adult/reduced €7/3; ⏰ 2.30-5.50pm Mon, 10am-12.40pm & 3-6.20pm Tue-Sun), has been preserved as it was during Puccini's residence and is hence fascinating to visit (by guided tour every 40 minutes). In summer the villa grounds and lakeshore buzz with the world-famous **Puccini Festival** (www.puccini festival.it), which sees three or four of the great man's operas perfomed in a purpose-built outdoor theatre. Tickets are like gold dust and sell out months in advance.

Puccini was a frequent visitor to **Montecatini Terme**, a charming spa resort 56km east, known for its mineral-rich waters. May to October, spa lovers still flock here to wallow in warm waters and indulge in beauty treatments at its *terme* (thermal baths) in grand old buildings overlooking a beautiful park. The **tourist office** (☎ 0573 77 22 44; www.montecatiniturismo.it; Viale Verdi 66-68, Montecatini Terme; ⏰ 9am-12.30pm & 3-6pm Mon-Sat, plus 9am-noon Sun summer) has details.

In 1921 Puccini and Elvira moved to a villa in nearby **Viareggio** where the composer became a regular fixture at **Gran Caffè Margherita** (Viale Regina Margherita 30). He worked on his last opera, the unfinished *Turandot,* here. After Puccini's death in 1924, Elvira and son Antonio added a chapel to the Torre del Lago villa; Puccini's remains were interred there in 1926.

NORTHWESTERN TUSCANY LUCCA

NORTHWESTERN TUSCANY LUCCA

Lucca

200 m
0.1 miles

Orto Botanico

Baluardo Santa Croce

Porta San Donato

Passeggiata della Mura

Via delle Conce

Piazza Sant'Agostino

Palazzo Pfanner

Via del Bachchettoni

Baluardo San Salvatore

Via della Quarquonia

Piazza San Francesco

Via Paoli

Porta Elisa

Via Elisa

Orto Botanico

Baluardo della Libertà

Via del Bachchettoni

Baluardo San Regolo

Via Santa Chiara

Via San Michetto

Via del Fosso

Via del Fosso

Via San Nicolao

Porta San Gervasio

Via del Giardino Botanico

Via Santa Gemma Galgani

Via Rosi

Via della Fratta

Via della Quarquonia

Via Filungo

Piazza San Pietro

Via Canuleia

Via dell'Angelo Custode

Via Guinigi

Torre Guinigi

Via Mordini

Via Sant'Andrea

Via Santa Croce

Piazza dei Servi

Via Vallisneri

Via della Rosa

Piazza Anfiteatro

Piazza Scarpellini

Via della Anfiteatro

Piazza del Carmine

Piazza Bernardini

Museo della Cattedrale

Piazza Antelminelli

Cattedrale di San Martino

Passeggiata della Mura

Piazza San Frediano

Via della Cavallerizza

Via degli Angeli

Via del Moro

Via Buia

Via Filungo

Via Cenami

Via del Battistero

Via del Molinetto

Piazza San Giovanni

Piazza San Michele

Piazza San Romano

Via Battisti

Via degli Asili

Via Santa Lucia

Via Santa Lucia

Via Roma

Piazza San Giovanni

Via San Giorgio

Via del Loreto

Via Tegrimi

Via Caldera

Via di Poggio

Piazza San Michele

Corte Campana

Via Veneto

Piazza Napoleone

Piazza del Giglio

Via Santa Giustina

Via della Cervia

Via Vittorio Emanuele II

Via Galli Tassi

Via del Toro

Porta San Donato

Orto Botanico

Passeggiata della Mura

Mura

Piazza Verdi

Piazzale San Donato

Via San Paolino

Piazzale Boccherini

Porta Sant'Anna

Lucca

◎ **Top Sights**
1 Cattedrale di San Martino D4
2 Museo della Cattedrale D4
3 Palazzo Pfanner C2
4 Torre Guinigi E3

◎ **Sights**
5 Chiesa di San Michele in Foro C3
6 Chiesa e Battistero dei SS
   Giovanni e Reparata D4
7 City Wall C1
8 Lucca Centre of Contemporary
   Art E2
9 Museo Nazionale di Palazzo Mansi B3
10 Puccini Museum C3
11 Torre Civica delle Ore D3

🛏 **Sleeping**
12 2italia D2
13 Alla Corte degli Angeli C2
14 Ostello San Frediano D1
15 Piccolo Hotel Puccini C3

🍴 **Eating**
16 Buca di Sant'Antonio C3
17 Cantine Bernardini 1586 .... D3
18 Da Felice C3
19 Forno Amedeo Giusti C3
20 Grom D2
21 Local Food Market A3
22 Port Ellen Clan F1
23 Ristorante Giglio C4
24 Trattoria da Leo C2

🎭 **Entertainment**
25 Teatro del Giglio C4

🛍 **Shopping**
26 Antica Bodega di Prospero C3
27 Antica Farmacia Massagli C3
28 Caniparoli B3
29 De Cervesia D2
30 Taddeucci C3

over the left doorway of the portico are believed to be by Nicola Pisano, while inside, treasures include the **Volto Santo** (literally, Holy Countenance) crucifix sculpture and a wonderful 15th-century tomb in the **sacristy**. The cathedral interior was rebuilt in the 14th and 15th centuries with a Gothic flourish.

Legend has it that the Volto Santo, a simply fashioned image of a dark-skinned, life-sized Christ on a wooden crucifix, was carved by Nicodemus, who witnessed the crucifixion. In fact, it has been dated to the 13th century. A major object of pilgrimage, the sculpture is carried through the streets every 13 September at dusk during the **Luminaria di Santa Croce**, a solemn torchlit procession marking its miraculous arrival in Lucca.

The cathedral's many other works of art include a magnificent *Last Supper* by Tintoretto above the third altar of the south aisle and Domenico Ghirlandaio's 1479 *Madonna Enthroned with Saints*. This impressive work by Michelangelo's master is currently located in the sacristy. Opposite lies the exquisite, gleaming marble tomb of Ilaria del Carretto carved by Jacopo della Quercia in 1407. The young second wife of the 15th-century lord of Lucca, Paolo Guinigi, Ilaria died in childbirth aged only 24. At her feet lies her faithful dog.

⭐ **Museo della Cattedrale**   MUSEUM
(www.museocattedralelucca.it; Piazza San Martino; adult/reduced €4/3, with cathedral sacristy & Chiesa e Battistero dei SS Giovanni & Reparata €7/5; ⏱10am-6pm) The cathedral museum safeguards elaborate gold and silver decorations made for the cathedral's Volto Santo, including a 17th-century crown and a 19th-century sceptre.

**Chiesa e Battistero dei
SS Giovanni e Reparata**   CHURCH
(Piazza San Giovanni; adult/reduced €4/3, with cathedral museum & sacristy €7/5; ⏱10am-6pm summer, 10am-5pm Sat & Sun winter) The 12th-century interior of this deconsecrated church is a hauntingly atmospheric setting for summertime opera recitals; buy tickets in advance inside the church. In the north transept, the Gothic baptistry crowns an **archaeological area** comprising five building levels going back to the Roman period. Don't miss the hike up the red-brick **bell tower**.

> ℹ **CENT SAVER**
>
> If you plan to visit the Museo della Cattedrale, Chiesa de SS Giovanni e Reparata and the sacristy inside Cattedrale di San Martino, buy a cheaper combined ticket (adult/reduced €7/5) at any of the sights.

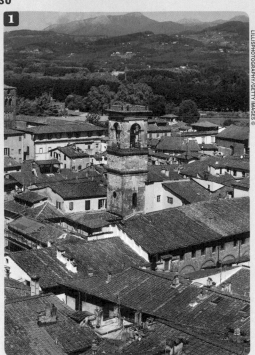

SEPP PUCHINGER/GETTY IMAGES ©

JOHN HESELTINE/GETTY IMAGES ©

3

PHILIP GAME/GETTY IMAGES ©

1. Lucca (p226)

Lovely Lucca is a precious pearl of a city that endears itself to everyone who visits.

2. Arno river (p222), Pisa

Pisa comes into its own along the peaceful banks of the Arno.

3. Castelnuovo di Garfagnana (p243)

Fresh *porcini*, chestnuts and sacks of *farro* (spelt) fill Castelnuovo di Garfagnana's autumnal markets.

4. Serchio river (p243)

Three stunning valleys have been formed by Serchio and its tributaries.

A GOURMET WALLTOP PICNIC

When in Lucca, picnicking atop its city walls – on grass or at a wooden picnic table – is as lovely (and typical) a Lucchesi lunch as any.

Buy fresh-from-the-oven pizza and focaccia with a choice of fillings and toppings from fabulous bakery **Forno Amedeo Giusti** (Via Santa Lucia 20; pizzas & filled focaccias per kg €9-16; ☻7am-7.30pm Mon-Sat, 4-7.30pm Sun), then nip across the street for a bottle of Lucchesi wine and Garfagnese *biscotti al farro* (spelt biscuits) at **Antica Bodega di Prospero** (Via Santa Lucia 13; ☻9am-1pm & 4-7.30pm); look for the old-fashioned shop window stuffed with sacks of beans, lentils and other local pulses.

Complete the perfect picnic with a slice of *buccellato*, a traditional sweetbread loaf with sultanas and aniseed seeds, baked in Lucca since 1881. Devour the rest at home, with butter, dipped in egg and pan-fried, or dunked in sweet Vin Santo. Buy it at pastry shop **Taddeucci** (www.taddeucci.com; Piazza San Michele 34; buccellato per 300/600/900g loaf €4.50/9/13.50; ☻8.30am-7.45pm, closed Thu winter). Or seduce tastebuds with truffles, white chocolate spread and other artisanal chocolate creations almost too beautiful to eat from **Caniparoli** (www.caniparolicioccolateria.it; Via San Paolino 96; ☻9.30am-1pm & 3.30-7.30pm Mon-Sat, to 7pm Sun), the finest chocolate shop in town.

Swill down the picnic with your pick of Italian craft beers at microbrewery **De Cervesia** (Via Fillungo 90; ☻10am-1pm & 3.30-7.30pm Tue-Sat), with a small shop on Lucca's main shopping street and tap room for serious tasting (open 5pm to 10pm Tuesday to Sunday) a few blocks away at Via Michele Rosi 20. Should a shot of something stronger be required to aid digestion, nip into historic pharmacy **Antica Farmacia Massagli** (Piazza San Michele; ☻9am-7.30pm) for a bottle of China elixir, a heady liqueur of aromatic spices and herbs first concocted in 1855 as a preventive measure against the plague. Lucchese typically drink the natural alcoholic drink (no colouring or preservatives) at the end of a meal.

★**Palazzo Pfanner**　　PALACE
(www.palazzopfanner.it; Via degli Asili 33; palace or garden adult/reduced €4.50/4, both €6/5; ☻10am-6pm Apr-Nov) Fire the romantic in you with a stroll around this beautiful 17th-century palace where parts of *Portrait of a Lady* (1996) starring Nicole Kidman and John Malkovich were shot. Its baroque-styled garden – the only one of substance within the city walls – enchants with ornamental pond, lemon house and 18th-century statues of Greek gods posing between potted lemon trees. Summertime chamber music concerts hosted here are absolutely wonderful.

Climb the grand outdoor staircase to the frescoed and furnished piano *nobile* (main reception room), home to Felix Pfanner, an Austrian émigré who first brought beer to Italy – and brewed it in the mansion's cellars from 1846 until 1929. From the copperpots strung above the hearth in the kitchen to the dining-room table laid for lunch, the rooms vividly evoke daily life in an early 18th-century Lucchese *palazzo*.

**Chiesa di
San Michele in Foro**　　CHURCH
(Piazza San Michele; ☻7.40am-noon & 3-6pm summer, 9am-noon & 3-5pm winter) One of Lucca's many architecturally significant churches, this glittering Romanesque edifice marks the spot where the city's Roman forum was. The present building, with its exquisite wedding-cake facade, was constructed on the site of its 8th-century precursor over 300 years, beginning in the 11th century. Crowning the structure is a figure of the archangel Michael slaying a dragon. Inside the dimly lit interior, don't miss Filippino Lippi's 1479 painting of Sts Helen, Jerome, Sebastian and Roch (complete with plague sore) in the south transept.

★**Torre Guinigi**　　TOWER
(Via Guinigi; adult/reduced €4/3; ☻9.30am-6.30pm summer, 10.30am-4.30pm winter) The bird's-eye view from the top of this medieval, 45m-tall red-brick tower adjoining 14th-century **Palazzo Guinigi** is predictably magnificent. But what impresses even more are the seven oak trees planted in a U-shaped flower bed at the top of the tower.

Legend has it that upon the death of powerful Lucchese ruler Paolo Guinigi (1372–1432) all the leaves fell off the trees. Count 230 steps to the top.

Torre Civica delle Ore   TOWER
(Via Fillungo; adult/reduced €4/3; ⊙9.30am-6.30pm summer) Break from the boutiques of Via Fillungo with a hike up the 207 wooden steps of Lucca's 13th-century clock tower – at 50m tall, the highest of the city's 130 medieval towers. Legend has it the tower is inhabited by the ghost of Lucida Mansi, a Lucchese lass who sold her soul to the devil in exchange for remaining young and beautiful for three decades.

On 14 August 1623 the devil came after her to pay her debt, only for Lucida to climb up the clock tower to try and stop time. The devil caught her and took her soul.

**Lucca Centre of
Contemporary Art**   MUSEUM
(www.luccamuseum.com; Via della Fratta 36; adult/reduced €9/7; ⊙10am-7pm Tue-Sun) FREE Lucca's contemporary art museum hosts some riveting contemporary art exhibitions; check its website for details.

**Museo Nazionale
di Palazzo Mansi**   MUSEUM
(Via Galli Tassi 43; adult/reduced €4/2; ⊙8.30am-7.30pm Tue-Sat) This 16th-century mansion built for a wealthy Luccan merchant is a wonderful piece of rococo excess. The private apartments are draped head to toe in tapestries, paintings and chintz. The elaborate, gilded bridal suite must have inspired such high jinks in its time.

✷ Festivals & Events

Lucca Summer Festival   MUSIC
(www.summer-festival.com; ⊙Jul) This month-long festival brings rock and pop stars to Lucca.

⊨ Sleeping

★ **Piccolo Hotel Puccini**   HOTEL €
(☑0583 5 54 21; www.hotelpuccini.com; Via di Poggio 9; s/d €75/100; ❄🔊) In a brilliant central location, this welcoming three-star hotel hides behind a discreet brick exterior. Its small guest rooms are attractive, with wooden floors, vintage ceiling fans and colourful, contemporary design touches. Breakfast, optional at €3.50, is served at candlelit tables behind the small reception area. Rates are around 30% lower in winter.

Ostello San Frediano   HOSTEL €
(☑0583 46 99 57; www.ostellolucca.it; Via della Cavallerizza 12; dm/d €23/68; ⊙mid-Feb–Dec; 🔊) Slap-bang in the centre of walled Lucca, inside a historic building, hostellers won't get closer to the action than this. Top-notch in comfort and service, this HI-affiliated hostel with 141 beds in voluminous rooms is serviced with a bar and grandiose dining room (breakfast €5, lunch or dinner €11). Non-HI members can buy a welcome stamp for €2.

★ **Locanda Vigna Ilaria**   B&B €€
(☑0583 33 20 91; www.locandavignailaria.it; Via della Pieve Santo Stefano 967c, St Alessio; d/q €110/120; P) Those on a Tuscan road trip or who love easy parking will be smitten with this stone house in a wealthy suburb, 4km north of Lucca's walled city in St Alessio

NORTHWESTERN TUSCANY LUCCA

LOCAL KNOWLEDGE

VILLA BONGI
....

Ask anyone from Lucca where to lunch on Sunday or flee the city to escape the stifling summer heat and the reply is invariably **Villa Bongi** (☑347 4955383, 348 7340143; www.villabongi.it; Via di Cocombola 640, Montuolo; 3-/6-course tasting menu €35/45, meals €30-35; ⊙dinner Mon & Wed-Sat, lunch Sun; 🪑), a dreamy salmon-pink mansion with stone-balustrade verandah, 7km west of town. The grand old villa overlooks olive groves and has a wonderful tree-shaded terrace on which diners feast alfresco on Tuscan cuisine and green views of soft rolling Lucchesi hills.

Pasta is strictly homemade and traditional dishes enjoy a creative seasonal twist – red-cabbage risotto with gorgonzola fondue, saffron-scented *tagliatelle* (ribbon pasta) with prosciutto and prawns. Come winter, dining is all about snuggling up, glass of wine in hand, in front of a roaring fire. Advance reservations essential, especially on Sunday when Lucchese families flock here for Villa Bongi's outstanding-value lunch.

WORTH A TRIP

A VILLA TOUR

Between the 15th and 19th centuries, successful Lucchesi merchants flouted their success to the world by building opulent summer residences in the hills around the city, and though a few have crumbled away or been abandoned, many are still inhabited.

Villa Reale (☑ 0583 3 01 08; www.parcovillareale.it; Via Fraga Alta 2, Marlia, Capannori; adult/reduced €8/7; ◷ 10am-6pm Tue-Sun summer) Elisa Bonaparte, Napoleon's sister and short-lived ruler of Tuscany, once lived in handsome Villa Reale, 7km north of Lucca in Marlia. The house isn't open to the public, but the statuary-filled gardens can be visited.

Villa Grabau (☑ 0583 40 60 98; www.villagrabau.it; Via di Matraia 269, San Pancrazio; guided tour €7; ◷ 10am-1pm & 3-7pm Tue-Sun summer, 10am or 11am-1pm & 2-5.30pm or 6pm winter) Neoclassical Villa Grabau, just north of Lucca in San Pancrazio, sits among a vast parkland with sweeping traditional English- and Italian-styled gardens, splashing fountains, more than 100 terracotta pots with lemon trees and a postcard-pretty lemon house – host to fashion shows, concerts and the like – dating from the 17th century. It even has a clutch of self-catering properties to rent in its grounds should you happen to fall in love with the estate. Guided villa and garden visits last 45 minutes.

Villa Oliva (☑ 0583 40 64 62; www.villaoliva.it; San Pancrazio; ◷ 9.30am-12.30pm & 2-6pm summer) In San Pancrazio, the gardens of Villa Oliva, a 15th-century country residence designed by Lucchesi architect Matteo Civitali, demand a springtime stroll. Retaining its original design, the fountain-rich park staggers across three levels and includes a romantic cypress alley and stables reckoned to be even more beautiful than those at Versailles. Watch out for concerts held here.

To reach these villas, take the SS12 northeast from Lucca (direction Abetone) and exit onto the SP29 to Marlia. From Marlia, San Pancrazio is a mere 1.2km north.

(dump the car, then meander along green lanes, past vast villas bathed in olive groves). The *locanda* (inn) has five rooms furnished with a mix of old, new and upcycled – lots of wine boxes!

Its downstairs restaurant, open evenings, is a gastronomic fish-driven treat (meals €45). In summer, dining is alfresco in the pretty walled garden with wooden decking.

2italia　　　　　　　　　　APARTMENT €€
(☑ 392 9960271; www.2italia.com; Via della Anfiteatro 74; apt for 2 adults & up to 4 children €190; ☎) Not a hotel but several family-friendly self-catering apartments overlooking Piazza Anfiteatro, with a communal kids' playroom in the attic. Available on a nightly basis (minimum two nights), the project is the brainchild of well-travelled parents-of-three, Kristin (English) and Kaare (Norwegian). Spacious apartments sleep up to six, have a fully equipped kitchen and washing machine, and come with sheets and towels.

Kristin and Kaare have several other apartments and villas to rent in and around Lucca. They also organise cycling tours, cooking courses, wine tastings and olive pickings for guests.

Alla Corte degli Angeli　　BOUTIQUE HOTEL €€€
(☑ 0583 46 92 04; www.allacortedegliangeli.com; Via degli Angeli 23; s/d/ste €150/250/400; ✳@☎) This boutique hotel sits in a couple of 15th-century townhouses, with a stylish beamed lounge leading to 21 sunny rooms adorned with frescoed ceilings, patches of exposed brick and landscape murals. Every room is named after a different flower, and up-to-the-minute bathrooms have jacuzzi tubs and power-jet showers. Breakfast €10.

✗ Eating & Drinking

Lucca is known for its traditional cuisine and prized olive oil. Garfagnana is not far away and local chestnuts, *porcini* mushrooms, honey, *farro* (spelt), sheep's-milk cheese and *formenton* (ground corn) are abundant – and a perfect match with a delicate white Colline Lucchesi or a red Montecarlo di Lucca wine.

★ Da Felice　　　　　　　　　　PIZZA €
(www.pizzeriadafelice.it; Via Buia 12; focaccias €1-3, pizza slices €1.30; ◷ 11am-8.30pm Mon, 10am-8.30pm Tue-Sat) This buzzing spot behind Piazza San Michele is where the locals come for wood-fired pizza, *cecina* and *castagnacci*. Eat in or take away, a *castagnaccio*

comes wrapped in crisp white paper, and my it's good married with a chilled bottle of Moretti beer.

Grom
GELATERIA €

(www.grom.it; Via Fillungo 56; cone €2.20-3.30; ☺ 11.30am-10pm Sun-Thu, to 11pm or midnight Fri & Sat) Natural and organic is the philosophy of this master ice-cream maker. Join the line of locals for a tub of caramel and pink Himalayan salt, yoghurt, tiramisu or seasonal fruit sorbet.

Trattoria da Leo
TRATTORIA €

(☑ 0583 49 22 36; Via Tegrimi 1; meals €25; ☺ 12.30-2pm & 7.30-10.30pm Mon-Sat) A much-loved veteran, Leo is famed for its friendly ambience and cheap food – ranging from plain-Jane acceptable to grandma delicious. Arrive in summer to snag one of 10 checked-tableclothed tables crammed beneath parasols on the narrow street outside. Otherwise, it's noisy dining inside among typically nondescript 1970s decor. No credit cards.

Local Food Market
DELI €€

(☑ 0583 31 10 77; Via San Paolino 116; meals €30; ☺ 10am-11.30pm Tue-Sun) This bright, modern address is hidden in a courtyard, complete with potted lemon plants and tables in the sun. In keeping with the seemingly latest trend sweeping through Tuscany, Local Food Market is just that – an upmarket food market, deli and health food shop where you can eat between shelves stacked high with local Tuscan products.

★ Ristorante Giglio
TUSCAN €€

(☑ 0583 49 40 58; www.ristorantegiglio.com; Piazza del Giglio 2; meals €35; ☺ 12.30-2pm & 7.30-10pm Thu-Mon, 7.30-10pm Wed) Don't let the tacky plastic-covered pavement terrace deter. Splendidly at home in the frescoed 18th-century Palazzo Arnolfini, Giglio is stunning. Dine at white-tableclothed tables, sip a complimentary *prosecco* (sparkling wine), watch the fire crackle in the marble fireplace and savour traditional Tuscan cuisine with a modern twist: think fresh artichoke salad served in an edible Parmesan wafer 'bowl', or risotto simmered in Chianti.

End with Lucchese *buccellato* (sweetbread) filled with ice cream and berries.

Port Ellen Clan
TUSCAN €€

(☑ 0583 49 39 52; www.portellenclan.com; Via del Fosso 120; meals €30; ☺ 7.30pm-1am Wed-Fri, noon-3pm & 7.30pm-1am Sat & Sun) 'Ristorante, Enoteca, Design Ideas' is the strapline of this romantic candlelit space named after the town in the Scottish Hebrides where the owner holidays. Cuisine is imaginative with homemade *tortelli* stuffed with stewed oxtail and pork tenderloin with fennel mash jostling for attention on the creative menu. Excellent artisan beer and whisky list.

Cantine Bernardini 1586
TUSCAN €€

(☑ 0583 49 43 36; www.cantinebernardini.com; Via del Suffragio 7; meals €30; ☺ 7-11pm Mon, Wed & Thu, noon-2.30pm & 7-11pm Fri-Sun) This hybrid *osteria-enoteca* in the red-brick vaulted cellars of 16th-century Palazzo Bernardini has the balance just right. Seasonal Tuscan dishes such as chestnut-flour ravioli in a wild-boar sauce or a springtime flan of violet artichokes tempt on the menu, and the wine list is exceptional. Extra kudos for the children's menu, veggie burgers, cooking classes and tastings, occasional DJs and live music.

Buca di Sant'Antonio
TUSCAN €€€

(☑ 0583 5 58 81; www.bucadisantantonio.com; Via della Cervia 3; meals €40; ☺ lunch & dinner Tue-Sat, lunch Sun) Gosh, what a fabulous collection of copper pots strung from the wood-beamed ceiling! This atmosphere-laden restaurant has wooed romantic diners since 1782 and is still going strong. The Tuscan cuisine does not quite live up to the exceptional wine list, but it remains a favourite nonetheless. Service is formal – think gents of a certain age in black suits and dicky-bows – and opens with a glass of *prosecco* on the house as an aperitif.

ℹ Information

Tourist Office (☑ 0583 58 31 50; www.lucca itinera.it; Piazzale Verdi; ☺ 9am-7pm summer, to 5pm winter) Free hotel reservations, left-luggage service (two bags €2.50/4.50/7 per hour/half-day/day) and guided city tours in English departing daily at 2pm (€10, two hours).

ℹ Getting There & Away

BUS

From the bus stops around Piazzale Verdi, **Vaibus Lucca** (www.lucca.cttnord.it) runs services throughout the region, including to the following three destinations:

Bagni di Lucca (€3.40, 25 to 45 minutes, eight daily)

Castelnuovo di Garfagnana (€4.20, 1½ hours, eight daily)

Pisa airport (€3.40, 45 minutes to one hour, 30 daily)

CAR & MOTORCYCLE

The A11 runs westwards to Pisa and Viareggio and eastwards to Florence. To access the Garfagnana, take the SS12 and continue on the SS445.

The easiest option is to park at Parcheggio Carducci, just outside Porta Sant'Anna. Within the walls, most car parks are for residents only, indicated by yellow lines. Blue lines indicate where anyone, including tourists, can park (€2 per hour). If you are staying within the city walls, contact your hotel ahead of your arrival and enquire about the possibility of getting a temporary resident permit during your stay.

TRAIN

The train station is south of the city walls: take the path across the moat and through the (dank, grungy) tunnel under Baluardo San Colombano. Regional train services:

Florence (€7.20, 1¼ to 1¾ hours, hourly)
Pietrasanta (€5.90, 50 minutes, hourly)
Pisa (€3.40, 30 minutes, every 30 minutes)
Pistoia (€5.30, 45 minutes to one hour, half-hourly)
Viareggio (€3.40, 25 minutes, hourly)

❶ Getting Around

BICYCLE

Rent wheels, ID required, to pedal the 4.2km circumference of Lucca's romantic city walls from a couple of outlets on Piazza Santa Maria or try the following:

Tourist Center Lucca (☑ 0583 49 44 01; www.touristcenterlucca.com; Piazzale Ricasoli 203; bike per hr/3hr/day €4/8/12; ☺ 8.30am-7.30pm summer, 9am-6pm winter) Exit the train station and bear left to find this handy bike rental outlet, with kids' bikes, tandems, trailers and various other gadgets. It also has left-luggage facilities.

PISTOIA

POP 90,200

Pretty Pistoia sits snugly at the foot of the Apennines. An easy day trip from Pisa, Lucca or Florence, it deserves more attention than it gets. A town that has grown well beyond its medieval ramparts, its *centro storico* is tranquil, well preserved and guardian to some striking contemporary art.

On Wednesdays and Saturdays a morning market transforms Pistoia's vast main square, Piazza del Duomo, as well as its surrounding streets into a lively sea of blue awnings and jostling shoppers. Otherwise, from Monday to Saturday you'll find open-air stalls heaped with seasonal fruit and vegetables on tiny Piazza della Sala, west of the cathedral.

◉ Sights

Pistoia's key sights are clustered around its beautiful cathedral square, Piazza del Duomo, hemmed by a maze of narrow pedestrian streets made for meandering.

★**Cattedrale di San Zeno** CATHEDRAL
(Piazza del Duomo; adult/reduced chapel €2/1.50, bell tower €6/4; ☺ 8.30am-12.20pm & 3.30-6.45pm, chapel 9-10am, 11.30am-12.30pm & 3.30-6pm) This cathedral with beautiful Pisan-Romanesque facade and sky-high brick **campanile** safeguards a lunette of the Madonna and Child between two angels by Andrea della Robbia. Its other highlight, in **Cappella di San Jacopo** off the north aisle, is the silver Dossale di San Giacomo (Altarpiece of St James) begun in 1287 and finished two centuries later by Brunelleschi. Buy tickets for the bell tower and chapel in the Battistero di San Giovanni.

★**Battistero di San Giovanni** RELIGIOUS SITE
(Piazza del Duomo; ☺ 10am-1pm & 3-6pm Tue-Sun) **FREE** Across the square from the cathedral is this 14th-century octagonal baptistry, elegantly banded in green-and-white marble to a design by Andrea Pisano. An ornate square marble font and soaring dome enliven the otherwise bare, red-brick interior.

Museo dell'Antico Palazzo dei Vescovi MUSEUM
(☑ 0573 36 92 75; Piazza del Duomo; adult/reduced €5/3; ☺ guided tours 10.15am, 11.45am, 1.15pm & 2.45pm Tue, Thu & Fri, 10.15am, 11.45am, 1.15pm, 3pm & 4.30pm Sat & Sun) The bishops' palace, the oldest building in Pistoia, is wedged next to the cathedral and provides a fascinating tour of Pistoia's urban history, ranging from touchable scale models of key architectural gems such as Pistoia's cathedral and baptistry on the 1st floor, and a subterranean tour of archaeological treasures hidden in the basement.

Museo Civico GALLERY
(Piazza del Duomo 1; adult/reduced €3.50/2; ☺ 10am-6pm Thu-Sun) Pistoia's Gothic **Palazzo Communale** is strung with works by Tuscan artists from the 13th to 20th centuries. Don't miss Bernardino di Antonio

Detti's *Madonna della Pergola* (1498) with its modern treatment of St James, the Madonna and baby Jesus; spot the mosquito on Jesus' arm.

★**Chiesa di Sant'Andrea** CHURCH
(Via Sant'Andrea 21; ☉ variable) This 12th-century church was built outside the original city walls, hence its windowless (fortified) state. The partly white-and-green marble-striped facade is enlivened by a relief of the *Journey and Adoration of the Magi* (1166) by Gruamonte and Adeodato. But the highlight – Pistoia's most prized art work – is within the gloomy interior: an imposing marble pulpit carved by Giovanni Pisano (1298–1301). Two lions and a bent human figure bear the heavy load of the seven-columned masterpiece, and Sibyls and the Prophets decorate the capitals.

Try to decipher the story of the Annunciation, Nativity, Adoration of the Kings, Slaughter of the Innocents, Crucifixion and Last Judgment in the sculpted relief panels around the pulpit.

Palazzo Fabroni MUSEUM
(✑ 0573 37 18 17; Via Sant'Andrea 18; adult/reduced €3.50/2; ☉ 10am-6pm Thu-Sun) Take a breather from the ancient with this spacious and airy contemporary art museum, host to riveting temporary exhibitions and a permanent collection amassed through exhibiting artists donating works to the gallery. Highlights include the shadow wall painting *Scultura d'Ombra* (2007) by iconoclastic Italian artist Claudio Parmiggiani (b 1943) and rooms dedicated to Pistoia-born artists Mario Nigro (1917–92) and Fernando Melani (1907–85). Don't miss the photo of sculptor Marino Marini on the beach with his horse at Forte dei Marmi in 1973.

Should you get completely hooked, upon advance request it is possible to visit the nearby **casa-studio** (✑ 0573 37 18 17; Corso Gramsci 159) of Fernando Melani, where the abstract artist lived and worked.

Piazzetta degli Ortaggi PIAZZA
Don't miss this beautiful bijou square with its laid-back cafe life and striking, life-size sculpture of three blindfolded men, **Giro di Sole** (Around the Sun; 1996) by contemporary Pistoia artist Roberto Barni (b 1939). In the 18th century the market square, adjoining Piazza della Sala and once home to a brothel, was the entrance to Pistoia's Jewish ghetto.

Ospedale del Ceppo MONUMENT
(✑ 0573 36 80 23; www.irsapt.it; Piazza Giovanni XXIII 13; underground tour adult/reduced €9/8; ☉ 10am-7pm summer, to 6pm winter) The facade of this former hospital, sparkling after recent renovation works, stuns with its 16th-century polychrome terracotta frieze by Giovanni della Robbia. It depicts the *Sette Opere di Misericordia* (Seven Works of Mercy), and the five medallions represent the *Virtù Teologali* (Theological Virtues). Although the 13th-century hospital building cannot be visited, you can delve into its underground belly of passageways and subterranean rivers decorated with old surgical tools, scalpels and all sorts with a one-hour **Pistoia Sotteranea** guided tour.

★**Museo Marino Marini** MUSEUM
(✑ 0573 3 02 85; www.fondazionemarinomarini.it; Corso Silvano Fedi 30; adult/reduced €3.50/2; ☉ 10am-6pm Mon-Sat summer, to 5pm winter, chapel 8.15am-1.30pm Mon-Sat plus 2-7pm 1st Sun of month) This gallery inside Palazzo del Tau is devoted to Pistoia's most famous modern son, eponymous sculptor and painter Marino Marini (1901–80). Dozens of his drawings and paintings – mainly of female nudes (pear-shaped, evoking goddess of fertility Pomona) and horses – hang here. Visit in the morning to see **Cappella del Tau**, the tiny 14th-century chapel, frescoed by the School of Giotto and dramatic guardian to

---

WORTH A TRIP

A (SERIOUS) ART LOVER'S DETOUR

A tea house, aviary and other romantic 19th-century follies mingle with some cutting-edge art installations created by the world's top contemporary artists at **Fattoria di Celle** (✑ 0573 47 99 07; www.goricoll.it; Via Montalese 7, Santomato di Pistoia; ☉ by appointment only May-Sep), 5km from Pistoia. The extraordinary private collection and passion of local businessman Giuliano Gori, this unique sculpture park showcases 70 site-specific installations sprinkled around his vast family estate.

Visits – reserved for serious art lovers – require reservation via email at least 30 days in advance and entail a guided four- to five-hour hike around the estate (no rest stops!).

Pistoia

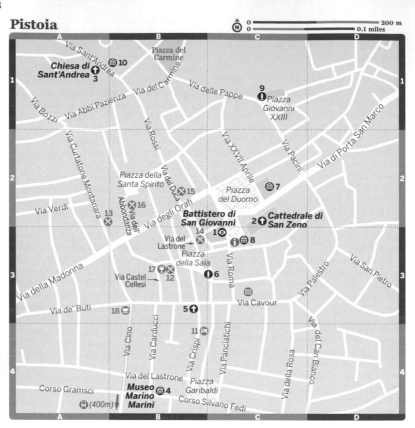

Marini's monumental equestrian sculpture *The Miracle* (1952).

Families, look out for the hands-on family tours (€5, advance reservation by telephone) organised in English once a month by the museum.

★ Festivals & Events

Giostra dell'Orso   CULTURAL
(⊙25 Jul) Translated as Joust of the Bear, medieval jousting and other equestrian pranks fill Piazza del Duomo during Pistoia's celebration of its patron saint, San Giacomo.

Pistoia Blues   MUSIC
(www.pistoiablues.com; ⊙ Jul) Going strong for at least three decades, Pistoia's annual blues festival lures big names. BB King, Miles Davis, Sting and Santana have all taken to the stage here – an electrical fresco affair that packs out Piazza del Duomo. Tickets costs €25 to €75.

🛏 Sleeping

Hotel Patria   HOTEL €€
(☑0573 35 88 00; www.patriahotel.com; Via Francesco Crispi 8-12; s/d €109/129; ❊@🛜) Perfectly placed down a side street by the distinctively striped Chiesa di San Giovanni Fuorcivitas, this swish 27-room hotel is within easy strolling distance of all the main sights. Carpeted corridors open on to comfortable rooms dressed in creams, sage greens and other soft neutral hues.

Tenuta di Pieve a Celle   HOTEL €€
(☑0573 91 30 87; www.tenutadipieveacelle.it; Via di Pieve a Celle 158; d €160; P❊🛟) The out-of-town option; a driveway lined with cypress trees leads to this 1850s country estate with olive grove and pool, in the hills 3km outside Pistoia. Five pretty rooms with canopy beds overlook expansive gardens, and host Fiorenza cooks evening meals on request using seasonal produce fresh from her organic vegetable garden.

Pistoia

✗ Eating & Drinking

Pistoia's eat street is pedestrian **Via del Lastrone**, lined with cafes, wine bars and traditional restaurants serving *carcerato* (a type of offal), *frittata con rigatino* (omelette with salt-cured bacon), *farinata con cavalo* (chickpea pancake with cabbage), *migliacci* (fritters made with pig's blood) and other local specialities. End your meal with *berlingozzo*, a sweet traditionally served with a glass of local Vin Santo.

Car-free market square **Piazza della Sala** and its surrounding web of narrow streets is the other hot spot in town for a good meal or atmospheric drink at trendy bars.

★ Magno Gaudio   CAFE €
(☑0573 2 69 05; Via Curtatone e Montanara 12; meals €20; ☉7am-midnight Mon-Sat; 🛜) If it is local Pistoians you're looking for, snag a table at this brilliant all-rounder. Be it breakfast, brunch or dinner, this cafe delivers with free wi-fi, creative cuisine by chef Maurizio – lots of fish and sesame seed-encrusted tuna carpaccio to die for – and friendly unpretentious service. *Panini* to take away, too.

Osteria Pizzeria Apicio   PIZZA €
(☑334 7581991; Via del Duca 8; meals €20; ☉7pm-12.30am Tue-Sun) Squirrelled away in yet another wonderful old building down a side street, this hybrid pizzeria-*osteria* is a staunchly local affair. Its cavernous, chapel-like interior is a mesmerising collage of original features – sky-high vaulted ceiling, exposed stone, red brick, water well – and the oven-fired pizzas are the best in town. A tip-top choice of craft beers is the icing on the cake.

★ Osteria La BotteGaia   OSTERIA €€
(☑0573 36 56 02; www.labottegaia.it; Via del Lastrone 17; meals €28; ☉noon-3pm & 7-11pm Tue-Sat, 7-11pm Sun) Dishes range from staunchly traditional to experimental at this Slow Food–hailed *osteria*, famed for its finely butchered cured meats and interesting wine list. Aubergine and ribcotta strudel in tomato sauce is one of a few interesting vegetarian options. Reserve in advance or, if you don't get a table, opt for wine and snacks at La BotteGaia's *vineria* (wine bar) on the same street.

I Salaioli   DELI €€
(☑0573 2 02 25; www.isalaioli.it; Piazza della Sala 20-22; meals €30; ☉7am-11pm) One glance at the delectable wedges of salami and rounds of cheese on the counter begging to be eaten and you'll be smitten. This is one of those fabulous deli-restaurants that suits naturally gourmet Tuscany so, so well: products are fresh, local, seasonal and can be bought to take home or eaten in situ – in the deli interior or on the people-watching pavement terrace.

Trattoria dell'Abbondanza   TRATTORIA €€
(☑0573 36 80 37; Via dell'Abbondanza 10; meals €25; ☉12.15-2.15pm & 7.15-10.30pm Fri-Tue, 7.15-10.30pm dinner Thu) Dine beneath coloured parasols in an atmospheric alley outside or plump for a table inside where homey collections of door bells, pasta jars and so on catch the eye. The cuisine, once you've deciphered the handwriting on the menu, is simple tasty Tuscan.

Fiaschetteria La Pace   WINE BAR
(☑0573 2 31 39; Via dei Fabbri 7-9; meals €25) 'Everything is going to be alright' is the strapline of this hip bar and bistro. And indeed, be it shelling free peanuts around a wood scrubbed table in the vintage interior or perched on a stone slab of a window sill outside, everything *is* good at this trendy

PRATO

It is off the beaten tourist track, yes. But the historical town of Prato (pop 191,268) is conveniently 'on the track' when it comes to savouring this unexplored town as a crowd-free foray by train from Pistoia (€2.50, 15 minutes) or Florence (€2.30, 30 minutes).

Tuscany's second-largest town after Florence, this traditional textile-producing centre has a compact old town girded by near-intact city walls. From Prato's **Stazione Porta al Serraglio** it is a five-minute walk to **Piazza Duomo** and 12th-century **Cattedrale di Santo Stefano** (Piazza Duomo; ⊘9am-3am Mon-Sat) **FREE**, with magnificent frescoes by Filippo Lippi behind the altar and Agnolo's fresco cycle of the *Legend of the Holy Girdle* (1392–95) in the chapel to the left of the entrance. The unusual protruding pulpit (1428) on the cathedral's Pisan-Romanesque facade was designed by Donatello and Michelozzo to publicly display the *sacra cintola*, a deeply venerated girdle believed to have been given to St Thomas by the Virgin and brought to Prato from Jerusalem after the Second Crusade. Brought out five times a year today, the fine wool rope brocaded with gold thread is locked away in the chapel in a gold reliquary with three keys.

Learn more about the Virgin's girdle at nearby **Museo di Palazzo Pretorio** (☑0574 193 49 96; www.palazzopretorio.prato.it; Piazza del Commune; adult/reduced €8/6; ⊘10.30am-6.30pm Wed-Mon), an impressive bulk of a history museum that reopened as one of Tuscany's smartest museums after a record 20-year-long renovation job. The **tourist office** (☑0574 2 41 12; www.pratoturismo.it; Piazza Buonamici 7; ⊘9am-1pm & 3-6pm Mon-Fri, 10am-1pm Sat & Sun) is just around the corner from here. Dedicated museum buffs can continue to local textile museum **Museo del Tessuto** (☑0574 61 15 03; www.museodel tessuto.it; Via Puccetti 3; adult/reduced €6/4; ⊘10am-3pm Tue-Fri, to 7pm Sat, 3-7pm Sun), at home in the former Campolmi textile mill.

Post-sightseeing, excite tastebuds with a sweet shopping spree at **Antonio Mattei** (www.biscottimatteideseo.it; Via Ricasoli 20; ⊘8am-7.30pm Tue-Fri, 8am-1pm & 3.30-7.30pm Sat, 8am-1pm Sun, closed Jul), Prato's famed *biscottificio* where the city's signature *biscotti di Prato* (twice-baked almond biscuits made for dunking in sweet wine) have been made since 1858. To see the bakers in action, visit in the morning. The biscuits (€16 per kg), not sealed but simply wrapped in waxy royal-blue paper and tied with string, are best eaten within five days.

Round off your Prato visit with a memorable glass of wine and lunch, *apericena* (meal-sized *aperitif* buffet) from 6pm or dinner at **Le Barrique** (☑0574 3 01 51; www.lebarrique winebar.it; Corso Mazzoni 19; ⊘noon-12.30am). The wine bar, with stylish red-brick interior and excellent Tuscan kitchen, is one of the few places in town to taste **mortadella di Prato**, a heavily seasoned, rose-coloured sausage spiced up with Alchermes liqueur and only produced by two butchers in Prato today.

eating-drinking address. Creative Tuscan cuisine and traditional tasting boards of salami and cheese keep everyone happy any time of day.

Caffètteria Marini
CAFE

(www.fondazionemarinomarini.it; Corso Silvano Fedi 32; ⊘8am-8pm) This warm, vibrant cafe with its own bakery (superb breads) and garden buzzes with local life. Sip an espresso at the bar, chat with friends over cappuccino at one of four tables in the cosy interior, or flop on a country-style sofa in the covered porch and admire the blooming hydrangeas in the fabulous cloister garden – utterly gorgeous in summer.

Grand Café du Globe
CAFE

(Piazza Gavinana; ⊘7.30am-8.30pm Mon-Sat, 7.30am-1pm & 3.30-8.30pm Sun) This old-world cafe and *pasticceria* with genteel, black-tie and suited waiting staff is a lovely spot to drink coffee and eat delicious cakes – sitting down or standing up (with the local police who pop in here for espresso shots). It also has well-filled *panini* and focaccia (€2.50) to eat in or take away.

ℹ Information

Tourist office (☑0573 2 16 22; www.pistoia. turismo.toscana.it; Piazza del Duomo 4; ⊘9am-1pm & 3-6pm)

ⓘ Getting There & Around

TRAIN

From the train station, head straight along Viale XX Settembre, across the roundabout, and beyond along Via Atto Vannucci to get to the Old Town. Regional train services:

Florence (€4.30, 45 minutes, every 20 minutes)

Lucca (€5.30, 45 minutes to one hour, half-hourly)

Pisa (€9.20, two hours, one daily or change at Lucca)

Prato (€2.50, 15 minutes, every 20 minutes)

Viareggio (€6.60, one hour, hourly)

SAN MINIATO & AROUND

POP 28,100

There is one delicious reason to visit this enchantingly sleepy, medieval hilltop town almost equidistant (50km) between Pisa and Florence: to eat, hunt and dream about the *tuber magnatum pico* (white truffle).

San Miniato town's ancient cobbled streets, burnt soft copper and ginger in the hot summer sun, are a delight to meander. Savour a harmonious melody of magnificent palace facades, 14th- to 18th-century churches and an impressive Romanesque cathedral, ending with the stiff hike up San Miniato's reconstructed medieval fortress tower, **Torre di Frederico II** (Tower of Frederick II; admission €3.50; ☺11am-5pm Tue-Sun), to enjoy a great panorama. Before setting off buy a combined ticket to all the key sites (€5) at the tourist office.

Then knuckle down to the serious business of lunch. Many local restaurants buy their meat from **Sergio Falaschi** (www.sergiofalaschi.it; Via Augusto Conti 18-20, San Miniato; ☺7.30am-1pm & 4-8pm Mon, Tue & Thu-Sat, 7.30am-1pm Sun), the local *macelleria* (butcher) specialising in products made from *cinta senese* (indigenous Tuscan pig from the area around Siena), including the Slow Food favourite, *mallegato* (blood sausage). Other local products worth looking for on menus are *carciofo San Miniatese* (locally grown artichokes) in April and May; chestnuts and wild mushrooms in autumn (fall); *formaggio di capra delle colline di San Miniato* (the local goat's cheese); and locally raised Chianina beef.

Don't leave town without nipping into **Slow Food** (Via Augusto Conti 39; ☺variable) to ask about tastings, tours, cellar visits, wine itineraries and other great tastebud-tempting activities. It also organises the fabulous **Mercati della Terra di San Miniato** (www.mercatidellaterra.it; Piazzale Dante Alighieri; ☺9am-2pm 3rd Sun of month), a vibrant farmers market humming with fresh fruit, veg, meat, raw milk and other local produce from small-scale farmers and artisan producers. It's held on the third Sunday of the month.

🛏 Sleeping & Eating

★ **Barbialla Nuova** FARMSTAY €
(☎0571 67 70 04; www.barbiallanuova.it; Via Casastada 49, Montaione; 2-/4-/6-/8-person apt from €90/145/180/290, minimum 2/7 nights winter/summer; P ⓢ ⊠) 𝄞 Creamy Chianina cows graze on the hillside and wild boars ferret for white truffles between tree roots on this heavily wooded, 500-hectare biodynamic farm with just the right mix of adventure (unpaved roads) and panache (stylish decor). Apartments in old farmhouses dotted around the property offer self-catering accommodation and, most memorably, guests can buy fresh truffles in season at the farm shop.

Staying here is all about feeding the pigs, admiring the livestock, walking (guests get a map of trails around the estate), stocking up on fresh organic produce and truffles at the farm shop – and cooking them up! Barbialla is 20km south of San Miniato on the SP76; look for the white sign on your right 3km after the village of Carrazano.

Podere del Grillo TUSCAN €
(☎0571 40 93 79; www.poderedelgrillo.eu; Via Serra 3, La Serra; meals €25, tasting platters €10-15; ☺6-11pm Mon-Sat, 12.30-3.30pm & 6-11pm Sun) 𝄞 The quality of ingredients here is so extraordinary most dishes hardly need cooking or culinary intervention. Everything is sourced from local organic farms and it shows. Top off tasty salads, cold meats and cheeses with an artsy crowd, stylish location in a red-brick farmhouse and a positively urban bar vibe. Occasional live music, art shows and cultural events. Dinner from 8pm.

From San Miniato, head south towards Montaione and after a couple of kilometres, play 'Spot pretend cows' (in the parking area opposite the red-brick farm).

★ **Osteria Il Papero** TUSCAN €€
(☎338 4302267; www.osteriailpapero.it; Piazza 1 Maggio 1, Balconevisi; meals €35; ☺8-11pm Wed-Sat, noon-3pm Sun) Lost in the hills above San Miniato, in the hamlet of Balconevisi, this

DON'T MISS

HUNTING WHITE TRUFFLES

An integral part of local culture since the Middle Ages, some 400 *tartufaio* (truffle hunters) in the trio of small valleys around San Miniato snout out the precious fungus, pale ochre in colour, from October to mid-December. The paths and trails they follow are a family secret, passed between generations. The truffles their dogs sniff out are worth a small fortune after all, selling for €1500 per kilogram in Tuscany and four times as much in London and other European capitals.

There is no better time to savour the mystique of this cloak-and-dagger truffle trade than during San Miniato's **Mostra Mercato Nazionale del Tartufo Bianco** (National White Truffle Market), during the last three weekends in November, when restaurateurs and truffle tragics come from every corner of the globe to purchase supplies, sample truffle-based delicacies in the town's shops and restaurants, and breathe in one of the world's most distinctive aromas. San Miniato tourist office has a list of truffle dealers and can help you join a truffle hunt.

The best are the early morning truffle hunts at **Barbialla Nuova** (p241), a 500-hectare farm, 20km south of San Miniato near Montaione, run by new-generation farmer Guido Manfredi. Truffle hunts (€80 per person, 2½ hours) on the estate with truffle-hunter Giovanni end with a glass of Chianti and tasting of local organic cheese and salami – or go to a local restaurant and savour your truffle shaved over pasta and after, a *bistecca alla fiorentina* (chargrilled T-bone steak). Famed far and wide for its enviable success rate when it comes to uncovering these nuggets of 'white' gold, Barbialla's *tartufaio* and its dogs unearth some 20kg or so of edible booty in a season.

humble family-run *osteria* completely stuns with its unexpectedly creative – and delicious – Tuscan cuisine. Local farm products rule in the kitchen where young chef Leandro Gaccione applies his artistic talent with astonishing effect. Don't miss the fabulous themed tastings accompanied by live music the first Thursday evening of each month; reserve in advance.

Pepenero TUSCAN €€€
(☏ 0571 41 95 23; www.pepenerocucina.it; Via IV Novembre 13, San Miniato; meals €50; ☉ 7.30-10pm Sat, 12.30-2pm & 7.30-10pm Sun & Wed-Fri) Chef and TV star Gilberto Rossi is one of the new breed of innovative Tuscan chefs using traditional products to create modern, seasonally driven dishes at this much-lauded restaurant. To share some of his secrets, sign up for one of his half-day cooking classes followed by an informal lunch on the restaurant's terrace. Advance reservations essential.

Peperino TUSCAN €€€
(☏ 0571 41 95 23; Via IV Novembre 1, San Miniato; menu incl bottle champagne & wine €250; ☉ by appointment only) Book the only table – a table for two – at Peperino, the world's smallest restaurant plump in the heart of Tuscany's most gourmet village, next to big brother, Pepenero. Decor is in-your-face romantic (think pink silk), furnishings are period and

the waiter only comes when diners ring the bell. Reserve months in advance.

ℹ️ Information

Tourist office (☏ 0571 4 27 45; www.san miniatopromozione.it; Piazza del Popolo 1; ☉ 9am-1pm Mon, 9am-1pm & 2-5pm Tue-Sun)

ℹ️ Getting There & Away

CAR
From Pisa or Florence, take the FI-PI-LI (SS67); there is car parking on Piazza del Popolo.

TRAIN
Train it to San Miniato then hop on a shuttle bus (€1, every 20 minutes) to the Old Town.

Regional train services:
Florence (€5.30, 45 minutes, hourly)
Pisa (€4.30, 30 minutes, hourly)

THE APUANE ALPS & GARFAGNANA

Rearing up inland from the Versilian Riviera are the Apuane Alps, a rugged mountain range protected by the Parco Regionale delle Alpi Apuane (www.parcapuane.it), and beckoning hikers with a trail of isolated farmhouses, medieval hermitages and hilltop villages.

Continue inland, across the Alps' eastern ridge and three stunning valleys formed by the Serchio and its tributaries – the low-lying Lima and Serchio Valleys and the higher Garfagnana Valley, collectively known as the **Garfagnana** – take centre stage. Thickly forested with chestnut woods and unknown to most, this is an unexplored land where fruits of the forest (chestnuts, *porcini* mushrooms and honey) create a rustic and fabulous cuisine.

The main gateway to this staunchly rural part of Tuscany is Castelnuovo di Garfagnana, home to the regional park visitors centre. If faintly more 'cosmopolitan' rocks your boat as a base, consider Pietrasanta on the Apuane Alps' southern fringe.

Castelnuovo di Garfagnana

POP 6020

The medieval eyrie of Castelnuovo crowns the confluence of the Serchio and its smaller tributary, the Turrite. Its heart is pierced by the burnt-red **Rocca Ariostesca** (Ariosto's Castle), built in the 12th century and named after Italian poet Ariosto who lived here between 1522 and 1525 as governor of the Garfagnana for the House of Este. Opposite, historic cake shop and chocolate-maker **Fronte delle Rocca** (Piazza Ariosto 1; ⊘9am-1pm & 3-7.30pm Tue-Sun) has been the hub of local life since 1885. Indulge in a glass of *prosecco,* then follow Via Fulvio Testi to the **duomo** (Piazza del Duomo), with its lovely *Madonna and Two Saints* by Michele di Ridolfo del Ghirlandaio.

Footsteps away, across from the old city gate, sacks of beans, chickpeas, walnuts and *porcini* sit outside grocer's shop **Alimentari Poli Roberto** (Via Olinto Dini 6; ⊘8.30am-1pm & 3.30-8.30pm) – his chestnut beer, beer made from locally grown *farro, farro*-encrusted pecorino and honey are prerequisites for any respectable Garfagnana picnic, as is the *castagnaccio* and *biroldo* (a type of pork salami spiced with wild fennel). Or sit down to a mind-blowing symphony of cold dishes crafted from local products and brought to shared tables one at a time at 160-year-old **Osteria Vecchia Mulino** (✆0583 6 21 92; www.vecchiomulino.info; Via Vittorio Emanuele 12; tasting menu incl wine €25; ⊘11am-9pm Tue-Sun) – advance reservations essential. End with a chestnut, fig and honey or *crema di farro* ice cream (complete with whole grains of *farro*) from **Fuori dal Contro** (www.fuoridalcentro.com; Piazza Olinto Dini 1f; cones €1-4; ⊘1-8pm Mon-Sat, 11am-8pm Sun).

Thursday morning is market day.

ℹ Information

Centro Visite Parco Alpi Apuane (✆0583 6 51 69; www.turismo.garfagnana.eu; Piazza delle Erbe 1; ⊘9am-1pm & 3-7pm summer, to 5.30pm winter; ☎) Regional park visitors centre with bags of info on farm accommodation, walking, mountain biking, horse riding and other activities in the Apuane Alps; sells maps and has lists of local guides and mountain huts. Free wi-fi hot spot complete with sofas for connecting in comfort.

NORTHWESTERN TUSCANY CASTELNUOVO DI GARFAGNANA

OFF THE BEATEN TRACK

AN OPERA BUFF'S DETOUR

Some 35km west of both Barbialla Nuova and San Gimignano, ringed by a natural amphitheatre of soul-stirring hills, is **Lajatico** (population 1390). This tiny village is the birthplace and family home of opera singer Andrea Bocelli (b 1958) who, each year in July or August, returns to his village to sing – for just one evening.

His stage is the astonishing **Teatro del Silenzio** (www.teatrodelsilenzio.it), a specially constructed, open-air 'Theatre of Silence' built in a green meadow on the fringe of the village where the natural silence is broken once a year – by the Tuscan tenor and his friends (Placido Domingo, José Carreras, Sarah Brightman and Chinese pianist Lang Lang have all performed here). Each year different sculptures by contemporary artists are added to the ensemble, to striking effect. Gently rolling, fresh green hills as far as the eye can see is the astonishing 360-degree backdrop and listening to the tenor sing to an audience of 10,000 is an overwhelming experience. Tickets, usually released each year in March, cost €80 to €400 and are sold by **Vivaticket** (www.vivaticket.it).

Opera buffs with a penchant for a fine vintage can continue 5km to **La Sterza** to buy wine and olive oil produced on Bocelli's family estate at **Cantina Bocelli**, a red-brick vaulted cellar at the southern end of the village on the SR439.

Apuane Alps & Garfagnana

EMILIA-ROMAGNA

SS63

The Apuane Alps

Fivizzano

Monte Vecchio (1982m)

Giuncugnano

Casola

Serchio

SS445

Monte Frignone (1331m)

Monte Bocca di Scala (1846m)

Pania di Corfino (1602m)

Monte Alto (1538m)

San Romano in Garfagnana

Corfino

SS324

Piazza al Serchio

Villa Collemandina

Castiglione di Garfagnana

Pizzo d'Uccello (1781m)

Monte Umbriano (1229m)

Poggio

Monte Sagro (1749m)

Monte Pisanino (1945m)

Lago di Vagli

Lago di Pontecosi

Sillico

Pontecosi

Pieve Fosciana

Monte Crondilice (1805m)

Monte Tambura (1890m)

Vagli di Sotto

Gragnana

Colonnata

Monte Sella (1839m)

Castelnuovo di Garfagnana

Carrara

Monte Sumbra (1764m)

SP13

Cascio

Pian della Fioba

Antona

Altagnana

SP4

Passo del Vestito (1151m)

Isola Santa

Gallicano

Marina di Massa

Massa

Monte Altissimo (1589m)

Monte Corchia (1677m)

Vergemoli

Grotta del Vento

SS1

Levigliani

Pania della Croce (1858m)

Fornovolasco

Azzano

A12

Monte Croce (1314m)

Parco Regionale delle Alpi Apuane

Seravezza

Stazzema

Forte dei Marmi

Santa Anna

Monte Matanna (1317m)

Pietrasanta

Monte Piglione (1232m)

Monte Prano (1220m)

Ligurian Sea

Versilian Riviera

Marina di Pietrasanta

Camaiore

Tourist Office (☑ 0583 64 10 07; www.
castelnuovagarfagnana.org; Piazza delle
Erbe; ⊙ 9.30am-1pm & 3.30-7pm Mon-Sat,
10am-1pm & 3.30-6.30pm Sun, shorter
hours winter) Opposite the park visitors
centre.

ℹ Getting There & Away

CAR

Take the SS12 from Lucca (direction Abetone)
and turn off onto the SS445. There's a car park
at Piazza del Genio, off Via Roma on the opposite
side of the river to the walled *centro storico*.

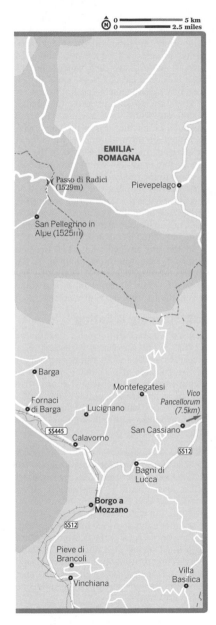

TRAIN
Regional train services:
Lucca (€5.30, one hour, nine daily)
Pisa (€6.60, 1½ hours, four daily)

Barga

POP 10,200

This chic village, 12km south of Castelnuovo di Garfagnana, is an irresistibly slow Tuscan hilltop town with a disproportionately large and dynamic English-speaking community. Churches, artisan workshops, attractive stone houses and palaces built by rich merchants between the 15th and 17th centuries lace the steep streets leading up to the Romanesque **Duomo di San Cristoforo**.

🛏 Sleeping & Eating

⭐ **Al Benefizio** AGRITURISMO €

(☑ 0583 72 22 01; www.albenefizio.it; apt per night €90-115; 🅿 @ 🤶 🐕) Squeeze your car along the narrow road to this olive farm, framed by acacia and chestnut woods 2km from Barga. It has two well-equipped apartments for two to four people in the old stables, both with spectacular views. Guests can swim, mountain bike and have use of a BBQ. But the real reason to visit is to get acquainted with owner Francesca, a walking guide and beekeeper.

With her you can visit the apiary, see how honey is extracted, and sign up for an olive oil workshop. Husband Francesco, equally fascinating, is a sound engineer (hence the welcome presence of a state-of-the-art home theatre). No credit cards.

Casa Cordati HOMESTAY €

(☑ 0583 72 34 50; www.casacordati.it; Via di Mezzo 17; s/d €30/48; ⏺ Mar-Oct; @ 🤶) This atmospheric townhouse is an ode to art, fittingly so given it languishes in the former home and studio of painter Bruno Cordati (1890–1979). The ground-floor gallery (free admission) shows off some of his works, while rooms above tout wooden floors, period decor and an artsy feel. Some bathrooms are shared.

⭐ **Locanda di Mezzo** TUSCAN €€

(☑ 0583 171 75 25; Piazza dell'Annunziata 7; meals €25; ⏺ 12.30-2.30pm Mon, 12.30-2.30pm & 7.45-10.30pm Tue-Sun) Local lads Giulio and Francesco provide the creative fun and energy behind Barga's most recent opening, tables enviably sprawled out in summer across photogenic Piazza dell'Annunziata. Traditional Tuscan dishes get a distinctly creative kick, while paying homage to the ravishing local farm products they're invariably made from: think *farro* ravioli in sage butter or *maltagliati* (pasta diamonds) with baby squid in chickpea cream.

ⓘ Information

Tourist office (☑ 0583 72 47 45; www. comune.barga.lu.it; Via di Mezzo 47; ☺9am-1pm Mon-Fri, 9am-1pm & 3-5.30pm Sat, shorter hours winter)

ⓘ Getting There & Away

CAR

Take the SS12 from Lucca (direction: Abetone), veer left onto the SS445 and then turn right onto the SP7 at Fornacci di Barga. Barga is 5km further on.

Bagni di Lucca

POP 6270

Small-town Bagni di Lucca is 28km south of Castelnuovo di Garfagnana on the banks of the Lima river. Famed in the early 19th century for its thermal waters enjoyed by the gentry of Lucca and an international set (Byron, Shelley, Heinrich Heine and Giacomo Puccini were among the celebrity guests to take the waters), the spa town today is a pale shadow of its former splendid neoclassical self. In past years it had its own beautiful neoclassical **casino** (1837) with music room where Strauss, Puccini and Liszt all performed, as well as a theatre and atypically ornate Anglican church, now the municipal library (look for the stucco lion and unicorn motif above each window on the vivid burnt-red facade). In the small British cemetery baroque tombs speak volumes.

There are two distinct areas: the smaller casino-clad **Ponte a Serraglio**, clustered around a bridge that crosses the Lima river; and the main town, 2km north, where most shops, restaurants and hotels are. In the former, a few doors down from the riverside casino, the **Sorgente La Cova** (Viale Casino Municipale 84) spouting out of an old stone roadside wall is a natural spring believed to be the cure of all ills. Its water, fabulously, is hot. Park up like a local and wash your hands in it, bathe tired feet in it, drink it, bottle it.

In the tiny riverside hamlet of Borgo a Mozzano, 2km southwest of town, is the medieval stone **Ponte del Diarolo** – the so-called 'Devils' Bridge' with ancient stone paving dating from the 14th century.

🛏 Sleeping & Eating

Bagni di Lucca Terme   HOTEL, SPA €

(☑ 0583 8 72 21; www.termebagnidilucca.it; Piazza San Martino 11; d €106) Pampering is part of the package at this hotel spa that is equipped with a pool, fitness centre, two natural steam grottoes and a wellness centre offering various steam and thermal mud baths, massages with salt, stone or olive oil and so on.

★**Buca di Baldabò**   TUSCAN €

(☑ 0583 8 90 62; www.labucadibaldabo.it; Via Prati 11, Vico Pancellorum; meals €20; ☺noon-3pm & 7-10pm Jun-Aug, lunch with reservation & 7-10pm Wed-Sun Sep-May) Perched on a hillock above chestnut and walnut forests, this is an iconic address every local foodie knows about. Hidden at the back of the village bar, it has no printed menu. Find out what's cooking that day and take your pick from homemade pastas and sauces cooked up daily by chef Giovanni. Game is particularly big and side dishes are creative.

To get to Vico Pancellorum from Bagni di Lucca, head 9km north along the scenic SS12 to Abetone and at the northern end of Ponte Coccia take the sharp turning on the left signposted 'Vico Pancellorum'; the restaurant is another 3km from here, at the foot of the hamlet, along a steep, narrow, curvaceous road. Advance reservations are essential.

GET ORGANISED: HIKING, BIKING & EATING

Tuscany Walking (www.tuscanywalking.com) Family-run, English-speaking set-up in Barga offering guided and self-guided hikes.

Eco Guide (www.eco-guide.it) Guided nature tours on foot and by bicycle, by this creative Lucca-based set-up, including magical night walks in the Garfagnana, kids' walks and a 'Spectacular Apuane Alps' day hike.

Sapori e Saperi Gastronomic Adventures (www.sapori-e-saperi. com) Embark on a culinary tour of the Garfagnana with passionate foodie Heather Jarman: learn how bread is traditionally baked, sausages made, *pecorino* cheese produced as it's been done for generations; visit olive farms, harvest chestnuts, hunt truffles, meet local cheesemakers and savour age-old recipes in local-endorsed restaurants.

THREE PERFECT ROAD TRIPS

Nerves and stomach depending, dozens of narrow roads spaghetti from Castelnuovo into the Garfagnana's rural depths.

Alpine Flora & Marble Mountain

Head west towards the Med. The first 17km along the SP13 is straightforward, but once you fork right 2km south of Arni (follow signs for Massa along the SP4), motoring becomes a relentless succession of hairpins, unlit tunnels and breathtaking vistas of Carrara's marble quarries as you cross the Apuane Alps over the **Passo del Vestito** (1151m). Stop in **Pian della Fioba** to discover alpine flora in the **Orto Botanico Pietro Pellegrini** (Botanical Garden; www.parcapuane.toscana.it/ob; Pian della Fioba; admission €3; ⊙9am-noon & 3-6pm Jun-Oct). From here the road drops down, through **Antona** and **Altagnana** clinging to the hillside, to **Massa** on the Versilian coast. The entire drive is 42km.

Subterranean Rivers & Lakes

The SS445 is a twisting route that leads you through lush green hills pocked with caves. The most accessible and spectacular is **Grotta del Vento** (☑ 0583 72 20 24; www.grotta delvento.com; Grotta del Vento 1, Vergemoli; adult/reduced 1hr guided visit €9/7, 2hr €14/11, 3hr €20/16; ⊙10am-noon & 2-6pm), 9km west of the SS445 along a horribly narrow road. Inside is a world of underground abysses, lakes and caverns. April to October, choose between a one-, two- or three-hour guided tour – if you're up to the 800/1200 steps involved in the two-/three-hour tour (!) it's worth it. November to March, the one-hour tour (300 steps) is the only choice.

Across a Mountain Pass

Spiralling north from Castelnuovo, a concertina of hairpin bends (the SS324) lifts you to **Castiglione di Garfagnana** and over the scenic **Passo di Radici** mountain pass, across the Apennines, into Emilia-Romagna. A minor parallel road to the south of the pass takes you to **San Pellegrino in Alpe**, a hilltop village (at 1525m) with a monastery and, in the old hospital, a **Museo Etnografico** (Ethnographic Museum; ☑ 0583 64 90 72; www.sanpellegrinoinalpe.it; Via del Voltone 14, San Pellegrino in Alpe; adult/reduced €2.50/1.50; ⊙10am-1pm & 2-6.30pm summer, closed Mon & shorter hours winter) that brings traditional mountain life, scarcely changed for centuries, to life.

Circolo dei Forestieri TUSCAN €
(☑ 0583 8 60 38; Piazza Jean Varraud 10; meals €20; ⊙noon-3pm & 7.30-10pm Tue-Sun) Quell hunger pangs at the former home of the Foreigners' Club, an elegant belle époque building on the river side of Viale Umberto I, southeast of the casino. Its grand dining room, chandeliers et al, provides a splendid setting in which to enjoy good-value Tuscan cuisine.

❶ Information

Tourist office (☑ 0583 80 57 45; www.comunebagnidilucca.it; Viale Umberto I 93; ⊙10am-1pm Mon & Wed-Sat)

❶ Getting There & Away

TRAIN
Regional train services:
Lucca (€3.40, 30 minutes, seven daily)
Pisa (€5.30, 1¼ hours, five daily)

Carrara

POP 64,234

Many first-time visitors assume the white mountain peaks forming Carrara's backdrop are capped with snow. In fact, the vista provides a breathtaking illusion – the white is 2000 hectares of marble gouged out of the foothills of the Apuane Alps in vast quarries that have been worked since Roman times.

The texture and purity of Carrara's white marble (derived from the Greek *marmaros,* meaning shining stone) is unrivalled and it remains the world's most sought-after. It was here that Michelangelo selected marble for masterpieces including *David* (actually sculpted from a dud veined block). Carrara marble was also used for London's iconic Marble Arch and by Rodin to sculpt *The Kiss*.

WORTH A TRIP

MARBLE MOUNTAIN

Zipping down a dank, wet, unlit tunnel in a dusty white minibus, grubby headlights blazing, driver incongruously dolled up in a shiny shocking-pink bomber jacket, it is all somewhat surreal. Five minutes into the pitch-black marble mountain, everyone is told to get out.

It is 16°C, foggy, damn dirty and slippery on foot and far from being a polished pearly white, it's grey – cold, wet, miserable grey. Rough cut blocks, several metres long and almost as wide, are strewn about the place like toy bricks and marble columns prop up the 15m-high ceiling, above which a second gallery, another 17m tall, stands. The place is bigger than several football pitches, yet amazingly there is still plenty of marble left for the five workers employed at **Cava di Fantiscritti** (p248), 5km north of Carrara, to extract – with the aid of water and mechanical diamond-cutting chains that slice through the rock like butter – 10,000 tonnes of white marble a month. The current market price, said to have risen by 30% in the last five years, is up to €3000 per tonne.

To learn how the Romans did it (with chisels and axes – oh my!), visit the surprisingly informative, open-air **Cava Museo** (www.cavamuseo.com; Cava di Fantiscritti; ◷11am-6pm) **FREE**, adjoining the souvenir shop across from the quarry entrance. Don't miss the B&W shots of marble blocks being precariously slid down the *lizza* (mountain pathway) to the bottom of the mountain where 18 pairs of oxen would pull the marble to Carrara port. In the 1850s tunnels were built for trains to do the job (hence the tunnel tour groups use to drive into the mountain) – which they did until the 1960s.

The quarries, 5km out of town, have long been the area's biggest employers, with a workforce of 5000. It's hard, dangerous work and on Carrara's central Piazza XXVII Aprile a monument remembers workers who lost their lives up on the hills. These tough men formed the backbone of a strong leftist and anarchist tradition in Carrara, something that won them no friends among the Fascists or, later, the occupying German forces.

Carrara mines export 1.4 million tonnes of marble a year, worth a handsome €330 million. In 2014 a Saudi Arabian construction group controlled by the Bin Laden family – already a chief client – acquired a majority 50% stake in Marmi Carrara, buying out the stakes held by four local families for €45 million. Environmentalists, meanwhile, fear the mines are being over-exploited and are campaigning for stricter regulations to to limit how much of their precious mountains can be carved out.

Bar the thrill of seeing its mosaic marble pavements, marble street benches, decorative marble putti and marble everything else, the old centre of Carrara doesn't offer much for the visitor.

◉ Sights & Activities

The tourist office has information on walking trails with magnificent quarry views and also on a three-hour 'Michelangelo in White' biking itinerary – a 24km route that sees cyclists climb 550m up from Carrara-Avenza train station to the quarries and beyond to Colonnata.

Museo del Marmo   MUSEUM
(Marble Museum; ☑0585 84 57 46; www.museo delmarmo.com; Viale XX Settembre; adult/ reduced €4.50/2.50; ◷9am-1pm & 3.30-6pm Mon-Sat May-Sep) Opposite the tourist office, Carrara's Marble Museum tells the full story of the marble quarries outside town, from the old chisel-and-hammer days to the 21st-century's high-powered industrial quarrying. A fascinating audiovisual history presentation documents the lives of quarry workers in the 20th century.

Cava di Fantiscritti   HISTORIC SITE
(Fantiscritti Quarry; Via Fantiscritti) Head up the mountain to this dusty, truck-busy *cava de marmo* (marble quarry), through a dramatic series of tunnels used by trains to transport marble until the 1960s when trucks took over. At the Fantiscritti Quarry entrance, pick a 40-minute guided tour by minibus/ on foot of the **Ravaccione 84 gallery** inside the quarry, run by **Marmotour** (www. marmotour.com; adult/reduced €10/5), or a Bond-style 4WD tour of the open-cast quarry run by various operators on site. Yes, the Bond movie *Quantum of Solace* was shot here. Tours are dramatic.

✗ Eating

The *only* place to lunch is in the hamlet of **Colonnata**, 2km from Fantiscritti, where one of Tuscany's greatest gastronomic treats, *lardo di colonnata* (thinner-than-wafer-thin slices of local pig fat) sits ageing in marble vats of herby olive oil. Once you're hooked, purchase a vacuum-packed slab (from €13.50 per kg) to take home from one of the many *larderie* (shops selling *lardo*) in the village.

Locanda Apuana   TUSCAN €
(☑ 0585 76 80 17; www.locandaapuana.com; Via Communale 1, Colonnata; meals €20; ☺ noon-2.30pm & 7.30-10pm Tue-Sat, noon-2.30pm Sun) The address, just off central Piazza Palestro, to feast on *crostini caldi con lardo* (warm toasts topped with lardo) et al.

Ristorante Venanzio   TUSCAN €€
(☑ 0585 75 80 62; www.ristorantevenanzio.com; Piazza Palestro 3, Colonnata; meals €30; ☺ noon-2.30pm & 7-11pm Mon-Wed, Fri & Sat, noon-2.30pm Sun) Even those who initially find the idea of noshing on a hunk of fat off-putting are bound to be won over when sampling it melted over piping-hot *focaccette* (small, flat buns made of wheat flour and cornmeal) at this family-run restaurant with classical decor on Colonnata's central, marble-paved square. Its €40 *menu degustazione* (tasting menu; minimum two people) is a treat.

ℹ Information

Tourist office (☑ 0585 84 41 36; www.turismomassacarrara.it; Viale XX Settembre; ☺ 8.30am-4.30pm summer, 9am-4pm Thu-Sun winter) Opposite the stadium; stop here to pick up a map of Carrara, its marble workshops and out-of-town quarries.

ℹ Getting There & Away

TRAIN

The nearest station is Carrara-Avenza, between Carrara and Marina di Carrara. Regional train services:
Pietrasanta (€2.50, 15 minutes, at least twice hourly)
Viareggio (€3.40, 25 minutes, twice hourly)

THE VERSILIAN COAST

The beaches from Viareggio northwards to Liguria are popular with local holiday-makers and some tourists, but have been blighted by beachfront strip development and get unpleasantly packed with Italy's beach-loving hoi polloi during summer. We suggest steering clear of this coastal strip and instead heading inland to explore the hinterland town of Pietrasanta, known for its vibrant arts culture and *centro storico*.

Versilia is a major gateway to the Apuane Alps, Garfagnana and Lunigiana, with roads from the coastal towns snaking their way deep into the heart of the mountains and connecting with small villages and walking tracks.

Pietrasanta

POP 24,200

Often overlooked by Tuscan travellers, this refined art town is a real unexpected surprise. Its bijou historic heart, originally walled, is car-free and loaded with tiny art galleries, workshops and fashion boutiques – perfect for a day's amble broken only by lunch.

Founded by Guiscardo da Pietrasanta, *podestà* (governing magistrate) of Lucca, in 1255, Pietrasanta was seen as a prize by Genoa, Lucca, Pisa and Florence, all of whom jostled for possession of its marble quarries and bronze foundries. As was so often the case, Florence won out and Leo X (Giovanni de' Medici) took control in 1513. Leo put the town's famous quarries at the disposal of Michelangelo, who came here in 1518 to source marble for the facade of San Lorenzo in Florence. The artistic inclination of Pietrasanta dates from this time, and today it is the home of many artists, including internationally lauded Colombian-born sculptor Fernando Botero, whose work can be seen here.

Pietrasanta is a great base for exploring the Apuane Alps and a lovely day trip from Pisa or Viareggio.

◉ Sights & Activities

From Pietrasanta train station on Piazza della Stazione head straight across Piazza Carducci, through the Old City gate and onto **Piazza del Duomo**, the main square that poses as an outdoor gallery for sculptures and other large works of art.

Duomo di San Martino   CATHEDRAL
(Piazza del Duomo; ☺ variable) It is impossible to miss Pietrasanta's attractive cathedral, dating from 1256, on the central square. Its distinctive 36m-tall, red-brick bell tower is

actually unfinished; the red brick was meant to have a marble cladding.

Chiesa di Sant'Agostino
CHURCH

(Piazza del Duomo; ⊘variable) The far end of Piazza del Duomo is dominated by the 13th-century stone hulk of this deconsecrated church. Once dedicated to St Augustine, the Romanesque space hosts seasonal art exhibitions today.

Museo dei Bozzetti
MUSEUM

(✉0584 79 55 00; www.museodeibozzetti.it; Via Sant'Agostino 1; ⊘9am-1pm & 2-7pm Tue-Fri, 2-7pm Sat, 4-7pm Sun) FREE Inside the convent adjoining Chiesa di Sant'Agostino dozens of moulds of famous sculptures cast or carved in Pietrasanta are showcased by this small museum.

Via della Rocca
VIEWPOINT

(Piazza del Duomo) Next to Chiesa di Sant'Agostino, a steep path known as Via della Rocca leads up to what remains of Pietrasanta's ancient fortifications. The crenallated city walls date to the early 1300s and what remains of **Palazzo Guinigi** was built as a residence for *signore* of Lucca, Paolo Guinigi, in 1408. Views of the city and deep blue Mediterranean beyond are predictably worth the short climb.

Battistero
RELIGIOUS SITE

(Baptistry; Via Garibaldi 12; ⊘variable) Around the corner from the cathedral on pedestrian Via Garibaldi is this old-world atmospheric baptistry. The pair of baptismal fonts – one originally in the cathedral in the 16th century and the other a hexagonal tub (1389) used two centuries before for full immersion baptisms – form a dramatic ensemble in the tiny candlelit space.

Via Garibaldi
STREET

This quaint pedestrian strip is peppered with chic fashion boutiques and stylish art galleries. Highlights guaranteed to tempt include fashion designer **Paolo Milani** (Via Garibaldi 11; ⊘variable), whose studio is a riot of bold vibrant prints and a wild mix of textures covering the whole sombre to sequin-sparkly spectrum; multibrand fashion queen and trendsetter **Zoe** (www.zoecompany.eu; Via Garibaldi 29-33 & 44-46; ⊘10am-1pm & 4-8pm); vintage furniture design boutique **Lei** (Via Garibaldi 22); and concept store **Dada** (www.dadaconcept.it; Via Garibaldi 39; ⊘10am-1pm & 3.30-7.30pm Tue-Sun).

Chiesa della Misericordia
CHURCH

(Via Mazzini 103; ⊘variable) Squirrelled away on Via Mazzini is this precious chapel. Tucked between shops, the superb Chiesa della Misericordia is frescoed with the Gate of Paradise and Gate of Hell by Fernando Botero (b 1932). Spot the self-portrait of the Colombian artist – who lives in Pietrasanta – in Hell.

🛏 Sleeping

★ Le Camere di Filippo
B&B

(✉0584 7 00 10; www.filippolondon.it; Via Stagio Stagi 22; d €120-150; 🅿❄@🛜) A fabulous address with two kitchens and four fantastic rooms, each with a different colour scheme and crisp design.

★ Albergo Pietrasanta
BOUTIQUE HOTEL €€€

(✉0584 79 37 26; www.albergopietrasanta.com; Via Garibaldi 35; d €310; 🅿❄@🛜) Should you find yourself totally smitten with Pietrasanta and unable to leave, this chic 17th-century *palazzo* – a perfect fusion of old and new – is among Tuscany's loveliest boutique town hotels. After a day spent sightseeing, its gorgeous courtyard, conservatory and beautifully appointed, classically elegant rooms are made for relaxing and pampering.

🍴 Eating & Drinking

The historic heart spoils for choice with its many artsy addresses spilling onto flowerpot-adorned summer terraces. Pedestrian Via Stagio Stagi, parallel to main street Via Mazzini, has several appealing restaurants; Piazza del Duomo with its many cafes is the alfresco favourite for a coffee or sundowner.

★ Filippo
TUSCAN €€

(✉0584 7 00 10; http://ristorantefilippo.com; Via Stagio Stagi 22; meals €40; ⊘12.30-2.30pm & 7.30pm-2am, closed Mon winter) 🌿 This exceptional foodie address never disappoints. From the homemade bread (all six or so varieties) and focaccia brought warm to your table throughout the course of your meal, to the contemporary fabric on the walls, giant wicker lampshades and modern open kitchen, this bistro is chic. The cuisine is seasonal and as creative as the interior design.

Pinocchio
SEAFOOD €€

(✉0584 7 05 10; Vicolo San Biagio 5; meals €40; ⊘12.30-2pm & 7.30-10pm Tue-Sun) This contemporary restaurant is a hip-crowd favourite. Fish and seafood in various creative guises – spicy octopus ragout, black-and-white seafood-spiked spaghetti, seed-crusted cod stockfish – are its raison d'être, served in a casually refined interior or beneath parasols on its Via Stagio Stagi pavement terrace; the entrance is in the alley around the corner.

Osteria Barsanti 54   TUSCAN €€
(☑0584 7 15 14; www.osteriabarsanti54.com; Via Barsanti 54; meals €35; ⊙noon-2.30pm & 7-10.30pm) Tucked away on a quiet lane near the city gate is this new-kid-on-the-block *osteria*, refined temple to good slow food and wine. 'Cook with love' is the strapline of culinary creatives Alessandro and Marco, and quality seasonal dishes packed with anchovies, sardines, purple potatoes, kale and the like seduce every time. Lunch on Thursday is posh *lampredotto* (tripe sandwich), served with a glass of red and bean salad.

★L'Enoteca Marcucci   WINE BAR
(☑0584 79 19 62; www.enotecamarcucci.it; Via Garibaldi 40; ⊙10am-1pm & 5pm-1am Tue-Sun) Taste fine Tuscan wine on bar stools at high wooden tables or beneath big parasols on the street outside. Whichever you pick, the distinctly funky, artsy spirit of Pietrasanta's best-loved *enoteca* enthrals.

ℹ Information

Tourist Office (☑0584 28 33 75; www.comune.pietrasanta.lu.it; Piazza Statuto; ⊙10am-12.15pm & 5-7.15pm Tue-Sun summer)

ℹ Getting There & Away

TRAIN

Regional train services:
Lucca (with change of train in Pisa or Viareggio; €5.90, one hour, every 30 minutes)
Pisa (€4.30, 30 minutes, every 30 minutes)
Viareggio (€2.50, 10 minutes, every 10 minutes)

Viareggio

POP 63,400

This hugely popular sun-and-sand resort is known as much for its flamboyant Mardi Gras Carnevale, second only to Venice for party spirit, as for its dishevelled line-up of old art-nouveau facades, once grand, on its seafront that recall the town's 1920s and '30s heyday.

◎ Sights

Viareggio's vast golden sandy **beachfront** is laden with cafes, climbing frames and other kids' amusements and, bar the short public stretch opposite fountain-pierced **Piazza Mazzini**, is divided into *stabilimenti* (individual lots where you can hire cabins, umbrellas, sun lounges etc). Only a handful of waterfront buildings retain the ornate stylishness of the 1920s and '30s, notably Puccini's favourite cafe, 1929 Gran Caffè Margherita (p227) and neighbouring wooden **Chalet Martini** (1899).

Literature lovers might like to pass by **Piazza Shelley**, the only tangible reference to the romantic poet who drowned in Viareggio; his body was washed up on the beach and his comrade-in-arts, Lord Byron, had him cremated on the spot.

La Citadella di Carnevale   MONUMENT
(☑0584 5 30 48; Via Santa Maria Goretti; ⊙10am-noon Mon-Fri summer, 10am-noon Mon, Wed & Fri winter) **FREE** A couple of kilometres from the seafront is 'Carnival City', aka 16 gargantuan hangars which serve as workshops and garage space for the fantastic floats, crafted with a passion by each highly skilled and prized *carrista* (float-builder) for Viareggio's annual carnival. Carnevale history and the art of making *teste in capo* (the giant heads worn in processions) and *mascheroni a piedi* (big walking masks) is explained in the on-site **Museo del Carnevale** (Carnival Museum). Ask about its hands-on papier-mâché workshops.

The largest floats featuring a papier-mâché merry-go-round of clowns, opera divas, skeletons, kings etc are a staggering 20m wide and 14m tall. They take five months to build and carry 200 people each during processions. Stroll around the complex and a *carrista* will inevitably invite you into their workshop.

★彡 Festivals & Events

Carnevale di Viareggio   CULTURAL
(http://viareggio.ilcarnevale.com)   Viareggio's annual moment of glory lasts four weeks in February to early March when the city goes wild during Carnevale – a festival of floats, many featuring giant satirical effigies of political and other topical figures, which also includes fireworks and rampant dusk-to-dawn spirit.

Tickets for the 3pm Sunday processions (adult/reduced €18/13) can be bought on the same day from ticket kiosks on the procession circuit or in advance via email.

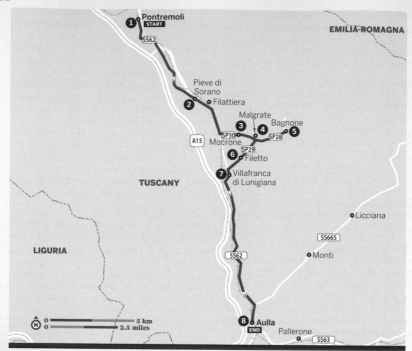

Driving Tour
The Via Francigena

START PONTREMOLI
END AULLA
LENGTH 32KM; TWO TO THREE HOURS

This medieval pilgrimage route connected Canterbury with Rome. It was so popular with pilgrims that in the 8th century the Lombard kings built churches, hospices and monasteries offering shelter for pilgrims along its Lunigiana length. This tour, perfectly viable by car or bicycle, explores some of them.

From **①Pontremoli** take the SS62 (direction La Spezia and Villafranca) and follow it 8km towards Filattiera. In a field on the left, admire the Romanesque **②Pieve di Sorano** (1148), with *piagnaro* (stone slab) roof and watchtower to signal its presence as a fortified stop on the pilgrimage route. Beyond the church is the old hilltop village. Continue for 2.5km along the SS62 then turn left onto the SP30 (direction Bagnone) and drive 2.3km. In **③Mocrone** enjoy great views of **④Malgrate** teetering on the hillside on your left; break for lunch at old-world village inn Locanda Gavarini.

About 4km after Mocrone, the road brings you into **⑤Bagnone**, an important trading stop on the Via Francigena and distinctive for its castle, church and eateries. Stretch your legs with a scenic walk above the fiercely gushing river and its dramatic gorges; pick up the easy 15- or 30-minute trail from Piazza Roma and end on main street Via della Repubblica. The final leg across the medieval, stone-paved Ponte Vecchio (Old Bridge) is the stuff of poetry.

From Bagnone backtrack towards Mocrone and onwards towards Villafranca, veering slightly left onto the SP29 to reach the walled medieval hamlet of **⑥Filetto**. Park outside the monumental gate and wander through its tiny piazzas and narrow lanes.

Arriving in **⑦Villafranca di Lunigiana** 1.5km south, you're on another key stop on the pilgrim route. Set on the Magra river, it is an unassuming place with a small ethnographical museum in an old 15th-century flour mill.

End the tour 12km south in **⑧Aulla**, known for its abbey founded in AD 884 and housing the remains of St Caprasio, the monk who inspired monastic life in Provence from the 5th century.

🍴 Eating & Drinking

⭐ La Barchina
FISH & CHIPS €

(📞347 7212848; Lungomolo Corraldo del Greco; ⊙noon-3pm Tue-Fri, noon-11pm Sat & Sun) Join locals standing in line at this small white boat, moored at the harbour, which cooks up the morning's catch for lunch. The hot item to order is *fritto misto* (€8), a mix of squid, prawns and octopus battered, deep-fried and served with a huge friendly smile in plastic punnets. Friday cooks up *baccalà* (cod; €8) and veggie lovers are catered for with punnets of fried mushrooms.

To find the *barchina* (boat), walk to the harbour end of seafront promenade Viale Regina Margherita and duck under the white iron footbridge crossing the canal.

Lettera 22
CAFE

(Via Giuseppe Mazzini 84; 📶) Mid-afternoon, lounge with hip locals at Lettera 22, a refreshingly stylish and up to the minute literary cafe between the beach and the train station with free wi-fi, armchairs, books to browse, kids' corner, cakes and wonderful pots of herbal and flavoured teas.

ℹ️ Information

Tourist Office (📞0584 96 22 33; www.apt versilia.it; Viale Regina Margherita 20; ⊙9am-1pm & 3-6pm Mon-Sat) Across from the clock on the waterfront.

ℹ️ Getting There & Away

TRAIN

To hit the seafront from the **train station** (Piazza Dante Alighieri), exit and walk straight ahead along Via Guiseppe Mazzini for 10 minutes to Piazza Giuseppe Mazzini and the sandy beach-fringed promenade beyond. Regional train services:

Florence (€9.20, 1½ hours, at least hourly)

Livorno (€5.30, 45 minutes, 16 daily)

Lucca (€3.40, 17 minutes, every 20 minutes)

Pietrasanta (€2.50, 10 minutes, every 10 minutes)

Pisa (€3.40, 18 minutes, every 20 minutes)

Pontremoli (€7.20, 1¼ hours, hourly)

THE LUNIGIANA

This landlocked enclave of territory is bordered to the north and east by the Apennines, to the west by Liguria and to the south by the Apuane Alps and the Garfagnana.

The few tourists who make their way here tend to be lunching in Pontremoli, a real off-the-beaten-track gastronomic gem, or following in the footsteps of medieval pilgrims along the Via Francigena.

Autumnal visits reward with fresh, intensely scented *porcini* mushrooms that sprout under chestnut trees in fecund woods and hills. Wild herbs cover fields, and 5000 scattered hives produce the region's famous chestnut and acacia honey. These fruits of the forest and other regional delicacies, including Zeri lamb, freshly baked *focaccette*, crisp and sweet *rotella* apples, boiled pork shoulder, *caciotta* (a delicate cow's-milk cheese), *bigliolo* beans, local olive oil and Colli di Luni wines, are reason alone to visit.

Pontremoli

POP 7520

It may be small, but this out-of-the-way town presided over by the impressive bulk of Castello del Piagnaro has a decidedly grand air – a legacy of its strategic location on the pilgrimage and trading route of Via Francigena. Its merchants made fortunes in medieval times, and adorned the *centro storico* with palaces, piazzas and graceful stone bridges.

The *centro storico* is a long sliver stretching north–south between the Magra and Verde rivers, which have historically served as defensive barriers. Meandering its streets takes you beneath colonnaded arches, through former strongholds of opposing Guelph and Ghibelline factions, and past a 17th-century cathedral and an 18th-century theatre.

◉ Sights

Castello del Piagnaro
CASTLE

(www.statuestele.org; adult/reduced €4/2; ⊙9am-12.30pm & 3-6pm Tue-Sun summer, to 5.30pm winter) From central Piazza della Repubblica and adjacent Piazza del Duomo, walk along Via Garibaldi then bear left along Vietata l'Affissione or Sdrucciolo del Castello, two pretty alleys and staircases that stagger uphill to this ramshackle castle. Former military barracks, it takes its name from the *piagnaro* (stone slabs) that were once widely used to roof Lunigianese buildings.

Views across town from the castle are impressive and inside is a small museum showcasing primitive stelae statues found nearby. No one knows exactly what these stelae, which have been found throughout the Lunigiana, were for – most depict male and female idols and date from around 3000 BC.

🛏 Sleeping & Eating

In summer, come 5pm, what feels like the entire Pontremoli population congregates on central **Piazza della Repubblica** to mingle on the terrace of **Caffè degli Svizzeri** (📞0187 83 01 60; Piazza della Repubblica 22; ☉7am-8pm Tue-Sun summer, shorter hours winter), around since 1842, to eat gelato and lap up the general old-world charm that this tiny, overtly rural town exudes. Do the same.

★ Locanda Gavarini   HOTEL €
(📞0187 49 55 04; www.locandagavarini.it; Via Benedicenti 50, Mocrone; s/d €60/80; P ✿) This country restaurant and inn, in the village of Mocrone at the end of the narrowest street you're ever likely to drive along, is a rural idyll where the only noise is twittering birds and the sunrise cry of the village cockerel. The restaurant (meals €20) is a culinary homage to Lunigianese tradition and is the best local dine for miles around.

Trattoria Da Bussè   TRATTORIA €
(📞0187 83 13 71; Piazza del Duomo 31; meals €25; ☉8-10pm Mon-Thu, 12.30-2.30pm & 8-10pm Sat & Sun) This Slow Food favourite footsteps from the cathedral has been run by the same family since the 1930s. It has all its original decor and could not be more old-world in vibe. Its regional menu includes *torta d'erbe della Lunigiana* (herb pie cooked over coals in a cast-iron pan lined with chestnut leaves to keep the mixture from sticking). Delicious.

Trattoria Pelliccia   TRATTORIA €€
(📞0187 83 05 77; Via Garibaldi 137; meals €30; ☉noon-2pm & 7.30-10pm) Tucked at the end of the *centro storico* is this trattoria, perfect for eating local. Start with *testaroli della lunigiana al pesto* (a type of savoury crepe cut into diamonds, cooked like pasta and served with pesto), followed by oven-baked *agnello di Zeri* (€13; lamb). End with an unjustly good sorbet (lemon and sage, pistachio and pepper, strawberry and port ...).

ℹ Information

Tourist Office (📞0187 83 20 00; Piazza della Repubblica 33; ☉10am-noon & 3.30-6pm Sat & Sun)

ℹ Getting There & Away

TRAIN
Regional train services:
La Spezia (€5.30, 50 minutes, frequent)
Pisa (€8.70, 90 minutes, hourly)

Eastern Tuscany

Best Places to Eat

➡ Antica Osteria Agania (p261)

➡ Ristorante Da Ventura (p266)

➡ Toscana Twist (p270)

➡ Ristorante Da Muzzicone (p273)

➡ La Bucaccia (p274)

Off the Beaten Track

➡ Osteria dell'Acquolina (p263)

➡ Piero della Francesco's *Madonna del Parto* (p266)

➡ Museo Michelangeliolesco (p267)

➡ Borgo Corsignano (p267)

➡ Santuario della Verna (p269)

Why Go?

The eastern edge of Tuscany is beloved by film directors who have immortalised its landscape and medieval hilltop towns in several critically acclaimed and visually splendid films. Yet the region remains refreshingly bereft of tourist crowds and offers uncrowded trails for those savvy enough to explore here. Attractions are many and varied: spectacular mountain scenery and walks in the Casentino; magnificent art and architecture in the medieval cities of Arezzo, Sansepolcro and Cortona; one of Italy's most significant Catholic pilgrimage sites; and Tuscany's best *bistecca alla fiorentina* (chargrilled T-bone steak) in the Val di Chiana. Your travels may be solitary, and for the most part, you'll need your own wheels to get around – but they'll always be rewarding.

Road Distances (km)

	Assisi	Arezzo	Cortona	Sansepolcro
Arezzo	94			
Cortona	65	29		
Sansepolcro	76	38	52	
Poppi	132	36	62	71

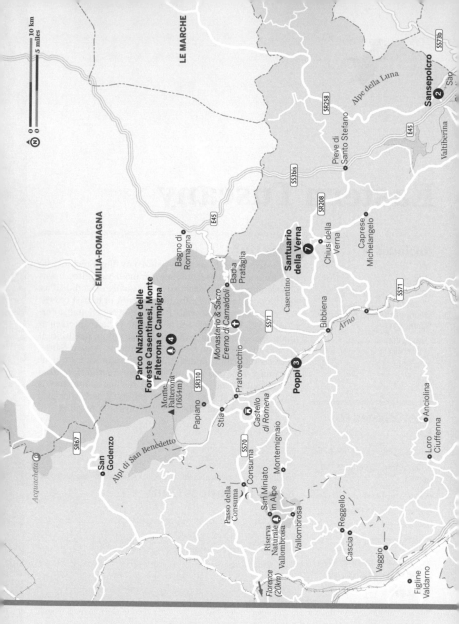

Eastern Tuscany Highlights

1 Marvelling at frescoes in **Cappella Bacci** (p258) and one of Tuscany's most beautiful squares, **Piazza Grande** (p258), in Arezzo.

2 Admiring the work of Renaissance painter Piero della Francesca at the **Museo Civico** (p263) in traditional lace-making centre Sansepolcro.

3 Exploring a well-preserved medieval castle in the fortified hamlet of **Poppi** (p267).

4 Communing with nature on a pilgrimage to secluded medieval monasteries in **Parco Nazionale delle Foreste Casentinesi, Monte Falterona e Campigna** (p269).

EMILIA-ROMAGNA

LE MARCHE

Parco Nazionale delle Foreste Casentinesi, Monte Falterona e Campigna

Monte Falterona (1654m)

Bagno di Romagna

Badia Prataglia

Monastero & Sacro Eremo di Camaldoli

Casentino

Santuario della Verna 7

Chiusi della Verna

Caprese Michelangelo

Sansepolcro 2

Alpe della Luna

Pieve di Santo Stefano

Valtiberina

San Godenzo

Alpi di San Benedetto

Acquacheta

Papiano

Stia

Castello di Romena

Pratovecchio

Bibbiena

Arno

Poppi 3

Consuma

Passo della Consuma

Montemignaio

San Miniato in Alpe

Riserva Naturale Vallombrosa

Vallombrosa

Florence (20km)

Reggello

Cascia

Vaggio

Loro Ciuffenna

Anciolina

Figline Valdarno

SR67

SR310

SS70

SS71

SR258

SS3bis

SR208

SR571

E45

0 10 km
0 5 miles

⑤ Admiring churches and sensational religious art at the **Museo Diocesano** (p271) in spectacular hilltop town Cortona.

⑥ Feasting on the finest *bistecca alla fiorentina* (T-bone steak) of your life in **Castiglion Fiorentino** (p273) in the Val di Chiana, home to Tuscany's famed Chianina cow.

⑦ Trailing pilgrim-revered St Francis from the Umbrian hilltop town of **Assisi** (p274) to the exquisitely remote **Santuario della Verna** (p269).

AREZZO

POP 99,200

Arezzo may not be a Tuscan centrefold, but those parts of its historic centre that survived merciless WWII bombings are as compelling as any destination in the region – the city's central square is as beautiful as it appears in Roberto Benigni's classic film *La vita è bella* (Life is Beautiful).

Once an important Etruscan trading post, Arezzo was later absorbed into the Roman Empire. A free republic as early as the 10th century, it supported the Ghibelline cause in the violent battles between pope and emperor and was eventually subjugated by Florence in 1384.

Today, the city is known for its churches, museums and fabulously sloping Piazza Grande, across which a huge antiques fair spills during the first weekend of each month. Come dusk, Arentini (locals of Arezzo) spill along the length of shop-clad Corso Italia for the ritual late-afternoon *passeggiata*.

◉ Sights & Activities

★Cappella Bacci   CHURCH

(📲0575 35 27 27; www.pierodellafrancesca.it; Piazza San Francesco; adult/reduced €8/5; ⊙9am-6.30pm Mon-Fri, to 5.30pm Sat, 1-5.30pm Sun) This chapel, in the apse of 14th-century Basilica di San Francesco, safeguards one of Italian art's greatest works: Piero della Francesca's fresco cycle of the *Legend of the True Cross*. Painted between 1452 and 1466, it relates the story of the cross on which Christ was crucified. Only 25 people are allowed in every half-hour, making advance booking (by telephone or email) essential in high season. The ticket office is down the stairs by the basilica's entrance.

This medieval legend is as entertaining as it is inconceivable. The illustrations follow the story of the tree that Seth plants on the grave of his father, Adam, and from which the True Cross is made. Another scene shows the long-lost cross being rediscovered by Helena, mother of the emperor Constantine; behind her, the city of Jerusalem is represented by a medieval view of Arezzo.

❶ CENT SAVER

A combined ticket (adult/reduced €12/7) covers admission to Cappella Bacci, Museo Archeologico Nazionale and Museo di Casa Vasari.

Other scenes show the victory of Heraclius over the Persian king Khosrau, who had been accused of stealing the cross; Constantine sleeping in a tent on the eve of his battle with Maxentius (note Piero's masterful depiction of the nocturnal light); and Constantine carrying the cross into battle.

Two of the best-loved scenes depict the meeting of the Queen of Sheba and King Solomon. In the first half she is kneeling on a bridge over the Siloam River and meeting with the king; she and her attendants are depicted wearing rich Renaissance-style gowns. In the second half, King Solomon's palace seems to be modelled on the designs of notable architect Leon Battista Alberti.

★Chiesa di
Santa Maria della Pieve   CHURCH

(Corso Italia 7; ⊙8am-12.30pm & 3-6.30pm) FREE This 12th-century church – Arezzo's oldest – has an exotic Romanesque arcaded facade adorned with carved columns, each uniquely decorated. Above the central doorway are 13th-century carved reliefs called *Cyclo dei Mesi* representing each month of the year. The plain interior's highlight – removed for restoration work at the time of writing – is Pietro Lorenzetti's polyptych *Madonna and Saints* (1320–24), beneath the semidome of the apse. Below the altar is a 14th-century silver bust reliquary of the city's patron saint, San Donato. Other treasures include a 13th-century crucifix by Margarito di Arezzo (left of the altar by the door to the sacristy) and a fresco on a column (across from the sacristy door) of Sts Francesco and Domenico by Andrea di Nerio (1331–69).

Piazza Grande   PIAZZA

This lopsided and steeply sloping piazza is overlooked at its upper end by the porticoes of the Palazzo delle Logge Vasariane (Piazza Grande), completed in 1573. The church-like Palazzo della Fraternità dei Laici (Piazza Grande) in the northwest corner was started in 1375 in the Gothic style and finished after the onset of the Renaissance.

★Duomo di Arezzo   CATHEDRAL

(Cattedrale di SS Donato e Pietro; Piazza del Duomo; ⊙7am-12.30pm & 3-6.30pm) FREE Construction started in the 13th century but Arezzo's cathedral wasn't completed until the 15th century. In the northeast corner, left of the intricately carved main altar, is an exquisite fresco of *Mary Magdalene* (c 1459) by Piero della Francesca. Also notable are five glazed

Arezzo

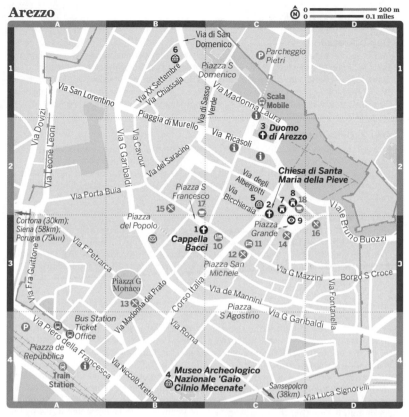

Arezzo

terracottas by Andrea della Robbia and his studio. Behind the cathedral is the pentagonal **Fortezza Medicea** (1502) atop the crest of one of Arezzo's two hills – the *duomo* was built on the crest of the other.

★**Museo Archeologico Nazionale 'Gaio Cilnio Mecenate'**   MUSEUM
(www.museistatistaliarezzo.it; Via Margaritone 10; adult/reduced €6/3; ☉ 8.30am-7.30pm, to 1.30pm Nov) Overlooking the remains of a Roman amphitheatre that once seated up to 10,000

THREE PERFECT DAYS

Day 1: Arezzo

Two major films are set in Arezzo. Explore the historic streets and piazzas where Roberto Benigni filmed La vita è bella (Life is Beautiful). Pop into the **Duomo** and **Chiesa di Santa Maria della Pieve**; see where Arezzo-born painter, architect and art historian Vasari lived and worked; and pay homage to Piero della Francesca's genius in Basilica di San Francesco's **Capella Bacci**, where Anthony Minghella shot the most memorable scene of The English Patient.

Day 2: Della Robbia Trail

This famous family of sculptors took ceramics way beyond teacups in the 15th century, creating magnificent devotional sculptures for churches throughout Tuscany. Visit the medieval monasteries at **Camaldoli** and La Verna in the Parco Nazionale delle Foreste Casentinesi, Monte Falterona e Campigna to admire masterpieces in glazed terracotta by the most famous member of the family, Andrea (1435–1525).

Day 3: Val di Chiana

Home to apple orchards, olive groves and lush pastures where creamy-white Chianina cattle graze, the huge Val di Chiana is worth dipping into en route between Arezzo and Cortona or to central Tuscany. Meander off the beaten track to hilltop towns **Castiglion Fiorentino** (exceptional and very meaty lunch stop), **Foiano della Chiana** and **Lucignano**.

---

spectators, this museum in a 14th-century convent building exhibits Etruscan and Roman artefacts. The highlight is the *Cratere di Euphronios,* a 6th-century-BC Etruscan vase decorated with vivid scenes showing Hercules in battle. Also of note is an exquisite tiny portrait of a bearded man from the second half of the 3rd century AD, executed in chrysography whereby a fine sheet of gold is engraved then encased between two glass panes.

Casa Museo di Ivan Bruschi   MUSEUM
(www.fondazionebruschi.it; Corso Italia 14; adult/reduced €5/3; ☺10am-7pm Tue-Sun summer, 10am-1pm & 2-6pm Tue-Sun winter) Ivan Bruschi, a wealthy antiques dealer, restored 13th-century **Palazzo del Capitano del Popolo** in the 1960s. After his death, the Palazzo became a house-museum showcasing Bruschi's eclectic collection of furniture, art, coins, jewellery, costumes and ceramics dating from the prehistoric, Etruscan, Greek, Roman, medieval and Renaissance periods. Admission costs €1 if you have a ticket for the Cappella Bacci.

Museo di Casa Vasari   MUSEUM
(Vasari House Museum; www.museistataliarezzo.it; Via XX Settembre 55; adult/reduced €4/2; ☺9am-7pm Mon & Wed-Sat, to 1pm Sun) Built and sumptuously decorated by Arezzo-born painter, architect and art historian Giorgio Vasari (1511–74), this museum is where Vasari lived and worked, and where the original manuscript of his *Lives of the Most Excellent Painters, Sculptors and Architects* (1550) – still in print under the title *The Lives of the Artists* – is kept. End on the bijou, Renaissance-style roof garden with flower beds, box hedges and fountain in its centre. To get in the museum, ring the bell.

The most important room in the Mannerist residence is the **Sala della Virtu** (Room of Virtue), which he decorated in 1548 while writing *Lives*. It features episodes in the lives of the most famous painters of antiquity. Vasari's contemporaries were celebrated in the **Camera della Fama con le Quattro Arti** (Room of Fame and the Four Arts), where the seven portraits include Michelangelo, Andrea del Sarto and – in a display of hubris – Vasari himself.

✪ Festivals & Events

Fiera Antiquaria di Arezzo   ANTIQUES
(Arezzo Antique Fair) Tuscany's most famous antiques fair is held in Piazza Grande on the first Sunday and preceding Saturday of every month.

Giostra del Saracino   CULTURAL
(Joust of the Saracino; www.giostradelsaracino arezzo.it; Piazza Grande) This medieval jousting competition, held on Piazza Grande on the third Saturday of June and first Sunday of September, sees the city's four *quartieri* (quarters) put forward a team of 'knights'.

🛏 Sleeping

Palazzo dei Bostoli
B&B €

(☑ 334 1490558; www.palazzobostoli.it; Via G Mazzini 1; s/d €55/75; ❉ ◈) This old-fashioned place offers five simple but comfortable rooms on the 2nd floor of a 13th-century *palazzo* (mansion) near Piazza Grande. Breakfast – a coffee and *cornetto* (croissant) – is served at a bar on nearby Corso Italia.

Casa Volpi
HOTEL €

(☑ 0575 35 43 64; www.casavolpi.it; Via Simone Martini 29; s/d €65/95; P @ ◈) This 18th-century manor is a delicious 1.5km bicycle ride away from the cobbled streets of downtown Arezzo (the hotel lends guests wheels). Its 15 rooms are decorated in a classical style, with plenty of original features – beamed ceilings, red-brick flooring, parquet – to charm. Family-run, the hotel restaurant spills in to the pretty garden in summer. Breakfast €9.

Graziella Paliu Hotel
BOUTIQUE HOTEL €€

(☑ 0575 40 19 62; www.hotelpatio.it; Via Cavour 23; s/d €130/180, ste €200-320; ❉ @ ◈) A delightful mix of ancient (15th-century cellars) and contemporary design, this 10-room hotel has themed rooms named after Bruce Chatwin's travel books – with decor to match. Pink-kissed Arkady is the 'Australia room', Fillide exudes a distinctly Moroccan air, and Cobra Verde is a green Amazon-inspired loft. Every room has a Macbook for guests to go online and service is first-class.

🍴 Eating & Drinking

★ Antica Osteria Agania
TUSCAN €

(☑ 0575 29 53 81; www.agania.com; Via G Mazzini 10; meals €25; ◷ noon-3pm & 6-10.30pm Tue-Sun) Agania has been around for years and her fare is die-hard traditional – the tripe and *grifi con polenta* (lambs' cheeks with polenta) are sensational. But it is timeless, welcoming addresses such as this, with potted fresh herbs on the doorstep, that remain the cornerstone of Tuscan dining. Begin with *antipasto misto* (mixed appetisers) followed by your choice combo of six pastas and eight sauces. Agania's *pici* (fat spaghetti) with wild boar sauce is legendary. Arrive by 1pm to beat the crowd of regulars or join the crowd waiting outside.

La Bottega di Gnicche
SANDWICHES €

(www.bottegadignicche.com; Piazza Grande 4; panini €3.50-5; ◷ 11am-8pm Thu-Tue) Choose from a delectable array of artisan meats and cheeses to stuff in a *panini* (sandwich) at this old-fashioned *alimentari* (grocery store) on Arezzo's main piazza. Eat next to bright yellow bags of artisan Martelli pasta stacked up on the front porch, or perch on a stool inside.

La Torre di Gnicche
TUSCAN €

(www.latorredignicche.it; Piaggia San Martino 8; soup €7, meat & cheese platters €10; ◷ noon-3pm & 6pm-midnight Thu-Tue) This cosy bottle-lined room just off Piazza Grande offers a huge choice of Tuscan wine (by the glass or bottle), platters of cheese and meat, and rustic tummy-fillers including *pappa al pomodoro* (a thick bread and tomato soup served in summer) and *ribollita* (a 'reboiled' bean, vegetable, cabbage and bread soup served in winter).

Il Cantuccio
TUSCAN €€

(☑ 0575 2 68 30; www.il-cantuccio.it; Via Madonna del Prato 76; meals €25; ◷ noon-3pm & 7-11.30pm Thu-Tue) Tucked away from Arezzo's churches and museums, this much-loved trattoria is particularly cosy in winter when its vaulted, red-brick cellar setting comes into its own. Cuisine is Tuscan, seasonal, and cooked up with much love and pride. Begin with fresh artichoke salad in spring, followed by your tastebuds' pick of a dozen-odd 'mix-and-match' pasta types and sauces, tomato simple to truffle extravagant.

La Cantina del Doc
TUSCAN €€

(☑ 0575 2 20 90; Via Cavour 61; meals €25; ◷ 12.30-3pm Mon, Wed & Thu, 12.30-3pm & 7-10pm Fri-Sun) The gargantuan cooking pots and baking trays brazenly displayed in the window are a bold statement. And most wonderfully of all, the traditional Tuscan cuisine dished up at this modern two-room trattoria do not

---

TERRE DI AREZZO
....

The Arezzo region boasts one DOCG and five DOC wines: Chianti Colli Arentini DOCG, Vinsanto del Chianti Colli Arentini DOC, Vinsanto del Chianti Colli Arentini Occhio di Pernice DOC, Valdichiana DOC, Cortona DOC and Pietraviva DOC. To investigate these fully, follow the **Strada del Vino Terre di Arezzo** (www.stradadelvino.arezzo.it) or take full advantage of their regular appearances on the wine menus of restaurants across the region. For information and a map, pop into the **Strada del Vino Terre di Arezzo Information Point** (☑ 0575 29 40 66; Via Ricasoli 38-40; ◷ 9.30am-3pm Mon-Fri) in Arezzo.

disappoint. Pasta is strictly *fatta in casa* (homemade) – the *maltagliatti* (a rough-cut type of pasta made from pasta scraps) with kale and crispy bacon is delicious.

Caffè Vasari
CAFE

(✆0575 04 36 97; www.caffevasari.it; Piazza Grande 15; ⊙6.30am-9pm summer, 8.30am-6pm winter) Bathed in Tuscan sun rays from dawn to dusk, this traditional cafe really is the perfect spot for lapping up the ancient elegance and beauty of Piazza Grande over a coffee or *aperitivo*. Find it enviously squirrelled away beneath the cinematic porticoes of Palazzo delle Loggia Vasariane.

Caffè dei Costanti
CAFE

(www.caffedeicostanti.it; Piazza San Francesco 19-20; ⊙8.30am-9.30pm Wed-Sun, to 2am summer) Arezzo's oldest and most atmospheric cafe is located directly opposite the Basilica di San Francesco, so it's a perfect coffee stop before or after a visit to the Cappella Bacci. The coffee is excellent, as are the home-baked pastries. The outdoor tables are popular with the *aperitivo* set.

❶ Information

Tourist Office (✆0575 40 19 45; www.benvenutiadarezzo.it; Palazzo Comunale, Via Ricasoli; ⊙10am-1pm & 2-7pm Mon-Fri, 10am-1pm Sat & Sun Jun-Sep, to 4pm Oct-May) Find a branch (Piazza del Repubblica 22-23; ⊙10.30am-12.30pm & 2-4pm) of the tourist office to the right as you exit the train station.

OFF THE BEATEN TRACK

VILLA FONTELUNGA

Gorgeous is the only word to use when describing **Villa Fontelunga** (✆0575 66 04 10; www.fontelunga.com; Via Cunicchio 5, Foiano della Chiana; d €295-350, ste €395; ⊙Mar-Oct; P❄@ ❂❧), a 19th-century villa with fiery burnt-orange facade in Foiano della Chiana, 30 minutes southwest of Arezzo. Restored, decorated and run by three charming friends (one an architect, one a landscape designer and one a former international banker), its nine rooms are the perfect balance of traditional Tuscan elegance and jet-set pizazz.

There's a two-night minimum stay, service is first class, and the hotel has a couple of additional naturally stylish self-catering villas to rent.

Una Vetrina per Arezzo e Le Sue Vallate (✆0575 182 27 70; ⊙9am-7pm) Private tourist office on the *scala mobile* leading up to Piazza del Duomo; toilet facilities (€0.50).

❶ Getting There & Away

BUS

Buses operated by Siena Mobilità (www.siena mobilita.it) serve Siena (€6.80, 1½ hours, seven daily). **Etruria Mobilità** (www.etruriamobilita.it) buses serve Sansepolcro (€4.10, one hour, hourly) and Cortona (€3.40, one hour, frequent). Buy tickets from the **ticket office** (Piazzale della Repubblica; ⊙6.10am-8pm Mon-Sat, 8am-12.30pm & 2.30-7pm Sun) to the left as you exit the train station; buses leave from the bus bay opposite.

CAR & MOTORCYCLE

To drive here from Florence, take the A1; the SS73 heads west to Siena. Parking at the train station costs €2 per hour.

TRAIN

Arezzo is on the Florence–Rome train line – there are frequent services to Florence (*Regionale* €8, one to 1½ hours) and Rome (Intercity €26.50, 2¼ hours; *Regionale* €14.15, 2¾ hours). There are twice-hourly regional trains to Cortona (€3.40, 20 minutes).

ANGHIARI

This unspoilt medieval hill town looms over the plain where the army of the Italian League, spearheaded by the Republic of Florence, famously defeated the numerically superior forces of Milan in 1440. Enclosed by massive walls, it is an easy detour for those travelling between Arezzo and Sansepolcro. The walls enclose steep cobbled lanes lined by houses, shops, churches and the **Museo Statale di Palazzo Taglieschi** (Piazza Mameli 16; adult/child €2/1; ⊙10am-7pm Tue-Sun summer, 9am-6pm Tue-Sun winter), which has a modest collection of 15th- and 16th-century sculptures and paintings. The **tourist office** (✆0575 74 92 79; www.anghiari.it; Corso Giacomo Matteotti 103; ⊙9.30am-12.30pm & 4-6.30pm), on the almost vertical Corso Giacomo Matteotti just outside the walls, has accommodation lists. Find convenient parking on Piazza Baldaccio (aka Piazza del Mercato), just opposite.

SANSEPOLCRO

POP 16,100

This 'hidden gem' is a town that truly deserves the description. Dating from the year 1000, Sansepolcro (called 'Borgo' by locals) reached its current size in the 15th century and was walled in the 16th. Its historic centre is littered with *palazzi* and churches hiding Renaissance works of art or bejewelled with exquisite terracotta Andrea della Robbia medallions. Spend a day wandering from dimly lit church to church, following in the footsteps of Sancepolcro's greatest son, Renaissance artist Piero della Francesca.

⊙ Sights

★ Museo Civico   MUSEUM
(www.museocivicosansepolcro.it; Via Niccolò Aggiunti 65; adult/reduced €8/5; ⊘10am-1.30pm & 2.30-7pm summer, 10am-1pm & 2.30-6pm winter) The town's flagship museum is home to a small but top-notch collection of artworks, including three Piero della Francesca masterpieces: *Resurrection* (1458–74), the *Madonna della Misericordia* polyptych (1445–56) and *Saint Julian* (1455–58). Admire also works by the studio of Andrea della Robbia: a polychrome terracotta called *The Nativity and Adoration of the Shepherds* (1485) and a beautiful tondo (circular sculpture) known as the *Virgin and Child with Manetti Coat of Arms* (1503).

Cattedrale di
San Giovanni Evangelista   CATHEDRAL
(Duomo di Sansepolcro; Via Giacomo Matteotti 4; ⊘10am-noon & 4-7pm) Sansepolcro's 14th-century *duomo* contains an *Ascension* by Perugino, a *Resurrection* by Raffaellino del Colle and a polyptych by Niccolò di Segna that is thought to have influenced Piero's *Resurrection*. Left of the main altar is the striking *Il Volto Santo* (Sacred Face), a wooden crucifix with a wide-eyed Christ in a blue gown that dates to the 9th century, and – nearby – a beautiful ceramic tabernacle (unfortunately badly chipped) by Andrea della Robbia. Leaving the cathedral, turn right onto Piazza Garibaldi to admire the 16 medallions by Andrea della Robbia on the facade of **Palazzo Preterio**.

Chiesa di San Lorenzo   CHURCH
(Via di Santa Croce 2; ⊘9am-6pm Mon-Fri, to 5pm Sat & Sun) Pop a €1 coin in the slot to illuminate Rosso Fiorentino's masterpiece *Deposition of Christ* (1528), behind the altar in 16th-century Chiesa di San Lorenzo. The church was built in 1556 for Benedictine nuns whose previous seat had been razed when Sansepolcro's new city walls were built in 1554. Find it at the southern end of foodie street Via Lucca Pacioli.

LUNCH EN ROUTE FROM FLORENCE

Heading east from Florence to Arezzo, vivid pink villa, **Osteria dell'Acquolina** (☑055 97 74 97; www.acquolina.it; Via Setteponti Levante 26, Terranuova Bracciolini; meals €30; ⊘noon-4pm & 7-11pm Tue-Sun), in an olive grove is the perfect lunch stop, especially in summer when the dining action spills out onto the terracotta-brick terrace with 360-degree views of olive trees, vines and hills beyond. Cuisine is Tuscan and there's no written menu – the chef cooks different dishes every day.

The mixed platter of *antipasti* (delicious bread and tomato 'soup') is a mainstay, as are imaginative *primi* (green pepper and mint risotto) and the classic T-bone steak, *bistecca alla fiorentina* (€45 per kilogram). Advance reservations are recommended at weekends when Florentines flock here for a taste of the Tuscan countryside.

To find Acquolina, take the Valdarno exit off the A1 and follow signs for 'Terranuova Bracciolini' and 'Arezzo' until you pick up 'Osteria dell'Acquolina' signs.

Chiesa di Santa Maria delle Grazie   CHURCH
(Piazza Beato Ranieri; ⊘8.30am-1pm & 3-6pm) This 16th-century church was built by members of the Fraternity of Death (men who cared for plague sufferers). Inside, the *Madonna delle Grazie* (1555) is a painting of a pregnant Madonna that may slightly predate Piero's *Parto* in Monterchi. The artist was Raffaellino del Colle, a member of the fraternity, who included a skull at the Madonna's feet as a reference to the fraternity's sombre work.

Aboca Museum   MUSEUM
(www.abocamuseum.it; Via Niccolò Aggiunti 75; adult/reduced €8/4; ⊘10am-1pm & 3-7pm Tue-Sun summer, 10am-1pm & 2.30-6pm Tue-Sun winter) When magnificent art and churches tire, take a break in this medicinal plant museum inside 18th-century **Palazzo Bourbon del Monte**. Exhibits provide a fascinating insight into the relationship between man and herbs from prehistoric times to present, with rooms dedicated to mortars, weighing scales, glassware and antique books chronicling ancient remedies. In the Poison Cellar deadly ingredients were skillfully crafted into medicinal remedies.

KEN WELSH/GETTY IMAGES ©

1. Basilica di San Francesco, Assisi (p274) **2.** Abbazia di Monte Oliveto Maggiore (p134) **3.** Abbazia di Sant'Antimo (p161), near Montalcino

Magnificent Monasteries

Consider yourself warned: after visiting these medieval monasteries in Tuscany and nearby Umbria, you may well find yourself entertaining serious thoughts about leaving your fast-paced urban existence to embrace the contemplative life.

Basilica di San Francesco, Assisi

Every year, more than five million pilgrims make their way to the medieval hilltop town of Assisi, St Francis' birthplace (p274) in the Umbria region to visit the huge basilica and monastery that is dedicated to his legacy. Don't miss his ornamental tomb in the basilica crypt.

Abbazia di Monte Oliveto Maggiore

The Benedictine monks living in this medieval abbey (p134) southeast of Siena tend the vineyard and olive grove, study in one of Italy's most important medieval libraries and walk through a cloister frescoed by Luca Signorelli and Il Sodoma.

Monasterio & Sacro Eremo di Camaldoli

Deep in the forest of the Casentino, amid a landscape that has changed little for centuries, lie this Benedictine monastery and hermitage (p270). Treasures include paintings by Vasari and Bronzino, as well as one of Andrea della Robbia's greatest terracotta sculptures.

Santuario della Verna

St Francis of Assisi is said to have received the stigmata at this spectacularly located monastery (p269) on the southeastern edge of the Casentino. Pilgrims flock here to worship in the Cappella delle Stimmate and to admire the della Robbia artworks in the church.

Eremo Francescano Le Celle

A babbling stream, old stone bridge and terraces of olive trees contribute to the fairy-tale feel of this picturesque Franciscan hermitage (p273) just outside Cortona.

PIERO DELLA FRANCESCA

Though many details about his life are hazy, it is believed that the great Renaissance painter Piero della Francesca was born around 1420 in Sansepolcro and died in 1492. Trained as a painter from the age of 15, his distinctive use of perspective, mastery of light and skilful synthesis of form and colour set him apart from his artistic contemporaries, and the serene grace of his figures remains unsurpassed to this day. In his book *The Lives of the Artists*, Piero's fellow townsman Giorgio Vasari called him the 'best geometrician of his time' and lamented the fact that so few of his works were preserved for posterity, leading to him being 'robbed of the honour that [was] due to his labours'.

Piero's most famous works are the *Legend of the True Cross* in Arezzo's **Cappella Bacci** (p258), his *Resurrection* in Sansepolcro's **Museo Civico** (p263) and his panel featuring *Federico da Montefeltro and Battista Sforza, the Duke and Duchess of Urbino* in the Uffizi. But he is perhaps most fondly remembered for his luminous *Madonna del Parto* showcased in a **museum** (Pregnant Madonna Museum; ☑ 0575 7 07 13; www. madonnadelparto.it; Via della Reglia 1, Monterchi; adult/reduced €5.50/4; ☉ 9am-1pm & 2-7pm summer, to 5pm Wed-Mon winter) in **Monterchi**, a village in the remote Tiber Valley between Sansepolcro (15km north) and Arezzo (28km west).

For a complete itinerary, pick up the brochure **Terre di Piero** at tourist offices or consult it online at http://terredipiero.it.

⚡ Festivals & Events

Palio della Ballestra   CULTURAL
(☉ 2nd Sun Sep) Crossbow tournament between local archers and rivals from nearby Gubbio, with contestants and onlookers in medieval costumes.

🛏 Sleeping

Guidi, Da Ventura and Fiorentino all offer a couple of B&B rooms up top as well as memorable dining.

Relais Palazzo Magi   B&B €
(☑ 0575 74 04 77; www.hotelmagisansepolcro. it; Via XX Settembre 160-162; s/d €70/80; ❄ 🐾) Comfort and charm are perfectly aligned at Sansepolcro's best sleeping option, in a 15th-century *palazzo*. Some of its 16 rooms have frescoed walls, and guests can socialise in a billiard room and TV lounge.

✕ Eating & Drinking

★ **Ristorante Da Ventura**   TUSCAN €€
(☑ 0575 74 25 60; www.albergodaventura.it; Via Niccolò Aggiunti 30; meals €25; ☉ 12.30-2.15pm & 7.30-9.45pm Tue-Sat) This old-world eatery is a culinary joy. Trolleys laden with fiesty joints of pork, beef stewed in Chianti Classico and roasted veal shank are pushed from table to table, bow-tied waiters intent on piling plates high. The veal filet topped with wafer-thin slices of *lardo di colonnata* (local pig fat) and the veal carpaccio with black truffle shavings are glorious.

Vegetarians are well catered for with a feast of a mixed house *antipasti* followed by black truffle omelette or buttered *tagliatelle* (ribbon pasta). Cartoons on the walls are by Livornoborn hotshot satirist Alberto Fremura.

Ristorante Fiorentino   ITALIAN €€
(☑ 0575 74 20 33; www.ristorantefiorentino.it; Via Luca Pacioli 60; meals €35; ☉ noon-3pm & 7.30-10.30pm Thu-Tue) An iconic address, this grandiose dining room dates to 1807. Sweep up the marble staircase and into a historic world of glass chandeliers, Renaissance wooden coffered ceiling and original fireplace. Food is traditional with an occasional modern twist.

Enoteca Guidi   WINE BAR
(☑ 0575 74 19 07; www.locandaguidi.it; Via Luca Pacioli 44-46; meals €20; ☉ 11am-midnight Thu-Tue) Owner Saverio presides over the *enoteca* (wine bar) and rear dining space where simple meals are served. Enjoy a local beer or some *vino* (everything from local drops to fashionable Super Tuscans).

ℹ Information

Tourist Office (☑ 0575 74 05 36; www. valtiberinaintoscana.it; Via Giacomo Matteotti 8; ☉ 9.30am-1pm & 2.30-6.30pm summer, shorter hours winter; 🐾)

ℹ Getting There & Away

BUS
Etruria Mobilità (www.etruriamobilita.it) buses link Sansepolcro with Anghiari (€1.50, 10 minutes)

and Arezzo (€4.20, one hour). **Sulga** (www.sulga. it) operates a daily service to Rome and Fiumicino Airport (€19.50, 3½ to 4¼ hours); check schedules and buy tickets online. Buses use the bus station off Via G Marconi, near Porta Fiorentina.

CAR & MOTORCYCLE

A Zona a Traffico Limitato (ZTL; Limited Traffic Zone) applies within the city walls; you'll find free parking just outside.

THE CASENTINO

The northeastern corner of Tuscany is home to spectacular mountains, historic monasteries and hamlets where traditional customs and cuisine are proudly maintained. The website www.casentino.net is a handy resource, with plenty of information on mountain biking and hiking.

Poppi

POP 6260

Seeming to float in the clouds above the Arno plain, Poppi Alta (the historic upper section of the town) is crowned by the commanding presence of the Castello dei Conti Guidi. The kiosk in the piazza outside the castle is the social hub during the summer months; at other times locals tend to socialise in Ponte a Poppi (the lower town).

⊙ Sights

Castello dei Conti Guidi   CASTLE
(✆0575 52 05 16; www.buonconte.com; Piazza Repubblica 1; adult/reduced €6/5; ⊙10am-7pm summer, to 5pm Thu-Sun winter) Castello dei Conti

Guidi was built in the 13th century by Count Simone da Battifolle, head of the Guidi family. Inside, there's a fairy-tale courtyard, a handsome staircase, a library full of medieval manuscripts and a chapel with frescoes by Taddeo Gaddi. The scene of Herod's feast shows Salome apparently clicking her fingers as she dances, accompanied by a lute player, while John the Baptist's headless corpse lies slumped in the corner.

🛏 Sleeping

★ Borgo Corsignano   AGRITURISMO €€
(✆0575 50 02 94; www.borgocorsignano.it; Località Corsignano; d €80-120; P@☎❋) In a *borgo* (medieval village) once home to Camaldoli monks, this gorgeous country hotel is the Casentino's finest accommodation option. A 5km drive from Poppi, it has a mix of self-catering apartments and houses spread among 13 old stone properties. Voluptuous sculptures collected by the art-loving owners pepper the vast grounds, and weeping mountain views are magnificent. Facilities include two large pools, a playground suitable for teens as well as tots, a wellness centre with sauna and jacuzzi, and a tennis court.

Fattorie de Celli   AGRITURISMO €€
(✆0575 52 99 17; www.borgocorsignano.it; Via de Becarino 32a, Celli, Poppi; d €80-120; ⊙May-Oct; P☎❋) For a complete Tuscan getaway, this vast green estate offers 16 traditional farmhouses in the countryside, 5km northwest of Poppi. Self-catering properties sleep two to 11 guests, and mix traditional with contemporary Tuscan decor. Sustainable Villa Chimera is built solely from natural

---

OFF THE BEATEN TRACK

MICHELANGELO

Art lovers can have a field day in the remote Tuscan outback of Casentino. *David*'s creator was born in the lost village of Caprese (today called **Caprese Michelangelo**, population 1491), 17km south of Chiusi della Verna, and the small stone house where the artist grew up can be visited. Right at the top of the hilltop village, next to Caprese's medieval castle, the **Museo Michelangeliolesco** (Via Capoluogo 1, Castello di Caprese; adult/reduced €4/3; ⊙10am-7.30pm Mon-Fri, 9.30am-7.30pm Sat & Sun) tells the tale of Michelangelo's childhood roamings in the countryside here and his subsequent artistic career through a series of plaster casts.

So deeply was the artist inspired by the landscape here that he used the silhouette of Mount Penna, as seen from Chiusa della Verna, as the backdrop for the *Tondo Doni* in Florence's Uffizi and the *Creation of Adam* fresco in Rome's Sistine Chapel. Driving downhill from the Santuario della Verna towards Ciusa della Verna village, look for a brown sign on the left indicating 'La Roccia di Adamia'. Adam's Rock is just that – the rock that Michelangelo painted and on which he set a reclining Adam holding out his left arm, fingers almost touching, towards a bearded God.

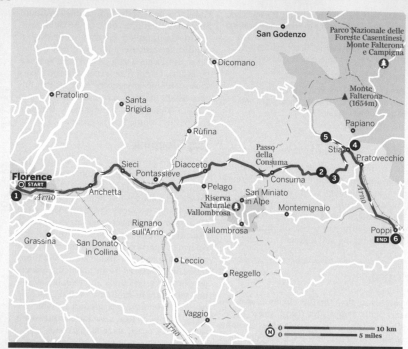

Driving Tour
The Casentino

START FLORENCE
END POPPI
LENGTH 59KM; SIX HOURS

For a foray into this corner of Tuscany, head southeast (direction Firenze Sud) from **❶ Florence** and drive alongside the Arno river through Pontassieve and over the Passo della Consuma (SS70), a mountain pass over this Tuscan section of the Apennine Mountains (follow the signs for Consuma and Bibbiena). The road will eventually bring you to the turn-off to the **❷ Castello di Romena**, on the left-hand side of the road. After wandering around this ruined 11th-century castle that Dante once visited, walk or drive down the hill to **❸ Pieve di Romena**, a Romanesque church with interior capitals featuring primitive carvings of human and animal figures. To gain entry, try knocking on the door of the adjoining building. Next, follow the road signs to the town of **❹ Stia**. This is where the Arno meets its first tributary, the Staggia, and the town was for many years the centre of the local wool industry. It's now home to the Museo dell'Arte della Lana – Lanificio di Stia, a wool museum that occupies a centuries-old mill that was the Casentino's major employer from the 1800s until 2000 when it closed down. Near the museum's entrance is Tessilnova, a shop selling examples of the brightly coloured and 'nubby' woollen blankets and clothing that the Casentino is famous for, as well as other top-quality, Italian-made woollen clothing.

From Stia, drive 4km northwest along the P556 (direction Fornace and Londa) to the **❺ Santuario di Santa Maria delle Grazie**, a beautiful Renaissance church dating from 1432 – if the church is not open, try to find a local who might be able to let you inside to admire a fresco by Ghirlandaio and two very pretty ceramic lunettes by Benedetto Buglioni. Backtracking to Stia, proceed south through Pratovecchio and continue on to the regional centre of **❻ Poppi**, where you can visit the magnificent Castello dei Conti Guidi and wander the picturesque streets of the upper town before heading to your accommodation for the night.

materials and has its own pool staring at the entire Casentino valley.

Four shared pools, playgrounds and a tree-climbing course for older children make Celli a real favourite with families.

✖️ Eating

La Vite   TUSCAN €
(☑0575 56 09 62; www.ristorantelavite.net; Piazza della Repubblica, Soci; meals €25; ⊙noon-2.30pm & 6.30-10.30pm Wed-Mon) This easy dine in Soci, 5km east of Poppi, is run by young dynamic sommelier Barbara and chef Cesare. It's a real favourite with locals – and travellers hungry for a good-value feast of top-quality Tuscan food in the company of great wine. Under no circumstances skimp on *dolci* (dessert) – all homemade and fabulous.

L'Antica Cantina   TUSCAN €€
(☑0575 52 98 44; www.anticacantina.com; Via Lapucci 2; meals €40; ⊙noon-2.30pm & 8-11pm Tue-Sun, closed Jan) This old-fashioned dining experience cooks up traditional Tuscan beneath a vaulted ceiling. Find it on a steep side street off Via Cesare Battisti in Poppi Alta.

ℹ️ Information

Tourist Office (☑0575 52 05 11; www.casentino.ar.it; Via Roma 203, Ponte a Poppi; ⊙8am-6pm Mon-Fri)

ℹ️ Getting There & Away

CAR & MOTORCYCLE
From Florence, take the SR67 and SR69 (Via Aretina) and veer onto the SS70 (Passo della Consuma). To Arezzo, take the SR70 and SS71.

TRAIN
Frequent trains run by **Trasporto Ferroviario Toscano** (www.trasportoferroviariotoscano.it) link Poppi with Arezzo (€3.70, one hour), Bibbiena (€1.50, 10 minutes) and Stia (€1.50, 15 minutes).

Parco Nazionale delle Foreste Casentinesi, Monte Falterona e Campigna

One of three national parks in Tuscany, the **Foreste Casentinesi, Monte Falterona & Campigna National Park** (www.parcoforestecasentinesi.it) straddles the Tuscany–Emilia-Romagna border and protects scenic stretches of the Apennines and Italy's largest forest and woodlands.

One of the highest peaks, **Monte Falterona** (1654m), marks the source of the Arno. The park is home to a rich assortment of wildlife, including nearly 100 bird species. Nine self-guided nature trails criss-cross the park: the most popular is the 4.5km uphill hike (4½ hours) from San Benedetto in Alpe to the spectacular **Acquacheta waterfall**, made famous by Dante's *Divine Comedy*.

The major settlement in the park is **Badia Pratáglia**, a small village in the Alpe di Serra, near the border with Emilia-Romagna.

⊙ Sights

★**Santuario della Verna**   MONASTERY
(☑0575 53 41; www.laverna.it; Via del Santuario 45, Chiusi della Verna; ⊙Cappella delle Stimmate 8am-7pm summer, to 5pm winter, Museo della Verna 10am-noon & 2-5pm) FREE This remote Franciscan monastic complex is where St Francis of Assisi is said to have received the stigmata and is a major pilgrimage destination. The **Corridoio delle Stimmate**, decorated with modern frescoes recounting St Francis' life, leads to the **Cappella delle Stimmate**, built in 1263 on the spot where the saint supposedly received the stigmata two years before his death, aged 44. The monumental *Crucifixion* by Andrea della Robbia here is magnificent.

Across from the door to the chapel, steps lead outside to the **Precipicio**, the precipice – literally – from which the devil supposedly tried to hurl Francis down onto the rocks below. The narrow path is not for those prone to vertigo.

The monastery **basilica** houses remarkably fine polychrome glazed ceramics by Andrea della Robbia and his studio – a *Madonna and Child Enthroned between Saints* to your right as you enter the church, a *Nativity* on the right before the altar, an *Adoration* in the small chapel to the right of the altar, saints on either side of the altar, a huge *Ascension* (c 1480) in the chapel to the left of the altar, and a beautiful *Annunciation* in the second chapel to the left.

Don't miss the **Cappella delle Reliquie**, a small chapel on the right side of the basilica, safeguarding the habit that Francis wore when he recieved the stigmata in 1224. Other relics include the saint's girdle, a blood-stained cloth used to clean his stigmatic wounds, a whip used by Francis as an instrument of penance, and the stick he walked with when roaming the mountains.

In the interesting **Museo della Verna**, monastic life is evoked with ancient bibles and song books, manuscripts, sacred art, the re-creation of an old pharmacy, a huge cauldron above the old kitchen chimney, and so on.

By car, follow signs just outside the hamlet of Chiusi della Verna for the sanctuary or take the way of the pilgrims along the taxing 30-minute uphill footpath from Chiusi della Verna. The sanctuary is 23km east of Bibbiena, accessed via the SP208. There is a pilgrim guesthouse (€53 per person) with refectory (set breakfast/lunch/dinner €4.50/16/16), and cafe-bar selling monk-made products (chocolate, honey, liqueur, jams, conserved fruit) on site. Parking is €1/7 per hour/day.

Monasterio & Sacro Eremo di Camaldoli   MONASTERY
(www.camaldoli.it; ⊘monastery 8am-1pm & 3.30-6pm, hermitage 9am-noon & 3-5pm, pharmacy 9am-12.30pm & 2.30-6pm) **FREE** Hidden in the dense forest of the national park are the Benedictine monastery and hermitage of Camaldoli, founded between 1024 and 1025 by St Romuald and now home to a community of 20 or so monks.

From Poppi, take Via Camaldoli (SR67) and follow it up through the forest. You will come to a fork in the road – the hermitage is uphill to the right and the monastery is downhill to the left.

You can visit the monastery's church, which houses three paintings by Vasari. Down a set of stairs off the main road are the forbidding 11th-century cloisters and the austere Cappella dello Spirito Santo, a stone space with an exhibition about daily life in the monastery. Pop into the 16th-century *farmacia* (pharmacy), accessed from the side of the main building, which sells soap, perfumes and other items made by members of the monastic community.

The hermitage has a small church with a Bronzino altarpiece of the *Crucifixion and Four Saints,* but the highlight is the Cappella di San Antonio Abate, to the left as you enter the church building. Inside is an exquisite altarpiece by Andrea della Robbia.

ℹ Information

Badia Prataglia Visitor Centre (☑ 0575 55 94 77; www.parcoforestecasentinesi.it; Via Nazionale 14a, Badia Prataglia; ⊘9am-12.30pm & 3.30-6pm summer, 9am-12.30pm Sat & Sun winter) Wealth of information about the national park.

VAL DI CHIANA

This wide green valley stretches south from Arezzo and is punctuated by gently rolling hills crowned with medieval villages. Its prized agricultural land is rich in orchards and olive groves, but is primarily known as the home of Tuscany's famed Chianina cows, one of the oldest breeds of cattle in the world and the essential ingredient in Tuscany's signature dish, *bistecca alla fiorentina.*

LOCAL KNOWLEDGE

TASTY PRATOVECCHIO

The town itself is unremarkable, but Pratovecchio does have two tasty addresses well worth the 8km drive from Poppi.

La Tana degli Orsi (☑ 0575 58 33 77; Via Roma 1, Pratovecchio; meals €40; ⊘7.30-10.30pm Thu-Mon) In the evening the dozen tables at La Tana degli Orsi (The Lair of the Bear), an unusual chalet-style building, are hotly contested, rendering advance reservations essential. Decor hovers between classy and kitsch, but cuisine is top-quality Tuscan with many traditional Casentino dishes created here with local produce. An outstanding wine list lures oenophiles.

Toscana Twist (☑ 0575 58 21 20; Via della Libertà 3; meals €30; ⊘6am-7.30pm Tue-Thu, to 11pm Fri, to 9pm Sat) Toscana Twist is a rare and wonderful breed in rural Tuscany. This exceptionally contemporary address near the train station is a pedigree hybrid. Its day begins with breakfast – delicious cakes, cookies and pastries – and closes with dinner on Friday, and an *aperitivo* banquet (from 6.30pm) on Saturday. Both evenings set the place buzzing with savvy hobnobbing locals from surrounding villages. Decor is an appealing mix of 'vintage tea room' and 'contemporary artsy'.

Cuisine is creative Tuscan packed with fresh seasonal veggies. The Chianina beef carpaccio with Parmesan shavings or liver with onions (followed by a mixed salad of cherry tomatoes and spicy green raducchio leaves) are exceptional.

OFF THE BEATEN TRACK

BIBBIENA

One of the Casentino's oldest settlements, Bibbiena (population 12,512) proffers a quiet charm in its ancient upper town. The 12th-century **Pieve dei SS Ippolito e Cassiano** (closed for renovation), downhill from central square Piazza Roma, safeguards a 14th-century crucifix by the Master of San Polo in Rosso and a 15th-century *Madonna and Child Enthroned with Angels* by Arcangelo di Cola da Camerino.

Cafe pavement terraces sit pretty beneath the porticoes on Piazza Roma, and quintessential Slow Food address **Il Tirabusciò** (The Corkscrew; ☑ 0575 59 54 74; www. tirabuscio.it; Via Rosa Scoti 12; meals €30; ◷ noon-2pm & 7.30-10pm Wed-Sun, 7.30-10pm Mon) is a refined and classical lunch option with its linen window drapes, white tablecloths and modern Tuscan kitchen.

After lunch pop into **ExpArt** (www.expartgallery.com; Via Borghi 80; ◷ no fixed hours), an exciting art gallery and studio displaying contemporary art by local and Tuscan artists, a few doors away on the same street. Invariably someone is at work on front of an easel in the bright, white, hybrid gallery-studio space.

Should you be persuaded to linger longer, **Lo Chalet** (☑ 0575 59 32 85; Viale Giuseppe Garibaldi 4; ◷ 11am-midnight) in the lower reaches of the old town is the cutting-edge contemporary choice for an *aperitivo* with a view. Overnight at **Hotel Borgo Antico** (☑ 0575 53 64 45; www.borgoantico-bibbiena.com; Via Cappucci 5; s/d €45/75).

If you're in the valley on the third Sunday in June, don't miss the **Palio dei Rioni** – imagine Siena's *palio* on a smaller scale – that sees jockeys on horseback race around Piazza Garibaldi in Castiglion Fiorentino.

Castiglion Fiorentino

POP 13,400

Driving from Arezzo to Cortona, break in this picturesque walled town crowned with the impressively restored Cassero, a bulky medieval fortress with panoramic views of the Val di Chiana both from its grassy green grounds and also the top of its half-ruined medieval *torre* (tower). Buy tickets to scale the **tower** (Cassero; adult/reduced €3/1.50; ◷ 10am-6pm Fri-Sun summer, 10am-12.30pm & 3.30-6pm Fri-Sun winter) from the ticket desk inside the neighbouring **Museo Civico Archeologico** (Cassero; adult/reduced €3/2; ◷ 10am-6pm Fri-Sun summer, 10am-12.30pm & 3.30-6.30pm Fri-Sun winter), a well put-together archaeological museum that incorporates medieval prison cells and the subterranean remains of a 6th-century-BC Etruscan temple and an Etruscan house from the late 4th century BC.

The lower part of Castiglion Fiorentino's fortress plays sentry to a small collection of art including Taddeo Gaddi's *Virgin and Child* in the **Pinacoteca Comunale** (Cassero; adult/reduced €3/2; ◷ 10am-12.30pm & 4-6.30pm Thu-Sat summer, 10am-12.30pm & 3.30-6pm Thu-Sat winter). A combined adult/reduced ticket for both museums is available for €5/3.

A Zona Traffico Limitata (ZTL) applies in the streets immediately surrounding the Cassero, but there is ample free parking on Piazza Garibaldi. Walk down the hill to Porta Fiorentina to find the **tourist information booth** (☑ 0575 65 82 78; www.proloco castiglionfiorentino.it; Porta Fiorentina; ◷ 10am-noon Tue-Sun, 4-6pm Wed & Fri).

Cortona

POP 22,600

Rooms with a view are the rule rather than the exception in this spectacularly sited hilltop town. In the late 14th century Fra' Angelico lived and worked here, and fellow artists Luca Signorelli and Pietro da Cortona were both born within the walls – all three are represented in the Museo Diocesano's small but sensational collection. Large chunks of *Under the Tuscan Sun,* the soap-in-the-sun film of the book by Frances Mayes, were shot here.

◉ Sights

★ **Museo Diocesano**   MUSEUM

(Piazza del Duomo 1; adult/reduced €5/3; ◷ 10am-7pm Tue-Sun summer, to 5pm Tue-Sun winter) Little is left of the original Romanesque character of Cortona's cathedral, rebuilt several times in a less-than-felicitous fashion. Fortunately, its wonderful artworks have been saved and displayed in this museum. Highlights include a moving *Crucifixion* (1320) by Pietro Lorenzetti and two beautiful works

Cortona

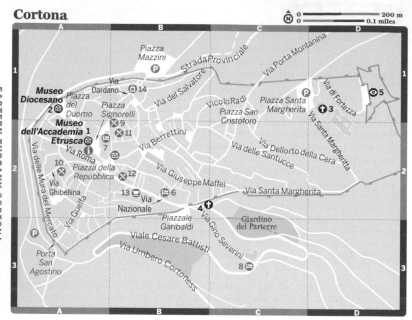

Cortona

by Fra' Angelico: *Annunciation* (1436) and *Madonna with Child and Saints* (1436–37). Room 1 features a remarkable Roman sarcophagus decorated with a frenzied battle scene between Dionysus and the Amazons.

★ Museo dell'Accademia Etrusca   MUSEUM
(MAEC; www.cortonamaec.org; Piazza Signorelli 9; adult/reduced €10/7; ⊙10am-7pm summer, to 5pm Tue-Sun winter) The plain facade of 13th-century Palazzo Casali was added to the original building in the 17th century. Inside, this fascinating museum displays substantial local Etruscan and Roman finds, Renaissance globes, 18th-century decorative arts and contempo-

rary paintings. The Etruscan collection is the highlight, particularly those objects excavated from the tombs at Sodo, just outside town.

Chiesa di San Domenico   CHURCH
(Largo Beato Angelico; ⊙9am-6pm) At the eastern end of Via Nazionale is this 15th-century church, home to a 1515 painting of the *Madonna and Saints* by luminary Luca Signorelli.

Basilica di Santa Margherita   CHURCH
(Piazza Santa Margherita; ⊙8am-noon & 3-7pm summer, 9am-noon & 3-6pm winter) For an effective cardiovascular workout, hike up to this largely 19th-century church through Cortona's warren of steep cobbled lanes. Inside, the

remains of St Margaret, patron saint of Cortona, lie in a 14th-century glass-sided tomb above the altar.

Fortezza del Girifalco   LANDMARK
(Via per Santa Margherita; adult/child €3/1.50; ⊙10am-1pm & 3-6pm Sat & Sun May & Jun, 10am-1pm & 4-7pm Jul-Sep) There's a stupendous view over the Val di Chiana to Lago Trasimeno in Umbria from the remains of this Medici fortress atop the highest point in town.

Eremo Francescano Le Celle   MONASTERY
(☑0575 60 33 62; www.lecelle.it; Strada dei Cappuccini 1; ⊙dawn-dusk) This Franciscan hermitage is hidden in dense woodland 3km north of Cortona. Its buildings sit next to a picturesque stream with an 18th-century stone bridge, and the only sounds to disturb the tranquil atmosphere are the bells that call the resident friars to vespers and mass in the cave-like Chiesa Cella di San Francesco.

✦ Festivals & Events

Giostra dell'Archidado   CULTURAL
(www.giostraarchidado.com; ⊙May or Jun) A full week of medieval merriment (the date varies to coincide with Ascension Day) culminates in a crossbow competition.

Cortonantiquaria   FAIR
(www.cortonantiquaria.it; ⊙late Aug or early Sep) Cortona's antiques market sets up in the 18th-century halls of Palazzo Vagnotti.

🛏 Sleeping

Casa Chilenne   B&B €
(☑0575 60 33 20; www.casachilenne.com; Via Nazionale 65; d €110; 🅿@🛜) Run by San Francisco-born Jeanette and her Cortonese husband Luciano, this welcoming B&B scales a narrow townhouse on Cortona's main pedestrian street. Five spacious rooms have access to a small rooftop terrace, complete with bijou cooking area and chairs to lounge on.

★La Corte di Ambra   B&B €€
(☑0575 178 82 66; www.cortonaluxuryrooms.com; Via Benedetti 23; d €150-300; 🅿@🛜) Squirrelled away in Palazzo Fierli-Petrella, this contemporary guesthouse has five luxurious rooms with whitewashed beamed ceilings, chandelier lighting and beautiful linens in mellow neutral tones. En suite bathrooms are up-to-the-minute and – unusually for a Renaissance Tuscan palace – the B&B has a lift; one room is genuinely wheelchair-friendly.

THE PERFECT STEAK

Ask any local where to sink your teeth into the perfect *bistecca alla fiorentina*, aka Tuscany's iconic T-bone steak, and the answer is always **Ristorante Da Muzzicone** (☑348 9356616, 0575 65 84 03; Piazza San Francesco 7; meals €30; ⊙12.15-2.15pm & 7.30-9.30pm). In business for over a decade next to Chiesa di San Francesco, the restaurant is famed for its succulent, cooked-to-perfection beef (€45 per kilogram) grilled above a wood fire.

If T-bone traditionally butchered from the Val di Chiana's famed Chianina cow is not your cup of tea, there are grilled beef filets in green pepper sauce or balsamic vinegar to tempt. In summer, tables spill onto the pretty square outside. Advance reservations essential.

Villa Marsili   HOTEL €€
(☑0575 60 52 52; www.villamarsili.net; Viale C Battisti 13; s €110-360; 🅿🅿@🛜) Service is the hallmark at this attractive villa wedged against the city walls. Guests rave about the helpful staff, lavish breakfast buffet and early evening *aperitivo* served in the garden. Pricer suites have jacuzzis and wonderful views across the Val di Chiana to Lago Trasimeno. The cheapest rates are nonrefundable online.

🍴 Eating & Drinking

Pedestrian main street Via Nazionale has plenty of places where you can linger over coffee or cocktails.

Fiaschetteria La Fett'unta   TUSCAN €
(☑0575 63 05 82; www.winebarcortona.com; Via Giuseppe Maffei 3; meals €15) This tiny, deli-style *fiaschetteria* (wine bar) with tempting cold cuts and pre-prepared dishes sitting beneath glass, begging to be gobbled up, cooks up first-class budget dining. Service is overwhelmingly friendly; there's a kids' corner; and the traditional Tuscan cuisine – fresh from the kitchen of big sister Osteria del Teatro across the street – is spot-on.

Pasticceria Banchelli   PASTRIES €
(☑0575 60 10 52; Via Nazionale 11; ⊙10am-8pm Tue-Sun) For sinful cakes with coffee, this cake shop with cafe has been the place to go since 1930.

WORTH A TRIP

ASSISI

Thanks to St Francis, who was born here in 1182, the hilltop town of Assisi (population 28,132) in the neighbouring region of Umbria is a major destination for millions of pilgrims. Its major drawcard is the **Basilica di San Francesco** (www.sanfrancescoassisi.org; Piazza di San Francesco; ⊘upper church 8.30am-6.45pm, lower church & tomb 6am-6.45pm) **FREE**, which comprises two churches filled with magnificent Renaissance art. The **upper church** was built between 1230 and 1253 in the Italian Gothic style and features a superb fresco cycle by Giotto. Downstairs, in the dimly lit **lower church**, there's a series of colourful frescoes by Simone Martini, Cimabue and Pietro Lorenzetti. Stairs lead down to the crypt where the tomb of St Francis lies.

To book English-language guided tours of the basilica, contact its **information office** (☑075 819 00 84; www.sanfrancescoassisi.org; Piazza di San Francesco 2; ⊘9am-noon & 2-5.30pm Mon-Sat) or fill out the form on the website.

Assisi is a popular overnight destination, so book ahead during peak times: Easter, August, September and the Feast of St Francis (4 October). Contact the **tourist office** (☑075 813 86 80; www.assisi.regioneumbria.eu; Piazza del Comune 22; ⊘9.30am-7pm daily summer, 8am-2pm & 3-6pm Mon-Fri, 9am-7pm Sat, 9am-6pm Sun winter) for accommodation lists. For lunch, consider seasonal Umbrian cuisine at **Osteria Eat Out** (☑075 81 31 63; www.nunassisi.com; Via Eremo delle Carceri 1a; meals €35-50; ⊘12.30-2.30pm & 7.30-10.30pm Tue-Sun), or stylish **Vinò** (Piazza del Comune 38; panini/salads €5/8; ⊘10am-midnight) for gourmet panini, creative salads and salami-and-cheese platters in the company of fine wine.

Sulga buses connect Assisi with Florence (€13, 2½ hours, twice weekly). A Zona a Traffico Limitato (ZTL; Limited Traffic Zone) applies in the historic centre, but there are plenty of paid car parks just outside the walls.

★**La Bucaccia**   TUSCAN €€
(☑0575 60 60 39; www.labucaccia.it; Via Ghibellina 17; meals €32, set tasting menu €29; ⊘12.45-3pm & 7-10.30pm Tue-Sun) Cortona's finest address, this gourmet gem is at home in the old medieval stable of a Renaissance *palazzo*. Cuisine is Tuscan and Cortonese, and the cheese course is superb, thanks to owner Romano Magi who ripens his own. Dedicated gourmets won't be able to resist the six *pecorino* types to taste with fruit sauces, salsas and honeys. Reservations essential.

Osteria del Teatro   ITALIAN €€
(☑0575 63 05 56; www.osteria-del-teatro.it; Via Giuseppe Maffei 2; meals €32; ⊘noon-2.30pm & 7-10pm Thu-Tue) The walls are clad with photos of actors who have dined here after performing in the nearby theatre, and service is suitably theatrical – waiters wield what could well be the biggest pepper grinder in the world, and blocks of locally produced chocolate are attacked with a butcher's knife for a sweet finale.

Taverna Pane e Vino   TUSCAN, WINE BAR €€
(☑0575 63 10 10; www.pane-vino.it; Piazza Signorelli 27; meals €25; ⊘noon-11pm Tue-Sun) This vaulted cellar is a hot spot with locals who come here to indulge in Tuscan and Italian wines with *bruschette*, terracotta dishes of baked cheese and bacon, and Tuscan soups and meats.

Caffè degli Artisti   CAFE
(Via Nazionale 18) This vintage cafe on Cortona's pedestrian main street is wonderful for mellowing out over an aromatic pot of white, black or green leaf tea, with honey if so desired.

 Shopping

I Tre Toscani   FOOD & DRINK
(Via Dardano 35) There is no tastier shop in Cortona for tasting and buying wine, olive oil and cheese aged in *farro* (spelt) or straw.

 Information

Tourist Office (☑0575 63 72 21; www.comunedicortona.it; Piazza Signorelli; ⊘9am-12.30pm Mon, Wed & Fri, 9am-12.30pm & 3-5.30pm Tue & Thu)

ⓘ Getting There & Away

Car is by far the easiest way to access hilltop Cortona. The nearest train station is 6km southwest in Camucia, accessible via bus (€1.40, 15 minutes, hourly). Camucia train station has no ticket office, only machines (if you need assistance purchasing tickets, go to the station at Terontola, south of Camucia, instead). Destinations include the following:

Arezzo (€3.40, 25 minutes, hourly)
Florence (€10.20, 1¾ hours, hourly)
Rome (€11.15, 2¾ hours, eight daily)

Understand Florence & Tuscany

Florence & Tuscany Today

It is not all fabled romance in this land of super wines and old stone farmsteads lost in cinematic rushes of rolling hills, vineyards and cypress alleys. The Tuscan cart still turns around the same 'go slow' spindle it did three millennia ago – but with bank troubles, diminishing state coffers and modern new regulations to dodge en route.

Best in Print

The Stones of Florence (Mary McCarthy; 1956) A timeless portrait of Florence.

Tuscan Cities (William Dean Howells) Wonderful travel narrative penned by the American consul to Venice in 1883.

The Birth of Venus (Sarah Dunant; 2003) The daughter of a wealthy merchant falls in love with a fresco painter in 15th-century Florence.

The Decameron (Giovanni Boccaccio; 1353) A bawdy masterpiece.

A Tabernacle for the Sun (Linda Proud; 1997) Book One of the Botticelli Trilogy.

Best on Film

Life is Beautiful (Robert Benigni; 1998) Oscar-winning Holocaust comedy set in Arezzo.

A Room with a View (James Ivory; 1985) Exquisitely rendered screen version of EM Forster's 1908 novel.

Tea with Mussolini (Franco Zeffirelli; 1999) Semi-autobiographical film, opening in Florence in 1935.

The English Patient (Anthony Minghella; 1996) Romantic drama starring Arezzo's Cappella Bacci.

A Tough Sell

Tuscany, like every *regione* in Italy and beyond, is feeling the strain of ongoing financial crisis in Europe. With economies floundering for over five years now, it's increasingly tough. In 2013 Tuscans had already been shaken to the core by the near-collapse and subsequent government bail-out of their oldest financial institution, in business since 1472, the Banca Monte dei Paschi di Siena. Restructuring and raising capital through a €5 billion share sale 12 months later seemed to right matters at the bank, but late 2014 dealt a new blow to Tuscan morale: Banca Monte dei Paschi di Siena failed European regulator stress tests – the largest bank in Europe to do so. In May 2015 the Sienese bank announced it would raise another €3 billion from its shareholders, but with all confidence lost, and promised 8% return on equity by 2018 only, it will clearly be a tough sell.

Chest of Treasures

As state coffers diminish, museums are increasingly unable to afford a full quota of staff; hence opening certain floors or rooms to visitors for limited hours only. Yet milestones have been reached in Tuscany's endless quest to safeguard its treasures, unmatched in Europe. In Prato the Museo di Palazzo Pretorio reopened as one of Italy's smartest museums after 20 years of renovation. And hopes are high for a 2015 opening of the Centro per l'Arte Contemporanea Luigi Pecci in Prato – a 1980s contemporary art museum expected to dazzle once its much-delayed €9 million renovation job is completed.

In Florence the €65 million 'New Uffizi' refurbishment project continues to move two steps forwards, one step backwards: dozens more rooms on the 1st floor have opened, but the radical exit loggia designed by Japanese architect Arato Isozaki is off the agenda for the foreseeable future (find it pigeonholed on *pala-*

zzo backburners*)*. Old-school Florence has, however, woken up to the value of its modern assets: state-of-the-art displays using multimedia, sound and film at Florence's new Museo Novecento put the Uffizi to shame, while the €2.5 million contemporary art centre planned for 2019 in a derelict power station in Florence Novoli promises to be equally groundbreaking.

War on Winemakers
The weather gods decimated Tuscany's 2014 olive harvest – a rainy summer, mild winter and too many olive flies ruined more than 50% of the crop, with many farmers not bothering to harvest what little survived. But the region's wealth of vines withstood the year's adverse meteorological conditions. Wine production in 2014 was down 15% to 20% on the previous year, but the quality stayed strong. Big-bodied wines like Montacino and Bolgheri promise to be less structured but as aromatic as ever.

But in mid-2014 Tuscan vines, vital to the Tuscan economy (180 million bottles a year, from vineyards covering 8% of agricultural land), took a battering from a different direction. The regional government approved a landscape protection plan introducing limitations on wine production – specifically, the creation of new vineyards – to encourage biodiversity and reduce environmental risks (landslides, soil erosion etc). Local wine producers condemned the sustainability plan, as did the media, as a 'war on winemakers', and an attack on their land rights. Tuscan president Enrico Rossi retaliated by pledging to attempt to inscribe the Tuscan landscape on Unesco's World Heritage list.

Back to Grass Roots
Sustainability and Slow Food have always been at home in the Tuscan world, a region born out of agriculture. And as modernity accelerates at an increasingly swift pace, Tuscany tenaciously digs in to preserve an extraordinary grass-roots heritage that begs travellers to sit beneath dangling hams in the local butcher's shop tasting fennel salami and Chianti Classico, or to fall asleep at night on the neighbourhood farm. Hipster farm-to-table dining has always existed in this rich green part of the world, yet even Tuscans are taking it one step further as they open Michelin-starred restaurants with organic farms, and food boutiques with shop-floor dining. Tuscany produces the bulk of Italy's organic wine, and in spring 2015 the Fattoria Casabianca winery, in the Chianti Colli Senesi near Siena, produced Tuscany's first certified vegan Chianti wine.

POPULATION: **3.69 MILLION**

AREA: **22,994 SQ KM**

GDP: **€107 BILLION**

ANNUAL INFLATION: **0.1%**

UNEMPLOYMENT RATE: **10.4%**

if Tuscany were 100 people
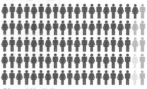
91 would be Italian
2 would be Albanian
2 would be Romanian
5 would be Other

belief systems
(% of population)

85 Roman Catholic
15 Other

population per sq km

FLORENCE TUSCANY ITALY

= 200 people

History

Tuscan history is an opera that quietly opens with the wine-loving Etruscans around the 9th century BC, staccatos with feisty clashes between medieval city-states, and crescendos with Florence's powerful Medici dynasty and the birth of the Renaissance. To this day, it is the Renaissance, with its extraordinary art and architecture, that defines the region's largest city and remains its greatest moment; Tuscany has not been at the cusp of such momentous change since.

The Etruscans

Best Etruscan Ruins

Vie Cave, Pitigliano

Parco Archeologico di Baratti e Populonia, Golfi di Baratti

Necropoli, Sovana

No one knows exactly why the ancient Etruscans headed to Tuscany in the 9th century BC, but Etruscan artefacts give clues as to why they stayed: dinner. The wild boar roaming the Tuscan hills was a favourite on the menu, and boar hunts are a recurring theme on Etruscan ceramics and tomb paintings. In case the odd boar bristle tickled the throat while eating, Etruscans washed down their meals with plenty of wine, thereby introducing viticulture to Italy.

Tomb paintings show Etruscan women keeping pace with men in banquets so decadent they scandalised even the orgy-happy Romans. Many middle-class and aristocratic women had the means to do what they wished, including indulging in music and romance, participating in politics and overseeing a vast underclass of servants. Roman military histories boast of conquests of Etruscan women along with Etruscan territory, starting in the 3rd century BC. According to recent genetic tests, Etruscans did not mingle much with their captors – their genetic material is distinct from modern Italians, who are the descendants of ancient Romans.

Etruscans didn't take kindly to Roman authority, nor were they keen on being enslaved to establish Roman plantations. They secretly allied with Hannibal to bring about the ignominious defeat of the Romans – one of the deadliest battles in all of Roman history – at Lago Trasimeno in neighbouring Umbria: 16,000 Roman soldiers were lost in approximately three hours.

After that Rome took a more hands-off approach with the Etruscans, granting them citizenship in 88 BC to manage their own affairs in the

TIMELINE	9th century BC	265 BC	88 BC
	Etruscans bring highly civilised wine, women and song to the hills of Tuscany – never has life been so good. Unfortunately, they fail to invite the Romans and war ensues.	Etruria falls to Rome, but remains unruly and conspires with Hannibal against Rome during the Punic Wars.	The Romans establish the province of Tuscia (Tuscany), grant Etruscans citizenship and give them a free hand to run the province as they deem fit.

new province of Tuscia (Tuscany), and in return securing safe passage along the major inland Roman trade route via the Via Flaminia. Little did the Romans realise when they paved the road that they were also paving the way for their own replacements in the 5th to 8th centuries AD: first came German emperor Theodoric, then Byzantine emperor Justinian, then the Lombards and finally Charlemagne in 800.

Medieval Scandal

Political power constantly changed hands in medieval Tuscany. Nevertheless, two notorious women wielded power effectively against a shifting backdrop of kings and popes. The daughter of a Roman senator and notorious prostitute-turned-senatrix, Marozia already had one illegitimate son by her lover Pope Sergius III and was pregnant when she married the Lombard duke of Spoleto, Alberic I, in 909 AD. He was hardly scrupulous himself: he'd achieved his position by murdering the previous duke, and he soon had Sergius III deposed. When Alberic was in turn killed, Marozia married Guy of Tuscany and conspired with him to smother Pope John X and install (in lethally rapid succession) Pope Leo VI and Pope Stephen VIII.

After Guy's death, she wooed his half-brother Hugh of Arles, the new king of Italy. No matter that he already had a wife: his previous marriage was soon annulled. But at the wedding ceremony, Marozia's son, Alberic II, who had been named Pope John XI, had the happy couple arrested. Marozia spent the rest of her life in prison, but her legacy lived on: five popes were her direct descendants.

Countess Matilda of Tuscany (1046–1115) was another power woman. Rumour has it that she was more than just an ally to Pope Gregory VII, and there's no doubt she was a formidable strategist. To consolidate her family's Tuscan holdings, she married her own stepbrother, Godfrey the Hunchback. She soon arranged for him to be sent off to Germany, annulling the marriage and marrying a powerful prince 26 years her junior.

When Matilda's ally Pope Gregory VII excommunicated Holy Roman Emperor Henry IV in 1077 for threatening to replace him with an antipope, the emperor showed up outside her castle barefoot and kneeling in the snow to beg the pope's forgiveness. Gregory, who was Matilda's guest, kept him waiting for three days before rescinding the excommunication. Henry retaliated for what he saw as Matilda's complicity in his humiliation by conspiring with Matilda's neighbours to seize her property, and even turned her trophy husband against her – but Matilda soon dislodged Henry's power base in the north with the support of his own son, Conrad. Disgraced by his own family and humbled on the battlefield by a woman, Henry died in 1106.

Learn to speak Etruscan at Etruscology: www.etruskisch.de/pgs/vc.htm. Favourite words: *netshvis* (a fortune teller who reads animal entrails) and *thuta* (which can mean either 'chaste' or 'only married once').

Best Roman Relics

Area Archeologica, Fiesole

Roman theatre, Volterra

Vetulonia

59 BC	AD 570–774	773–74	1080
After emerging victorious from a corrupt election campaign for the position of Roman consul, Julius Caesar establishes a soldier-retiree resort called Florentia.	The Lombards rule Italy as far south as Florence, and manage to turn the tiny duchy of Spoleto into a booming trade empire.	Charlemagne crosses the Alps into Italy, fighting the Lombards and having his ownership of Tuscany, Emilia, Venice and Corsica confirmed by Pope Hadrian I.	Henry IV deposes Pope Gregory VII for the second time, installing Clement III in his place and marching against Gregory's supporter Matilda of Tuscany, confiscating her territory.

A New Law & Order

By the 13th century Tuscans wanted change. Farmers who had painstakingly reclaimed their fields wanted to get their produce to market alive; merchants needed peaceful piazzas in which to conduct their business; and the populace at large began to entertain hopes of actually living past the age of 40.

In a bid to reorganise their communities in a more civilised fashion, *comuni* (city-states) were established in Florence, Siena and other towns. In this new power-sharing arrangement, representatives were drawn from influential families, guilds and the merchant classes. Building projects were undertaken to give citizens a new sense of shared purpose and civic identity. Hospitals and public charities helped serve the needy, and new public squares, marketplaces and town halls became crucial meeting places for civic society.

Law and order was kept by a *podestà*, an independent judiciary often brought in from outside the city for limited terms of office to prevent corruption. Each *comune* developed its own style of government: Siena's was the most imaginative. To curb bloody turf battles among its *contrade* (neighbourhoods), Siena channelled its fighting spirit into organised boxing matches, bullfights and Il Palio, an annual horse race. Anyone who broke the peace was fined and the city's coffers soon swelled with monies collected in the city's *osterie* (casual taverns or eateries presided over by a host) for cursing.

Medieval Tuscany was criminal: leaders of powerful families were stabbed by rivals while attending Mass; peasants were ambushed by brigands; and bystanders were maimed in neighbourhood disputes that all too easily escalated to murderous brawls. Petty crimes were punished with steep fines, corporal punishment and public flogging or mutilation.

FLAGELLATING MONKS & NUNS

The first known case of religious self-flagellation dates from the mid-13th century in Perugia in neighbouring Umbria, when a strange, spontaneous parade of believers began whipping themselves while singing.

By 1260 roving bands of Flagellants appeared in major Tuscan cities, stripped to the waist, hooded and ecstatically whipping themselves while singing *laudi* (songs about the passion of Christ). They made quite an impression in Florence and Siena where adherents formed *scuole di battuti* (schools of beatings) to build *case di Dio* (houses of God) that served as charity centres, hospices and hosts to mass flagellation sessions.

The Church remained neutral on the issue until the fledgling Flagellants claimed their activities could grant temporary relief from sin. This posed direct competition to the Church's practice of confession, not to mention its steady business in indulgences, pardons and tithes. The Flagellant movement was banned in 1262, only to regain momentum a century later during the plague and recur periodically until the 15th century, when the Inquisition subjected Flagellants to the ultimate mortification of the flesh: burning at the stake.

Self-flagellation processions continued to be held in Tuscany under the Church's guidance into the late 19th century.

1082	1136	1167	1296
Florence picks a fight with Siena over ownership of the Chianti region, starting a bitter rivalry that will last the next 400 years.	Scrappy, seafaring Pisa adds Amalfi to its list of conquests, which included Jerusalem, Valencia, Tripoli and Mallorca, and colonies in Constantinople and Cairo, among others.	Siena's *comune* (city-state) establishes a written constitution, declaring that elected terms should be short and money should be pretty; it's soon amended to guarantee Sienese public boxing matches.	Building work begins on Florence's *duomo*. The cathedral takes 150 years to complete and, once capped with the largest dome in Italy since antiquity, becomes the ultimate symbol of Renaissance Florence.

After Florence won yet another battle against Siena by cutting off the town's water supply, Siena's *comune* was faced with a funding choice: build an underground aqueduct to fend off Florence or a cathedral to establish Siena as the creative capital of the medieval world. The council voted unanimously for the latter.

Dante's Circle of Hell

'Midway on our life's journey, I found myself in dark woods, the right road lost...' So begins the ominous year 1300 in Dante Alighieri's *Inferno,* where our hero Dante (1265–1321) escapes from one circle of hell only to tumble into the next. In the 14th century, Dante and his fellow Tuscans endured a hellish succession of famine, economic collapses, plague, war and tyranny.

When medieval mystics predicted the year 1300 would bring doom, they were off by barely 50 years. Approximately two-thirds of the population were decimated in cities across Tuscany in the bubonic plague outbreak of 1348, and since the carriers of the plague (fleas and rats) weren't identified or eradicated, the Black Death ravaged the area for decades. Entire hospital and monastery populations were wiped out, leaving treatment to opportunists promising miracle cures. Flagellation, liquor, sugar and spices were prescribed, as was abstinence from bathing, fruit and olive oil.

Painful though those days must have been to record, writers such as Boccaccio, Dante and Marchione di Coppo Stefani (c 1336–85) wrote frank assessments of their time, believing their critiques might one day serve the greater good. More than any painterly tricks of perspective or shading, it's this rounded view of humanity that brought truth to Renaissance art.

Renaissance Belligerence & Beauty

The Renaissance was a time of great art and great tyrants, between which there was an uneasy relationship. The careful balance of power of the *comuni* became a casualty of the plague in the 14th century; political control was mostly left to those who survived and were either strong enough or unscrupulous enough to claim it. In *comuni* such as Florence and Siena, powerful families assumed control of the *signorie,* the city councils ostensibly run by guild representatives and merchants.

Cities, commercial entities and individual families took sides with either the Rome-backed Guelphs or the imperial Ghibellines, loyalists of the Holy Roman Empire. Since each of these factions was eager to put itself on the map, this competition might have meant a bonanza for artists and architects – but shifting fortunes in the battlefield meant funds for pet art projects could disappear just as quickly as they appeared.

Relive 14th-century Florence: visit Dante's Florentine home, including the chapel where he met his muse and a traditional tripe shop. For Dante with a pop-culture twist, read Sandow Birk's and Marcus Sanders' *The Divine Comedy,* which sets *Inferno* in Los Angeles' traffic, *Purgatorio* in foggy San Francisco and *Paradiso* in New York.

America was named after Amerigo Vespucci, a Florentine navigator who, from 1497 to 1504, made several voyages of discovery in what would one day be known as South America.

1314–21	1348–50	1375–1406	1378
Dante Alighieri writes his *Divina Commedia,* told in the first person, using Tuscan dialect instead of the usual formal Latin. It's peppered with political satire, pathos, adventure and light humour.	The Black Death ravages Tuscany, wiping out approximately two-thirds of the population in dense urban areas, and it doesn't stop there: further outbreaks are recorded until 1500.	Coluccio Salutati serves as chancellor of Florence, promoting a secular civic identity to trump old feudal tendencies; it's a bold, new model of citizenship for Europe that occasionally even works.	The Florentine *signoria* (city council) ignores a petition from the city's *ciompi* (wool carders), who want guild representation: cue the Revolt of Ciompi, an ultimately unsuccessful democratic uprising.

Tuscany began to resemble a chess game, with feudal castles appearing only to be overtaken, powerful bishops aligning with nobles before being toppled, and minor players backed by key commercial interests occasionally rising to power. Nowhere was the chess game harder to follow than in the Ghibelline *comune* of Pistoia: first it was conquered by the Florentine Guelphs, then it split into White and Black Guelph splinter groups, then it was captured by Lucca (which was at that time Ghibelline backed) before being reclaimed by the Florentines.

The Medici have nothing to hide – at least, not anymore. Dig your own dirt on Florence's dynamic dynasty in the archives at www.medici.org.

The Medici

The Medici family were not exempt from the usual failings of Renaissance tyrants, but early on in his rise to power Cosimo the Elder (1389–1464) revealed a surprisingly enlightened self-interest and an exceptional

HOW MACHIAVELLIAN!

Few names have such resonance as Niccolò Machiavelli (1469–1527), the Florentine scholar and political thinker who said 'the times are more powerful than our brains'. He was born into a poor offshoot of one of Florence's leading families and his essential premise – 'the end justifies the means' – is one that continues to have a disturbing impact five centuries on.

Impoverished as Machiavelli's family was, his father had a well-stocked library, which the young Niccolò devoured. When he was 29, Machiavelli landed a post in the city's second chancery (religious court). By 1500 he was in France on his first diplomatic mission in the service of the Republic. Indeed, so impressed was he by the martial success of Cesare Borgia and the centralised state of France that Machiavelli concluded Florence, too, needed a standing army – which he convinced the Republic to establish in 1506. Three years later it was bloodied in battle against the rebellious city of Pisa.

The return to power of the Medici family in 1512 was a blow for Machiavelli. Suspected of plotting against the Medici, he was thrown into Florence's Le Stinche (the earliest known jail in Tuscany, dating from 1297 and among the first in Europe) in 1513 and tortured with six rounds of interrogation on the prison's notorious rack. Yet he maintained his innocence. Once freed, he retired a poor man to a small property outside Florence.

But it was during these years that Machiavelli did his greatest writing. *Il Principe* (The Prince) is his classic treatise on the nature of power and its administration, a work reflecting the confusing and corrupt times in which he lived and his desire for strong and just rule in Florence and beyond. He later wrote an official history of Florence, the *Istorie Fiorentine*.

In 1526 Machiavelli joined the papal army in its futile fight against imperial forces. By the time the latter had sacked Rome in 1527, Florence had again rid itself of Medici rule. Machiavelli hoped he would be restored to a position of dignity, but to no avail. He died frustrated and, as in his youth, impoverished.

1469–92	1478–80	1494	1497
Lorenzo de' Medici unofficially rules Florence, despite the 1478 Pazzi Conspiracy, an attempted overthrow that left his brother Giuliano torn to shreds in the *duomo*.	A confusing set of overlapping wars breaks out among the papacy, Siena, Florence, Venice, Milan and Naples, as individual families broker secret pacts and the dwindling Tuscan population pays the price.	The Medici are expelled by Charles VIII of France, and Savonarola declares a theocratic republic with his Consiglia di Cinquecento.	Savonarola sets fire to art in Florence. Books, paintings, musical instruments et al go up in flames on the pious preacher's 'Bonfire of Vanities' on Florence's Piassa della Signoria.

A BLOW TO INTELLECTUAL THOUGHT

Savonarola's theocratic rule over Florence (1494–98) lasted just four years. His denunciation of decadence got him excommunicated and executed by Pope Alexander VI, who didn't appreciate Savonarola criticising his extravagant spending, illegitimate children and pursuit of personal vendettas. But Savonarola's short reign had an impact on Tuscany for centuries to come: it made the Church see a need to exert more direct control over the independent-minded region, and to guard against humanist philosophies that might contradict the Church's divine authority. This led to the Inquisition: heretical ideas were made punishable by death, which had an understandably chilling effect on intellectual inquiry. Celebrated universities in Pisa and Siena were subject to close scrutiny, and the University of Pisa was effectively closed for about 50 years until Cosimo I de' Medici (1519–74) reinaugurated it in 1543.

eye for art. Although he held no elected office, he served as ambassador for the Church, and through his behind-the-scenes diplomatic skills managed to finagle a rare 25-year stretch of relative peace for Florence. When a conspiracy led by competing banking interests exiled him from the city in 1433, some of Cosimo's favourite artists split town with him, including Donatello and Fra' Angelico.

But they weren't gone long: Cosimo's banking interests were too important to Florence, and after just a year he returned triumphant to crush his rivals, exert even greater behind-the-scenes control and sponsor masterpieces such as Brunelleschi's legendary dome for Florence's Duomo.

But sponsorship from even the most enlightened and powerful patrons had its downside: their whims could make or break artists and they attracted powerful enemies. Lorenzo de' Medici (Lorenzo Il Magnifico; 1449–92) was a legendary supporter of the arts and humanities, providing crucial early recognition and support for Leonardo da Vinci, Sandro Botticelli and Michelangelo Buonarroti, among others.

But after Lorenzo escaped an assassination attempt by a conspiracy among the rival Florentine Pazzi family, the king of Naples and the pope, the artists he supported had to look elsewhere for sponsorship until Lorenzo could regain his position. Religious reformer Savonarola took an even darker view of Lorenzo and the classically influenced art he promoted, viewing it as a sinful indulgence in a time of great suffering. When Savonarola ousted the Medici in 1494, he decided that their decadent art had to go, too, and works by Botticelli, Michelangelo and others are said to have gone up in flames in the massive 'Bonfire of the Vanities' on Florence's Piazza della Signoria.

Tuscany's Renaissance legacy was almost lost in the 1966 Great Flood of Florence that left thousands homeless and three million manuscripts and thousands of artworks under mud, stone and sewerage. Those heroes who helped dig the treasures from the mud are honoured as *gli angeli del fango* (angels of mud).

1498	1527–30	1633	1656
To test Savonarola's beliefs, rival Franciscans invite him to a trial by fire. He sends a representative to be burned in his place, but he is eventually tortured, hung and burned as heretic.	Florentines run the Medici out of town. The Republic of Florence holds out for three years, until the emperor's and pope's combined cannon power reinstalls the Medici.	Galileo Galilei is condemned for heresy in Rome. True to his observations of a pendulum in motion, the Inquisition's extreme measures yielded an opposite reaction: Enlightenment.	The plague kills at least 300,000 people across central and southern Italy.

Galileo

One of the most notable faculty members at the revitalised University of Pisa was a professor of mathematics named Galileo Galilei (1564–1642). To put it in mathematical terms, Galileo was a logical paradox: a Catholic who fathered three illegitimate children; a man of science with a poetic streak, who lectured on the dimensions of hell according to Dante's *Inferno;* and an inventor of telescopes whose head was quite literally in the clouds, yet who kept in close contact with many friends who were the leading intellectuals of their day.

Galileo's meticulous observations of the physical universe attracted the attention of the Church, which by the 16th century had a difficult relationship with the stars. Pope Paul III kept several astrologers on hand, and no major papal initiative or construction project could be undertaken without first using an astrolabe to search the sky for auspicious signs. Nevertheless, theologian (and sometime astrologer) Tommaso Campanella was found guilty of heresy for his views that emphasised observation.

Research into the universe's guiding physical principles was entrusted by Paul III to his consulting theologians, who determined from close examination of the scriptures that the sun must revolve around the earth.

Equipped with telescopes that he'd adjusted and improved, Galileo came to a different conclusion. His observations supported Nicolaus Copernicus' theory that the planets revolved around the sun, and a cautious body of Vatican Inquisitors initially allowed him to publish his findings as long as he also presented a case for the alternate view. But when Galileo's research turned out to be dangerously convincing, the Vatican reversed its position and tried him for heresy, too.

By then Galileo was quite ill, and his weakened state and widespread support may have spared him the usual heresy sentence of execution. Under official threat of torture, Galileo stated in writing that he may have overstated the case for the Copernican view of the universe, and was allowed to carry out his prison sentence under house arrest. Pope Urban VIII alternately indulged his further studies and denied him access to doctors, but Galileo kept on pursuing scientific research even after he began losing his sight. Meanwhile, Tommaso Campanella was taken out of prison and brought to Rome, where he became Urban VIII's personal astrologer in 1629.

Gold Gilt: Going for Baroque

With his astrologers on hand, the pope might have seen Italy's foreign domination coming. Far from cementing the Church's authority, the Inquisition created a power vacuum on the ground while papal authorities were otherwise occupied with lofty theological matters. While local Italian nobles and successful capitalists vied for influence, the Austrian Holy

See Galileo's preserved middle finger (and other body parts) in Florence's superb and wholly interactive Museo Galileo, next to the Uffizi. Online, explore Galileo's life, times, religious context and scientific advances in The Galileo Project (http://galileo. rice.edu).

1737	1760s	1765–90	1796–1801
Austrian empress Maria Theresa ends the Medici dynastic rule by installing her husband as grand duke of Tuscany. She remains the brains of the operation, reforming Tuscany from behind the scenes.	Florence, along with Venice, Milan and Turin, becomes an essential stop for British aristocrats on the Grand Tour, a trend that continues until the 1840s.	Enlightenment leader Leopold I continues his mother Maria Theresa's reforms. Moved by Cesare Beccaria's case for criminal justice reform, he makes Tuscany the first sovereign state to outlaw the death penalty.	Italy becomes a battleground between Napoleon, the Habsburgs and their Russian allies: Tuscans witness much of their cultural patrimony divvied up as spoils of war.

Roman Empress Maria Theresa took charge of the situation in 1737, and set up her husband Francis as the grand duke of Tuscany.

Napoleon Bonaparte took over swathes of Tuscany in 1799. So appreciative was Napoleon of the area's cultural heritage, in fact, that he decided to take as much as possible home with him. What he couldn't take he gave as gifts to various relatives – never mind that all those Tuscan villas and church altarpieces were not technically his to give. Following Napoleon's fall from grace in 1814, the emperor was ceremoniously exiled to the island of Elba in the Tuscan Archipelago, and Habsburg Ferdinando III took over the title of grand duke of Tuscany. However, Napoleon's sister Elisa Bonaparte and various other relations refused to budge from the luxe Lucchesi villas they had usurped; concessions were made to accommodate them all.

Still more expats arrived in Tuscany with the inauguration of Italy's cross-country train lines in 1840. Soon no finishing-school education could be complete without a Grand Tour of Italy, and the landmarks and museums of Tuscany were required reading. Train-loads of debutantes, dour chaperones and career bachelors arrived, setting the stage for EM Forster novels, Tuscan time-share investors and George Clooney wannabes.

Red & Black: A Chequered Past

While an upper-crust expat community was exporting Romantic notions about Italy, the country was facing harsh realities. Commercial agriculture provided tidy sums to absentee royal Austrian landlords while reducing peasants to poverty and creating stiff competition for small family farms. In rural areas, three-quarters of the family income was spent on a meagre diet of mostly grains. The promise of work in the burgeoning industrial sector lured many to cities, where long working

HABSBURG & MEDICI LEGACIES

Austrian Holy Roman Empress Maria Theresa (mother of 16 children – including the now-notorious Marie Antoinette) was a self-taught military strategist who put local potentates in check and pushed through reforms. She curbed witch burning, outlawed torture, established mandatory education and allowed Italian peasants to keep a modest share of their crops. She also ended the Medici dynastic rule and brought the Habsburgs' signature flashy style to Tuscany, kicking off a frenzy of redecoration that included flamboyant frescoes packed with cherubs, ornate architectural details (that were surely a nightmare to dust), and gilding whenever and wherever possible.

Perhaps fearing that her family's priceless art collection might factor into Maria Theresa's redecorating plans, the last Medici heiress, Anna Maria Luisa de' Medici, willed everything to the city of Florence upon her death in 1743, on the condition that it all must remain in the city.

1805–14	1840	1861	1871
Napoleon establishes himself as king of Italy, with the military assistance of Italian soldiers he'd conscripted; when his conscripts desert, Napoleon loses Tuscany to Grand Duke Ferdinando III in 1814 and is exiled to Elba.	Tourism arrives in Tuscany with the opening of the Leopolda railway, a 101km-long line connecting the Tuscan cities of Florence, Pisa and Livorno.	Two decades of insurrections culminate in a new Italian government, with a parliament and a king. Florence becomes Italy's capital in 1865, despite widespread poverty and periodic bread riots.	After French troops are withdrawn from Rome, the forces of the Kingdom of Italy defeat the Papal States to take power in Rome; the capital moves there from Florence.

hours and dangerous working conditions simply led to another dead end, and 70% of family income was still spent on food. Upward mobility was rare, since university admissions were strictly limited, and the Habsburgs were cautious about allowing locals into their imperial army or bureaucratic positions. Increasingly, the most reliable means for Tuscans to support their families was emigration to the Americas.

Austrian rule provided a common enemy that united Italians across provinces and classes. The Risorgimento (reunification period) was not so much a reorganisation of some previously unified Italian states (which hadn't existed since Roman times) as a revival of city-state ideals of an independent citizenry. The secret societies that had flourished right under the noses of the French as a local check on colonial control formed a network of support for nationalist sentiment. In 1848 and 1849 revolution broke out, and a radical government was temporarily installed in Florence.

Nervous that the Austrians would invade, conservative Florentine leaders invited Habsburg Leopold II to return as archduke of Tuscany. But when rural unrest in Tuscany made Austria's return to power difficult, Austrian retaliation and brutal repression galvanised nationalist sentiment in the region. Although Italy was united under one flag in 1861, this early split between radicals and conservatives would define the region's future political landscape.

Unification didn't end unemployment or unrest; only 2% of Italy's population gained the right to vote in 1861. Strikes were held to protest working conditions, and their brutal suppression gave rise to a new Socialist Party in 1881. The new Italian government's money-making scheme to establish itself as a colonial power in Abyssinia (modern-day Ethiopia and Eritrea) proved a costly failure: 17,000 Italian soldiers were lost near Adowa in 1896. When grain prices were raised in 1898, many impoverished Italians could no longer afford to buy food, and riots broke out. Rural workers unionised, and when a strike was called in 1902, 200,000 rural labourers came out en masse.

Finally Italian politicians began to take the hint and initiated some reforms. Child labour was banned, working hours set and the right to vote extended to all men over the age of 30 by 1912 (women would have to wait until 1945). But as soon as the government promised the Socialists to fund an old-age pension scheme, it reneged, and invaded Tunisia instead.

Italy got more war than it had budgeted for in 1914, when WWI broke out. A prominent young Socialist firebrand named Benito Mussolini (1883–1945) led the call for Italy to intervene in support of the Allies, though most Socialists were opposed to such an action. As a result, Mussolini was expelled from the Socialist Party and went on to join the Italian army. After being injured and discharged, he formed the Italian Combat Squad in 1919, the forerunner of the National Fascist Party.

Best Historical Reads

Renaissance Florence on Five Florins a Day (2010), Charles FitzRoy

Tuscany: A History (2011), Alistair Moffat

Queen Bee of Tuscany: The Redoubtable Janet Ross (2013), Ben Downing

1915	1921	1940–43	1943–45
Italy enters WWI fighting a familiar foe: the Austro-Hungarian Empire. War casualties, stranded POWs, heating-oil shortages and food rationing make for a hard-won victory by 1918.	Mussolini forms the Fascist Party, and Tuscan supporters fall in line by 1922. The 1924 elections are 'overseen' by Fascist paramilitary groups, and the Fascists win a parliamentary majority.	The Fascist Italian Empire joins Germany in declaring war on Great Britain and France. Italy surrenders in 1943; Mussolini refuses to comply and war continues.	The Italian Resistance joins the Allies against Mussolini and the Nazis; Tuscany is liberated. When civil warfare ends in 1945, a national coalition government is formed.

Inter-War Blues

Though Italy had been on the winning side in WWI, Tuscans were not in the mood to celebrate. In addition to war casualties, 600,000 of their fellow countrymen served time as prisoners of war, and 100,000 died primarily due to the Italian government's failure to send food, clothing and medical supplies to its own soldiers. Wartime decrees that extended working hours and outlawed strikes had made factory conditions so deplorable that women led mass strikes. Bread shortages and bread riots spread, and in 1919 violent uprisings broke out in the industrial towns of Viareggio and Piombino: the dismissal of 500 workers at the Piombino steel mills sparked off a general strike which rapidly degenerated into full-scale bloodshed between workers and armed forces.

Mussolini had clearly found support for his call to order in disgruntled Tuscany, and by 1922 his black-shirted squads could be seen parading through Florence, echoing his call for the ousting of the national government and the purging of socialists and communists from all local positions of power. In 1922 the Fascists marched on Rome and staged a coup d'etat, installing Mussolini as prime minister.

No amount of purging prevented the country from plunging into recession in the 1930s, after Mussolini demanded a revaluation of the Italian lira. While the free-fall of wages won Mussolini allies among industrialists,

THE CYCLIST, THE FRIAR & THE ACCOUNTANT

Unbelievable as it may sound, this trio became heroes of the Italian Resistance during WWII. Giorgio Nissim was a Jewish accountant in Pisa who belonged to a secret Tuscan Resistance group that helped Jewish Italians escape from fascist Italy. The network was discovered by the Fascists, and everyone involved was sent to concentration camps, except for Giorgio, who remained undetected. It seemed nowhere was safe for Jewish refugees – until Franciscan friar Rufino Niccacci helped organise the Assisi Underground, which hid hundreds of Jewish refugees from all over Italy in convents and monasteries across Umbria in 1943 and 1944. In Assisi, nuns who'd never met Jewish people before learned to cook kosher meals for their guests, and locals risked their lives to provide shelter to total strangers.

The next problem was getting forged travel documents to the refugees, and quickly. Enter Gino Bartali, world-famous Tuscan cyclist, Tour de France winner and three-time champion of the Giro d'Italia. After his death in 2003, documents revealed that during his 'training rides' during the war years, Bartali had carried Resistance intelligence and falsified documents that were used to transport Jewish refugees to safe locations. Suspected of involvement, Bartali was once interrogated at the dreaded Villa Triste in Florence, where political prisoners were held and tortured – but he revealed nothing. Until his death he refused to discuss his efforts to save Jewish refugees, even with his children, saying, 'One does these things, and then that's that.'

1946	1959–63	1966	1969
Umberto II is exiled after a referendum to make Italy a republic is successful; 71.6% of Tuscans vote for a republic.	Italy's economy revives via industrialisation, entrepreneurship and US Marshall Plan investments designed to stop it from joining the Soviet Bloc.	The Arno bursts its banks, submerging Florence in metres of mud and water. Some 5000 people are left homeless and thousands of art works and manuscripts destroyed.	Strikes and university-student uprisings demand social change and promote sweeping reforms, not just in working conditions but also housing, social services, pensions and civil rights.

it created further desperation among his power base. New military conquests in Libya and Ethiopia initially provided a feeble boost to the failing economy, but when the enormous bill came due in the late 1930s, Mussolini hastily agreed to an economic and military alliance with Germany. Contrary to the bold claims of Mussolini's propaganda machine, Tuscany and the rest of Italy was ill-prepared for the war it entered in 1940.

WWII & Tuscan Resistance

Florence was badly damaged during WWII, but it was not until the end of the war, following the occupation of the city by German troops on 11 September 1943, that the first bombs were dropped. Allied forces broke through the German line south of Rome in May 1944 and promptly rushed north to liberate Rome and all the territory in between. Forced to retreat, the Germans built a new defensive line using forced labour further north: the Gothic Line ran east from the Pisan coast – via Pisa, Lucca, Florence and eastern Tuscany – to the Adriatic Coast. Allied bombers immediately retaliated by taking out Florence's Campo di Marte train station and with it a precious supply line for the Germans; several hundred Florentine civilians were also killed. In neighbouring Pisa, the cathedral and Leaning Tower remained intact but the Camposanto was ruined, along with much of the old town.

A powerful Resistance movement emerged in Tuscany during WWII, but not soon enough to prevent hundreds of thousands of Italian casualties, plus a still-unknown number of Italians shipped to death camps in Germany and to 23 concentration camps in Italy, including one near Arezzo; in Florence, a stone in front of the city synagogue memorialises the 248 Jews from Florence who died in camps. Similar fates were shared by Jews in Siena, Pisa and other Tuscan towns.

German forces' final gift to Florence before leaving in August 1944 was to destroy all the bridges across the Arno in order to slow advancing Allied troops. Every bridge was blown up except for Ponte Vecchio, which Hitler ordered to be spared: the timelessly seductive view down the Arno from the new window Mussolini had specially punched in the bridge section of the Vasarian Corridor in anticipation of Hitler's visit to Florence in 1941 had obviously made a lasting impression on the Nazi leader.

Rise of the Tuscan Left

A new Italian government surrendered to the Allies in 1943, but Mussolini refused to concede defeat, and dragged Italy through two more years of civil war, Allied campaigns and German occupation. Tuscany emerged from these years redder than ever, and became a staunch Socialist power base.

Immediately after the war, three coalition governments succeeded one another. Italy became a republic in 1946 and the newly formed right-

The Light in the Ruins (2013) by New York best-selling author Chris Bohjalian paints a vivid portrait of the 'innermost ring of Dante's inferno' that was Tuscany during WWII. It tells the tale of the doomed love between an Italian noblewoman and a German soldier.

1970s–'80s	1993	1995	2005
The Anni di Piombo (Years of Lead) terrorise the country with extremist violence and reprisals; police kill anarchist Franco Serantini in Pisa, and Red Brigades kill Florence's mayor in 1986.	A car bomb at the Uffizi kills six and causes US$10 million damage to artworks. The Mafia is suspected, but never indicted. The same year 200,000 people protest Mafia violence.	Maurizio Gucci, heir to the Florence-born Gucci fashion empire, is gunned down outside his Milan offices. Three years later, his estranged wife Patrizia Reggiani is jailed for ordering his murder.	Regional elections see centre-left president Claudio Martini win a second term in office, confirming Tuscany as Italy's bastion of the left. He forges closer ties with the rest of Europe and with Tuscans abroad.

wing Democrazia Cristiana (Christian Democrats) won the first elections under the new constitution in 1948.

Until the 1980s the Partito Comunista Italiano (Italian Communist Party), despite being systematically kept out of government, played a crucial role in Tuscany's social and political development. The party was founded in the Tuscan port town of Livorno in 1921, and its huge popularity prompted the so-called Anni di Piombo (Years of Lead) in the 1970s, dominated by terrorism and social unrest. In 1978 the Brigate Rosse (Red Brigades, a group of young left-wing militants responsible for several bomb blasts and assassinations) claimed their most important victim – former Christian Democrat prime minister Aldo Moro. He was kidnapped in Rome, kept hostage for 54 days, then shot. A memorial next to Chiesa di San Francesco al Prato in Pistoia in northwestern Tuscany remembers Moro, his two bodyguards and three policemen killed during the initial kidnapping.

During the 1970s divorce and abortion became legal, and legislation was passed allowing women to keep their own names after marriage. The Regione Toscana was one of 15 regional governments with limited powers to be formed across the country, and from then on it was the red left in Tuscany that dominated local political debate.

Trouble at the Bank

Europe's ailing economy limped from bad to dire in 2012 in a financial crisis considered to be the worst since the 1930s Great Depression – and Tuscany found itself sucked in. The Tuscan crunch came with the Monte dei Paschi di Siena bank scandal. In 2013 the Banca Monte dei Paschi di Siena – Italy's third-largest lender and the world's longest-operating bank, in business in a gorgeous *palazzo* in Siena since 1472 – revealed losses of €730 million on a trio of derivative deals, made between 2007 and 2009 and hidden from regulators. While former high-ranking officials at the pedigree bank grappled with corruption, fraud and bribery allegations, the government came to the rescue with a €4.1 billion bail-out. Tuscan taxpayers, still reeling from the new home property tax and other tough austerity measures introduced by short-lived prime minister Mario Monti in 2011 and 2012, were far from impressed with such government 'spending'.

Restructuring at the bank, essential for survival, saw hundreds of the bank's 1900 branches close countrywide. But the fallout of the scandal reached far beyond job cuts. For decades 'il Monte' (as Tuscans know the bank) sustained Siena's vibrant cultural life. Through the foundation, Fondazione Monte dei Paschi di Siena, it funded part of the city's university, hospital, football team, Palio horse race and so on – effectively providing around 10% of Siena's local government budget. For Siena (and Tuscany) the social and economic impact of their sugar daddy's dramatic fall from grace was a grave cause for concern.

HISTORY TROUBLE AT THE BANK

Tuscany's regional government is headed by the president, elected every five years. In turn he is aided by 10 ministers and a legislative regional council comprising 65 members, also elected by proportional representation for the same five-year term. Keep tabs on regional government and council at www.regione.toscana.it and www.consiglio.regione.toscana.it respectively.

2008	2010	2012	2015
Silvio Berlusconi and his right-wing allies win a second seven-year term in office. Tuscany's traditional support of leftist candidates and parties is diluted, with support for the Rainbow Left coalition falling dramatically.	In regional elections famously red Tuscany stands firm against Berlusconi's governing centre-right coalition: Enrico Rossi becomes Tuscan's new centre-left president.	Italian cruise ship *Costa Concordia* sinks off the Tuscan coast, claiming 32 lives. The eventual removal of the wreckage in 2015 from the island of Giglio is the most costly in maritime salvage history.	The left emerges stronger than ever in Tuscany in regional elections. Incumbent centre-left president Enrico Rossi's Democratic Party (PD) lands 48.03% of votes, ensuring Rossi a second term in office.

The Tuscan Way of Life

Romanticised the world over, Tuscany has impassioned more writers, designers and filmmakers than any other region. Yet what is it that makes the birthplace of Gucci, Cavalli and the Vespa scooter so inspiring, so *dolce*? Florence takes the lead with its artistic heritage and tradition of master craftsmanship, its inhabitants whose natural style, grace and appreciation of beauty finds expression in an extraordinary attention to detail, quest for perfection and pride in local dialect and history. Enter the cornerstones of Tuscan lifestyle...

Rural Roots

Deeply attached to their patch of land, people in this predominantly rural neck of the woods, where there is only a sugar-dusting of small towns, are not simply Italian or Tuscan. Harking back to centuries of coexistence as rival political entities with their own styles of architecture, schools of painting, bell towers and so on, it is the *paese* (home town) or, in the case of Siena and other towns, the *contrada* (neighbourhood) in which one is born that reigns supreme. For most, such *campanilismo* (literally, loyalty to one's bell tower) is all-consuming. 'Better a death in the family than a Pisan at the door' says an old Florentine proverb, referencing the historic rivalry between the Tuscan towns.

Passionate, proud, reserved, hard-working, family-oriented, fond of food and wine, thrifty, extremely self-conscious and proud of their appearance are characteristics attributed to Tuscans across the board.

Brash, no, but in Florence Florentines like to make it known where they stand in society. From oversized doorknobs to sculpted stonework, overt statements of wealth and power are everywhere in this class-driven city, whose dialect – penned for the world to read by literary greats Dante, Boccaccio and Petrarch in the 14th century – is deemed the purest form of Italian.

Titled Florentines are still alive and well, accounting for a tiny fraction of contemporary Florentine society. From the 12th century until the

A PEASANT'S LIFE

Mezzadria (share-cropping), a medieval form of land management in place until 1979, was the key to success in the Tuscan countryside. *Contadini* (peasants) lived and worked on the land, receiving in return a home for their traditionally large families (typically numbering 10 – the more hands the better) and 50% of the crops or profit reaped from the land they worked. The other half went to the *padrone* (landowner) who often did not live on his *fattoria* (agricultural estate) but in the city.

Post-WWII industrialisation saw the invention of the tractor and the first shift in the equal balance between landowner and peasant: farmers had no money to buy tractors, obliging owners to invest instead and so upsetting the apple cart in terms of who gave how much. Gradually farm workers gravitated towards towns in search of better-paid jobs, the 1960s witnessing a particularly large exodus and so prompting the eventual collapse of share-cropping and many a Tuscan farm with it.

COFFEE CULTURE

Coffee is not just a drink but a way of life for Tuscans, whose typical day is regimentally punctuated with caffeine, the type of coffee depending wholly on time of day and occasion.

The number-one cardinal rule: cappuccino (espresso topped with hot, frothy milk), *caffè* latte (milkier version with less froth) and latte macchiato (warmed milk 'stained' with a spot of coffee) are only ever drunk at breakfast or in the early morning. If you're truly Tuscan, though, the chances are you'll probably grab a speed espresso (short, sharp shot of strong, black coffee) or *caffè doppio* (double espresso) standing up at the bar with everyone else at your favourite cafe on the way to work.

Lunch and dinner only end one way, with *un caffè* (literally 'a coffee', meaning an espresso and nothing else), although come dusk it is quite acceptable to perhaps finish with *un caffè corretto* (espresso with a dash of grappa or other spirit).

Sitting down at a table in a cafe to have a coffee is four times more expensive than drinking it standing at the bar.

Renaissance when wealth and ability overtook aristocratic ranking, titles of nobility – prince, duke, marquis, count, viscount, baron, patrician and noble – ruled the roost. Florentine nobility derived mainly from bankers and merchants, and many of the city's most wonderful properties and countryside estates remain in the hands of counts and barons – Europe's largest private walled garden, the Giardini di Torrigiani, is a prime example.

In the city, elderly nobles still gather each week at Florence's exclusive, elusive Circolo dell' Unione (aka 'club of nobles'), enthroned since 1852 in a *palazzo* on Florence's most aristocratic street Via de' Tournabuoni. Membership is not hereditary and costs (a lot). Some 60% of the club's 400-odd members (of which just a handful are female) bear a title – titles not actually recognised by the Italian state since 1948, following the fall of the Italian monarchy.

La Dolce Vita

Life is *dolce* (sweet) for this privileged pocket of Italy, one of the country's wealthiest enclaves where the family reigns supreme, and tradition and quality reign over quantity. From the great names in viticulture to the flower-producing industry of Pescia and the small-scale farms of rural Tuscany, it is family-run businesses handed down the generations that form the backbone of this proud, strong region.

In Florence – the only city with a faint hint of the cosmopolitan – daily life is the fastest paced. Florentines rise early, drop their kids at school by 8am then flit from espresso to the office by 9am. Lunch is a lengthy affair for these food- and wine-loving people, as is the early-evening *aperitivo*, enjoyed in a bar with friends to whet the appetite for dinner. For younger Florentines, who bear the biggest brunt of Florence's ever-rising rent and salaries that scarcely rise, it is quite common to treat the lavish *aperitivo* spread like dinner – enter *apericena*. Smokers, fast dwindling, puff on pavements outside.

There is no better time of day or week than late Sunday afternoon to witness the *passeggiata* (early evening stroll), a wonderful tradition that sees Tuscans in towns don a suitable outfit and walk – to get a gelato, chat, meet friends, mooch, contemplate the sunset and, quite simply, relish the close of the day at an exceedingly relaxed pace.

Theatre, concerts, art exhibitions (the free opening on Thursday evenings at Florence's Palazzo Strozzi is always packed) and *il calcio* (football) entertain after hours. Tuscany's top professional football club, ACF Fiorentina, has a fanatical fan base (check the memorabilia in Florence's Trattoria Mario).

Unesco World Heritage Sights

Historic centre of Florence

Piazza dei Miracoli, Pisa

Historic centre of Siena

Val d'Orcia

Historic centre of San Gimignano

Historic centre of Pienza

Medici villas and gardens, Tuscany

Weekends see many flee their city apartments for less urban climes, where the din of *motorini* (scooters) whizzing through the night lessens and there's more space and light: green countryside is a mere 15-minute getaway from lucky old Florence, unlike many urban centres where industrial sprawl really sprawls.

Casa Dolce Casa

By their very nature, family-orientated Tuscans travel little (many spend a lifetime living in the town of their birth) and place great importance on *casa dolce casa* (home sweet home) – the rate of home ownership in Tuscany is among Europe's highest.

Rural lifestyle is slavishly driven by close-knit, ancient communities in small towns and villages, where local matters and gossip are more important than national or world affairs. Everyone knows everyone to the point of being clannish, making assimilation for outsiders hard – if not impossible. Farming is the self-sufficient way of life, albeit one that is becoming increasingly difficult – hence the mushrooming of *agriturismi* (farm-stay accommodation), as farmers stoically utilise every resource they have to make ends meet.

At one time the domain of Tuscany's substantial well-off British population (there's good reason why playwright John Mortimer dubbed Chianti 'Chiantishire' in his 1988 novel and 1989 TV adaptation *Summer's Lease*), the region's bounty of stylish stone villas and farmhouses with terracotta floors, wood-burning fireplaces and terraces with views are now increasingly passing back into the hands of Tuscans eagerly rediscovering their countryside.

Urban or rural, children typically remain at home until they reach their 30s, often only fleeing the nest to wed. In line with national trends, Tuscan families are small – one or two kids; around 20% of families are childless and 25% of households consist of singles. Despite increasing numbers of women working, chauvinistic attitudes remain well entrenched in more rural areas.

La Festa

Delve into the mindset of a Tuscan and a holy trinity of popular folklore, agricultural tradition and religious rite of passage dances before your eyes – which pretty much translates as *la festa* (party!). No cultural agenda is more jam-packed with ancient festivity than theirs: patron saints

---

VIRTUAL TUSCAN LIFESTYLE

Girl in Florence (http://girlinflorence.com) Insider musings, reflections, practical tips and (excellent) recommendations from an American gal called Georgette, who's very much at home in Florence.

Emiko Davies (www.emikodavies.com) Travel, lifestyle and Tuscan musings and recipes by food photographer and cookbook author Emiko Davies; her exceedingly beautiful images of food transport you straight to her kitchen table in Florence.

One Hundred Years Later in Florence (http://bellabiker.blogspot.com) A New York executive follows her Italian ancestors to Florence and settles down to live and love the country her family abandoned in 1904.

Maple Leaf Mamma (www.mapleleafmamma.com) Sharp, pithy prose on navigating motherhood in a traditionally macho country, from a feminist perspective; penned by a Canadian in Florence.

A Dusty Olive Green (www.adustyolivegreen.com) A captivating photoblog by a Florence-based Danish photographer with a penchant for travel, portraits and interiors.

TUSCAN DESIGN

Never has Italian design been so expressive as in 1963 when Piaggio in Pontedera, 25km east of Pisa, launched the Vespa 50, a motorised scooter requiring no driving license. Overnight it became a 'must-have' item as Italy's young things snapped up the machine and the freedom and independence it gave. All of Europe's Vespas are still made in the Tuscan plant where the original 'wasp' was born in 1946.

While Audrey Hepburn was cruising around Rome side-saddle on a Vespa for Hollywood, a group of anti-establishment artists and architects were busy building a reputation for Florence as the centre of 1960s avant-garde design: design groups Radical Design, Archizoom and Superstudio were all founded in Florence in 1966, and included hot shots Florentines Massimo Morozzi (b 1941; buy his pasta set from Alessi) and Andrea Branzi (b 1938), whose furniture designs are timeless.

As with fashion, the design scene moved to Milan in the 1970s, starving Tuscany of its cutting edge.

alone provide weeks of celebration given that every village, town, profession, trade and social group has a saint they call their own and venerate.

La festa climaxes, not once but twice, with Siena's soul-stirring Il Palio, a hot-blooded horse race conceived in the 12th century to honour the Virgin Mary and revamped six centuries on to celebrate the miracles of the Madonna of Provenzano (2 July) and Assumption (16 August). Deeply embroiled in its religious roots is a fierce *contrada* rivalry, not to mention a fervent penchant for dressing up and a widespread respect of tradition. Horses are blessed before the race; jockeys ride bareback; and the silk banner for the winner of August's race is ritually designed by local Sienese artists, while July's is by non-Sienese.

Although it's by no means the social force it once was, Catholicism (the religion of 85% of the region) and its rituals nevertheless play a key role in daily lives: first Communions, church weddings and religious feast days are an integral part of Tuscan society.

Bella Figura

A sense of style is vital to Tuscans, who take great pride in their dress and appearance to ensure their *bella figura* (good public face). Dressing impeccably comes naturally to most, and for most Florentines, chic is a byword. Indeed, it was in their naturally beautiful city that the Italian fashion industry was born and bred.

Guccio Gucci and Salvatore Ferragamo got the haute-couture ball rolling in the 1920s with boutiques in Florence. And in 1951 a well-heeled Florentine nobleman called Giovanni Battista Giorgini held a fashion soirée in his Florence home to spawn Italy's first prêt-à-porter fashion shows. The catwalk quickly shifted to Florence's Palazzo Pitti, where Europe's most prestigious fashion shows dazzled until 1971 (when the women's shows moved to Milan). The menswear shows stayed put, though, and top designers still leg it to Florence twice a year to unveil their menswear collections at the Pitti Immagine Uomo fashion shows and their creations for *bambini* (kids) at Pitti Bimbo.

THE TUSCAN WAY OF LIFE BELLA FIGURA

Tuscan Icons

The Vespa scooter

Gucci

Chianti wine

Michelangelo's David

Renaissance art

The Tuscan Table

Be it by sinking your teeth into a beefy blue *bistecca alla fiorentina* (chargrilled T-bone steak), wine tasting in Chianti, savouring Livorno fish stew or devouring white truffles unearthed around San Miniato, travelling Tuscany is a memorable banquet of gastronomic and viticultural experiences.

A Country Kitchen

It was above an open wood fire in *la cucina contadina* (the farmer's kitchen) that Tuscan cuisine was cooked up. Its basic premise: don't waste a crumb.

During the 13th and 14th centuries, when Florence prospered and the wealthy started using silver cutlery instead of fingers, simplicity remained the hallmark of dishes served at lavish banquets thrown by feuding families as a show of wealth. And while the Medici passion for flaunting the finer things in life during the Renaissance gave Tuscan cuisine a fanciful kick, with spectacular sugar sculptures starring alongside spit-roasted suckling pig, ordinary Tuscans continued to rely on the age-old *cucina povera* (poor dishes) to keep hunger at bay.

Contemporary Tuscan cuisine remains faithful to these humble roots, using fresh local produce and eschewing fussy execution.

A Bloody Affair: Meat & Game

The icon of Tuscan cuisine is Florence's *bistecca alla fiorentina,* a chargrilled T-bone steak rubbed with olive oil, seared on the chargrill, seasoned, and served *al sangue* (blue and bloody). A born-and-bred rebel, this feisty cut of meat is weighed before it's cooked and priced on menus by *l'etto* or 100g. Traditionally it is from creamy Chianina cows, one of the oldest breeds of cattle originating from the wide green Val de Chiana in eastern Tuscany.

Tuscan markets conjure up animal parts many wouldn't dream of eating. In the past, prime beef cuts were the domain of the wealthy and offal was the staple peasant fare: tripe was simmered for hours with onions, carrots and herbs to make *lampredotto* or with tomatoes and herbs to make *trippa alla fiorentina* – two classics still going strong.

Pasto, an ancient mix of *picchiante* (cow's lungs) and chopped potatoes, is not even a gastronomic curiosity these days – due to lack of demand it has died a quiet death and it is no longer possible to find it on restaurant menus. Equally ancient *cibrèo* (chicken's kidney, liver, heart and cockscomb stew) and *colle ripieno* (stuffed chicken's neck) are both still cooked up, though. Another golden oldie featured on many a medieval fresco is *pollo al mattone* – boned chicken splattered beneath a brick, rubbed with herbs and baked beneath the brick. The end result is handsomely crispy.

Cinghiale (wild boar), hunted in autumn, is turned into *salsicce di cinghiale* (wild-boar sausages) or simmered with tomatoes, pepper and herbs to create a rich stew.

Best Bistecca alla Fiorentina

Trattoria Mario, Florence

All'Antico Ristoro di' Cambi, Florence

Ristorante Da Muzzicone, Castiglion Fiorentino

Officina della Bistecca, Panzano in Chianti

Osteria Acquacheta, Montepulciano

In Tuscany the family pig invariably ends up on the plate as a salty slice of *soprassata* (head, skin and tongue boiled, chopped and spiced with garlic, rosemary and other herbs and spices), *finocchiona* (fennel-spiced sausage), prosciutto, nearly black *mallegato* (spiked with nutmeg, cinnamon, raisins and pine kernels from San Miniato) or *mortadella* (a smooth-textured pork sausage speckled with cubes of white fat). *Lardo di colonnata* (thin slices of local pork fat aged in a mix of herbs and oils for at least six months) is a treat hard to find outside of Tuscany.

Best on Friday: Fish

Livorno leads the region in seafood: *cacciucco* (one 'c' for each type of fish thrown into it) is the signature dish. Deriving its name from the Turkish *kukut*, meaning 'small fry', *cacciucco* is a stew of five fish simmered with tomatoes and red peppers, served atop stale bread. *Triglie alla livornese* is red or white mullet cooked in tomatoes, and *baccalà alla livornese*, also with tomatoes, features cod traditionally salted aboard the ships en route to the old Medici port. *Baccalà* (salted cod), not to be confused with *stoccofisso* (unsalted air-dried stockfish) is a trattoria mainstay, served on Fridays as tradition and old-style Catholicism demands.

Poor Man's Meat: Pulses, Grains & Vegetables

Poor man's meat was precisely what pulses were to Tuscans centuries ago. Jam-packed with protein, cheap and available year-round (eaten fresh in summer, dried in winter), pulses go into traditional dishes like *minestra di fagioli* (bean soup), *minestra di pane* (bread-and-bean soup) and *ribollita* (a 'reboiled' bean, vegetable and bread soup with black cabbage, left to sit for a day before being served).

Of the dozens of bean varieties, *cannellini* and dappled *borlotti* are the most common; both are delicious drizzled with olive oil to accompany meat. The round yellow *zolfino* from Pratomagno and silky smooth

---

GO SLOW TUSCANY

Born out of a desire to protect the world from McDonaldisation, **Slow Food** (www .fondazioneslowfood.com) preserves local food traditions and encourages interest in the food we eat, its origins and how it tastes. Created by Italian wine writer Carlo Petrini, it works in over 130 countries and has also spawned **Slow City** (www.cittaslow.blogspot. com). Slow City towns – Anghiari, Barga, Castelnuovo Berardenga, Civitella in Val di Chiana, Greve in Chianti, Massa Marittima, Pratovecchio, San Miniato, San Vincenzo and Suvereto in Tuscany – have a visible and distinct culture: they rely on local resources rather than mass-produced food and culture; work to reduce pollution; and increasingly rely on sustainable development, such as organic farming and public transport.

Industrialisation, globalisation and environmental dangers threaten traditional, indigenous edibles. Enter Slow Food's **Ark of Taste**, a project born and headquartered in Florence that aims to protect and promote endangered food products including, in Tuscany: Chianina beef, *lardo di colonnata,* Certaldo onions, Casola chestnut bread, Cetica red potatoes, Garfagnana potato bread and *farro* (spelt), Carmignano dried figs, *cinta senese* (the indigenous Tuscan pig), Londa Regina peaches, Pistoian Mountain *pecorino* cheese, Orbetello *bottarga* (salted mullet roe) and Zeri lamb. Among the many cured meats that make the list: San Miniato *mallegato,* Prato mortadella (smooth-textured pork sausage made dull-pink with drops of alkermes liqueur and speckled white with cubes of fat), Sienese *buristo* (a type of pork salami made in the province of Siena), Valdarno *tarese* (a 50cm- to 80cm-long pancetta spiced with red garlic, orange peel and covered in pepper), Florentine *bardiccio* (fresh fennel-flavoured sausage encased in pig intestine and eaten immediately) and *biroldo* (spiced blood sausage made in Garfagnana from pig's head and blood).

Sampling any of these Tuscan items guarantees an authentic tasting experience.

sorano bean from Pescia are prized. Of huge local pride to farmers in Garfagnana is *farro della garfagnana* (spelt), an ancient grain grown in Europe as early as 2500 BC.

Tuscany's lush vegetable patch sees medieval vegetables grow alongside tomatoes. Wild fennel, black celery (braised as a side dish), sweet red onions (delicious oven-baked), artichokes and zucchini flowers (stuffed and oven-baked), black cabbage, broad beans, chicory, chard, thistle-like cardoons and green tomatoes are among the more unusual ones to look out for.

Prized as one of the most expensive spices, saffron is all the rage around San Gimignano where it was enthusiastically traded in medieval times. Fiery red and as fine as dust by the time it reaches the kitchen, saffron in its rawest state is the dried flower stigma of the saffron crocus.

Where's the Salt: Bread

One bite and the difference is striking: Tuscan *pane* (bread) is unsalted, creating a disconcertingly bland taste many a bread lover might never learn to love.

Yet it is this centuries-old staple, deliberately unsalted to ensure it lasted for a good week and to complement the region's salty cured meats, that forms the backbone of Tuscany's most famous dishes: *pappa al pomodoro* (bread-and-tomato soup), *panzanella* (tomato and basil salad mixed with a mush of bread soaked in cold water) and *ribollita*. None sound or look particularly appetising, but their depth of flavour is extraordinary.

Thick-crusted *pane toscana* is the basis of two antipasti delights: *crostini* (lightly toasted slices of bread topped with liver pâté) and *fettunta* or Tuscan bruschetta (also called *crogiantina*; toast fingers doused in garlic, salt and olive oil).

A Dowry Skill: Cheese

So important was cheesemaking in the past, it was a dowry skill. Still respected, the sheep's-milk *pecorino* crafted in Pienza ranks among Italy's greatest *pecorini*: taste it young and mild with fava beans, fresh pear or

Best Creative Tuscan

Il Santo Bevitore, Florence

La Bottega del Buon Caffè, Florence

Filippo, Pietrasanta

Osteria di Passignano, near Greve in Chianti

Antica Trattoria Aurora, Magliano in Toscana

DINING ETIQUETTE

➡ **Dress** Smart-casual is best, particularly in Florence and other cities and large towns where working urbanites go home to freshen up between *aperitivo* and dinner.

➡ **Courses** Don't feel obliged to order the Tuscan Full Monty; it's quite acceptable to order just one or two courses such as an *antipasto* (starter) and *primo* (pasta course), or even just a *secondo* (main course).

➡ **Bread** Is plentiful, unsalted and served without butter – or side plate (put it on the table).

➡ **Spaghetti** Twirl it around your fork as if you were born twirling – no spoons please.

➡ **Young children** It is perfectly acceptable to ask for a plate of plain pasta with butter and Parmesan.

➡ **Coffee** Never order a cappuccino after 11am, and certainly not after a meal when an espresso is the only respectable way to end a meal (with, perhaps, a digestive of grappa or other fiery liqueur).

➡ **Il conto** (the bill) Whoever invites pays.

➡ **Splitting the bill** Common enough.

➡ **Tipping** If there is no *servizio* (service charge included), leave 10% to 15% tip.

OLIVE OIL

Olive oil heads Tuscany's culinary trinity (bread and wine are the other two) and epitomises the earthy simplicity of Tuscan cuisine: dipping chunks of bread into pools of this liquid gold or biting into a slice of oil-doused *fettunta* (bruschetta) are sweet pleasures here.

The Etruscans were the first to cultivate olive trees and press the fruit to make oil, a process refined by the Romans. As with wine, strict rules govern when and how olives are harvested (October to December), the varieties used, and so on.

The best Tuscan oils wear a Chianti Classico DOP or Terre di Siena DOP label and have an IGP certificate of quality issued by the region's Consortium of Tuscan Olive Oil. In Florence look out for prize-wining oils from local olive oil producer Marchesi de' Frescobaldi.

chestnuts and honey; or try it mature and tangy, spiked with *toscanello* (black peppercorns) or as *pecorino di tartufo* (infused with black-truffle shavings). *Pecorino* massaged with olive oil during the ageing process turns red and is called *rossellino*.

Festive Frolics: Sweets, Chocolate & Ice

Be it the honey, almond and sugar-cane sweets served at the start of 14th-century banquets in Florence, or the sugar sculptures made to impress at the flamboyant 16th- and 17th-century feasts of the power-greedy Medici, *dolci* (sweets) have always been reserved for festive occasions. In more humble circles, street vendors sold *bomboloni* (doughnuts) and *pandiramerino* (rosemary-bread buns), while carnival in Florence was marked by *stiacchiata* (Florentine flat bread made from eggs, flour, sugar and lard, then dusted with icing sugar).

As early as the 13th century, servants at the Abbazia di Montecelso near Siena paid tax to the nuns in the form of *panpepato* (a pepper-and-honey flat bread), although legend tells a different tale: following a siege in Siena, Sister Berta baked a revitalising flat cake of honey, dried fruit, almonds and pepper to pep up the city's weakened inhabitants. Subsequently sweetened with spices, sprinkled with sugar and feasted on once a year at Christmas, Siena's *panforte* (literally 'strong bread') – a flat, hard cake with nuts and candied fruit – is now eaten year-round. An old wives' tale says it stops couples quarrelling.

Unsurprisingly, it was at the Florentine court of Catherine de' Medici that Italy's most famous product, gelato, first appeared thanks to court maestro Bernardo Buontalenti (1536–1608), who engineered a way of freezing sweetened milk and egg yolks. For centuries, ice cream and sherbets – a mix of shaved ice and fruit juice served between courses at Renaissance banquets to aid digestion – only appeared on wealthy tables.

Tuscan *biscotti* (biscuits) – once served with candied fruits and sugared almonds at the start of and between courses at Renaissance banquets – are dry, crisp and often double-baked. *Cantucci* are hard, sweet biscuits studded with almonds. *Brighidini di lamporecchio* are small, round aniseed-flavoured wafers; *ricciarelli* are almond biscuits, sometimes with candied orange; and *lardpinocchiati* are studded with pine kernels. In Lucca, locals are proud of their *buccellato* (a sweet bread loaf with sultanas and aniseed seeds), a treat given by godparents to their godchild on their first Holy Communion and eaten with alacrity at all other times.

Cibo biologico (organic food) is increasingly popular in farm-rich Tuscany, where stand-out dining choices (like Podere del Grillo near San Miniato, La Cerreta near Sassetta, Pisa's biOsteria 050) are designed around organic farm produce. In Florence 5 e Cinque is an outstanding vegetarian eatery; Vivanda marries organic cuisine with organic wine.

Buone Feste

Be it harvest, wedding, birth or religious holiday, traditional celebrations are intrinsically woven into Tuscan culinary culture. They are not as raucous as festivals of the past, when an animal was sacrificed, but most remain meaty affairs.

Tuscans have baked breads and cakes such as ring-shaped *berlingozzo* (Tuscan sweet bread) and *schiacciata alla fiorentina* (a flattish, spongey bread-cum-cake best made with old-fashioned lard) for centuries during Carnevale, the period of merrymaking leading up to Ash Wednesday. Fritters are another sweet Carnevale treat: *cenci* are plain twists (literally 'rags') of fried, sweet dough sprinkled with icing sugar; *castagnole* look like puffed-up cushions; and *fritelle di mele* are slices of apple battered, deep fried and eaten warm with sugar.

On Easter Sunday families take baskets of hard-boiled white eggs covered in a white-cloth napkin to church to be blessed, and return home to a luncheon feast of roast lamb gently spiced with garlic and rosemary, pre-empted by the blessed eggs.

September's grape harvest sees grapes stuck on top of *schiacciata* to make *schiacciata con l'uva* (grape cake), and autumn's chestnut harvest brings a flurry of chestnut festivals and *castagnaccio* (chestnut cake baked with chestnut flower, studded with raisins, topped with a rosemary sprig and served with a slice of ricotta) to the Tuscan table.

Come Christmas, *bollito misto* (boiled meat) with all the trimmings is traditional for many families: various animal parts, trotters et al, are thrown into the cooking pot and simmered for hours with a vegetable and herb stock. The meat is later served with mustard, green salsa and other sauces. A whole pig, notably the recently revived ancient white-and-black *cinta senese* indigenous breed, roasted on a spit, is the other option.

> Pasta is as much Tuscan as it is Italian, and no Tuscan banquet would be quite right without a *primo* (first course) of home-made *maccheroni* (wide, flat ribbon pasta), *pappardelle* (wider flat ribbon pasta) or Sienese *pici* (a thick, hand-rolled version of spaghetti) served with a duck, hare, rabbit or boar sauce.

On the Wine Trail

There's far more to this vine-rich region than cheap, raffia-wrapped bottled Chianti – *that* was the 1970s, darling! Something of a viticulture powerhouse, Tuscany excites oenophiles with its myriad full-bodied, highly respected reds. Wine tasting is an endless pleasure and the region is peppered with *enoteche* (wine bars) and *cantine* (wine cellars) designed especially for tasting and buying.

Many are planted on Tuscany's *strade del vino* (wine roads), signposted itineraries that lead motorists and cyclists along wonderfully scenic back roads into the heart of Tuscan wine country.

TOP THREE WINE & OIL ROADS

Meander past olive groves, vines and farms plump with local produce with these delightful *Strade del Vino & dell'Olio*.

Strada del Vino e dei Sapori Colli di Maremma (www.stradavinimaremma.it) This route southeast of Grosseto highlights several DOC and DOCG wines, extra-virgin olive oil Toscano IGP, and the Maremma breed of cattle.

Strada del Vino e dell'Olio Lucca Montecarlo e Versilia (www.stradavinoeoliolucca.it) Seravezza in the Apuane Alps to Lucca, then east to Montecarlo and Pescia: features Lucca's famous DOP olive oil and the Colline Lucchesi and Montecarlo di Lucca DOCs.

Strada del Vino e dell'Olio Costa degli Etruschi (www.lastradadelvino.com) Scenic 150km itinerary along the Etruscan Coast from Livorno to Piombino and then over to the Tuscan island of Elba: super Tuscan Sassicaia is the big tasting highlight.

LABELS OF QUALITY

....

Quality and origin of Tuscan wine is flagged with these official classifications:

DOC (Denominazione d'Origine Controllata; Protected Designation of Origin) Must be produced within a specified region using defined methods to meet a certain quality; the rules spell out production area, grape varietals and viticultural/bottling techniques.

DOCG (Denominazione d'Origine Controllata e Garantita; Protected Designation of Origin and Quality) The most prestigious stamp of quality, DOCG wines are particularly good ones, produced in subterritories of DOC areas. Of Italy's 44 DOCGs, eight are Tuscan – Brunello di Montalcino, Carmignano, Chianti, Chianti Classico, Morellino di Scansano, Vernaccia di San Gimignano, Vino Nobile di Montepulciano and Elba Aleatico Passito.

IGT (Indicazione Geografica Tipica; Protected Geographical Indication) High-quality wines that don't meet DOC or DOCG definitions, such as Super Tuscans.

Tuscan white amounts to one label loved by Renaissance popes and artists alike: the aromatic Vernaccia di San Gimignano, best drunk as an *aperitif* on a terrace in or around San Gimignano.

Brunello di Montalcino

Brunello is up there at the top with Italy's most prized: count on up to €15 for a glass, €30 to €100 for an average bottle and €5000 for a 1940s collectible. The product of Sangiovese grapes grown south of Siena, it must spend at least two years ageing in oak. It is intense and complex with an ethereal fragrance, and is best paired with game, wild boar and roasts. Brunello grape rejects go into Rossi di Montalcino, Brunello's substantially cheaper but wholly drinkable kid sister.

Vino Nobile di Montepulciano

Prugnolo Gentile grapes (a clone of Sangiovese) form the backbone of the distinguished Vino Nobile di Montepulciano. Its intense but delicate nose and dry, vaguely tannic taste make it the perfect companion to red meat and mature cheese.

Chianti

This cheery, full and dry fellow is known the world over as being easy to drink, suited to any dish and wholly affordable. More famous than good in the 1970s, contemporary Chianti gets the thumbs up from wine critics today. Produced in seven subzones from Sangiovese and a mix of other grape varieties, Chianti Classico – the traditional heart of this long-standing wine-growing area – is the best known, with a DOCG (Denominazione d'Origine Controllata e Garantita; Protected Designation of Origin and Quality) guarantee of quality and a Gallo Nero (Black Cockerel) emblem that once symbolised the medieval Chianti League. Young, fun Chianti Colli Senesi from the Siena hills is the largest subzone; Chianti delle Colline Pisane is light and soft in style; and Chianti Rùfina comes from the hills east of Florence.

Super Tuscans

One result of Chianti's 'cheap wine for the masses' reputation in the 1970s was the realisation by some Tuscans – including the Antinoris, Tuscany's most famous wine-producing family – that wines with a rich, complex, internationally acceptable taste following the New World tradition of blending varieties could be sold for a lot more than local wines. Thus, innovative, exciting wines were developed and cleverly marketed to appeal to buyers both in New York and in Florence. And when an

Best Wine Tasting in situ

....

Antinori nel Chianti Classico, Chianti

....

Badia a Passignano, Chianti

....

Castello di Ama, Chianti

....

Poggio Antico, Montalcino

....

Cantina del Redi, Montepulciano

English-speaking scribe dubbed the end product 'Super Tuscans', the name stuck. (Although Italian winemakers prefer the term IGT – Indicazione Geografica Tipica.) Sassacaia, Solaia, Bolgheri, Tignanello and Luce are all superhot Super Tuscans.

More and more international wine producers are turning to Tuscan soil to blend Super Tuscans and other modern wines. American-owned Castello Banfi, in the Tuscan biz for over three decades, scooped the prestigious Vinitaly wine prize in 2011 and continues to impress the international wine world, quietly underscoring the demise of wine-making as the exclusive domain of old, blue-blooded Tuscan wine-making families. These days, in this ancient land first cultivated by the Etruscans, Tuscany's oldest craft is open to anyone with wine-wizardry nous.

Celebrity Wine

With the birth of Super Tuscans, a gaggle of celebrity-backed wine was born: Sting owns an estate near Figline Valdarno in Chianti, where he produces a Chianti Colli Aretini known as Il Serrestori (after the silk-weaving family who once owned his pad), sold under his own private label, in a limited number of signed bottles.

Sinatra Family Estates (yes, that's Frank) owns a 3-hectare vineyard in the Fiesole hills near Florence, where grapes are grown to make La Voce (literally 'the Voice'), a limited-edition Super Tuscan blend of Colorino and Sangiovese grapes.

Other celebrity wines to look out for are the Super Tuscan reds produced by the son of Florentine designer Roberto Cavalli at Tenuta degli Dei outside Panzano in Chianti (top-of-the-range bottles are packaged in a typical Cavalli, flashy leopard-skin box); and those produced southeast of Pisa on the family estate of opera singer Andrea Bocelli, sold at Cantina Bocelli in La Sterza.

If celebrity design is more your cup of tea, taste wine at the subterranean, design-driven **Rocca di Frassinello** (www.roccadifrassinello.it) winery near Grossetto by architect Renzo Piano; or the equally breathtaking **Petra** (www.petrawine.it) winery by Swiss architect Mario Botta in the Etruscan hills near Suvereto.

Then, of course, there is the spectacular Antinori cellar in Bargino, ground-breaking in design – quite literally: an entire hillside in the heart of Chianti Classico was dug up, a designer cellar was popped inside and earthed over, and new vines were planted leaving just two giant slashes (the panoramic terraces of the 26,000 sq metre building) visible from the opposite rolling Chianti hill.

Best Wine Bars

....

Le Volpi e l'Uva, Florence

....

Il Santino, Florence

....

Enoteca Marcucci, Pietrasanta

....

Enoteca Tognoni, Bolgheri

....

Enoteca dei Difficili, Suvereto

....

Tuscany on Page & Screen

It's no wonder that so many books, films and television productions are set in Tuscany. Few places have such a rich history and landscape to draw on for inspiration, and even fewer offer authors, actors and crews such a sybaritic location in which to research, write and shoot their works. The birthplace of Italian literature (courtesy of the great Dante Alighieri) and the setting for the greatest Italian film of recent decades (*Life is Beautiful*), Tuscany offers the visitor plenty of options when it comes to pre-departure reading and viewing.

Tuscany in Print

The region's literary heritage and culture is rich, varied and one that continues to nurture both local and foreign writers to this day.

Local Voices

Prior to the 13th century, Italian literature was written in Latin – but all that changed with Florentine-born Dante Alighieri (c 1265–1321). One of the founders of the Dolce Stil Novo (Sweet New Style) literary movement, whose members wrote lyric poetry in the Tuscan vernacular, Dante went on to use the local language when writing the epic poem that was to become the first, and greatest, literary work published in the Italian language: *La grande commedia* (The Great Comedy), published around 1317 and later renamed *La divina commedia* (The Divine Comedy) by his fellow poet Boccaccio. Divided into three parts – *Inferno, Purgatorio* and *Paradiso* – The Divine Comedy delivered an allegorical vision of the afterlife that made an immediate and profound impression on readers and, through its wide-reaching popularity, established the Tuscan dialect as the new standardised form of written Italian.

Another early adaptor to the new language of literature was Giovanni Boccaccio (1303–75), who hailed from Certaldo. His masterpiece, *The Decameron*, was written in the years following the plague of 1348. A collection of 100 allegorical tales recounted by 10 characters, it delivered a vast panorama of personalities, events and symbolism to contemporary readers and was nearly as popular and influential as *The Divine Comedy*.

The remaining member of the influential triumvirate that laid down the course for the development of a rich literature in Italian was Petrarch (Francesco Petrarca; 1304–74), born in Arezzo to Florentine parents. Although most of his writings were in Latin, he wrote his most popular works, the poems, in Italian. *Il canzoniere* (Songbook; c 1327–68) is the distilled result of his finest poetry. Although the core subject is his unrequited love for a woman named Laura, the breadth of human grief and joy is treated with a lyrical quality hitherto unmatched. His influence spread far and across time: the Petrarchan sonnet form, rhyme scheme and even subject matter was adopted by English metaphysical poets of 17th-century England such as John Donne.

> Food forms the subject of many Tuscan memoirs. Two worth reading are *A Culinary Traveller in Tuscany: Exploring & Eating Off The Beaten Track* (Beth Elon; 2006) and *The Tuscan Year: Life and Food in an Italian Valley* (Elizabeth Romer; 1985).

TUSCAN MEMOIRS

Many people visit Tuscany and dream of purchasing their own piece of paradise. The following writers did just that, some establishing wildly successful literary franchises in the process.

Kinta Beevor (*A Tuscan Childhood;* 1993) A beautiful evocation of life in the Tuscan countryside between the two world wars, by the daughter of an English painter who bought a castle in Tuscany and hobnobbed with the likes of DH Lawrence, Aldous Huxley et al.

Eric Newby (*A Small Place in Italy;* 1994) The original Tuscan memoir: Newby bought a farmhouse in northeast Tuscany in the 1960s and so came to pen this sensitive portrait of rural Tuscany, its people, seasons and ancient rituals.

Frances Mayes (*Under the Tuscan Sun: At Home in Italy; Bella Tuscany; In Tuscany; Every Day in Tuscany;* 1996–2010) Following the end of her marriage, American writer and poet (and subsequent Tusan bard) bought a dilapidated house in Cortona, did it up and wrote about it in *Under the Tuscan Sun* – a classic today.

Ferenc Máté (*The Hills of Tuscany; A Vineyard in Tuscany: A Wine-Lover's Dream; The Wisdom of Tuscany;* 1999–2009) The author and his wife, a painter, left New York for Tuscany's Montalcino vineyards in 1990 – the abandoned farm they bought anchors a wine-producing estate today.

Mark Gordon Smith (*Tuscan Echoes; Tuscan Light: Memories of Italy;* 2003–2007) It's the tiny details of nature, season and cuisine that stand out in the short-story prose of this English writer who spent his early childhood in Tuscany.

Another outstanding writer of this period was Niccolò Machiavelli (1469–1527), known above all for his work on power and politics, *Il Principe* (The Prince; 1532).

The 19th Century Onwards

After its stellar start during the Renaissance, Tuscany took a literary break in the 17th and 18th centuries. It wasn't until the 19th century that the scene started to regain some momentum.

Giosue Carducci (1835–1907) was one of the key figures of 19th-century Tuscan literature. Born in the Maremma, he spent the second half of his life in Bologna. The best of his poetry, written in the 1870s, ranged in tone from pensive evocation of death (such as in 'Pianto antico') or memories of youthful passion ('Idillio Maremmano') to a historic nostalgia harking back to the glories of ancient Rome.

Florence's Aldo Palazzeschi (1885–1974) was in the vanguard of the Futurist movement during the pre-WWI years. In 1911 he published arguably his best work, *Il codice di Perelà* (Perelà's Code), an at times bitter allegory that in part becomes a farcical imitation of the life of Christ.

Another Florentine, Vasco Pratolini (1913–91), set four highly regarded Neorealist novels in his birthplace: *Le ragazze di San Frediano* (1949), *Cronaca familiare* (1947), *Cronache di poveri amanti* (1947) and *Metello* (1955).

Tuscan-born Dacia Maraini (b 1936), for many years the partner of author Alberto Moravia, is one of Italy's most lauded contemporary writers, with novels, plays and poetry to her credit. Her best-known works include *Buio* (1999), which won the Premio Strega, Italy's most prestigious literary award, and *La lunga vita di Marianna Ucrìa* (published in English as *The Silent Duchess;* 1990).

Britons Abroad

Pictures from Italy (Charles Dickens; 1846)

Along the Road (Aldous Huxley; 1925)

Etruscan Places (DH Lawrence; 1932)

Through Foreign Eyes

The trend of setting English-language novels in Tuscany kicked off during the era of the Grand Tour, when wealthy young men from Britain and Northern Europe travelled around Europe to view the cultural legacies of classical antiquity and the Renaissance, completing their liberal educations and being introduced to polite society in the process. The Grand Tour's heyday was from the mid-17th century to the mid-19th century.

With the advent of rail travel in the 1840s, the prospect of a cultural odyssey opened to the middle classes. Wealthy travellers from Britain, America and Australasia flocked to Italy, some of whom wrote about their experiences. Notable among these were Henry James, who set parts of *The Portrait of a Lady* (1881) and *Roderick Hudson* (1875) here; George Eliot, whose *Romola* (1862) was set in 15th-century Florence; and EM Forster, who set *A Room with a View* (1908) in Florence and *Where Angels Fear to Tread* (1905) in San Gimignano (fictionalised as Monteriano).

Things slowed down in the early 20th century, with only a few major novelists choosing to set their work here. These included Somerset Maugham (*Up at the Villa;* 1941) and Aldous Huxley (*Time Must Have a Stop;* 1944).

Americans Abroad
....
Italian Hours (Henry James; 1909)
....
The Stones of Florence (Mary McCarthy; 1956)
....
The City of Florence (RWB Lewis; 1995)

TUSCANY ON PAGE & SCREEN TUSCANY IN PRINT

MURDER IN TUSCANY

Tuscany features as the setting for some compelling crime fiction written by local and foreign authors.

Michael Dibdin His popular Aurelio Zen novels include *And Then You Die* (2002), set on the Tuscan coast.

Michele Giuttari A former high-ranking Florentine policeman, Giuttari has set five of his Michele Ferrara novels here: *A Florentine Death* (2008), *A Death in Tuscany* (2009), *Death of a Mafia Don* (2010), *The Black Rose of Florence* (2012) and *Death Under a Tuscan Sun* (2015).

Lucretia Grindle The Inspector Pallioti novels – *The Faces of Angels* (2006), *The Villa Triste* (2010) and *The Lost Daughter* (2011) – are set in Florence.

John Spencer Hill The late Canadian writer set two historical crime titles here: *The Last Castrato* (1995) in Florence and *Ghirlandaio's Daughter* (1996) in Lucca.

Christobel Kent Her Florentine-based private detective Sandro Cellini features in *A Florentine Revenge* (2006), *A Time of Mourning* (aka *The Drowning River;* 2009), *A Fine and Private Place* (aka *Murder in Tuscany;* 2010), *The Dead Season* (2012) and *A Darkness Descending* (2013).

Magdalen Nabb The prolific British crime writer wrote 14 novels featuring Florentine policeman Marshal Guarnaccia.

Iain Pears The Jonathan Argyll/Flavia di Stefano series includes *The Raphael Affair* (1991), set in Siena; *Giotto's Hand* (1994), set in Florence; and *The Immaculate Deception* (2000), set in various Tuscan locations.

Marco Vichi This Florence-born writer is best known for his Inspector Bordelli series, set in 1960s Florence. The fifth, most recent book, *Death in the Tuscan Hills* (2015), moves into the surrounding countryside.

Elizabeth George In *Just One Evil Act* (2013), the first of the Lynley books to be set outside Britain, Detective Sergeant Havers travels to Lucca and Barga in search of a kidnapped child.

THE REAL ADVENTURES OF PINOCCHIO

A timeless tale of a wooden puppet that turns into a boy, Le avventure di Pinocchio (The Adventures of Pinocchio) is among the most widely read and internationally popular pieces of literature ever to emerge from Italy.

In the early 1880s, Carlo Collodi (1826–90), a Florentine journalist, wrote a series for Il Giornale dei Bambini, the first Italian newspaper for children. Entitled Storia di un burattino (Story of a Puppet) and subsequently renamed, it would have made Collodi (real name Lorenzini) a multimillionaire had he lived to exploit the film and translation rights.

The character of Pinocchio is a frustrating mix of the likeable and the odious. At his worst he's a wilful, obnoxious, deceitful little monster who deserves just about everything he gets. Humble and blubbering when things go wrong, he has the oh-so-human tendency to resume his wayward behaviour when he thinks he's in the clear.

The story, weaving between fantasy and reality, is a mine of references, some more veiled than others, to the society of late-19th-century Italy – a troubled country with enormous socio-economic problems compounded by the general apathy of those in power. Pinocchio waits the length of the story to become a real boy. But, while his persona may provoke laughter, his encounters with poverty, petty crime, skewed justice and just plain bad luck constitute a painful education in the machinations of the 'real' world.

Disney made a much-loved animated film of the story in 1940. It won two Academy Awards – one for Best Original Score and one for Best Original Song ('When You Wish Upon a Star'). A number of Italian adaptations have also been made, including one directed by Roberto Benigni in 2002.

In recent decades, a number of highly regarded novels have been set in Tuscany. Perhaps the best known of these is the Renaissance fiction by English writer Linda Proud, whose Botticelli trilogy – A Tabernacle for the Sun, Pallas and the Centaur and The Rebirth of Venus – is set in Renaissance Florence during the Pazzi Conspiracy, the Medici exile and the rise of Savonarola. The historical detail in all three is exemplary, and each is a cracking good read. Her novel about Botticelli's master Fra' Filippo Lippi, A Gift for the Magus, was published in 2012.

Other writers who have used Renaissance Florence as a setting include Sarah Dunant (The Birth of Venus; 2003), Salman Rushdie (The Enchantress of Florence; 2008), Michaela-Marie Roessner-Hermann (The Stars Dispose; 1997, and The Stars Dispel; 1999) and Jack Dann (The Memory Cathedral; 1995). Of these, Dann wins the prize for constructing the most bizarre plot, setting his novel in a version of the Renaissance in which Leonardo da Vinci actually constructs a number of his inventions (eg the flying machine) and uses them during a battle in the Middle East while in the service of a Syrian general.

Also set in Florence are Innocence (1986) by Booker Prize–winning novelist Penelope Fitzgerald, which is set during the 1950s; The Sixteen Pleasures (1994) by Robert Hellenga, set after the devastating flood of 1966; The English Patient (1992) by Michael Ondaatje; and Inferno (2013) by Dan Brown of The De Vinci Code fame (or should that be infamy?).

Don't Miss

Life is Beautiful

A Room with a View

The Night of the Shooting Stars

Tuscany on Film

Cinema heavyweight Franco Zeffirelli was born in Florence in 1923 and has set many of his films in the region. His career has taken him from radio and theatre to opera (both stage productions and film versions) and his films include Romeo and Juliet (1968), Brother Sun, Sister Moon (1972), Hamlet (1990) and the semi-autobiographical Tea with Mussolini

(1999). Watch snippets of the latter as part of an engaging cinematic montage of films set in Florence at the city's Museo Novecento.

Actor, comedian and director Roberto Benigni was born near Castiglion Fiorentino in 1952. He picked up four Oscars and created a genre all of his own – Holocaust comedy – with the extraordinarily powerful *La vita é bella* (Life is Beautiful; 1998), a film shot in the east Tuscan town of Arezzo that he directed, co-wrote and starred in. Often compared with Charlie Chaplin and Buster Keaton, he has directed nine films (two set in Tuscany) and acted in many more, including three directed by American independent film-maker Jim Jarmusch.

Four films based on neo-realist novels by Vasco Pratolini were shot in Florence: *Le ragazze di San Frediano* (The Girls of San Frediano; Valerio Zurlini; 1954), *Cronache di poveri amanti* (Chronicle of Poor Lovers; Carlo Lizzani; 1954), *Cronaca familiare* (Family Diary; Valerio Zurlini; 1962) and *Metello* (Mauro Bolognini; 1970).

Award-winning film-makers Paolo and Vittorio Taviani were born in San Miniato and have set parts of three of their films in Tuscany: *La notte di San Lorenzo* (The Night of the Shooting Stars; 1982), *Le affinità elettive* (Elective Affinities; 1996) and *Good Morning Babylon* (1987).

Decameron on Screen

Decameron Nights (Hugo Fregonese; 1953)

⋯⋯⋯⋯⋯⋯⋯

Decameron (Pier Paolo Pasolini; 1971)

⋯⋯⋯⋯⋯⋯⋯

Virgin Territory (David Leland; 2007)

ON LOCATION IN TUSCANY

Tuscany has long been a popular location for international film and TV shoots. The following are among the best:

➜ *The English Patient* (Anthony Minghella; 1996) Includes scenes shot in a monastery outside Pienza but is predominantly remembered for its lyrically beautiful sequence when Kip (Naveen Andrews) takes Hana (Juliette Binoche) into Arezzo's Cappella Bacci and hoists her aloft on ropes so that she can see Piero della Francesca's frescoes in the illumination of a flare.

➜ *Gladiator* (Ridley Scott; 2000) Those glorious shots of fields of wheat rippling in the breeze were shot near Pienza.

➜ *Hannibal* (Ridley Scott; 2001) Parts of the sequel to *The Silence of the Lambs* were shot in Florence.

➜ *Much Ado about Nothing* (Kenneth Branagh; 1993) Branagh, Emma Thompson and Keanu Reeves star in this adaptation of Shakespeare's comedy; shot in Chianti.

➜ *Quantum of Solace* (Marc Forster; 2008) The 22nd Bond film featured great action sequences shot in Carrara and Siena.

➜ *A Room with a View* (James Ivory; 1985) Hugely popular period adaptation of EM Forster's 1908 novel set in Florence; there was also a 2007 UK ITV adaptation by Andrew Davies.

➜ *September Affair* (William Dieterle; 1950) Joseph Cotten and Joan Fontaine fall in love in Florence; features Kurt Weill's famous 'September Song'.

➜ *Stealing Beauty* (Bernardo Bertolucci; 1996) In her first film role, Liv Tyler grapples with her grief and burgeoning sexuality in the lush Tuscan countryside.

➜ *Up at the Villa* (Philip Haas; 2000) Sean Penn and Kristin Scott Thomas star in an adaptation of Somerset Maugham's novel.

➜ *Where Angels Fear to Tread* (Charles Sturridge; 1991) A fine cast including Helen Mirren, Judy Davis and Helena Bonham Carter stars in this period film shot in San Gimignano.

➜ *Inferno* (Ron Howard; 2016) Film adaptation of Dan Brown's 2013 novel, starring Tom Hanks waking up in a Florentine hospital; shot on location in Florence, Venice and Istanbul.

Art & Architecture

In many respects, the history of Tuscan art is also the history of Western art. Browse through any text on the subject and you'll quickly develop an understanding of how influential the Italian Renaissance, which kicked off and reached its greatest flowering in Florence, has been over the past 500 years. Indeed, it's no exaggeration to say that architecture, painting and sculpture rely on its technical innovations and take inspiration from its major works to this very day.

The Etruscans

Top Etruscan Museums

Museo Etrusco Guarnacci, Volterra

Museo dell'Accademia Etrusca, Cortona

Museo Civico Archeologico 'Isidoro Falchi', Vetulonia

Museo Archeologico Nazionale 'Gaio Cilnio Mecenate', Arezzo

Roughly 2800 years before we all started dreaming of a hilltop getaway in Tuscany, the Etruscans had a similar idea: hill towns that they founded are dotted throughout the countryside.

From the 8th to the 3rd centuries BC, Etruscans held their own against friends, Romans and countrymen, worshipped their own gods and goddesses, and farmed lowlands using sophisticated drainage systems of their own invention. How well they lived between sieges and war is unclear, but they sure knew how to throw a funeral. Etruscan *necropoli* (tombs) are found throughout southern, central and eastern Tuscany. Excavation of these tombs often yields a wealth of jewellery, cinerary urns (used for body ashes) made from terracotta and alabaster, earthenware pottery (particularly the glossy black ceramic known as *bucchero*) and bronze votive offerings.

Of course, the Romans knew a good thing when they plundered it. After conquering swathes of Etruscan territory in Tuscany in the 3rd century BC, they incorporated the Etruscans' highly refined, geometric style into their own art and architecture.

Enter Christianity

Roman centurions weren't in the area for long before Christianity began to take hold. After abandoning his studies and a promising career in Rome to adopt the contemplative life around AD 500, a young man from the region named Benedict went on to achieve a number of miracles, personally establish 12 monasteries and inspire the founding of many more. His story is visually narrated in great detail in the stunning fresco series (1497–1505) by Il Sodoma and Luca Signorelli in the Great Cloister at Abbazia di Monte Oliveto Maggiore, near Siena.

One early Benedictine monastery, San Pietro in Valle, was built in neighbouring Umbria by order of the Lombard duke of Spoleto, Faroaldo II. It kick-started a craze for the blend of Lombard and Roman styles known as Romanesque, and many local ecclesiastical structures were built in this style. The basic template was simple: a stark nave stripped of extra columns ending in a domed apse, surrounded by chapels usually donated by wealthy patrons.

In the 11th century the Romanesque style acquired a distinctly Tuscan twist in Pisa, when the coloured marble banding and veneering of the city's *duomo* (cathedral) set a new gold standard for architectural decoration. This new style (sometimes described as Pisan) was then applied to a swath of churches throughout the region, including the Chiesa di San Miniato al Monte, in Florence, and the Chiesa di San Michele in Foro and Cattedrale di San Martino, both in Lucca.

Siena was not about to be outdone in the architectural stakes by its rivals, Florence and Pisa, and so in 1196 its city council approved a no-expenses-spared program to build a new *duomo*. They certainly got their money's worth, ending up with a spectacular Gothic facade by Giovanni Pisano, a pulpit by Nicola Pisano and a rose window designed by Duccio di Buoninsegna.

While Tuscany's churches were becoming increasingly more spectacular, nothing prepared pilgrims for what they would find inside the upper and lower churches of the Basilica di San Francesco in Assisi, Umbria. Not long after St Francis' death in 1226, an all-star team of Tuscan artists was hired to decorate these churches in his honour, kicking off a craze for frescoes that wouldn't abate for centuries. Cimabue, Giotto, Pietro Lorenzetti and Simone Martini captured the life and gentle spirit of St Francis while his memory was still fresh in the minds of the faithful. For medieval pilgrims unaccustomed to multiplexes and special effects, entering a space that had been covered from floor to ceiling with stories told in living colour must have been a dazzling, overwhelming experience.

The Middle Ages: the Rise of the Comune

While communities sprang up around hermits and holy men in the hinterlands, cities began taking on a life of their own from the 13th and 14th centuries. Roman road networks had been serving as handy trade routes starting in the 11th century, and farming estates and villas began to spring up outside major trading centres as a new middle class of merchants, farmers and skilled craftspeople emerged. Taxes and donations sponsored the building of hospitals such as the Ospedale Santa Maria della Scala in Siena. Streets were paved, town walls erected and sewerage systems built to accommodate an increasingly sophisticated urban population not keen on sprawl or squalor.

Once townsfolk came into a bit of money, they weren't necessarily keen to part with it, and didn't always agree how their tax dollars should be spent. *Comuni* (local governments) were formed to represent the various interests of merchants, guilds and competing noble families, and the first order of business on the agenda in major medieval cities, such as Siena, Florence and Volterra, was the construction of an impressive town hall to reflect the importance and authority of the *comune*. The greatest example is Siena's Palazzo Comunale.

In addition to being savvy political lobbyists and fans of grand architectural projects that kept their constituents gainfully employed, medieval *comuni* were masters of propaganda, and perfectly understood the influence that art and architecture could wield. A perfect case in point is Ambrogio Lorenzetti's *Allegories of Good and Bad Government* fresco series in Siena's Palazzo Comunale, which is better and bigger than any political billboard could ever be. In the *Allegory of Good Government,* Lorenzetti's grey-bearded figure of Legitimate Authority is flanked by an entourage who'd certainly put White House interns to shame: Peace, Fortitude, Prudence, Magnanimity, Temperance and Justice. Above them flit Faith, Hope and Charity, and to the left Concord sits confidently on her throne while the reins of justice are held taut overhead.

Next to this fresco is another depicting the effects of good government: townsfolk make their way through town in an orderly fashion, pausing to do business, greet one another, join hands and dance a merry jig. But things couldn't be more different in the *Allegory of Bad Government,* where horned and fanged Tyrannia rules over a scene of chaos

Best Art Galleries

Uffizi Gallery, Florence

Galleria dell'Accademia, Florence

Pinacoteca Nazionale, Siena

Museo Nazionale di San Matteo, Pisa

Galleria Palatina, Palazzo Pitti, Florence

RICHARD I'ANSON/GETTY IMAGES ©

1. Fresco in Basilica di San Francesco (p274), Assisi
Assisi's major drawcard is this basilica, which comprises two churches filled with magnificent Renaissance art.

2. Pinturicchio's frescoes in the *duomo* (p126), Siena
Inside Siena's *duomo*, the small Libreria Piccolomini's walls are decorated with vividly coloured narrative frescoes.

3. Masaccio's frescoes in Basilica di Santa Maria del Carmine (p83), Florence
Masaccio's fresco cycle illustrating the life of St Peter is considered among his greatest works, representing a definitive break with Gothic art and a plunge into new worlds of expression.

4. Museo di San Marco (p77), Florence
Fra' Angelico's frescoes portray religious figures in all-too-human moments of uncertainty, reflecting the humanist spirit of the Renaissance.

JULIET COOMBE/GETTY IMAGES ©

surrounded by winged vices and Justice lies unconscious, her scales shattered. Like the best campaign speeches, this cautionary tale was brilliantly rendered, but not always heeded.

On the World Stage

When they weren't busy politicking, late-medieval farmers, craftspeople and merchants did quite well for themselves. Elegant, locally made ceramics, tiles and marbles were showcased in churches across Tuscany and became all the rage throughout Europe and the Mediterranean when pilgrims returned home to England and France with examples after following the Via Francigena pilgrimage route from Canterbury to Rome. Artisans were kept busy applying their skills to civic works projects and churches, which had to be expanded and updated to keep up with the growing numbers and rising expectations of pilgrims in the area.

With outside interest came outside influence, and local styles adapted to international markets. Florence became famous for lustrous, tin-glazed *maiolica* (majolica ware) tiles and plates painted with vibrant metallic pigments that were inspired by the Islamic ceramics of Majorca (Spain). The prolific della Robbia family started to create richly glazed ceramic reliefs that are now enshrined at the Museo del Bargello in Florence and in churches and museums across the region.

Gothic Churches

····························

Duomo, Siena

····························

Abbazia di San Galgano, south of Siena

····························

Chiesa di Santa Maria della Spina, Pisa

Modest Romanesque cathedrals were given an International Gothic makeover befitting their appeal to pilgrims of all nations, but the Italian take on the French style was more colourful than the grey-stone spires and flying buttresses of Paris. The local version often featured a simple layout and striped stone naves fronted by multilayer birthday-cake facades, which might be frosted with pink paint, glittering mosaics and rows of arches capped with sculptures. The most famous example of this confectionary approach is the *duomo* in Siena.

The evolution from solid Romanesque to airy Gothic to a yin and yang balance of the two can be witnessed in buildings throughout the region, many of which blend a relatively austere Romanesque exterior with high Gothic drama indoors. This set a new ecclesiastical architecture standard that was quickly exported into Tuscany and on to the rest of Europe.

GIOTTO DI BONDONE

The 14th-century Tuscan poet Giovanni Boccaccio wrote in the *Decameron* that his fellow Tuscan Giotto di Bondone (c 1266–1337) was 'a genius so sublime that there was nothing produced by nature...that he could not depict to the life'.

Boccaccio wasn't the only prominent critic of the time to consider Giotto extraordinary – Giorgio Vasari was also a huge fan, arguing that Giotto initiated the 'rebirth' (*rinascità* or *renaissance*) in art. In his paintings, Giotto abandoned popular conventions such as the three-quarter view of head and body, and presented his figures from behind, from the side or turning around, just as the story demanded. Giotto had no need for lashings of gold paint and elaborate ornamentation to impress the viewer with the significance of the subject. Instead, he enabled the viewer to feel the dramatic tension of a scene through a naturalistic rendition of figures and a radical composition that created the illusion of depth.

Giotto's important works in Tuscany include an altarpiece portraying the Madonna and Child among angels and saints in Florence's Uffizi Gallery, a painted wooden crucifix in the Basilica di Santa Maria Novella and frescoes in the Basilica di Santa Croce. His magnificent *Life of St Francis* fresco cycle graces the walls of the upper church of the Basilica di San Francesco in Assisi, Umbria.

Many Renaissance painters included self-portraits in their major works. Giotto didn't, possibly due to the fact that friends such as Boccaccio described him as the ugliest man in Florence. With friends like those...

Dark Times

By the 14th century the smiling Sienese townsfolk of Ambrogio Lorenzetti's *Allegory of Good Government* must have seemed like the figment
of a fertile imagination. After a major famine in 1329 followed by a bank
collapse, Siena's *comune* went into debt to maintain roads, continue work
on the *duomo,* help the needy and jump-start the local economy. But just
when it seemed set for a comeback, the plague devastated the city in 1348.
Three-quarters of Siena's population – including Pietro and Ambrogio
Lorenzetti – died, and virtually all economic and artistic activity ground to
a halt. Another plague hit in 1374, killing 80,000 Sienese, and was swiftly
followed by a famine. It was too much – the city never entirely recovered.

Florence was also hit by the plague in 1348, and despite fervent public
prayer rituals, 96,000 Florentines died in just seven months. Those who
survived experienced a crisis of faith, making Florence fertile territory
for humanist ideals – not to mention macabre superstition, attempts to
raise the dead, and a fascination with corpses that the likes of Leonardo
da Vinci would call science and others morbid curiosity.

At plague's end, a Florentine building boom ensued when upstart merchants such as Cosimo I de' Medici (Cosimo the Elder) and Palla Strozzi
competed to put their stamp on a city that needed to be reimagined after
the horrors it had undergone.

As madness and
profligacy often
run through fam-
ilies, so too does
artistic genius.
Italian artistic
dynasties include
the della Robbias
(Luca, Marco,
Andrea, Giovanni
and Girolamo),
the Lorenzettis
(Ambrogio and
Pietro) and the
Pisanos (Nicola
and Giovanni, An-
drea and Nino).

The Renaissance

It wasn't only merchants who were jockeying for power at this time. To
put an end to the competing claims of the Tuscan Ghibelline faction
that was allied with the Holy Roman Empire, the Rome-backed Guelph
faction had marked its territory with impressive new landmarks, predominantly in Florence. Giotto – often described as the founding artist
of the Renaissance – had been commissioned to design the city's iconic
85m-tall square *campanile* (bell tower) and one-up the 57m-tall tower
under construction in Ghibelline Pisa that was already looking a bit off
kilter. And this was only one of many such projects.

'Mess with Florence, and you take on Rome' was the not-so-subtle hint
delivered by Florentine architects, who made frequent reference to the
glories of the ancient power and its classical architecture when designing
the new churches, *palazzi* and public buildings that started sprouting
across the city during the *Trecento* (14th century) and proliferated in the
Quattrocento (15th century). This new Florentine style became known as
Renaissance or 'rebirth', and really started to hit its swing after architect
Filippo Brunelleschi won a competition to design the dome of Florence's
duomo. Brunelleschi was heavily influenced by the achievements of the
classical masters, but he was able to do something that they hadn't been
able to do themselves – discover and record the mathematical rules by
which objects appear to diminish as they recede from us. In so doing,
he gave local artists and architects a whole new visual perspective and a
means to glorious artistic ends.

To decorate the new buildings, artists enjoyed a bonanza of commissions to paint heroic battle scenes, fresco private chapels and carve busts
of the latest power players – works that sometimes outlived their patrons'
clout. A good example is the Peruzzi family, whose members had risen to
prominence in 14th-century Florence as bankers with interests reaching
from London to the Middle East, and who set the trend for art patronage by commissioning Giotto to fresco the family's memorial chapel in
Santa Croce, completed in 1320. When Peruzzi client King Edward III of
England defaulted on loans the family went bankrupt – but as patrons
of Giotto's precocious experiments in perspective and Renaissance illu-
sionism, their legacy set the tone for the artistic flowering of Florence.

As well as en-
dowing churches,
building palaces
and funding fres-
coes, the wealthy
merchant families
of the Renais-
sance commis-
sioned plenty of
portraits. Cosimo
I de' Medici's
favourite portrait
painter was
Agnolo di Cosimo
(1503–72), called
Bronzino because
of his dark
complexion. Look
for his Medici
portraits in the
Uffizi, Florence.

Tuscan Artists

Plenty of big names jostle for precedence in the pantheon of Tuscan artists, so narrowing any list down to a 'Top Five' is a near impossible task. Here's our best attempt.

Michelangelo Buonarroti (1475–1564)

The quintessential Renaissance man. A painter, sculptor and architect with more masterpieces to his credit than any other artist either before or since. In Florence, view his *David* in the Galleria dell'Accademia and his *Tondo Doni* (Holy Family) in the Uffizi.

Sandro Botticelli (c 1444–1510)

His Renaissance beauties charmed commissions out of the Medicis and continue to exert their siren call on the millions who visit the Uffizi Gallery each year. Don't miss his *Primavera* and *Birth of Venus*.

Giotto di Bondone (c 1266–1337)

Giotto kick-started the Renaissance with action-packed frescoes in which each character pinpoints emotions with facial expressions and poses that need no translation. Make the pilgrimage to Assisi to see his *Life of St Francis* fresco cycle.

Fra' Angelico (c 1395–1455)

Few artists are saints – they're far more likely to be sinners. One of the exceptions was Il Beato Angelico, who was canonised in 1982. His best-loved work is the *Annunciation*, versions of which are on display in Florence's Museo di San Marco and Cortona's Museo Diocesano.

Duccio di Buoninsegna (c 1255–1318)

Head honcho of the Sienese school; known for his riveting Madonnas with level gazes and pale-green skin against glowing gold backgrounds. His masterwork is the *Maestà* in the Museo dell'Opera in Siena.

1. Fra' Angelico's *Annunciation* 2. Botticelli's *Primavera*
3. Di Buoninsegna's *Madonna with Child and Six Angels*

FILIPPO BRUNELLESCHI

Many Renaissance men left their mark on Florence, but few did so with as much grace and glory as Filippo Brunelleschi (1377–1446). An architect, mathematician, engineer and sculptor, Brunelleschi trained as a master goldsmith and showed early promise as a sculptor – he was an entrant in the 1401 competition to design the doors of the baptistry in Florence (won by fellow goldsmith Lorenzo Ghiberti) and shortly after travelled to Rome with Donatello, another goldsmith by training, to study that city's ancient architecture and art. When he returned to Florence in 1419, he took up an architectural commission from the silk merchant's guild to design a hospital for foundlings on Piazza della Santissima Annunziata in San Marco. Known as the Ospedale degli Innocenti (Hospital of the Innocents), his classically proportioned and detailed building featured a distinctive nine-arched loggia and was a radical departure from the High Gothic style that many of his artistic contemporaries were still embracing. Its design was sober, secular and sophisticated, epitomising the new humanist age.

In 1419, after completing his work on the foundling hospital, Brunelleschi moved on to a commission that was to occupy him for the next 42 years – the dome of Florence's *duomo*. His mathematical brain and talent for devising innovative engineering solutions enabled him to do what many Florentines had thought impossible: deliver the largest dome to be built in Italy since antiquity.

Brunelleschi's other works in Florence include the Basilica di San Lorenzo, the Basilica di Santo Spirito and the Cappella de' Pazzi in the Basilica di Santa Croce. Vasari said of him: 'The world having for so long been without artists of lofty soul or inspired talent, heaven ordained that it should receive from the hand of Filippo the greatest, the tallest, and the finest edifice of ancient and modern times, demonstrating that Tuscan genius, although moribund, was not yet dead.' He is buried in the *duomo*, under the dome that was his finest achievement.

Filippo Lippi (1406–69) entered the Carmelite order as a monk aged 14 but renounced his vows after eloping with a novice who was sitting for the figure of the Madonna in a fresco he was painting for Prato's *duomo*. Their son Filippino (1457–1504) became a painter, too.

One Florentine family to follow the Peruzzis' lead was the prominent Brancacci, who commissioned Masolino da Panicale and his precocious assistant Masaccio to decorate a chapel in the Basilica di Santa Maria del Carmine in Florence. After Masaccio's premature death aged only 27, the frescoes were completed by Filippino Lippi. In these dramatic frescoes, framed in astonishingly convincing architectural sets, scenes from the life of St Peter allude to pressing Florentine concerns of the day: the new income tax, unfair imprisonment and hoarded wealth. Masaccio's image of the expulsion of Adam and Eve from the Garden of Eden proved especially prophetic: the Brancacci were allied with the Strozzi family, and were similarly exiled by the Medici before they could see the work completed.

But the patrons with the greatest impact on the course of art history were, of course, the Medici. Patriarch Cosimo the Elder was exiled in 1433 by a consortium of Florentine families who considered him a triple threat: powerful banker, ambassador of the Church, and consummate politician with the savvy to sway emperors and popes. But the flight of capital from Florence after his departure created such a fiscal panic that the banishment was hastily rescinded and within a year the Medici were well and truly back in town. To announce his return in grand style, Cosimo funded the 1437 rebuilding of the Convento di San Marco (now Museo di San Marco) by Michelozzo, and commissioned Fra' Angelico to fresco the monks' quarters with scenes from the life of Christ. Another artist pleased to see Cosimo return was Donatello, who had completed his lithe bronze statue of *David* (now in the city's Museo del Bargello) with his patronage.

Through such commissions, early Renaissance innovations in perspective, closely observed realism and chiaroscuro (the play of light and dark) began to catch on throughout the region. In Sansepolcro, a painter named Piero della Francesca earned a reputation for figures who were glowing with otherworldly light, and who were caught in personal pre-dicaments that people could relate to: Roman soldiers snoozing on the job, crowds left goggle-eyed by miracles, bystanders distressed to witness cruel persecution. His fresco series *Legend of the True Cross,* commis-sioned by the Bacci family for a chapel in Arezzo's Chiesa di San Frances-co, was one of the supreme artistic achievements of the time.

The High Renaissance

The decades leading up to and starting the *Cinquecento* (16th century) are often seen as a kind of university faculty meeting, with genteel, silver-haired sages engaged in a collegial exchange of ideas. A bar brawl might be closer to the metaphorical truth, with artists, scientists, politicians and clergy mixing it up and everyone emerging bruised. The debate was never as simple as Church versus state, science versus art or seeing ver-sus believing; in those days, politicians could be clergy, scientists could be artists, and artists could be clergy. There were many artistic super-stars during this period, and most were locals who ended up honing their skills in Florence and then moving elsewhere in Italy. Their careers were documented by Giorgio Vasari in his gossipy *Lives of the Artists.*

Inspired by Masaccio, tutored by Fra' Filippo Lippi and backed by Lorenzo de' Medici, Sandro Botticelli was a rising Florentine art star who was sent to Rome to paint a fresco celebrating papal authority in the Sistine Chapel. The golden boy who'd painted the *Birth of Venus* for Lorenzo de' Medici's private villa in 1485 (now in Florence's Uffizi Gal-lery) could do no wrong until he was accused of sodomy in 1501. The charges didn't stick but the rumours did, and Botticelli's work was cri-tiqued as too decadently sensual for religious subjects. When religious reformer Savonarola ousted the Medici and began to purge Florence of decadent excess in the face of surely imminent Armageddon, Botticelli paintings went up in flames in the massive 'Bonfire of the Vanitics'. Botti-celli repudiated mythology and turned his attention to Madonnas, some of whom bear a marked family resemblance to his Venus.

Michelangelo, a village lad from Caprese (today Caprese Michelangelo) in the remote Tuscan outback of Casentino in eastern Tuscany, was an-other of Lorenzo de' Medici's protégées. His classically inspired work was uniformly admired until the Medici were ousted by Savonarola in 1494.

Masaccio's *Trinity,* a wall painting in the Basilica di Santa Maria Novella in Florence, is often described as one of the founding works of Renais-sance painting and the inspira-tion for Leonardo da Vinci's *Last Supper* fresco.

GIORGIO VASARI'S 'LIVES OF THE ARTISTS'

Painter, architect and writer Giorgio Vasari (1511–74) was one of those figures rightfully described as a 'Renaissance man'. Born in Arezzo, he gew up in what is now the small but fascinating house-museum Museo di Casa Vasari. He later trained as a painter in Florence, working with artists such as Andrea del Sarto and Michelangelo (he idolised the latter). As a painter, he is best remembered for his floor-to-ceiling frescoes in the Salone dei Cinquecento in Florence's Palazzo Vecchio. As an architect, his most accomplished work was the elegant loggia of the Uffizi Gallery (he also designed the enclosed, elevated corri-dor that connected the Palazzo Vecchio with the Uffizi and Palazzo Pitti and was dubbed the 'Corridoio Vasariano' in his honour). But posterity remembers him mainly for his work as an art historian. His *Lives of the Most Excellent Painters, Sculptors and Architects, from Cimabue to Our Time,* an encyclopaedia of artistic biographies published in 1550 and ded-icated to Cosimo I de' Medici, is still in print (as *The Lives of the Artists*) and is full of won-derful anecdotes and gossip about his artistic contemporaries in 16th-century Florence.

Memorable passages include his recollection of visiting Donatello's studio one day only to find the great sculptor staring at his extremely life-like statue of the *Prophet Hab-akkuk* and imploring it to talk (we can only assume that Donatello had been working too hard). Vasari also writes about a young Giotto painting a fly on the surface of a work by Cimabue that the older master then tried to brush away.

By some accounts, Savonarola tossed rare early paintings by Michelangelo onto his bonfires. Without his Medici protectors, Michelangelo seemed unsure of his next move: he briefly hid in the basement of San Lorenzo and then roamed around Italy. In Rome he carved a Bacchus for Cardinal Raffaele Riaro that the patron deemed unsuitable – which seemed to spur Michelangelo to make a bigger and still more sensuous statue of *David* in 1501. It's now exhibited in Florence's Galleria dell'Accademia.

Leonardo, who hailed from Vinci, southwest of Florence, had so many talents that it is hard to isolate only a few for comment. In his painting, he took what some critics have described as the decisive step in the history of Western art – namely, abandoning the balance that had previously been maintained between colour and line and choosing to modulate his contours using shading. This technique is called sfumato and it is perfectly displayed in his *Mona Lisa* (now in the Louvre in Paris). Few of his works remain in his birthplace; the exceptions are his *Adoration of the Magi* and *Annunciation,* both in the Uffizi.

In 1542 the Inquisition arrived in Italy, marking a definitive end to the Renaissance exploration of humanity in all its glorious imperfections. Tuscan art and architecture would never again lead the world by example.

Critics believe the rock Adam reclines against in Michelangeo's *Creation of Adam* fresco in Rome's Sistine Chapel was inspired by a rock from the artist's childhood home in eastern Tuscany. Track down the rock in Caprese Michelangelo, 40km north of Arezzo.

RENAISSANCE FRESCOES

They may look like ordinary bible stories now, but in their heyday, Renaissance frescoes provided running social commentary as well as religious inspiration. In them, human adversity looked divine, and vice versa.

Fantastic examples are found throughout Tuscany, but to see the very best head to the following churches and museums:

Collegiata, San Gimignano (p146) There are hardly any undecorated surfaces in this cathedral, with every wall sporting huge, comic-strip-like frescoes by Bartolo di Fredi, Lippo Memmi, Domenico Ghirlandaio and Benozzo Gozzoli. The highlight is Taddeo di Bartolo's gleefully grotesque *Final Judgment* (1396).

Libreria Piccolomini, Duomo, Siena (p126) Umbrian artist Bernardino Pinturicchio extols the glory of Siena in 10 vibrant fresco panels (c 1502–1507) celebrating Enea Silvio Piccolomini, aka the humanist Pope Pius II. St Catherine of Siena makes a cameo appearance.

Museo di San Marco, Florence (p77) Fra' Angelico's frescoes portray religious figures in all-too-human moments of uncertainty, reflecting the humanist spirit of the Renaissance. The highlight is his *Annunciation* (c 1440).

Museo Civico, Siena (p125) Magnificent is the only word to use when describing Ambrogio Lorenzetti's *Allegories of Good and Bad Government* (1338–40) and Simone Martini's *Maestà* (Virgin Mary in Majesty; 1315).

Cappella Brancacci, Florence (p83) Masaccio's *The Expulsion of Adam and Eve from Paradise* and *The Tribute Money* (c 1427) showcase architectural perspective and sly political satire.

Cappella Bacci, Chiesa di San Francesco, Arezzo (p258) Piero della Francesca's *Legend of the True Cross* (c 1452–66) displays a veritable encyclopaedia of Renaissance painting tricks (directional lighting, steep perspective etc).

Chiesa di Sant'Agostino, San Gimignano (p148) Benozzo Gozzoli's bizarre fresco of San Sebastian (c 1464) shows the fully clothed saint protecting the citizens of San Gimignano, helped by a bare-breasted Virgin Mary and semi-robed Jesus. Wins the prize for weirdest religious iconography.

Cappella dei Magi, Palazzo Medici-Riccardi, Florence (p77) More Gozzoli, but this time there's nothing strange about his subject matter, which has members of the Medici family making a guest appearance in the *Procession of the Magi to Bethlehem* (c 1459–63).

A Stop on the Grand Tour

A 'Grand Tour' of Italy became an obligatory display of culture and class status by the 18th century, and Tuscany was a key stop on the itinerary. German and English artists enraptured with Michelangelo, Perugino and other early High Renaissance painters took the inspiration home, kick-starting a neoclassicist craze. Conversely, trends from northern Europe (impressionism, plein-air painting and romanticism) became trendy among Italian artists, as witnessed in the collection at Florence's Galleria d'Arte Moderna in the Palazzo Pitti, which is dominated by late-19th-century works by artists of the Tuscan Macchiaioli school (the local equivalent of impressionism). These include Telemaco Signorini (1835–1901) and Giovanni Fattori (1825–1908).

In architecture, the most fascinating case of artistic import-export is Italian art nouveau, often referred to as Liberty after the London store that put William Morris' Italian-inspired visual ideals into commercial action.

The 20th Century

After centuries under the thumbs of popes and sundry imperial powers, Tuscany had acquired a certain forced cosmopolitanism, and local artists could identify with Rome, Paris or other big cities in addition to their own *contrada* (neighbourhood). The two biggest stars in the early decades of this century were Livorno-born painter and sculptor Amedeo Modigliani (1884–1920), who lived most of his adult life in Paris, and Greek-born painter Giorgio de Chirico (1888–1978), who studied in Florence and painted the first of his 'Metaphysical Town Square' series there.

Other than Modigliani and di Chirico, no Tuscan painters of note were represented within the major artistic movements of the century: Futurismo (Futurism), Pittura Metafisica (Metaphysical Painting), Spazialismo (Spatialism) and Arte Povera (conceptual art using materials of little worth). Architecture didn't have many local stars either, with the only exception being Giovanni Michelucci (1891–1990), whose buildings include Santa Maria Novella Railway Station in Florence (1932–34).

In the field of abstract art, installation art and sculpture, it was small town Pistoia that made itself heard in the 1950s and 1960s through a trio of artists: Pistoia-born Fernando Melani (1907–85) lived all his life in Pistoia, rarely exhibiting elsewhere other than his home town. His playful works utilised an abundance of recycled materials, thin metal wire being shaped and twisted in all directions to create the most extraordinary forms and models. Contemporary Mario Nigro (1917–1992) moved to Livorno when he was 12 and later, once the abstract art bug bit, to the brighter lights of Milan. In the field of sculpture, Pistoia's Marino Marini (1901–80) drew on Tuscany's Etruscan heritage in his work, developing a strong equestrian theme – nudes and men on horseback is what Marini did best.

In the 1980s there was a return to painting and sculpture in a traditional (primarily figurative) sense. Dubbed 'Transavanguardia', this movement broke with the prevailing international focus on conceptual art and was thought by some critics to signal the death of avant-garde – view works at Prato's top-billing contemporary art centre, Centro per l'Arte Contemporanea 'Luigi Pecci'. Tuscan artists who were part of this movement include Sandro Chia (b 1946).

Contemporary Art

A heritage of rich artistic traditions spanning three millennia means job security for legions of Tuscan art conservation specialists and art historians, but can have a stultifying effect on artists attempting to create something wholly new. Fortunately, there's more going on than the daubs being created by sidewalk artists outside major museums and tourist attractions would seem to indicate.

The term 'Macchiaioli' (the name given to a 19th-century group of Tuscan plein-air artists) was coined by a journalist in 1862. It mockingly implied that the artists' finished works were no more than sketches, and was drawn from the phrase *'darsi alla macchia'* (to hide in bushes or scrubland).

ART & ARCHITECTURE A STOP ON THE GRAND TOUR

Best Sculpture Gardens

Fattoria di Celle, near Pistoia

Giardino dei Tarocchi, southern Tuscany

Castello di Ama, Chianti

Tuscan Architecture

Italy has more than its share of great buildings, and a large percentage of these are in Tuscany. Brunelleschi and Michelangelo both designed masterpieces here, and every town and city seems to have at least one notable Romanesque, Gothic or Renaissance structure.

Churches

Tuscany's *chiese* (churches) are headline attractions where worship can take many forms. Every village, town and city has at least one church, and many are repositories of great art. Florence has masterpieces galore (don't miss Santa Maria Novella, Santa Croce and San Lorenzo), but Siena, Pisa and San Gimignano are richly endowed, too, with their respective *duomos* (cathedrals) being the best-loved and most distinctive buildings in town. On the border of Tuscany and Umbria, Orvieto's *duomo* is one of the most beautiful in the country.

Baptistries

Important cathedrals often have a detached *battistero* (baptistry) with a dedicated altar and font. Pisa's cupcake-shaped example in the Piazza dei Miracoli, with its exquisite hexagonal marble pulpit carved by Nicola Pisano, is wonderful, as is Florence's Romanesque version with its famous door panels sculpted by Lorenzo Ghiberti.

1. Aerial view of Piazza del Campo (p124), Siena **2.** Orvieto's *duomo* (cathedral; p167)

Hospitals

Funded by the church, the *comune* (municipality) or wealthy philanthropists, *ospedali* (hospitals) have historically been among the largest and grandest of civic buildings. Siena's Santa Maria della Scala is perhaps the best known, but architecture buffs adore Brunelleschi's Ospedale degli Innocenti in Florence.

Palaces

The Medicis weren't the only dynasty with a penchant for building *palazzi* (palaces). In the medieval and Renaissance periods, wealthy families in every city built houses aimed to impress, as did ambassadors, popes, cardinals and *podestàs* (chief magistrates). Architecturally notable examples include Palazzo Strozzi, Palazzo Pitti and Palazzo Medici-Riccardi in Florence; Palazzo Piccolomini, Palazzo Salimbeni and Palazzo Chigi-Saracini in Siena; and Palazzo Piccolomini in Pienza.

Piazzas

These triumphs of town planning are the lifeblood of every Tuscan community, the places where locals come to connect with their neighbours and where important institutions such as churches and town halls are almost inevitably situated. The two most famous examples, Piazzo Pio II in Pienza and Piazza dei Miracoli in Pisa, feature in Unesco's World Heritage List. Worthy of an honourable mention are Livorno's Piazza dei Domenicani, Arezzo's Piazza Grande and Massa Marittima's Piazza Garibaldi.

Town Halls

Built to showcase wealth and civic pride, the *palazzo comunale* (municipal palace) is often the most impressive secular building in a Tuscan town. Noteworthy examples include those on Siena's Piazza del Campo, Volterra's Piazza dei Priori and Florence's Piazza della Signoria.

One of contemporary architecture's greatest achievements is the Antinori wine cellars (2013) in Bargino, Chianti. Designed by Florentine architect Marco Casamonti, the futuristic glass-fronted cellars are literally built into a hillside, subsequently planted with vines.

One of the most notable visual artists working here is Massimo Bartolini (b 1962), who radically alters the local landscape with just a few deceptively simple (and quintessentially Tuscan) adjustments of light and perspective that fundamentally change our experience: a bedroom where all the furniture appears to be sinking into the floor, Venice style, or a gallery where the viewer wears special shoes that subtly change the lighting in the gallery with each step. Bartolini has also changed the local flora of the tiny Tuscan town of Cecina, near Livorno, where he lives and works, attracting colourful flocks of contemporary art collectors and curators.

The bijou town of Pietrasanta in the hinterland of the Versilian coast in northwestern Tuscany has a vibrant arts community and is home to the much-lauded Colombian-born sculptor Fernando Botero (b 1932).

Also notable is San Gimignano's Galleria Continua, a world-class commercial gallery whose portfolio of artists includes Tuscans Giovanni Ozzola (b 1982) and Luca Pancrazzi (b 1961).

Art & Architecture Glossary

Annunciation	the appearance of the Angel Gabriel to Mary to tell her that she will bear the Son of God
apse	a vaulted semicircular or polygonal recess, especially at the end of a choir in a church
architrave	1. the part of the *entablature* that holds columns in place; 2. a band of mouldings or other ornamentation atop or around openings or panels
atrium	forecourt
badia	abbey
baldacchino	canopy, usually over a high altar in a *basilica*
basilica	an early or medieval Christian church with a ground plan similar to or derived from the Roman basilica
bas-relief	sculpture in low relief
battistero	a church building in which baptism was/is administered
Byzantine	art and architecture of the Byzantine Empire; predated the Romanesque, Gothic and Renaissance movements
campanile	bell tower
cappella	chapel
cartoon	a full-size preparatory drawing for a painting or *fresco*
cella	sanctuary of a temple
cenacolo	scene of the Last Supper (often in the refectory of a convent or monastery)
chiaroscuro	literally 'light-dark'; artistic distribution of light and dark areas in a painting
chiostro	cloister; a rectangular open space surrounded by a covered walkway
clerestory	upper part of the nave wall of a church featuring windows
coffer	ornamental sunken panel in a ceiling
colonnade	a series of columns set at regular intervals, and usually supporting an *entablature*, a roof or a series of arches
cornice	1. a horizontal moulded projection that crowns or finishes a wall or building; 2. the uppermost division of an *entablature*, resting on the *frieze*; 3. the moulding(s) between the walls and ceiling of a room
cortile	courtyard
cruciform	cross-shaped
crypt	underground chamber or vault used as a burial place
cupola	a rounded vault or dome

diptych	painting or carving with two panels; usually small and portable and often used as an altarpiece
duomo	cathedral
entablature	sits on top of a row of columns on a classical facade; includes an *architrave*, the decorative *frieze* atop that and the triangular *pediment* to cap it off
exedra	semicircular recess
ex-voto	tablet or small painting expressing gratitude to a saint
font	receptacle, usually made of stone, that holds the water used in baptisms
fresco	painting executed on wet plaster
frieze	the part of an *entablature* between the *architrave* and the *cornice*, commonly ornamented with sculpture
Gothic	style of art and architecture in the late medieval period; popular from the 12th century
grisaille	technique of monochrome painting in shades of grey
loggia	covered area on the side of a building; porch; lodge
lunette	semicircular space in a vault or ceiling or above a door or window; often decorated with a *fresco* or painting
Madonna della Misericordia	literally 'Madonna of Mercy'; in art, an iconic formula showing a group of people seeking protection under the outspread cloak of the Madonna
Maestà	literally 'Majesty'; in art, an iconic formula of the enthroned Madonna with Christ Child, often surrounded by angels and saints
mausoleo	mausoleum; stately and magnificent tomb
narthex	vestibule along the facade of an early Christian church
nave	the main body, or middle part (lengthwise), of a church, flanked by aisles and extending typically from the entrance to the *apse*
necropolis	ancient cemetery or burial site
oculus	round window
pediment	a low triangular gable crowned with a projecting *cornice*, especially over a *portico* or porch at the end of a gable-roofed building
piano nobile	main floor of a palace
Pietà	literally 'pity' or 'compassion'; sculpture, drawing or painting of the dead Christ being held by the Madonna
pietra forte	fine sandstone used as a building material
pietra serena	greenish-grey 'serene stone'
pieve	parish church, usually in a rural setting
pinacoteca	art gallery
podium	a low continuous structure serving as a base or terrace wall
polyptych	painting or carving consisting of more than three panels; usually used as an altarpiece
porphyry	dark blue-, purple- or red-coloured rock
portico	a structure consisting of a roof supported by columns or piers forming the entrance to a church or other building
predella	small painting or panel attached below a large altarpiece
presbytery	eastern part of a church chancel, beyond the choir
pulpit	a platform or raised structure in a church from which a priest delivers a sermon
quadriporto	four-sided porch
quatrefoil	four-lobed design
relief	an apparent projection of parts in a sculpture or *frieze* giving the appearance of the third dimension
Renaissance	cultural movement that started in Florence; c 14th to 17th centuries

Romanesque	architecture of the early Western Christian empire c 6th to 12th centuries
rose window	circular window divided into sections by stone mullions and tracery; usually found in Gothic churches
rustification	stone with a chiselled, rough-hewn look
sacristy	room in a church where the sacred vessels, vestments etc are kept
sanctuaio	sanctuary; the part of a church above the altar
sfumato	hazy blending of colours and blurring of outlines; used in painting
sgraffito	a surface covered with plaster, then scratched away to create a 3D trompe l'œil effect of carved stone or brick
sinopia	working sketch for a *fresco*
spolia	creative reuse of ancient monuments in new structures
stele	upright stone with carved inscription or image
stemma	coat of arms
stigmata	marks appearing on a saint's body in the same places as the wounds of Christ
stucco	plasterwork
tabernacle	in Christian worship, a locked box in which the communion wafers and wine are stored
tempera	powdered pigment bound together with a mixture of egg and water; used in painting
tesoro	treasury
tesserae	small cubes of marble, stone or glass used in mosaic work
tondo	circular painting or relief
transept	the transverse portion(s) of a cruciform church
travertine	limestone used in paving and building
triptych	painting or carving over three panels, hinged so that the outer panels fold over the middle one; often used as an altarpiece
tufa	soft volcanic rock
vault	arched structure forming a ceiling or roof
vestibule	passage, hall or antechamber between the outer door and interior parts of a building

Survival Guide

Directory A–Z

Accommodation

See p33 for information on accommodation in Tuscany.

Customs Regulations

Visitors coming into Italy from non-EU countries can import the following duty free:

➡ 1L spirits (or 2L wine)

➡ 200 cigarettes

➡ up to a total of €430 (€150 for travellers aged under 15) for other goods, including perfume and eau de toilette.

Anything over these limits must be declared on arrival and the appropriate duty paid. On leaving the EU, non-EU citizens can reclaim any Value Added Tax (VAT) on any purchases over €154.94. For more information, visit www.italia.it.

Discount Cards

Free admission to many galleries and cultural sites is available to youths under 18 and seniors over 65 years. EU citizens aged between 18 and 25 also often qualify for a 50% discount. In our reviews, we have indicated this by using

the description 'reduced' when citing admission charges. When in Florence, consider purchasing a **Firenze Card** (€72), valid for 72 hours and covers admission to 67 museums, villas and gardens in Florence, as well as unlimited use of public transport.

You can also often save money by purchasing a *biglietto cumulativo*, a ticket that allows admission to a number of associated sights for less than the combined cost of separate admission fees.

Youth, Student & Teacher Cards

➡ The European Youth Card (*Carta Giovani Europea*; www.cartagiovani.it, http://eyca.org; €5 to €19, depending on where purchased) is available to anyone, worldwide, under 30. It offers thousands of discounts on Italian hotels, museums, restaurants, shops and clubs and can be bought online.

➡ Student, teacher or youth travel cards (www.isic.org) can save money on accommodation, travel, food and drink. They're available online and worldwide from student unions, hostelling organisations and youth travel agencies such as **STA Travel** (www.statravel.com). Options include the International Student Identity Card (ISIC; for full-time students), International Teacher Identity Card (for full-time teachers) and the

Climate

Florence

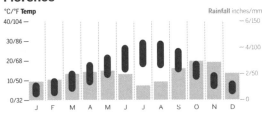

Elba

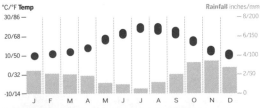

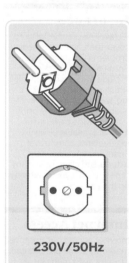

230V/50Hz

230V/50Hz

International Youth Travel Card (for travellers under 31).

➡ Note many places in Italy give discounts according to age rather than student status. An ISIC may not always be accepted without proof of age (eg passport). In our reviews, we use 'reduced' rather than 'student' when citing admission charges.

Electricity

Embassies & Consulates

For foreign embassies and consulates in Italy that are not listed here, look under 'Ambasciate' or 'Consolati' in the telephone directory. In addition to the following, some countries run honorary consulates in other cities.

Australian Embassy (☑emergencies 800 877790, info 06 85 27 21; www.italy. embassy.gov.au; Via Antonio Bosio 5, Rome; ⏰9am-5pm Mon-Fri)

Australian Consulate (☑02 776 741; Via Borgogna 2, Milan; Ⓜ San Babila)

Austrian Embassy (☑06 844 01 41; www.aussenminis terium.at/rom; Via Pergolesi 3, Rome)

Austrian Consulate (☑02 78 37 43; www.aussenministe rium.at/mailandgk; Piazza del Liberty 8/4, Milan)

Canadian Embassy (☑06 854 44 29 11; www.canada international.gc.ca/italy-italie; Via Zara 30, Rome)

French Embassy (☑06 68 60 11; www.ambafrance-it.org; Piazza Farnese 67, Rome)

French Consulate (☑02 655 91 41; http://www.amba france-it.org/-Consulat-de-Milan-; Via della Moscova 12, Milan; Ⓜ Turati)

German Embassy (☑06 49 21 31; www.rom.diplo.de; Via San Martino della Battaglia 4, Rome)

German Consulate (☑02 623 11 01; www.mailand.diplo .de; Via Solferino 40, Milan; Ⓜ Moscova)

Irish Embassy (☑06 585 23 81; www.ambasciata-irlanda.it; Villa Spada, Via Giacomo Medici 1, Rome)

Japanese Embassy (☑06 48 79 91; www.it.emb-japan. go.jp; Via Quintino Sella 60, Rome)

Japanese Consulate (☑02 624 11 41; www.milano. it.emb-japan.go.jp; Via Cesare Mangili 2/4, Milan; Ⓜ Turati)

Netherlands Embassy (☑06 3228 6001; www.olanda. it; Via Michele Mercati 8, Rome)

New Zealand Embassy (☑06 853 75 01; www.nz embassy.com/italy; Via Clitunno 44, Rome)

New Zealand Consulate (☑02 7217 0001; www.nz embassy.com/italy; Via Terraggio 17, Milan; Ⓜ Cadorna)

Slovenian Embassy (☑06 8091 4310; www.rim.velepo slanistvo.si; Via Leonardo Pisano 10, Rome)

Swiss Embassy (☑06 80 95 71; www.eda.admin.ch/roma; Via Barnaba Oriani 61, Rome)

Swiss Consulate (☑02 777 91 61; www.eda.admin.ch/ milano; Via Palestro 2, Milan; Ⓜ Turati)

UK Embassy (☑06 4220 0001; http://ukinitaly.fco.gov. uk; Via XX Settembre 80a, Rome)

UK Consulate (☑06 4220 2431; Via San Paolo 7, Milan; Ⓜ San Babila)

US Embassy (☑06 4 67 41; http://italy.usembassy.gov; Via Vittorio Veneto 121, Rome)

US Consulate (☑055 26 69 51; http://italy.usembassy. gov; Lungarno Vespucci 38, Florence)

Food

For detailed information about eating in Tuscany, see Eat & Drink Like a Local (p36).

Gay & Lesbian Travellers

Homosexuality is legal in Italy and well accepted in the major cities. On the Tuscan coast, Torre del Lago has a lively gay scene, best expressed by **Friendly Versilia** (www.friendlyversilia.it), a summer campaign that encourages gays and lesbians to revel in Torre del Lago's fun-in-the-sun frolics from late April to September.

Resources include the following:

Arcigay (www.arcigay.it) Bologna-based national organisation for the LGBTI community.

Azione Gay e Lesbica Firenze (☏055 22 02 50; www.azione-gayelesbica.it; Via Pisana 32r) Active Florence-based organisation for gays and lesbians.

GayFriendlyItaly.com (www.gayfriendlyitaly.com) English-language site produced by Gay. it, featuring events and information on homophobia issues and the law.

Gay.it (www.gay.it) Website featuring LGBT news, feature articles and gossip.

Pride (www.prideonline.it) National monthly magazine of art, music, politics and gay culture.

Health

Recommended Vaccinations

No jabs are required to travel to Italy. However, the World Health Organization (WHO) recommends that all travellers should be covered for diphtheria, tetanus, measles, mumps, rubella and polio, as well as hepatitis B.

Health Insurance

➡ The free European Health Insurance Card (EHIC) covers EU citizens and those from Switzerland, Norway and Iceland for most medical care in public hospitals free of charge.

➡ The EHIC does not cover emergency repatriation home or non-emergencies.

➡ EHIC is available from health centres and, in the UK, online (www.ehic.org.uk) and from post offices.

➡ Citizens from other countries should check whether there's a reciprocal arrangement for free medical care between their country and Italy – Australia, for instance, has such an agreement; carry your Medicare card.

➡ Additional health insurance should cover the worst possible scenario, such as an accident requiring an emergency flight home.

➡ Check in advance whether your insurance plan will make payments directly to providers or reimburse you later for overseas health expenditures.

Availability of Health Care

Pharmacists can give you valuable advice and sell over-the-counter medication for minor illnesses. They can also advise you when more specialised help is required and point you in the right direction.

Pharmacies generally keep the same hours as other shops, closing at night and on Sundays. However, in big cities a handful remain open on a rotation basis *(farmacie di turno)* for emergency purposes. These are listed online at www.miniportale.it/mini

portale/farmacie/Toscana. htm. You can also check the door of any pharmacy that is closed for business – it will display a list of the nearest emergency pharmacies.

If you need an ambulance, call ☏118. For emergency treatment, head straight to the *pronto soccorso* (casualty) section of a public hospital, where you can also get emergency dental treatment.

Insurance

A travel-insurance policy to cover theft, loss and medical problems is a good idea. Some policies specifically exclude dangerous activities, which can include scuba diving, motorcycling and even hiking – read the fine print.

Worldwide travel insurance is available at www.lonelyplanet.com/travel-insurance. You can buy, extend and claim online any time – even if you're already on the road.

Internet Access

Internet access has improved markedly in the past couple of years, with many locals now having home connections and a large percentage of hotels, B&Bs, hostels and *agriturismi* (accommodation on working farms or wine estates) now offering free wi-fi. As a result, specialised internet cafes are thin on the ground.

Legal Matters

The average tourist will only have a brush with the law if robbed by a bag-snatcher or pickpocket, or if their car is towed away.

In an emergency (to report theft, robbery, assault or accidents) call ☏113 or ☏112 – the latter has a reply service in a number of languages.

Maps

You can choose from a number of sheet maps covering the region, including Michelin's *Toscana* (1:200,000), Marco Polo's *Toscana/Tuscany* (1:200,000) and Touring Editore's *Toscana* (1:200,000). You can buy them from book shops and some petrol stations, though it's a good idea to buy maps before leaving home.

Money

The euro is Italy's currency. Notes come in denominations of €500, €200, €100, €50, €20, €10 and €5. Coins are in denominations of €2 and €1, and 50, 20, 10, five, two and one cents.

ATMs

Bancomats (ATM machines) are widely available throughout Tuscany and are the best way to obtain local currency.

Credit Cards

International credit and debit cards can be used at any *bancomat* displaying the appropriate sign. Cards are also good for payment in most hotels, restaurants, shops, supermarkets and tollbooths.

If your card is lost, stolen or swallowed at an ATM, you can telephone toll free to have an immediate stop put on its use:

Amex (☑06 7290 0347)
Diners Club (☑800 393939)
MasterCard (☑800 870866)
Visa (☑800 819014)

Moneychangers

You can change money in banks, at the post office or in a *cambio* (exchange office). Post offices and banks tend to offer the best rates; exchange offices keep longer hours, but watch for high commissions and inferior rates.

Taxes & Refunds

A Value Added Tax (VAT) of around 22%, known as IVA (Imposta di Valore Aggiunto), is slapped on most goods and services in Italy; a discounted rate of 10% applies in restaurants, bars and hotels. If you are a non-EU resident and spend more than €155 (€154.94 to be precise!) on a purchase, you can claim a refund when you leave. The refund only applies to purchases from affiliated retail outlets that display a 'tax free for tourists' (or similar) sign. You have to complete a form at the point of sale, then have it stamped by EU customs as you leave the zone (if you are visiting one or more EU countries after visiting Italy, you'll need to submit the form at your final port of exit). For information, visit Tax Refund for Tourists (www.taxrefund.it) or pick up a pamphlet on the scheme from participating stores.

Opening Hours

As a general rule, opening times for most individual businesses are as follows:

Banks 8.30am to 1.30pm and 3.30pm to 4.30pm Monday to Friday

Bars and pubs 10am to 1am

Cafes 7.30am to 8pm

Nightclubs 10pm to late

Post offices (main) 8am to 7pm Monday to Friday, 8.30am to noon Saturday

Post offices (branch) 8am to 2pm Monday to Friday, 8.30am to noon Saturday

Restaurants 12.30pm to 2.30pm and 7.30pm to 10pm

Shops 9am to 1pm and 3.30pm to 7.30pm (or 4pm to 8pm) Monday to Saturday

Post

Le Poste (www.poste.it), Italy's postal system, is reasonably reliable but if you are sending a package you might want to use DHL or FedEx, which can be safer.

Francobolli (stamps) are available at post offices and authorised *tabacchi* (tobacconists; look for the official sign: a big 'T', often white on black). Since letters often need to be weighed, what you get at the tobacconist for international airmail will occasionally be an approximation of the proper rate. If

---

ITALY'S POLICE FORCES

There are six national police forces in Italy, as well as a number of local police forces. The main services are shown in the table.

ORGANISATION	JURISDICTION	UNIFORM
polizia di stato (civil national police)	thefts, visa extensions and permits; based at the local *questura* (police station)	powder blue trousers with a fuchsia stripe and a navy blue jacket
arma dei carabinieri (military police)	general crime, public order and drug enforcement (often overlapping with the *polizia di stato*)	black uniforms with a red stripe
polizia municipale (aka *vigili urbani*; municipal police)	parking tickets, towed cars, public order, petty crime	varies according to province

you've any concerns about ensuring an accurate stamp price, use a post office. *Tabacchi* keep regular shop hours.

Public Holidays

Most Italians take their annual holiday in August, with the busiest period occurring around 15 August, known locally as Ferragosto. This means that many businesses and shops close for at least a part of that month. Settimana Santa (Easter Week) is another busy holiday period for Italians.

Individual towns have public holidays to celebrate the feasts of their patron saints. National public holidays:

New Year's Day (Capodanno or Anno Nuovo) 1 January

Epiphany (Epifania or Befana) 6 January

Easter Sunday (Domenica di Pasqua) March/April

Easter Monday (Pasquetta or Lunedì dell'Angelo) March/April

Liberation Day (Giorno della Liberazione) 25 April – marks the Allied Victory in Italy, and the end of the German presence in 1945.

Labour Day (Festa del Lavoro) 1 May

Republic Day (Festa della Repubblica) 2 June

Feast of the Assumption (Assunzione or Ferragosto) 15 August

All Saints' Day (Ognissanti) 1 November

Feast of the Immaculate Conception (Immaculata Concezione) 8 December

Christmas Day (Natale) 25 December

Boxing Day (Festa di Santo Stefano) 26 December

Telephone
Domestic Calls

➡ Italian telephone area codes all begin with 0 and consist of up to four digits. The area code is followed by a number of anything from four to nine digits. The area code is an integral part of the telephone number and must always be dialled, even when calling from next door.

➡ Mobile-phone numbers begin with a three-digit prefix such as ⏎330.

➡ Toll-free (free-phone) numbers are known as *numeri verdi* and usually start with ⏎800.

➡ Nongeographical numbers start with ⏎840, 841, 848, 892, 899, 163, 166 or 199.

➡ Some six-digit national rate numbers are also in use (such as those for Alitalia, rail and postal information). As elsewhere in Europe, Italians choose from a host of providers of phone plans and rates, making it difficult to make generalisations about costs.

International Calls

➡ The cheapest options for calling internationally are free or low-cost computer programs such as Skype and Viber.

➡ Cut-price call centres can be found in all of the main cities, and rates can be considerably lower than from Telecom Italia payphones for international calls. You simply place your call from a private booth inside the centre and pay for it when you've finished.

➡ International calling cards, sold at newsstands and *tabacchi*, also offer cheaper rates. They can be used at public telephones.

➡ To call another country from Italy, first dial ⏎00, then the relevant country and area codes, followed by the telephone number.

➡ To call Italy from abroad, call the international access number (⏎011 in the USA, ⏎00 from most other countries), Italy's country code (⏎39) and then the area code of the location you want, including the leading 0.

Mobile Phones

➡ Italy uses GSM 900/1800, which is compatible with the rest of Europe and Australia but not with North American GSM 1900 or the totally different Japanese system.

➡ Many modern smartphones are multiband, meaning they are compatible with a number of international networks – check with your service provider about using yours in Italy.

➡ Beware of mobile calls being routed internationally; it can be very expensive for a 'local' call.

➡ You can get a temporary or prepaid account from several companies if you already own a GSM, dual- or multiband mobile phone.

➡ Always check with your mobile-service provider in your home country to

---

PRACTICALITIES

Weights and measurements Italy uses the metric system for weights and measures.

Smoking Banned in all enclosed public spaces.

Newspapers The major daily newspapers are *Corriere della Sera* (www.corriere.it/english), which publishes in both Italian and English, and the Florentine edition of *La Repubblica* (www.firenze.repubblica.it), which is only in Italian. For news, views and classifieds in English, pick up a copy of the free monthly newspaper *The Florentine* (www.theflorentine.net) from select hotels, cafes, bookshops and bars in Florence.

see whether your handset allows use of another SIM card. If yours does, it can cost as little as €20 to activate a local prepaid SIM card (sometimes with €10 worth of calls on the card). You'll need to register with a mobile-phone shop, bring your passport and wait for about 24 hours for your account to be activated.

➜ You can easily top up an Italian account with *ricarica* (prepaid minutes) from your selected mobile company at *tabacchi*, supermarkets and banks.

➜ **TIM** (www.tim.it), **Vodafone** (www.vodafone.it) and **Wind** (www.wind.it) have the densest networks of outlets across the country.

➜ If you have an internet-enabled phone turn off data roaming when you're not using it, otherwise it devours credit.

Payphones & Phonecards

➜ Telecom Italia payphones can be found on the streets, in train stations and in Telecom offices.

➜ Most payphones accept only *carte/schede telefoniche* (phonecards), although some also accept credit cards.

➜ Telecom offers a wide range of prepaid cards for both domestic and international use; for a full list, see www.telecomitalia.it/telefono/carte-telefoniche.

➜ You can buy phonecards (most commonly €5 or €10) at post offices, *tabacchi* and newsstands. Break off the top left-hand corner of the card before use. All phonecards have an expiry date, printed on the face of the card.

Time

Italy operates on a 24-hour clock. It is one hour ahead of GMT/UTC. Daylight-saving time starts on the last Sunday in March, when clocks are put forward one hour. Clocks are put back an hour on the last Sunday in October. This is especially valuable to know in Italy, as 'summer' and 'winter' hours at museums and other sights are usually based on daylight-saving time.

Tourist Information

➜ Tuscany's regional tourist authority is www.turismo.toscana.it.

➜ Tourist offices operate under a variety of names but are often known as 'Pro Loco'.

➜ The economic downturn and ensuing budget cuts have impacted on Tuscany's tourism sector. Some tourist information offices have closed, others operate on reduced hours, and hours are often subject to change.

Travellers with Disabilities

Italy is not an easy country for travellers with disabilities and getting around can be a problem for wheelchair users. Even a short journey in a city or town can become a major expedition if cobblestone streets have to be negotiated. Although many buildings have lifts, they are not always wide enough for wheelchairs.

Not an awful lot has been done to make life any easier for the hearing impaired and partially sighted.

Italy's national rail company, Trenitalia, offers a helpline for disabled passengers at ☑199 303060.

Two companies that focus on accessible travel:

Accessible Italy (www.accessibleitaly.com) Based in the Republic of San Marino, this outfit specialises in holiday services for people with disabilities, ranging from tours and hiring adapted transport to organising weddings.

Sage Traveling (www.sagetraveling.com) European accessible travel specialists who run customised tours; its website offers tips and advice on accessible travel in Florence.

Visas

➜ European citizens of the 26 countries in the Schengen Area can enter Italy with nothing more than a valid identity card or passport. British nationals only need a passport.

➜ Residents of 28 non-EU countries, including Australia, Brazil, Canada, Israel, Japan, New Zealand and the USA, do not require visas for tourist visits of up to 90 days.

➜ All non-EU and non-Schengen nationals entering Italy for more than 90 days, or for any reason other than tourism (such as study or work) may need a specific visa. For details, visit www.esteri.it or contact an Italian consulate.

➜ EU citizens do not require any permits to live or work in Italy but, after three months' residence, are supposed to register themselves at the municipal registry office where they live and offer proof of work or sufficient funds to support themselves.

➜ Non-EU foreign citizens with five years' continuous legal residence may apply for permanent residence.

➜ You should have your passport stamped on entry as, without a stamp, you could encounter problems if trying to obtain a residence permit (*permesso di soggiorno*). If you enter the EU via another member state, get your passport stamped there.

Permesso di Soggiorno

Non-EU citizens planning to stay at the same address

for more than one week are supposed to report to the police station to receive a *permesso di soggiorno*. Tourists staying in hotels are not required to do this.

A *permesso di soggiorno* only really becomes a necessity if you plan to study, work (legally) or live in Italy. Obtaining one is never a pleasant experience; it often involves long queues and the frustration of arriving at the counter only to find you don't have the necessary documents.

The exact requirements, such as specific documents and *marche da bollo* (official stamps), can change. In general, you will need a valid passport (if possible containing a stamp with your date of entry into Italy), a special visa issued in your own country if you are planning to study (for non-EU citizens), four passport photos and proof of your ability to support yourself financially. You can apply at the *ufficio stranieri* (foreigners' bureau) of the police station closest to where you're staying.

EU citizens do not require a *permesso di soggiorno*.

Study Visas

Non-EU citizens who want to study at a university or language school in Italy must have a study visa. These can be obtained from your nearest Italian embassy or consulate. You will normally require confirmation of your enrolment, proof of payment of fees and adequate funds to support yourself. The visa covers only the period of the enrolment. This type of visa is renewable within Italy but, again, only with confirmation of ongoing enrolment and proof that you are able to support yourself (bank statements are preferred).

Transport

GETTING THERE & AWAY

Flights, cars and tours can be booked online at lonely planet.com/bookings.

Entering the Country

➡ EU and Swiss citizens can travel to Italy with their national identity card alone. All other nationalities must have a valid passport and may be required to fill out a landing card at airports.

➡ By law you are supposed to have your passport or ID card with you at all times. You'll need one of these documents for police registration every time you check into a hotel.

➡ In theory, there are no passport checks at land crossings from neighbouring countries, but random customs controls do occasionally still take place between Italy and Switzerland.

Air

➡ High season for air travel to Italy is mid-April to mid-September.

➡ Shoulder season runs from mid-September to the end of October and from Easter to mid-April.

➡ Low season is November to March.

➡ Tickets around Christmas and Easter often increase in price or sell out in advance.

Airlines

Domestic flights in and out of the region:

Air One (www.flyairone.com) Pisa International Airport to/from Olbia and Catania.

Alitalia (www.alitalia.it) Pisa International Airport, Florence Airport and Bologna Airport to/from Rome and Catania.

Meridiana Fly (www.meridiana.it) Bologna Airport to/from Olbia and Cagliari.

Ryanair (www.ryanair.com) Pisa International Airport to/from Trapani, Palermo, Bari, Brindisi and Cagliari; Umbria International Airport to/from Brindisi, Cagliari and Trapani; Bologna Airport to Bari, Brindisi, Trapani and Palermo.

Land

Border Crossings

If you are entering Italy from a neighbouring EU country, you do not require a passport check.

Bus

Buses are the cheapest overland option to Italy, but services are less frequent, less comfortable and significantly slower than the train.

Car & Motorcycle

Every vehicle travelling across the border should

AIRPORTS SERVICING TUSCANY

AIRPORT	ALTERNATIVE NAMES	LOCATION	WEBSITE
Pisa International Airport (PSA)	Aeroporto Galileo Galilei	Pisa	www.pisa-airport.com
Florence Airport (FLR)	Amerigo Vespucci; Peretola	Florence	www.aeroporto.firenze.it
Umbria International Airport (PEG)	Perugia San Francesco d'Assisi	Perugia, Umbria	www.airport.umbria.it
Bologna Airport (BLQ)	Aeroporto G Marconi	Bologna, Emilia-Romagna	www.bologna-airport.it

display a valid national licence plate and an accompanying registration card.

Train

➡ Milan is the major rail hub in northern Italy; most European services arrive there; onward connections include Florence and Pisa.

➡ The Thello sleeper train travels from Paris-Gare de Lyon to Milan.

➡ From France, you can also change at Turin for connecting services to Pisa.

➡ For train times, go to the Eurail website (www.eurail.com). It also provides a free, searchable timetable app, which works offline.

Sea

Ferries connect Italy with its islands and countries all across the Mediterranean. However, the only options for reaching Tuscany directly by sea are the ferry crossings to Livorno from Spain, Sardinia and Corsica.

For a comprehensive guide to all ferry services into and out of Italy, check out Traghettionline (www.traghettionline.com). The website lists every route and includes links to ferry companies, where you can buy tickets or search for deals.

GETTING AROUND

To/From the Airport

Bologna Airport Appennino Shuttle (www.appenninoshuttle.it) buses go to Florence (€25, 90 minutes, 10 daily). Tickets are €5 cheaper online.

Florence Airport Buses run into central Florence (€6, 30 minutes, half-hourly).

Pisa International Airport From 2016 the PisaMover light train (every 10 minutes) is due to link the airport to Pisa Central train station; buses ply the route until then. From the station, hourly trains run to Florence (€8, one hour). One bus (€14, daily 11.45am, two hours) links the airport with Siena.

Umbria International Airport A couple of buses a day go to Perugia (€3, 30 minutes), with bus and train connections onto Tuscany from there.

Bicycle

Cycling is a national pastime in Italy. Bikes are prohibited on the autostrada (expressway), but there are few other special road rules.

Bikes can be taken on any train that carries the bicycle logo. The cheapest option is to buy a separate bicycle ticket: €3.50 for *regionale* (slow local train) services and €12 for international services. Tickets are valid for

24 hours. Ferries allow free bicycle passage.

Boat

Year-round, regular ferries connect Piombino on the mainland with Portoferraio on Elba, and the smaller ports of Cavo and Rio Marina. From Livorno, ferries run to the islands of Capraia (year-round) and Gorgona (summer-only).

Bus

Although trains are the most convenient and economical way to travel between major towns, a bus is often the best public transport link between small towns and villages. For a few intercity routes, such as between Florence and Siena, the bus is your best bet.

➡ Dozens of regional companies are loosely affiliated under the **Tiemme** (www.lfi.it) network.

➡ Most companies reduce or even drop services on holidays and weekends, especially Sundays.

➡ Local tourist offices often carry bus timetables.

➡ Buy tickets at ticket booths and dispensing machines at bus stations, or from most *tabacchi* (tobacconists) and newsstands. They can usually also be bought on board at a slightly higher cost.

➡ Validate tickets in the machine on board.

EXPRESS TRAINS FROM CONTINENTAL EUROPE

FROM	TO	FREQUENCY	DURATION (HR)	COST (€)
Geneva	Milan	4 daily	4	80
Munich	Verona	5 daily	5½	79
Paris	Milan	4 daily	7-10	60-95
Ventimiglia	Milan	6 daily	4	10-20
Vienna	Florence	nightly	11	90
Zurich	Milan	7 daily	3¾	72

BUS COMPANIES IN TUSCANY

REGIONAL BUS COMPANY	WEBSITE (MOST IN ITALIAN ONLY)	SERVICES
ATL	www.atl.livorno.it	Livorno
CAT	www.catspa.it	Lunigiana & Massa-Carrara
CPT	www.cpt.pisa.it	Pisa & Volterra
Etruria Mobilità	www.etruriamobilita.it	eastern Tuscany
Siena Mobilità	www.sienamobilita.it	Siena & around
SITA	www.sitabus.it	Florence & Chianti
Tiemme	www.tiemmespa.it	southern Tuscany
Vaibus	www.vaibus.it	Lucca, Garfagnana & Versilia

➡ In larger cities, ticket companies often have offices at the bus terminal; some offer good-value daily tourist tickets.

➡ Turn up on time: in defiance of deep-seated Italian tradition, buses are almost always punctual.

Car & Motorcycle

Automobile Associations

The **Automobile Club d'Italia** (ACI; ☑803 116, from a foreign mobile 800 116 800; www.aci.it) is a driver's best resource in Italy. For 24-hour roadside emergency service, dial 803 116. Foreigners do not have to join but instead pay a per-incident fee.

Car Hire

To rent a car you must be at least 25 years old and have a credit card. Car-rental agencies expect you to bring the car back with a full tank of petrol and will charge astronomically if you don't. You should also make sure that the office where you are returning your car will be open when you arrive – if not you will face fines.

Make sure you understand what is included in the price (unlimited kilometres, tax, insurance, collision damage waiver and so on). Also consider vehicle size carefully: high fuel prices, extremely narrow streets and tight parking conditions mean that smaller is always better.

Motorcycle Hire

Agencies throughout Tuscany rent everything from small Vespas to larger touring bikes.

Helmets are compulsory. Most firms won't hire motorcycles to under 18s. Many require a sizeable deposit, and you could be responsible for reimbursing part of the cost of the bike if it is stolen.

You don't need a licence to ride a scooter under 50cc. The speed limit is 45km/h, you must be 14 or over and you can't carry passengers. To ride a motorcycle or scooter between 50cc and 125cc, you must be aged 16 or over and have a licence (a car licence will do). For motorcycles over 125cc you will need a motorcycle licence.

Scooters below 150cc can't be ridden on motorways. Motorcycles can access some Zona a Traffico Limitato (ZTLs; Limited Traffic Zones).

Driving Licence

All EU member states' driving licences are fully recognised throughout Europe. Drivers with a non-EU licence are supposed to obtain an International Driving Permit (IDP) to accompany their national licence, though anecdotal testimonies indicate that this rule is rarely enforced.

Fuel & Spare Parts

Italy's petrol (gas) prices are among the highest in Europe and vary from one service station (benzinaio, stazione di servizio) to another.

During the time of research, lead-free gasoline (senza piombo; 95 octane) averaged €1.50 per litre, with diesel (gasolio) averaging €1.40 per litre. Many petrol stations are unattended at lunchtime, at night and on weekends; at these times credit cards can often be used for payment (note, though, that not all foreign cards are accepted).

Spare parts are available at many garages or via the 24-hour ACI motorist assistance number (☑803 116).

Insurance

Always carry proof of vehicle ownership and evidence of third-party insurance. If driving an EU-registered vehicle, your home country insurance is sufficient. Ask your insurer for a European Accident Statement (EAS) form, which can simplify matters in the event of an accident.

Parking

Parking spaces outlined in blue are designated for paid parking (look for a nearby ticket machine and display the ticket on your dashboard). White outlines indicate free parking; yellow outlines indicate that residential permits are needed. Traffic police generally turn a blind eye to motorcycles or scooters parked on footpaths.

Road Network

Tuscany has an excellent road network, including autostradas, superstradas (dual carriageways) and

SPEED LIMITS

For cars and motorbikes the following speed limits apply:

➡ Urban areas: 50km/h

➡ Secondary roads: 70km/h to 90km/h (look for signs)

➡ Main roads: 110km/h (90km/h in rain)

➡ Autostradas: 130km/h (110km/h in rain)

Speed limits are lower for towing vehicles (including caravans) and camper vans.

major highways. Most of these are untolled, with the main exceptions being the A11 and A12 (FI-PI-LI) autostrada connecting Florence, Pisa and Livorno and the A1 autostrada linking Milan and Rome via Florence and Arezzo. For information about driving times and toll charges on these, check www.auto strade.it/en.

There are several minor road categories, listed here in descending order of importance:

Strade statali (state highways) Represented on maps by 'S' or 'SS'. Vary from toll-free, four-lane highways to two-lane main roads. The latter can be extremely slow, especially in mountainous regions.

Strade regionali (regional highways connecting small villages) Coded SR or R.

Strade provinciali (provincial highways) Coded SP or P.

Strade locali Often not even paved or mapped.

Road Rules

➡ Cars drive on the right and overtake on the left.

➡ Unless otherwise indicated, always give way to cars entering an intersection from a road on your right.

➡ Seatbelts (front and rear) are required by law; violators are subject to an on-the-spot fine.

➡ Children under 12 must travel in the back seat, those under four must use child seats, and those under 1.5m must be either in an approved restraint system or suitable seat.

➡ Cars must carry a warning triangle and reflective vest; they must be used in rural areas in the event of a breakdown or accident.

➡ Italy's blood-alcohol limit is 0.05% and random breath tests take place. Penalties can be severe.

➡ Speeding fines follow EU standards and are proportionate with the number of kilometres per hour over the speed limit. The maximum is €2000 and the suspension of your driving licence.

➡ Headlights are compulsory day and night for all vehicles on the autostradas, and advisable for motorcycles even on smaller roads. Many Tuscan towns and cities have a ZTL in their historic centre. This means only local vehicles with parking permits can enter – all other vehicles must stay outside the ZTL or face fines. Hire cars are not exempt – travellers who unknowingly breach ZTLs can end up with hefty charges (fine plus administrative fee) on their credit cards.

Local Transport

Taxi

You can usually find taxi ranks at train and bus stations, or you can telephone for taxis. It's best to go to a designated taxi stand, as it's illegal for taxis to stop in the street if hailed. If you phone a taxi, bear in mind that the meter starts running from the moment of your call rather than when the taxi picks you up.

Tram

Florence has a tram network, but it services residential areas rather than tourist hot spots.

CLIMATE CHANGE & TRAVEL

Every form of transport that relies on carbon-based fuel generates CO_2, the main cause of human-induced climate change. Modern travel is dependent on aeroplanes, which might use less fuel per kilometre per person than most cars but travel much greater distances. The altitude at which aircraft emit gases (including CO_2) and particles also contributes to their climate change impact. Many websites offer 'carbon calculators' that allow people to estimate the carbon emissions generated by their journey and, for those who wish to do so, to offset the impact of the greenhouse gases emitted with contributions to portfolios of climate-friendly initiatives throughout the world. Lonely Planet offsets the carbon footprint of all staff and author travel.

Train Routes

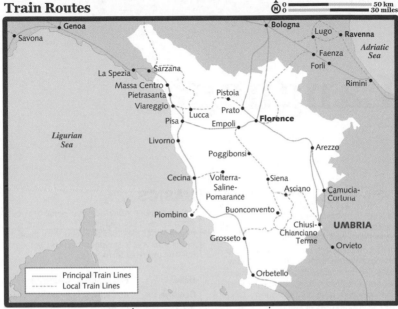

Principal Train Lines
Local Train Lines

Train

➡ **Trenitalia** (☎Italian speaking 199 89 20 21; www. trenitalia.com) is the partially privatised state train system, which runs most of the services in Italy.

➡ **Eurail** (www.eurail.com) offers a free timetable app which is searchable offline.

➡ The train network throughout Tuscany is limited.

➡ Tickets can be purchased from the ticket office or automated ticket machines at stations.

➡ Validate tickets before boarding using the yellow *convalida* machines installed at the entrance to train platforms.

➡ Travelling without a validated ticket risks a fine of at least €50. It's paid on the spot to an inspector who will escort you to an ATM if you don't have the cash on you.

➡ Train timetables at stations generally display *arrivi* (arrivals) on a white background and *partenze* (departures) on a yellow one. Italy has several types of trains:

Regionale (R) Slow and cheap, they stop at nearly all stations; *regionale veloce* (fast regional) trains stop at fewer stations.

InterCity (IC) Faster, more-expensive services operating between major cities.

Alta Velocità (AV) State-of-the-art high-speed services travelling up to 350km/hr. More expensive than InterCities but journey times can be cut by half. The AV *Frecciarossa* stops at Florence, en route between Turin, Milan, Bologna, Rome and Salerno. Advance reservations are required.

Classes & Costs

There are 1st and 2nd classes on most Italian trains; a 1st-class ticket costs just less than double the price of a 2nd-class one. There's not a huge amount of difference between the two – just a bit more space in 1st class, along with complimentary tea and coffee.

If you are taking a short trip, check the difference between the *regionale* and IC/AV ticket prices, as *regionale* tickets are always considerably cheaper – you might arrive 10 minutes earlier on an IC or AV service, but you'll also pay at least €5 more. Check up-to-date prices of routes on www.trenitalia.com.

Left Luggage

Most sizeable train stations have either a guarded left-luggage office or self-service lockers. The guarded offices are usually open 24 hours or 6am to midnight and charge around €5 per 12 hours for each piece of luggage.

Train Passes

Trenitalia offers various discount passes, including the *Carta Verde* (€40) for those aged 12 to 26 years and *Carta d'Argento* (€30) for seniors (60+ years). They give 10% to 15% off basic fares and 25% off international connections. See www.trenitalia.com for details.

Language

Modern standard Italian began to develop in the 13th and 14th centuries, predominantly through the works of Dante, Petrarch and Boccaccio – all Tuscans – who wrote chiefly in the Florentine dialect. The language drew on its Latin heritage and many dialects to develop into the standard Italian of today. Although many dialects are spoken in everyday conversation in Italy, standard Italian is understood throughout the country. Despite the Florentine roots of standard Italian – and the fact that standard Italian is widely used in Florence and Tuscany – anyone who has learned some Italian will notice the peculiarity of the local accent. In Florence, as in other parts of Tuscany, you are bound to hear the hard 'c' pronounced as a heavy 'h'. For example, *Voglio una cannuccia per la Coca Cola* (I want a straw for my Coca Cola) sounds more like *Voglio una hannuccia per la Hoha Hola*.

Italian pronunciation is relatively easy as the sounds used in spoken Italian can all be found in English. If you read our coloured pronunciation guides as if they were English, you'll be understood. The stressed syllables are indicated with italics. Note that ai is pronounced as in 'aisle', ay as in 'say', ow as in 'how', dz as the 'ds' in 'lids', and that r is a strong and rolled sound. Keep in mind that Italian consonants can have a stronger, emphatic pronunciation – if the consonant is written as a double letter, it should be pronounced a little stronger, eg *sonno son*·no (sleep) versus *sono so*·no (I am).

WANT MORE?

For in-depth language information and handy phrases, check out Lonely Planet's *Italian Phrasebook*. You'll find it at **shop.lonelyplanet.com**, or you can buy Lonely Planet's iPhone phrasebooks at the Apple App Store.

BASICS

Italian has two words for 'you' – use the polite form *Lei* lay if you're talking to strangers, officials or people older than you. With people familiar to you or younger than you, you can use the informal form *tu* too.

Hello.	*Buongiorno.*	bwon·*jor*·no
Goodbye.	*Arrivederci.*	a·ree·ve·*der*·chee
Yes./No.	*Sì./No.*	see/no
Excuse me.	*Mi scusi.* (pol)	mee *skoo*·zee
	Scusami. (inf)	*skoo*·za·mee
Sorry.	*Mi dispiace.*	mee dees·*pya*·che
Please.	*Per favore.*	per fa·*vo*·re
Thank you.	*Grazie.*	*gra*·tsye
You're welcome.	*Prego.*	*pre*·go

How are you?
Come sta/stai? (pol/inf)　　*ko*·me sta/stai

Fine. And you?
Bene. E Lei/tu? (pol/inf)　　*be*·ne e lay/too

What's your name?
Come si chiama?　　*ko*·me see *kya*·ma

My name is …
Mi chiamo …　　mee *kya*·mo …

Do you speak English?
Parla/Parli inglese? (pol/inf)　　*par*·la/*par*·lee een·*gle*·ze

I don't understand.
Non capisco.　　non ka·*pee*·sko

ACCOMMODATION

Do you have a … room?	*Avete una camera …?*	a·*ve*·te *oo*·na *ka*·me·ra …
double	*doppia con letto matrimoniale*	*do*·pya kon *le*·to ma·*tree*·mo·*nya*·le
single	*singola*	*seen*·go·la

How much is it per ...?	Quanto costa per ...?	kwan·to kos·ta per ...
night	una notte	oo·na no·te
person	persona	per·so·na

Is breakfast included?

La colazione è compresa?	la ko·la·tsyo·ne e kom·pre·sa

air-con	aria condizionata	a·rya kon·dee·tsyo·na·ta
bathroom	bagno	ba·nyo
campsite	campeggio	kam·pe·jo
guesthouse	pensione	pen·syo·ne
hotel	albergo	al·ber·go
youth hostel	ostello della gioventù	os·te·lo de·la jo·ven·too
window	finestra	fee·nes·tra

DIRECTIONS

Where's ...?

Dov'è ...?	do·ve ...

What's the address?

Qual'è l'indirizzo?	kwa·le leen·dee·ree·tso

Could you please write it down?

Può scriverlo, per favore?	pwo skree·ver·lo per fa·vo·re

Can you show me (on the map)?

Può mostrarmi (sulla pianta)?	pwo mos·trar·mee (soo·la pyan·ta)

at the corner	all'angolo	a·lan·go·lo
at the traffic lights	al semaforo	al se·ma·fo·ro
behind	dietro	dye·tro
far	lontano	lon·ta·no
in front of	davanti a	da·van·tee a
left	a sinistra	a see·nee·stra
near	vicino	vee·chee·no
next to	accanto a	a·kan·to a
opposite	di fronte a	dee fron·te a
right	a destra	a de·stra
straight ahead	sempre diritto	sem·pre dee·ree·to

EATING & DRINKING

What would you recommend?

Cosa mi consiglia?	ko·za mee kon·see·lya

What's in that dish?

Quali ingredienti ci sono in questo piatto?	kwa·li een·gre·dyen·tee chee so·no een kwe·sto pya·to

KEY PATTERNS

To get by in Italian, mix and match these simple patterns with words of your choice:

When's (the next flight)?

A che ora è (il prossimo volo)?	a ke o·ra e (eel pro·see·mo vo·lo)

Where's (the station)?

Dov'è (la stazione)?	do·ve (la sta·tsyo·ne)

I'm looking for (a hotel).

Sto cercando (un albergo).	sto cher·kan·do (oon al·ber·go)

Do you have (a map)?

Ha (una pianta)?	a (oo·na pyan·ta)

Is there (a toilet)?

C'è (un gabinetto)?	che (oon ga·bee·ne·to)

I'd like (a coffee).

Vorrei (un caffè).	vo·ray (oon ka·fe)

I'd like to (hire a car).

Vorrei (noleggiare una macchina).	vo·ray (no·le·ja·re oo·na ma·kee·na)

Can I (enter)?

Posso (entrare)?	po·so (en·tra·re)

Could you please (help me)?

Può (aiutarmi), per favore?	pwo (a·yoo·tar·mee) per fa·vo·re

That was delicious!

Era squisito!	e·ra skwee·zee·to

Cheers!

Salute!	sa·loo·te

Please bring the bill.

Mi porta il conto, per favore?	mee por·ta eel kon·to per fa·vo·re

I'd like to reserve a table for ...	Vorrei prenotare un tavolo per ...	vo·ray pre·no·ta·re oon ta·vo·lo per ...
(two) people	(due) persone	(doo·e) per·so·ne
(eight) o'clock	le (otto)	le (o·to)

I don't eat ...	Non mangio ...	non man·jo ...
eggs	uova	wo·va
fish	pesce	pe·she
nuts	noci	no·chee
(red) meat	carne (rossa)	kar·ne (ro·sa)

Key Words

bar	locale	lo·ka·le
bottle	bottiglia	bo·tee·lya
breakfast	prima colazione	pree·ma ko·la·tsyo·ne

cafe	*bar*	bar
cold	*freddo*	*fre*·do
dinner	*cena*	*che*·na
drink list	*lista delle bevande*	*lee*·sta de·le be·*van*·de
fork	*forchetta*	for·*ke*·ta
glass	*bicchiere*	bee·*kye*·re
grocery store	*alimentari*	a·lee·men·*ta*·ree
hot	*caldo*	*kal*·do
knife	*coltello*	kol·*te*·lo
lunch	*pranzo*	*pran*·dzo
market	*mercato*	mer·*ka*·to
menu	*menù*	me·*noo*
plate	*piatto*	*pya*·to
restaurant	*ristorante*	ree·sto·*ran*·te
spicy	*piccante*	pee·*kan*·te
spoon	*cucchiaio*	koo·*kya*·yo
vegetarian (food)	*vegetariano*	ve·je·ta·*rya*·no
with	*con*	kon
without	*senza*	*sen*·tsa

Meat & Fish

beef	*manzo*	*man*·dzo
chicken	*pollo*	*po*·lo
(dried) cod	*baccalà*	ba·ka·*la*
crab	*granchio*	*gran*·kyo
duck	*anatra*	*a*·na·tra
fish	*pesce*	*pe*·she
(cured) ham	*prosciutto*	pro·*shoo*·to
herring	*aringa*	a·*reen*·ga
lamb	*agnello*	a·*nye*·lo
lobster	*aragosta*	a·ra·*gos*·ta
meat	*carne*	*kar*·ne
mussels	*cozze*	*ko*·tse
octopus	*polpi*	*pol*·pee
oysters	*ostriche*	o·*stree*·ke
pork	*maiale*	ma·*ya*·le

prawn	*gambero*	*gam*·be·ro
rabbit	*coniglio*	ko·*nee*·lyo
salmon	*salmone*	sal·*mo*·ne
sausage	*salsiccia*	sal·*see*·cha
scallops	*capasante*	ka·pa·*san*·te
seafood	*frutti di mare*	*froo*·tee dee *ma*·re
shrimp	*gambero*	*gam*·be·ro
squid	*calamari*	ka·la·*ma*·ree
thinly sliced raw meat	*carpaccio*	kar·*pa*·cho
tripe	*trippa*	*tree*·pa
trout	*trota*	*tro*·ta
tuna	*tonno*	*to*·no
turkey	*tacchino*	ta·*kee*·no
veal	*vitello*	vee·*te*·lo

Vegetables

artichokes	*carciofi*	kar·*cho*·fee
asparagus	*asparagi*	as·*pa*·ra·jee
aubergine/ eggplant	*melanzane*	me·lan·*dza*·ne
beans	*fagioli*	fa·*jo*·lee
black cabbage	*cavolo nero*	*ka*·vo·lo *ne*·ro
cabbage	*cavolo*	*ka*·vo·lo
capsicum	*peperone*	pe·pe·*ro*·ne
carrot	*carota*	ka·*ro*·ta
cauliflower	*cavolfiore*	ka·vol·*fyo*·re
cucumber	*cetriolo*	che·tree·o·lo
fennel	*finocchio*	fee·*no*·kyo
lentils	*lenticchie*	len·*tee*·kye
lettuce	*lattuga*	la·*too*·ga
mushroom	*funghi*	*foon*·gee
nuts	*noci*	*no*·chee
olive	*oliva*	o·*lee*·va
onions	*cipolle*	chee·*po*·le
peas	*piselli*	pee·*ze*·lee
potatoes	*patate*	pa·*ta*·te
rocket	*rucola*	*roo*·ko·la
salad	*insalata*	een·sa·*la*·ta
spinach	*spinaci*	spee·*na*·chee
tomatoes	*pomodori*	po·mo·*do*·ree
vegetables	*verdura*	ver·*doo*·ra

Fruit & Gelato Flavours

apple	*mela*	*me*·la
cherry	*ciliegia*	chee·lee·*e*·ja
chocolate	*cioccolata*	cho·ko·*la*·ta

chocolate and hazelnuts	bacio	ba·cho
forest fruits (wild berries)	frutta di bosco	froo·ta dee bos·ko
fruit	frutta	froo·ta
grapes	uva	oo·va
hazelnut	nocciola	no·cho·la
lemon	limone	lee·mo·ne
melon	melone	me·lo·ne
orange	arancia	a·ran·cha
peach	pesca	pe·ska
pear	pere	pe·re
pineapple	ananas	a·na·nas
plum	prugna	proo·nya
strawberry	fragola	fra·go·la
trifle	zuppa inglese	tsoo·pa een·gle·ze
vanilla	vaniglia	va·nee·ya
wild/sour cherry	amarena	a·ma·re·na

Other

bread	pane	pa·ne
butter	burro	boo·ro
cheese	formaggio	for·ma·jo
cream	panna	pa·na
cone	cono	ko·no
cup	coppa	ko·pa
eggs	uova	wo·va
honey	miele	mye·le
ice	ghiaccio	gya·cho
jam	marmellata	mar·me·la·ta
noodles	pasta	pas·ta
oil	olio	o·lyo
pepper	pepe	pe·pe
rice	riso	ree·zo
salt	sale	sa·le
soup	minestra	mee·nes·tra
soy sauce	salsa di soia	sal·sa dee so·ya
sugar	zucchero	tsoo·ke·ro

Question Words

How?	Come?	ko·me
What?	Che cosa?	ke ko·za
When?	Quando?	kwan·do
Where?	Dove?	do·ve
Who?	Chi?	kee
Why?	Perché?	per·ke

truffle	tartufo	tar·too·fo
vinegar	aceto	a·che·to

Drinks

beer	birra	bee·ra
coffee	caffè	ka·fe
(orange) juice	succo (d'arancia)	soo·ko (da·ran·cha)
milk	latte	la·te
red wine	vino rosso	vee·no ro·so
soft drink	bibita	bee·bee·ta
tea	tè	te
(mineral) water	acqua (minerale)	a·kwa (mee·ne·ra·le)
white wine	vino bianco	vee·no byan·ko

For additional food and drink terms, check out the Eat & Drink Like a Local chapter (p36).

EMERGENCIES

Help!
Aiuto! — a·yoo·to

Leave me alone!
Lasciami in pace! — la·sha·mee een pa·che

I'm lost.
Mi sono perso/a. (m/f) — mee so·no per·so/a

There's been an accident.
C'è stato un incidente. — che sta·to oon een·chee·den·te

Call the police!
Chiami la polizia! — kya·mee la po·lee·tsee·a

Call a doctor!
Chiami un medico! — kya·mee oon me·dee·ko

Where are the toilets?
Dove sono i gabinetti? — do·ve so·no ee ga·bee·ne·tee

I'm sick.
Mi sento male. — mee sen·to ma·le

It hurts here.
Mi fa male qui. — mee fa ma·le kwee

I'm allergic to ...
Sono allergico/a a ... (m/f) — so·no a·ler·jee·ko/a a ...

SHOPPING & SERVICES

I'd like to buy ...
Vorrei comprare ... — vo·ray kom·pra·re ...

I'm just looking.
Sto solo guardando. — sto so·lo gwar·dan·do

Can I look at it?
Posso dare un'occhiata? — po·so da·re oo·no·kya·ta

How much is this?
Quanto costa questo? — kwan·to kos·ta kwe·sto

It's too expensive.
È troppo caro/a. (m/f)   e *tro·*po ka·ro/a

Can you lower the price?
Può farmi lo sconto?   pwo *far·*mee lo *skon·*to

There's a mistake in the bill.
C'è un errore nel conto.   che oo·*ne·*ro·re nel *kon·*to

ATM	*Bancomat*	ban·ko·mat
post office	*ufficio*	oo·*fee·*cho
	postale	pos·*ta·*le
tourist office	*ufficio del*	oo·*fee·*cho del
	turismo	too·*reez·*mo

TIME & DATES

What time is it?	*Che ora è?*	ke o·ra e
It's one o'clock.	*È l'una.*	e *loo·*na
It's (two) o'clock.	*Sono le (due).*	so·no le (*doo·*e)
Half past (one).	*(L'una) e mezza.*	(*loo·*na) e me·dza
in the morning	*di mattina*	dee ma·*tee·*na
in the afternoon	*di pomeriggio*	dee po·me·*ree·*jo
in the evening	*di sera*	dee *se·*ra
yesterday	*ieri*	ye·ree
today	*oggi*	o·jee
tomorrow	*domani*	do·*ma·*nee
Monday	*lunedì*	loo·ne·*dee*
Tuesday	*martedì*	mar·te·*dee*
Wednesday	*mercoledì*	mer·ko·le·*dee*
Thursday	*giovedì*	jo·ve·*dee*
Friday	*venerdì*	ve·ner·*dee*
Saturday	*sabato*	sa·ba·to
Sunday	*domenica*	do·me·*nee·*ka
January	*gennaio*	je·*na·*yo
February	*febbraio*	fe·*bra·*yo
March	*marzo*	mar·tso
April	*aprile*	a·*pree·*le
May	*maggio*	ma·jo
June	*giugno*	joo·nyo
July	*luglio*	loo·lyo
August	*agosto*	a·*gos·*to
September	*settembre*	se·*tem·*bre
October	*ottobre*	o·*to·*bre
November	*novembre*	no·*vem·*bre
December	*dicembre*	dee·*chem·*bre

Numbers

1	*uno*	oo·no
2	*due*	doo·e
3	*tre*	tre
4	*quattro*	kwa·tro
5	*cinque*	cheen·kwe
6	*sei*	say
7	*sette*	se·te
8	*otto*	o·to
9	*nove*	no·ve
10	*dieci*	dye·chee
20	*venti*	ven·tee
30	*trenta*	tren·ta
40	*quaranta*	kwa·*ran·*ta
50	*cinquanta*	cheen·*kwan·*ta
60	*sessanta*	se·*san·*ta
70	*settanta*	se·*tan·*ta
80	*ottanta*	o·*tan·*ta
90	*novanta*	no·*van·*ta
100	*cento*	chen·to
1000	*mille*	mee·lel

TRANSPORT

Public Transport

At what time does the ... leave/arrive?	*A che ora parte/ arriva ...?*	a ke o·ra par·te/ a·ree·va ...
boat	*la nave*	la na·ve
bus	*l'autobus*	low·to·boos
ferry	*il traghetto*	eel tra·*ge·*to
metro	*la metro- politana*	la me·tro· po·lee·*ta·*na
plane	*l'aereo*	la·e·re·o
train	*il treno*	eel *tre·*no
... ticket	*un biglietto ...*	oon bee·*lye·*to
one-way	*di sola andata*	dee so·la an·*da·*ta
return	*di andata e ritorno*	dee an·*da·*ta e ree·*tor·*no
bus stop	*fermata dell'autobus*	fer·*ma·*ta del ow·to·boos
platform	*binario*	bee·*na·*ryo
ticket office	*biglietteria*	bee·lye·te·*ree·*a
timetable	*orario*	o·*ra·*ryo
train station	*stazione ferroviaria*	sta·*tsyo·*ne fe·ro·*vyar·*ya

Does it stop at ...?
Si ferma a ...?   see *fer*·ma a ...

Please tell me when we get to ...
Mi dica per favore   mee *dee*·ka per fa·*vo*·re
quando arriviamo a ...   kwan·do a·ree·*vya*·mo a ...

I want to get off here.
Voglio scendere qui.   vo·lyo *shen*·de·re kwee

Driving & Cycling

I'd like	*Vorrei*	vo·*ray*
to hire	*noleggiare*	no·le·*ja*·re
a/an ...	*un/una ...* (m/f)	oon/*oo*·na ...
bicycle	*bicicletta* (f)	bee·chee·*kle*·ta
car	*macchina* (f)	*ma*·kee·na
motorbike	*moto* (f)	*mo*·to
bicycle pump	*pompa della bicicletta*	*pom*·pa de·la bee·chee·*kle*·ta
child seat	*seggiolino*	se·jo·*lee*·no
helmet	*casco*	*kas*·ko

mechanic	*meccanico*	me·*ka*·nee·ko
petrol/gas	*benzina*	ben·*dzee*·na
puncture	*gomma bucata*	go·ma boo·*ka*·ta
service station	*stazione di servizio*	sta·*tsyo*·ne dee ser·*vee*·tsyo

Is this the road to ...?
Questa strada porta a ...? kwe·sta stra·da por·ta a ...

(How long) Can I park here?
(Per quanto tempo)   (per kwan·to tem·po)
Posso parcheggiare qui? po·so par·ke·*ja*·re kwee

The car/motorbike has broken down (at ...).
La macchina/moto si è   la ma·kee·na/*mo*·to see e
guastata (a ...).   gwas·*ta*·ta (a ...)

I have a flat tyre.
Ho una gomma bucata.   o oo·na go·ma boo·*ka*·ta

I've run out of petrol.
Ho esaurito la   o e·zow·*ree*·to la
benzina.   ben·*dzee*·na

I've lost my car keys.
Ho perso le chiavi della   o *per*·so le *kya*·vee de·la
macchina.   ma·*kee*·na

GLOSSARY

For art and architecture terms, see p320.

abbazia – abbey

affittacamere – rooms for rent in private houses

agriturismo – farm-stay accommodation

albergo – hotel

alimentari – grocery shop

alto – high

ambulanza – ambulance

anfiteatro – amphitheatre

aperitivo – predinner drinks accompanied by cocktail snacks

autostazione – bus station/ terminal

autostrada – motorway, highway

basilica – Christian church with a rectangular hall, aisles and an apse at the end

battistero – baptistry

biblioteca – library

biglietto – ticket

biglietto cumulativo – combined ticket that allows entrance to a number of associated sights

borgo – ancient town or village; farm hamlet

cabinovia – two-seater cable car

calcio – football

camera doppia – room with twin beds

camera matrimoniale – room with a double bed

camera singola – single room

campanile – bell tower

campeggio – camping

campo – field

cantinetta – small cellar where wine is served

cappella – chapel

carabinieri – military police

Carnevale – carnival period between Epiphany and Lent

casa – house, home

castello – castle

cattedrale – cathedral

cava – quarry

centro – city centre

centro storico – literally, 'historical centre'; old town

chiesa – church

colle – hill

colonna – column

comune – equivalent to a municipality; town or city council; historically, a commune (self-governing town or city)

contrada – town district

convalida – ticket-stamping machine

coperto – cover charge

corso – main street, avenue

deposito bagagli – left luggage

dolce – sweet; also dessert course

duomo – cathedral

enoteca – wine bar (see also *fiaschetteria*)

fattoria – farmhouse

ferrovia – train station

festa – festival

fiaschetteria – small tavern serving wine and snacks (see also *enoteca*)

fontana – fountain

forno – bakery

foro – forum

gelateria – ice-cream shop

golfo – gulf

grotta – cave

isola – island

lago – lake

largo – small square

libreria – bookshop
locanda – inn, small hotel
loggia – covered area on the side of a building; porch
lungomare – seafront road, promenade

macchia – scrub, bush
macellerìa – butcher shop
mare – sea
mercato – market
monte – mountain, mount
motorino – scooter
municipio – town hall
museo – museum

nave – ship
necropoli – ancient cemetery, burial site

osteria – casual tavern or eatery presided over by a host

palazzo – palace; a large building of any type, including an apartment block
parcheggio – car park
parco – park

passeggiata – traditional evening stroll
pasticceria – shop selling cakes and pastries
pensione – small hotel
permesso di soggiorno – residence permit
piazza – square
piazzale – large open square
pinacoteca – art gallery
ponte – bridge
porta – door, city gate
portico – walkway, often on the outside of buildings
porto – port

questura – police station

rifugio – mountain hut
rocca – fort

sagra – festival (usually with a culinary theme)
sala – room in a museum or a gallery
santuario – sanctuary
scalinata – flight of stairs
scavi – excavations
spiaggia – beach

stazione – station
stazione di servizio – service/petrol station
stazione marittima – ferry terminal
strada – street, road
superstrada – expressway; highway with divided lanes

tabaccheria/tabaccaio – tobacconist's shop/tobacconist
teatro – theatre
tempio – temple
terme – thermal bath
torre – tower
trattoria – simple restaurant

ufficio stranieri – foreigners' bureau
uffizi – offices

via – street, road
vicoli – alley, alleyway

ZTL – *(Zona a Traffico Limitato)* Limited Traffic Zone

Behind the Scenes

SEND US YOUR FEEDBACK

We love to hear from travellers – your comments keep us on our toes and help make our books better. Our well-travelled team reads every word on what you loved or loathed about this book. Although we cannot reply individually to your submissions, we always guarantee that your feedback goes straight to the appropriate authors, in time for the next edition. Each person who sends us information is thanked in the next edition – the most useful submissions are rewarded with a selection of digital PDF chapters.

Visit **lonelyplanet.com/contact** to submit your updates and suggestions or to ask for help. Our award-winning website also features inspirational travel stories, news and discussions.

Note: We may edit, reproduce and incorporate your comments in Lonely Planet products such as guidebooks, websites and digital products, so let us know if you don't want your comments reproduced or your name acknowledged. For a copy of our privacy policy visit lonelyplanet.com/privacy.

OUR READERS

Many thanks to the travellers who used the last edition and wrote to us with helpful hints, useful advice and interesting anecdotes:

Alexander and Caroline Wrigley, David Kerrigan, Iain Mann, Isabel Vollers, Jim Noviello, Jochen Thielen, Josef Sørensen, Kelley Eckmair, Margaret Simpson, Pedro Pacheco, Peter Gaskell, Samantha Tollerson, Sara Viti

AUTHOR THANKS

Nicola Williams

Grazie to those who shared their Tuscan love with me: in Florence, Betty Soldi and Matteo Perduca, Alessio and Assumi, Doreen and Carmello, Fabrizio Rangone, Judy Witts aka Divina Cucina, Roberto Romoli and gals' about town Nardia Plumridge (@lostinflorence), Georgette Jupe (@girlinflorence), Flavia Cori (@Tuscanyicious) and Coral Sisk (@curious appetite). Heartfelt thanks to Pistoia experts Dr Paolo Bresci and Molly McIlwrath, Ilaria Leccarelli (Castiglion Fiorentino) and Elisabetta Pandolfini (Prato). My chunk of this book is dedicated to kid team supreme Niko, Mischa and Kaya Lüfkens, and super papa Matthias.

Belinda Dixon

The kindness of strangers enriches travels – thank you to all who transformed my on-the-road days. To Anna Tyler my gratitude for the opportunity; to Nicola Williams the same for wisdom and support. Jo and Liz: I raise a glass of prosecco. JL: my thanks for still making me smile.

ACKNOWLEDGMENTS

Climate map data adapted from Peel MC, Finlayson BL & McMahon TA (2007) 'Updated World Map of the Köppen-Geiger Climate Classification', *Hydrology and Earth System Sciences*, 11, 1633–44.

Illustration pp62-3 by Javier Zarracina.

Cover photograph: *Duomo*, Florence, Pietro Canali / 4Corners ©.

THIS BOOK

This 9th edition of Lonely Planet's *Florence & Tuscany* guidebook was researched and written by Nicola Williams and Belinda Dixon. The 8th edition was written by Virginia Maxwell and Nicola Williams.

This guidebook was produced by the following:

Destination Editor Anna Tyler

Product Editors Briohny Hooper, Alison Ridgway

Regional Senior Cartographer Anthony Phelan

Book Designer Wendy Wright

Coordinating Editor Andrea Dobbin

Assisting Editors Imogen Bannister, Kate Chapman, Melanie Dankel, Kate James, Jodie Martire, Anne Mulvaney, Susan Paterson, Vicky Smith

Assisting Cartographers Mick Garrett, Rachel Imeson, Corey Hutchison

Cover Researcher Naomi Parker

Thanks to Sarah Billington, Grace Dobell, Andi Jones, Claire Murphy, Catherine Naghten, Karyn Noble, Samantha Russell-Tulip, Dianne Schallmeiner, Lauren Wellicome

Index

Map Legend

Sights
- Beach
- Bird Sanctuary
- Buddhist
- Castle/Palace
- Christian
- Confucian
- Hindu
- Islamic
- Jain
- Jewish
- Monument
- Museum/Gallery/Historic Building
- Ruin
- Shinto
- Sikh
- Taoist
- Winery/Vineyard
- Zoo/Wildlife Sanctuary
- Other Sight

Activities, Courses & Tours
- Bodysurfing
- Diving
- Canoeing/Kayaking
- Course/Tour
- Sento Hot Baths/Onsen
- Skiing
- Snorkelling
- Surfing
- Swimming/Pool
- Walking
- Windsurfing
- Other Activity

Sleeping
- Sleeping
- Camping

Eating
- Eating

Drinking & Nightlife
- Drinking & Nightlife
- Cafe

Entertainment
- Entertainment

Shopping
- Shopping

Information
- Bank
- Embassy/Consulate
- Hospital/Medical
- Internet
- Police
- Post Office
- Telephone
- Toilet
- Tourist Information
- Other Information

Geographic
- Beach
- Gate
- Hut/Shelter
- Lighthouse
- Lookout
- Mountain/Volcano
- Oasis
- Park
- Pass
- Picnic Area
- Waterfall

Population
- Capital (National)
- Capital (State/Province)
- City/Large Town
- Town/Village

Transport
- Airport
- Border crossing
- Bus
- Cable car/Funicular
- Cycling
- Ferry
- Metro station
- Monorail
- Parking
- Petrol station
- S-Bahn/Subway station
- Taxi
- T-bane/Tunnelbana station
- Train station/Railway
- Tram
- Tube station
- U-Bahn/Underground station
- Other Transport

Routes
- Tollway
- Freeway
- Primary
- Secondary
- Tertiary
- Lane
- Unsealed road
- Road under construction
- Plaza/Mall
- Steps
- Tunnel
- Pedestrian overpass
- Walking Tour
- Walking Tour detour
- Path/Walking Trail

Boundaries
- International
- State/Province
- Disputed
- Regional/Suburb
- Marine Park
- Cliff
- Wall

Hydrography
- River, Creek
- Intermittent River
- Canal
- Water
- Dry/Salt/Intermittent Lake
- Reef

Areas
- Airport/Runway
- Beach/Desert
- Cemetery (Christian)
- Cemetery (Other)
- Glacier
- Mudflat
- Park/Forest
- Sight (Building)
- Sportsground
- Swamp/Mangrove

Note: Not all symbols displayed above appear on the maps in this book

OUR STORY

A beat-up old car, a few dollars in the pocket and a sense of adventure. In 1972 that's all Tony and Maureen Wheeler needed for the trip of a lifetime – across Europe and Asia overland to Australia. It took several months, and at the end – broke but inspired – they sat at their kitchen table writing and stapling together their first travel guide, *Across Asia on the Cheap*. Within a week they'd sold 1500 copies. Lonely Planet was born.

Today, Lonely Planet has offices in Franklin, London, Melbourne, Oakland, Beijing and Delhi, with more than 600 staff and writers. We share Tony's belief that 'a great guidebook should do three things: inform, educate and amuse'.

OUR WRITERS

Nicola Williams

Florence; Northwestern Tuscany; Eastern Tuscany British writer Nicola Williams lives on the southern shore of Lake Geneva. Thankfully for her Italianate soul, it is an easy hop through the Mont Blanc Tunnel to Italy where she has spent years eating her way around and revelling in its extraordinary art, architecture, cuisine and landscape. Hunting Tuscan white truffles is an annual October ritual. Nicola has worked on numerous titles for Lonely Planet, including *Italy*, *Milan, Turin & Genoa* and *Piedmont*. She shares her travels on Twitter at @Tripalong. Nicola also wrote most of the Plan Your Trip section and the Understand section.

Read more about Nicola at:
http://auth.lonelyplanet.com/profiles/nicolawilliams

Belinda Dixon

Siena & Central Tuscany; Central Coast & Elba; Southern Tuscany Having cut her teenage travel teeth on Italy's trains, rarely has a year passed when Belinda hasn't been back. Highlights of this title's research include perfecting off-road driving skills on Chianti's lanes, tasting silky green olive oil in Elba and getting thoroughly spooked in Pitigliano's night-time streets (think dark alleys, meowing cats and suddenly-extinguished lights). And everywhere, very, very diligently researching Tuscan food and wine. Belinda also wrote the Outdoor Experiences chapter and the Survival Guide section.

Read more about Belinda at:
http://auth.lonelyplanet.com/profiles/belindadixon

Published by Lonely Planet Publications Pty Ltd
ABN 36 005 607 983
9th edition – January 2016
ISBN 978 1 74321 683 5
© Lonely Planet 2016   Photographs © as indicated 2016
10 9 8 7 6 5 4 3 2 1
Printed in China

Although the authors and Lonely Planet have taken all reasonable care in preparing this book, we make no warranty about the accuracy or completeness of its content and, to the maximum extent permitted, disclaim all liability arising from its use.

32953012479210